# LISTEN 'N' LEARN
# SPANISH
## *with your Favorite Movies*

SCOTT THOMAS AND GABY THOMAS

**Mc
Graw
Hill**

New York   Chicago   San Francisco   Lisbon   London   Madrid   Mexico City
Milan   New Delhi   San Juan   Seoul   Singapore   Sydney   Toronto

In memory of
**Dr. Bill Stivers**
Pepperdine University Professor of Spanish
*teacher, travel companion, and friend*

**Library of Congress Cataloging-in-Publication Data**

Thomas, Scott (Daniel Scott)
     Listen 'n' learn Spanish with your favorite movies : boost your language skills
from the comfort of your couch / Scott Thomas and Gaby Thomas.
          p.   cm.
     ISBN-10 0-07-147565-6 (acid-free paper)
     ISBN-13 978-0-07-147565-5 (acid-free paper)
     1. Spanish language—Textbooks for foreign speakers—English.    2. Spanish language—
Self-instruction.     3. Spanish language—Spoken Spanish—Audio-visual aids.    4. Motion pictures—
United States—Plots, themes, etc.     I. Thomas, Gaby.     II. Title.     III. Title: Listen and learn Spanish
with your favorite movies.

     PC4129.E5T48     2010
     468.2'421—dc22                                                      2009013546

1 2 3 4 5 6 7 8 9 0    FGR/FGR    2 1 0

ISBN    978-0-07-147565-5
MHID        0-07-147565-6

Interior design by Village Bookworks, Inc.

Photo credits are listed on page iv.

**Bonus Summaries Online**
Additional movie profiles can be obtained from mhprofessional.com for the following titles:
   *In Memoriam: New York City, 9/11/01* (2002)
   *The Bishop's Wife* (1947)
   *Facing the Giants* (2006)
   *Rudy* (1993)
Locate the *Listen 'n' Learn Spanish with Your Favorite Movies* web page for these free PDF downloads.

McGraw-Hill books are available at special quantity discounts to use as premiums and sales promotions
or for use in corporate training programs. To contact a representative, please visit the Contact Us pages
at www.mhprofessional.com.

# Contents

Photo Credits    iv

Acknowledgments    v

How to Use This Book    vi

Core Vocabulary    xi

## BEGINNER

Eight Below (2006)    1

The Fox and the Hound (1981)    13

March of the Penguins (2005)    21

The Princess Bride (1987)    32

## ADVANCED BEGINNER

The Absent-Minded Professor (1961)    50

Eragon (2006)    67

The Chronicles of Narnia:
The Lion, the Witch and the Wardrobe (2005)    79

Tarzan (1999)    92

## INTERMEDIATE

Holes (2003)    103

Home Alone (1990)    123

Hoosiers (1986)    138

Rocky III (1982)    154

## ADVANCED

Anne of Green Gables (1985)    171

Finding Nemo (2003)    212

The Incredibles (2004)    229

Mary Poppins (1964)    251

# Photo Credits

# Acknowledgments

We wish to express our appreciation to the following people for their assistance in the preparation of this book:

Chris Haddan, for working through the night and well into the early morning hours to help us come up with meaningful vocabulary lists

Christopher Brown of McGraw-Hill Professional, for his patience and always valuable suggestions from the earliest stages of the project

Greg Johnson, for his insight into language acquisition and valuable suggestions in organizing the vocabulary lists for practical use

Tim and Shelley Znamenacek, for giving us many of the tools needed to complete this project and for proofreading our drafts

Alison Rigney and Glenn Bradie of the Everett Collection, for helping us select and obtain the movie photographs

Daniel Delgado and Isabel Baltazar, for helping us clarify several Spanish words and phrases

Isabel Delgado, for her diligent and excellent work transcribing many of the movies

Terry Yokota and Daniel Franklin of Village Bookworks, for their top-notch editorial and design work

# How to Use This Book

Watching foreign language movies has long been a way for students to learn a new language, and many language instructors show movies in the target language as a means of helping their students learn. Foreign language experts recommend watching movies or television in the target language as a way to improve language skills, with the following benefits in mind:

- Native speakers can be heard and imitated.
- The rhythm and sound of the language becomes familiar.
- Grammar and vocabulary are used in a natural context.
- The student is immersed in the language for extended periods of time.
- It's an entertaining and fun way to learn.

Now that familiar English language movies are readily available with foreign language audio tracks through DVD and other digital formats, foreign language enthusiasts can take advantage of this technology to improve their language acquisition and to learn Spanish and other languages more quickly and easily than ever before.

But before you turn on the television to a Spanish station or sit down to watch your favorite movie using the Spanish audio track, you may want to consider a couple of things. While there is some benefit to watching movies and trying to pick out familiar words, it is easy to become over-whelmed as the wave of unintelligible, indistinct, and meaningless syllables crashes over you. It's also not very efficient: You can spend many hours listening to a lot of dialogue and come away with only small gains in understanding. That could be boring and frustrating, but it wouldn't be if you could progress more rapidly—and mark the progress you've made.

Our approach helps you solve these problems. For instance, let's take a line from *The Chronicles of Narnia: The Lion, the Witch and the Wardrobe*.

The untrained ear hears something like what the eye sees here:

**Mevoyatenerquehacerunpeludosombrerodecastor**

But if you already know this:

| | |
|---|---|
| **me voy a** | I'm going to |
| **tener que** | to have to |
| **hacer** | to make |
| **un** | a, an, one |
| **peludo** | furry |
| **sombrero** | hat |
| **de** | of, from |
| **castor** | beaver |

You will hear this:

**Me voy a tener que hacer un peludo sombrero de castor.**

And understand this:

*I'm going to have to make a furry hat out of that beaver.*
(LIT *I'm going to have to make a furry hat of beaver.*)

It's that simple!

1. **Words and phrases.** By knowing the words and phrases ahead of time, your ear will be pre-disposed to identify them. This allows you to avoid the frustration of being unable to distinguish, without tremendous effort, what you are hearing.

2. **Definitions.** By knowing the definitions for the words and phrases ahead of time, you can attach meaning to them without having to search a traditional dictionary.

3. **Marking progress.** Being able to refer to lists of common words and phrases that occur in a specific movie allows you to monitor your progress and increases your motivation.

4. **Familiar movies.** When you watch movies you're familiar with—like those that are a part of this collection—not only does your comprehension go up, but you have more fun learning!

Following are the steps for putting this approach into practice.

## Step 1. Learn Core Vocabulary

Eighty percent of the Spanish used in these 20 movies is made up of about 600 words and phrases, which are listed in the Core Vocabulary that begins on page xi. If you know these words and phrases, you'll understand 80 percent of the Spanish words being spoken. This gives you a huge head start in being able to enjoy the movies as you watch them.

The Core Vocabulary is comprised of 52 short lists, none longer than 20 items, organized in eight categories. Each vocabulary entry consists of a main entry followed by its English translation, including a grammar tag where appropriate (see p. x). Usage is illustrated in a sentence or phrase from one of the movies included in this collection, together with its English translation and the title and chapter of the movie in which it appears.

We used the transcripts of 40 movies to develop the Core Vocabulary and found that it closely matches the frequency list developed for *The Big Red Book of Spanish Vocabulary* (McGraw-Hill, 2005). The time you invest in making sure that you know this Core Vocabulary is time well spent, because this list consists of the words you will encounter when you

- watch movies in Spanish beyond those included in this collection
- watch Spanish television programs
- listen to Spanish music
- read Spanish novels and nonfiction books
- participate in everyday conversation

In short, these words are the foundation on which you will build your fluency in Spanish.

## Step 2. Select a Movie by Level of Difficulty, Genre, or Chronology

For most people, starting with one of the four Beginner movies is the best choice, because the pace of the dialogue or narration is considerably slower than in the more challenging movies. Starting with one of the Advanced movies will likely present problems, because these movies include more and noticeably faster dialogue and, generally, a more extensive vocabulary. However, you should be able to start with one of the Advanced Beginner or Intermediate movies if you already own it with Spanish audio, and especially if you are familiar with the story line.

When purchasing DVDs or other movie formats, be aware that more than one edition may exist, and not all of them include the Spanish audio track. Check for confirmation that Spanish audio is included.

## Movies Listed by Genre

| Category | Movie |
|---|---|
| Adventure | *Eight Below* (2006)<br>*Eragon* (2006)<br>*The Fox and the Hound* (Animated, 1981)<br>*The Incredibles* (Animated, 2004)<br>*The Princess Bride* (1987) |
| Drama | *Facing the Giants* (2006)<br>*Holes* (2003)<br>*Hoosiers* (1986)<br>*Rocky III* (1982) |
| Biography/History/Documentary | *In Memoriam: New York City, 9/11/01* (Documentary, 2002)<br>*March of the Penguins* (Documentary, 2005)<br>*Rudy* (1993) |
| Classic Literature Adaptation | *Anne of Green Gables* (1985)<br>*The Chronicles of Narnia: The Lion, the Witch and the Wardrobe* (2005)<br>*Tarzan* (Animated, 1999) |
| Comedy/Musical | *The Absent-Minded Professor* (1961)<br>*The Bishop's Wife* (1947)<br>*Finding Nemo* (Animated, 2003)<br>*Home Alone* (1990)<br>*Mary Poppins* (1964) |

## Movies Listed by Chronology

| Category | Movie |
|---|---|
| 1940–1959 | *The Bishop's Wife* (1947) |
| 1960–1979 | *The Absent-Minded Professor* (1961)<br>*Mary Poppins* (1964) |
| 1980–1989 | *The Fox and the Hound* (1981)<br>*Rocky III* (1982)<br>*Anne of Green Gables* (1985)<br>*Hoosiers* (1986)<br>*The Princess Bride* (1987) |
| 1990–1999 | *Home Alone* (1990)<br>*Rudy* (1993)<br>*Tarzan* (1999) |

| Category | Movie |
|---|---|
| 2000–2009 | *In Memoriam: New York City, 9/11/01* (2002)<br>*Finding Nemo* (2003)<br>*Holes* (2003)<br>*The Incredibles* (2004)<br>*The Chronicles of Narnia: The Lion, the Witch and the Wardrobe* (2005)<br>*March of the Penguins* (2005)<br>*Eight Below* (2006)<br>*Eragon* (2006)<br>*Facing the Giants* (2006) |

## Step 3. Study the Vocabulary Guide and Watch the Movie

After you have reviewed the Core Vocabulary and selected a movie appropriate to your interest and ability level, you will be ready to work with the vocabulary guides in each movie profile. Each vocabulary entry provides the English translation. The infinitive is given for a spoken verb form, and a verb that appears in either the subjunctive or imperative form is marked as such. The gender is provided for a masculine noun with an ending other than **-o** or **-dor**, and for a feminine noun with an ending other than **-a**, **-dad**, or **-ión**. When a spoken noun is in the plural form, its singular form is also given. For an overview of what is available in each guide, see the explanatory chart on the following page.

Each movie profile begins with basic vocabulary that occurs in that specific movie. Take the time to memorize these words, because they will occur frequently. Although memorizing vocabulary may not be the most exciting part of learning a language, it is motivating to know that these are words you will definitely use.

You are now ready to approach the movie as a whole, a chapter at a time, or even scene by scene if you choose. Because you can bookmark and replay sections of a digitally recorded movie, you can approach it in whatever way is most beneficial to you.

You might choose to study the vocabulary for a movie chapter and memorize it, then watch the chapter to see how well you understand what is being said. You may also watch the movie chapter and follow along with the text, which includes brief scene markers to help you locate the new vocabulary as it occurs. Mark the checkbox for each listed word or phrase that you have learned. Once you have mastered a chapter or scene, you can move on to the next one.

The payoff for this incremental approach comes when you are able to watch the entire movie and understand what is being said almost as easily as if you were hearing it in English. That's a good time to celebrate!

If you like this approach to learning Spanish vocabulary and are interested in using this method for learning from television shows, novels, nonfiction books, and music videos, visit *www.language safari.com* or *www.languagesafari.com/mcgraw-hill* for special products and promotions.

# Explanatory Chart

Names of characters and places in the movie

Words that occur frequently throughout the movie, arranged by part of speech

Grammar tag (where useful); English translation; sentence from the movie that uses the word or phrase

Singular form of plural noun used in the movie

Number, title, and length of DVD chapter

Notable phrases that occur in the chapter

Scene marker

Vocabulary listed in order of occurrence within the scene

Checkbox for monitoring progress

Grammar tag for noun

Infinitive of conjugated verb form used in the movie

Grammar tag for verb

## BASIC VOCABULARY

### Names

Lucy, Edmund, Ed, Narnia, Aslan, Susan, Tumnus, Adán, Pevensie

### Nouns

□ **castillo** castle · *Debe estar en el **castillo** de la bruja y ya saben lo que dicen.* He must be in the witch's castle, and you all know what they say.

□ **castor** *NM* beaver · *También el **castor** me dijo que planeas hacerte un sombrero con él.* The beaver also told me that you plan to make him into a hat for yourself.

□ **fauno** faun · *Soy un **fauno**, y tú, ¿qué eres?* I'm a faun, and you, what are you?

□ **tropas** troops · *tropa* troop · *¿Nuestras **tropas**?* Our troops?

## 1 Introduction                                      7:09

### Phrases to Listen For

**tenemos que** we have to
**¿por qué?** why?

🎬 Edmund is watching the bombing through a window.

□ **refugio** shelter
□ **¡agáchate!** *IMP* get down! · *agachar* to crouch, to get down
□ **nos matas** you kill us · *matar* to kill
□ **egoísta** selfish

🎬 At a train station, Lucy, Susan, Edmund, and Peter say good-bye to their mother.

□ **personal** *NM* personnel
□ **evacuación** evacuation
□ **¿te abriga?** are you dressed warmly? · *abrigarse* to dress warmly
□ **obligaría** he would force · *obligar* to force, to obligate
□ **pórtate** *IMP* behave yourself · *portarse* to behave oneself

## Grammar Tags Used in This Book

| ADJ | adjective | INT | interjection | NMF | masculine or feminine noun |
|---|---|---|---|---|---|
| ADV | adverb | LIT | literally | NMPL | masculine plural noun |
| DIM | diminutive | M | masculine | OBJ | object |
| ENG | English | NF | feminine noun | PEJ | pejorative |
| EXP | expression | NFPL | feminine plural noun | PRO | pronoun |
| IMP | imperative | NM | masculine noun | SUBJ | subjunctive |

# Core Vocabulary

The 614 vocabulary items in this section represent 80 percent of the words spoken in most movies in Spanish. Each word or phrase is followed by an illustrative example. Note that these examples come from both the movies covered in this book and from those available as bonus downloads (see page ii).

## COMMON PHRASES

### POLITE CONVERSATION

**a ver**  let's see · *A ver, déjame pensar.*  Let's see, let me think. [The Fox and the Hound, ch. 2]

**así es**  that's right, yes indeed, that's how it is · *Así es, adiós.*  That's right, good-bye. [Home Alone, ch. 1]

**buenas noches**  good night · *Buenas noches, Westley.*  Good night, Westley. [The Princess Bride, ch. 11]

**buenas tardes**  good afternoon, good evening · *Buenas tardes, joven.*  Good afternoon, young man. [Mary Poppins, ch. 2]

**buenos días**  good morning, good day · *Señorita Fleener, buenos días.*  Miss Fleener, good morning. [Hoosiers, ch. 4]

**de acuerdo**  agreed, all right · *estar de acuerdo* to be in agreement, to agree · *Estoy de acuerdo con Fezzik.*  I agree with Fezzik. [The Princess Bride, ch. 4]

**de nada**  you're welcome · *De nada.*  You're welcome. [Rudy, ch. 25]

**feliz navidad**  Merry Christmas · *Oye, Johnny, ¿no quieres decirle feliz navidad a tu hermanito?* Hey, Johnny, don't you want to say Merry Christmas to your little brother? [Rudy, ch. 16]

**hasta la vista**  see you later · *Hasta la vista, Julia.*  See you later, Julia. [The Bishop's Wife, ch. 13]

**hasta luego**  see you later (*LIT* until later) · *Hasta luego, Mamá Búho.*  See you later, Mama Búho. [The Fox and the Hound, ch. 10]

**hasta pronto**  see you soon (*LIT* until soon) · *Hasta pronto, muchachos.*  See you soon, guys. [The Princess Bride, ch. 21]

**lo siento**  I'm sorry · *Como lo siento, querido.* I'm so sorry, dear. [The Chronicles of Narnia: The Lion, the Witch and the Wardrobe, ch. 11]

**muchas gracias**  thank you very much · *Gracias, muchas gracias.*  Thank you, thank you very much. [The Bishop's Wife, ch. 2]

**muy bien**  very well, quite fine · *No lo hice muy bien la última vez.*  I didn't do it very well last time. [Eight Below, ch. 12]

**por favor**  please · *¿Quieres esperar un momento, por favor, Sylvester?*  Do you want to wait a moment, please, Sylvester? [The Bishop's Wife, ch. 11]

**por supuesto**  of course · *Por supuesto, aunque usualmente sé para quien voy a trabajar.* Of course, although I usually know who I'm going to work for. [The Incredibles, ch. 9]

### QUESTIONS

**¿cómo se llama?**  what is your name?, what is it called? · *¿Cómo se llama este lugar?*  What is this place called? [Anne of Green Gables, ch. 3]

**¿cómo te llamas?**  what is your name? · *¿Cómo te llamas, tú?*  What is your name? [The Fox and the Hound, ch. 6]

**¿no es así?**  isn't that right? · *¿No es así?*  Isn't that right? [Anne of Green Gables, ch. 1]

**¿por qué?**  why? · *¿Por qué lo haces?*  Why do you do it? [Home Alone, ch. 11]

**¿por qué no?**  why not? · *Y, ¿por qué no?*  And why not? [The Bishop's Wife, ch. 6]

**¿qué pasa?**  what's happening?, what's going on? · *¿Qué pasa contigo?*  What's going on with you? [Rocky III, ch. 11]

**¿qué pasó?**  what happened?, what's been going on?, what's up? · *¿Qué pasó?*  What happened? [Rocky III, ch. 8]

**¿qué tal...?**  hello, what about ...?, how's it going?, what's up?, what do you think of that? [EXAMPLES: *¿qué tal el trabajo?* how's your work going?, *¿qué tal tu novia?* what's up with your girlfriend?, *qué tal, ¿eh?* what do you think of that?] · *¿Qué tal? Mi nombre es Inigo Montoya.*  Hello, my name is Inigo Montoya. [The Princess Bride, ch. 26]

**¿qué te pasa?**  what's the matter?, what's the matter with you? · *Oye, ¿qué te pasa?*  Hey, what's the matter with you? [Holes, ch. 6]

## MISCELLANEOUS

**a pesar de** in spite of · *A pesar de eso, todo ha marchado bien.* In spite of that, everything has gone well. [Holes, ch. 12]

**antes de que** before · *Será mejor que lleguemos antes de que oscurezca.* It will be better if we arrive before it gets dark. [Holes, ch. 19]

**así que** so, therefore · *¿Así que viajarán a París?* So you'll be traveling to Paris? [Home Alone, ch. 4]

**claro que...** of course ... · *¡claro que sí!* of course! · *claro que no* of course not · *Pero claro que tengo una identidad secreta.* But of course I have a secret identity. [The Incredibles, ch. 13]

**hasta que** until · *Nos prometió quedarse hasta que el viento cambiara. ¿No es verdad, Mary Poppins?* You promised us you would stay until the wind changed. Isn't that right, Mary Poppins? [Mary Poppins, ch. 21]

**hay que** it is necessary · *¡Hay que salir!* We have to leave! (*LIT* It is necessary to leave!) [The Chronicles of Narnia: The Lion, the Witch and the Wardrobe, ch. 1]

**lo que** what, that · *Nadie en Guilder sabe lo que hicimos.* Nobody in Guilder knows what we did. [The Princess Bride, ch. 5]

**para que** so that, in order to · *Hay que pagar para que no hablen en la compañía.* It's necessary to pay so that they don't talk at the company. [The Incredibles, ch. 7]

**sin embargo** however · *Sin embargo, el campeón es un hombre muy fuerte.* However, the champion is a very strong man. [Rocky III, ch. 14]

**tal vez** maybe, perhaps · *Tal vez sobrevivan.* Maybe they'll survive. [Eight Below, ch. 6]

**tener que** to have to · *Tengo que limpiar el tanque antes de que Darla llegue.* I have to clean the tank before Darla arrives. [Finding Nemo, ch. 20]

# NUMBERS

## NUMERALS

**cero** zero · *La temperatura ahora es de sesenta grados bajo cero.* The temperature now is sixty degrees below zero. [March of the Penguins, ch. 7]

**uno** one · *Uno para nosotros, uno para el buen Zeroni.* One for us, one for good old Zeroni. [Holes, ch. 24]

**dos** two · *Dos tiros.* Two shots. [Hoosiers, ch. 24]

**tres** three · *Invertimos tres años en ellos.* We invested three years in them. [Facing the Giants, ch. 2]

**cuatro** four · *Cinco niños, seis niñas, cuatro padres, dos choferes y una montaña de valijas.* Five boys, six girls, four parents, two drivers, and a mountain of suitcases. [Home Alone, ch. 6]

**cinco** five · *Cinco más.* Five more. [Facing the Giants, ch. 12]

**seis** six · *Tiene seis dedos en la mano derecha.* He has six fingers on his right hand. [The Princess Bride, ch. 13]

**siete** seven · *Setenta y dos, setenta y tres, setenta y cuatro, setenta y cinco, setenta y seis, setenta y siete...* Seventy-two, seventy-three, seventy-four, seventy-five, seventy-six, seventy-seven ... [The Chronicles of Narnia: The Lion, the Witch and the Wardrobe, ch. 3]

**ocho** eight · *Boda a las ocho treinta en punto.* Wedding at eight thirty sharp. [The Absent-Minded Professor, ch. 1]

**nueve** nine · *Aún espero nueve hoyos.* I still expect nine holes. [Holes, ch. 17]

**diez** ten · *Diez pasos más, diez más, diez más, diez más.* Ten more steps, ten more, ten more, ten more. [Facing the Giants, ch. 12]

**veinte** twenty · *Han pasado veinte años.* Twenty years have passed. [Hoosiers, ch. 2]

**treinta** thirty · *South Bend Central va a la cabeza, cuarenta – treinta y cuatro.* South Bend Central is in the lead, forty – thirty-four. [Hoosiers, ch. 30]

**cuarenta** forty · *En cuarenta años he visto a los mejores jugadores que ha tenido el estado.* In forty years I have seen the best players that this state has had. [Hoosiers, ch. 3]

**cincuenta** fifty · *Debe haber sido cincuenta.* It must have been fifty. [Facing the Giants, ch. 12]

**ciento** one hundred · *Si eso sucede se unirá a otros cientos que han muerto esperándote a ti.* If that happens, she will join hundreds of others who have died waiting for you. [Eragon, ch. 14]

**mil** thousand, one thousand · *Tres mil cuarenta y siete personas murieron en los ataques terroristas en Nueva York, Virginia y Pennsylvania.* Three thousand forty-seven people died in the terrorist attacks in New York, Virginia, and Pennsylvania. [In Memoriam, ch. 13]

**primer** first · *¿Qué tal tu primer día, Yelnats?* How was your first day, Yelnats? [Holes, ch. 6]

# CONNECTORS

## ARTICLES

**el** M the · *Es el presidente del banco, el anciano señor Dawes.* He's the president of the bank, old Mr. Dawes. [Mary Poppins, ch. 15]

**la** the · *El agua es el más preciado lujo en la faz de la tierra.* Water is the most precious luxury on the face of the earth. [Holes, ch. 14]

**las** the · *Las sábanas están duras.* The sheets are scratchy. [The Chronicles of Narnia: The Lion, the Witch and the Wardrobe, ch. 2]

**los** the · *Su fotografía aparecerá en todos los diarios.* Your photo will appear in all the daily newspapers. [Mary Poppins, ch. 11]

## INTERJECTIONS

**adelante** come in, proceed, go ahead · *Aquí Victoria, **adelante** McMurdo.* Victoria here, go ahead McMurdo. [Eight Below, ch. 4]

**adiós** good-bye · ***Adiós.*** Good-bye. [Rudy, ch. 12]

**ay** ay · *Ay, mira lo que hiciste—lo molestaste, hermano.* Ay, look what you did—you annoyed him, brother. [Facing the Giants, ch. 4]

**bravo** bravo · ***Bravo.*** Bravo. [The Absent-Minded Professor, ch. 5]

**cuidado** be careful · ***Cuidado**, los tiburones comen peces.* Be careful, sharks eat fish. [Finding Nemo, ch. 10]

**entonces** then · ***Entonces** nos vemos temprano.* Then we'll see you bright and early. [Eight Below, ch. 2]

**felicidades** congratulations · ***Felicidades**, Rudy.* Congratulations, Rudy. [Rudy, ch. 19]

**gracias** thank you, thanks · ***Gracias**, señor.* Thank you, sir. [Mary Poppins, ch. 4]

**hola** hi, hello · ***Hola**, Mamá Búho.* Hi, Mama Búho. [The Fox and the Hound, ch. 15]

## CONJUNCTIONS

**aunque** although · ***Aunque** creo que un periodo de prueba sería muy prudente.* Although I think a trial period would be very prudent. [Mary Poppins, ch. 6]

**cuando** when · *Vendrá **cuando** esté listo, no antes.* He'll come when he's ready, not before. [Hoosiers, ch. 10]

**e** and [used instead of *y* when the following word begins with *i* or *hi*] · *Fezzik **e** Inigo se reunieron.* Fezzik and Inigo met up. [The Princess Bride, ch. 18]

**mientras** while · *¿Y es por eso que trataron de matarme **mientras** dormía?* And that's why you tried to kill me while I was sleeping? [Anne of Green Gables, ch. 14]

**ni** neither, nor · *Pero, sabes muy bien que **ni** a la señora Brougham **ni** a mí nos gustan los postres elaborados.* But you know very well that neither Mrs. Brougham nor I like fancy desserts. [The Bishop's Wife, ch. 8]

**o** or · *No podemos dejar que correteen solos en los tejados, ¿**o** sí?* We can't allow them to run alone over the rooftops, or can we? [Mary Poppins, ch. 17]

**pero** but · *Lo que muchos hombres están buscando está frente a su nariz, **pero** para algunos lo desconocido es difícil de resistir.* What many men are searching for is right in front of their nose, but for some the unknown is hard to resist. [Eragon, ch. 3]

**porque** because · *Dan, tenemos un programa débil **porque** hay un entrenador débil.* Dan, we have a weak program because there is a weak coach. [Facing the Giants, ch. 8]

**pues** well · ***Pues** te diré una cosa, Mary Poppins.* Well, I'll tell you one thing, Mary Poppins. [Mary Poppins, ch. 23]

**que** that, than · *¿Crees **que** es divertido?* Do you think that it's fun? [Holes, ch. 2]

**si** if · *No sé **si** me gustará eso.* I don't know if I will like that. [The Fox and the Hound, ch. 20]

**u** or [used instead of *o* when the following word begins with *o* or *ho*] · *En pocas semanas, de una forma **u** otra, la mayoría de los animales encuentran a quien estaban buscando.* Within a few weeks, one way or another, the majority of the animals find whom they were looking for. [March of the Penguins, ch. 4]

**y** and · *Cuando lleguen a la fosa, naden a través **y** no sobre ella.* When you arrive at the trench, swim through and not over it. [Finding Nemo, ch. 13]

## PREPOSITIONS

**a** at, to · *Estoy seguro de que llegar **a** las finales está más allá de sus sueños, así que no hablemos de eso.* I'm sure that making it to the finals is the furthest thing from your dreams, so let's not even talk about that. [Hoosiers, ch. 23]

**al** [a + el] to the, at the · *Mejor leer en donde van **al** pantano.* Better to read where they go to the swamp. [The Princess Bride, ch. 10]

**bajo** under · *Quiero los extremos ahí en cada lugar, en cada juego, pero **bajo** control.* I want the ends there in each place, in each play, but under control. [Rudy, ch. 1]

**como** like, how · *Peleas **como** cabra loca.* You fight like a crazy goat. [Eragon, ch. 3]

**con** with, to · *Negocia **con** tu cuerpo—que te dé más fuerza.* Negotiate with your body—to give you more strength. [Facing the Giants, ch. 12]

**contra** against · *Hoy jugaremos **contra** Verdi.* Today we'll play against Verdi. [Hoosiers, ch. 15]

**de** of, from · *Por favor, quiero comprar un lindo ramo **de** flores para mi esposa.* Please, I'd like to buy a pretty bouquet of flowers for my wife. [Facing the Giants, ch. 18]

**del** [de + el] of the, from the · *Bueno, algo que he entendido es que no importa cuanto trate, nunca pasaré **del** equipo de entrenamiento.* Well, something that I have understood is that it doesn't matter how much I try, I will never get off of the training squad. [Rudy, ch. 22]

**desde** from, since · *¿Y qué ha hecho **desde** entonces?* And what have you done since then? [Hoosiers, ch. 4]

**durante** during, for · *Fue a su habitación y cerró la puerta, y **durante** días no durmió ni comió.* She went to her room and closed the door, and for days she neither slept nor ate. [The Princess Bride, ch. 2]

**en** in, at, on · *Ha nadado cientos de metros en la oscuridad.* He's swum hundreds of meters in the dark. [Finding Nemo, ch. 17]

**entre** between · *Hay una gran diferencia entre estar casi muerto y totalmente muerto.* There is a big difference between being almost dead and totally dead. [The Princess Bride, ch. 21]

**hacia** toward · *Ese es un sendero propio para viajar hacia grandes aventuras.* That is a path just right for traveling toward great adventures. [Mary Poppins, ch. 8]

**hasta** until, up to · *Algún día llegaré hasta cinco, pero no sé qué tanto daño te causaría.* Someday I will get up to five, but I don't know how much damage that would cause you. [The Princess Bride, ch. 17]

**para** for · *Entrenador, esto es para Rudy.* Coach, this is for Rudy. [Rudy, ch. 25]

**por** for, by · *Ve por agua.* Go for water. [Holes, ch. 6]

**sin** without · *No sabría qué hacer sin usted.* I wouldn't know what to do without you. [The Absent-Minded Professor, ch. 1]

**sobre** over, about · *Llama por radio a Katie y que te informe sobre la tormenta, Doc.* Call Katie on the radio to get a report about the storm, Doc. [Eight Below, ch. 5]

## COGNATES
### Nouns
FAMILY AND FRIENDS

**bebé** NM baby · *¿Todavía quieres tener un bebé?* Do you still want to have a baby? [Facing the Giants, ch. 4]

**esposo/esposa** husband/wife, spouse · *Eres peor que mi esposo cuando se baña.* You are worse than my husband when he takes a bath. [The Chronicles of Narnia: The Lion, the Witch and the Wardrobe, ch. 11]

**familia** family · *Mi familia fue asesinada por los hombres del rey cuando era pequeño.* My family was killed by the king's men when I was a little boy. [Eragon, ch. 17]

**mamá** mom, mama, mother · *Sí, mi mamá dejará el trago y mi padre regresará pronto.* Yeah, my mom will stop drinking and my dad will come back any time now. [Holes, ch. 19]

**papá** NM dad, papa, father · *Papá, tal vez en la escuela vea un tiburón.* Dad, maybe at school I'll see a shark. [Finding Nemo, ch. 3]

**persona** person · *Parece que esa persona no te ha pedido que bailes con él.* It looks like that person has not asked you to dance with him. [Anne of Green Gables, ch. 14]

JOBS AND ROLES

**almirante** NM admiral · *Este imponente edificio que ven ustedes ahora es el hogar del almirante Boom, retirado de la marina real.* This imposing building that you all see now is the home of Admiral Boom, retired from the Royal Navy. [Mary Poppins, ch. 2]

**ángel** NM angel · *¿Cómo supo David que era un ángel?* How did David know that it was an angel? [The Bishop's Wife, ch. 9]

**campeón** NM champion · *Eres el campeón.* You are the champion. [Rocky III, ch. 14]

**capitán** NM captain · *El capitán hace todo lo que puede, pero su teléfono sigue averiado.* The captain is doing everything that he can, but your telephone is still out of order. [Home Alone, ch. 8]

**comandante** NMF commander · *Disculpe, Comandante.* Excuse me, Commander. [Eight Below, ch. 6]

**defensa** defense, defensive player [SPORTS] · *Logra evadir la defensa y continúa.* He manages to avoid the defense and he keeps going. [Facing the Giants, ch. 23]

**doctor/doctora** doctor · *Doctora Rosemary Paris, coordinadora.* Doctor Rosemary Paris, coordinator. [Eight Below, ch. 2]

**enemigo/enemiga** enemy · *¿Eres el tipo de hombre que pondría veneno en su propia copa o en la de su enemigo?* Are you the kind of man who would put poison in his own cup or in that of his enemy? [The Princess Bride, ch. 9]

**general** NMF general [ARMED FORCES] · *General, prepare sus tropas para la batalla.* General, prepare your troops for the battle. [The Chronicles of Narnia: The Lion, the Witch and the Wardrobe, ch. 17]

**jefe** NMF boss, chief, manager · *Al jefe de bomberos.* To the fire chief. [In Memoriam, ch. 9]

**líder** NMF leader · *Se elije a un líder por su corazón.* A leader is chosen for his heart. [Eragon, ch. 20]

**oficial** NMF official, officer · *Bueno, hasta pronto, oficial.* Well, see you later, officer. [The Absent-Minded Professor, ch. 6]

**policía** NMF policeman, policewoman · *policía* police force · *Enviarán a un policía a la casa a ver a Kevin.* They will send a policeman to the house to see Kevin. [Home Alone, ch. 9]

**presidente** NMF president · *Puedo asegurarle, señor, que el presidente está muy interesado en cualquier desarrollo que tenga que ver con nuestra prosperidad nacional.* I can assure you, sir, that the president is very interested in any development that has to do with our national prosperity. [The Absent-Minded Professor, ch. 7]

**profesor/profesora** professor, teacher · *Ah, profesor, usted está aquí para buscar gorilas, no para seguir una fantasía infantil.* Ah, professor, you are here to look for gorillas, not to chase a childhood fantasy. [Tarzan, ch. 22]

## PLACES AND THINGS

**auto** auto, car · *¿Auto? ¿Qué le pasó al auto?* Car? What happened to the car? [The Incredibles, ch. 5]

**balón** *NM* ball · *Ahora envía el balón entre esos postes.* Now send the ball between those posts. [Facing the Giants, ch. 14]

**chocolate** *NM* chocolate · *Descuide, señora Macready, habrá alguna explicación, pero primero creo que ella necesita una taza de chocolate.* Don't worry, Mrs. Macready, there must be some explanation, but first I believe that she needs a cup of hot chocolate. [The Chronicles of Narnia: The Lion, the Witch and the Wardrobe, ch. 7]

**dólar** *NM* dollar · *¿Un dólar ochenta y cinco por un triste arbusto anémico?* A dollar eighty-five for a sad, anemic shrub? [The Bishop's Wife, ch. 2]

**escuela** school · *Canté en el coro de mi escuela.* I sang in my school choir. [Rudy, ch. 14]

**forma** form · *¿De cuál forma?* In what way? [Rudy, ch. 12]

**frente** *NM* front · *Si le va a acercar a los perros, debe ser por el frente siempre.* If you're going to approach the dogs, it must always be from the front. [Eight Below, ch. 3]

**grupo** group · *¿Hablas del grupo de música country?* Are you talking about the country music group? [Facing the Giants, ch. 19]

**habitación** bedroom, room · *Revisa la habitación.* Check the bedroom. [Holes, ch. 1]

**línea** line · *Los llevé hasta la línea.* I took them to the line. [Hoosiers, ch. 27]

**proyecto** project · *Este proyecto ha confiscado completamente mi vida, cariño.* This project has completely taken over my life, darling. [The Incredibles, ch. 14]

**punto** period, dot, point, spot [PLACE] · *Nadie huye de este punto.* Nobody escapes from this spot. [Eragon, ch. 19]

**tren** train · *¿Viene a tiempo el tren de la tarde?* Is the afternoon train on time? [Anne of Green Gables, ch. 3]

**universidad** university · *El profesor y yo nos conocemos de la universidad de Viena.* The professor and I know each other from the University of Vienna. [The Bishop's Wife, ch. 6]

## THOUGHTS AND FEELINGS

**deseo** desire · *Es mi deseo que limpies el bosque antes de mi matrimonio.* It is my desire that you clear the forest before my wedding. [The Princess Bride, ch. 17]

**duda** doubt · *No hay duda de que perdimos a muchos policías y bomberos.* There is no doubt that we lost many police officers and firefighters. [In Memoriam, ch. 5]

**felicidad** happiness, joy · *Tiene usted pasaje para viajar, qué felicidad.* You have a ticket for travel, what joy. [Home Alone, ch. 13]

**historia** history, story · *Esta noche quiero contarles la historia de la calceta vacía.* Tonight I want to tell you the story of the empty stocking. [The Bishop's Wife, ch. 12]

**idea** idea · *Oigan, tengo una gran idea.* Listen, I have a great idea. [The Fox and the Hound, ch. 2]

**opinión** opinion · *cambiar de opinión* to change one's mind · *¿Alguien ha cambiado de opinión?* Has anyone changed his mind? [Rudy, ch. 20]

**oportunidad** opportunity · *Primero, quiero darle las gracias por la oportunidad de estar en el equipo.* First, I want to thank you for the opportunity to be on the team. [Rudy, ch. 22]

**perdón** *NM* pardon, forgiveness · *Siempre he dicho, es mejor pedir perdón que permiso.* I've always said, it's better to ask for forgiveness than for permission. [Eragon, ch. 6]

**problema** *NM* problem · *¿Cuál es el problema?* What is the problem? [Eragon, ch. 6]

**razón** *NF* reason · *tener razón* to be right · *Jerry, tiene razón.* Jerry, he's right. [Eight Below, ch. 5]

**realidad** reality · *en realidad* really, in reality · *En realidad no quieres contarme, ¿eh?* You really don't want to tell me, eh? [Holes, ch. 10]

## TIME AND NUMBERS

**día** *NM* day · *Llegó el día de la boda.* The day of the wedding arrived. [The Princess Bride, ch. 18]

**hora** hour, time · *Ya es hora.* It's time. [Rocky III, ch. 14]

**minuto** minute · *No tenemos un minuto.* We don't have a minute. [The Chronicles of Narnia: The Lion, the Witch and the Wardrobe, ch. 12]

**momento** moment · *En este momento parece que la casa está vacía.* At this moment, it appears that the house is empty. [Home Alone, ch. 12]

**número** number · *Bloquea el número cuarenta y uno en la línea.* Block number forty-one at the baseline. [Hoosiers, ch. 23]

**par** *NM* pair, couple · *En un par de días seremos padres!* In a couple of days, we'll be parents! [Finding Nemo, ch. 1]

## MISCELLANEOUS

**ataque** *NM* attack · *Y en ese momento concluimos que obviamente era un ataque terrorista.* And at that moment we concluded that obviously it was a terrorist attack. [In Memoriam, ch. 4]

**atención** attention · *poner atención* to pay attention · *Pongan atención.* Pay attention. [Anne of Green Gables, ch. 12]

**caso** case, attention · *No me hagas mucho* **caso.** Don't pay much attention to me. [The Chronicles of Narnia: The Lion, the Witch and the Wardrobe, ch. 14]

**clase** NF class, type, kind · *Jimmy, no te vi en la* **clase** *hoy.* Jimmy, I didn't see you in class today. [Hoosiers, ch. 7]

**color** NM color · *¿De qué* **color** *tenía la panza?* What color was the belly? [Holes, ch. 7]

**compañía** company · *La* **compañía** *quiere que vaya a una conferencia.* The company wants me to go to a conference. [The Incredibles, ch. 8]

**estado** state · *En cuarenta años he visto a los mejores jugadores que ha tenido el* **estado.** In forty years I have seen the best players that the state has had. [Hoosiers, ch. 3]

**favor** NM favor · *Que me haga el* **favor** *de explicar todo esto.* Do me the favor of explaining all this. [Mary Poppins, ch. 19]

**fiesta** party · *Oye, las* **fiestas** *son buenas y divertidas, pero no podemos.* Listen, parties are good and fun, but we can't. [Finding Nemo, ch. 8]

**orden** NM order · *en* **orden** all right · *¿Todo en* **orden?** Is everything all right? [Facing the Giants, ch. 5]

**parte** NF part · *Forman* **parte** *del comité de la catedral.* They make up part of the cathedral committee. [The Bishop's Wife, ch. 6]

**silencio** silence · *Cuando te retiras hay* **silencio.** When you retire, there is silence. [Rocky III, ch. 9]

## Verbs

### -ar CONJUGATION · GENERAL ACTIVITIES

**atacar** to attack · *Primero oriéntense antes de* **atacar.** First, get yourselves set before attacking. [Hoosiers, ch. 10]

**atrapar** to trap · *La bruja quiere* **atrapar** *a los cuatro.* The witch wants to trap all four. [The Chronicles of Narnia: The Lion, the Witch and the Wardrobe, ch. 10]

**avanzar** to advance, to move forward · *Sigue* **avanzando.** Keep moving forward. [Facing the Giants, ch. 12]

**comenzar** to commence, to begin, to start · *Sólo quiero saber cuando* **comenzaremos.** I just want to know when we are going to start. [Hoosiers, ch. 5]

**contar** to count, to tell · *Ustedes me* **contaron** *que amasó una fortuna en la bolsa.* You told me that he amassed a fortune in the stock market. [Holes, ch. 4]

**encontrar** to find · *Pero angosta es la entrada y estrecho el camino que guía a la vida, y tú lo puedes* **encontrar.** But narrow is the gate and straight is the way that leads to life, and you can find it. [Facing the Giants, ch. 14]

**entrar** to enter, to get in, to go in · *Harry, voy a* **entrar.** Harry, I'm going in. [Home Alone, ch. 18]

**explicar** to explain · *No puedo* **explicar** *eso.* I can't explain that. [Hoosiers, ch. 25]

**funcionar** to function, to work, to run · *Ah, usted sabe como suenan los Modelos T. Algunas veces podría jurar que* **funcionan** *sin válvulas.* Ah, you know how these Model Ts sound. Sometimes you'd swear that they run without valves. [The Absent-Minded Professor, ch. 6]

**presentar** to present, to introduce · *¿La* **presentaron** *con el primer ministro?* Did they introduce you to the prime minister? [Anne of Green Gables, ch. 2]

**retirarse** to retire · *No puedo* **retirarme** *ahora, Mick.* I can't retire now, Mick. [Rocky III, ch. 5]

**robar** to rob, to steal · *¡Tu zorro ladrón fue a* **robar** *mis gallinas!* Your thieving fox went to steal my hens! [The Fox and the Hound, ch. 8]

**salvar** to save · *Kerchak, lo he* **salvado** *de Sabor.* Kerchak, I have saved him from Sabor. [Tarzan, ch. 4]

**terminar** to finish · *Las* **terminé** *tan pronto que fue como un milagro.* I finished them so fast that it was like a miracle. [The Bishop's Wife, ch. 6]

**usar** to use · *Y hay otros más que de* **usarlos** *antes de estar listo te aniquilarán.* And there are others that if you use them before you are ready, they will kill you. [Eragon, ch. 11]

### -ar CONJUGATION · THOUGHTS AND FEELINGS

**aceptar** to accept · *Ahora que si eso me da a ganar unos dólares extra es algo que tienes que aprender a* **aceptar.** Now if that lets me win a few extra dollars, that's something that you have to learn to accept. [The Absent-Minded Professor, ch. 4]

**desear** to desire · *Su aspecto deja mucho que* **desear.** Her appearance leaves much to be desired. [Anne of Green Gables, ch. 5]

**dudar** to doubt · **Dudo** *que las anguilas asesinas le hagan una oferta como ésta.* I doubt that the killer eels will make you an offer like this. [The Princess Bride, ch. 5]

**estudiar** to study · *¿No ha hecho nada más que* **estudiar** *esgrima?* You haven't done anything but study sword fighting? [The Princess Bride, ch. 7]

**imaginar** to imagine · *No quiero* **imaginar** *el daño que ya sufrió el tejido.* I don't want to imagine the damage that's been done to the tissue. [Eight Below, ch. 5]

**importar** to be important to, to matter to, to concern · *No te metas en lo que no te* **importa.** Don't get involved in matters that don't concern you. [Rudy, ch. 5]

**molestar** to bother · *Cletus, lamento tener que* **molestarte,** *pero ¿podrías hacerme un favor?* Cletus, I'm sorry to have to bother you, but would you do me a favor? [Hoosiers, ch. 6]

**ocupar** to occupy, to take care of · *Nos **ocupamos** de todo, créeme.* We took care of everything, believe me. [Home Alone, ch. 8]

**ordenar** to order, to command · *Como **ordene**.* As you wish. (LIT As you command.) [The Princess Bride, ch. 10]

**perdonar** to pardon, to forgive · *Considero que debo **perdonar** a Diana y permitir que tome sus lecciones de piano.* I think I ought to forgive Diana and let her take her piano lessons. [Anne of Green Gables, ch. 14]

**preparar** to prepare · *Pues más vale que lo sean porque Aslan está **preparando** sus tropas.* Well you'd better be, because Aslan is preparing his troops. [The Chronicles of Narnia: The Lion, the Witch and the Wardrobe, ch. 9]

**significar** to mean, to signify · *Olvidaste lo que **significa** ser jinete.* You've forgotten what it means to be a rider. [Eragon, ch. 14]

## -er CONJUGATION

**aparecer** to appear · *En la excavación de Cavernícola **apareció** algo.* Something appeared in Caveman's excavation. [Holes, ch. 15]

**comprender** to comprehend, to understand · *Tú me **comprendes**, Henry.* You understand me, Henry. [The Bishop's Wife, ch. 4]

**detener** to detain, to arrest, to stop · *Algunas veces pienso que pude **detener** mi puño para no lastimar a ese muchacho.* Sometimes I think that I could stop my fist so as not to hurt that kid. [Hoosiers, ch. 25]

**mantener** to maintain, to stay · *¿Cómo se han **mantenido** de pié?* How have they stayed on their feet? [Rocky III, ch. 1]

**mover** to move · *moverse* to move oneself · *No **te muevas**, voy a curarte.* Don't move, I'm going to fix you up. [Eight Below, ch. 5]

**ofrecer** to offer · *Anne Shirley, ¿qué le **ofreciste** de tomar a mi Diana?* Anne Shirley, what did you offer my Diana to drink? [Anne of Green Gables, ch. 11]

**prometer** to promise · *Le **prometí** a la señorita Stacy que no lo haría para que los nervios no me traicionaran.* I promised Miss Stacy that I wouldn't do it so that my nerves don't betray me. [Anne of Green Gables, ch. 15]

**suponer** to suppose · *Si Lucy no miente y no está loca, entonces debemos **suponer** que dice la verdad.* If Lucy doesn't lie and isn't crazy, then we must suppose that she's telling the truth. [The Chronicles of Narnia: The Lion, the Witch and the Wardrobe, ch. 7]

## -ir CONJUGATION

**cumplir** to complete, to accomplish · *Amigos, él tiene un trabajo que **cumplir**.* Friends, he has a job to complete. [Hoosiers, ch. 5]

**dirigir** to direct, to guide · *Va a **dirigir** el trineo.* You are going to guide the sled. [Eight Below, ch. 3]

**existir** to exist · *Peter, **existe** una gran magia más poderosa que cualquiera de nosotros y que rige sobre toda Narnia.* Peter, there exists a great magic more powerful than any of us, and it reigns over all Narnia. [The Chronicles of Narnia: The Lion, the Witch and the Wardrobe, ch. 14]

**ocurrir** to occur, to happen, to be going on · *No sé donde estoy, no sé qué **ocurre**.* I don't know where I am, I don't know what's going on. [Finding Nemo, ch. 27]

**permitir** to permit, to allow · *Michael, no **permitiré** que derroches tu dinero.* Michael, I will not allow you to squander your money. [Mary Poppins, ch. 15]

**preferir** to prefer · ***Prefiero** morir en la brega.* I prefer to die working. [Anne of Green Gables, ch. 19]

**recibir** to receive · *El profesor Kirke no está acostumbrado a **recibir** niños en su casa.* Professor Kirke is not accustomed to receiving children in his house. [The Chronicles of Narnia: The Lion, the Witch and the Wardrobe, ch. 2]

**referirse** to refer, to mean · *Nadie y **me refiero** a nadie viene a nuestra casa y nos pone en ridículo.* Nobody, and I mean nobody, comes to our house and makes fools of us. [Rudy, ch. 25]

**servir** to serve, to work, to help, to be useful to · *¿Cómo puede **servirle** esto a un granjero?* How can this be useful to a farmer? [The Absent-Minded Professor, ch. 7]

**unir** to unite, to join, to come together · ***Únanse** todos.* Come together, everyone. [Rudy, ch. 1]

## Adjectives and Adverbs
### THOUGHTS AND FEELINGS

**amable** kind · *Es usted muy **amable**.* You are very kind. [The Bishop's Wife, ch. 2]

**cierto** certain, true · *¿Es **cierto** que ya no estás cavando?* Is it true that you aren't digging any more? [Holes, ch. 16]

**especial** special · *¿Acaso es muy **especial**?* Are you saying he's something special? [The Bishop's Wife, ch. 6]

**extraño** strange · *Hay algo **extraño**.* There's something strange. [The Bishop's Wife, ch. 14]

**feliz** happy · *Y, Profesor, le deseo una **feliz** luna de miel.* Professor, I wish you a happy honeymoon. [The Absent-Minded Professor, ch. 1]

**horrible** horrible · *Es una experiencia **horrible**.* It's a horrible experience. [In Memoriam, ch. 6]

**importante** important · *¿A un hombre tan **importante** y ocupado?* To a man so important and busy? [Mary Poppins, ch. 20]

**imposible** impossible · *Es **imposible**.* It's impossible. [Tarzan, ch. 8]

**increíble** incredible · *Mister **Increíble**.*
Mr. Incredible. [The Incredibles, ch. 1]

**justo** fair, just · *No será **justo** para ti, anciano.*
This won't be fair to you, old man. [Eragon, ch. 9]

**maravilloso** marvelous, wonderful · *Ah, esto es **maravilloso**, señor Clayton.* Ah, this is wonderful, Mr. Clayton. [Tarzan, ch. 26]

**perfecto** perfect · *Zach Avery engañó a la defensa y logró un pase **perfecto**.* Zach Avery tricked the defense and made a perfect pass. [Facing the Giants, ch. 20]

**posible** possible · *Ahora debemos concentrarnos en salvar la mayor cantidad de vidas **posible**.* Now we must concentrate on saving the greatest number of lives possible. [In Memoriam, ch. 8]

**santo** holy, good, saintly · *Oh, **santo** cielo.* Oh, good heavens. [The Bishop's Wife, ch. 9]

**suficiente** sufficient, enough · *No tienes la fuerza **suficiente**.* You don't have enough strength. [Eragon, ch. 16]

MISCELLANEOUS

**final** final · *Cada uno trata de levantarse antes de la cuenta **final**.* Each one is trying to get up before the final count. [Rocky III, ch. 1]

**gran** great · *Ganamos un **gran** juego.* We won a great game. [Hoosiers, ch. 27]

**grande** large, big, great · *No es mi culpa ser el más **grande** y fuerte.* It's not my fault for being the biggest and the strongest. [The Princess Bride, ch. 8]

**igual** equal, the same, just the same · *Pide tiempo fuera, **igual** están perdidos.* Ask for time out, they are out of it just the same. [Facing the Giants, ch. 22]

**medio** half · *Cuatro metros y **medio**.* Four and a half meters. [Hoosiers, ch. 28]

**mucho** a lot, many · *Ya sé **mucho** de mi mismo.* I already know a lot about myself. [The Bishop's Wife, ch. 6]

**nuevo** new · *Es un **nuevo** baile que se llama "retar."* It's a new dance called "The Challenge." [Rocky III, ch. 11]

**rápido** fast, quick, rapid · *Corre, Rocky. **Rápido**, **rápido**, **rápido**. Muévete, **rápido**. Corre.* Run, Rocky. Fast, fast, fast. Move it, fast. Run. [Rocky III, ch. 11]

**segundo** second · *En el **segundo**.* In the second. [Rocky III, ch. 8]

**último** last, latest, ultimate · *Es la **última** vez que elegimos gol de campo.* That's the last time we choose a field goal. [Facing the Giants, ch. 25]

# NOUNS
## People
### FAMILY

**abuelo/abuela** grandfather/grandmother · *Bueno, tal vez me preocupé un poco, pero eso no es lo mismo, **abuelo**.* Well, maybe I was a little bit concerned, but that's not the same thing, Grandpa. [The Princess Bride, ch. 5]

**hermano/hermana** brother/sister · *Matthew siempre fue el mejor de los **hermanos**.* Matthew was always the best of brothers. [Anne of Green Gables, ch. 19]

**hijo/hija** son, daughter · *¿Están buscando a mi **hijo**? ¿Sabe dónde está?* Are they looking for my son? Do you know where he is? [Home Alone, ch. 11]

**madre** NF mother · *Y la **madre** de todas las ventiscas está a punto de llegar.* And the mother of all snowstorms is about to arrive. [March of the Penguins, ch. 9]

**mujer** NF woman, wife · *Y, ¿qué valor tiene—la promesa de una **mujer**?* And of what value is that—the promise of a woman? [The Princess Bride, ch. 10]

**padre** NM father · *Lo siento, **padre**. Lo intenté. Lo intenté.* I'm sorry, father. I tried. I tried. [The Princess Bride, ch. 26]

**tío/tía** uncle/aunt · *Kevin, si el **tío** Frank dice que no la veas, es que debe ser muy mala.* Kevin, if Uncle Frank says not to see it, it must be very bad. [Home Alone, ch. 1]

## ROLES AND TITLES

**amo/ama** master/mistress, owner · *El **amo** está loco de remate.* The master is completely crazy. [Mary Poppins, ch. 21]

**caballero** gentleman, knight · *Bueno, seguramente, **caballeros**, entienden este tipo de cosas.* Well, surely, gentlemen, you understand this kind of thing. [The Absent-Minded Professor, ch. 9]

**dama** lady · *Por una **dama** hermosa.* To a beautiful lady. [The Bishop's Wife, ch. 7]

**Dios** God · *Para nosotros inspiración divina no significa que **Dios** se posesiona de alguien y le dicta las escrituras.* To us divine inspiration does not mean that God takes possession of someone and dictates the scriptures. [Rudy, ch. 11]

**entrenador/entrenadora** coach · *Seguro, **entrenador**.* Sure, Coach. [Facing the Giants, ch. 28]

**jugador/jugadora** player · *Tenemos noventa y cinco **jugadores** aquí.* We have ninety-five players here. [Rudy, ch. 20]

**maestro/maestra** master, teacher · *Gilbert será **maestro** de escuela de Avonlea.* Gilbert will be the teacher at Avonlea school. [Anne of Green Gables, ch. 8]

**reina** queen · *Si puedo enseñarle a un perico a cantar "Dios Salve a la **Reina**," sin duda enseñaré a este salvaje una cosa o dos.* If I can teach a parrot to sing "God Save the Queen," I can no doubt teach this savage a thing or two. [Tarzan, ch. 22]

**rey** NM king · *Mi **rey**, Galbatorix, como temía, el dragón ha nacido.* My king, Galbatorix, as you feared, the dragon has hatched. [Eragon, ch. 5]

**señor/señora** sir, Mr. / ma'am, Mrs. · *Oh, será mejor que lo haga, **señor** Hawk.* Oh, it will be better if you do it, Mr. Hawk. [The Absent-Minded Professor, ch. 9]

**señorita** unmarried woman, Miss · *Si me quiere hacer el favor, **señorita** Cassaway, aquí tiene el manuscrito de mi sermón de navidad.* If you would do me the favor, Miss Cassaway, here is the manuscript of my Christmas sermon. [The Bishop's Wife, ch. 11]

### MISCELLANEOUS

**amigo/amiga** friend · *¿Mi **amigo** Toby va a ser mi enemigo?* My friend Toby is going to be my enemy? [The Fox and the Hound, ch. 10]

**chico/chica** boy/girl · *Buena **chica**.* Good girl. [Eight Below, ch. 5]

**gente** NF people · *Y había **gente** joven en ellos.* And there were young people in them. [In Memoriam, ch. 1]

**hombre** NM man · *Sólo porque un **hombre** de traje rojo te dio una espada no significa que seas un héroe.* Just because a man in a red suit gave you a sword doesn't mean that you are a hero. [The Chronicles of Narnia: The Lion, the Witch and the Wardrobe, ch. 13]

**joven** NMF young man, young woman · *No sé lo que siente una **joven** desde hace cuarenta y siete años y prefiero olvidarlo.* I haven't known what a young woman feels for forty-seven years and I prefer to forget it. [Anne of Green Gables, ch. 14]

**muchacho/muchacha** boy/girl, child, kid · *Disculpe, estos buenos **muchachos** han trabajado duro.* Excuse me, these good boys have worked hard. [Holes, ch. 11]

**niño/niña** boy/girl, child · *Amo a mi **niña**, muy orgulloso de ti.* I love my girl, very proud of you. [Anne of Green Gables, ch. 19]

## Places and Things
### NATURE AND THE OUTDOORS

**agua** water · *Naturalmente, después de su larga marcha, están ansiosas por volver al **agua**, algunas veces demasiado ansiosas.* Naturally, after their long march, they are anxious to return to the water, sometimes too anxious. [March of the Penguins, ch. 8]

**árbol** NM tree · *Todos juntos en un gran **árbol**.* All together in a big tree. [Tarzan, ch. 20]

**calle** NF street · *En sólo una **calle**, cinco familias no están.* On just one street, five families are gone. [Home Alone, ch. 8]

**camino** road, path · *No sabemos con certeza como encuentran su **camino**.* We don't know with any certainty how they find their path. [March of the Penguins, ch. 2]

**campo** country, field · *Tenemos que buscar el gol de **campo**.* We have to go for a field goal. [Facing the Giants, ch. 26]

**cielo** sky, heaven · *¡**Cielos**!* Heavens! [The Fox and the Hound, ch. 7]

**fuego** fire · *Detengan el **fuego**.* Hold your fire. [The Absent-Minded Professor, ch. 12]

**lugar** NM place · *Porque en este **lugar** ya no es el mismo ídolo que era en la preparatoria.* Because in this place he's no longer the same idol he was in high school. [Rudy, ch. 6]

**luz** NF light · *En pocas semanas, los días comienzan a transcurrir prácticamente sin **luz** alguna.* In a few weeks, the days start to go by with practically no light at all. [March of the Penguins, ch. 5]

**mar** NM sea · *El pingüino emperador es técnicamente un ave, aunque viva en el **mar**.* The emperor penguin is technically a bird, although he lives in the sea. [March of the Penguins, ch. 2]

**mundo** world · *El **mundo** perdió un joven y brillante compositor cuando murió.* The world lost a young and brilliant composer when he died. [The Bishop's Wife, ch. 13]

**sol** NM sun · *Al igual que sucede con el **sol**, los polluelos son mas fuertes cada día.* Just like what happens with the sun, the chicks are stronger each day. [The March of the Penguins, ch. 13]

**tierra** earth, land, soil, dirt · *Bienvenido al fondo de la **tierra**, Doc.* Welcome to the bottom of the earth, Doc. [Eight Below, ch. 2]

### HOUSE AND HOME

**cabeza** head · *Tengo que contar **cabezas**.* I have to count heads. [Home Alone, ch. 6]

**cama** bed · *Vamos afuera a preparar sus **camas**.* We're going outside to make your beds. [Eight Below, ch. 2]

**casa** house · *No quiero que recorras la **casa** vanagloriándote como un pavo real.* I don't want you running through the house strutting like a peacock. [Anne of Green Gables, ch. 14]

**corazón** NM heart · *Su **corazón** no responde como antes.* His heart is not responding like before. [Anne of Green Gables, ch. 3]

**cuarto** room · *Hay goteras en el **cuarto** de servicio.* There are leaks in the back room. [Facing the Giants, ch. 2]

**gato** cat · *¡Ven **gatito**, gatito! ¿Quieres tu comida?* Here kitty, kitty! Do you want your food? [The Chronicles of Narnia: The Lion, the Witch and the Wardrobe, ch. 17]

**juego** game [SPORTS] · *Ustedes regalaron el **juego**.* You gave the game away. [Facing the Giants, ch. 6]

**juguete** *NM* toy · *Son herramientas, no juguetes.* They are tools, not toys. [The Chronicles of Narnia: The Lion, the Witch and the Wardrobe, ch. 12]

**libro** book · *Es el libro que mi padre solía leerme cuando estaba enfermo.* It's the book that my father used to read me when I was sick. [The Princess Bride, ch. 1]

**mano** *NF* hand · *Creed con su mano izquierda.* Creed with his left hand. [Rocky III, ch. 1]

**ojo** eye · *Cierra los ojos y cuenta.* Close your eyes and count. [The Fox and the Hound, ch. 6]

**perro** dog · *Son perros fuertes.* They are strong dogs. [Eight Below, ch. 6]

**pié** *NM* foot · *Para mis fanáticos soy dulces pies, pero mi esposa me decía el... pie oloroso.* To my fans I'm Sweetfeet, but my wife called me ... Stinky Foot. [Holes, ch. 24]

**puerta** door, gate · *Las derrotas de Increíble en la corte cuesta millones al gobierno y abren las puertas a docenas de demandas a superhéroes en todo el mundo.* Incredible's defeats in court cost the government millions and open the gates for dozens of lawsuits against superheroes everywhere. [The Incredibles, ch. 2]

**regalo** gift, present · *Bueno, con Princeton Heights descalificado, esto es un regalo navideño adelantado para Shiloh.* Well, with Princeton Heights disqualified, this is an early Christmas present for Shiloh. [Facing the Giants, ch. 20]

**traje** *NM* suit · *Necesitas otro traje.* You need another suit. [The Incredibles, ch. 10]

**vino** wine · *El vino debe beberse lentamente y no vaso tras vaso.* Wine should be drunk slowly, and not glass after glass. [Anne of Green Gables, ch. 11]

MISCELLANEOUS

**avión** *NM* airplane · *La situación es que dos aviones atacaron al parecer.* The situation is that apparently two planes attacked. [In Memoriam, ch. 2]

**barco** boat, ship · *Pronto será sólo un recuerdo porque el barco de Roberts,* Venganza, *está anclado al otro lado.* Soon it will be only a memory, because Roberts' ship, the *Vengeance,* is anchored on the other side. [The Princess Bride, ch. 11]

**cambio** change, variation, change [MONEY] · *Tal vez podría hacer un cambio gradual.* Maybe we could make a gradual change. [Hoosiers, ch. 5]

**ciudad** city · *Un objeto volador no identificado está sobre la ciudad.* An unidentified flying object is over the city. [The Absent-Minded Professor, ch. 12]

**cosa** thing · *Mucha gente donaba cosas viejas para el refugio de los indigentes.* Many people donated old things to the homeless shelter. [Holes, ch. 21]

**cuenta** bill, count · *Pero cuando Cleopatra visitó Roma, se supone que las cien monedas se usaron para pagar la cuenta de hotel.* But when Cleopatra visited Rome, it is supposed that the one hundred coins were used to pay the hotel bill. [The Bishop's Wife, ch. 7]

**dinero** money · *A ver, joven, déme hasta el último centavo de mi dinero.* Let's see, young man, give me up to the last penny of my money. [Mary Poppins, ch. 16]

**equipo** team · *Me propuse ayudar al equipo de cualquier forma que me fuera posible, pero no me aceptarán porque no estudio aquí.* I set out to help the team in any way possible, but they won't accept me because I don't study here. [Rudy, ch. 13]

**país** *NM* country, nation · *Es un país libre.* It's a free country. [Rocky III, ch. 10]

**pueblo** town, townspeople, people · *Amado pueblo ... la Princesa Buttercup.* Beloved people ... the Princess Buttercup. [The Princess Bride, ch. 3]

## Abstract Nouns

TIME

**año** year · *Quiere por favor decirle que en vez de obsequios este año, sólo quiero recuperar a mi familia.* Will you please tell him that instead of gifts this year, I just want to have my family back. [Home Alone, ch. 14]

**fin** *NM* end · *Hasta el fin.* Until the end. [The Chronicles of Narnia: The Lion, the Witch and the Wardrobe, ch. 19]

**mañana** morning · *Saldremos de la casa a las ocho de la mañana en punto.* We will leave the house at eight o'clock in the morning on the dot. [Home Alone, ch. 4]

**mes** *NM* month · *Oye, si me hubieras dicho hace dos meses que jugaríamos contra Princeton Heights en los play-offs no te lo hubiera creído.* Listen, if you had told me two months ago that we would be playing against Princeton Heights in the play-offs, I wouldn't have believed you. [Facing the Giants, ch. 19]

**navidad** Christmas · *¡Feliz navidad!* Merry Christmas! [The Chronicles of Narnia: The Lion, the Witch and the Wardrobe, ch. 12]

**noche** *NF* night · *Las lunas vienen y se van en la noche que pronto será interminable.* The moons come and go in the night that soon will be endless. [The March of the Penguins, ch. 5]

**pasado** past · *No volteo al pasado, nene, me distrae del ahora.* I don't look to the past, darling, it distracts from the now. [The Incredibles, ch. 10]

**prisa** hurry · *Date prisa, Anne, ¿acaso piensas que el tren va a esperarte?* Hurry up, Anne, do you think the train is going to wait for you? [Anne of Green Gables, ch. 18]

**semana** week · *En pocas **semanas**, los días comienzan a transcurrir prácticamente sin luz alguna.* In a few weeks, the days will begin to pass with practically no light at all. [March of the Penguins, ch. 5]

**tarde** NF afternoon · *Ha estado trabajando toda la **tarde**.* You have been working all afternoon. [The Absent-Minded Professor, ch. 1]

**tiempo** time, season, weather · *Banks, no me sorprendería que usted navegara hacia un mal **tiempo** ahora.* Banks, it wouldn't surprise me if you were heading for some foul weather today. [Mary Poppins, ch. 3]

**vez** NF time · *Esta **vez** no escapará.* This time he won't escape. [The Fox and the Hound, ch. 5]

### THOUGHTS AND FEELINGS

**amor** NM love · *Su verdadero **amor** se casa con otro esta noche así que por eso sufre tanto.* His true love is marrying another tonight, so that's why he is suffering so much. [The Princess Bride, ch. 19]

**ayuda** help · *Necesito su **ayuda**.* I need your help. [Hoosiers, ch. 16]

**culpa** blame, fault · *Claro que fue tu **culpa**.* Of course it was your fault. [The Fox and the Hound, ch. 5]

**deber** NM duty · *Tu **deber** es llegar a los varden con vida.* Your duty is to get to the Varden alive. [Eragon, ch. 13]

**fuerza** strength · *Es el Señor. Siento su **fuerza**.* It's the Lord. I feel His strength. [Hoosiers, ch. 23]

**gusto** pleasure · *Si tiene que ir a Chicago, con **gusto** la llevaremos.* If you have to go to Chicago, we'll take you there, with pleasure. [Home Alone, ch. 13]

**miedo** fear · *¿Estás diciendo que no te interesa? O, ¿te gustaría intentarlo pero tienes **miedo**?* Are you saying you are not interested, or you would like to try it, but you are afraid? [Facing the Giants, ch. 5]

**placer** NM pleasure · *Con **placer** y gran sentido del deber cumplido, los declaro marido y mujer.* With pleasure and a great sense of accomplishment, I pronounce you husband and wife. [The Absent-Minded Professor, ch. 12]

**suerte** NF luck · *Le deseo **suerte**.* I wish you luck. [Anne of Green Gables, ch. 19]

### MISCELLANEOUS

**acuerdo** agreement · *Es un **acuerdo**.* It's an agreement. [Holes, ch. 16]

**derecho** right · *Nuestros **derechos** hay que defender.* It's necessary to defend our rights. [Mary Poppins, ch. 2]

**falta** miss, lack · *La **falta** de disciplina es escandalosa.* The lack of discipline is scandalous. [Anne of Green Gables, ch. 9]

**frío** cold · *Oh, el **frío** no me afecta mucho.* Oh, the cold doesn't affect me much. [The Bishop's Wife, ch. 5]

**guerra** war · *Mamá nos alejó de una **guerra** y ahora estamos en otra.* Mom moved us away from one war, and now we're in another. [The Chronicles of Narnia: The Lion, the Witch and the Wardrobe, ch. 9]

**izquierda** left · *En la siguiente calle, dé vuelta a la **izquierda** hacia la carretera nueve.* At the next street, turn left toward Highway 9. [The Absent-Minded Professor, ch. 9]

**lado** side, place · *Las ventanas del **lado** oeste del edificio habían estallado.* The windows on the west side of the building had shattered. [In Memoriam, ch. 4]

**ley** NF law · *Entonces sabes ya que todo traidor por **ley** es mío.* Then you know already that every traitor by law is mine. [The Chronicles of Narnia: The Lion, the Witch and the Wardrobe, ch. 16]

**modo** manner, way, custom · *No hay **modo** de bajar.* There's no way to get down. [Mary Poppins, ch. 13]

**muerte** NF death · *Bueno, supongo que fue una **muerte** romántica para un ratón.* Well, I suppose it was a romantic death for a mouse. [Anne of Green Gables, ch. 12]

**nombre** NM name · *Mi **nombre** es… es Tod.* My name is … is Tod. [The Fox and the Hound, ch. 16]

**palabra** word · *Lo más curioso es que en todo ese tiempo no he escrito una **palabra**, ni una **palabra**.* The strangest thing is that in all that time I haven't written one word, not one word. [The Bishop's Wife, ch. 7]

**paso** step · *Con el tiempo, después de ser transportados sobre las patas de sus madres durante mil pasos como un niño que aprende a bailar sobre los zapatos de su madre, el polluelo da sus primeros **pasos** sin ayuda.* In time, after being transported atop their mothers' feet for a thousand paces like a child who learns to dance atop his mother's shoes, the chick takes its first steps without assistance. [March of the Penguins, ch. 13]

**pelea** fight · *Si inicias una **pelea** la directora vendrá y será dura con nosotros.* If you start a fight, the director will come and will be hard on us. [Holes, ch. 10]

**pregunta** question · *Le pregunté a la señora Spencer que por qué era rojo, y dijo que no lo sabía, que sería mejor que no hiciera más **preguntas**.* I asked Mrs. Spencer why it was red, and she said that she didn't know, that it would be better not to ask more questions. [Anne of Green Gables, ch. 3]

**sueño** dream · *Dieron su vida en busca del **sueño** americano.* They gave their lives in search of the American dream. [In Memoriam, ch. 12]

**trabajo** work · *Buen **trabajo**, Rade.* Good work, Rade. [Hoosiers, ch. 10]

**verdad** truth · *¿Quieres la **verdad**?* Do you want the truth? [Rocky III, ch. 12]

**viaje** NM trip · *Gracias por el **viaje**.* Thanks for the ride. (LIT Thanks for the trip.) [Holes, ch. 2]

**vida** life · *Lo que aún tenga de **vida** en mi, te la daré.* Whatever life I still have within me, I give it to you. [Eragon, ch. 22]

# PRONOUNS AND ADJECTIVES
## Pronouns
### SUBJECTS AND OBJECTS OF PREPOSITIONS

**conmigo** with me · *¿Quién está **conmigo**?* Who is with me? [Facing the Giants, ch. 26]

**contigo** with you · *Apuesto que no podrías conseguir que baile **contigo**.* I bet you can't get him to dance with you. [Anne of Green Gables, ch. 14]

**él** M he · *él* OBJ him · ***Él** no llegó.* He didn't arrive. [Anne of Green Gables, ch. 3]

**ella** she · *ella* OBJ her · ***Ella** le llamará después.* She'll call you later. [Home Alone, ch 8]

**nosotros/nosotras** we · *nosotros/nosotras* OBJ us · ***Nosotros** atacamos el fuerte y ellos lo defienden.* We attack the fort and they defend it. [The Bishop's Wife, ch. 6]

**ti** OBJ you · *Estoy orgulloso de **ti**.* I'm proud of you. [Rocky III, ch. 6]

**tú** you · *Oh, ¡qué glorioso el día haces **tú**, Bert!* Oh, how glorious you make the day, Bert! [Mary Poppins, ch. 9]

**usted** you · ***Usted** lo mencionó y yo sólo estaba tratando de animarla.* You mentioned it and I was just trying to encourage you. [Home Alone, ch. 21]

**ustedes** you · *Ha sido un placer hablar con **ustedes**. Adiós.* It's been a pleasure talking with you. Good-bye. [Hoosiers, ch. 4]

**yo** I · *Tal vez tú quieras ponernos en peligro pero **yo** no.* Maybe you want to put us in danger, but I don't. [Tarzan, ch. 21]

### DIRECT AND INDIRECT OBJECTS

**la** her, you, it · *La reja tiene una llave y yo **la** tengo.* The castle gate has a key, and I have it. [The Princess Bride, ch. 19]

**las** them, you · *La experiencia y la cabeza más dura, **las** tiene Rocky Balboa.* Concerning experience and the hardest head, Rocky Balboa has them. [Rocky III, ch. 7]

**le** you, him, her; to you, to him, to her · *Nada **le** daba tanto placer como ordenar al joven.* Nothing gave her as much pleasure as ordering the young man around. [The Princess Bride, ch. 11]

**les** you, them; to you, to them · *¿Qué **les** sucede?* What's the matter with you?, What's happening to you? [Facing the Giants, ch. 6]

**lo** him, you, it · *Yo **lo** arreglaré.* I'll fix it. [Tarzan, ch. 7]

**los** them, you · *Nadie **los** conoce mejor que yo.* Nobody knows them better than I. [Hoosiers, ch. 13]

**me** me; to me, of me · *Le ¿O **me** tienes miedo, eh?* Oh, you're afraid of me, are you? [Rocky III, ch. 7]

**nos** us; to us · *Y **nos** rodearon.* And they surrounded us. [Tarzan, ch. 20]

**se** to him, to her, to you, to them · *Tampoco **se** lo dije a ella.* I didn't tell her either. [The Bishop's Wife, ch. 7]

**te** you; to you · *¿Qué **te** hice?* What did I do to you? [Rocky III, ch. 3]

### MISCELLANEOUS

**algo** something · *Una chimenea es **algo** maravilloso.* A chimney is something wonderful. [Mary Poppins, ch. 17]

**alguien** somebody, someone · *¿Esperaba a **alguien** más?* Were you expecting someone else? [Hoosiers, ch. 2]

**nada** nothing · ***Nada**.* Nothing. [Holes, ch. 16]

**nadie** nobody, no one · ***Nadie** dormirá esta mañana.* Nobody will sleep this morning. [Mary Poppins, ch. 12]

**qué** what? · *¿**Qué** le pasó en la aleta?* What happened to the fin? [Finding Nemo, ch. 3]

**quién** who? · *¿**Quién** te ha metido esas ideas en la cabeza?* Who put those ideas in your head? [Anne of Green Gables, ch. 3]

**todo** all · *Sí, es **todo** lo que tengo.* Yes, that's all that I have. [Eight Below, ch. 6]

## Adjectives
### POSSESSIVES

**mi** my · *Fue **mi** culpa, Kerchak.* It was my fault, Kerchak. [Tarzan, ch. 10]

**mío** mine, my, of mine · *¿Es tu papá, o el **mío**?* Is that your father, or mine? [Finding Nemo, ch. 27]

**nuestro** our · *Hacen proezas de destreza y habilidad ante **nuestros** ojos.* They perform feats of dexterity and skill right before our eyes. [Mary Poppins, ch. 8]

**su** his, her, your, their · ***Su** padre los llama.* Your father is calling you. [Mary Poppins, ch. 21]

**sus** his, her, your, their · ***Sus** hermanas me envían con una triste noticia.* Your sisters send me with sad news. [The Chronicles of Narnia: The Lion, the Witch and the Wardrobe, ch. 17]

**suyo** his, her, its, your, their; his, hers, yours, theirs · *El Señor puso una necesidad en nuestras vidas, y ahora pondremos una en la **suya**.* The Lord filled a need in our lives, and now we fill one in yours. [Facing the Giants, ch. 17]

**tu** your · *No sabes como desearía que algunos jugadores tuvieran **tu** corazón.* You don't know how much I would love for some players to have your heart. [Rudy, ch. 22]

**tus** your · *Hay un traidor en **tus** tropas, Aslan.*
There is a traitor among your troops, Aslan.
[The Chronicles of Narnia: The Lion, the Witch and the
Wardrobe, ch. 16]

**tuyo** yours · *La idea ha sido **tuya**.* The idea has
been yours. [Anne of Green Gables, ch. 16]

PHYSICAL CHARACTERISTICS

**alto** tall, high · *Has pagado un **alto** precio por tu
valor.* You have paid a high price for your courage.
[Eragon, ch. 23]

**bajo** low, short · *¿Entonces por qué me hizo tan
**bajo** y débil?* Then why did he make me so short
and weak? [Facing the Giants, ch. 7]

**bello** beautiful · *Oh, señora Semental, se ve usted
muy **bella**.* Oh, Mrs. Stallion, you look very
beautiful. [Rocky III, ch. 5]

**blanco** white · *El ciervo **blanco** se está alejando.*
The white stag is moving away. [The Chronicles of
Narnia: The Lion, the Witch and the Wardrobe, ch. 23]

**bonito** beautiful, pretty · *El de Robert es un traje
tan **bonito** que tenía que continuar.* Robert's
is such a beautiful suit that I had to continue.
[The Incredibles, ch. 14]

**claro** clear, bright, light · *¿Está **claro**?* Is that clear?
[Holes, ch. 16]

**dulce** sweet · *Debes reservar un espacio en tus
planes para el romance, **dulce** Anne.* You must
leave room in your plans for romance, sweet Anne.
[Anne of Green Gables, ch. 18]

**duro** hard · *No sea **duro** con ellos.* Don't be hard
on them. [Mary Poppins, ch. 4]

**frío** cold · *Ahí está en ese **frío** y triste banco día
tras día, siempre rodeado de grandes montones de
**frío** y cruel dinero.* There he is in that cold and sad
bank, day after day, always surrounded by huge
mountains of cold and cruel money. [Mary Poppins,
ch. 16]

**fuerte** strong · *A pesar de haberse conocido hace
pocos días, el vínculo entre madre e hijo es
sorprendentemente **fuerte**.* In spite of having met
each other only a few days before, the bond
between mother and child is surprisingly strong.
[March of the Penguins, ch. 15]

**hermoso** beautiful · *¿Si fuera muy **hermosa**
y tuviera el cabella castaño, podría aceptarme?*
If I was very beautiful and had nut-brown hair,
would you accept me? [Anne of Green Gables,
ch. 3]

**largo** long · *Y por lo que veo, será un viaje **largo**.*
And from what I can see, it will be a long trip.
[The Fox and the Hound, ch. 9]

**lindo** pretty, handsome, wonderful · *¿Dejará que
esa **linda** niña vaya con alguien más?* You'll allow
that pretty girl to go with someone else? [The
Absent-Minded Professor, ch. 7]

**lleno** full · *Y pronto el estómago del polluelo
estará nuevamente **lleno** de alimento.* And soon
the chick's stomach will again be full of food.
[March of the Penguins, ch. 17]

**negro** black · *El caballero **negro** lo siente ahora.*
The Black Knight ("the Man in Black") feels it now.
[The Princess Bride, ch. 19]

**pequeño** small, little · *Oh, éste es muy **pequeño**.*
Oh, this one is very small. [Mary Poppins, ch. 6]

**solo** alone, single, lonely · *A partir de aquí debo
continuar **solo**.* Starting here I must continue
alone. [The Chronicles of Narnia: The Lion, the Witch
and the Wardrobe, ch. 16]

**viejo** old · *Viena, la **vieja** y bella Viena.*
Vienna, old and beautiful Vienna. [The Bishop's
Wife, ch. 2]

ATTITUDE AND SOCIAL CHARACTERISTICS

**bueno** good · *Una **buena** cometa necesita una
**buena** cola, ¿no es cierto?* A good kite needs
a good tail, isn't that right? [Mary Poppins, ch. 22]

**difícil** difficult, hard · *Es **difícil** decir, el yeso
es una obra de arte gracias a Eric.* It's hard to say,
the cast is a work of art, thanks to Eric. [Eight Below,
ch. 6]

**fácil** easy · *No será **fácil**, Alteza.* It won't be easy,
Your Highness. [The Princess Bride, ch. 17]

**listo** ready · *Tu armadura está **lista**, Eragon.*
Your armor is ready, Eragon. [Eragon, ch. 19]

**loco** crazy · *¿Estás **loco**?* Are you crazy?
[Tarzan, ch. 18]

**mal** bad · *Sólo quería que supieras que tal vez
hiciste cosas **malas** antes, pero eso no te convierte
en un **mal** chico.* I just want you to know that
perhaps you did bad things before, but that does
not make you a bad young man. [Holes, ch. 3]

**maldito** cursed, damned, condemned · *Si olvidas
volver por Madame Zeroni, tú y tu familia estarán
**malditos** toda la eternidad.* If you forget to return
for Madame Zeroni, you and your family will be
cursed for all eternity. [Holes, ch. 6]

**mayor** best, top · *Creo que tengo el premio **mayor**.*
I think I've got the top prize. [The Incredibles,
ch. 24]

**mejor** better, best · *Porque soy el **mejor** y necesitas
que alguien te enseñe algo diferente.* Because I
am the best, and you need someone to teach you
something different. [Rocky III, ch. 9]

**peor** worse · *Oye, Bert, tú eres **peor** que los niños.*
Listen, Bert, you are worse than the children.
[Mary Poppins, ch. 10]

**pobre** poor · *Un granjero, **pobre**, **pobre** y perfecto.*
A farm boy, poor, poor and perfect. [The Princess
Bride, ch. 10]

**querido** beloved, dear · *Pase, mi **querido** amigo.*
Come in, my dear friend. [The Bishop's Wife, ch. 14]

**quieto** still · *Quieto, Trabalenguas, creo que estoy oyendo algo.* Keep still, Trabalenguas, I think I am hearing something. [The Fox and the Hound, ch. 5]

**ridículo** ridiculous · *No seas ridículo.* Don't be ridiculous. [Rudy, ch. 25]

**seguro** sure, safe · *¿Está seguro de que no nos siguen?* Are you sure they are not following us? [The Princess Bride, ch. 5]

**serio** serious · *en serio* seriously · *¿En serio no lo conocen?* Seriously, you don't know him? [The Chronicles of Narnia: The Lion, the Witch and the Wardrobe, ch. 9]

**tonto** foolish, silly · *Superca… Super… o como sea esa expresión tonta.* Superca… super… or however that silly expression goes. [Mary Poppins, ch. 12]

**tranquilo** tranquil, quiet, easy · *Es tan bello y tranquilo aquí, como si fuéramos los únicos en el mundo.* It's so beautiful and calm here, as if we were the only ones in the world. [The Absent-Minded Professor, ch. 12]

**triste** sad · *Oh, se ve tan, no sé, tan triste, Mamá Búho.* Oh, he looks, I don't know, so sad, Mama Búho. [The Fox and the Hound, ch. 15]

MISCELLANEOUS

**cada** each, every · *Mañana tus hombres nos escoltarán al canal de Florín donde cada barco de mi armada nos esperará para acompañarnos en nuestra luna de miel.* Tomorrow your men will escort us to the Channel of Florin where each ship of my fleet will await us in order to accompany us on our honeymoon. [The Princess Bride, ch. 19]

**diferente** different · *Me siento diferente.* I feel different. [The Incredibles, ch. 31]

**menos** except, less · *¿Crees que podrías hacer menos ruido, eh?* Do you think that you could make less noise, eh? [Home Alone, ch. 10]

**mismo** same · *Hay dos clases de tontos—el hombre que se desnuda y corre por la nieve, aullando bajo la luna, y él que hace lo mismo en mi habitación.* There are two classes of dumb—the man who gets naked and runs through the snow howling at the moon, and the one who does the same thing in my bedroom. [Hoosiers, ch. 5]

**otro** other, another · *No caigas otra vez.* Don't fall again. [Finding Nemo, ch. 8]

**propio** own · *Está generando su propia energía.* It's generating its own energy. [The Absent-Minded Professor, ch. 2]

**próximo** next · *Oiga, ¿va a jugar sólo con tres la próxima vez?* Hey, are you going to play with just three next time? [Hoosiers, ch. 12]

**qué** what · *¿Qué clase de lugar es este?* What kind of place is this? [Holes, ch. 21]

**único** only, unique · *Soy hijo único.* I am an only child. [Home Alone, ch. 12]

## Other Pronouns and Adjectives

DEMONSTRATIVES

**aquel/aquella** ADJ that · *aquél/aquélla/aquello* PRO that one · *¿Recuerdas aquel tubo?* Do you remember that tube? [Holes, ch. 16]

**esa** ADJ that · *ésa* PRO that one · *¿Ves esa montaña?* Do you see that mountain? [Holes, ch. 18]

**ese** M ADJ that · *ése* M PRO that one · *Ese sujeto es una máquina trituradora, y tiene hambre.* That guy is a crushing machine, and he's hungry. [Rocky III, ch. 5]

**eso** PRO that · *¿Qué controlas con eso?* What do you control with that? [The Incredibles, ch. 29]

**esta** ADJ this · *ésta* PRO this one · *Ésta es la primera tormenta para los polluelos y muchos de ellos no sobrevivirán.* This is the first storm for the young penguins and many of them will not survive. [March of the Penguins, ch. 14]

**este** M ADJ this · *éste* M PRO this one · *En este mundo de amor.* In this world of love. [Tarzan, ch. 1]

**esto** PRO this · *Para ser honesto, ver esto me tiene angustiado.* To be honest, seeing this has me very upset. [In Memoriam, ch. 7]

MISCELLANEOUS

**algún/alguno/alguna** ADJ · *alguno/alguna* PRO some · *Algunas parejas, tal vez muy jóvenes, son demasiado impulsivas o apresuradas y en tan solo un momento su relación llega a su fin.* Some couples, perhaps very young, are too impulsive or hurried, and in only a moment their relationship comes to its end. [March of the Penguins, ch. 5]

**cual** PRO which · *cuál* ADJ, PRO which, what (among several options) · *Alcalde, ¿cuál es la situación?* Mayor, what is the situation? [In Memoriam, ch. 2]

**cualquier/cualquiera** ADJ, PRO whatever, whichever, any · *Ah, Jefe, puedo burlar a ese perro tonto en cualquier momento.* Ah, Chief, I can fool that silly dog at any moment. [The Fox and the Hound, ch. 9]

**demás** ADJ, PRO the other, the others · *¿Dónde están todos los demás?* Where are all the others? [Home Alone, ch. 22]

**ningún/ninguno/ninguna** ADJ · *ninguno/ninguna* PRO no, any · *Hablar o no hablar no hace ninguna diferencia.* Speaking or not speaking doesn't make any difference. [Eragon, ch. 6]

**tal** ADJ, PRO someone called, such, as such · *Ella se hizo amiga de un fauno, un tal Tumnus.* She has made friends with a faun, someone called Tumnus. [The Chronicles of Narnia: The Lion, the Witch and the Wardrobe, ch. 6]

# VERBS
## -ar Conjugation
### GENERAL ACTIVITIES

**arreglar** to fix · *arreglarse* to get ready, to get dressed · *Creí que no lo mencionarías. **Arréglate.*** I didn't think you would mention it. Get dressed. [Eragon, ch. 23]

**ayudar** to help · *¡**Ayúdame!*** Help me! [Tarzan, ch. 24]

**buscar** to look for, to seek · *Oigan, ¿saben que los hemos **buscado** desde hace mucho?* Hey, did you know we've looked for them for a long time? [Home Alone, ch. 21]

**callar** to quiet, to silence · *callarse* to be quiet · ***Cállate**, esta vez lo atraparemos.* Be quiet, this time we'll trap him. [The Fox and the Hound, ch. 20]

**cerrar** to close · *Fue a su habitación y **cerró** la puerta, y durante días no durmió ni comió.* She went to her room and closed the door, and for days she neither slept nor ate. [The Princess Bride, ch. 2]

**comprar** to buy · ***Compre** sus golosinas, goma de mascar...* Buy your candy, chewing gum ... [The Absent-Minded Professor, ch. 11]

**cuidar** to care for, to take care of · *Prométeme que los vas a **cuidar.*** Promise me that you will take care of them. [The Chronicles of Narnia: The Lion, the Witch and the Wardrobe, ch. 1]

**dar** to give · *Ven acá, tenemos que **darte** la medalla.* Come here, we have to give you the medal. [The Bishop's Wife, ch. 6]

**despertar** to wake up · *Ay, va a **despertar** a las cinco.* Ay, he's going to wake up at five. [Eight Below, ch. 9]

**empezar** to begin, to start · *Quisiera poder **empezar** el ensayo pero no sé cómo.* I would like to be able to begin the rehearsal, but I don't see how. [The Bishop's Wife, ch. 10]

**enviar** to send · *Mi querido Stanley, tus cartas me hacen sentir como una de esas madres que pueden **enviar** a sus hijos de campamento.* My dear Stanley, your letters make me feel like one of those mothers who is able to send her children off to camp. [Holes, ch. 10]

**escuchar** to hear, to listen · *Ah, **escucha**, Bob, te reubico si quieres.* Ah, listen, Bob, I'll relocate you if you want. [The Incredibles, ch. 7]

**hablar** to speak, to talk · *Cuando termine de **hablar** con ellos, vendrán de rodillas a implorarnos con bolsas de dinero, barriles de dinero.* When I finish talking to them, they'll come on their knees begging with bags of money, barrels of money. [The Absent-Minded Professor, ch. 7]

**levantar** to lift, to raise up · *levantarse* to get up · *Si ninguno **se levanta** sería empate.* If neither gets up, it will be a tie. [Rocky III, ch. 1]

**llamar** to call · *¿Puedo **llamarte** por tu nombre?* May I call you by your name? [The Fox and the Hound, ch. 16]

**mirar** to look at · *Kala, **mira**, no es como nosotros.* Kala, look, he isn't like us. [Tarzan, ch. 4]

**pagar** to pay · *Trabajo para Vizzini para **pagar** las deudas y gano muy poco.* I work for Vizzini in order to pay my debts and I make very little. [The Princess Bride, ch. 7]

**probar** to try, to test, to taste · *Entonces voy a **probarlo** enseguida.* Then I'm going to try it right away. [Anne of Green Gables, ch. 1]

**quitar** to remove · *quitarse* to take off · *Será mejor que **me quite** el zapato.* It will be better if I take off my shoe. [The Absent-Minded Professor, ch. 10]

**sentarse** to sit down · ***Siéntate**, Marion, otra vez estás bajo arresto.* Sit down, Marion, you are under arrest again. [Holes, ch. 23]

### MOVEMENT AND MOTION

**acercarse** to move close, to draw nearer · *Se **acerca** una fuerte tormenta.* A powerful storm is moving closer. [Eight Below, ch. 4]

**alcanzar** to reach, to catch up to · *¡Si me **alcanzas!*** If you catch up to me! [Tarzan, ch. 13]

**alejarse** to move farther away, to distance, to get away from · *¡**Aléjate** de eso!* Get away from that! [Tarzan, ch. 10]

**andar** to walk, to move forward, to associate (with friends) · *Ya oyeron. ¡A cavar, muchachos! ¡**Andando**! ¡**Andando**! ¡**Andando**! ¡**Andando**!* You heard it. Dig, boys! Move it! Move it! Move it! Move it! [Holes, ch. 13]

**bajar** to go down, to come down, to lower · *Y luego me obligué a **bajar** para lavar mi ropa, y descubrí que no es tan malo.* And then I forced myself to go down to wash my clothes, and I discovered that it's not so bad. [Home Alone, ch. 15]

**caminar** to walk, to step · *Qué bueno que encontraste tu roca, pero tienes que regresar, **camina** por donde ya pasaste, sobre tus pisadas.* That's great that you found your rock, but you have to come back, walk back the way you came, right on your footprints. [Eight Below, ch. 4]

**llegar** to arrive · ***Llega** tarde, como siempre.* He arrives late, like always. [The Absent-Minded Professor, ch. 5]

**llevar** to carry, to take, to lead · *Eso nos **llevaría** a descubrimientos inimaginables.* That could lead us to unimaginable discoveries. [Eight Below, ch. 4]

**marchar** to march, to walk · *marcharse* to leave · *Si alguno de ustedes no quiere estar en el equipo, puede **marcharse**.* If any of you doesn't want to be on the team, you can leave. [Hoosiers, ch. 5]

**parar** to stop · *Y cuando empiezo a reír no puedo **pararme**.* And when I start to laugh, I can't stop myself. [Mary Poppins, ch. 13]

**regresar** to return · *Al **regresar** las madres rodean la multitud y gritan con fuerza y esperan a que su pareja les responda.* On returning, the mothers surround the multitude and cry loudly and hope that their mate responds to them. [March of the Penguins, ch. 12]

**viajar** to travel · *Si te interesa saberlo, **viajaba** en el bote de Diana pero se empezó a hundir.* If you are interested in knowing, I was traveling in Diana's boat but it began to sink. [Anne of Green Gables, ch. 16]

**volar** to fly · *Sí, **volaremos** mañana temprano.* Yes, we fly early tomorrow. [Home Alone, ch. 4]

### EMOTIONS AND FEELINGS

**amar** to love · *Las últimas palabras de mi padre fueron "**ámala** como amé a tu madre, y entonces habrá felicidad."* The final words of my father were "Love her as I loved your mother, and then you will find happiness." [The Princess Bride, ch. 15]

**asustar** to frighten · *No me **asustas**.* You don't scare me. [Rocky III, ch. 3]

**calmar** to calm · *Ya **cálmense** chicos.* Calm down right now, boys. [The Absent-Minded Professor, ch. 10]

**confiar** to trust, to rely on, to depend on · *Nunca más volveré a **confiar** en ti.* I'll never trust you again. [The Fox and the Hound, ch. 5]

**disculpar** to excuse · *Por supuesto, y ahora si me **disculpa**, mañana será un importante día para los niños y sólo deben pensar en dormir.* Of course, and now if you will excuse me, tomorrow is going to be an important day for the children and they must think only about sleeping. [Mary Poppins, ch. 14]

**encantar** to enchant, to charm, to delight · *Simple, elegante sí, intrépido, te **encantará**.* Simple, yes elegant, daring, it will delight you. [The Incredibles, ch. 14]

**esperar** to wait, to hope, to expect · *Doc, **espera** un minuto.* Doc, wait a minute. [Eight Below, ch. 4]

**gustar** to like (LIT to please; commonly used with an indirect object [EXAMPLES: *Me gusta la película.* I like the movie., *¿Te gustan los tamales?* Do you like tamales?]) · *¿Te **gustaría** averiguarlo?* Would you like to find out? [The Incredibles, ch. 16]

**lamentar** to be sorry · *Lo **lamento**.* I'm sorry. [The Absent-Minded Professor, ch. 3]

**preocupar** to concern, to worry, to bother · *preocuparse* to be worried · *¡No **te preocupes**, vamos a estar bien!* Don't worry, we're going to be all right! [The Chronicles of Narnia: The Lion, the Witch and the Wardrobe, ch. 1]

**vengar** to avenge · *Galbatorix tratará de **vengar** su derrota.* Galbatorix will try to avenge his defeat. [Eragon, ch. 23]

### WORK AND PLAY

**cantar** to sing · *Vine a oír **cantar** a mi nieta.* I came to hear my granddaughter sing. [Home Alone, ch. 15]

**descansar** to rest · *Debes **descansar**.* You must rest. [The Princess Bride, ch. 16]

**enseñar** to teach · *¿No oíste la razón de que hagas hoyos? Eso te sirve. Te **enseña** una lección.* Didn't you hear the reason for making holes? It helps you. It teaches you a lesson. [Holes, ch. 16]

**ganar** to win · *Así que era mi trabajo mantenerte **ganando**, y mantener tu salud.* So it was my job to keep you winning, and to keep you healthy. [Rocky III, ch. 5]

**golpear** to hit · *¡No te **golpees**! ¡No te **golpees**! ¡No te **golpees**! ¡No te **golpees**!* Don't hit yourself! Don't hit yourself! Don't hit yourself! Don't hit yourself! [Tarzan, ch. 7]

**jugar** to play (a game) · *¿Por qué no **jugamos** a las escondidas?* Why don't we play hide-and-seek? [The Chronicles of Narnia: The Lion, the Witch and the Wardrobe, ch. 7]

**lanzar** to throw, to launch · *No sé **lanzar**.* I don't know how to throw. [The Bishop's Wife, ch. 6]

**pelear** to fight · *Aprendí esgrima, a **pelear**, todo lo que quiso enseñarme.* I learned fencing, to fight, everything that he wanted to teach me. [The Princess Bride, ch. 11]

**sacar** to take out, to pull out · *Esa es la forma de **sacar** un diente.* That's the way to pull out a tooth. [Finding Nemo, ch. 17]

**soltar** to let go, to let loose, to free · *soltarse* to get loose, to get free · *¡Todos se **soltaron**!* They all got free! [Eight Below, ch. 13]

**tocar** to touch, to play (an instrument) · *Pero, George, no sabes **tocar**.* But, George, you don't know how to play. [Mary Poppins, ch. 12]

**trabajar** to work · *He tenido que **trabajar** en Paris.* I have had to work in Paris. [The Bishop's Wife, ch. 6]

### THOUGHTS

**asegurar** to assure, to ensure, to make sure · *Te puedo **asegurar** que sin importar a qué nivel entrenes, es irreal siempre que llegas al partido final.* I can assure you that no matter at what level you coach, it seems unreal when you make it to the championship game. [Facing the Giants, ch. 22]

**dejar** to allow, to let, to permit · ***Deja** que queme.* Let it burn. [Facing the Giants, ch. 12]

**equivocarse** to mistake, to be mistaken, to be wrong · *A menos que me **equivoque**, y nunca me* *equivoco, se dirigieron hacia al pantano.* Unless I'm wrong, and I'm never wrong, they are heading toward the swamp. [The Princess Bride, ch. 10]

**intentar** to try · *Déjame intentar.* Let me try. [Holes, ch. 1]

**jurar** to swear · *¿Y no es pecado jurar?* And isn't it a sin to swear? [Anne of Green Gables, ch. 11]

**olvidar** to forget, to leave behind · *olvidarse* to forget, to forget about · *No te olvides de nosotros.* Don't forget about us. [Mary Poppins, ch. 23]

**pensar** to think · *Pienso que cerca de las siete estará en graves problemas.* I think that about seven o'clock he will be in serious difficulty. [The Absent-Minded Professor, ch. 11]

**preguntar** to ask (a question) · *preguntarse* to wonder · *Así que si se preguntan qué está haciendo aquí en el hielo, bueno, eso es parte de nuestra historia.* So if you wonder what it is doing here in the ice, well, that is part of our story. [March of the Penguins, ch. 2]

**recordar** to remember, to remind · *Recuerda de dónde vienes, lo que te costó llegar aquí.* Remember where you come from, what it cost you to get here. [Rocky III, ch. 14]

**soñar** to dream · *¿Que por soñar con su catedral se ha apartado de la gente que amaba?* That by dreaming about his cathedral, he has moved away from the people that he loved? [The Bishop's Wife, ch. 10]

MISCELLANEOUS

**acabar** to finish, to exhaust · *Así acabaríamos al mismo tiempo.* That way we would finish at the same time. [Holes, ch. 16]

**apostar** to bet · *Apuesto a que sí. Las batallas son algo repugnante.* I bet you can. Battles are ugly affairs. [The Chronicles of Narnia: The Lion, the Witch and the Wardrobe, ch. 12]

**bastar** to be enough · *¡Ya basta! ¡Ya basta! ¿Por qué están haciendo esto? ¡Ya basta! ¡Basta! ¡Ayúdenme!* Enough already! Enough already! Why are you doing this? Enough already! Enough! Help me! [Holes, ch. 12]

**cambiar** to change · *En cuanto a los otros, la relación está a punto de cambiar.* Concerning the others, the relationship is about to change. [March of the Penguins, ch. 6]

**cansar** to tire · *cansarse* to get tired · *Cuando se cansan de caminar, hacen descansar las patas, y usan el vientre en su lugar.* When they get tired of walking, they give their feet a rest and use their belly instead. [March of the Penguins, ch. 2]

**casar** to marry, to perform a marriage ceremony · *casarse* to marry, to get married · *Si me dices que debemos casarnos en diez días, por favor cree que moriré al amanecer.* If you tell me that we must marry in ten days, please believe that I will die at dawn. [The Princess Bride, ch. 16]

**continuar** to continue · *Sin importar el frío que haga, o lo hambrientos que estén, los padres deben continuar moviéndose.* No matter how cold it gets, or how hungry they are, the parents must continue moving. [March of the Penguins, ch. 11]

**estar** to be · *Yo sé donde está el veneno.* I know where the poison is. [The Princess Bride, ch. 9]

**faltar** to be lacking, to be missing · *Te falta la barba para ser un enano.* You're missing the beard to be a dwarf. [The Chronicles of Narnia: The Lion, the Witch and the Wardrobe, ch. 3]

**interesar** to interest, to matter · *No le interesa lo que nos pase.* It doesn't matter to you what happens to us. [Mary Poppins, ch. 21]

**llorar** to cry, to weep · *Bueno, no es la Real Academia de pintura, pero tampoco hacen llorar.* Well, it's not the Royal Academy of painting, but they don't cause one to cry either. [Mary Poppins, ch. 8]

**lograr** to achieve, to reach a goal, to accomplish · *En un segundo se terminó todo lo que había logrado.* In one second, everything that I had accomplished ended. [Hoosiers, ch. 25]

**matar** to kill · *Tu Westley está muerto. Yo lo maté.* Your Westley is dead. I killed him. [The Princess Bride, ch. 23]

**necesitar** to need · *¡Lo necesito!* I need it! [The Incredibles, ch. 26]

**pasar** to pass, to spend (time), to enter · *Me invitaron a pasar la noche.* They invited me to spend the night. [Anne of Green Gables, ch. 13]

**quedar** to remain · *quedarse* to remain, to stay · *Bien, supongo que puedo quedarme un ratito, sólo si tienes sardinas.* Well, I suppose that I can stay a little while, only if you have sardines. [The Chronicles of Narnia: The Lion, the Witch and the Wardrobe, ch. 3]

**sonar** to sound, to ring · *No suena tan mal.* It doesn't sound so bad. [The Princess Bride, ch. 1]

**tomar** to take, to drink · *Toma tiempo, pero lo harás.* It takes time, but you will do it. [Rocky III, ch. 11]

**tratar** to try · *Mientras las madres llenan por fin sus estómagos vacíos, los padres se aferran a la vida en la superficie, tratando de mantener los huevos calientes y a salvo.* While the mothers finally fill their empty stomachs, the fathers cling to life on the surface, trying to keep their eggs warm and safe. [March of the Penguins, ch. 9]

## -er Conjugation
### GENERAL ACTIVITIES

**aprender** to learn · *Creo que **aprendimos** una invaluable lección.* I think we learned an invaluable lesson. [Holes, ch. 16]

**comer** to eat · *Oh, ¿no se los habrá **comido** el león del zoológico?* Or, won't the lion from the zoo have eaten them? [Mary Poppins, ch. 2]

**conocer** to know (a person or place), to be familiar with (something), to meet · *Es porque **conoces** a muy pocos como yo.* That's because you know very few like me. [The Chronicles of Narnia: The Lion, the Witch and the Wardrobe, ch. 4]

**creer** to believe · *No puedo **creerlo**.* I can't believe it. [Eight Below, ch. 13]

**deber** to ought, must · ***Debemos** escapar.* We must escape. [Finding Nemo, ch. 8]

**entender** to understand · *Lo **entiendo**, pero tú tienes que **entender** que te amaba y que ese era su trabajo, protegerte.* I understand, but you have to understand that he loved you and that that was his job, to protect you. [Rocky III, ch. 12]

**hacer** to do, to make · *Kevin, ¿qué **hiciste** en mi habitación?* Kevin, what did you do to my room? [Home Alone, ch. 23]

**leer** to read · *Puedes **leer** un poco más, si quieres.* You can read a little more, if you want. [The Princess Bride, ch. 5]

**parecer** to seem, to look like · ***Parece** que muchas personas se han atrasado en sus pagos.* It looks like a lot of people have gotten behind on their payments. [The Absent-Minded Professor, ch. 10]

**poder** to be able to [often "can" in English] · *No **puedo** hablar.* I can't speak. [In Memoriam, ch. 11]

**poner** to put, to set · *Elige a un mal muchacho, **ponlo** a hacer hoyos todo el día en el sol ardiente y se convierte en un chico bueno.* Take a bad boy, put him to digging holes all day in the burning hot sun, and he turns into a good kid. [Holes, ch. 5]

**saber** to know · *Cuando quiera **saber** de una mujer, pregunte a los viejos.* When you want to know about a woman, ask the old men. [The Bishop's Wife, ch. 7]

**suceder** to happen · *¿Qué **sucede**?* What's happening? [The Princess Bride, ch. 10]

**tener** to have · *Parece que **tenemos** algo en común.* It seems that we have something in common. [Rudy, ch. 15]

**traer** to bring · *Has sido tan amable en **traer** a los niños a casa.* You have been so kind in bringing the children home. [Mary Poppins, ch. 17]

**ver** to see · *Ah, sí, algo **vi** respecto a él en el periódico.* Ah, yes, I saw something about him in the newspaper. [The Incredibles, ch. 6]

**volver** to return, to go back · ***Volveremos** mañana.* We'll go back tomorrow. [Home Alone, ch. 11]

### EMOTIONS AND FEELINGS

**agradecer** to thank, to give thanks · *Y también le **agradezco** que no se haya acercado a Jimmy.* I also thank you for not having approached Jimmy. [Hoosiers, ch. 17]

**merecer** to deserve · *Él no **merece** una oportunidad.* He doesn't deserve a chance. [Hoosiers, ch. 16]

**querer** to want, to love · *Así es, mi amigo, ¿ya **quieres** salir a sentir el calor?* That's it, my friend, do you want to go out and feel the heat? [Eight Below, ch. 1]

**temer** to fear, to be afraid of · *David, no puedes **temer** al fracaso.* David, you can't be afraid of failure. [Facing the Giants, ch. 5]

### WORK AND PLAY

**caer** to fall · **caerse** to fall · *Me **caí** del techo de la casa de los Spurgeon.* I fell off the roof at the Spurgeons' house. [Anne of Green Gables, ch. 10]

**correr** to run · *A Diana jamás se le habría ocurrido **correr** a la cama y saltar sobre ella.* It never would have occurred to Diana to run to the bed and leap into it. [Anne of Green Gables, ch. 14]

**perder** to lose · ***Perdiste** la pelea por las peores razones.* You lost the fight for the worst reasons. [Rocky III, ch. 9]

**romper** to break · **romperse** to break, to be broken · *Esa es una frágil promesa que se hace y **se rompe** fácilmente.* That is a fragile promise that is made and is easily broken. [Mary Poppins, ch. 11]

**vencer** to conquer, to defeat, to beat · *No puedo **vencerlo**.* I can't beat him. [Rocky III, ch. 7]

### MISCELLANEOUS

**deber** to ought, must · *Esto **debe** ser una broma.* This must be a joke. [The Absent-Minded Professor, ch. 9]

**haber** to have [HELPING VERB] · *Lamento **haber** llegado tarde.* I'm sorry to have arrived late. [Anne of Green Gables, ch. 3]

**ser** to be · *Ah, hola, mi nombre **es** Marlin.* Ah, hi, my name is Marlin. [Finding Nemo, ch. 8]

## -ir Conjugation
### GENERAL ACTIVITIES

**abrir** to open · *Anda, sé buen niño y **abre** la puerta.* Come on, be a good boy and open the door. [Home Alone, ch. 17]

**conseguir** to get, to acquire · *Creo que si se esfuerza lo suficiente, puede **conseguir** una beca para ir a la universidad de Wabash y salir de aquí.* I think that if he tries hard enough, he can get a scholarship to go to Wabash College and get out of here. [Hoosiers, ch. 8]

**decidir** to decide · *Ustedes dos **decidan** si se queda.* You two decide if he stays. [Rudy, ch. 20]

**decir** to say, to tell · *Te **dije** que volvería.* I told you I was coming back. [Eight Below, ch. 13]

**dormir** to sleep · *Creo que debes **dormir** ahora.* I think you ought to sleep now. [The Princess Bride, ch. 27]

**escribir** to write · ***Escribirás** cuatro veces una carta.* You will write a letter four times. [The Princess Bride, ch. 16]

**ir** to go · *Ahora **voy** a lanzarlo como un trapo sucio.* Now I'm going to toss him like a dirty rag. [Rocky III, ch. 4]

**morir** to die · *Mi nombre es Inigo Montoya, tú mataste a mi padre, prepárate para **morir**.* My name is Inigo Montoya, you killed my father, prepare to die. [The Princess Bride, ch. 16]

**oír** to hear · *¡**Oye**, Adrian, lo logré!* Listen, Adrian, I did it! [Rocky III, ch. 1]

**pedir** to ask for, to request · *No hay nada a Chicago, Nueva York, Nashville. Lo que **pidas**, todo está vendido.* There's nothing to Chicago, New York, Nashville. Whatever you ask for, everything is sold out. [Home Alone, ch. 9]

**salir** to leave · *¿Van a **salir** de la ciudad?* Are you going to leave town? [Home Alone, ch. 6]

**seguir** to continue, to follow · *Tienen el fin de semana para pensar si quieren **seguir** en este equipo o no...* You have the weekend to think about whether you want to continue on this team or not … [Hoosiers, ch. 11]

**sentir** to feel · **sentirse** to feel, to be feeling · *Kari, en serio no **me siento** cómoda con esto.* Kari, seriously, I don't feel comfortable about this. [The Incredibles, ch. 17]

**subir** to go up, to get on, to board · ***Sube** al caballo.* Get on the horse. [Eragon, ch. 7]

**venir** to come · *¿Quiere **venir** a Washington?* You want to come to Washington? [The Absent-Minded Professor, ch. 7]

**vestir** to dress, to put on (clothes) · **vestirse** to get dressed · *El único uniforme que **vestirás** será el mismo que estás vistiendo ahora.* The only uniform that you will put on will be the same one that you are putting on now. [Rudy, ch. 21]

**vivir** to live · *Yo les pregunto, "¿para qué están **viviendo**?"* I ask you, "What are you living for?" [Facing the Giants, ch. 11]

## ADVERBS

### TIME

**ahora** now · ***Ahora** toma una siesta, muchacho.* Now, take a siesta, young man. [Holes, ch. 7]

**antes** before · *Y seré como **antes**.* And I will be like before. [Rocky III, ch. 4]

**aún** still, yet, even · ***Aún** no estás listo para atacar a nadie.* You are still not ready to attack anybody. [Eragon, ch. 9]

**cuando** when · *cuándo* when · *¿Pero **cuándo** atrapamos a Bomb Voyage?* But when do we capture Bomb Voyage? [The Incredibles, ch. 1]

**después** later · *después de* after · *Vamos profesor, **después de** tantos años.* Come on, professor, after so many years. [The Bishop's Wife, ch. 2]

**hoy** today · *Lo que hagas tú **hoy**, lo haré también.* What you do today, I will do, too. [Tarzan, ch. 23]

**jamás** never · ***Jamás** lo había visto.* I never saw it. [The Bishop's Wife, ch. 2]

**luego** later, afterward, then · *Voy a llamar a Maya y **luego** quiero que suelte el freno.* I'm going to call Maya, and then I want you to let go of the brake. [Eight Below, ch. 3]

**nunca** never · *Yo **nunca** podría amar a alguien como te amo a ti, Anne.* I could never love anyone like I love you, Anne. [Anne of Green Gables, ch. 11]

**pronto** soon · *Muy **pronto** vendrá Westley.* Westley will come very soon. [The Princess Bride, ch. 23]

**siempre** always · *Mary Poppins dice que ella está **siempre**.* Mary Poppins says that she always is. [Mary Poppins, ch. 15]

**tarde** late · *Corre, cielo, o vas a llegar **tarde** al trabajo.* Run along, sweetie, or you are going to arrive late for work. [The Incredibles, ch. 10]

**todavía** still · *Estás lento **todavía**.* You're still slow. [Rocky III, ch. 13]

**ya** already, now, right away · *Sí, **ya** lo tengo.* Yes, I have it already. [The Absent-Minded Professor, ch. 10]

### LOCATION

**abajo** down, below, under · *Era 1933, **abajo** por un punto—cinco, cuatro, tres, dos, uno... lancé el balón.* It was 1933, down by one point—five, four, three, two, one … I took the shot. [Hoosiers, ch. 6]

**acá** here, over here · *¡Vengan **acá**!* Come here! [Eight Below, ch. 13]

**adonde** where · *adónde* where, to where · *¿Y **adónde** va el cohete?* Where is the rocket going? [Eight Below, ch. 6]

**ahí** there · ***Ahí** estaré.* I'll be there. [Rudy, ch. 21]

**allá** there, over there · *más allá* beyond · ***Más allá** de esas fronteras hay reminiscencias de resistencia.* Beyond those borders there are remnants of resistance. [Eragon, ch. 5]

**allí** there · *Creo que está **allí** adentro.* I think it's inside there. [The Fox and the Hound, ch. 2]

**aquí** here · *¿Qué fue lo que pasó **aquí**?* What was it that happened here? [Mary Poppins, ch. 19]

**arriba** up, above · *Dice que descubrió un mundo encantado, en el ropero de **arriba**.* She says that she discovered an enchanted world in the upstairs wardrobe. [The Chronicles of Narnia: The Lion, the Witch and the Wardrobe, ch. 7]

**atrás** back, behind · *Hágalos que lancen desde muy **atrás** y cuidado con el purgatorio al que ellos llaman gimnasio.* Make them shoot it from far back and take care of that purgatory that they call a gym. [Hoosiers, ch. 13]

**cerca** near, close · *Eso estuvo **cerca**.* That was close. [The Incredibles, ch. 6]

**dentro** inside · *Control quiere a todos **dentro** para estar seguros, cambio.* Control wants everyone inside in order to be safe, over. [Eight Below, ch. 4]

**donde** where · *dónde* where · *Anne, no tenías porqué haber tomado mi broche. ¿En **dónde** lo dejaste?* Anne, you had no reason to have touched my brooch. Where did you leave it? [Anne of Green Gables, ch. 6]

**junto** together · *Descuide, irán todos **juntos** en grupo.* Don't worry, they will all go together in a group. [Finding Nemo, ch. 3]

**lejos** far away, far · *Ahora quiero que te vayas, **lejos** de mi hogar, **lejos** de mi vida, y **lejos** de Julia.* Now I want you to go, far from my home, far from my life, and far from Julia. [The Bishop's Wife, ch. 11]

### HOW AND HOW MUCH

**así** like this, like that, in this way, in that way · *Y **así**, habiendo llegado, se disponen a cumplir con el propósito de su viaje, encontrar una pareja.* And in that way, having arrived, they get ready to complete the purpose of their trip, to find a mate. [March of the Penguins, ch. 3]

**bien** well, fine · *Ah, **bien** hecho, Jane.* Ah, well done, Jane. [Tarzan, ch. 23]

**casi** almost · *Se puso así de cerca, **casi** acechándome.* He put himself very close like this, almost threatening me. [Tarzan, ch. 21]

**¿cómo?** how? · *¿Y **cómo** te atreves a venir sin ellos?* And how dare you come without them? [The Chronicles of Narnia: The Lion, the Witch and the Wardrobe, ch. 10]

**cuánto** how much · *No se imagina **cuánto**.* You have no idea how much. [Rudy, ch. 21]

**demasiado** too much · *Es **demasiado** tarde para eso.* It's too late for that. [Eragon, ch. 15]

**más** more · *Cada día la temperatura desciende un poco **más**, y el sol se pone **más** temprano.* Each day the temperature drops a little more, and the sun sets earlier. [March of the Penguins, ch. 3]

**muy** very · *Pueden causarte daños **muy** severos.* They can cause you some very severe damage. [Rocky III, ch. 4]

**poco** little · *Escucha amigo, ven aquí, tenemos una situación un **poco** complicada, ¿entiendes?* Listen, friend, come here, we have a situation that's a little complicated, you understand? [Tarzan, ch. 7]

**qué** how, what a · *Qué glorioso es un día con Mary.* How glorious is a day with Mary. [Mary Poppins, ch. 9]

**tan** so, such · *Le agradezco que cambiara de opinión **tan** rápidamente.* I thank you for changing your mind so quickly. [Anne of Green Gables, ch. 14]

**tanto** so much · *Papá se rió **tanto** que murió.* Dad laughed so much that he died. [Mary Poppins, ch. 22]

### MISCELLANEOUS

**acaso** perhaps, maybe · *¿Acaso vino del cielo?* Perhaps it came from heaven? [Holes, ch. 14]

**además** in addition, furthermore, plus · *Además, si lo analizas con lógica, ni siquiera van a salir del ropero.* Plus, if you analyze it logically, they aren't even going to leave the wardrobe. [The Chronicles of Narnia: The Lion, the Witch and the Wardrobe, ch. 8]

**aun** even · *Sí, **aun** sin motor.* Yes, even without a motor. [The Absent-Minded Professor, ch. 6]

**no** no, not · *Los goles de campo **no** son una opción.* Field goals are not an option. [Facing the Giants, ch. 26]

**quizá** perhaps, maybe · *Peter, el tiempo de usar esto **quizá** llegue pronto.* Peter, the time to use this may perhaps arrive soon. [The Chronicles of Narnia: The Lion, the Witch and the Wardrobe, ch. 12]

**sí** yes · *Sí, fue … fue terrible.* Yes, it was … it was terrible. [Home Alone, ch. 21]

**siquiera** at least · *ni siquiera* not even · *Ni siquiera movió los pies.* He didn't even move his feet. [Hoosiers, ch. 21]

**sólo** only · *Me lo puse ayer, **sólo** para ver como lucía.* I put it on yesterday, just to see how it looked. [Anne of Green Gables, ch. 6]

**también** also · *Pues si tú das amistad a las damas, sí, ellas **también** te van a dar amistad.* Well, if you give friendship to the ladies, yes, they will also give you friendship. [The Fox and the Hound, ch. 17]

**tampoco** neither, either · *Tampoco hueles bien.* You don't smell good either. [The Princess Bride, ch. 18]

# Eight Below

¿Qué tal tu chica?
*How's your girl?*

GENRE      Adventure
YEAR       2006
DIRECTOR   Frank Marshall
CAST       Paul Walker, Bruce Greenwood, Moon Bloodgood, Jason Biggs
STUDIO     Walt Disney Pictures

Jerry Shepard is a wilderness guide who specializes in leading expeditions in Antarctica—expeditions that are often exciting, but sometimes dangerous. After being forced to leave his dogs behind in an evacuation of the base due to a heavy snowstorm, he is determined to rescue the dogs. Action scenes are divided between the dogs' efforts to survive and his efforts to rescue them. Although the Spanish dialogue is spoken at a faster clip than in the other Beginner movies, the dialogue is evenly paced, easy to follow, and spaced throughout the film to give the student frequent and visually impressive breaks.

## BASIC VOCABULARY

### Nouns

☐ **Antártida** Antarctica · *Es la mayor tormenta en **Antártida** en veinticinco años.* It's the biggest storm in Antarctica in twenty-five years.

☐ **base** NF base · *Aquí **base** a Melbourne, respondan.* Base here to Melbourne, come in.

☐ **guía** NMF guide [PERSON] · *Mi deber siendo el **guía** es llevarte de regreso vivo.* My duty as guide is to bring you back alive.

☐ **hielo** ice · *Un témpano se rompió de un banco de **hielo** y bloqueó la ruta que los pingüinos de Adelia siguen para ir a pescar.* An ice floe broke off from a bank of ice and blocked the route that the Adélie penguins follow in order to go fishing.

☐ **invierno** winter · *Sólo me queda una semana para volver antes de que llegue el **invierno**.* I only have one week left to get back before winter arrives.

☐ **tormenta** storm · *Una **tormenta** se aproxima.* A storm is approaching.

☐ **trineo** sled · *¿En **trineo**?* By sled?

### Verbs

☐ **empacar** to pack · *Tengo que **empacar**.* I have to pack.

☐ **partir** to leave · *Hora de **partir**.* Time to leave.

## 1 Opening Credits 4:24

### Phrases to Listen For

**ya basta** enough already
**el suspenso me mata** the suspense is killing me
**hay que** it's necessary
**tal vez** maybe, perhaps

### Names

Shorty, Dewey, Truman, Jack

▆ Voices are heard over a darkened screen. A penguin thermometer shows the temperature inside.

☐ **grados** degrees · *grado* degree

☐ **centígrados** centigrade · *centígrado* centigrade

☐ **aguanto** I can stand · *aguantar* to be able to stand, to tolerate, to put up with

☐ **suspenso** suspense

☐ **mata** it kills · *matar* to kill

☐ **tibios** lukewarm · *tibio* lukewarm

☐ **calor** NM heat

☐ **sudor** NM sweat

☐ **rostro** face

▆ The two men run to the outside thermometer. Opening credits.

☐ **récord** NM record

☐ **está helando** it's freezing · *helar* to freeze

▆ Jerry Shepard holds a baseball bat in his hands.

☐ **odio** I hate · *odiar* to hate

☐ **salmón** NM salmon

☐ **congelado** frozen · *congelar* to freeze

☐ **ejercitarte** to train, to practice · *ejercitarse* to train, to practice

☐ **desayunar** to eat breakfast

☐ **jardín derecho** right field · *jardín* NM garden · *derecho* ADJ right

☐ **batear** to bat, to swing a bat

☐ **cuidándolos** caring for them · *cuidar* to care for, to take care of

☐ **tráela** IMP bring it · *traer* to bring

☐ **no griten** IMP don't shout · *gritar* to shout

☐ **desayuno** breakfast

## 2 Bottom of the Planet 10:35

### Phrases to Listen For

**gusto de verla** it's a pleasure to see you, it's nice to see you
**me siento con suerte** I feel lucky
**mucha suerte** good luck
**vas a caer** you're going down (LIT you are going to fall)
**¿no le falta algo...?** isn't something missing ...?
**ya sé** I already know, I know already
**tiene que ir** he has to go
**lo que pasa** what's happening
**en trineo** by sled
**lo que tú digas** SUBJ whatever you say
**¿eso te agrada?** you like that?
**es que** it's that, it's just that
**¿qué pasó?** what happened?
**desde entonces** since then
**eso creo** I think so
**tienes que** you have to
**apuesto a que** I bet

### Names

Davis McClaren, UCLA, Jerry Shepard, Charlie Cooper, Andy Harrison, Rosemary Paris, Katie, Melbourne, FNC, Coop, Buck, Max, Rosie

▆ An airplane lands. Katie, the pilot, gets out of the plane. Her passenger is Dr. Davis McClaren.

☐ **piloto** pilot

☐ **licencia** license

☐ **soportó** it withstood · *soportar* to withstand, to tolerate

- **dieciséis** sixteen
- **kilómetros** kilometers · *kilómetro* kilometer
- **metros** meters · *metro* meter
- **científico** scientist
- **bienvenido** *ADJ* welcome
- **fondo** bottom
- **igualmente** same to you, equally
- **sur** *NM* south
- **se resbala** you'd slide off (*LIT* you slide off) · *resbalarse* to slip, to slide
- **planeta** *NM* planet
- **cartógrafo** cartographer
- **mecánico** mechanic
- **limpio** I clean · *limpiar* to clean
- **pistas** runways · *pista* runway

Andy Harrison and Rosemary Paris greet the new arrivals.

- **director** *NM* director
- **honor** *NM* honor
- **coordinadora** coordinator · *coordinador* coordinator
- **resto** the rest, the remainder
- **adentro** inside

Inside the base, several members of the team are playing poker.

- **póquer** *NM* poker
- **veinticinco** twenty-five
- **centavos** cents · *centavo* cent
- **de entrada** entry
- **traducción** translation
- **novia** bride, girlfriend · *novio* groom, boyfriend
- **preciosa** precious · *precioso* precious
- **científica** scientist · *científico* scientist
- **italiana** Italian · *italiano* Italian
- **foto** *NF* photograph · *fotografía* photograph
- **paciencia** patience
- **¿cuántas?** how many? *¿cuántos?* how many?
- **emocionado** excited · *emocionarse* to be excited
- **valles** valleys · *valle* *NM* valley
- **secos** dry · *seco* dry
- **época** season, time
- **monte** *NM* mount, mountain
- **meteorito** meteorite
- **dedicamos** we dedicate · *dedicar* to dedicate
- **secreto** secret

Jerry leaves the poker game to join McClaren and Andy at the map table.

- **mapa** *NM* map
- **correcto** correct
- **dirección** direction
- **opuesta** opposite · *opuesto* opposite
- **doble** double

- **distancia** distance
- **recorrí** I covered · *recorrer* to cover [DISTANCE]
- **ruta** route
- **tanteando** carefully examining · *tantear* to examine carefully
- **terreno** terrain
- **no me he parado** I haven't stopped · *pararse* to stop
- **complacerlo** to accommodate him · *complacer* to accommodate, to please
- **enero** January
- **vehículos** vehicles · *vehículo* vehicle
- **nieve** *NF* snow
- **peligroso** dangerous
- **delgado** thin, slim
- **afuera** outside

Jerry puts the dogs to bed outside.

- **te agrada** it pleases you · *agradar* to please
- **te esfuerces** *SUBJ* you make an effort · *esforzarse* to make an effort, to force
- **estrella** star

Jerry knocks on Katie's open door.

- **calenté** I heated up · *calentar* to heat
- **helado** ice cream
- **favorito** favorite
- **fresa** strawberry
- **horario** schedule
- **no me quejo** I can't complain (*LIT* I don't complain) · *quejarse* to complain
- **fantástica** fantastic · *fantástico* fantastic
- **está envejeciendo** he is getting old, he is growing old · *envejecer* to get old, to grow old

Rosie joins them.

- **no interrumpo** I'm not interrupting · *interrumpir* to interrupt
- **charla** chat, light conversation
- **temprano** early
- **detalle** *NM* detail

McClaren and Coop prepare their bunks.

- **con permiso** excuse me (*LIT* with permission) · *permiso* permission
- **golpe** *NM* a hit, a blow
- **piso** floor
- **cómodo** comfortable
- **exactamente** exactly
- **cartografía** cartography
- **exploré** I explored · *explorar* to explore
- **tracé** I mapped · *trazar* to map, to draw up (plans)
- **milímetro** millimeter
- **territorio** territory

🎬 Jerry joins McClaren and Coop in their quarters.

- ☐ **¿anotaste?** did you score? · *anotar* to score
- ☐ **no llegué al bat** I didn't get up to bat · *llegar* to get (somewhere), to arrive · *bat NM* baseball bat
- ☐ **calefacción** heating system
- ☐ **congelar** to freeze
- ☐ **botella** bottle
- ☐ **sugiero** I suggest · *sugerir* to suggest
- ☐ **torpedo** torpedo

🎬 Jerry and McClaren prepare to leave with the dogs.

- ☐ **regla** rule
- ☐ **arnés** *NM* harness
- ☐ **tenso** tense, taut
- ☐ **se enreda** it becomes tangled · *enredarse* to become tangled
- ☐ **depende** it depends · *depender* to depend
- ☐ **vigilarlos** to watch over them · *vigilar* to watch over
- ☐ **les fascina** it fascinates them · *fascinar* to fascinate
- ☐ **desfallecer** to faint
- ☐ **presentaciones** introductions · *presentación* introduction
- ☐ **cachorro** puppy
- ☐ **entrenamiento** training
- ☐ **talento** talent
- ☐ **gemelos** twins · *gemelo* twin
- ☐ **mordió** he bit · *morder* to bite
- ☐ **cicatriz** *NF* scar
- ☐ **finalmente** finally
- ☐ **malamutes** malamutes · *malamute NM ENG* malamute
- ☐ **gris** gray
- ☐ **rojo** red
- ☐ **cerebro** brain

🎬 Andy, Katie, and Cooper join Jerry and McClaren.

- ☐ **excelente** excellent
- ☐ **cuida** *IMP* take care of · *cuidar* to take care of
- ☐ **descuida** *IMP* don't worry · *descuidar* to not worry
- ☐ **alimentar** to feed, to nourish
- ☐ **graciosa** funny · *gracioso* funny
- ☐ **intrépidos** intrepid · *intrépido* intrepid
- ☐ **exploradores** explorers · *explorador* explorer
- ☐ **despedirte** to say good-bye · *despedirse* to say good-bye
- ☐ **causar** to cause
- ☐ **complejo** complex
- ☐ **despídete** *IMP* say good-bye · *despedirse* to say good-bye
- ☐ **despedirme** to say good-bye · *despedirse* to say good-bye
- ☐ **qué asco** *EXP* yuck, gross, sick

- ☐ **asqueroso** gross, sickening
- ☐ **baba** slobber
- ☐ **boca** mouth
- ☐ **nariz** *NF* nose
- ☐ **gracioso** funny
- ☐ **no sé qué les divierte** I don't know why that's so funny (*LIT* I don't know what is so entertaining to you) · *divertir* to entertain

**3  The Expedition**                          7:56

## Phrases to Listen For
**al frente** up ahead, in front
**hay que** it's necessary
**tenemos que** we have to
**por poco** that was close, close call
**no hay por qué** you're welcome, not at all
**qué suerte tiene** he's lucky
**estilo de vida** lifestyle
**ya es tarde** it's already late

## Name
Eric

🎬 Jerry and McClaren leave with the dogs. They stop. Jerry surveys the ice field through binoculars.

- ☐ **grueso** thick
- ☐ **vehículos** vehicles · *vehículo* vehicle
- ☐ **nieve** *NF* snow
- ☐ **arnés** *NM* harness
- ☐ **formación** formation
- ☐ **abanico** fan
- ☐ **lento** slow
- ☐ **distribuye** it distributes · *distribuir* to distribute
- ☐ **peso** weight
- ☐ **se hunde** it sinks · *hundirse* to sink

🎬 Jerry and McClaren watch leopard seals through their binoculars.

- ☐ **focas leopardo** leopard seals · *foca* seal · *leopardo* leopard
- ☐ **rodeamos** we go around · *rodear* to go around, to avoid
- ☐ **espacio** space

🎬 Jerry stops the dogs and puts McClaren behind the sled to control the brakes.

- ☐ **glaciar** *NM* glacier
- ☐ **controle** *SUBJ* you control · *controlar* to control
- ☐ **freno** brake
- ☐ **pisadas** footsteps · *pisada* footstep · *pisar* to step on, to walk on
- ☐ **guíe** *IMP* guide · *guiar* to guide
- ☐ **rastro** track, trail
- ☐ **tantear** to examine carefully

- **terreno** terrain
- **ambos** both
- **necesario** necessary
- **estabilícelo** *IMP* stabilize it · *estabilizar* to stabilize

🎬 Jerry finds a fissure in the glacier.

- **presione** *IMP* press · *presionar* to press
- **fisura** fissure
- **rodearla** to avoid it · *rodear* to avoid
- **guiarlos** to guide them · *guiar* to guide
- **lentamente** slowly
- **ligeramente** lightly
- **¡deténgalos!** *IMP* stop them! · *detener* to stop

🎬 The sled breaks through the ice.

- **resista** *IMP* hang in there, hold on · *resistir* to hang on, to resist
- **sujételo** *IMP* hold on to it · *sujetar* to hold on
- **planee** *SUBJ* you plan · *planear* to plan
- **excursión** excursion
- **no empaque** *IMP* don't pack · *empacar* to pack
- **accedió** you agreed · *acceder* to agree, to concede

🎬 Andy and McClaren camp in their tent.

- **artista** *NMF* artist
- **novia** girlfriend · *novio* boyfriend
- **broma** joke
- **guiando** guiding · *guiar* to guide
- **científicos** scientists · *científico* scientist
- **soportaría** would tolerate, would put up with · *soportar* to tolerate, to put up with
- **no resultó** it didn't work out · *resultar* to work out, to turn out, to result in
- **relaciones** relationships · *relación* relationship
- **estilo** style
- **temprano** early
- **afuera** outside

## 4 Melbourne 7:16

### Phrases to Listen For
**cambio y fuera** over and out
**cambio** over
**vamos de vuelta** we're going back
**lo siento** I'm sorry
**tenemos que** we have to
**a primera hora** first thing
**lo que** what
**en busca de** in search of
**tienes que** you have to
**es un trato** it's a deal
**se nos acaba el tiempo** time is running out

**qué bueno** that's great
**mediodía** noon, midday

### Names
Doc, Melbourne, Andy, Steve, Jerry, McMurdo

🎬 The next day, Jerry and McClaren climb a mountain and look into the distance at Melbourne.

- **presione** *IMP* press · *presionar* to press
- **freno** brake
- **sorprendente** surprising
- **hogar** *NM* home
- **precioso** precious

🎬 A storm brews. Victoria station receives a radio message from McMurdo.

- **estación** station
- **enormes** enormous · *enorme* enormous
- **sistemas de baja presión** low pressure systems · *sistema* *NM* system · *bajo* low · *presión* pressure
- **sur** *NM* south
- **control** *NM* control
- **alerta** *IMP* alert · *alertar* to alert
- **radio** radio

🎬 At camp, Jerry prepares a hot drink.

- **taza** cup
- **evidencia** evidence
- **apunta** it points to · *apuntar* to point to
- **siguientes** following, next · *siguiente* following, next
- **respondan** *IMP* respond · *responder* to respond
- **repetir** to repeat
- **recepción** reception
- **¿me copias?** do you copy me? · *copiar* to copy
- **se acerca** it is getting close · *acercarse* to get close, to draw near
- **vamos de vuelta** we're going back, we're returning · *ir* to go · *vuelta* return

🎬 Jerry and McClaren are inside the tent.

- **decisión** decision
- **se aproxima** it is approaching · *aproximarse* to approach
- **menor** minor
- **advierto** I warn · *advertir* to warn
- **diferencia** difference
- **llevarte de regreso** to take you back · *llevar* to carry · *regreso* return
- **roca** rock
- **planeta** *NM* planet
- **lejano** distant, far-away
- **témpano** ice floe
- **meteorito** meteorite
- **Mercurio** Mercury

□ **descubrimientos** discoveries · *descubrimiento* discovery
□ **inimaginables** unimaginable · *inimaginable* unimaginable
□ **montaña** mountain
□ **navegas** you navigate · *navegar* to navigate
□ **emociona** it excites · *emocionar* to excite
□ **he cruzado** I have crossed · *cruzar* to cross
□ **arriesgarte** to take a risk · *arriesgarse* to take a risk
□ **trato** deal

🎬 The next day, Jerry and McClaren climb through rocks and snow.
□ **zona** zone
□ **peligrosa** dangerous · *peligroso* dangerous
□ **enorme** enormous
□ **once** eleven
□ **centímetros** centimeters · *centímetro* centimeter
□ **ancho** width
□ **intacto** intact
□ **basalto** basalt
□ **área** area
□ **revisada** checked, reviewed · *revisar* to check, to review
□ **pisadas** footsteps · *pisada* footstep · *pisar* to step on, to walk on

🎬 At Victoria, the team receives another radio message.
□ **aumentó** it gained, it grew, it became bigger · *aumentar* to gain, to grow, to become bigger
□ **velocidad** velocity, speed
□ **intensidad** intensity
□ **coordenadas** coordinates · *coordenada* coordinate

## 5 Impending Storm 9:42

### Phrases to Listen For
**tal vez** maybe, perhaps
**bien hecho** well done
**justo así** just like that
**tienes que** you have to
**no te preocupes** IMP don't worry
**¿estás bien?** are you all right?
**no me gusta** I don't like (*LIT* it doesn't please me)
**hay que** it's necessary
**lo siento** I'm sorry
**está por partir** it's about to leave

### Names
Doc, Maya, Buck, Shadow, Rosemary, Jerry, Katie, McClaren

🎬 On the sled once more, Jerry notices blood in the snow.
□ **herido** hurt, wounded · *herir* to hurt, to wound
□ **radio** radio
□ **informe** SUBJ she reports, she informs · *informar* to report, to inform
□ **responda** IMP respond · *responder* to respond, to answer
□ **pata** paw, leg [OF AN ANIMAL]
□ **curarte** to treat you · *curar* to treat, to heal, to cure
□ **posición** position

🎬 The ice gives way beneath McClaren.
□ **pierna** leg
□ **no tragues** IMP don't swallow · *tragar* to swallow
□ **orilla** edge
□ **sostente** IMP hold on · *sostenerse* to hold on
□ **pegado** stuck, attached · *pegar* to stick
□ **congelado** frozen · *congelar* to freeze
□ **duras** you last · *durar* to last
□ **ahogado** drowned · *ahogarse* to drown
□ **resiste** IMP hang in there, don't give up, hold on · *resistir* to hang in, to not give up, to hold on, to resist
□ **respirar** to breathe
□ **profundo** deep

🎬 Jerry places a rope in Maya's mouth.
□ **muerde** IMP bite · *morder* to bite
□ **soga** rope
□ **lento** slow
□ **tranquila** EXP easy, take it easy, be calm
□ **alerta** alert
□ **suave** soft, smooth
□ **encima** on top
□ **brazo** arm
□ **trata** IMP try · *tratar* to try
□ **derecho** right
□ **codo** elbow
□ **lazo** lasso, rope
□ **ténsenla** IMP tighten it up · *tensar* to tighten, to tighten up
□ **alinéalos** IMP line them up · *alinear* to line up

🎬 Jerry secures McClaren in the sled.
□ **resistir** to hold on, to hang on
□ **regrésanos** IMP take us back · *regresar* to take back, to return
□ **ayúdala** IMP help her · *ayudar* to help

🎬 Back at the base, the team discusses the storm. Jerry and McClaren continue.
□ **capacidad** ability
□ **tormentas** storms · *tormenta* storm

▣ Katie calls Jerry on the radio. Jerry and McClaren continue. The team waits.

- □ **respondan** *IMP* answer, respond, come in [RADIO] · *responder* to answer, to respond
- □ **contesten** *IMP* answer · *contestar* to answer
- □ **contéstame** *IMP* answer me · *contestar* to answer
- □ **dieciséis** sixteen
- □ **kilómetros** kilometers · *kilómetro* kilometer

▣ Katie spots the sled. The team receives them outside.

- □ **camilla** stretcher
- □ **tos** *NF* cough
- □ **revisar** to check
- □ **adentro** inside

▣ Inside the base camp, Andy attends McClaren.

- □ **botiquín** *NM* first-aid kit
- □ **hipotermia** hypothermia
- □ **mete** *IMP* put in · *meter* to put in, to insert
- □ **descongelarlas** to thaw them out · *descongelar* to thaw, to unfreeze
- □ **alimenté** I fed · *alimentar* to feed
- □ **roca** rock
- □ **descubrieron** they discovered · *descubrir* to discover
- □ **meteoro** meteor
- □ **alístate** *IMP* get ready · *alistarse* to get ready
- □ **despegar** to take off [AIRCRAFT]
- □ **enseguida** right away, at once
- □ **médica** medical · *médico* medical
- □ **encargarme** to take charge · *encargarse* to take charge
- □ **recoger** to pick up
- □ **ni siquiera lo discutiré** I won't even discuss it · *ni siquiera* *ADV* not even · *discutir* to discuss, to argue
- □ **quemadura de tercer grado** third-degree burn · *quemadura* burn · *tercer* third · *grado* degree
- □ **daño** damage
- □ **sufrió** it suffered · *sufrir* to suffer
- □ **tejido** tissue
- □ **regreso** I'll return (*LIT* I return) · *regresar* to return

## 6 Evacuation  14:35

### Phrases to Listen For
**tienes algo de miedo** you are a little afraid
**qué bien** excellent, very good
**qué suerte** what luck
**todo el tiempo** all the time

**todo el mundo** everyone
**de vuelta** return
**¿cómo que no?** what do you mean?
**qué cosa** that's something, I've got bigger problems
**tenemos que** we have to
**lo siento** I'm sorry
**de verdad lo siento** I'm really sorry
**lo que** what
**tal vez** maybe, perhaps
**lo lamento** I'm sorry
**tengo que** I have to
**antes de** before
**piénselo bien** think about it, think again, think through it
**¿qué tal?** what's up?, how's it going?
**tienes a todos en tu bolsillo** you have them all in your pocket
**a lo mucho** at most
**tengo que** I have to
**tratar de olvidarte** to try to forget

### Names
Dodgers, Shepard, NFS, Andy Harrison, Rosie, Cooper

▣ Several members of the team lift McClaren up into the airplane.

- □ **pierna** leg
- □ **camilla** stretcher
- □ **sujetar** to fasten
- □ **collares** collars · *collar* *NM* collar

▣ Jerry and Coop secure the dogs.

- □ **no tardará** it won't be long · *tardar* to be long [TIME]
- □ **resiste** *IMP* hang on · *resistir* to hang on, to resist, to oppose

▣ Jerry and Coop board the plane.

- □ **cinturón** *NM* seat belt

▣ At McMurdo Station, Coop sits at Jerry's bedside.

- □ **desmayaste** you fainted · *desmayar* to faint
- □ **brincando** jumping · *brincar* to jump
- □ **pelota de playa** beach ball · *pelota* ball · *playa* beach
- □ **botando** bouncing · *botar* to bounce
- □ **estadio** stadium
- □ **horror** *NM* horror
- □ **gritar** to shout, to scream
- □ **intenso** intense
- □ **locura** craziness
- □ **se llenó** it filled up · *llenarse* to fill up, to become full

☐ **se curó** he recovered · *curarse* to recover
☐ **grandioso** terrific, magnificent
☐ **estupendo** stupendous, wonderful
☐ **no ha parado de nevar** it hasn't stopped snowing · *parar* to stop · *nevar* to snow

🎬 Katie spots Jerry in the hallway.

☐ **clima** *NM* weather
☐ **cancelaron** they canceled · *cancelar* to cancel
☐ **vuelos** flights · *vuelo* flight
☐ **mejore** *SUBJ* it improves · *mejorar* to improve
☐ **primavera** spring [SEASON]

🎬 Jerry enters the McMurdo command center.

☐ **de vuelta** back
☐ **evacuados** evacuated · *evacuado* evacuated · *evacuar* to evacuate
☐ **doscientas** two hundred · *doscientos* two hundred
☐ **Nueva Zelanda** New Zealand
☐ **motores** motors · *motor* *NM* motor
☐ **congelarse** to become frozen
☐ **dura** it lasts · *durar* to last
☐ **provisiones** *NFPL* provisions · *provisión* provision, supply
☐ **movamos** *SUBJ* we move · *mover* to move
☐ **transportó** it transported · *transportar* to transport
☐ **lo regreso** I'll return it (*LIT* I return it) · *regresar* to return
☐ **C ciento treinta** C-130 [AIRCRAFT]
☐ **aterrizarían** they would land · *aterrizar* to land [AIRCRAFT]
☐ **abandonarlos** to abandon them · *abandonar* to abandon
☐ **enseguida** at once
☐ **gráficas** graphics · *gráfica* graphic

🎬 Katie visits Jerry in his quarters.

☐ **beber** to drink
☐ **abandonamos** we abandoned · *abandonar* to abandon
☐ **no te dañes** *IMP* don't hurt yourself · *dañarse* to hurt oneself
☐ **sobrevivan** *SUBJ* they survive · *sobrevivir* to survive
☐ **aseguré** I secured · *asegurar* to secure
☐ **no se soltarán** they won't get free · *soltarse* to get free
☐ **hallara** *SUBJ* I find · *hallar* to find
☐ **manera** manner, way
☐ **decepcioné** I disappointed · *decepcionar* to disappoint
☐ **elevar** to elevate, to raise

☐ **expectativas** expectations · *expectativa* expectation

🎬 A plane lands in Washington, D.C. Jerry visits several officials.

☐ **llene** *IMP* fill · *llenar* to fill
☐ **formulario** blank form
☐ **entréguelo** *IMP* turn it in · *entregar* to turn in, to deliver
☐ **administración** administration
☐ **roja** red · *rojo* red
☐ **piso** floor
☐ **financiamiento** financing, funding
☐ **agosto** August
☐ **sur** *NM* south
☐ **veinticinco** twenty-five
☐ **reporte** *NM* report

🎬 The dogs escape. Jerry visits McClaren in Pasadena, California.

☐ **cohete** *NM* rocket
☐ **sorpresa** surprise
☐ **Marte** Mars
☐ **viajero** traveler
☐ **dedos** fingers · *dedo* finger
☐ **conservo** I keep, I have · *conservar* to keep, to have, to conserve
☐ **excelente** excellent
☐ **yeso** cast
☐ **obra de arte** work of art · *obra* work · *arte* *NM* art
☐ **café** *NM* coffee
☐ **cocina** kitchen

🎬 Jerry and McClaren speak in the dining room.

☐ **obsequio** gift
☐ **agencias** agencies · *agencia* agency
☐ **visité** I visited · *visitar* to visit
☐ **fundaciones** foundations · *fundación* foundation
☐ **cadenas de televisión** television networks · *cadena* network · *televisión* television
☐ **convencerlos** to convince them · *convencer* to convince
☐ **cámara** camera
☐ **juntar el dinero** to raise the money · *juntar* to raise, to collect · *dinero* money
☐ **se cierra** it is closed · *cerrar* to close
☐ **bolsillo** pocket
☐ **fundación** foundation
☐ **fondos** *NMPL* funds
☐ **siguiente** next
☐ **desperdiciar** to waste
☐ **realista** realistic
☐ **averiguarlo** to find it out · *averiguar* to find out

**7** **On Your Own** 7:09

🎬 The dogs chase a bird. Jerry lives in a trailer on the coast. Katie leaves several messages for him.

**8** **Deep Winter** 5:23

🎬 March 30: The dogs have spent 50 days on their own.

**9** **Can't Let Go** 12:21

## Phrases to Listen For

**a la vez** at a time
**tengo que** I have to
**burlarte de mí** to make fun of me
**tal como** just like
**que tal** how well
**no hay nada que hablar** there's nothing to say
**ya basta** enough already
**tal vez** maybe, perhaps
**debes dejar de culparte** you've got to stop
　blaming yourself
**no te disculpes** IMP don't apologize
**lo que** what
**tenía que** he had to
**lo importante** the important thing
**dar la bienvenida** to welcome
**cacerías tontas** wild goose chases, foolish
　hunting expeditions
**ya que** since
**whiskey en las rocas** whiskey on the rocks
**no tenía que** I didn't have to
**tienes que** you have to
**que tengas mucha suerte** SUBJ good luck,
　that you may have good luck
**por favor** please
**buena suerte** good luck

## Names

Al, Jerry Shepard, Brandy, McKinley, Mindo,
Davis McClaren, Eve, Eric, Christchurch,
Bailey's

🎬 Jerry teaches kayaking to a group of children.

☐ **océano** ocean
☐ **mente** NF mind
☐ **respeten** IMP respect · *respetar* to respect
☐ **estén alertas** IMP be on the alert · *estar alerta*
　to be on the alert
☐ **remo** oar, paddle
☐ **exacto** exactly, exact
☐ **alternando** alternating · *alternar* to alternate
☐ **cubrirme** to cover for me · *cubrir* to cover

🎬 Katie arrives and talks to Jerry.

☐ **pájaro** bird
☐ **chapoteadero** wading pool
☐ **burlarte** to make fun of · *burlarse* to make fun
　of
☐ **conduje** I drove · *conducir* to drive
☐ **ha crecido** she has grown · *crecer* to grow
☐ **entrenaron** they trained · *entrenar* to train

🎬 Jerry and Katie walk along the shore.

☐ **tráela** IMP bring it · *traer* to bring
☐ **obvio** obvious
☐ **contestaste** you answered · *contestar* to answer
☐ **se nota** it's obvious, it's clear
☐ **últimamente** recently, lately
☐ **apenas** barely
☐ **agradable** pleasant, nice
☐ **opuesto** opposite
☐ **intelectual** intellectual
☐ **ingeniero** engineer
☐ **ingenioso** ingenious, clever
☐ **rechazaste** you rejected · *rechazar* to reject
☐ **expedición** expedition
☐ **tema** NM subject
☐ **escondiéndote** hiding · *esconderse* to hide
　(oneself)
☐ **mírate** IMP look at yourself · *mirarse* to look at
　oneself
☐ **rentas** you rent · *rentar* to rent
☐ **kayak** NM kayak
☐ **culparte** to blame yourself · *culparse* to blame
　oneself

🎬 Jerry visits Mindo's dog training compound.

☐ **reconoce** he recognizes · *reconocer*
　to recognize
☐ **amante** NMF lover
☐ **obsequio** gift

🎬 Sitting at a table by the fireplace, Jerry and Mindo
　discuss the dogs.

☐ **disculparte** to apologize · *disculparse*
　to apologize
☐ **criaste** you raised · *criar* to raise (a child or
　animal)
☐ **Yukón** Yukon
☐ **verano** summer
☐ **pasear** to go for a walk
☐ **se toparon** they came across · *toparse* to come
　across
☐ **oso pardo** grizzly bear · *oso* bear ·
　*pardo* brown, dark gray
☐ **enorme** enormous
☐ **mordió** it bit · *morder* to bite
☐ **mata** it kills · *matar* to kill

☐ **notó** he noticed · *notar* to notice
☐ **resto** the rest, the remainder
☐ **recuperó** recovered · *recuperar* to recover
☐ **salud** *NF* health
☐ **te cuento** I tell you · *contar* to tell
☐ **honrando** honoring · *honrar* to honor
☐ **paz** *NF* peace

🎬 Jerry packs. Day 133: The dogs continue on their own. A black tie dinner is being held in honor of McClaren's discovery.

☐ **les invito** I invite you all · *invitar* to invite
☐ **honrar** to honor
☐ **bienvenida** welcome
☐ **meteorito** meteorite
☐ **documentado** documented · *documentar* to document
☐ **Mercurio** Mercury

🎬 McClaren speaks to the dinner attendees.

☐ **apoyo** support
☐ **paciencia** patience
☐ **alrededor de** around
☐ **expediciones** expeditions · *expedición* expedition
☐ **descritas** described · *descrito* described · *describir* to describe
☐ **cacerías tontas** wild goose chases, foolish hunting expeditions · *cacería* hunting · *tonto* foolish
☐ **continuo** continuous
☐ **descubrimiento** discovery
☐ **realizó** he made, he did · *realizar* to make real, to realize a goal, to achieve a goal or objective
☐ **no habrían vuelto** they wouldn't have returned · *volver* to return

🎬 McClaren finds Jerry after his speech.

☐ **whiskey en las rocas** whiskey on the rocks · *whiskey* *NM* whiskey · *roca* rock
☐ **te felicito** I congratulate you · *felicitar* to congratulate
☐ **me alegra** it makes me happy, I'm happy · *alegrar* to make happy
☐ **pasarte** to hand you, to pass over to you · *pasar* to hand over, to pass over
☐ **Nueva Zelanda** New Zealand
☐ **conseguiste** did you get · *conseguir* to get
☐ **arriesgarte** to take a risk · *arriesgarse* to take a risk
☐ **saluda** *IMP* say hello · *saludar* to say hello, to greet

🎬 McClaren and his wife put their son to bed.

☐ **niñera** sitter, nanny
☐ **excelente** excellent

☐ **héroes** heroes · *héroe* *NM* hero
☐ **cierre** *NM* closing out, closing down [ACCOUNTING]

## **10** Teamwork                              9:11

### Phrases to Listen For
**bote de pesca** fishing boat
**lo que** what, that
**lo más seguro** the most probable, the most likely
**en su sano juicio** in his right mind
**lo siento** I'm sorry
**no lo creo** I don't believe it
**¿todo bien?** everything all right?
**¿qué pasa?** what's happening?
**¿cómo estás?** how are you?
**gusto verte** good to see you
**es una locura** it's crazy
**¿cómo te sientes?** how do you feel?

🎬 July 10: The dogs find a whale and a leopard seal. In Christchurch, New Zealand, Jerry speaks with a boat captain.

☐ **bote** *NM* boat, ship
☐ **se alquila** it is for rent · *alquilarse* to be for rent
☐ **bote de pesca** fishing boat · *bote* *NM* boat · *pesca* fishing
☐ **bar** *NM* bar
☐ **ni de broma** don't even joke about it · *broma* joke

🎬 In a bar, Jerry talks with another boat captain.

☐ **pagarte** to pay you · *pagar* to pay
☐ **poseo** I possess · *poseer* to possess
☐ **no soporta** it doesn't tolerate · *soportar* to tolerate
☐ **temperaturas** temperatures · *temperatura* temperature
☐ **se parta** *SUBJ* it splits · *partirse* to split, to break
☐ **por la mitad** in half · *mitad* *NF* half
☐ **desesperado** desperate
☐ **opción** option
☐ **en su sano juicio** in his right mind · *sano* healthy · *juicio* judgment, considered opinion
☐ **rompehielos** *NM* icebreaker

🎬 A waitress interrupts Jerry and places a drink in front of him.

☐ **manda** she sends · *mandar* to send
☐ **disculpa** excuse (me) · *disculpar* to excuse, to forgive

🎬 Jerry talks to Katie at the bar.

- □ **piloto** pilot
- □ **expedición** expedition
- □ **libre** free
- □ **temporada** season
- □ **te extrañé** I missed you · *extrañar* to miss

🎬 Cooper joins Jerry and Katie at the bar. McClaren joins them as well.

- □ **se acortó** it was cut short · *acortarse* to be cut short
- □ **fondos** *NMPL* funds

🎬 Jerry, Cooper, and McClaren join Katie aboard a helicopter.

- □ **locura** craziness
- □ **elevar** to raise
- □ **expectativas** expectations · *expectativa* expectation
- □ **aterrizar** to land [AIRCRAFT]

## 11 Hope                                    9:24

### Phrases to Listen For

**estrellas fugaces** shooting stars
**de buena suerte** good luck
**tal vez** maybe
**pase lo que pase** *SUBJ* whatever happens
**me alegra** I'm glad (*LIT* it makes me happy)
**tenía que** I had to
**¿qué pasó...?** what happened ...?
**ya se acabó** it finished
**qué lástima** what a pity, that's too bad
**echar un vistazo** to take a look
**lo que** what
**la recta final** the final stretch
**lo lamento** I'm sorry
**de ida y vuelta** round trip
**tiene mucha razón** he's quite right, he makes a lot of sense
**en serio** seriously
**hay que** it's necessary
**de ese modo** that way
**sin ofender** no offense

### Names

Jerry, Hansen, Simonetta Pirelli, Lamborghini, Polarsyssel

🎬 The helicopter approaches a ship.

- □ **helicóptero lima noviembre Oscar Mike bravo** helicopter Lima November Oscar Mike Bravo [AVIATION CODE IDENTIFICATION] · *helicóptero* helicopter
- □ **solicito** I request · *solicitar* to request, to solicit

- □ **aterrizar** to land [AIRCRAFT]
- □ **nave** *NF* ship
- □ **afirmativo** affirmative
- □ **sosténganse bien** *IMP* hold on tight · *sostenerse* to hold on

🎬 Jerry joins Katie on deck.

- □ **acompaño** I accompany · *acompañar* to accompany
- □ **cuántas** how many · *cuántos* how many
- □ **estrellas** stars · *estrella* star
- □ **estrellas fugaces** shooting stars · *estrella* star · *fugaz* fleeting
- □ **consciente** conscious, aware
- □ **me alegra** I'm happy (*LIT* it makes me happy) · *alegrar* to make happy
- □ **entendiste** you understood · *entender* to understand
- □ **calma** *EXP* easy, take it easy, calm down
- □ **adulto** adult
- □ **ingenioso** ingenious, clever
- □ **ingeniero** engineer
- □ **qué lástima** what a pity, too bad

🎬 The dogs wait. The ship breaks through the ice and comes to a halt.

- □ **echar un vistazo** to take a quick glance · *echar* to throw · *vistazo* quick glance

🎬 The team joins the captain on the ice; comments are barely audible. Shortly, the team joins the captain on the bridge.

- □ **grueso** thick
- □ **sorprendernos** to surprise us · *sorprender* to surprise
- □ **hemos cruzado** we have crossed · *cruzar* to cross
- □ **recta final** home stretch · *recta* straight line · *final* final
- □ **novia** girlfriend · *novio* boyfriend
- □ **italiana** Italian
- □ **témpano** ice floe
- □ **banco** bank
- □ **bloqueó** it blocked · *bloquear* to block
- □ **ruta** route
- □ **pingüinos de Adelia** Adélie penguins · *pingüino* penguin · *Adelia* Adélie
- □ **pescar** to fish
- □ **relevancia** relevance
- □ **paciencia** patience
- □ **trazar** to map, to trace
- □ **investigadores** researchers · *investigador* researcher
- □ **pista** track, trail
- □ **taza** cup

□ **sabroso**  delicious
□ **oficina**  office

🎬 While the team views a map, Cooper continues to explain his idea.

□ **de ida y vuelta**  round trip
□ **mitad** *NF*  half
□ **distancia**  distance
□ **bases**  bases · *base NF* base
□ **equipada**  equipped · *equipado* equipped · *equipar* to equip
□ **vehículos de tracción**  tractors, Caterpillar® · *vehículo* vehicle · *tracción* traction
□ **cohete** *NM*  rocket
□ **resuelto**  resolved · *resolver* to resolve
□ **sin ofender** *EXP*  no offense · *ofender* to offend

## 12 Return to the Base                    5:03

### Phrases to Listen For
**todos a bordo**  all aboard
**¡qué lindo!**  beautiful!, how beautiful!
**en cuanto a**  concerning
**la revancha es dulce**  revenge is sweet
**¿verdad que sí?**  isn't that right?

### Name
Geraldo

🎬 The team arrives at the Italian base in the helicopter.

□ **llaves**  keys · *llave NF* key
□ **bodega**  warehouse
□ **palas**  shovels · *pala* shovel
□ **cavar**  to dig

🎬 Cooper drives the snow tractor out of the storage unit. Jerry, Katie, and McClaren join Cooper on board. Later, the dogs wait as the snow tractor crosses the ice.

□ **todos a bordo**  all aboard
□ **extraordinario**  extraordinary
□ **grazie, Geraldo**  thank you, Jerry [ITALIAN]
□ **vuelos**  flights · *vuelo* flight
□ **soporté**  I tolerated · *soportar* to tolerate
□ **revancha**  revenge
□ **venganza**  revenge

## 13 One More                    9:51

### Phrases to Listen For
**por favor**  please
**lo siento**  I'm sorry
**no está tan mal**  it's not that bad
**¿qué tal...?**  what about ...?
**hora de irnos**  time to go

### Names
Buck, Truman, Shorty

🎬 The team arrives at Victoria. Jerry follows the chains.

□ **liberarse**  to get free
□ **cadena**  chain
□ **precioso**  precious
□ **cara**  face
□ **quítamelo** *IMP*  get him off · *quitar* to remove
□ **estrellas**  stars · *estrella* star

🎬 The dogs board. Max refuses.

□ **obediente**  obedient
□ **calma** *EXP*  easy, take it easy, be calm
□ **encendemos**  we start · *encender* to start [MOTOR]
□ **espacio**  space

## 14 End Credits                    7:30

🎬 End credits.

# The Fox and the Hound

**Apuesto que sabes jugar a las escondidas.**
*I bet you'd be good playing hide-and-seek.*

GENRE      Adventure/Animation
YEAR       1981
DIRECTORS  Ted Berman, Richard Rich, Art Stevens
CAST       Arturo Mercado, Juan Antonio Edwards, Carmen Donadío
STUDIO     Walt Disney Productions

Can the childhood friendship that develops between a fox named Tod and a hound named Toby last? After a time, these two friends go their separate ways. When they meet up years later as hunter and hunted, it's bound to be interesting. Though told as a serious story, the comedic relief provided by Dinky and his pal Trabalenguas as they hunt the caterpillar is delightful and clever. This is an excellent Beginner film for the student who is just starting to use Spanish in context, because the dialogue has a fairly slow pace, the accents are easy to understand, and the grammar is simple.

## BASIC VOCABULARY

### Names

Abigail, Amos, Búho, Dinky, Slade, Toby, Trabalenguas (Tongue Twister), Vixey

### Nouns

- ☐ **amistad** friendship · *Cuando el tiempo haya pasado, ¿durará esa **amistad** o se olvidará?* When time has passed, will that friendship last or will it be forgotten?
- ☐ **bosque** NM forest · *¿Te parece bien andar por el **bosque** a medianoche despertando a los demás?* Does it seem all right to you to travel through the forest in the middle of the night waking up others?
- ☐ **cazador** hunter · *Te vimos volver con Jefe y el **cazador**.* We saw you return with Chief and the hunter.
- ☐ **demonios** INT demons [used as an exclamation, along the lines of "rats," "nuts," or "holy cow"] · *demonio* demon · ***Demonios**, mujer, me estás lastimando el pie.* For gosh sakes, woman, you're hurting my foot.
- ☐ **diantres** INT demons, devils, evil spirits [used as an exclamation, along the lines of "rats," "nuts," or "holy cow"] · *diantre* demon, devil, evil spirit · *¡O, **diantres**! Creo que se torció mi p-p-pico.* Oh, shucks! I think I bent my b-b-beak!
- ☐ **gusano** worm · *Que no escape ese **gusano**.* Don't let that worm escape.
- ☐ **propiedad** property · *¡Fuera de mi **propiedad**!* Get off my property!
- ☐ **zorrito** little fox · *Eres un **zorrito** muy glotón.* You are a very gluttonous little fox.
- ☐ **zorro** fox · *Liberto a ese **zorro** en alguna parte del bosque.* She let that fox go in some part of the forest.

### Verbs

- ☐ **cazar** to hunt · *Prohibido **Cazar*** No Hunting (LIT Hunting Prohibited)
- ☐ **escapar** to escape · *Jefe no lo dejará **escapar**.* Chief won't let him escape.

### Other

- ☐ **adentro** ADV inside · *Sé que está **adentro**.* I know that he is inside.

## 1 Opening Credits 4:33

🎬 Opening credits. A mother fox flees with her pup in an effort to escape barking dogs.

## 2 Orphaned 3:13

### Phrases to Listen For

**a ver** let's see
**no te preocupes** IMP don't worry
**me encargaré de todo** I'll handle everything

### Name

Mama Búho

🎬 Mama Búho approaches the young fox by the fence.

- ☐ **tranquilízate** IMP calm down · *tranquilizarse* to calm down
- ☐ **no tardaré** I won't take long · *tardarse* to take long, to be delayed

🎬 Trabalenguas pecks at a tree. Mama Búho soon joins them.

- ☐ **encuentro** I find · *encontrar* to find, to encounter

🎬 The three birds hold council together.

- ☐ **me encargaré** I'll take charge · *encargarse* to take charge

## 3 Widow Tweed Adopts Tod 2:16

### Phrases to Listen For

**hacerte daño** to hurt you
**me parece que** it seems to me that
**tener miedo** to be afraid

🎬 Widow Tweed sees the birds carrying her clothes.

- ☐ **ropa** clothes
- ☐ **diablillos** little devils · *diablillo* DIM little devil [TERM OF ENDEARMENT] · *diablo* devil
- ☐ **traviesas** mischievous · *travieso* mischievous, pesky
- ☐ **aves** birds · *ave* NF bird
- ☐ **¡válgame Dios!** INT oh dear!, good heavens!
- ☐ **daño** damage
- ☐ **pequeño pillo** little rascal · *pequeño* little · *pillo* rascal

🎬 Widow Tweed sits in the rocking chair with the young fox.

- ☐ **glotón** gluttonous, greedy

## 4 A Surprise for Chief 1:30

### Phrases to Listen For

**¿qué te parece...?** what do you think about ...?
**más vale** you'd better, you might as well
**a partir de hoy** beginning today

🎬 Amos presents a small dog to old Chief.

- ☐ **sorpresa** surprise
- ☐ **cachorro** puppy
- ☐ **crecerá** he will grow · *crecer* to grow
- ☐ **más vale** you'd better
- ☐ **te acostumbres** *SUBJ* you get used to · *acostumbrarse* to get used to
- ☐ **a partir de hoy** starting today · *a partir de* starting, beginning · *hoy* today

## 5 | Mischief in the Barn 6:02

### Phrases to Listen For
**tendrás que** you will have to
**por supuesto** of course
**ya entiendo** now I understand
**ya basta** enough already
**lo que** what
**dale duro** *IMP* give it to him hard
**no es asunto tuyo** it's none of your business
**duro con él** be tough with him
**¿por dónde se fue?** where'd he go?
**¿qué te pasó?** what happened to you?
**tuviste la culpa** it was your fault
**tienes la culpa** it is your fault
**confiar en ti** to trust you
**a ver** let's see
**tienes mucho que aprender** you have a lot to learn

### Names
Abigail, Tod, Toby

🎬 The widow Tweed is milking a cow. Tod is with her.

- ☐ **paciente** patient
- ☐ **labores** chores · *labor NM* chore, labor, work

🎬 Tod frightens the hen.

- ☐ **leche** *NF* milk
- ☐ **tranquilízate** *IMP* calm down, easy · *tranquilizarse* to calm down
- ☐ **tranquila** *EXP* easy, take it easy, be calm
- ☐ **zalamerías** flattery · *zalamería* flattery
- ☐ **enojarme** to get angry, to become angry · *enojarse* to get angry, to become angry
- ☐ **pillo** rascal
- ☐ **travesuras** pranks · *travesura* prank, mischief

🎬 Outside the barn, Tod speaks for the first time. Dinky and Trabalenguas fly toward a tree.

- ☐ **olvido** I forget · *olvidar* to forget
- ☐ **no escapará** he will not escape · *escapar* to escape
- ☐ **raro** strange

- ☐ **cierra** *IMP* close · *cerrar* to close
- ☐ **pico** beak

🎬 Tod joins Dinky and Trabalenguas at the tree.

- ☐ **no te metas** *IMP* don't interfere · *meterse* to interfere, to become involved in
- ☐ **asunto** matter
- ☐ **que no escape** *SUBJ* don't let it escape · *escapar* to escape
- ☐ **tras** after
- ☐ **recto** direct hit, straight hit
- ☐ **quijada** jaw
- ☐ **se torció** it was bent · *torcerse* to bend
- ☐ **desayuno** breakfast
- ☐ **gusanos** worms · *gusano* worm
- ☐ **desayunar** to eat breakfast
- ☐ **guácala** gross, sick

🎬 Tod chases a butterfly. Toby sniffs a scent.

- ☐ **estás olfateando** are you sniffing · *olfatear* to sniff
- ☐ **había olfateado** I had sniffed · *olfatear* to sniff
- ☐ **olor** smell, odor
- ☐ **está cocinando** he is cooking · *cocinar* to cook
- ☐ **pollo** chicken
- ☐ **patatas** potatoes · *patata* potato
- ☐ **hueles** you smell · *oler* to smell
- ☐ **huelo** I smell · *oler* to smell
- ☐ **olores** smells, odors · *olor NM* smell, odor
- ☐ **averiguar** to investigate, to find out
- ☐ **olfato** sense of smell
- ☐ **guiará** it will guide · *guiar* to guide

## 6 | Tod and Copper Meet 1:15

### Phrases to Listen For
**¿cómo te llamas?** what is your name?
**claro que sí** of course

🎬 Tod speaks to Toby inside the fallen tree.

- ☐ **estás oliendo** are you smelling · *oler* to smell
- ☐ **rastrear** to look for signs or clues, to follow a trail
- ☐ **jugar a las escondidas** to play hide-and-seek
- ☐ **olfato** sense of smell
- ☐ **voltéate** *IMP* turn around · *voltearse* to turn around
- ☐ **cierra** *IMP* close · *cerrar* to close

## 7 | "The Best of Friends" 4:15

### Phrases to Listen For
**otra vez** again
**ni siquiera verás** you will not even see
**tengo que irme** I have to go

**hay que** it's necessary
**mi mejor amigo** my best friend
**a ver** let's see
**tiene que hacer** he has to do
**claro que no** of course not
**¿por qué no?** why not?

Toby and Tod play hide-and-seek while "Best of Friends" is sung in Spanish in the background.

☐ **alegría** happiness
☐ **tengo que irme** I have to go · *irse* to go away
☐ **rara** strange · *raro* strange
☐ **ideal** ideal
☐ **durará** it will last · *durar* to last

Toby and Tod swim as Mama Búho looks on. Amos and Chief look for Toby.

☐ **nadar** to swim
☐ **travieso** mischievous
☐ **cachorro** puppy
☐ **escaparse** to escape
☐ **obedecer** to obey
☐ **nos estamos divirtiendo** we're having fun · *divertirse* to have fun
☐ **enojado** angry · *enojarse* to get angry

Toby is tied up. Tod and Toby play.

☐ **amarrado** tied up · *amarrar* to tie
☐ **divertido** fun · *divertirse* to have fun
☐ **ruido** noise

## 8 | Tod Gets into Trouble 4:37

### Phrase to Listen For
**ya basta** enough already

Tod observes Chief as he sleeps.

☐ **¡caracoles!** *INT* jeepers!, yikes!, holy smokes!, good grief! · *caracol NM* snail
☐ **orejas** ears · *oreja* ear
☐ **¡caray!** *INT* good heavens!
☐ **dientotes** big teeth · *diente NM* tooth
☐ **no escapará** he will not escape · *escapar* to escape
☐ **está persiguiendo** he is pursuing · *perseguir* to pursue
☐ **acorralado** pinned down, cornered · *acorralar* to corral, to surround, to pin down, to corner
☐ **malvado** evil
☐ **tejón** *NM* badger

Chief discovers Tod and the chase begins.

☐ **que no te alcance** *SUBJ* don't let him catch you (*LIT* may he not reach you) · *alcanzar* to reach

The widow Tweed slams the brakes on her car and faces up to Amos.

☐ **escopetero** shotgun shooter
☐ **lunático** *ADJ* crazy
☐ **radiador** radiator
☐ **endiablada** devilish · *endiablado* devilish
☐ **está cargada** it's loaded · *cargar* to load
☐ **ladrón** *ADJ* thieving
☐ **gallinas** hens · *gallina* hen
☐ **mentiroso** liar
☐ **torpe** clumsy
☐ **testaruda** stubborn · *testarudo* stubborn
☐ **carácter** *NM* character
☐ **causar** to cause
☐ **dispararé** I will shoot · *disparar* to shoot
☐ **no fallaré** I will not fail · *fallar* to fail

## 9 | Cooped Up 2:56

### Phrases to Listen For
**otra vez** again
**lo que** what
**a ver** let's see
**tienes que** you have to

Tod looks out the window as the widow Tweed cooks.

☐ **me apena** it grieves me · *apenar* to grieve
☐ **encerrado** locked up, enclosed · *encerrar* to lock up, to enclose
☐ **causaste** you caused · *causar* to cause
☐ **ayer** yesterday
☐ **cacería** hunting

Amos starts his car and prepares to leave.

☐ **endemoniada** fiendish, demon-possessed · *endemoniado* fiendish, demon-possessed
☐ **arruinar** to ruin
☐ **radiador** radiator
☐ **enseñaremos** we will teach you · *enseñar* to teach
☐ **perseguir** to pursue
☐ **zorros** foxes · *zorro* fox
☐ **novato** beginner, rookie
☐ **derecho** right
☐ **primavera** spring [SEASON]

After Toby, Chief, and Amos drive away, Tod talks to Mama Búho.

☐ **despedirme** to say good-bye · *despedirse* to say good-bye
☐ **burlar** to outsmart, to outwit, to evade
☐ **educación** education

## 10 "Lack of Education" 7:14

### Phrases to Listen For
**¿por qué?** why?
**haces amistad** you make friends (*LIT* you make friendship)
**mejor amigo** best friend
**lo que** what
**para que** so that
**lo siento** I'm sorry
**¡al ataque!** attack!
**por aquí** over here
**hasta luego** see you later (*LIT* until later)

▶ Mama Búho sings "Lack of Education."

- [ ] **eliminación** elimination
- [ ] **can** *NM* canine, dog
- [ ] **persigue** he pursues · *perseguir* to pursue
- [ ] **rencor** *NM* rancor
- [ ] **educación** education
- [ ] **mas** but
- [ ] **alerta** alert
- [ ] **piel** *NF* skin
- [ ] **localizar** to find
- [ ] **torva** stern · *torvo* stern
- [ ] **mirada** look · *mirar* to look at
- [ ] **arma** weapon
- [ ] **cargada** loaded · *cargar* to load

▶ The birds show Tod the animal hides.

- [ ] **asesino** killer
- [ ] **cariño** dear, sweetie

▶ The "worm" breaks through the snow. Dinky and Trabalenguas chase him.

- [ ] **se está congelando** it is freezing · *congelarse* to freeze, to be freezing
- [ ] **pico** beak
- [ ] **odioso** hateful
- [ ] **cómodo** comfortable
- [ ] **caliente** hot
- [ ] **abrigado** protected · *abrigar* to protect, to shelter
- [ ] **picos** beaks · *pico* beak
- [ ] **se congelan** they become frozen · *congelarse* to become frozen, to freeze
- [ ] **afuera** outside
- [ ] **quejándonos** complaining · *quejarse* to complain
- [ ] **temblando** trembling · *temblar* to tremble

▶ Dinky and Trabalenguas say good-bye to Mama Búho. Toby and Chief hunt through the winter.

- [ ] **invierno** winter
- [ ] **sur** *NM* south
- [ ] **primavera** spring [SEASON]

## 11 The Next Spring 5:23

### Phrases to Listen For
**a ver** let's see
**lo siento** I'm sorry
**lo que** what
**claro que** of course
**ya basta** enough already
**hasta luego** see you later (*LIT* until later)
**qué grande está** how big he is
**no importa** it doesn't matter
**hace mucho tiempo** it's been a long time
**está bien** it's fine, okay
**hay que** it's necessary
**de acuerdo** agreed, all right

### Name
Mama Búho

▶ Mama Búho talks to Tod as Dinky and Trabalenguas arrive.

- [ ] **bienvenidos** welcome · *bienvenido ADJ* welcome
- [ ] **solitario** lonely
- [ ] **pillos** rascals · *pillo* rascal
- [ ] **seguramente** surely
- [ ] **flaco** skinny
- [ ] **feo** ugly
- [ ] **fino** fine
- [ ] **elegante** elegant
- [ ] **collar** *NM* collar
- [ ] **cola** tail
- [ ] **están molestándome** you are bothering me · *molestar* to bother

▶ The widow Tweed carries a plant outside. Dinky and Trabalenguas spot the "worm" and give chase.

- [ ] **asunto** matter
- [ ] **pendiente** pending
- [ ] **tubo** tube, pipe
- [ ] **¿lo atrapaste?** did you trap him? · *atrapar* to trap
- [ ] **se escondió** he hid himself · *esconderse* to hide
- [ ] **¡recórcholis!** *INT* double wow! · *córcholis* wow

▶ Amos, Toby, and Chief arrive home in the truck filled with pelts.

- [ ] **cruel** cruel
- [ ] **artero** crafty
- [ ] **enojado** angry · *enojarse* to get angry

▶ Mama Búho talks to Tod about the pelts.

- [ ] **cuántas** how many · *cuántos* how many
- [ ] **pieles** skins · *piel NF* skin

□ **se va a alegrar** he is going to be happy ·
*alegrarse* to be happy
□ **no te apures** IMP don't hurry · *apurarse*
to hurry

🎬 Toby tries to play with Chief.

□ **divertirnos** to have fun · *divertirse* to have
fun
□ **falla** failure
□ **cacería** hunting
□ **novato** rookie, beginner
□ **olfatear** to sniff
□ **rastrear** to look for signs or clues, to follow
a trail
□ **zorros** foxes · *zorro* fox
□ **olfatearlos** to sniff them · *olfatear* to sniff
□ **rastrearlos** to track them · *rastrear* to track
□ **odiarlos** to hate them · *odiar* to hate

## 12  A Difficult Reunion                    4:56

**Phrases to Listen For**
  **de acuerdo** agreed, all right
  **antes de que** before
  **hay que** it's necessary
  **otra vez** again
  **gracias a Dios** thank God

🎬 Tod visits Toby in the night.

□ **oí** I heard · *oír* to hear
□ **has crecido** you have grown · *crecer* to grow
□ **me agrada** I'm happy (LIT it pleases me) ·
*agradar* to please
□ **dificultades** difficulties · *dificultad* NF
difficulty

🎬 Chief discovers Tod. Amos chases. The widow
Tweed leaves her house.

□ **están persiguiendo** they are pursuing ·
*perseguir* to pursue
□ **atrápenlo** IMP trap him · *atrapar* to trap
□ **que no escape** SUBJ don't let him escape ·
*escapar* to escape

🎬 The train crosses the bridge.

□ **salta** IMP jump · *saltar* to jump

## 13  The Aftermath                          2:31

🎬 Amos Slade threatens Tod at the widow Tweed's
house.

□ **encerrado** locked up · *encerrar* to lock up,
to enclose

## 14  "Good-bye May Seem Forever"          6:55

**Phrases to Listen For**
  **para siempre** forever
  **lo que** what
  **¿te parece bien...?** does it seem all right ...?
  **ni siquiera preguntaron** they didn't even ask
  **por aquí** over here

🎬 Widow Tweed places Tod in the car.

□ **por casualidad** by coincidence
□ **soledad** loneliness
□ **mas** but
□ **tristeza** sadness
□ **alegría** happiness
□ **nació** was born · *nacer* to be born
□ **descubrí** I discovered · *descubrir* to discover
□ **recuerdo** I remember · *recordar* to remember
□ **lluviosos** rainy · *lluvioso* rainy
□ **nos calentábamos** we warmed up ·
*calentarse* to warm up

🎬 Tod seeks shelter from the storm.

□ **ajena** belonging to someone else · *ajeno*
belonging to someone else

🎬 Amos spies the widow Tweed arriving in the storm.

□ **libertó** she set free · *libertar* to set free

🎬 Chief recovers from his injury.

□ **pata** leg [OF AN ANIMAL], paw
□ **comida** food
□ **suave** soft
□ **almohada** pillow
□ **comodidad** comfort
□ **calor** NM heat
□ **barril** NM barrel
□ **visitar** to visit
□ **inválido** ADJ invalid
□ **qué ingratos** how ungrateful · *ingrato* ungrateful

🎬 Amos shows Toby the trap.

□ **sin sospechar** without suspecting · *sospechar*
to suspect

## 15  Big Mama Comes Looking for Tod       3:47

**Phrases to Listen For**
  **me alegra** I'm happy (LIT it makes me happy)
  **no tengo nada que hacer** I have nothing to do
  **¿qué pasó?** what happened?
  **lo siento** I'm sorry

**¿por qué...?** why ...?
**se ve** he looks
**tal vez** maybe, perhaps
**te ves bellísima** you look beautiful
**buenos días** good morning

### Name
Mama Búho

🎬 Mama Búho searches for Tod and talks to Vixey.

- □ **alas** wings · *ala* wing
- □ **más vale** you'd better
- □ **kilos** kilograms · *kilo* kilogram
- □ **edad** age
- □ **guapo** handsome, good-looking
- □ **caray** INT yikes, good heavens
- □ **me alegra** I'm happy (LIT it makes me happy) · *alegrar* to make happy
- □ **seguramente** surely

🎬 Tod falls out of the tree.

- □ **anoche** last night
- □ **intención** intention
- □ **revolviste** you mixed up · *revolver* to mix up
- □ **hueca** empty, hollow · *hueco* empty, hollow
- □ **accidente** NM accident
- □ **excusas** excuses · *excusa* excuse
- □ **no te metas** IMP don't interfere, don't meddle · *meterse* to interfere, to meddle
- □ **alfiletero ambulante** walking pincushion · *alfiletero* pincushion · *ambulante* walking
- □ **gruñón** NM grump, grouch
- □ **vecindario** neighborhood
- □ **forastero** outsider, stranger

🎬 Mama Búho and Vixey find Tod.

- □ **cariño** dear, sweetie
- □ **completamente** completely
- □ **mágicas** magic · *mágico* magic

## 16   Tod Meets Vixey                3:33

### Phrases to Listen For
**¿por qué no?** why not?
**claro que sí** of course
**por favor** please
**claro que no** of course not
**así es** that's how, that's the way, that's right
**lo siento** I'm sorry

🎬 Mama Búho approaches Tod.

- □ **terrible** terrible
- □ **anímate** IMP cheer up · *animarse* to cheer up

- □ **mira a tu alrededor** IMP look at your surroundings, look around you · *mirar* to look at · *alrededor* surroundings
- □ **bello** beautiful, pretty
- □ **anoche** last night

🎬 Tod sees Vixey.

- □ **zorrita** DIM little fox · *zorro* fox
- □ **sorpresa** surprise

🎬 Tod hunts fish for Vixey.

- □ **río** river
- □ **truchas** trout · *trucha* trout
- □ **pescar** to fish
- □ **experto** expert
- □ **pescador** ADJ fish-catching
- □ **alardear** to boast, to brag
- □ **trucos** tricks · *truco* trick
- □ **nunca fallo** I never fail · *fallar* to fail
- □ **que pesque una** SUBJ may he catch one · *pescar* to catch fish, to fish
- □ **enorme** enormous
- □ **observa** IMP observe · *observar* to observe
- □ **la atrapé** I caught it! · *atrapar* to catch, to trap

🎬 Tod catches a stick instead of a fish.

- □ **granja** farm
- □ **pesca** fishing
- □ **gracioso** funny
- □ **ríanse** IMP laugh · *reírse* to laugh
- □ **evitarlo** to avoid it · *evitar* to avoid
- □ **hueca** empty · *hueco* empty
- □ **enojarte** to get angry · *enojarse* to get angry
- □ **no me regañes** IMP don't scold me · *regañar* to scold

## 17   "Appreciate the Lady"          3:17

### Phrases to Listen For
**no te enojes** IMP don't get angry
**estoy segura de que** I'm sure that

🎬 Tod is dripping wet. Mama Búho sings.

- □ **no te enojes** IMP don't be angry · *enojarse* to get angry
- □ **simpatía** sympathy
- □ **satisfacciones** satisfaction · *satisfacción* satisfaction
- □ **sincero** sincere
- □ **afecto** affection
- □ **simular** to fake, to feign
- □ **alardear** to brag, to boast
- □ **halagar** to compliment, to flatter
- □ **natural** natural

🎬 Dinky and Trabalenguas laugh.

□ **interesante** interesting

🎬 Vixey shows Tod the forest.

□ **te mostraré** I will show you · *mostrar* to show
□ **ideal** ideal

## 18 The Hunter Seeks Revenge 5:36

### Phrase to Listen For

**tengo miedo** I'm afraid

🎬 Amos reads the "No Hunting" sign.

□ **prohibido cazar** no hunting · *prohibido* prohibited · *cazar* to hunt · *prohibir* to prohibit
□ **rastréalo** IMP track him down, track him · *rastrear* to track

🎬 Amos places the trap.

□ **beberla** to drink it · *beber* to drink

🎬 Tod and Vixey play. Amos reviews his traps.

□ **astuto** clever, astute
□ **diablo** devil

🎬 Tod steps on the traps.

□ **se está escapando** he's escaping · *escaparse* to escape

🎬 Tod and Vixey run away.

□ **refugio** refuge, den

🎬 Tod and Vixey are inside the den.

□ **por detrás** through the back
□ **salida** exit
□ **no tardarán** they won't be long · *tardar* to be long [TIME]

## 19 An Unexpected Turn of Events 3:10

🎬 Amos falls into his own trap. Tod saves Toby from the bear.

## 20 Copper Saves Tod 5:37

### Phrases to Listen For

**¿qué pasó?** what happened?
**buena suerte** good luck
**ten cuidado** be careful
**mi mejor amigo** my best friend

### Name

Slade

🎬 Toby saves Tod from Amos. Dinky and Trabalenguas find a butterfly. The widow Tweed dresses Amos' wounds.

□ **te estás portando** you are behaving · *portarse* to behave
□ **estás lastimando** you are hurting · *lastimar* to hurt
□ **pie** NM foot
□ **tonterías** foolishness
□ **está mejorando** it is improving · *mejorar* to improve

🎬 Chief speaks to Toby.

□ **alboroto** racket, uproar, fuss
□ **está armando** he is kicking up · *armar* to kick up
□ **pierna** leg
□ **lastimada** injured · *lastimado* injured · *lastimar* to injure, to hurt

🎬 Toby remembers when he and Tod first met. Tod and Vixey look over the farm.

# March of the Penguins

**El rigor del invierno se debilita con lentitud y los polluelos comienzan a correr libremente.**
*Winter's grip slowly weakens and the chicks begin to run free.*

GENRE      Documentary/Nature
YEAR       2005
DIRECTOR   Luc Jacquet
CAST       Emperor penguins
STUDIO     Warner Independent Pictures

Who would think you could turn a film about penguins into a tense drama of love and survival? Luc Jacquet and his team combine tremendous cinematography with brilliant storytelling to bring the story of the emperor penguins of Antarctica to life. This Academy Award winner will hold your attention as you witness the perils these penguins face year after year. It's a great film for those who are just beginning to use Spanish in context, because the Spanish is precisely and deliberately spoken, contains limited complex grammar, and gives the student time to breathe in between narrations.

## BASIC VOCABULARY
### Nouns

□ **alimento** food, nourishment · *No falta mucho para que los padres regresen con sus estómagos llenos de alimento para los polluelos.* It won't be long before the fathers return with their stomachs filled with nourishment for the chicks.

□ **comida** food · *Durante los siguientes meses los padres se turnarán para viajar al mar en busca de comida.* During the following months, the parents will take turns traveling to the sea in search of food.

□ **hambre** NF hunger · *Ella está literalmente muriéndose de hambre.* She is literally dying of hunger.

□ **hielo** ice · *El hielo comienza a adelgazar y desquebrajarse.* The ice begins to thin and to break apart.

□ **huevo** egg · *Por ahora esperan al huevo y al brutal invierno que hará todo lo posible para destruir ese huevo y al polluelo que alberga.* For now, they wait for the egg and for the brutal winter that will do everything possible to destroy that egg and the chick it houses.

□ **invierno** winter · *El invierno podrá haber terminado, pero no así los peligros.* Winter may have ended, but not the dangers.

□ **machos** males · *macho* male · *Como hay menos machos que hembras, aquí las hostilidades entre las hembras son inevitables.* As there are fewer males than females, here the hostilities among the females are inevitable.

□ **marcha** march · *Naturalmente, después de su larga marcha, están ansiosas por volver al agua, algunas veces demasiado ansiosas.* Naturally, after their long march, they are anxious to return to the water, sometimes too anxious.

□ **millas** miles · *milla* mile · *Las madres exhaustas habrán caminado setenta millas.* The exhausted mothers will have walked seventy miles.

□ **océano** ocean · *Y para noviembre, el océano está a unos pocos centenares de yardas del criadero.* And by November, the ocean is a few hundred yards from the breeding ground.

□ **pareja** mate · *Al regresar, las madres rodean la multitud y gritan con fuerza y esperan a que su pareja les responda.* On their return, the mothers surround the multitude and they shout loudly and wait for their mate to answer them.

□ **patas** feet · *pata* foot [OF AN ANIMAL] · *Cuando se cansan de caminar hacen descansar las patas, y usan el vientre en su lugar.* When they get tired of walking, they rest their feet and use their bellies instead.

□ **pingüinos** penguins · **pingüino** penguin · *Para encontrarse entre la enorme multitud, los pingüinos dependen del sonido, no de la vista.* In order to find each other among the enormous crowd, the penguins depend on sound, not on sight. · *El pingüino solitario no tiene esperanzas contra el frío del invierno.* The lone penguin has no hope against the cold of winter.

□ **polluelos** fledglings, chicks · *polluelo* fledgling, chick · *Y con toda probabilidad sus polluelos no volverán a verlos.* And in all probability, their chicks will not return to see them.

□ **temperatura** temperature · *Cada día la temperatura desciende un poco más, y el sol se pone más temprano.* Every day the temperature drops a little more, and the sun goes down earlier.

### Verb

□ **alimentarse** to feed oneself, to nourish oneself · *Y las madres deben regresar para alimentarse una vez más.* And the mothers must return to nourish themselves once more.

### Other

□ **finalmente** ADV finally · *Y finalmente, un día a principios de junio recordamos por qué vinieron aquí.* And finally, one day at the beginning of June, we recalled why they came here.

□ **recién** ADV recently (EXAMPLE: *recién nacido* newborn [LIT recently born]) · *Y tal como lo hicieron con el huevo, los padres rápidamente entregan los recién nacidos a las madres.* And just like they did with the egg, the fathers quickly give the newborns to the mothers.

## 1 Antarctica                                    4:06

### Phrases to Listen For
**tiempo atrás** long ago
**tal vez** maybe, perhaps

🎬 Opening credits.

□ **promedio** average
□ **fondo** bottom
□ **moderada** moderate · *moderado* moderate
□ **grados** degrees · *grado* degree
□ **Fahrenheit** Fahrenheit
□ **Antártida** Antarctica
□ **tropical** tropical
□ **densos** dense · *denso* dense
□ **bosques** forests · *bosque* NM forest
□ **continente** NM continent
□ **desplazarse** to be displaced, to be moved
□ **sur** NM south
□ **desplazamiento** displacement, movement from one place to another

□ **reemplazados** replaced · *reemplazado*
  replaced · *reemplazar* to replace
□ **superficie** NF surface

🎬 A half-moon is visible above the ice.

□ **antiguos** ancient · *antiguo* ancient
□ **moradores** inhabitants · *morador* inhabitant
□ **leyenda** legend
□ **tribu** NF tribe
□ **clima** NM climate, weather
□ **temporal** temporary
□ **obstinados** obstinate · *obstinado* obstinate
□ **denodadas** stalwart, bold · *denodado* stalwart,
  bold
□ **almas** souls · *alma* soul
□ **rehusaron** they refused · *rehusar* to refuse
□ **partir** to depart, to leave
□ **millones** millions · *millón* NM million
□ **hogar** NM home
□ **oscuro** dark
□ **seco** dry
□ **ventoso** windy
□ **supervivencia** survival
□ **triunfo** triumph

## 2  On Foot and Stomach          5:42

### Phrases to Listen For

**así que** so
**habrá de comenzar** it will have begun
**a veces** sometimes
**sin embargo** however
**no obstante** however
**suele ser** it usually is
**lleno de gracia** graceful

🎬 An ice mountain is shown. Shortly, a penguin leaps
  out of the water.

□ **mayoría** majority
□ **acto** act
□ **disparatado** absurd
□ **emperador** emperor
□ **técnicamente** technically
□ **ave** NF bird
□ **época** season, time of year
□ **abandona** he abandons · *abandonar*
  to abandon
□ **comodidad** comfort
□ **hogar** NM home
□ **oceánico** oceanic
□ **emprender** to undertake
□ **formidable** formidable
□ **distancia** distance
□ **no nadará** he will not swim · *nadar* to swim

🎬 Several penguins leap out of the water.

□ **marzo** March
□ **verano** summer
□ **polar** polar
□ **aves** birds · *ave* NF bird
□ **alimentándose** feeding themselves, nourishing
  themselves · *alimentarse* to feed oneself,
  to nourish oneself
□ **estómago** stomach
□ **reproducción** reproduction
□ **setenta** seventy
□ **continuamente** continually
□ **peligroso** dangerous
□ **aparentemente** apparently
□ **no sobrevivirán** they will not survive ·
  *sobrevivir* to survive
□ **sin embargo** however
□ **clan** NM clan
□ **haya saltado** SUBJ he has jumped · *saltar*
  to jump

🎬 The camera pans over crowds of penguins
  marching toward the camera. Several penguins
  pause, one in the foreground.

□ **destino** destination, destiny
□ **no obstante** however
□ **bloques** blocks · *bloque* NM block
□ **desconcierta** it disconcerts · *desconcertar*
  to disconcert
□ **certeza** certainty
□ **estrellas** stars · *estrella* star
□ **habiendo realizado** having carried out,
  having completed, having accomplished ·
  *realizar* to carry out, to complete,
  to accomplish
□ **centenares** hundreds · *centenar* NM (about a)
  hundred
□ **generaciones** generations · *generación*
  generation
□ **guiados** guided · *guiado* guided · *guiar*
  to guide
□ **invisible** invisible
□ **brújula** compass
□ **interna** internal · *interno* internal
□ **permanecen** they remain · *permanecer*
  to remain
□ **indecisos** indecisive · *indeciso* indecisive
□ **retoma** he takes up again · *retomar* to take up
  again

🎬 A line of penguins crosses the ice in the distance;
  mountains of ice are in the background. Shortly,
  the penguins are shown sliding on their bellies.

□ **vientre** NM belly
□ **suele** it usually · *soler* to usually (+ VERB)

□ **desfile** *NM* parade
□ **gracia** grace, humor

## 3 Birthplace Gathering 4:35

### Phrases to Listen For
**a menudo** often
**lo que** what

The wind blows ice and snow into the air. The penguins appear tiny in the distance.

□ **desciende** it descends · *descender* to descend
□ **temprano** early
□ **clima** *NM* climate, weather
□ **notablemente** notably
□ **riguroso** rigorous
□ **caravanas** caravans · *caravana* caravan
□ **similares** similar · *similar* similar
□ **se aproximan** they draw near · *aproximarse* to draw near
□ **direcciones** directions · *dirección* direction
□ **a menudo** often
□ **nacieron** they were born · *nacer* to be born

The camera pans an immense line of marching penguins. Several penguins on their bellies cross in front of another penguin.

□ **aparearán** they will mate · *aparear* to mate
□ **relativa** relative · *relativo* relative
□ **seguridad** security
□ **orilla** edge
□ **merodea** it lurks · *merodear* to lurk, to prowl, to wander
□ **mayoría** majority
□ **depredadores** predators · *depredador* predator
□ **enormes** enormous · *enorme* enormous
□ **muros** walls · *muro* wall
□ **protección** protection
□ **vientos** winds · *viento* wind
□ **verdadera** true · *verdadero* true
□ **eligieron** they chose · *elegir* to choose
□ **yace** it lies · *yacer* to lie [POSITION]
□ **grueso** thick
□ **firme** *ADJ* firm
□ **verano** summer
□ **impedirá** it will impede, it will prevent · *impedir* to impede, to prevent
□ **accidentalmente** accidentally
□ **congelado** freezing, frozen · *congelar* to freeze

□ **se disponen** they set about, they prepare, they get ready · *disponerse* to set about, to prepare, to get ready
□ **propósito** purpose
□ **realmente** really

The camera continues to focus on one pair of penguins. Then a close-up shows a penguin marching to the right.

□ **pingüinos emperadores** emperor penguins · *pingüino* penguin · *emperador* emperor
□ **monógamos** monogamous
□ **aparean** they mate · *aparear* to mate
□ **estación** season [OF THE YEAR]
□ **búsqueda** search
□ **machos** males · *macho* male
□ **hembras** females · *hembra* female
□ **hostilidades** hostilities · *hostilidad* hostility
□ **inevitables** inevitable, unavoidable · *inevitable* inevitable, unavoidable
□ **comprometido** committed · *comprometerse* to commit oneself
□ **instantáneamente** instantaneously
□ **disponible** available
□ **ocasionalmente** occasionally
□ **hembra** female
□ **interrumpir** to interrupt
□ **cortejo** courtship
□ **objeción** objection
□ **aprovechan** they take advantage of · *aprovechar* to take advantage of
□ **ocasión** occasion
□ **acicalarse** to preen
□ **muecas** faces, facial gestures · *mueca* face, facial gesture
□ **braman** they bellow · *bramar* to bellow
□ **se pavonean** they strut · *pavonearse* to strut
□ **participan** they participate · *participar* to participate
□ **deportes** sports · *deporte* *NM* sport
□ **contacto** contact

## 4 Partnership 5:03

### Phrases to Listen For
**tiene éxito** it is successful
**todo lo posible** everything possible

A pair of penguins is shown walking in an open area, a crowd of penguins in the background.

□ **pocas** a few · *pocos* a few
□ **u** or
□ **mayoría** majority
□ **animales** animals · *animal* *NM* animal

🎬 A penguin couple caresses one another.

☐ **siguientes** next · *siguiente* next
☐ **participará** it will participate · *participar* to participate
☐ **antigua** ancient · *antiguo* ancient
☐ **complicada** complicated · *complicado* complicated · *complicar* to complicate
☐ **relación** relationship
☐ **demostrarán** they will demonstrate · *demostrar* to demonstrate
☐ **exquisita** exquisite · *exquisito* exquisite
☐ **ternura** tenderness
☐ **separación** separation
☐ **reuniones** meetings · *reunión* meeting
☐ **tiene éxito** it is successful · *tener éxito* to be successful · *tener* to have · *éxito* success
☐ **surgirá** it will spring forth · *surgir* to spring forth
☐ **brutal** brutal
☐ **destruir** to destroy
☐ **alberga** it houses · *albergar* to house

🎬 The silhouette of a lone penguin is shown with the orange sky in the background.

☐ **mayo** May
☐ **ha desaparecido** it has disappeared · *desaparecer* to disappear
☐ **continúa** it continues · *continuar* to continue
☐ **descendiendo** descending, dropping, going down · *descender* to descend, to drop, to go down
☐ **rezagados** stragglers · *rezagado* straggler
☐ **debilidad** weakness
☐ **esperanza** hope
☐ **sobrevivir** to survive
☐ **remota** remote · *remoto* remote
☐ **solitario** lone
☐ **esperanzas** hopes · *esperanza* hope
☐ **simplemente** simply
☐ **desaparecerá** he will disappear · *desaparecer* to disappear
☐ **absorbido** absorbed · *absorber* to absorb
☐ **blancura** whiteness
☐ **rodea** it surrounds him · *rodear* to surround

## 5 Life and Loss 3:30

### Phrases to Listen For
**en cuanto** as soon as
**a partir de** beginning
**tal vez** perhaps, maybe
**tan solo** only

🎬 A black screen fades into crowds of penguins huddling in the distance.

☐ **descender** to descend
☐ **tribu** *NF* tribe

☐ **congelación** freezing
☐ **agruparse** to come together as a group, to huddle together
☐ **crearan** *SUBJ* they create · *crear* to create
☐ **organismo** organism
☐ **animales** animals · *animal NM* animal
☐ **se apiñan** they crowd together · *apiñarse* to crowd together
☐ **formar** to form
☐ **masa** mass
☐ **movimiento** movement
☐ **diseñada** designed · *diseñado* designed · *diseñar* to design
☐ **propósito** purpose
☐ **conservar** to conserve
☐ **calor** *NM* heat, warmth
☐ **tormenta** storm
☐ **se precipita** it rushes · *precipitarse* to rush

🎬 The moon shines in the night sky.

☐ **pocas** a few · *pocos* a few
☐ **transcurrir** to pass [TIME]
☐ **prácticamente** practically
☐ **lunas** moons · *luna* moon
☐ **interminable** interminable
☐ **principios de junio** the first days of June · *principio* beginning · *junio* June
☐ **escondido** hidden · *esconder* to hide
☐ **rápidamente** rapidly, quickly
☐ **late** it beats · *latir* to beat
☐ **interior** *NM* interior
☐ **sobrevivir** to survive
☐ **expuesto** exposed · *exponer* to expose
☐ **congelante** freezing
☐ **aire** *NM* air, wind

🎬 The face of one penguin is shown in close-up.

☐ **a partir de ahora** from now on · *a partir de* beginning, starting · *ahora* now
☐ **hambrienta** hungry · *hambriento* hungry
☐ **enseguida** at once, right away
☐ **parejas** couples · *pareja* couple
☐ **impulsivas** impulsive · *impulsivo* impulsive
☐ **apresuradas** in a hurry · *apresurado* in a hurry · *apresurar* to hurry
☐ **relación** relationship
☐ **observar** to observe
☐ **reclama** it reclaims · *reclamar* to reclaim

## 6 Role Reversal 3:48

### Phrases to Listen For
**en cuanto a** concerning
**a punto de** about, at the point of
**a pesar de** in spite of

**hasta que** until
**a salvo** safe
**desde luego** of course
**a mucha distancia** far away, a long way away

🎬 A pair of penguins is shown, one with a feather in its mouth.

☐ **relación** relationship
☐ **en vano** in vain
☐ **parejas** couples · *pareja* couple
☐ **huevos** eggs · *huevo* egg
☐ **infinita** infinite · *infinito* infinite
☐ **paciencia** patience
☐ **ensaya** it rehearses · *ensayar* to rehearse
☐ **necesarios** necessary · *necesario* necessary
☐ **transferir** to transfer
☐ **implacable** relentless, implacable
☐ **practican** they practice · *practicar* to practice
☐ **torpe** uncoordinated
☐ **ballet** *NM* ballet
☐ **decenas** tens · *decena* (about) ten
☐ **memoria** memory
☐ **bailan** they dance · *bailar* to dance
☐ **cautivantes** captivating · *cautivante* captivating
☐ **papel** *NM* role
☐ **naturaleza** nature
☐ **macho** male
☐ **se alimenta** she feeds herself, she is nourished · *alimentarse* to feed oneself, to be nourished
☐ **almacena** she stores · *almacenar* to store
☐ **recién nacido** newborn · *recién* recently · *nacido* born · *nacer* to be born
☐ **protegerá** he will protect · *proteger* to protect
☐ **violencia** violence
☐ **viento** wind
☐ **nido** nest
☐ **encima de** on top of
☐ **manteniéndolo** maintaining it · *mantener* to maintain
☐ **caliente** warm
☐ **pliegue** *NM* fold
☐ **piel** *NF* skin
☐ **vientre** *NM* belly

🎬 An egg rests on the feet of a penguin.

☐ **entregar** to give, to deliver
☐ **hembra** female
☐ **agotada** exhausted · *agotado* exhausted · *agotar* to exhaust, to wear out
☐ **partir** to depart
☐ **rápidamente** rapidly, quickly
☐ **devoción** devotion
☐ **paterna** paternal · *paterno* paternal
☐ **sometida** submitted · *sometido* submitted · *someter* to submit

☐ **duras** tough, difficult · *duro* tough, difficult
☐ **pruebas** tests · *prueba* test
☐ **materna** maternal · *materno* maternal
☐ **viaje de regreso** return trip · *viaje NM* trip · *regreso* return
☐ **considerablemente** considerably
☐ **original** *ADJ* original
☐ **sitio** site
☐ **reproducción** reproduction
☐ **producir** to produce
☐ **tercera** one third · *tercero ADJ* one third
☐ **peso** weight
☐ **corporal** *ADJ* corporal, body
☐ **literalmente** literally
☐ **distancia** distance
☐ **vigilia** vigil
☐ **ciento veinticinco** one hundred twenty-five
☐ **habrán soportado** they will have tolerated, they will have withstood · *soportar* to tolerate, to withstand
☐ **inviernos** winters · *invierno* winter
☐ **violentos** violent · *violento* violent
☐ **mortíferos** deadly · *mortífero* deadly

## 7 Winter's Grip 4:59

### Phrase to Listen For
**tomar en cuenta** taking into account

🎬 The moon disappears behind the clouds.

☐ **se disponen** they prepare themselves · *disponerse* to prepare
☐ **sobrellevar** to put up with, to tolerate, to endure
☐ **criadero** breeding ground
☐ **se precipita** it rushes · *precipitarse* to rush
☐ **tormenta** storm
☐ **invernal** *ADJ* winter
☐ **sesenta** sixty
☐ **grados** degrees · *grado* degree
☐ **viento** wind
☐ **soplar** to blow
☐ **cien** one hundred
☐ **agresivos** aggressive · *agresivo* aggressive
☐ **resto** the rest, the remainder
☐ **época** season, time of year
☐ **completamente** completely
☐ **dóciles** docile · *dócil* docile
☐ **forman** they form · *formar* to form
☐ **colaborador** *ADJ* collaborating, working together
☐ **se enfrentan** they face · *enfrentarse* to face
☐ **cuerpos** bodies · *cuerpo* body
☐ **masa** mass
☐ **turno** turn
☐ **centro** center
☐ **calor** *NM* heat

■ The male penguins huddle close together, a few raising their heads to sound off. One penguin is shown walking slowly to huddle with the rest.

☐ **equilibrio** equilibrium, balance
☐ **huevos** eggs · *huevo* egg
☐ **acróbatas** acrobats · *acróbata NMF* acrobat
☐ **cuerda floja** tightrope · *cuerda* rope · *flojo* loose

## 8 Underwater Feeding 4:00

**Phrases to Listen For**
**a lo largo de** along
**lo que** what
**antes de** before
**tienen que** they have to
**después de** after
**por debajo de** beneath

■ The female penguins are shown marching in the distance.

☐ **exhaustas** exhausted · *exhausto* exhausted
☐ **setenta** seventy
☐ **orilla** edge
☐ **se formó** it was formed · *formarse* to form, to be formed
☐ **obligará** it will force · *obligar* to force, to obligate
☐ **varias** several · *varios* several
☐ **pocas** a few · *pocos* a few
☐ **pulgadas** inches · *pulgada* inch
☐ **debajo de** underneath, below
☐ **sobrevivir** to survive
☐ **abertura** opening
☐ **búsqueda** search
☐ **dura** it lasts · *durar* to last
☐ **varios** several

■ Several female penguins slide into the water.

☐ **naturalmente** naturally
☐ **ansiosas** anxious · *ansioso* anxious
☐ **contener la respiración** to hold one's breath · *contener* to hold, to contain · *respiración* breathing, respiration
☐ **quince** fifteen
☐ **sumergirse** to submerge
☐ **profundidad** depth
☐ **mil setecientos** one thousand seven hundred
☐ **fondo** depth
☐ **peces** fish · *pez NM* fish
☐ **camarón antártico** Antarctic shrimp · *camarón NM* shrimp · *antártico* Antarctic
☐ **calamares** squid · *calamar NM* squid
☐ **nadan** they swim · *nadar* to swim

☐ **superficie** *NF* surface
☐ **pez** *NM* fish
☐ **haberse alojado** to have found lodging, to have stayed · *alojarse* to find lodging, to stay

## 9 Blizzards and Seals 4:41

**Phrases to Listen For**
**a salvo** safe
**todo el tiempo** all the time, always
**a punto de** about, at the point of
**por encima de** on top of
**sin cesar** without ceasing

■ The male penguins continue huddling together.

☐ **llenan** they fill · *llenar* to fill
☐ **estómagos** stomachs · *estómago* stomach
☐ **vacíos** empty · *vacío* empty
☐ **se aferran** they cling · *aferrarse* to cling
☐ **superficie** *NF* surface
☐ **huevos** eggs · *huevo* egg
☐ **calientes** warm · *caliente* warm
☐ **a salvo** safe
☐ **ocasionalmente** occasionally
☐ **viento** wind
☐ **arrastrará** it will drag · *arrastrar* to drag
☐ **nieve** *NF* snow
☐ **saciar** to satisfy
☐ **sed** *NF* thirst
☐ **han sobrevivido** they have survived · *sobrevivir* to survive
☐ **acerca** it gets closer · *acercar* to get closer
☐ **agotamiento** exhaustion

■ One penguin is shown lying on the ice.

☐ **generalmente** generally
☐ **simplemente** simply
☐ **desaparecen** they disappear · *desaparecer* to disappear

■ The male penguins huddle in the dark.

☐ **oscuro** dark
☐ **ventiscas** blizzards, snowstorms · *ventisca* blizzard, snowstorm
☐ **verdadero** true
☐ **esfuerzo** effort
☐ **apiñar** to group together, to huddle together
☐ **cuerpos** bodies · *cuerpo* body
☐ **resistir** to resist
☐ **rigor** *NM* harshness

■ The aurora australis is shown in the night sky.

☐ **encima de** on top of
☐ **aurora austral** aurora australis, southern lights

☐ **danza** it dances · *danzar* to dance
☐ **virtualmente** virtually
☐ **sin cesar** without ceasing · *sin* without ·
*cesar* to cease
☐ **oscuridad** darkness
☐ **total** total

🎬 A leopard seal waits below the ice.

☐ **hambrientas** hungry · *hambriento* hungry
☐ **se alegran** they are happy · *alegrarse* to be happy
☐ **regreso** return
☐ **depredadores** predators · *depredador* predator
☐ **por desgracia** unfortunately
☐ **hayan vuelto** SUBJ they have returned ·
*volver* to return
☐ **fauces** NFPL jaws
☐ **leopardo marino** sea leopard, leopard seal ·
*leopardo* leopard · *marino* ADJ sea
☐ **cobra** it takes, it claims · *cobrar* to take, to claim
☐ **por nacer** about to be born · *nacer* to be born
☐ **alimentado** fed, nourished · *alimentar* to feed,
to nourish
☐ **julio** July
☐ **hembras** female · *hembra* female
☐ **nido** nest
☐ **tercera** third · *tercero* third
☐ **emprenden** they undertake · *emprender*
to undertake

## 10 Light of Day     3:47

### Phrases to Listen For
**al parecer** seemingly
**hasta que** until
**después de** after
**aun así** even so
**lo que** what
**para que** so that, in order for
**está por venir** is about to come

🎬 The female penguins march once again. One slips.

☐ **helada** freezing · *helado* freezing · *helar*
to freeze
☐ **voraz** ravenous
☐ **se prolonga** it lingers · *prolongarse* to linger
☐ **oscuridad** darkness
☐ **lenta** slow · *lento* slow

🎬 Dawn breaks over the South Pole.

☐ **polo sur** South Pole · *polo* pole · *sur* ADJ south
☐ **momentáneamente** momentarily
☐ **esfuerzos** efforts · *esfuerzo* effort
☐ **en vano** in vain
☐ **regreso** return

## 11 Hatchlings     3:41

### Phrases to Listen For
**sin importar** no matter
**a pesar de** in spite of
**tal vez** maybe, perhaps
**para que** so that, in order for

🎬 The huddling male penguins begin to move.

☐ **hambrientos** hungry · *hambriento* hungry

🎬 The hatchling has broken free.

☐ **cascarón** NM eggshell
☐ **estómago** stomach
☐ **obligado** forced · *obligar* to force, to obligate
☐ **abandonar** to abandon
☐ **cría** young
☐ **alternativa** alternative · *alternativo* alternative
☐ **arma secreta** secret weapon · *arma* weapon ·
*secreto* secret
☐ **recién nacido** newborn · *recién* recently ·
*nacido* born · *nacer* to be born
☐ **recurre** he resorts to · *recurrir* to resort to
☐ **lo más profundo** the deepest part · *profundo*
deep
☐ **cuerpo** body
☐ **regurgita** it regurgitates · *regurgitar*
to regurgitate
☐ **sustancia** substance
☐ **lechosa** milky · *lechoso* milky
☐ **íntima** intimate · *íntimo* intimate
☐ **porción** portion
☐ **relegada** relegated · *relegado* relegated ·
*relegar* relegate
☐ **pliegue** NM fold
☐ **garganta** throat
☐ **exclusivamente** exclusively
☐ **banquete** NM banquet
☐ **ojalá** hopefully

🎬 The female penguins continue their march.

☐ **aceleran** they accelerate, they speed up ·
*acelerar* to accelerate, to speed up
☐ **ritmo** rhythm
☐ **presintieran** SUBJ they have a feeling · *presentir*
to have a feeling about the future
☐ **urgencia** urgency, emergency

## 12 Reunion     5:49

### Phrases to Listen For
**hasta que** until
**sin embargo** however
**de algún modo** somehow
**por primera vez** for the first time

**por fin** finally
**tal como** just like, just as, in the same way
**uno al otro** to each other
**aun así** even so
**por la cual** for which

🎬 The female penguins march away, backs to the camera.

☐ **arrastran sus patas** they shuffle · *arrastrar* to drag · *pata* leg [OF AN ANIMAL], paw
☐ **velocidad** velocity, speed
☐ **acarreando** hauling · *acarrear* to haul, to transport
☐ **vientres** bellies · *vientre NM* belly
☐ **destino** destiny

🎬 The female penguins approach the huddled mass of males.

☐ **enorme** enormous
☐ **multitud** NF multitude, crowd
☐ **dependen** they depend · *depender* to depend
☐ **sonido** sound
☐ **vista** sight
☐ **rodean** they surround · *rodear* to surround
☐ **gritan** they shout · *gritar* to shout
☐ **responda** SUBJ he responds, he answers · *responder* to respond, to answer
☐ **ruido** noise
☐ **ensordecedor** deafening
☐ **sin embargo** however
☐ **reunida** reunited · *reunido* reunited · *reunir* to reunite
☐ **rápidamente** rapidly, quickly
☐ **entregan** they deliver, they give · *entregar* to deliver, to give
☐ **recién nacidos** newborns · *recién* recently · *nacido* born · *nacer* to be born
☐ **turno** turn
☐ **proteger** to protect
☐ **inclemente** inclement, harsh, severe, fierce
☐ **se cantan** they sing to each other · *cantar* to sing
☐ **ambos** both
☐ **reconozcan** SUBJ they recognize · *reconocer* to recognize
☐ **voz** NF voice

🎬 The hatchling eats from inside the mother's beak.

☐ **disfruta** he enjoys · *disfrutar* to enjoy
☐ **cortar** to cut, to sever
☐ **vínculo** bond, link, connection
☐ **han soportado** they have tolerated · *soportar* to tolerate
☐ **mitad** NF half
☐ **peso** weight
☐ **setenta** seventy

☐ **etapa** stage
☐ **hembras** females · *hembra* female

## 13 Youngsters 3:31

### Phrases to Listen For
**al igual que** just as, in the same way
**después de** after

🎬 The camera rises, showing the crowd of female penguins.

☐ **separarse** to leave, to separate oneself

🎬 Two hatchlings are shown atop their mothers' feet.

☐ **transportados** transported · *transportado* transported · *transportar* to transport
☐ **bailar** to dance
☐ **zapatos** shoes · *zapato* shoe

## 14 First Storm 4:08

🎬 The wind blows across the ice.

☐ **regreso** return
☐ **vientos** winds · *viento* wind
☐ **estrépito** bang, loud noise, racket

🎬 The female penguins huddle.

☐ **tormenta** storm
☐ **no sobrevivirán** they will not survive · *sobrevivir* to survive

🎬 Five young penguins face the camera.

☐ **amainan** they die down · *amainar* to die down
☐ **búsqueda** search
☐ **sobrevivieron** they survived · *sobrevivir* to survive
☐ **acurrucándose** snuggling, huddling · *acurrucarse* to snuggle, to huddle
☐ **afortunados** fortunate · *afortunado* fortunate
☐ **pérdida** loss
☐ **insoportable** intolerable

## 15 Tragic Response 1:56

### Phrases to Listen For
**de vuelta** returned, returning
**de nuevo** again
**a pesar de** in spite of

🎬 One female penguin stands next to another.

☐ **reaccionará** she will react · *reaccionar* to react
☐ **intensa** intense · *intenso* intense

☐ **agonía** agony
☐ **inimaginable** unimaginable
☐ **de vuelta** returned, returning · *volver* to return
☐ **ansioso** anxious
☐ **vínculo** bond
☐ **sorprendentemente** surprisingly
☐ **siguientes** next, following · *siguiente* next, following
☐ **se fortalecerá** it will become stronger · *fortalecerse* to become stronger

## 16 Bothersome Bird                4:22

🎬 The penguins cast long shadows.
☐ **rigor** *NM* severity, harshness

🎬 Several young penguins run.
☐ **se debilita** it weakens · *debilitarse* to weaken
☐ **lentitud** *NF* slowness
☐ **libremente** freely
☐ **alentados** encouraged · *alentado* encouraged · *alentar* to encourage

🎬 A bird flies.
☐ **peligros** dangers · *peligro* danger

## 17 Family Time                4:42

**Phrases to Listen For**
 **por primera vez** for the first time
 **no falta mucho** it won't be long
 **para que** in order for, in order to, so that
 **en busca de** in search of

🎬 One penguin begins walking amid a group of young penguins.
☐ **agosto** August
☐ **situación** situation
☐ **inaceptable** unacceptable
☐ **alternativa** alternative · *alternativo* alternative
☐ **ya tienen edad suficiente** they are old enough · *edad* age · *suficiente* sufficient
☐ **primavera** spring [SEASON]
☐ **témpanos** ice floes · *témpano* ice floe
☐ **cercanos** near · *cercano* near
☐ **orilla** edge
☐ **derretirse** to melt
☐ **reduciendo** reducing · *reducir* to reduce
☐ **distancia** distance
☐ **criadero** breeding grounds
☐ **estómagos** stomachs · *estómago* stomach

🎬 Several young penguins cast long shadows.
☐ **se reunirán** they will gather, they will meet · *reunirse* to gather, to meet
☐ **rodearán** they will surround · *rodear* to surround
☐ **ansiosos** anxious · *ansioso* anxious
☐ **recién nacido** newborn · *recién* recently · *nacido* born · *nacer* to be born
☐ **garras** claws · *garra* claw
☐ **depredador** predator
☐ **reunión** reunion
☐ **alegría** happiness
☐ **estómago** stomach
☐ **nuevamente** newly

🎬 A young penguin looks well fed. The male penguins begin their march.
☐ **siguientes** next, following · *siguiente* next, following
☐ **se turnarán** they will take turns · *turnarse* to take turns
☐ **ocasionalmente** occasionally
☐ **reunida** reunited · *reunido* reunited · *reunir* to reunite

## 18 Separate Ways                4:41

**Phrases to Listen For**
 **en busca de** in search of
 **idas y venidas** coming and going (*LIT* goings and comings)
 **por última vez** for the last time
 **con toda probabilidad** in all probability

🎬 The ice melts.
☐ **septiembre** September
☐ **adelgazar** to become thin
☐ **resquebrajarse** to crack
☐ **se acerca** it draws near, it gets closer · *acercarse* to draw near, to get closer
☐ **frecuencia** frequency
☐ **plumaje** *NM* plumage, coat of feathers
☐ **denso** dense, thick
☐ **compacto** compact, full
☐ **protegerlo** to protect him · *proteger* to protect
☐ **noviembre** November
☐ **centenares** hundreds · *centenar* *NM* (about a) hundred
☐ **yardas** yards · *yarda* yard
☐ **criadero** breeding ground
☐ **al derretirse el hielo** as the ice melts, at the melting of the ice · *derretirse* to melt · *hielo* ice
☐ **se dispone** it gets ready, it prepares · *disponerse* to get ready, to prepare

□ **separarse** to separate, to become separated, to go their separate ways
□ **parejas** couples · *pareja* couple
□ **dedicadas** dedicated · *dedicado* dedicated · *dedicar* to dedicate
□ **antiguo** ancient
□ **ritual** ritual
□ **idas y venidas** coming and going (*LIT* goings and comings)
□ **se separarán** they will part, they will leave each other, they will go their separate ways · *separarse* to part, to leave one another, to go their separate ways
□ **mirada** look · *mirar* to look at
□ **miembros** members · *miembro* member
□ **tribu** *NF* tribe
□ **hogar** *NM* home

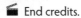 The penguins dive into the water.

□ **siguientes** next, following · *siguiente* next, following
□ **disfrutarán** they will enjoy · *disfrutar* to enjoy
□ **ricas** rich · *rico* rich
□ **tibias** lukewarm · *tibio* lukewarm
□ **corto** short
□ **verano** summer
□ **se alimentarán** they will feed themselves, they will nourish themselves · *alimentarse* to feed oneself, to nourish oneself

□ **probabilidad** probability
□ **permanecerán** they will remain · *permanecer* to remain
□ **supervisión** supervision
□ **creciendo** growing · *crecer* to grow
□ **fortaleciéndose** becoming stronger · *fortalecerse* to become stronger
□ **derritiéndose** melting · *derretirse* to melt
□ **devolviendo** returning · *devolver* to return, to give back
□ **pidió prestada** it borrowed · *pedir prestado* to borrow

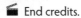 A group of young penguins stands near the sea.

□ **diciembre** December
□ **abandonar** to abandon
□ **nacieron** they were born · *nacer* to be born
□ **se zambullirán** they will dive into the water, they will take the plunge · *zambullirse* to dive, to plunge
□ **siglos** centuries · *siglo* century
□ **pingüino emperador** emperor penguin · *pingüino* penguin · *emperador* emperor
□ **inhóspito** inhospitable

## 19 End Credits
3:07

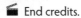 End credits.

# The Princess Bride

**Porque es verdadero amor. ¿Crees que pasa todos los días?**
*Because it's true love. Do you think that happens every day?*

| | |
|---|---|
| GENRE | Adventure/Fantasy/Literature Adaptation |
| YEAR | 1987 |
| DIRECTOR | Rob Reiner |
| CAST | Peter Falk, Fred Savage, Cary Elwes, Robin Wright |
| STUDIO | MGM |

When Grandfather answers his grandson's question about a bedtime story—"Has it got any sports in it?"—he sums up the story of *The Princess Bride*: "Are you kidding? Fencing. Fighting. Torture. Revenge. Giants. Monsters. Chases. Escapes. True love. Miracles." That's what you'll find in this terrific story by William Goldman. This is a relatively easy film for Spanish learners, though the Spanish is the most challenging of the Beginner films because the dialogue includes many complex sentence structures. Vocabulary topics include fencing, fighting, torture, revenge, and much more.

# BASIC VOCABULARY

## Names
Westley, Buttercup, Fezzik, Florin, Guilder, Humperdinck, Inigo Montoya, Roberts

## Nouns
- **alteza** highness, your highness · *De todos los que estamos, **Alteza**, lo que corre peligro es su cabeza.* Of all those here, Your Highness, your head is the one that is in danger.
- **boda** wedding · *Llegó el día de la **boda**.* The day of the wedding arrived.
- **espada** sword · *Mi cerebro, su **espada** y tu fuerza contra sesenta hombres, y crees que un ligero movimiento de cabeza me hace sentir feliz.* My brain, his sword, and your strength against sixty men, and you think that a slight movement of the head makes me feel happy.
- **odio** hate, hatred · *Si no es así cuando le encuentre, mi **odio** y mi furia no tendrán fin.* If it's not that way when I find her, my hatred and fury will have no end.
- **pantano** swamp · *Después de todo, fuiste tú quién se alejó en el **pantano**—sin mencionar que los piratas no son personas de confiar.* After all, it was you who left him at the swamp—not to mention that pirates are not to be trusted.
- **pirata** pirate · *Su barco fue atacado por el temible **pirata** Roberts, que nunca dejaba a alguien con vida.* His ship was attacked by the Dread Pirate Roberts, who has never left anyone alive.
- **princesa** princess · *Sólo la **princesa** importa.* Only the princess matters.
- **príncipe** prince · *Y sólo el **príncipe**, el conde y yo sabemos cómo entrar y salir.* And only the prince, the count, and I know how to enter and leave.
- **venganza** revenge · *Tuve la idea de **venganza** tanto tiempo que ahora que él ha muerto no sé qué hacer con el resto de mi vida.* I had the idea of revenge for so long that now that he has died, I don't know what to do with the rest of my life.

## Other
- **temible** dreadful, dreaded, fearsome · *Es el **temible** pirata Roberts.* He's the Dread Pirate Roberts.
- **verdadero** *ADJ* true · ***Verdadero** amor.* True love.

## 1 Main Title/Grandpa's Visit 2:14

### Phrases to Listen For
**tal vez** maybe, perhaps
**así es** that's right, yes indeed
**verdadero amor** true love

**trataré de estar atento** I'll try to pay attention
**muy amable de tu parte** very kind of you
**muy bien** very well

🎬 The grandson's mother enters his bedroom.
- **adivina** *IMP* guess · *adivinar* to guess
- **enfermo** sick, ill
- **me aprieta** he squeezes, he pinches · *apretar* to squeeze, to pinch
- **mejilla** cheek

🎬 Grandfather enters the bedroom.
- **obsequio** gift
- **ábrelo** *IMP* open it · *abrir* to open
- **edad** age
- **televisor** *NM* television
- **solía** he used to · *soler* to used to (+ *VERB*)
- **leerme** to read to me · *leer* to read
- **leértelo** to read it to you · *leer* to read
- **contiene** it contains · *contener* to contain
- **estás bromeando** are you joking, are you teasing · *bromear* to joke, to tease
- **esgrima** *NM* fencing
- **tortura** torture
- **gigantes** giants · *gigante NM* giant
- **monstruos** monsters · *monstruo* monster
- **persecución** pursuit
- **escapes** escapes · *escape NM* escape
- **milagros** miracles · *milagro* miracle
- **atento** attentive
- **voto** vote
- **confianza** confidence, trust
- **sorprendente** surprising

## 2 A Kissing Book 3:28

### Phrases to Listen For
**como ordene** *SUBJ* as you wish (*LIT* as you order)
**por favor** please
**te amo** I love you
**se dio cuenta** she noticed
**así que** therefore
**claro que sí** of course
**verdadero amor** true love
**todos los días** every day
**con vida** alive
**está bien** it's good, that's good, it's okay

### Name
S. Morgenstern

🎬 Grandfather begins to read.
- **capítulo** chapter
- **creció** she grew · *crecer* to grow

- ☐ **granja** farm
- ☐ **pasatiempos** pastimes · *pasatiempo* pastime
- ☐ **favoritos** favorite · *favorito* favorite
- ☐ **montar** to ride
- ☐ **caballo** horse
- ☐ **atormentar** to torture, to torment
- ☐ **mozo** servant, boy
- ☐ **magnífico** magnificent
- ☐ **comienzo** beginning

🎬 Buttercup dismounts and speaks to the farm boy.

- ☐ **pule** *IMP* polish · *pulir* to polish
- ☐ **silla** chair
- ☐ **rostro** face
- ☐ **se refleje** *SUBJ* it is reflected · *reflejarse* to be reflected
- ☐ **cubo** pail, bucket
- ☐ **se sorprendió** she was surprised · *sorprenderse* to be surprised
- ☐ **descubrir** to discover
- ☐ **sorprendente** surprising
- ☐ **jarro** jug

🎬 Billy interrupts the story. Then, sitting up in bed, he addresses his grandfather.

- ☐ **detente** *IMP* stop · *detener* to stop, to cease
- ☐ **engañarme** to trick me · *engañar* to trick, to deceive
- ☐ **deportes** sports · *deporte NM* sport
- ☐ **besos** kisses · *beso* kiss
- ☐ **interesante** interesting
- ☐ **empacó** he packed · *empacar* to pack
- ☐ **pertenencias** belongings · *pertenencia* belonging, possession

🎬 On the farm, Buttercup and the farm boy face each other. Soon they embrace.

- ☐ **emotivo** emotional
- ☐ **pasarte** to happen to you · *pasar* to happen
- ☐ **destino** destiny
- ☐ **asesinado** murdered, killed · *asesinar* to murder, to kill
- ☐ **piratas** pirates · *pirata NMF* pirate

## 3 Humperdinck's Bride                    1:42

### Phrase to Listen For
**a pesar de que** in spite of the fact that

🎬 Children run through the walkways.

- ☐ **plaza** plaza, town square
- ☐ **proclama** proclamation
- ☐ **pueblo** townspeople, people
- ☐ **aniversario** anniversary

- ☐ **quinientos** five hundred
- ☐ **fecha** date
- ☐ **me casaré** I will marry · *casarse* to marry, to get married
- ☐ **humilde** humble

🎬 Buttercup walks on red carpet into the courtyard.

- ☐ **vacío** emptiness
- ☐ **consumió** it consumed · *consumir* to consume
- ☐ **otorgaba** it permitted, it allowed *otorgar* to permit, to allow
- ☐ **derecho** right
- ☐ **escoger** to choose

🎬 Buttercup rides a horse outside the city.

- ☐ **alegría** happiness
- ☐ **montar** to ride

## 4 Three Circus Performers          2:36

### Phrases to Listen For
**lo que** what
**de gran prestigio** very prestigious
**estoy de acuerdo** I agree
**no lo olvides** *IMP* don't forget
**ya lo sé** I know
**me hartas** you make me sick

### Name
Vizzini

🎬 Three men stop Buttercup as she rides through a forest.

- ☐ **lady** *NF ENG* lady, noblewoman
- ☐ **actores** actors · *actor NM* actor
- ☐ **legua** league
- ☐ **aldea** small town
- ☐ **millas** miles · *milla* mile
- ☐ **gritar** to scream

🎬 Two men are on board a small ship. A third man stands in front of Buttercup's horse.

- ☐ **rasgas** you tear · *rasgar* to tear, to rip
- ☐ **tela** cloth
- ☐ **uniforme** *NM* uniform
- ☐ **caballo** horse
- ☐ **castillo** castle
- ☐ **sospeche** *SUBJ* he suspects · *sospechar* to suspect
- ☐ **guilderianos** people from Guilder · *guilderiano* person from Guilder
- ☐ **han capturado** they have captured · *capturar* to capture
- ☐ **cuerpo** body
- ☐ **frontera** border
- ☐ **sospechas** suspicions · *sospecha* suspicion

□ **confirmadas** confirmed · *confirmado*
confirmed · *confirmar* to confirm

🎬 The giant addresses the short bald man.

□ **asesinaríamos** we would murder · *asesinar*
to murder
□ **contraté** I hired · *contratar* to hire, to contract
□ **iniciar** to initiate
□ **prestigio** prestige
□ **gloriosa** glorious · *glorioso* glorious
□ **tradición** tradition
□ **correcto** correct
□ **asesinar** to murder, to kill
□ **inocente** innocent
□ **labios** lips · *labio* lip
□ **no se te contrató** you were not hired ·
*contratar* to hire, to contract
□ **cerebro** brain
□ **masa** mass
□ **hipopótamo** hippopotamus
□ **deforme** *ADJ* deformed

🎬 The man wearing a vest leaps onto the deck.

□ **ebrio** drunk
□ **no es de su incumbencia** it doesn't concern you,
it's none of your concern · *incumbencia* concern
□ **brandy** *NM ENG* brandy
□ **desvalido** helpless, without resources
□ **esperanza** hope
□ **perteneces** you belong · *pertenecer* to belong
□ **desempleado** unemployed
□ **Groenlandia** Greenland

🎬 The giant and the man wearing a vest talk on board
the ship.

□ **alardear** to boast, to brag
□ **fascina** it fascinates · *fascinar* to fascinate
□ **probablemente** probably
□ **lastimar** to hurt
□ **torturar** to torture
□ **poeta** *NMF* poet
□ **rocas** rocks · *roca* rock
□ **ahogándote** drowning yourself · *ahogarse*
to drown
□ **rimas** rhymes · *rima* rhyme
□ **me hartas** you make me sick, you annoy me,
you irritate me · *hartar* to make sick, to annoy,
to irritate
□ **tartas** cakes · *tarta* cake

## 5 The Shrieking Eels    3:23

### Phrases to Listen For
**¿por qué?** why?
**a pesar de** in spite of

**lo que** what
**ya basta** enough already
**te ves** you look
**tal vez** maybe, perhaps
**Dios mío** good heavens (*LIT* my God)
**lo siento** I'm sorry
**muy bien** very well
**tenía miedo** she was afraid
**te crees** you think you are

🎬 At night, Vizzini addresses the Spaniard on board
the ship.

□ **arrecife** *NM* reef
□ **al amanecer** at dawn · *amanecer NM* dawn
□ **inconcebible** inconceivable
□ **atraparán** they will catch · *atrapar* to catch
□ **colgará** he will hang · *colgar* to hang
□ **peligro** danger
□ **relajarnos** to relax · *relajarse* to relax
□ **absolutamente** absolutely
□ **totalmente** totally
□ **probablemente** probably
□ **pescador** fisherman
□ **infestadas** infested · *infestado* infested ·
*infestar* to infest
□ **animales** animals · *animal NM* animal
□ **hambrientos** hungry · *hambriento* hungry

🎬 Buttercup swims away from the ship.

□ **tras** after
□ **nadar** to swim
□ **babor** *NM* port side of a ship
□ **sonido** sound
□ **chillido** screech
□ **anguila** eel
□ **asesina** murderous · *asesino ADJ* murderous
□ **alimentar** to feed, to nourish
□ **carne** *NF* meat, flesh
□ **humana** human · *humano* human
□ **anguilas** eels · *anguila* eel
□ **asesinas** murderous · *asesino ADJ* murderous
□ **oferta** offer

🎬 Inside the bedroom, Grandfather addresses
his grandson.

□ **nervioso** nervous
□ **disculpa** excuse (me) · *disculpar* to excuse

🎬 The eel closes in on Buttercup.

□ **perseguirla** to pursue her · *perseguir*
to pursue

🎬 The giant pulls Buttercup from the water.

□ **suéltala** *IMP* let go of her · *soltar* to let go,
to release

□ **se acerca** it's getting close · *acercarse* to get closer, to draw near

□ **eso no nos concierne** that doesn't concern us · *concernir* to concern

□ **valiente** courageous, valiant

□ **comparada** compared · *comparado* compared · *comparar* to compare

## 6 Up a Cliff 5:43

### Phrases to Listen For

**estamos a salvo** we're safe
**tendrá que** he will have to
**date prisa** *IMP* hurry
**por favor** please
**lo que** what
**Dios mío** good heavens (*LIT* my God)
**debe de** he must
**tenemos mucha prisa** we are in a great hurry
**ten cuidado** *IMP* be careful
**tan fácil** so easy
**lo siento** I'm sorry
**tiene tanta prisa** you are in such a hurry
**de utilidad** useful
**de hecho** in fact
**ya que** since
**hasta que** until
**temo que** I'm afraid
**tendrá que** you will have to
**no basta** that's not good enough
**para que** so that, in order to

### Names

Vizzini, Domingo Montoya

🎬 The ship sails through the mist at dawn.

□ **se ha adelantado** he's made progress, he's moved forward · *adelantarse* to make progress, to move forward

□ **viento** wind

□ **quienquiera** whoever

□ **Acantilado de la Locura** Cliffs of Insanity · *acantilado* cliff · *locura* insanity, craziness

□ **apresúrense** *IMP* hurry up, speed up · *apresurarse* to hurry up, to speed up

🎬 The three men and Buttercup prepare to leave the ship at the Cliffs of Insanity.

□ **estamos a salvo** we are safe · *estar a salvo* to be safe

□ **suficientemente** sufficiently

□ **navegar** to sail, to navigate

□ **puerto** harbor

🎬 Fezzik climbs the Cliffs of Insanity.

□ **tras** after

□ **inconcebible** inconceivable

□ **date prisa** *IMP* hurry up · *dar prisa* to hurry, to rush

□ **coloso** colossus

□ **legendario** legendary

□ **no admito** I don't accept · *admitir* to accept

□ **excusas** *NFPL* apologies

□ **gigante** *NM* giant

□ **está a prueba** *EXP* it is on a trial basis · *estar a prueba* to be on a trial basis · *prueba* test, trial

🎬 Atop the Cliffs of Insanity, Vizzini cuts the rope.

□ **brazos** arms · *brazo* arm

□ **frontera** border

□ **alcánzanos** *IMP* catch up to us · *alcanzar* to catch up, to reach

□ **retaré** I will challenge · *retar* to challenge

□ **luchar** to struggle, to fight

□ **satisfecho** satisfied · *satisfacer* to satisfy

□ **uso** I use · *usar* to use

□ **enmascarados** masked · *enmascarado* masked · *enmascararse* to wear a mask

□ **estoy aguardando** I am waiting · *aguardar* to wait

🎬 The Spaniard addresses the Man in Black as he climbs up the cliff.

□ **lento** slow

□ **no pretendo** I don't want · *pretender* to want

□ **descortés** discourteous

□ **apreciaría** I would appreciate · *apreciar* to appreciate

□ **no me distrajera** *SUBJ* you don't distract me · *distraer* to distract

□ **apresurarse** to hurry up, to speed up

□ **arrojar** to throw forcefully

□ **soga** rope

□ **rama** branch

□ **utilidad** utility, usefulness

□ **impide** it gets in the way of · *impedir* to get in the way of, to impede

□ **relación** relation

□ **amistosa** friendly · *amistoso* friendly

□ **cima** top

□ **alentador** encouraging

□ **españoles** Spaniards · *español* Spaniard

□ **arroje** *IMP* throw · *arrojar* to throw

## 7 The Chatty Duelists 5:57

### Phrases to Listen For

**hasta que** until
**otra vez** again

**de esa forma**  like that
**tardó un año**  it took him a year
**así que**  so
**tenía once años**  I was eleven years old
**¿qué tal?**  what's up?, greetings
**algún día**  someday
**a no ser que**  it not being the case that
**¿por qué?**  why?
**tengo que**  I have to
**sin embargo**  however
**por favor**  please

## Names

Vizzini, Bonetti, Capo Ferro, Thibault

The Spaniard speaks to the Man in Black atop the Cliffs of Insanity.

☐ **aguardaré**  I will wait · *aguardar* to wait
☐ **indiscreto**  indiscreet
☐ **dedos**  fingers · *dedo* finger
☐ **conversación**  conversation
☐ **asesinado**  murdered · *asesinar* to murder
☐ **fabricaba**  he made, he fabricated · *fabricar* to make, to fabricate
☐ **estupendas**  stupendous · *estupendo* stupendous
☐ **espadas**  swords · *espada* sword
☐ **tardó**  it took · *tardar* to take (time)
☐ **décima**  tenth
☐ **precio**  price
☐ **prometido**  promised · *prometer* to promise
☐ **rehusó**  he refused · *rehusar* to refuse
☐ **cruzó**  crossed · *cruzar* to cross
☐ **reté**  I challenged · *retar* to challenge
☐ **asesino**  murderer
☐ **duelo**  duel
☐ **fallé**  I failed · *fallar* to fail
☐ **edad**  age
☐ **once**  eleven
☐ **dediqué**  I dedicated · *dedicar* to dedicate
☐ **entera**  entire · *entero* entire
☐ **estudio**  study
☐ **esgrima**  NM fencing, sword fighting
☐ **no fallaré**  I will not fail · *fallar* to fail
☐ **persecución**  pursuit, chasing
☐ **esperanza**  hope
☐ **deudas**  debts · *deuda* debt
☐ **decente**  decent

Inigo and the Man in Black draw their swords.

☐ **adecuada**  appropriate · *adecuado* appropriate
☐ **considerando**  considering · *considerar* to consider
☐ **terreno**  terrain
☐ **naturalmente**  naturally
☐ **anula**  it annuls, it cancels, it cancels out · *anular* to annul, to cancel, to cancel out

☐ **estrategia**  strategy
☐ **admito**  I admit · *admitir* to admit
☐ **sonríe**  you smile · *sonreír* to smile
☐ **zurdo**  left-handed

Inigo moves his sword into his right hand.

☐ **sorprendente**  surprising
☐ **dígamelo**  IMP tell it to me · *decir* to say, to tell
☐ **importancia**  importance
☐ **lástima**  pity
☐ **pérdida**  loss
☐ **sin embargo**  however
☐ **respeto**  respect

## 8  "Finish Him Your Way"  4:24

### Phrases to Listen For

**a tu estilo**  your way (LIT to your style)
**qué bien**  excellent
**en cuanto**  as soon as
**¿quieres decir?**  you mean?
**con franqueza**  frankly
**lo que**  what
**ni siquiera**  not even
**a mi favor**  in my favor
**¿por qué?**  why?
**hace mucho**  it's been a long time
**tiene que**  you have to
**mientras tanto**  meanwhile
**sueña con ángeles**  IMP dream about angels
**no cuenta**  he doesn't count
**lo que**  what

### Name

Vizzini

Vizzini addresses Fezzik.

☐ **inconcebible**  inconceivable
☐ **deshazte de él**  IMP get rid of him · *deshacerse de* to get rid of
☐ **estilo**  style
☐ **rocas**  rocks · *roca* rock
☐ **escóndete**  IMP hide · *esconder* to hide
☐ **detrás de**  behind
☐ **grandísimo**  great big

A rock shatters next to the Man in Black.

☐ **a propósito**  on purpose
☐ **fallar**  to fail
☐ **deportivamente**  sportingly
☐ **trucos**  tricks · *truco* trick
☐ **armas**  weapons · *arma* weapon
☐ **habilidad**  ability
☐ **piedras**  rocks · *piedra* rock
☐ **nos mataremos**  we will kill each other · *matar* to kill

□ **civilizada** civilized · *civilizado* civilized · *civilizar* to civilize
□ **con franqueza** frankly
□ **ventaja** advantage
□ **lucha** wrestling
□ **ejercicio** exercise

🎬 The Man in Black runs at Fezzik's midsection and bounces off.

□ **apenadas** ashamed · *apenado* ashamed · *apenarse* to be ashamed, to be embarrassed
□ **ágil** agile
□ **antifaz** *NM* mask
□ **¿te quemaste?** did you burn yourself? · *quemarse* to be burned
□ **ácido** acid
□ **cómodo** comfortable
□ **futuro** future

🎬 The Man in Black jumps on Fezzik's back.

□ **me he especializado** I have specialized · *especializarse* to specialize
□ **lucho** I wrestle, I fight · *luchar* to wrestle, to fight
□ **bandas de maleantes** criminal gangs · *banda* gang · *maleante NM* criminal
□ **movimientos** movements · *movimiento* movement
□ **media docena** half dozen
□ **no envidio** I don't envy · *envidiar* to envy
□ **dolor** *NM* pain
□ **enormes** enormous, large · *enorme* enormous, large

🎬 Prince Humperdinck simulates the duel atop the Cliffs of Insanity.

□ **duelo** duel
□ **cubrieron** they covered · *cubrir* to cover
□ **terreno** terrain
□ **grandes espadachines** master swordsmen · *espadachín NM* sword fighter
□ **perdedor** loser
□ **huyó** he fled · *huir* to flee
□ **vencedor** winner
□ **encaminó** he directed · *encaminar* to direct
□ **ambos** both
□ **planeado** planned · *planear* to plan
□ **guerreros** warriors · *guerrero* warrior
□ **trampa** trap

## 9   A Battle of Wits                         5:27

### Phrases to Listen For
**así que** so
**lo que** what

**temo que** I fear that
**así es** that's how it is
**tan hábil** that good
**¿de veras?** really?
**muy bien** very good
**tengo que** I have to
**así como** just like
**por lo tanto** therefore
**le estás dando largas al asunto** you're delaying the matter
**para que** so that, in order to
**no importa** it doesn't matter

### Names
Platón, Aristóteles, Sócrates, Australia, Asia, Siciliano

🎬 The Man in Black encounters Vizzini holding a knife to Buttercup's throat.

□ **arreglo** arrangement, agreement
□ **empate** *NM* tie
□ **competir** to compete
□ **físicamente** physically
□ **inferior** *NM* inferior
□ **cerebro** brain
□ **hábil** *ADJ* able
□ **deficientes** mentally handicapped people · *deficiente NMF* mentally handicapped person
□ **reto** I challenge · *retar* to challenge
□ **batalla de astucia** battle of wits · *batalla* battle · *astucia* astuteness, shrewdness

🎬 The Man in Black hands Vizzini a vial.

□ **inhala** *IMP* inhale · *inhalar* inhale
□ **no huelo** I don't smell · *oler* to smell
□ **no hueles** you don't smell · *oler* to smell
□ **polvo** dust, powder
□ **iocaína** iocane [fictional poison in *The Princess Bride*]
□ **inodoro** odorless
□ **insípido** tasteless
□ **disuelve** it dissolves · *disolver* to dissolve
□ **instantáneamente** instantaneously
□ **líquido** liquid
□ **venenos** poisons · *veneno* poison
□ **potentes** potent, powerful · *potente* potent, powerful
□ **ambos** both
□ **bebamos** *SUBJ* we drink · *beber* to drink
□ **descubriremos** we will discover · *descubrir* to discover
□ **acertó** he was right, he hit the mark · *acertar* to be right, to hit the mark
□ **falleció** he died · *fallecer* to die, to pass away
□ **simple** simple
□ **interpretar** to interpret

☐ **proyectas** you project · *proyectar* to project
☐ **tipo** type
☐ **copa** cup, goblet
☐ **sabio** wise, clever

🎬 The Man in Black asks Vizzini if he has decided.

☐ **decisión** decision
☐ **completamente** completely
☐ **proviene** it comes from · *provenir* to come from
☐ **habitada** inhabited · *habitar* to inhabit
☐ **criminales** criminals · *criminal NMF* criminal
☐ **escogeré** I will choose · *escoger* to choose
☐ **inteligencia** intelligence
☐ **extraordinaria** extraordinary · *extraordinario* extraordinary
☐ **haber sospechado** to have suspected · *sospechar* to suspect
☐ **origen** *NM* origin
☐ **escoger** to choose
☐ **asunto** the matter
☐ **gigante** *NM* giant
☐ **excepcionalmente** exceptionally
☐ **español** *NM* Spaniard
☐ **implica** it implies · *implicar* to imply
☐ **mortal** *ADJ* mortal
☐ **engañarme** to deceive me · *engañar* to deceive
☐ **me confunda** *SUBJ* I become confused · *confundirse* to become confused
☐ **escoge** *IMP* choose · *escoger* to choose

🎬 Vizzini switches the wine goblets.

☐ **gracioso** funny
☐ **no acertaste** you guessed wrong · *acertar* to guess correctly
☐ **cambié** I changed, I switched · *cambiar* to change
☐ **te volteaste** you turned around · *voltearse* to turn around
☐ **fácilmente** easily
☐ **trampa** trap
☐ **refrán** *NM* saying, proverb
☐ **famoso** famous
☐ **te inmiscuyas** *SUBJ* you interfere · *inmiscuirse* to interfere
☐ **terrestre** *ADJ* land
☐ **ligeramente** lightly, slightly

🎬 The Man in Black removes Buttercup's blindfold.

☐ **envenenada** poisoned · *envenenado* poisoned · *envenenar* to poison
☐ **inmunizándome** immunizing myself, building up an immunity · *inmunizar* to immunize

🎬 Prince Humperdinck kneels.

☐ **sufrimiento** suffering

## 10 Taker of Love & Lives 5:35

### Phrases to Listen For

**lo que** what
**no importa** it doesn't matter
**querrá decir** you mean, you will mean
**algún día** someday
**¿por qué?** why?
**alta mar** high seas
**quiero decir** I mean
**por favor** please
**verdadero amor** true love
**como ordene** *SUBJ* as you wish
**a menos que** unless
**¿qué pasa?** what's happening?
**otra vez** again
**tengo que** I have to

🎬 Buttercup sits on a rock and addresses the Man in Black.

☐ **me libera** you set me free · *liberar* to set free, to liberate
☐ **recompensa** reward
☐ **valor** *NM* value
☐ **promesa** promise
☐ **gracioso** funny
☐ **cazador** hunter
☐ **halcón** *NM* falcon
☐ **nublado** cloudy
☐ **admite** you admit · *admitir* to admit
☐ **prometido** fiancé · *prometida* fiancée
☐ **capaz** *ADJ* capable
☐ **asesino** murderer
☐ **advertencia** warning
☐ **se castiga** one punishes · *castigar* to punish
☐ **mienten** they lie · *mentir* to lie

🎬 Prince Humperdinck smells the vial the Man in Black had given to Vizzini.

☐ **iocaína** iocane [fictional poison in *The Princess Bride*]
☐ **huellas** footprints · *huella* footprint
☐ **furia** fury

🎬 A deep valley in the background, the Man in Black and Buttercup rest.

☐ **crueldad** cruelty
☐ **revela** it reveals · *revelar* to reveal
☐ **admítalo** *IMP* admit it · *admitir* to admit
☐ **orgullo** pride
☐ **despacio** slowly
☐ **pedazos** pieces · *pedazo* piece
☐ **apenas** barely, hardly
☐ **cruel** cruel
☐ **asesinó** murdered · *asesinar* to murder

□ **feo** ugly
□ **adinerado** wealthy
□ **ruin** mean, contemptible
□ **granjero** farmer
□ **tormenta** storm
□ **alta mar** high seas · *alto* high · *mar NM* sea
□ **prisioneros** prisoners · *prisionero* prisoner

🎬 The Man in Black reclines against a fallen log.

□ **excepciones** exceptions · *excepción* exception
□ **blando** soft
□ **la gente lo desobedece** people disobey him · *desobedecer* to disobey
□ **se mofa** you make fun of · *mofarse* to make fun of
□ **pena** grief
□ **dolor** *NM* pain
□ **lo contrario** the contrary
□ **está mintiendo** he is lying · *mentir* to lie

🎬 The Man in Black walks toward the seated Buttercup.

□ **recuerdo** I remember · *recordar* to remember
□ **¿la incomodo?** do I bother you? · *incomodar* to bother, to upset, to make uncomfortable
□ **incomodará** it will upset · *incomodar* to upset
□ **valientemente** courageously, valiantly
□ **conforta** it comforts · *confortar* to comfort
□ **humillaciones** humiliations · *humillación* humiliation
□ **súplicas** pleas, entreaties · *súplica* plea, entreaty
□ **belleza** beauty
□ **fidelidad** fidelity
□ **sobresalientes** *ADJ* the utmost
□ **realmente** really
□ **eterna** eternal · *eterno* eternal
□ **¿se comprometió?** did you become engaged? · *comprometerse* to become engaged
□ **por respeto a** out of respect for · *respeto* respect
□ **se burló** you mocked · *burlarse* to mock, to make fun of

🎬 Buttercup shoves the Man in Black into the valley below. On horseback, Prince Humperdinck speaks with his henchman.

□ **desaparecieron** they disappeared · *desaparecer* to disappear
□ **huyeron** they fled · *huir* to flee
□ **presa de** imprisoned by
□ **pánico** panic
□ **terror** *NM* terror

🎬 Lying on the grass, Westley, the Man in Black, takes Buttercup into his arms.

□ **no me esperaste** you didn't wait for me · *esperar* to wait
□ **no mata** it doesn't kill · *matar* to kill
□ **necesidad** necessity

🎬 Sandwich in hand, the grandson addresses his grandfather.

□ **besan** they kiss · *besar* to kiss
□ **no objetarás** you will not object · *objetar* to object
□ **enfermo** sick, ill
□ **te complaceré** I will please you · *complacer* to please

## 11  In the Fire Swamp                     4:59

### Phrases to Listen For
**estaremos a salvo** we will be safe
**se ven** they look, they appear
**ya que** since
**a veces** sometimes
**lo que** what
**por favor** please
**así como** just like
**muy bien** very well
**así que** so

### Names
Ryan, Roberts, Cummerbund, Patagonia

🎬 Westley and Buttercup run up the valley.

□ **cañada** gully
□ **desagradable** disagreeable, unpleasant, bothersome
□ **prometido** fiancé · *prometida* fiancée
□ **estaremos a salvo** we will be safe · *estar a salvo* to be safe
□ **no sobreviviremos** we won't survive · *sobrevivir* to survive
□ **tonterías** nonsense, foolishness · *tontería* nonsensical act, foolish act

🎬 Westley and Buttercup enter the Fire Swamp.

□ **construir** to construct
□ **verano** summer
□ **bellos** beautiful, pretty · *bello* beautiful, pretty

🎬 Buttercup's dress catches fire.

□ **aventura** adventure
□ **¿te quemaste?** did you burn yourself? · *quemarse* to burn oneself
□ **alerta** alert

- □ **recuerdo** memory
- □ **anclado** anchored · *anclar* to anchor
- □ **ha estado saqueando** he has been plundering · *saquear* to plunder, to sack
- □ **me sorprendo** I am surprised · *sorprenderse* to be surprised
- □ **excentricidades** oddities, eccentricities · *excentricidad* oddity, eccentricity
- □ **intrigó** it intrigued · *intrigar* to intrigue
- □ **descripción** description
- □ **belleza** beauty
- □ **finalmente** finally
- □ **valet** *NM* valet
- □ **probablemente** probably
- □ **época** season, time
- □ **esgrima** *NM* fencing
- □ **rico** rich
- □ **cabina** cabin
- □ **reveló** he revealed · *revelar* to reveal
- □ **secreto** secret

🎬 Westley carries Buttercup.

- □ **heredé** I inherited · *heredar* to inherit
- □ **anterior** previous
- □ **heredarás** you will inherit · *heredar* to inherit
- □ **quince** fifteen
- □ **causar** to cause
- □ **temor** *NM* fear
- □ **nadie se rendiría** nobody would surrender · *rendirse* to surrender
- □ **puerto** port, harbor
- □ **tripulación** crew
- □ **a bordo** aboard
- □ **marino** sailor

## 12 The R.O.U.S.s                                    2:38

### Phrases to Listen For
**así que** so
**no creo que** I don't believe that

🎬 After escaping from the quicksand, Buttercup embraces Westley.

- □ **no lo lograremos** we won't make it · *lograr* to achieve, to accomplish, to succeed
- □ **analízalo** *IMP* analyze it, think it through · *analizar* to analyze, to think through
- □ **terrores** terrors · *terror* *NM* terror
- □ **flamas** flames · *flama* flame
- □ **emiten** they emit · *emitir* to emit
- □ **sonido** sound
- □ **estallar** to explode
- □ **evitar** to avoid

- □ **descubriste** you discovered · *descubrir* to discover
- □ **arenas movedizas** quicksand · *arena* sand · *movedizo* mobile, unstable
- □ **roedores** rodents · *roedor* rodent
- □ **gigantescos** giant · *gigantesco* giant

## 13 Conditional Surrender                            2:16

### Phrases to Listen For
**¿quiere decir?** does it mean?
**otra vez** again
**¿qué sucede?** what happens?

🎬 After Westley and Buttercup exit the Fire Swamp, Prince Humperdinck and several men on horseback intercept them.

- □ **rendición** surrender
- □ **se rinde** you surrender · *rendirse* to surrender
- □ **ante** before
- □ **reconozco** I recognize · *reconocer* to recognize
- □ **valiente** courageous, valiant
- □ **capturará** you will capture · *capturar* to capture
- □ **secretos** secrets · *secreto* secret
- □ **felizmente** happily
- □ **repito** I repeat · *repetir* to repeat
- □ **ríndanse** *IMP* surrender · *rendirse* to surrender

🎬 After seeing that they are surrounded, Buttercup addresses Prince Humperdinck.

- □ **no lo lastimarás** you won't hurt him · *lastimar* to hurt
- □ **nos rendimos** we surrender · *rendirse* to surrender
- □ **regreso** I return · *regresar* to return
- □ **lastimar** to hurt, to injure
- □ **desgraciado** disgraced, miserable
- □ **marino** sailor
- □ **lo regresarás** you will return him · *regresar* to return
- □ **mételo** *IMP* put him in · *meter* to put in
- □ **calabozo** dungeon
- □ **no soportaré** I won't tolerate · *soportar* to tolerate, to stand for
- □ **evitarlo** to avoid it · *evitar* to avoid

🎬 Buttercup is taken away on horseback.

- □ **conducirlo** to take him · *conducir* to take, to drive
- □ **acción** action
- □ **mentiras** lies · *mentira* lie
- □ **dedos** fingers · *dedo* finger

## 14 The Pit of Despair 1:44

### Phrases to Listen For
**ni siquiera** not even
**hasta que** until
**¿para qué?** what for?
**así que** so

Westley is lying on a table, being nursed to health by an albino.

- ☐ **calabozo** dungeon
- ☐ **tormentos** tortures, torments • *tormento* torture, torment
- ☐ **escapar** to escape
- ☐ **cadenas** chains • *cadena* chain
- ☐ **gruesas** thick • *grueso* thick
- ☐ **tampoco sueñes en ser rescatado** IMP don't dream about being rescued either • *tampoco* neither • *soñar* to dream • *rescatar* to rescue
- ☐ **entrada** entrance
- ☐ **secreta** secret • *secreto ADJ* secret
- ☐ **conde** NM count
- ☐ **curarme** to cure me • *curar* to cure
- ☐ **insisten** they insist • *insistir* to insist
- ☐ **sana** healthy • *sano* healthy
- ☐ **destruirla** to destroy (the person) • *destruir* to destroy
- ☐ **tortura** torture
- ☐ **sobreviviste** you survived • *sobrevivir* to survive
- ☐ **valiente** courageous, valiant
- ☐ **nadie resiste** nobody resists, nobody withstands • *resistir* to resist, to withstand
- ☐ **máquina** machine

## 15 Queen of Garbage 2:36

### Phrases to Listen For
**desde luego** of course
**está bien** that's fine
**¿por qué?** why?
**verdadero amor** true love
**así que** so

Inside the castle, Prince Humperdinck speaks with Rugen, the six-fingered man.

- ☐ **salud** NF health
- ☐ **está afectando** it is affecting • *afectar* to affect
- ☐ **amanecer** NM dawn

The king's subjects are gathered in the courtyard at the castle.

- ☐ **mediodía** NM noon
- ☐ **ante** before
- ☐ **súbditos** subjects • *súbdito* subject

The grandson questions his grandfather.

- ☐ **injusto** unjust, unfair
- ☐ **escrito** written • *escribir* to write
- ☐ **estás revolviéndolo** you are mixing it up, you are messing it up • *revolver* to mix up, to mess up
- ☐ **léelo** IMP read it • *leer* to read
- ☐ **interrupciones** interruptions • *interrupción* interruption

The crowned Prince Humperdinck makes an announcement to his subjects. Buttercup steps into the courtyard. An old woman shouts at Buttercup.

- ☐ **basura** trash
- ☐ **rechazo** rejection
- ☐ **reverencia** reverence
- ☐ **putrefacción** putrefaction
- ☐ **fango** mud, slime
- ☐ **suciedad** filth

Buttercup gets out of bed.

- ☐ **faltaban diez días** it was ten days until • *faltar* to lack
- ☐ **pesadillas** nightmare • *pesadilla* nightmare
- ☐ **inteligente** intelligent

## 16 Alternative to Suicide 2:40

### Phrases to Listen For
**por favor** please
**así es** that's right
**después de todo** after all
**bandera blanca** white flag
**Dios lo bendiga** SUBJ God bless him
**¿de acuerdo?** agreed?
**tal vez** maybe, perhaps
**noche de bodas** wedding night
**debe de** he must

### Names
Rugen, Westley, Vizzini, Tyrone

Prince Humperdinck is seated at a table with a dog by his side when Buttercup enters.

- ☐ **al amanecer** at dawn • *amanecer* NM dawn
- ☐ **causarte** to cause you • *causar* to cause
- ☐ **pena** grief
- ☐ **considera** IMP consider • *considerar* to consider
- ☐ **cancelada** canceled • *cancelado* canceled • *cancelar* to cancel
- ☐ **le avisaremos** we will inform him • *avisar* to inform, to warn
- ☐ **sin mencionar** not to mention • *mencionar* to mention

- □ **piratas** pirates · *pirata NM* pirate
- □ **sugiero** I suggest · *sugerir* to suggest
- □ **trato** deal
- □ **carta** letter
- □ **dirección** direction
- □ **izaremos bandera blanca** we'll raise the white flag · *izar* to raise, to hoist · *bandera* flag · *blanca* white
- □ **mensaje** *NM* message
- □ **Dios lo bendiga** *SUBJ* God bless him · *bendecir* to bless
- □ **considérame** *IMP* consider me · *considerar* to consider
- □ **alternativa** alternative · *alternativo* alternative
- □ **suicidio** suicide

Rugen and Prince Humperdinck walk through a forest.

- □ **realmente** really
- □ **encantadora** enchanting, charming · *encantador* enchanting, charming
- □ **poco inteligente** not too intelligent · *inteligente* intelligent
- □ **atractiva** attractive · *atractivo* attractive
- □ **contraté** I hired · *contratar* to hire, to contract
- □ **compromiso** engagement
- □ **interesante** interesting
- □ **estrangularla** to strangle her · *estrangular* to strangle
- □ **noche de bodas** wedding night · *noche NF* night · *boda* wedding
- □ **se acuse** *SUBJ* one accuses, one blames · *acusar* to accuse, to blame
- □ **nación** nation
- □ **furiosa** furious · *furioso* furious
- □ **declaremos** *SUBJ* we declare · *declarar* to declare
- □ **botón secreto** secret button · *botón NM* button · *secreto* secret
- □ **calabozo** dungeon
- □ **recuperado** recovered · *recuperar* to recover
- □ **máquina** machine
- □ **planear** to plan
- □ **celebración** celebration
- □ **quinto centenario** five hundredth anniversary · *quinto* fifth · *centenario* hundredth anniversary
- □ **asesinar** to murder
- □ **condenar** to condemn

## 17 The Suction Machine 3:06

### Phrases to Listen For
**en lugar de** in place of
**algún día** someday
**así que** so

**lo que** what
**¿cómo te sientes?** how do you feel?
**por supuesto** of course
**antes de** before

### Name
Yellin

The Albino wheels Westley across the dungeon floor as Rugen rises to address Westley.

- □ **inventarla** to invent it · *inventar* to invent
- □ **has descubierto** you have discovered · *descubrir* to discover
- □ **profundo** profound, deep
- □ **enorme** enormous
- □ **interés** *NM* interest
- □ **dolor** *NM* pain
- □ **actualmente** currently, at present
- □ **estudio** I study · *estudiar* to study
- □ **efectos** effects · *efecto* effect
- □ **máquina** machine
- □ **sujeto** subject, person
- □ **totalmente** totally
- □ **honesto** honest
- □ **prueba** test
- □ **nivel** *NM* level

Water begins turning a wheel. Westley writhes in pain. Rugen turns off the machine.

- □ **concepto** concept
- □ **succión** suction
- □ **bomba** pump
- □ **antiguo** ancient, old
- □ **ocasión** occasion
- □ **succiona** it sucks out · *succionar* to suck out
- □ **daño** damage
- □ **te causaría** it would cause you · *causar* to cause
- □ **posteridad** posterity
- □ **interesante** interesting

Yellin enters Prince Humperdinck's office.

- □ **guardián** *NM* guardian
- □ **secreto** secret
- □ **asesinos** murderers · *asesino* murderer
- □ **se están infiltrando** they are infiltrating · *infiltrar* to infiltrate
- □ **bosque** *NM* forest
- □ **ladrones** thieves · *ladrón NM* thief
- □ **planean** they plan · *planear* to plan
- □ **prometida** fiancée · *prometido* fiancé
- □ **noche de bodas** wedding night · *noche NF* night · *boda* wedding
- □ **espías** spies · *espía NMF* spy
- □ **semejantes** similar · *semejante* similar
- □ **noticias** *NFPL* news

🎬 Buttercup joins Prince Humperdinck and Yellin.

☐ **paciencia** patience

🎬 Buttercup departs. Prince Humperdinck and Yellin continue their discussion.

☐ **asesinada** murdered · *asesinado* murdered · *asesinar* to murder
☐ **se vacíe** SUBJ it is emptied · *vaciarse* to be empty, to be emptied
☐ **se arreste** SUBJ one arrests · *arrestar* to arrest
☐ **moradores** inhabitants · *morador* inhabitant
☐ **resistirán** they will resist · *resistir* to resist
☐ **ayudantes** assistants · *ayudante* NMF assistant
☐ **escuadrón** NM squadron
☐ **limpies** SUBJ you clean · *limpiar* to clean
☐ **matrimonio** marriage
☐ **gobernar** to govern, to rule

## 18  A New Alliance                                         3:13

### Phrases to Listen For
**llevaba a cabo** he carried out
**hasta que** until
**¿qué tal?** what's up?
**te ves muy bien** you look great
**tal vez** maybe
**me siento** I feel
**basta** enough
**basta ya** enough already
**a pesar de** in spite of

### Names
Vizzini, Fezzik, Inigo, Rugen

🎬 A young man runs through a populated section of forest, chased by a man on horseback.

☐ **escuadrón** NM squadron
☐ **llevaba a cabo** he carried out · *llevar a cabo* to carry out
☐ **suéltame** IMP let go of me · *soltar* to let go of
☐ **español** NM Spaniard

🎬 Inigo leans against a hut.

☐ **inicio** beginning
☐ **no me moveré** I will not move · *moverse* to move
☐ **no me muevo** I'm not moving · *moverse* to move
☐ **obtuvimos** we obtained · *obtener* to obtain
☐ **principio** beginning
☐ **me quedo** I remain · *quedarse* to remain
☐ **torpe** clumsy, awkward
☐ **estoy aguardando** I am waiting · *aguardar* to wait

🎬 Fezzik lifts Inigo.

☐ **hueles** you smell · *oler* to smell
☐ **se reunieron** they met · *reunirse* to meet
☐ **reanimaba** he revived · *reanimar* to revive
☐ **existencia** existence
☐ **conde** NM count
☐ **dedos** fingers · *dedo* finger
☐ **considerando** considering · *considerar* to consider
☐ **búsqueda** search
☐ **noticia** news
☐ **satisfacción** satisfaction

🎬 Fezzik dunks Inigo's head in barrels of hot and cold water.

☐ **al revivir** in reviving · *revivir* to revive
☐ **castillo** castle
☐ **portón** NM castle gate
☐ **custodiado** guarded · *custodiar* to guard, to watch over
☐ **enfrentarías** would you face · *enfrentar* to face
☐ **planee** SUBJ he plans · *planear* to plan
☐ **estrategia** strategy
☐ **sino** but instead
☐ **planear** to plan
☐ **vámonos** let's go · *irse* to go away
☐ **tonterías** nonsense, foolishness · *tontería* nonsensical act, foolish act
☐ **alma** soul
☐ **paz** NF peace
☐ **sangre** NF blood

## 19  ... Like a King Scorned                               3:15

### Phrases to Listen For
**estar a salvo** to be safe
**luna de miel** honeymoon
**no importa** it doesn't matter
**de cualquier modo** in any way
**por no haberme dado cuenta** for not having noticed
**¿por qué no?** why not?
**lo que** what
**verdadero amor** true love
**así que** so
**con permiso** excuse me (LIT with permission)
**por favor** please

### Name
Florin

🎬 Yellin reports to Prince Humperdinck.

☐ **informa** IMP inform, report · *informar* to inform, to report
☐ **bosque** NM forest

☐ **vacío** empty
☐ **custodian** they guard · *custodiar* to guard, to watch over
☐ **reja** castle gate
☐ **duplica** *IMP* double it · *duplicar* to double
☐ **a salvo** safe
☐ **llave** *NF* key

Buttercup joins Yellin and Prince Humperdinck.

☐ **escoltarán** they will escort · *escoltar* to escort
☐ **canal** *NM* channel
☐ **armada** navy
☐ **acompañarnos** to accompany us · *acompañar* to accompany
☐ **luna de miel** honeymoon · *luna* moon · *miel* *NF* honey
☐ **con excepción de** with the exception of, except for · *excepción* exception
☐ **naturalmente** naturally
☐ **no me mientas** *IMP* don't lie to me · *mentir* to lie
☐ **cobarde** *NMF* coward
☐ **miserable** miserable
☐ **canalla** *NMF PEJ* swine
☐ **lastimarme** to hurt me · *lastimar* to hurt
☐ **destruirlo** to destroy it · *destruir* to destroy
☐ **sabuesos** bloodhounds, sleuths · *sabueso* bloodhound, sleuth
☐ **espadas** swords · *espada* sword
☐ **vil** vile
☐ **habitan** they inhabit · *habitar* to inhabit

Prince Humperdinck enters the dungeon, where Westley is still attached to the torture machine.

☐ **pareja** couple
☐ **cuentos** stories, tales · *cuento* story, tale
☐ **sufrir** to suffer

Hearing the cries of pain, Inigo calls to Fezzik.

☐ **sonido** sound
☐ **sufrimiento** suffering
☐ **sufre** he suffers · *sufrir* to suffer
☐ **con permiso** excuse me (*LIT* with permission) · *permiso* permission

## 20  Where is Westley?                3:07

### Phrases to Listen For
**lo siento** I'm sorry
**por favor** please
**¿por qué?** why?
**quieres decir** you mean
**Dios mío** good heavens (*LIT* my God)
**muy en serio** very seriously

### Name
Montoya

Inigo and Fezzik intercept the Albino.

☐ **refréscale la memoria** *IMP* refresh his memory · *refrescar* to refresh · *memoria* memory
☐ **intención** intention
☐ **te he fallado** I have failed you · *fallar* to fail
☐ **angustia** anguish, distress
☐ **guíes** *SUBJ* you guide · *guiar* to guide
☐ **guía** *IMP* guide · *guiar* to guide

The grandson questions his grandfather.

☐ **fingía** he was faking · *fingir* to fake
☐ **mata** he kills · *matar* to kill
☐ **enfermo** sick, ill
☐ **calabozo de los tormentos** dungeon of tortures [= Pit of Despair] · *calabozo* dungeon · *tormento* torture

Inside the dungeon, Inigo speaks.

☐ **derrota** defeat
☐ **cuerpo** body
☐ **milagro** miracle

## 21  Miracle Max                4:25

### Phrases to Listen For
**¿por qué?** why?
**en vez de** instead of
**tenemos una prisa espantosa** we're in a terrible hurry
**a punto de morir** about to die
**tiene que** he has to
**tal vez** maybe, perhaps
**así que** so
**verdadero amor** true love
**me encantan** I love them
**lo que** what
**tiene miedo** he is afraid
**hay que** it's necessary
**para que** so that, in order to
**por lo menos** at least

### Names
Max, Valerie, Humperdinck

Inigo knocks on the door of a hut.

☐ **milagroso** miraculous
☐ **me despidió** he fired me · *despedir* to fire, to dismiss
☐ **doloroso** painful
☐ **cortas** you cut · *cortar* to cut
☐ **daga** dagger

- **jugo de limón** lemon juice · *jugo* juice · *limón* NM lemon
- **escuadrón** NM squadron
- **milagro** miracle
- **interesante** interesting
- **lo revisaré** I'll look him over · *revisar* to look over, to examine, to check

🎬 Fezzik and Inigo place Westley on a table inside Miracle Max's hut.

- **espantosa** terrible, awful · *espantoso* terrible, awful
- **no me presiones** IMP don't rush me · *presionar* to pressure, to put pressure on
- **sesenta y cinco** sixty-five
- **excepto** except
- **noble** ADJ noble
- **causa** cause
- **lisiada** crippled · *lisiado* crippled
- **apunto de** about to
- **hambre** NF hunger
- **mentiroso** liar
- **asesinaron** they murdered · *asesinar* to murder
- **fuelle** NM bellows
- **deba** SUBJ he owes · *deber* to owe
- **preguntaré** I will ask · *preguntar* to ask
- **sabelotodo** know-it-all
- **diferencia** difference
- **totalmente** totally
- **ábrele su boca** IMP open his mouth · *abrir* to open · *boca* mouth
- **apenas** barely, hardly
- **ropa** clothes

🎬 Miracle Max addresses Westley.

- **valga la pena** SUBJ it is worth · *valer la pena* to be worth
- **emparedado** sandwich
- **ce** NF C [LETTER]
- **ele** NF L [LETTER]
- **te** NF T [LETTER]
- **cordero** lamb
- **lechuga** lettuce
- **tomate** NM tomato
- **carne magra de cordero** mutton · *carne* NF meat · *magra* lean · *cordero* lamb
- **maduros** ripe · *maduro* ripe
- **nutritivos** nutritious · *nutritivo* nutritious
- **claramente** clearly
- **trampa** trap
- **artimaña** trick
- **probablemente** probably
- **naipes** cards · *naipe* NM playing card

🎬 Miracle Max's wife challenges Max.

- **mentiras** lies · *mentira* lie
- **bruja** witch
- **su confianza se perdió** he lost his confidence · *confianza* confidence · *perderse* to lose
- **no oigo** I don't hear · *oír* to hear
- **decencia** decency
- **cállate** IMP be quiet, shut up · *callarse* to be quiet, to shut up
- **sufrirá** he will suffer · *sufrir* to suffer
- **humillación** humiliation

🎬 As Max paints a pill with chocolate, Inigo looks on.

- **píldora** pill, tablet
- **mágica** magic · *mágico* ADJ magic
- **cubierta** covering
- **se resbale** SUBJ it slides · *resbalar* to slide
- **quince** fifteen
- **nadar** to swim
- **diviértanse** IMP have fun · *divertirse* to have fun
- **castillo** castle

## 22 A Plan! 3:18

### Phrases to Listen For
**tenemos que** we have to
**cuanto antes** as soon as possible
**para que** so that
**lo que** what
**¿por qué?** why?
**volverte a la vida** to return to life
**tenemos que** we have to
**de acuerdo** agreed
**¿para qué?** what for?
**lo siento** I'm sorry

### Names
Buttercup, Humperdinck, Rugen

🎬 Fezzik observes the palace guard.

- **diferencia** difference
- **píldora** pill
- **quince** fifteen
- **castillo** castle
- **sostenle la cabeza** IMP hold his head up · *sostener* to hold up · *cabeza* head
- **ábrele la boca** IMP open his mouth · *abrir* to open · *boca* mouth

🎬 Inigo and Fezzik give Miracle Max's pill to Westley.

- **milagro** miracle
- **contestar** to answer
- **separados** separated · *separado* separate · *separar* to separate

☐ **brazos** arms · *brazo* arm
☐ **resumir** to summarize
☐ **impedir** to impede, to put a stop to
☐ **rescatar** to rescue
☐ **escapar** to escape
☐ **charlar** to chat
☐ **moviste** you moved · *mover* to move
☐ **dedo** finger
☐ **fantástico** fantastic
☐ **sano** I get well, I recover · *sanar* to get well, to recover
☐ **labor** *NM* task
☐ **portón** *NM* castle gate
☐ **mira** *IMP* look · *mirar* to look at
☐ **vigilado** watched over, guarded · *vigilar* to watch over, to guard
☐ **sesenta** sixty
☐ **ventaja** advantage
☐ **cerebro** brain
☐ **planear** to plan
☐ **ligero** light, slight
☐ **movimiento** movement
☐ **carretilla** wheelbarrow
☐ **albino** albino
☐ **no lo habían mencionado** you hadn't mentioned it · *mencionar* to mention
☐ **manto** cover
☐ **gigante** *NM* giant
☐ **¿dónde lo conseguiste?** where did you get it? · *conseguir* to get
☐ **milagroso** miraculous
☐ **obsequió** he gave · *obsequiar* to give a gift
☐ **necesitaré** I will need · *necesitar* to need
☐ **sostener** to sustain, to hold up
☐ **encuentro** I find · *encontrar* to find, to encounter
☐ **conde** *NM* count
☐ **escapamos** we escape · *escapar* to escape
☐ **agotador** tiring, exhausting

🎬 Prince Humperdinck stands behind Buttercup, fastening her necklace.

☐ **alegre** happy
☐ **novias** brides · *novia* bride · *novio* groom
☐ **no me casaré** I will not marry · *casarse* to marry

## 23 "Mawwiage!" 3:11

**Phrases to Listen For**
**lo que** what
**aún no** not yet
**verdadero amor** true love
**para siempre** forever
**tienen que** you have to

**así que** so
**¿por qué?** why?

**Names**
Roberts, Fezzik, Buttercup

🎬 The Impressive Clergyman addresses those gathered for the wedding.

☐ **matrimonio** marriage
☐ **reúne** it reunites · *reunir* to reunite
☐ **sagrado** sacred
☐ **sacramento** sacrament
☐ **bello** beautiful

🎬 Fezzik, dressed in black, is wheeled toward the guard at the castle gate by Inigo and Westley.

☐ **sobreviviente** survivor
☐ **pesadillas** nightmares · *pesadilla* nightmare
☐ **se harán realidad** they will come true · *hacerse realidad* to become reality

🎬 The Impressive Clergyman continues his remarks.

☐ **atesoren** *IMP* treasure · *atesorar* to treasure
☐ **sortija** ring

🎬 The gate nearly closes before Fezzik, Inigo, and Westley can enter.

☐ **reja** castle gate

🎬 Prince Humperdinck and Buttercup exchange words during the wedding.

☐ **terror** *NM* terror

🎬 Inigo demands the key from Yellin.

☐ **llave** *NF* key

🎬 The Impressive Clergyman finishes the wedding ceremony.

☐ **marido** husband
☐ **escolta** *IMP* escort · *escoltar* to escort
☐ **suite nupcial** honeymoon suite, bridal suite · *suite* *NF* suite · *nupcial* nuptial
☐ **enseguida** at once

## 24 "Prepare to Die" 3:33

**Phrases to Listen For**
**¿qué tal?** what's up?, greetings
**¿por qué?** why?
**ya que** since
**en cuanto** as soon as
**lo siento** I'm sorry

**Name**
Fezzik

🎬 Rugen and his men encounter Inigo, Fezzik, and Westley in the hallway.

☐ **gigante** *NM* giant
☐ **interrogarlo** to interrogate him · *interrogar* to interrogate

🎬 Inigo pursues Rugen.

☐ **está escapando** he is escaping · *escapar* to escape

🎬 The King and Queen escort Buttercup.

☐ **extraña** strange · *extraño* strange
☐ **suicidarme** to kill myself, to commit suicide · *suicidarse* to commit suicide
☐ **alcoba** bedroom, room
☐ **me besó** she kissed me · *besar* to kiss

🎬 Rugen hurls a knife at Inigo.

☐ **español** *NM* Spaniard
☐ **lección** lesson
☐ **hace ya varios años** all those years ago · *varios* several · *año* year
☐ **fallar** to fail
☐ **he presenciado** I have witnessed, I have seen · *presenciar* to witness

## 25  "Gently!"  0:55

**Phrase to Listen For**
**¿por qué?** why?

🎬 Buttercup holds a dagger in her hand.

☐ **escasez** *NF* scarcity, shortage
☐ **cuerpos** bodies · *cuerpo* body
☐ **pena** shame
☐ **dañar** to damage, to hurt
☐ **no me abrazas** you don't hug me, you don't embrace me · *abrazar* to hug, to embrace

## 26  On His Last Legs  1:55

**Phrases to Listen For**
**algún día** someday
**¿qué tal?** what's up?, greetings
**lo que** what
**por favor** please

**Name**
Inigo

🎬 Inigo stands to face Rugen.

☐ **sentido** sense
☐ **desarrollado** developed · *desarrollar* to develop
☐ **ofréceme** *IMP* offer me · *ofrecer* to offer

☐ **prométalo** *IMP* promise it · *prometer* to promise
☐ **rufián** *NM* ruffian

## 27  Bluffing  6:13

**Phrases to Listen For**
**algún día** someday
**¿no está de acuerdo?** don't you agree?
**primero lo primero** first things first
**enseguida** right away
**de una vez** at once, right away
**por qué** why
**para que** so that
**Dios mío** good heavens (*LIT* my God)
**quiere decir** that means
**para siempre** forever
**tal vez** maybe, perhaps
**así que** so
**así es** that's how it is
**al amanecer** at dawn
**estaban a salvo** they were safe
**otra vez** again
**de acuerdo** agreed
**muy bien** very well
**hasta pronto** see you soon (*LIT* until soon)
**como ordene** *SUBJ* as you wish

🎬 Buttercup confesses to Westley.

☐ **pecado** sin
☐ **has cometido** have you committed · *cometer* to commit
☐ **últimamente** recently, lately
☐ **contraje matrimonio** I got married · *contraer matrimonio* to marry · *contraer* to contract · *matrimonio* marriage
☐ **anciano** old man
☐ **marido** husband
☐ **nos saltamos** we skipped over · *saltarse* to skip over
☐ **casada** married · *casado* married · *casarse* to marry, to get married

🎬 Prince Humperdinck enters to join Westley and Buttercup in her bedroom.

☐ **tecnicismo** technicality
☐ **remediado** fixed · *remediar* to fix
☐ **dolor** *NM* pain
☐ **familiarizado** familiar · *familiarizar* to familiarize
☐ **frase** *NF* sentence
☐ **breve** brief
☐ **bufón** *NM* clown
☐ **cara** face
☐ **hipopótamo** hippopotamus
☐ **se atreve** he dares · *atreverse* to dare

- [ ] **insultarme** to insult me · *insultar* to insult
- [ ] **nariz** *NF* nose
- [ ] **lengua** tongue
- [ ] **error** *NM* error, mistake
- [ ] **volver a cometer** to make again · *volver* to return · *cometer* to commit, to make
- [ ] **derecho** right
- [ ] **orejas** ears · *oreja* ear
- [ ] **grito** scream, shout
- [ ] **deformidad** deformity
- [ ] **apreciar** to appreciate
- [ ] **llanto** crying, weeping
- [ ] **grite** *SUBJ* he shouts, he screams · *gritar* to shout, to scream
- [ ] **eco** echo
- [ ] **oídos** ears · *oído* ear
- [ ] **angustia** anguish
- [ ] **revolcándote** rolling around, wallowing · *revolcarse* to roll around, to wallow
- [ ] **terrible** terrible
- [ ] **miseria** misery
- [ ] **alardeas** you bluff, you boast, you brag · *alardear* to bluff, to boast, to brag
- [ ] **miserable** miserable
- [ ] **masa** mass
- [ ] **inmunda** filthy · *inmundo* filthy
- [ ] **mienta** *SUBJ* I lie · *mentir* to lie
- [ ] **ponerme de pie** to stand up · *ponerse de pie* to stand up

🎬 Westley rises from the bed and points his sword at Prince Humperdinck.

- [ ] **arrójala** *IMP* throw it · *arrojar* to throw
- [ ] **suelo** floor
- [ ] **átalo** *IMP* tie him · *atar* to tie
- [ ] **ayúdelo** *IMP* help him · *ayudar* to help
- [ ] **alardeaba** you were bluffing · *alardear* to bluff, to boast, to brag
- [ ] **cobardía** cowardice

🎬 Inigo, Westley, and Buttercup look out the window at Fezzik and four white horses.

- [ ] **establo** stable
- [ ] **caballos** horses · *caballo* horse
- [ ] **deduje** I figured · *deducir* to figure, to deduce
- [ ] **doncella** lady
- [ ] **descuida** *IMP* don't worry · *descuidar* to not worry, to neglect
- [ ] **vanidoso** vain

🎬 Buttercup leaps from the window into Fezzik's arms.

- [ ] **resto** the rest, the remainder
- [ ] **piratería** piracy
- [ ] **magnífico** magnificent

🎬 Inigo, Fezzik, Westley, and Buttercup ride out the castle gate.

- [ ] **cabalgaron** they rode · *cabalgar* to ride on horseback
- [ ] **libertad** liberty, freedom
- [ ] **al amanecer** at dawn · *amanecer* *NM* dawn
- [ ] **a salvo** safe
- [ ] **cubría** it covered · *cubrir* to cover
- [ ] **ola** wave
- [ ] **conforme** as

🎬 Grandfather closes the book.

- [ ] **besos** kisses · *beso* kiss
- [ ] **invención** invention
- [ ] **apasionados** passionate · *apasionado* passionate
- [ ] **puros** pure · *puro* pure
- [ ] **leérmelo** to read it to me · *leer* to read

## 28 End Credits 4:42

🎬 End credits.

# The Absent-Minded Professor

**Nunca habías lucido más bella.**
*You never looked more beautiful.*

GENRE        Comedy
YEAR         1961
DIRECTOR     Robert Stevenson
CAST         Fred MacMurray, Nancy Olson, Keenan Wynn, Tommy Kirk
STUDIO       Walt Disney Productions

When Professor Ned Brainard misses his wedding ceremony for the third time because one of his inventions explodes and leaves him unconscious, it allows his rival, Professor Shelby Ashton, to vie for the hand of his beloved Betsy. This absent-minded professor's plan to win back Betsy's heart provides rich comic fun on the basketball court, the dance floor, and all the way to the Pentagon. As the film progresses, Spanish students will learn vocabulary from conversations that cover a wide range of topics—from marriage to gambling, pep talks to UFO sightings, and confection sales to laws of energy and physics.

## BASIC VOCABULARY

### Names

Betsy Carlisle, Ned Brainard, Shelby, Biff, Ned, Rutland, Medfield, Washington, Alonzo Hawk

### Nouns

□ **aplicación** application · *Quiero que tengan en mente, caballeros, que ésta es una **aplicación** primitiva de mi descubrimiento.* I want you to keep in mind, gentlemen, that this is a primitive application of my discovery.

□ **colegio** college · *Esto puede salvar al **colegio**.* This can save the college.

□ **control** NM control · *Tendremos todo bajo **control** en un momento.* We'll have everything under control in a moment.

□ **descubrimiento** discovery · *Profesor, ¿qué rama de los servicios armados se le ha dado el control de su **descubrimiento**?* Professor, what branch of the armed services has been given control of your discovery?

□ **energía** energy · *Significa sólo una cosa—está generando su propia **energía**.* It means only one thing—it's producing its own energy.

□ **modelo T** Model T · *Es un **modelo T**, señor.* It's a Model T, sir.

□ **voligoma** flubber [INVENTED WORD] · ***Voligoma**, señor Hawk.* Flubber, Mr. Hawk.

### Other

□ **acerca de** about · *Betsy, ¿recuerdas lo que te dije esta mañana en la oficina **acerca de** mi descubrimiento?* Betsy, do you remember what I told you this morning at the office about my discovery?

□ **realmente** really · *Pero, ¿sabes lo que **realmente** son?* But do you know what they really are?

□ **tal vez** perhaps, maybe · ***Tal vez** puedas aprender algo.* Maybe you can learn something.

### 1 Opening Credits/ The Third Time's a Charm! 9:28

#### Phrases to Listen For

**de muchas formas** in many ways
**por ejemplo** for example
**a las ocho treinta de la noche** at 8:30 P.M.
**ya basta** enough already
**me da gusto verlo** I'm glad to see you (LIT it gives me pleasure to see you)
**la tercera es la vencida** the third time is the charm
**según dicen** as they say (LIT according to they say)

**por Dios** good heavens, dear God
**de hecho** in fact
**loco descabezado** wild and crazy man (LIT headless crazy man)
**tengo razón** I am right
**no tomo partido** I don't take sides
**buenas tardes** good afternoon
**parece que** it seems that
**lo que** what
**no se preocupe** IMP don't worry
**otra vez** again
**por amor de Dios** good heavens, for the love of God
**toda la tarde** all afternoon
**¿qué me pasa?** what's the matter with me?
**luna de miel** honeymoon
**espero que así sea** SUBJ I hope that's how it is
**bajo mi nariz** under my nose
**algunas veces** sometimes
**no se ve** one doesn't see
**lo siento** I'm sorry

### Names

Milan, Walt Disney, Fred MacMurray, Nancy Olson, Keenan Wynn, Tommy Kirk, Ashton, Carlisle, Chatsworth

🎬 Professor Brainard stands in front of a class.

□ **por ejemplo** for example
□ **acústica** acoustic · *acústico* acoustic
□ **descubierta** discovered · *descubierto* discovered · *descubrir* to discover
□ **famoso** famous
□ **científico** scientist
□ **crédito** credit
□ **tenor** NM tenor
□ **italiano** ADJ Italian
□ **estaba cantando** he was singing · *cantar* to sing
□ **aria** aria
□ **café** NM cafe
□ **nota** note, musical note
□ **alta** high · *alto* high
□ **ondas de sonido** sound waves · *onda* wave · *sonido* sound
□ **vaso** glass, drinking glass
□ **salón** NM classroom
□ **obsérvenme** IMP observe me · *observar* to observe
□ **mostraré** I will show · *mostrar* to show
□ **acción** action

🎬 Professor Brainard blows the trumpet. Credits and a song in English follow.

□ **distraído** absent-minded, distracted · *distraer* to distract

🎬 The smoke clears and the professor addresses the class.

□ **tarea** assignment, task
□ **boda** wedding

🎬 Shelby and Betsy park in front of a house.

□ **principio del fin** beginning of the end · *principio* beginning · *fin NM* end
□ **el punto sin regreso** the point of no return · *punto* point · *regreso* return
□ **milla** mile
□ **dichas de palabra** spoken · *dicha* said · *palabra* word · *decir* to say
□ **prometiste** you promised · *prometer* to promise
□ **supón** IMP suppose · *suponer* to suppose
□ **reverendo** reverend
□ **aburrido** bored · *aburrir* to bore
□ **múltiples** multiple · *múltiple* multiple
□ **bodas** weddings · *boda* wedding
□ **tercera** third · *tercero* third
□ **según dicen** as they say · *según* according to · *decir* to say
□ **sí me alegro** I am happy indeed · *alegrarse* to be happy
□ **novio** groom
□ **lenguas romances** Romance languages · *lengua* tongue, language · *romance* Romance [= DERIVED FROM LATIN]
□ **química física** physical chemistry · *química* chemistry · *físico* physical
□ **cometí** I committed · *cometer* to commit
□ **error** NM error
□ **cometerá** she will commit · *cometer* to commit
□ **descabezado** crazy, wild (LIT headless)
□ **ramo** bouquet
□ **olorosos** fragrant · *oloroso* fragrant
□ **jacintos** hyacinths · *jacinto* hyacinth
□ **detonador** detonator
□ **hidrógeno** hydrogen
□ **misa** mass
□ **no tomo partido** I don't take sides · *tomar* to take · *partido* side [OF AN ISSUE]

🎬 A couple answers the door and welcomes Betsy and the others.

□ **novia** bride · *novio* groom
□ **invitarme** to invite me · *invitar* to invite
□ **recuerdo** I remember · *recordar* to remember
□ **oí** I heard · *oír* to hear
□ **rival** NMF rival
□ **consecutiva** consecutive · *consecutivo* consecutive
□ **refrán** NM saying
□ **secretaria** secretary
□ **quedada** spinster

□ **invitados** guests · *invitado* guest
□ **instruí** I instructed, I gave instructions · *instruir* to instruct, to give instructions
□ **ama de llaves** housekeeper · *ama* mistress, supervisor · *llave NF* key
□ **se encargará** she will handle · *encargarse* to handle, to be in charge

🎬 Professor Brainard's housekeeper pulls a coat from the closet.

□ **anillo** ring
□ **bolsa** pocket

🎬 In his garage, Professor Brainard fiddles with scientific instruments. The housekeeper enters.

□ **raíz cuadrada** square root · *raíz NF* root · *cuadrado ADJ* square · *cuadrar* to square
□ **se cambie** SUBJ you change · *cambiarse* to change clothes
□ **resolver** to solve
□ **misterios** mysteries · *misterio* mystery
□ **universo** universe
□ **fallé** I failed · *fallar* to fail
□ **rotundamente** roundly, completely
□ **discúlpame** IMP excuse me · *disculpar* to excuse, to forgive
□ **alimentar** to feed
□ **qué torpe** how clumsy
□ **configuración** configuration
□ **molecular** molecular
□ **be** NF B [LETTER]
□ **libre** free
□ **permanecerá** it will remain · *permanecer* to remain
□ **grados** degrees · *grado* degree
□ **centígrados** centigrade · *centígrado* centigrade
□ **luna de miel** honeymoon · *luna* moon · *miel NF* honey
□ **cálculos** calculations · *cálculo* calculation
□ **nariz** NF nose
□ **bosque** NM forest
□ **cruza los dedos** IMP cross your fingers · *cruzar* to cross · *dedo* finger
□ **extraordinario** extraordinary
□ **excelente** excellent

🎬 The telephone rings. Betsy is calling.

□ **matrimonio** marriage
□ **fallaba** he didn't show · *fallar* to fail (to attend), to miss
□ **devolveré** I will return · *devolver* to return, to take back
□ **obsequios** gifts · *obsequio* gift
□ **devuelvan** SUBJ they return · *devolver* to return, to take back

□ **he causado** I have caused · *causar* to cause
□ **oficina** office
□ **acostumbrada** usual · *acostumbrado* usual · *acostumbrar* to usually (+ VERB)

## 2 Flubber! 7:15

### Phrases to Listen For

**¿qué pasó?** what happened?
**a tus órdenes** at your service
**por supuesto** of course
**tenemos que** we have to
**así que** so
**de la mañana** in the morning
**otra vez** again
**tengo que** I have to
**no se preocupe** IMP don't worry

### Names

Charlie, Chatsworth

Betsy addresses Shelby.

□ **guardián** NM escort

The dog kisses Professor Brainard.

□ **averiguarlo** to find it out, to check it out · *averiguar* to find out, to check out
□ **sino** but rather
□ **está generando** it is generating · *generar* to generate
□ **hemos descubierto** we have discovered · *descubrir* to discover
□ **tipo** type
□ **descubrí** I discovered · *descubrir* to discover
□ **sustancia** substance
□ **aparentemente** apparently
□ **suscribe** it subscribes · *suscribir* to subscribe
□ **requerimientos** requirements · *requerimiento* requirement
□ **clásicos** classic · *clásico* ADJ classic
□ **compuesto** compound
□ **meta-estable** meta-stable
□ **comportamiento** behavior
□ **clásico** ADJ classic
□ **hipótesis** NF hypothesis
□ **externa** external · *externo* external
□ **dispara** it fires, it triggers · *disparar* to fire, to trigger
□ **molecular** molecular
□ **libera** it frees · *liberar* to free, to liberate
□ **previamente** previously
□ **desconocido** unknown, unfamiliar · *desconocer* to not know, to not recognize
□ **bolas** round objects, balls · *bola* round object, ball

□ **goma** rubber
□ **voladoras** flying · *volador* flying
□ **sabrías** you would know · *saber* to know
□ **equis** NF X [LETTER OR VARIABLE]

Professor Brainard picks up a radioactive substance with tongs.

□ **útil** useful
□ **controlarla** to control it · *controlar* to control
□ **isótopo** isotope
□ **radioactivo** radioactive
□ **obturador** lever [TECHNICAL]
□ **liso** smooth
□ **obtener** to obtain
□ **cantidad** quantity
□ **correcta** correct · *correcto* correct
□ **rayos gamma** gamma rays · *rayo* ray
□ **bombardear** to bombard
□ **disparar** to fire, to trigger
□ **científico** scientific
□ **botarla** to bounce it · *botar* to bounce
□ **laboratorio** laboratory

Professor Brainard guides a cauldron on a tripod as it rises into the air.

□ **¡eureka!** INT eureka!
□ **suavizamos** we ease up · *suavizar* to ease, to ease up, to soften
□ **de vuelta** back · *volver* to come back, to go back
□ **suavemente** softly
□ **flor** NF flower
□ **peso** weight
□ **absolutamente** absolutely
□ **diferencia** difference
□ **boda** wedding
□ **faltan cinco minutos para las ocho** it's five minutes to eight · *faltar* to lack · *minuto* minute

## 3 Saving Medfield 6:59

### Phrases to Listen For

**cuello** neck
**sin embargo** however
**largo de aquí** get away from here, get out of here
**tengo que** I have to
**tienes que** you have to
**lo que** what
**estoy muy de acuerdo** I completely agree, I am completely in agreement
**por favor** please
**mis sueños de loco** my wildest dreams (LIT my crazy dreams)
**así es como** that's how

## Names
Alonzo Hawk, Syne, Carlisle, Daggett, Biffer

🎬 Betsy sits down at her desk.

- □ **perfectamente** perfectly
- □ **préstamos** loans · *préstamo* loan
- □ **etcétera** etcetera, etc.
- □ **perturbado** upset, disturbed, perturbed · *perturbar* to upset, to disturb, to perturb
- □ **rumores** rumors · *rumor NM* rumor
- □ **planea** you plan · *planear* to plan
- □ **posesión** possession
- □ **construir** to construct
- □ **albergue** *NM* shelter, hostel, inn
- □ **no lo harán** they will not do it · *hacer* to do
- □ **situación** situation
- □ **requiere** it requires · *requerir* to require
- □ **manejo** handling
- □ **delicado** delicate
- □ **alumno** student
- □ **estimado** esteemed · *estimar* to esteem, to respect
- □ **expresión** expression
- □ **impertinente** impertinent
- □ **cuello** neck

🎬 Professor Brainard climbs the stairs. President Daggett continues dictating a letter to Betsy.

- □ **sin embargo** however
- □ **confianza** confidence, trust
- □ **mostrarle** to show you · *mostrar* to show
- □ **plazo mayor** extension, longer term · *plazo* term, period · *mayor* greater
- □ **interés** *NM* interest
- □ **me atrevería** I would dare, I would be so bold · *atreverse* to dare, to be bold
- □ **sugerirle** to suggest to you · *sugerir* to suggest
- □ **pertinente** appropriate
- □ **lentes** *NMPL* glasses, eyeglasses
- □ **evitarlo** to avoid it · *evitar* to avoid
- □ **boda** wedding
- □ **laboratorio** laboratory
- □ **explotó** it exploded · *explotar* to explode
- □ **suelo** floor
- □ **sentido** consciousness
- □ **superfluo** superfluous
- □ **pelota** ball

🎬 Alonzo Hawk enters the president's office.

- □ **agradable** pleasant
- □ **sorpresa** surprise
- □ **charla** chat, talk
- □ **federal** federal

- □ **no vale la pena** it's not worth it · *valer la pena* to be worth it · *valer* to be worth · *pena* shame, embarrassment
- □ **reprobó** he failed · *reprobar* to fail, to give a failing grade to
- □ **estudiante** *NMF* student
- □ **atrasado** behind, slow · *atrasarse* to fall behind, to be slow
- □ **reunirse** to meet, to get together
- □ **mentes** minds · *mente NF* mind
- □ **fundaron** they founded · *fundar* to found
- □ **construyó** it constructed, it built · *construir* to construct, to build
- □ **atrevimiento** audacity
- □ **orgullosamente** proudly
- □ **retrasado** behind · *retrasarse* to fall behind, to be late
- □ **callarte** to be quiet · *callarse* to be quiet
- □ **examen** *NM* test, exam
- □ **no respondió** he didn't answer · *responder* to answer
- □ **sino** but furthermore, but rather
- □ **discutir** to argue
- □ **asunto** matter
- □ **a solas** alone
- □ **ánimo escolar** school spirit · *ánimo* spirit · *escolar ADJ* school
- □ **estrella** star
- □ **millón** *NM* million
- □ **principios** principles · *principio* principle
- □ **aprobar** to pass [EDUCATION]
- □ **vagas** vague · *vago* vague
- □ **promesas** promises · *promesa* promise
- □ **prestar** to loan, to lend
- □ **ha prestado** he has loaned · *prestar* to loan, to lend
- □ **me alegra** it makes me happy · *alegrar* to make happy
- □ **ética** ethics
- □ **directamente** directly
- □ **reclamar** to complain, to protest
- □ **déme** *IMP* give me · *dar* to give
- □ **oficina** office
- □ **alardea** you boast · *alardear* to boast
- □ **valen** they are worth · *valer* to be worth
- □ **efectivo** cash, money

🎬 Hawk leaves the president's office.

- □ **expediente** *NM* file
- □ **aluminio** aluminum
- □ **marcado** marked · *marcar* to mark
- □ **doble** double
- □ **emergencia** emergency
- □ **no acudí** I didn't go · *acudir* to go

- **complicadas** complicated · *complicado* complicated · *complicar* to complicate, to make complicated
- **simple** simple
- **términos** terms · *término* term
- **energía magnética** magnetic energy · *energía* energy · *magnético* magnetic
- **energía repulsiva** repulsive energy · *energía* energy · *repulsivo* repulsive
- **fija** set, fixed · *fijo* set, fixed
- **explosión** explosion
- **hubiera descubierto** SUBJ I would have discovered · *descubrir* to discover
- **energía termal** thermal energy · *energía* energy · *termal* thermal, heat
- **metros** meters · *metro* meter
- **previamente** previously
- **incompatibles** incompatible · *incompatible* incompatible
- **compuestos** compounds · *compuesto* compound
- **combustión** combustion
- **fusión** fusion
- **altas** high · *alto* high
- **temperaturas** temperatures · *temperatura* temperature
- **gases** gases · *gas* NM gas
- **explosivos** explosives · *explosivo* explosive
- **residuo** residue
- **adjunto** attached

At the file cabinet, Professor Brainard shows Betsy the flubber (*voligoma*).

- **qué conmovedor** how moving [EMOTION]
- **me disculpas** you forgive me · *disculpar* to forgive
- **compuesto** compound
- **meta-estable** meta-stable
- **cuya** whose · *cuyo* whose
- **configuración** configuration
- **molecular** molecular
- **entrega** delivery
- **diminutas** minute, tiny · *diminuto* NM minute, tiny
- **partículas** particles · *partícula* particle
- **superficie** NF surface
- **libera** it frees · *liberar* to free, to liberate
- **enormes** enormous · *enorme* enormous
- **cantidades** quantities, amounts · *cantidad* quantity, amount
- **actúan** they act · *actuar* to act
- **dirección** direction
- **opuesta** opposite · *opuesto* opposite
- **disparan** they fire, they trigger · *disparar* to fire, to trigger
- **al respecto** about it, with respect to it

- **bastante** quite
- **efecto** effect
- **total** total
- **trascendente** transcendent
- **lanzamiento** launching
- **externa** external · *externo* external
- **aplicada** applied · *aplicado* applied · *aplicar* to apply
- **elementales** elemental · *elemental* elemental
- **pseudo** pseudo
- **equilibrio** equilibrium

Betsy pulls some papers from the desk and addresses Professor Brainard.

- **claramente** clearly
- **salve** SUBJ it saves · *salvar* to save
- **valer** to be worth
- **millones** millions · *millón* NM million
- **botar** to bounce
- **calma** calm

## 4 The Test Drive 7:19

### Phrases to Listen For
- **¿qué es lo que quieres?** what is it that you want?
- **lo que** what
- **tienes que** you have to
- **corre la voz** there's a rumor, the word is out (LIT the voice runs)
- **en contra nuestra** against us
- **hacia adelante** forward
- **hacia la derecha** toward the right
- **hacia la izquierda** toward the left
- **así es** that's it
- **lo importante** the important thing
- **por supuesto** of course
- **a menos que** unless
- **acerca de** about
- **para que** so that
- **tengo que** I have to
- **¿por qué?** why?
- **si no le importa** if it doesn't matter to you
- **sí me importa** it really matters to me
- **antes de que** before
- **por favor** please
- **así que** so
- **dar un paseo** to go for a ride

### Names
Medfield, Lennie, Syne, Carlisle

Hawk and Biff ride in the back seat of a car.

- **presionar** to pressure
- **estás bromeando** you are joking · *bromear* to joke, to tease

- □ **convertirlo** to convert it · *convertir* to convert
- □ **albergues** shelters, hostels, inns · *albergue* NM shelter, hostel, inn
- □ **tienda** store
- □ **farmacia** pharmacy
- □ **se están hundiendo** they are sinking · *hundirse* to sink
- □ **supermercado** supermarket
- □ **supercolegios** super-colleges · *supercolegio* super-college
- □ **te graduaste** you graduated · *graduarse* to graduate
- □ **cierren** SUBJ they close · *cerrar* to close
- □ **alumnos** students · *alumno* student
- □ **leal** loyal
- □ **amistad** friendship
- □ **que se hagan cargo** that they take charge, that they take care · *hacerse cargo* to take charge, to take care
- □ **préstamo** loan
- □ **cariño** affection
- □ **caballo** horse
- □ **pierna** leg
- □ **rota** broken · *roto* broken · *romper* to break
- □ **miseria** misery
- □ **extra** extra
- □ **voz** NF voice
- □ **apuestas** bets, wagers · *apuesta* bet, wager
- □ **movimiento** movement
- □ **no le apostarás** you won't bet · *apostar* to bet
- □ **papilla** puree
- □ **acceso** access
- □ **información** information
- □ **valiosa** valuable · *valioso* valuable
- □ **refrán** NM saying
- □ **viento** wind
- □ **apostadores** gamblers, bettors · *apostador* gambler, bettor
- □ **préstamos** loans · *préstamo* loan
- □ **no vale** it isn't worth anything, it has no value · *valer* to be worth, to have value

🎬 Professor Brainard points to the apparatus he has designed and explains to Charlie how it works.

- □ **palanca** lever
- □ **chispas** sparks · *chispa* spark
- □ **obturador** lever [TECHNICAL]
- □ **salen** they leave, they get out · *salir* to leave
- □ **rayos gamma** gamma rays · *rayo* ray
- □ **pedal** NM pedal
- □ **gas** NM gas
- □ **delante** forward
- □ **pisamos** we step on · *pisar* to step on

- □ **freno** brake
- □ **en reversa** in reverse
- □ **supón** IMP suppose · *suponer* to suppose
- □ **giramos** we turn · *girar* to turn
- □ **volante** NM steering wheel
- □ **excepto** except
- □ **cofre** NM hood of a car
- □ **finalmente** finally

🎬 The professor fastens the seat belt for Charlie the dog.

- □ **cinturón de seguridad** seat belt · *cinturón* NM belt · *seguridad* safety
- □ **sonido** sound
- □ **sujétate bien** IMP hold on tight · *sujetarse* to hold on
- □ **se comporta** it behaves · *comportarse* to behave
- □ **bellamente** beautifully
- □ **novia** bride, girlfriend · *novio* groom, boyfriend
- □ **tierna** tender, affectionate · *tierno* tender, affectionate
- □ **confesar** to confess
- □ **confort** NM comfort

🎬 The professor lands the car in front of Betsy's house.

- □ **anciano** old man
- □ **mostrarte** to show you · *mostrar* to show
- □ **discúlpenos** IMP excuse us · *disculpar* to excuse, to forgive
- □ **acompáñame** IMP come with me, accompany me · *acompañar* to come with, to accompany
- □ **intento** I'm trying · *intentar* to try, to attempt
- □ **enfadarme** to become upset, to become annoyed · *enfadarse* to become upset, to become annoyed
- □ **escena** scene
- □ **no le ha causado** you haven't caused her · *causar* to cause
- □ **bastante** enough
- □ **pena** embarrassment, shame
- □ **no se meta** IMP stay out of, don't interfere · *meterse* to interfere, to become involved
- □ **sorpresa** surprise
- □ **obsequio de bodas** wedding gift · *obsequio* gift · *boda* wedding
- □ **mostrar** to show
- □ **merodeando** hanging around · *merodear* to hang around, to loiter
- □ **¿nos disculpa?** will you excuse us? · *disculpar* to excuse
- □ **oficina** office
- □ **fabuloso** fabulous
- □ **dar un paseo** to take a ride

## 5   A Basketball Wonder    12:43

### Phrases to Listen For

**tuve que** I had to
**premio del honor** prize of honor
**con permiso** excuse me (*LIT* with permission)
**por favor** please
**en contra de** against
**no importa** it doesn't matter
**me da pena** I feel sorry for
**no se da cuenta** he doesn't notice
**¿por qué?** why?
**lo siento** I'm sorry
**ni siquiera alcanza** it doesn't even reach
**me parece que** it seems to me
**zapatos de elevador** elevator shoes
**así que** so
**les están volando las orejas** they are yanking
    your ears out
**tenemos que** we have to
**tal vez** maybe, perhaps
**acerca de** about
**en lo absoluto** not at all
**de alguna forma** in some way, in a manner
    of speaking

### Names

Lenny, Medfield, Harper

🎬 Medfield and Rutland are playing basketball.

- [ ] **reto** challenge
- [ ] **apuestas** bets · *apuesta* bet
- [ ] **barato** cheap
- [ ] **precio** price
- [ ] **teléfono** telephone
- [ ] **obtener** to obtain
- [ ] **tipo** kind
- [ ] **premio** prize
- [ ] **honor** *NM* honor
- [ ] **derrotas** you defeat · *derrotar* to defeat
- [ ] **fiera** savage animal
- [ ] **con permiso** excuse me (*LIT* with permission) ·
    *permiso* permission

🎬 Professor Brainard sits behind Betsy and Shelby.

- [ ] **odio** I hate · *odiar* to hate
- [ ] **comprar en barata** to buy cheaply, to buy on
    sale · *comprar* to buy · *barato* cheap
- [ ] **oí** I heard · *oír* to hear
- [ ] **estaba expulsado** he was expelled · *expulsar*
    to expel
- [ ] **estrella** star
- [ ] **realistas** realistic · *realista* realistic
- [ ] **baloncesto** basketball
- [ ] **inglés** *NM* English
- [ ] **obtengo** I earn, I get · *obtener* to earn, to get

- [ ] **doble** double
- [ ] **discutirlo** to argue about it · *discutir* to argue
- [ ] **me da pena** it saddens me, it grieves me ·
    *dar pena* to sadden, to grieve · *dar* to give ·
    *pena* shame, embarrassment
- [ ] **sección** section
- [ ] **pertenece** he belongs · *pertenecer* to belong
- [ ] **pelota** ball
- [ ] **muchachillos** young men, boys · *muchacho*
    young man, boy
- [ ] **empujón** *NM* shove, push
- [ ] **zapatos** shoes · *zapato* shoe
- [ ] **elevador** elevator
- [ ] **gracioso** funny

🎬 The professor places flubber in the team's extra
    shoes.

- [ ] **pelar un gato** to skin a cat
- [ ] **no dio un paseo** she didn't take a ride ·
    *dar un paseo* to take a ride
- [ ] **sorprenderemos** we will surprise · *sorprender*
    to surprise
- [ ] **voligomizar** to flubbergast [*INVENTED WORD*]

🎬 The coach addresses the team at halftime.

- [ ] **orgulloso** proud
- [ ] **banca** bench
- [ ] **orejas** ears · *oreja* ear
- [ ] **déjenme** *IMP* allow me · *dejar* to allow
- [ ] **he entrenado** I have coached · *entrenar* to coach
- [ ] **luchen** *SUBJ* they fight, they struggle · *luchar*
    to fight, to struggle
- [ ] **verdadero** true
- [ ] **miren** *IMP* look · *mirar* to look at
- [ ] **no lucha** it doesn't fight, it doesn't struggle ·
    *luchar* to fight, to struggle

🎬 The coach addresses the professor.

- [ ] **conciencia** conscience
- [ ] **suspender** to suspend
- [ ] **disculpas** apologies · *disculpa* apology
- [ ] **mitad** *NF* half
- [ ] **calificaciones** grades · *calificación* grade
- [ ] **apalear** to beat
- [ ] **ignoran** you are unaware of · *ignorar*
    to be unaware of, to be ignorant of
- [ ] **en lo absoluto** not at all
- [ ] **salen** you go out · *salir* to go out, to leave
- [ ] **saltar** to jump
- [ ] **salten** *SUBJ* you jump · *IMP* jump · *saltar*
    to jump

🎬 Cheerleaders lead the crowd.

- [ ] **acábenlos** *IMP* finish them off · *acabar* to finish
- [ ] **plática** speech, talk

☐ **escondido** hidden · *esconder* to hide
☐ **arbitro** referee
☐ **dígamelo** *IMP* tell me what · *decir* to tell
☐ **reglas** rules · *regla* rule
☐ **míralos** *IMP* look at them · *mirar* to look at
☐ **ciego** blind
☐ **piedra** rock
☐ **dispara** *IMP* shoot · *disparar* to shoot
☐ **lanza** *IMP* shoot · *lanzar* to shoot, to throw

🎬 Medfield wins. Betsy, Shelby, and the professor discuss the victory.

☐ **descubrí** I discovered · *descubrir* to discover
☐ **seguramente** surely
☐ **crédito** credit
☐ **haya ganado** *SUBJ* it has won · *ganar* to win
☐ **exactamente** exactly

## 6  The Professor's Revenge  5:31

### Phrases to Listen For
**por favor** please
**por supuesto** of course
**buenas noches** good night
**lo que** what
**no lo sé** I don't know
**ahora mismo** right now
**no se preocupe** *IMP* don't worry
**tal vez** maybe, perhaps
**después de** after
**tuve que** I had to
**así es** that's right
**hasta pronto** see you soon (*LIT* until soon)

### Names
Charlie, Ashton, Hanson

🎬 Shelby escorts Betsy to her door.

☐ **respuesta** answer, response
☐ **baile** *NM* dance

🎬 Professor Brainard follows Shelby in his Model T.

☐ **probablemente** probably
☐ **anormal** strange, abnormal
☐ **desesperado** desperate
☐ **apago** I'm turning off · *apagar* to turn off, to switch off [MOTOR]
☐ **motor** *NM* motor

🎬 Shelby crashes into a police car.

☐ **apariencia** appearance
☐ **taza** cup
☐ **café** *NM* coffee
☐ **caliente** hot
☐ **describirla** to describe it · *describir* to describe

☐ **ruidos** noises · *ruido* noise
☐ **toldo** car roof
☐ **sople** *SUBJ* you blow · *soplar* to blow
☐ **averiguar** to find out
☐ **probable** probable
☐ **esté mirándonos** *SUBJ* it is looking at us · *mirar* to look at, to watch
☐ **oscuridad** darkness
☐ **saltar** to jump
☐ **sóplele** *IMP* blow into it · *soplar* to blow
☐ **ultrajante** insulting
☐ **se están portando** you are behaving · *portarse* to behave
☐ **salvajes** savages · *salvaje* *NMF* savage
☐ **director** *NM* director
☐ **departamento** department
☐ **inglés** *NM* English
☐ **se ha vuelto loco** have you gone mad?, have you gone crazy? · *volverse loco* to go mad, to go crazy
☐ **idiota** idiotic
☐ **cooperativo** cooperative
☐ **sople** *IMP* blow · *soplar* to blow
☐ **agradeceríamos** we would be grateful · *agradecer* to be grateful

🎬 Professor Brainard pulls up to speak to the police officers.

☐ **usual** usual
☐ **quinientos dos** 5-0-2 [LAW CODE] (*LIT* five hundred two) · *quinientos* five hundred
☐ **perdedores** losers · *perdedor* loser
☐ **idiotas** idiots · *idiota* *NMF* idiot
☐ **repararlo** to repair it · *reparar* to repair
☐ **válvula** valve
☐ **modelos T** Model Ts · *modelo* model
☐ **sargento** sergeant

## 7  A Business Proposition  10:39

### Phrases to Listen For
**tal vez** maybe, perhaps
**claro que sí** of course
**lo que** what
**acerca de** about
**algo así** something like that
**a menos que** unless
**¿por qué?** why?
**después de todo** after all
**así es** that's right
**para que** so that
**por completo** completely
**nada de nada** absolutely nothing, nothing at all (*LIT* nothing of nothing)
**por favor** please

**antes que** before
**para siempre** forever
**tienes razón** you are right
**tenga que ver con** SUBJ it has to do with
**claro que no** of course not
**de inmediato** immediately
**me doy cuenta** I notice
**ya basta** enough already
**lo que sea** SUBJ anything
**ni siquiera me verá** she won't even see me

## Names

Hawk, Daggett, Appleton, Lenny, Sam Willard, Chatsworth, Shelby Ashton

🎬 Dressed in a robe, Hawk shouts at his henchmen.

□ **ducha** shower, bath
□ **quince** fifteen
□ **averigüen** IMP find out · *averiguar* to find out, to research
□ **vitaminas** vitamins · *vitamina* vitamin
□ **pruebas** tests · *prueba* test
□ **saliva** saliva
□ **averiguaste** you found out · *averiguar* to find out
□ **vestidores** dressing rooms · *vestidor* dressing room
□ **intermedio** intermission, halftime
□ **charla** chat, talk
□ **grandioso** magnificent, awe-inspiring
□ **noticias** NFPL news
□ **felicito** I congratulate · *felicitar* to congratulate
□ **secreto** secret
□ **supremo** supreme
□ **información** information

🎬 Hawk sees the professor flying his Model T.

□ **dilo** IMP say it *decir* to say
□ **ése** that one
□ **genio** genius
□ **retacó** he stuffed · *retacar* to stuff
□ **oídos** ears · *oído* ear
□ **locura** craziness, crazy idea
□ **ligera** light, slight · *ligero* light, slight
□ **producir** to produce

🎬 The professor works on his Model T in the garage. Hawk and Biff enter.

□ **indulgencia** indulgence
□ **caber** to fit
□ **pedante** pedantic
□ **hombre de negocios** businessman · *hombre* NM man · *negocio* business
□ **planea** he plans · *planear* to plan
□ **tirar** to throw away
□ **visualice** IMP visualize · *visualizar* to visualize

□ **edificios** buildings · *edificio* building
□ **almacenes** warehouses · *almacén* NM warehouse
□ **edificio** building
□ **dedicado** dedicated · *dedicar* to dedicate
□ **enteramente** entirely
□ **ciencia** science
□ **revolucionario** revolutionary
□ **máquina** machine
□ **anoche** last night
□ **mutuamente** mutually
□ **nubes** clouds · *nube* NF cloud
□ **oler** to smell
□ **millones** millions · *millón* NM million
□ **ángulos** angles · *ángulo* angle
□ **gobierno** government
□ **era espacial** space age · *era* age · *espacial* space
□ **sucias** dirty · *sucio* dirty
□ **rodillas** knees · *rodilla* knee
□ **implorarnos** to beg us · *implorar* to beg, to implore
□ **bolsas** bags · *bolsa* bag
□ **barriles** barrels · *barril* NM barrel
□ **aclarar** to clarify
□ **chantajear** to blackmail
□ **crecer** to grow
□ **prosperar** to prosper
□ **lucha** struggle
□ **por completo** completely
□ **depende** it depends · *depender* to depend
□ **direcciones** directions · *dirección* direction
□ **no me malinterprete** IMP don't misunderstand me, don't misinterpret me · *malinterpretar* to misunderstand, to misinterpret
□ **apoyo** I support · *apoyar* to support
□ **está tirando** you are throwing · *tirar* to throw, to throw out
□ **bomba** bomb
□ **no intente volver a retroceder** IMP don't try to come back · *intentar* to try, to attempt · *volver* to return · *retroceder* to go back
□ **hierro** iron

🎬 Hawk and Biff ride in the back of their car.

□ **telefoneará** he will telephone · *telefonear* to telephone
□ **arpías** harpies · *arpía* harpy
□ **supón** IMP suppose · *suponer* to suppose
□ **si le echan mano** if they get hold of it, if they get their hands on it · *echar mano* to get hold of, to get one's hands on, to grab
□ **vehículo** vehicle
□ **volador** flying
□ **calla** IMP be quiet · *callarse* to be quiet
□ **intento** I'm trying · *intentar* to try, to attempt

☐ **idiota** *NMF* idiot
☐ **modelos T** Model Ts · *modelo* model

🎬 At the White House, O. J. Turnbull, Special
Assistant to the President, speaks on the telephone.

☐ **desarrollo** development
☐ **prosperidad** prosperity
☐ **nacional** national
☐ **insistir** to insist
☐ **naturaleza** nature
☐ **significativo** significant
☐ **rama** branch
☐ **nómbrelas** *IMP* name them · *nombrar* to name
☐ **transporte** *NM* transportation
☐ **industria** industry
☐ **agricultura** agriculture
☐ **no me cuelgue** *IMP* don't hang up on me ·
*colgar* to hang up [TELEPHONE]

🎬 A bespectacled man at the Department of
Agriculture answers the phone.

☐ **departamento** department
☐ **espléndido** splendid
☐ **granjero** farmer
☐ **cuántas** how many · *cuántos* how many
☐ **posibilidades** possibilities · *posibilidad*
possibility
☐ **fertilizante** *NM* fertilizer
☐ **vital** vital
☐ **sino** but also

🎬 At the Pentagon, a civilian addresses three
high-ranking military officers.

☐ **orgulloso** prideful
☐ **espíritu** *NM* spirit
☐ **cooperación** cooperation
☐ **ejército** Army
☐ **marina** Navy
☐ **fuerza aérea** Air Force · *fuerza* force ·
*aérea* air
☐ **columnistas** columnists · *columnista NMF*
columnist
☐ **periódicos** newspapers · *periódico* newspaper
☐ **diferencia** difference
☐ **real** real
☐ **mentiras** lies · *mentira* lie
☐ **teléfono** telephone
☐ **escriba** *SUBJ* he writes · *escribir* to write
☐ **carta** letter
☐ **conexión** connection
☐ **congresista** *NMF* member of Congress
☐ **comité** *NM* committee
☐ **apropiación** appropriations
☐ **influencia** influence
☐ **amigable** amicable, friendly

☐ **interesante** interesting
☐ **antigravedad** antigravity
☐ **cochera** garage
☐ **falso** false
☐ **investigaciones** research · *investigación*
research, investigation
☐ **vuelo** flight
☐ **de inmediato** immediately
☐ **doy** I give · *dar* to give
☐ **urgente** urgent
☐ **actualmente** currently, nowadays
☐ **piloto** pilot
☐ **breve** brief
☐ **contándonos** telling us · *contar* to tell,
to relate
☐ **llámanos** *IMP* call us · *llamar* to call

🎬 Professor Brainard hangs up the telephone.

☐ **planchado** ironed, pressed · *planchar* to iron,
to press
☐ **almidonado** starched · *almidonar* to starch
☐ **baile** *NM* dance
☐ **al respecto** about it
☐ **nariz** *NF* nose
☐ **metida** inserted · *metido* inserted ·
*meter* to insert, to put into
☐ **no le pertenecen** they don't pertain to you ·
*pertenecer* to pertain
☐ **misterios** mysteries · *misterio* mystery
☐ **universo** universe
☐ **intención** intention
☐ **simplemente** simply
☐ **me casaré** I will marry · *casarse* to marry,
to get married
☐ **desunir** to separate
☐ **átomos** atoms · *átomo* atom
☐ **hombro** shoulder
☐ **bailarines** dancers · *bailarín NM* dancer
☐ **compiten** they compete · *competir* to compete
☐ **se voltee** *SUBJ* he turns around · *voltearse* to turn
around
☐ **golpearé** I will hit · *golpear* to hit
☐ **exacto** exactly
☐ **civilizado** civilized · *civilizar* to civilize
☐ **brazos** arms · *brazo* arm
☐ **abrácela** *IMP* hug her, hold her, embrace her ·
*abrazar* to hug, to hold, to embrace
☐ **quítesela** *IMP* take her from him · *quitarse*
to take
☐ **mandril** *NM* mandrill
☐ **bestial** beastly
☐ **bailo** I dance · *bailar* to dance
☐ **chimpancé** *NM* chimpanzee
☐ **organillero** organ grinder
☐ **pareja** mate

## 8　The Dance　5:19

### Phrases to Listen For

**tengo que** I have to
**por favor** please
**tal vez** maybe, perhaps
**pensándolo bien** on the other hand, I take that back

◧ Professor Brainard drives under the "Welcome Alumni" sign. A military officer arrives at the airport.

□ **hundan** *IMP* sink · *hundir* to sink
□ **ejército** army
□ **gris** gray
□ **taxi** *NM* taxi
□ **ya tengo que irme** I have to go already, I have to go right away · *irse* to go away

◧ At the dance, Professor Brainard dances with Betsy.

□ **chimpancé** *NM* chimpanzee
□ **pareja** mate
□ **está mirándonos** it is looking at us · *mirar* to look at
□ **no los decepcionemos** *SUBJ* let's not disappoint them · *decepcionar* to disappoint
□ **baile** *NM* dance
□ **mira esto** *IMP* look at this · *mirar* to look at
□ **adentro** inside
□ **diversión** fun

## 9　Bait and Switch　9:01

### Phrases to Listen For

**por favor** please
**por supuesto** of course
**me doy cuenta** I notice
**de nuevo** again
**lo siento** I'm sorry
**ya lo verás** you will soon see
**¿por qué?** why?
**lo que** what
**pase lo que pase** *SUBJ* whatever happens
**es así como** it's just like how
**claro que** of course
**tenemos que** we have to
**creo en ti** I believe in you
**me alegro** I'm happy
**por completo** completely
**tiene razón** she is right
**muy bien** very good
**Dios mío** good heavens (*LIT* my God)
**he cambiado de opinión** I have changed my mind
**así es** that's right
**se ve** it looks

### Names

Bard, Shakespeare, Hawk, Betsy

◧ Professor Brainard escorts the military officers outside to the Model T.

□ **sorpresa** surprise
□ **doy** I give · *dar* to give
□ **tecnología** technology
□ **militar** *ADJ* military
□ **ha progresado** it has progressed · *progresar* to progress
□ **estoy utilizando** I am utilizing · *utilizar* to utilize
□ **medidas** measures · *medida* measure
□ **seguridad** security
□ **esconder** to hide
□ **en mente** in mind · *mente* *NF* mind
□ **primitiva** primitive · *primitivo* primitive
□ **obturador** lever [TECHNICAL]
□ **levitar** to levitate
□ **gas** *NM* gas
□ **delante** forward
□ **pedal** *NM* pedal
□ **freno** brake
□ **en reversa** in reverse, backwards
□ **absoluto** absolute, complete
□ **respiren profundo** *IMP* take a deep breath · *respirar* to breathe · *profundo* deep
□ **emociones** emotions · *emoción* emotion
□ **despegar** to take off [AIRCRAFT]
□ **firme** *ADJ* firm
□ **falla** it fails · *fallar* to fail
□ **seguramente** surely
□ **tipo** kind
□ **cohete** *NM* rocket
□ **probablemente** probably
□ **mecanismo** mechanism
□ **demora** delay
□ **demostración** demonstration
□ **aire** *NM* air
□ **broma** practical joke
□ **adentro** inside

◧ Professor Brainard and the military officers look inside the Model T engine.

□ **no me causa** it doesn't cause me, it doesn't provoke (in me) · *causar* to cause, to provoke
□ **risa** laughter
□ **ardilla** squirrel
□ **toque** *NM* touch
□ **libramos al aire** we've cleared the air · *librar* to clear, to free · *aire* *NM* air
□ **lástima** pity
□ **cierra la boca** *IMP* shut up, be quiet · *cerrar la boca* to shut up, to be quiet (*LIT* to close the mouth)

■ Betsy approaches Professor Brainard as he sits on the runner of the Model T.

- □ **burlarte** to make fun · *burlarse* to make fun
- □ **fraude** *NM* fraud
- □ **tornillo** screw
- □ **solemnemente** solemnly
- □ **he volado** I have flown · *volar* to fly
- □ **descanso** rest
- □ **mostrarte** to show you · *mostrar* to show
- □ **sostenla** *IMP* hold it · *sostener* to hold
- □ **bótala** *IMP* bounce it · *botar* to bounce
- □ **baloncesto** basketball
- □ **devolver** to return, to take back
- □ **radio** radio
- □ **cambió** he changed · *cambiar* to change
- □ **anoche** last night
- □ **trato** deal
- □ **lo mandé a volar** I sent him packing · *mandar a volar* to send packing · *mandar* to send · *volar* to fly
- □ **hurtó** he stole · *hurtar* to steal

■ Hawk sits in his chair and addresses the professor and Betsy.

- □ **me alegro** I'm glad · *alegrarse* to be glad, to be happy
- □ **proposición** proposition
- □ **estábamos discutiendo** we were discussing · *discutir* to discuss
- □ **zapatos** shoes · *zapato* shoe
- □ **voligomizados** flubberized [INVENTED WORD]
- □ **salto** jump
- □ **encima de** on top of
- □ **nubes** clouds · *nube* *NF* cloud
- □ **por completo** completely
- □ **poeta** *NMF* poet
- □ **suelo** ground
- □ **mortal** *ADJ* mortal
- □ **brinco** skip
- □ **canción** song
- □ **valiosos** valuable · *valioso* valuable
- □ **volador** flying
- □ **imagíneselo** *IMP* imagine it · *imaginar* to imagine
- □ **población** population
- □ **mundial** *ADJ* world
- □ **compra** it buys · *comprar* to buy
- □ **prácticamente** practically
- □ **tranquilícese** *IMP* calm down · *tranquilizarse* to calm down
- □ **mostraré** I will show · *mostrar* to show
- □ **presione** *IMP* press · *presionar* to press, to put pressure on
- □ **tacón** *NM* heel
- □ **equilibrio** equilibrium, balance

- □ **acostumbrarse** to get used to, to become accustomed to
- □ **salte** *IMP* jump · *SUBJ* I jump · *saltar* to jump
- □ **bastante** enough
- □ **ayúdame** *IMP* help me · *ayudar* to help
- □ **humanidad** humanity
- □ **incendio** fire
- □ **inmenso** immense
- □ **escaleras** stairs · *escalera* staircase
- □ **infierno** inferno
- □ **humo** smoke
- □ **por debajo de** from under
- □ **auxilio** help
- □ **soportar** to tolerate

■ Professor Brainard jumps off Hawk's balcony.

- □ **Gerónimo** Geronimo
- □ **turno** turn
- □ **divertido** fun · *divertirse* to have fun, to have a good time
- □ **aterrizará** you will land · *aterrizar* to land [AIRCRAFT]
- □ **suavemente** softly
- □ **pluma** feather
- □ **socio** associate, partner
- □ **fe** *NF* faith
- □ **producto** product
- □ **sensible** touchy, sensitive
- □ **cobarde** *NM* coward

■ Hawk jumps off the balcony.

- □ **miren** *IMP* look at, watch · *mirar* to look at, to watch
- □ **sencillo** simple
- □ **flexione** *IMP* flex · *flexionar* to flex
- □ **rodillas** knees · *rodilla* knee
- □ **tendió una trampa** you laid a trap · *tender* to lay, to set · *trampa* trap
- □ **escondió** you hid · *esconder* to hide
- □ **bodega** warehouse
- □ **aterrizaje** *NM* landing [AIRCRAFT]
- □ **departamento de bomberos** fire department · *departamento* department · *bombero* firefighter
- □ **haz algo** *IMP* do something · *hacer* to do · *algo* something
- □ **detenme** *IMP* stop me · *detener* to stop

# 10   Stealing the Car Back                    5:21

**Phrases to Listen For**
**¿por qué?** why?
**tenemos que** we have to
**lo que** what
**¿qué pasa?** what's up?

**bajo control** under control
**está dando un gran espectáculo** he's putting on a great show
**claro que** of course
**todo el mundo** everyone
**no se preocupe** *IMP* don't worry
**antes que** before
**con cuidado** carefully, be careful
**¿qué pasó?** what happened?
**no me gustaría** I wouldn't like (*LIT* it wouldn't please me)
**tener que** to have to
**lo de antes** the same as before, like before

## Names

Lenny, Betsy, Feisty McKenna, Marilou, Millie

🎬 Hawk's henchmen play cards in the warehouse.

□ **vigilar** to watch over
□ **lobo de mar** old salt (*LIT* sea wolf) · *lobo* wolf · *mar NM* sea

🎬 The professor and Betsy enter an alley near the warehouse.

□ **saltar** to jump
□ **se han atrasado** they have gotten behind · *atrasarse* to get behind, to be behind
□ **pagos** payments · *pago* payment
□ **ruidos** noises · *ruido* noise
□ **arpa** harp
□ **despacio** slowly
□ **bájalo** *IMP* put it down, lower it · *bajar* to put down, to lower
□ **zapato** shoe
□ **deshacer** to undo, to untie
□ **nudo** knot
□ **uña** fingernail, toenail
□ **cantos** songs · *canto* song
□ **pajaritos** *DIM* little birds · *pájaro* bird

🎬 The fire department arrives at Hawk's residence.

□ **jefe de bomberos** fire chief · *jefe NMF* chief · *bombero* firefighter
□ **calmarme** to calm down · *calmarse* to calm down
□ **idiota** *NMF* idiot
□ **espectáculo** show, spectacle
□ **red** *NF* net
□ **abran paso** *IMP* make way · *abrir paso* to make way · *abrir* to open · *paso* way
□ **de pie** standing · *pie NM* foot
□ **consejo** counsel
□ **autorización** authorization
□ **no se enoje** *IMP* don't get mad · *enojarse* to get mad

□ **mencioné** I mentioned · *mencionar* to mention
□ **mirones** curious onlookers · *mirón NM* curious onlooker
□ **área** area
□ **personalmente** personally
□ **experimentado** experienced · *experimentar* to experience
□ **cochero real** royal coachman · *cochero* coachman, driver of a carriage · *real ADJ* royal
□ **haz algo** *IMP* do something · *hacer* to do · *algo* something
□ **entrenamiento de primavera** spring training · *entrenamiento* training · *primavera* spring [SEASON]

🎬 Hawk's henchmen hear noise in the warehouse.

□ **canto** song
□ **astuto** astute, clever
□ **exactamente** exactly
□ **fallaron** you failed, you missed · *fallar* to fail
□ **no me acorralen** *IMP* don't corner me · *acorralar* to corner

## 11 Bringing Down Mr. Hawk  5:41

### Phrases to Listen For

**¿qué opina usted?** what do you think?
**cerca de las siete** about seven o'clock
**en graves problemas** in big trouble
**con permiso** excuse me (*LIT* with permission)
**por aquí** over here
**por favor** please
**tengo que** I have to
**jugar al tiro al blanco** to take target practice
**de hecho** in fact

### Names

Alonzo P. Hawk, Syne Lang, Hanson

🎬 Several onlookers watch Hawk jump higher and higher.

□ **golosinas** candies, sweets · *golosina* candy, sweet
□ **goma de mascar** chewing gum · *goma* gum · *mascar* to chew
□ **rosetas de maíz** popcorn · *roseta* rosette · *maíz* corn
□ **cigarros** cigarettes · *cigarro* cigarette
□ **baño** bath
□ **rostro** face
□ **se asomó** it suddenly appeared · *asomarse* to appear suddenly
□ **ventana** window
□ **calculo** I calculate · *calcular* to calculate

- ☐ **dieciocho** eighteen
- ☐ **pulgadas** inches · *pulgada* inch
- ☐ **salto** jump
- ☐ **¿qué opina usted?** what do you think? · *opinar* to think, to give an opinion
- ☐ **graves** grave, serious · *grave* grave, serious
- ☐ **con permiso** excuse me (*LIT* with permission) · *permiso* permission
- ☐ **touchdown** *ENG* touchdown

🎬 In the warehouse, Hawk's henchmen pursue the professor.

- ☐ **bodega** warehouse
- ☐ **no se vayan a rendir** *IMP* don't surrender · *rendirse* to surrender
- ☐ **golpe** *NM* hit, blow
- ☐ **pónganse de pie** *IMP* stand up · *ponerse de pie* to stand up
- ☐ **gorilas** gorillas · *gorila* gorilla
- ☐ **saltarín** *ADJ* hopping, jumping, bouncing

🎬 The professor and Betsy fly out of the warehouse.

- ☐ **paredes** walls · *pared* *NF* wall
- ☐ **idiotas** idiots · *idiota* *NMF* idiot
- ☐ **dímelo** *IMP* tell it to me, say it to me · *decir* to tell, to say
- ☐ **jugar al tiro al blanco** to take target practice · *tiro* shot · *blanco* target [SPORTS]
- ☐ **dispararles** to shoot at them · *disparar* to shoot
- ☐ **demostraré** I will demonstrate · *demostrar* to demonstrate
- ☐ **negocios** business · *negocio* business
- ☐ **patrulla** patrol car
- ☐ **apenas** barely, hardly
- ☐ **suelo** ground

🎬 Hawk and his men crash into a patrol car.

- ☐ **pajaritos** *DIM* little birds · *pájaro* bird
- ☐ **toldo** roof of a car
- ☐ **arma** weapon
- ☐ **disparada** fired · *disparado* fired · *disparar* to fire, to shoot
- ☐ **finanzas** *NFPL* finances
- ☐ **recuerdo** I remember · *recordar* to remember
- ☐ **patán** *NM* oaf
- ☐ **hielera** ice box, refrigerator
- ☐ **interrumpirlo** to interrupt you · *interrumpir* to interrupt
- ☐ **directo** direct
- ☐ **siguiente** next
- ☐ **dé vuelta** *IMP* turn, make a turn · *dar vuelta* to turn, to make a turn
- ☐ **carretera** highway
- ☐ **aire** *NM* air

- ☐ **millones** millions · *millón* *NM* million
- ☐ **seguramente** surely
- ☐ **no está acusando** you aren't accusing · *acusar* to accuse

## 12 Military Alert/End Credits   10:38

### Phrases to Listen For
- **lo que** what
- **otra vez** again
- **por lo tanto** therefore
- **¿por qué?** why?
- **por favor** please
- **no tengo con que arreglarlo** I don't have the stuff (the things, the tools, etc.) to fix it
- **tiene que** you have to
- **para que** so that
- **buena suerte** good luck

### Names
Mead, Stutz Bearcat, Papa Toledo, Singer, Myer, Anacostia

🎬 A radar operator reports to his commanding officer.

- ☐ **desconocido** unknown · *desconocer* to not know, to not be aware of
- ☐ **zona** zone, area
- ☐ **prohibida** prohibited · *prohibido* prohibited · *prohibir* to prohibit, to forbid
- ☐ **velocidad** velocity, speed
- ☐ **nudos** knots, nautical miles · *nudo* knot, nautical mile
- ☐ **pajarera** large birdcage, aviary
- ☐ **bandera** flag
- ☐ **alista** *IMP* prepare, get ready · *alistar* to prepare, to get ready
- ☐ **pájaros** birds · *pájaro* bird
- ☐ **azul** blue
- ☐ **en vuelo** in flight
- ☐ **vector** *NM* vector

🎬 The professor and Betsy fly quietly among the clouds. Shortly, two jets approach.

- ☐ **bello** beautiful, pretty
- ☐ **enterado** understood [RADIO COMMUNICATION]
- ☐ **artefacto** object
- ☐ **piloto** pilot
- ☐ **déme** *IMP* give me · *dar* to give
- ☐ **reporte** *NM* report
- ☐ **sugiero** I suggest · *sugerir* to suggest
- ☐ **se metió** it entered · *meterse* to enter, to insert, to go in
- ☐ **nube** *NF* cloud
- ☐ **procedimiento** procedure

□ **coronel** colonel
□ **se haga cargo** *SUBJ* he takes charge · *hacerse cargo* to take charge, to take care
□ **bromear** to play a practical joke, to joke, to tease
□ **no me interrumpa** *IMP* don't interrupt me · *interrumpir* to interrupt
□ **exactamente** exactly
□ **situación** situation

🎬 The professor and Betsy remain among the clouds.

□ **se está arruinando** it's ruining · *arruinarse* to be ruined
□ **peinado** hairdo, hairstyle
□ **nunca habías lucido** you have never looked · *lucir* to look, to look good

🎬 A group of officers discuss the Model T.

□ **sencillo** simple
□ **obviamente** obviously
□ **disfrazado** disguised · *disfrazar* to disguise
□ **declaro** I'm declaring · *declarar* to declare
□ **condición** condition
□ **amarilla** yellow · *amarillo* yellow

🎬 The professor and Betsy fly over Washington, D.C.

□ **orgulloso** proud
□ **no me sorprendería** it wouldn't surprise me · *sorprender* to surprise
□ **gritan** they shout, they are yelling · *gritar* to shout, to yell
□ **pica** it pokes · *picar* to poke
□ **tumba de Grant** Grant's tomb
□ **Nueva York** New York
□ **Monumento a Jefferson** Jefferson Monument
□ **Monticello** Monticello
□ **mapa** *NM* map
□ **turístico** tourist
□ **guantera** glove compartment
□ **edificio del Pentágono** Pentagon building
□ **estacionamiento** parking lot
□ **enorme** enormous
□ **mil novecientos diecisiete** 1917 [DATE], one thousand nine hundred seventeen
□ **capitolio** capitol
□ **causar** to cause
□ **alboroto** disturbance

🎬 The professor and Betsy listen to the radio.

□ **interrumpimos** we interrupt · *interrumpir* to interrupt
□ **programa** *NM* program
□ **boletín** *NM* bulletin
□ **urgente** urgent

□ **oficial en mando** commanding officer · *oficial NM* officer · *mando* command
□ **aérea** air
□ **radios** radios · *radio* radio
□ **comerciales** commercial · *comercial* commercial
□ **longitudes** longitudes · *longitud NF* longitude
□ **ondas** waves, frequencies · *onda* wave, frequency
□ **militares** military · *militar ADJ* military
□ **objeto volador no identificado (OVNI)** UFO, unidentified flying object · *objeto* object · *volador* flying · *no identificado* unidentified
□ **misil** *NM* missile
□ **área** area
□ **si no se identifica** if it doesn't identify itself · *identificarse* to identify oneself
□ **dispararemos** we will shoot · *disparar* to shoot
□ **inmediatamente** immediately
□ **atreverse** to dare
□ **se atreverán** they will dare · *atreverse* to dare
□ **advertencia** warning
□ **identifíquese** *IMP* identify yourself · *identificarse* to identify oneself
□ **abriremos fuego** we will open fire · *abrir* to open · *fuego* fire
□ **batería de misiles** missile battery · *batería* battery · *misil NM* missile
□ **directo** pointed
□ **repito** I repeat · *repetir* to repeat
□ **respuesta** answer, response
□ **estoy respondiendo** I am responding · *responder* to respond
□ **americano** American
□ **tarjetas de crédito** credit cards · *tarjeta* card · *crédito* credit
□ **reporta** it reports · *reportar* to report
□ **congreso** Congress
□ **en sesión** in session · *sesión* session
□ **congresistas** members of Congress · *congresista NMF* member of Congress

🎬 An official from the Department of Defense answers the telephone.

□ **asunto** matter
□ **bájelo** *IMP* take it down · *bajar* to take down, to bring down
□ **correcto** correct
□ **bájenlos** *IMP* take them down · *bajar* to take down, to bring down
□ **personal** personal
□ **identificarse** to identify yourself · *identificarse* to identify oneself
□ **directamente** directly
□ **estación** station
□ **naval** naval

□ **orden** *NF* order
□ **base** *NF* base
□ **ejército** army
□ **repórtese** *IMP* report · *reportarse* to report
□ **descender** to descend
□ **terreno** terrain
□ **césped** *NM* grass, lawn
□ **verde** green
□ **cabello** hair
□ **despeinado** messy [HAIR]

The professor and Betsy land on the White House lawn.

□ **dedicado** dedicated · *dedicar* to dedicate
□ **avance** *NM* advance
□ **ciencia** science
□ **entusiasmo** enthusiasm
□ **rama** branch
□ **servicios armados** armed services ·
*servicio* service · *armado* armed ·
*armar* to arm [WEAPONS]

□ **compartirán** they will share · *compartir* to share
□ **cimentará** it will strengthen · *cimentar* to strengthen
□ **lazos** ties · *lazo* tie
□ **tradicionales** traditional · *tradicional* traditional
□ **cooperación** cooperation
□ **interservicio** interservice
□ **conquistar** to conquer, to win the affections of someone

The professor and Betsy stand before the minister.

□ **repetirlo** to repeat it · *repetir* to repeat
□ **sentido** sense
□ **marido** husband
□ **novios** bride and groom
□ **novia** bride · *novio* groom
□ **recién** recently, newly
□ **finalmente** finally
□ **casados** married · *casado* married ·
*casarse* to marry, to get married

# Eragon

**Pobre Durza, ¿cómo le dirás al rey que fallaste?**
*Poor Durza, how will you tell the king you failed?*

GENRE      Adventure/Fantasy
YEAR       2006
DIRECTOR   Stefen Fangmeier
CAST       Ed Speleers, Sienna Guillory, Jeremy Irons, John Malkovich
STUDIO     Twentieth Century Fox

A simple farm boy who loves to hunt finds a mysterious rock in the king's forest. When that rock hatches, a fanciful adventure story unfolds, with its hero riding a flying dragon to protect the rebel forces of good against the well-established forces of evil. For the Spanish learner, *Eragon* is light on the use of the more difficult Spanish verb tenses, and the dialogue occurs at an easily manageable pace that allows time to process the new vocabulary.

## BASIC VOCABULARY

### Names

Eragon, Saphira, Brom, Durza, Arya, Galbatorix, Ra'zac, Varden, Shade

### Nouns

- **batalla** battle · *Y en una sangrienta **batalla** creyó que los había matado a todos, tanto a los jinetes como a sus dragones.* And in a bloody battle, he believed that he had killed all of them, the riders as well as their dragons.
- **campesino** peasant · *Un simple **campesino** de Carvajal.* A simple peasant from Carvajal.
- **dragones** dragons · **dragón** NM dragon · *Sabe de **dragones**.* He knows about dragons. · *Y cuando un **dragón** y su jinete son uno solo, llegan a ver como uno.* And when a dragon and his rider are as one, they begin to see as one.
- **ejército** army · *Dos patriotas voluntarios más para el **ejército** del rey.* Two more volunteer patriots for the army of the king.
- **jinetes** riders, knights · **jinete** rider, knight · *Y ahora, los días de los **jinetes** han regresado.* And now, the days of the riders have returned. · *Un **jinete** vivirá aunque su dragón muera, Eragon.* A rider will live on even though his dragon may die, Eragon.
- **montañas** mountains · *montaña* mountain · *Los que sobrevivieron huyeron a las **montañas**.* Those who survived fled to the mountains.

### Verb

- **cuida** IMP take care of · *cuidar* to take care of · ***Cuida** bien a Arya.* Take good care of Arya.

### Other

- **brisingr** [ELF LANGUAGE]
- **skulblakas ven** [ELF LANGUAGE]

---

## 1  Main Titles/The King's Stone  6:19

### Phrases to Listen For

**sin tener** not having (LIT without having)
**así que** so, therefore
**mi sufrir** my suffering

### Name

Alagaësia

🎬 Clouds and mountains are visible as the narrator begins the story.

- **época** age, epoch
- **imponente** imposing

---

- **gobernada** governed · *gobernado* governed · *gobernar* to govern
- **montaban** they rode, they mounted · *montar* to ride, to mount
- **poderosos** powerful · *poderoso* powerful
- **misión** mission
- **proteger** to protect
- **prosperó** it prospered · *prosperar* to prosper
- **arrogantes** arrogant · *arrogante* arrogant

🎬 As a dragon flies through the air, the narrator continues the story.

- **notando** noticing · *notar* to notice
- **debilidad** weakness
- **traicionó** he betrayed · *traicionar* to betray
- **sangrienta** bloody · *sangriento* bloody
- **rebelión** rebellion
- **incluyendo** including · *incluir* to include
- **defensores** defenders · *defensor* NM defender
- **libertad** NF liberty, freedom
- **sobrevivieron** they survived · *sobrevivir* to survive
- **huyeron** they fled · *huir* to flee
- **milagro** miracle
- **equilibrara** SUBJ it balances · *equilibrar* to balance

🎬 A woman on horseback and her escort ride swiftly through a forest.

- **aliada** allied · *aliado* allied · *aliar* to ally
- **huía** she fled · *huir* to flee
- **piedra** rock

🎬 The king sits on his throne addressing one of his henchmen.

- **sufro** I suffer · *sufrir* to suffer
- **no prolongues** IMP don't prolong · *prolongar* to prolong
- **sufrir** suffering · *sufrir* to suffer

🎬 A young man dresses and then blows out a candle.

- **se aventuraba** he was venturing · *aventurarse* to venture
- **cazar** to hunt

🎬 The woman on horseback is captured. The young man, Eragon, hunts a deer. Later, Eragon picks up the "stone."

- **mírenla** IMP look at her · *mirar* to look at
- **entrégamelo** IMP give it to me · *entregar* to give, to hand over
- **crea** SUBJ he believes · *creer* to believe
- **fallaste** you failed · *fallar* to fail

## 2  Eragon                                    2:36

### Phrases to Listen For

**¿cuánto vale?**  how much is it?, how much is it worth?

**se lo cambio por lo que tengo aquí**  I'll trade you for what I have here (*LIT* I'll trade it to you for what I have here)

**así que**  so, therefore

**perdón por no pelarlas**  pardon me for not plucking them

### Name
Spine

■ Soldiers escort young men in chains as the villagers protest.

- □ **patriotas**  patriots · *patriota NMF* patriot
- □ **voluntarios**  volunteers · *voluntario* volunteer
- □ **guerreros**  warriors · *guerrero* warrior
- □ **aldea**  small town
- □ **contribuir**  to contribute
- □ **alégrese** *IMP*  be happy · *alegrarse* to be happy
- □ **se convertirán**  they will become · *convertirse* to become
- □ **héroes**  heroes · *héroe NM* hero

■ Eragon enters a butcher shop.

- □ **caro**  expensive
- □ **carne** *NF*  meat
- □ **grasa**  fat
- □ **se desvanece**  it vanishes · *desvanecerse* to vanish, to disappear
- □ **corte** *NM*  cut
- □ **¿cuánto vale?**  how much is it worth? · *cuánto* how much · *valer* to be worth
- □ **especie** *NF*  type
- □ **roca**  rock
- □ **hurtaste**  you stole · *hurtar* to steal
- □ **estaba cazando**  I was hunting · *cazar* to hunt
- □ **devuélvela** *IMP*  return it · *devolver* to return
- □ **pertenece**  it belongs · *pertenecer* to belong
- □ **arriesgarías**  you would risk · *arriesgar* to risk

■ Eragon walks through the village streets and witnesses the soldiers talking to a man.

- □ **botín** *NM*  loot
- □ **apetitoso**  tempting
- □ **lazo de joyas**  string of jewels · *lazo* string, ribbon, thread · *joya* jewel
- □ **interesante**  interesting
- □ **senda**  trail, path
- □ **rama**  branch
- □ **relámpago**  lightning
- □ **tropezar**  to trip
- □ **colgué**  I hung · *colgar* to hang

- □ **ladrón** *NM*  thief
- □ **embustero**  cheat, liar
- □ **las confiscaré**  I will confiscate them · *confiscar* to confiscate
- □ **pelarlas**  plucking them · *pelar* to pluck
- □ **huesos**  bones · *hueso* bone
- □ **se ahogaran** *SUBJ*  they suffocate · *ahogarse* to suffocate, to drown

## 3  Roran Leaves Home                         5:01

### Phrases to Listen For

**¿qué pasó?**  what happened?

**lo que**  that, what

**antes de que**  before

**ya lo sabe**  he already knows

**aún no lo sé**  I still don't know

**me gusta**  I like (*LIT* it pleases me)

**por eso**  that's why

**hay que**  it's necessary

**por otro lado**  on the other hand (*LIT* on the other side)

**cuídate mucho** *IMP*  take care, be very careful

### Name
Roran

■ Eragon meets his brother on the family farm.

- □ **saluden** *IMP*  greet · *saludar* to greet
- □ **poderoso**  powerful
- □ **cazador**  hunter
- □ **invisible**  invisible
- □ **presa**  catch
- □ **¿te asustaste?**  were you afraid? · *asustarse* to be afraid, to be frightened
- □ **venado**  deer
- □ **gruñó**  it snorted · *gruñir* to snort, to grunt

■ Eragon and his brother Roran enter the barn. The two practice fighting.

- □ **respeto**  respect
- □ **cabra**  female goat
- □ **lento**  slow
- □ **iluso**  gullible
- □ **cráneo**  cranium, skull

■ Eragon and Roran talk while working in the field.

- □ **edad**  age
- □ **reclutado**  recruited, conscripted · *reclutar* to recruit, to conscript
- □ **soldados**  soldiers · *soldado* soldier
- □ **te avisaré**  I'll let you know · *avisar* to let know, to apprise
- □ **me establezca** *SUBJ*  I get settled · *establecerse* to get settled, to be established

🎬 At night, Eragon speaks with his uncle.

☐ **decidirás** you will decide · *decidir* to decide

☐ **nariz** *NF* nose

☐ **desconocido** unknown · *desconocer* to not know, to not recognize

☐ **resistir** to resist, to oppose

☐ **urgencia** urgency, emergency

☐ **no habría ganado** I wouldn't have gained · *ganar* to gain, to earn, to win

🎬 In the morning, with his travel bag on his shoulder, Roran bids farewell.

☐ **ahorré** I saved · *ahorrar* to save

☐ **bendición** blessing

🎬 Eragon walks with him into town.

☐ **practica** *IMP* practice · *practicar* to practice

☐ **tiro** shooting

## 4 Hatched                                  3:17

### Phrases to Listen For

**¿tienes hambre?** are you hungry? (*LIT* do you have hunger?)

**lo siento** I'm sorry

**lo que** what

**por lo que veo** as far as I can see (*LIT* for what I see)

🎬 The "rock" hatches.

☐ **roca** rock

☐ **ave** *NF* bird

🎬 Several react to the hatching.

☐ **ha nacido** it has been born · *nacer* to be born

🎬 Eragon shows the dragon his scar.

☐ **mira** *IMP* look · *mirar* to look at

☐ **labores** chores · *labor NM* chore

☐ **¿tienes hambre?** are you hungry? · *tener hambre* to be hungry (*LIT* to have hunger)

☐ **bebe** *IMP* drink · *beber* to drink

☐ **tibia** lukewarm · *tibio* lukewarm

☐ **ratas** rats · *rata* rat

## 5 Death Order                              2:16

### Phrase to Listen For

**antes de que** before

🎬 Inside the dark castle, Durza approaches the throne of Galbatorix.

☐ **ha nacido** it has been born · *nacer* to be born

☐ **simple** simple

☐ **asunto** subject, issue

☐ **leyenda** legend

☐ **real** real

☐ **valor** *NM* courage, bravery

☐ **desafiarme** to challenge me · *desafiar* to challenge

☐ **me desafíe** he challenges me · *desafiar* to challenge

☐ **fronteras** borders · *frontera* border

☐ **hay reminiscencias de resistencia** there are influential pockets of resistance · *reminiscencia* influence · *resistencia* resistance

☐ **enanos** dwarfs · *enano* dwarf

☐ **duendes** elves · *duende NM* elf

☐ **esperanza** hope

🎬 Eragon looks at his hand and then talks to the dragon.

☐ **urgencia** urgency, emergency

🎬 Durza calls forth the Ra'zac.

☐ **asesinen** *IMP* kill · *asesinar* to kill, to murder

## 6 Dragons and Dragon Riders         6:25

### Phrases to Listen For

**¿para qué?** what for?

**tienes mucha razón** you are quite right

**no me hagan caso** *IMP* don't pay any attention to me

**hasta que** until

**para sí mismo** for himself

**largo de aquí** get out of here

**tiene razón** he's right

**lo que** what

**por favor** please

**hasta aquí** to here, to this point

### Names

Horst, Galbatorix

🎬 Eragon walks through town at night. Horst, Brom, and others are seated at a table eating.

☐ **roto** broken · *romper* to break

☐ **sufrimiento** suffering

☐ **soldados** soldiers · *soldado* soldier

☐ **diferencia** difference

☐ **florecía** it flourished · *florecer* to flourish

☐ **crueldad** cruelty

☐ **época** age, epoch

☐ **aniquiló** he annihilated · *aniquilar* to annihilate

☐ **se oponía** he was opposed · *oponerse* to be opposed

🎬 Soldiers approach Brom.

- □ **te cuelgo** I hang you · *colgar* to hang
- □ **crimen** *NM* crime
- □ **sordo** deaf

🎬 The dragon flies for the first time.

- □ **ha vuelto** it has returned · *volver* to return
- □ **pensamientos** thoughts · *pensamiento* thought

🎬 At night, Eragon enters a house and opens a book.

- □ **¡lárgate!** *IMP* go away!, get lost! · *largarse* to go away, to get lost, to clear out
- □ **tamaño** size
- □ **escupen** they spit · *escupir* to spit
- □ **te burlaste** you made fun, you ridiculed · *burlarse* to make fun, to ridicule
- □ **permiso** permission
- □ **cultivo** crop
- □ **te meterás** you'll get yourself involved · *meterse* to get involved, to meddle
- □ **¿en qué te conviertes?** what are you turning into? · *convertirse* to turn into, to become
- □ **mentiroso** liar
- □ **cobarde** *NM* coward
- □ **real** real

## 7  Life in Danger                          4:50

### Phrases to Listen For
**estás en peligro** you are in danger
**¿por qué?** why?
**lo lamento** I'm sorry
**¿cómo que…?** what do you mean …?
**hasta que** until

🎬 Eragon walks the village streets, hearing cries of pain.

- □ **granja** farm
- □ **valle** *NM* valley

🎬 Eragon runs. Saphira picks him up.

- □ **peligro** danger
- □ **advertirle** to warn him · *advertir* to warn
- □ **sujétate** *IMP* hold on · *sujetarse* to hold on
- □ **me resbalo** I'm slipping · *resbalarse* to slip
- □ **bájame** *IMP* put me down, let me off · *bajar* to put down, to let off
- □ **necio** foolish
- □ **alternativa** alternative · *alternativo* alternative

🎬 Eragon lands in a haystack.

- □ **habrías sufrido** you would have suffered · *sufrir* to suffer

🎬 Brom arrives at the farm.

- □ **sepulte** *SUBJ* I bury · *sepultar* to bury
- □ **hoguera** bonfire
- □ **funeraria** funeral
- □ **asesinaron** they murdered · *asesinar* to murder
- □ **caballo** horse
- □ **cabalga** *IMP* ride · *cabalgar* to ride a horse

## 8  Chosen                                   5:00

### Phrases to Listen For
**¿por qué?** why?
**una porción de valentía, tres porciones de tonto** one part courage, three parts stupid
**ya que** since
**uno al otro** to each other
**lo que** what
**aun así** even so

### Name
Beor

🎬 Eragon and Brom ride a ridge trail. They dismount in the forest.

- □ **asesinado** murdered · *asesinar* to murder
- □ **protegiéndote** protecting you · *proteger* to protect
- □ **porción** portion
- □ **valentía** courage, bravery
- □ **asesinan** they murder · *asesinar* to murder
- □ **sin piedad** without mercy · *piedad* mercy
- □ **quince** fifteen
- □ **dieciséis** sixteen
- □ **diecisiete** seventeen
- □ **probablemente** probably
- □ **durarías** you would last · *durar* to last
- □ **asesinos** murderers · *asesino* murderer
- □ **asesinaré** I will kill · *asesinar* to kill, to murder
- □ **hechicero** sorcerer
- □ **poseído** possessed · *poseer* to possess
- □ **espíritus** spirits · *espíritu* *NM* spirit
- □ **demoniacos** demonic · *demoniaco* demonic
- □ **ruega** *IMP* pray · *rogar* to pray
- □ **esperanza** hope
- □ **rebeldes** rebels · *rebelde* rebel
- □ **parias** outcasts · *paria* *NMF* outcast
- □ **valientes** courageous, valiant · *valiente* courageous, valiant
- □ **dementes** demented · *demente* demented
- □ **oponerse** to oppose
- □ **fortaleza** strength
- □ **imaginarías** you would imagine · *imaginar* to imagine
- □ **trato** deal

□ **no mentirnos** not to lie to each other ·
*mentir* to lie
□ **pensamientos** thoughts · *pensamiento* thought

🎬 Eragon calls Saphira.

□ **abandoné** I abandoned · *abandonar* to abandon
□ **juzgaré** I will judge · *juzgar* to judge
□ **tranquila** *EXP* easy, take it easy, be calm

🎬 Brom approaches Saphira.

□ **musculosa** muscular · *musculoso* muscular
□ **proporciones** proportions · *proporción*
proportion
□ **garras** claws · *garra* claw
□ **torneadas** shapely · *torneado* shapely
□ **patas** legs · *pata* leg [OF AN ANIMAL]
□ **delgadas** thin · *delgado* thin
□ **voz** *NF* voice
□ **suave** soft
□ **anciano** old man
□ **puntas** points · *punta* point
□ **filosas** sharp · *filoso* sharp

🎬 Brom addresses Eragon.

□ **cargar** to carry
□ **destino** destiny
□ **elegido** chosen · *elegir* to choose
□ **nace** it is born · *nacer* to be born
□ **presencia** presence
□ **necesario** necessary
□ **riesgo** risk
□ **elegirme** to choose me · *elegir* to choose
□ **destruya** *SUBJ* he destroys · *destruir* to destroy
□ **asesinarte** to kill you · *asesinar* to kill,
to murder

## 9 The Journey Begins    4:35

### Phrases to Listen For

**peor aún** even worse
**de noche** at night
**haz lo que dice** *IMP* do what he says
**ten cuidado** *IMP* be careful
**cerca de** near
**lo que** what
**tal vez** maybe, perhaps
**por suerte para ti** lucky for you
**a final del día** at the end of the day

### Names

Urgals, Daret, Roran, Beor

🎬 Durza appears as the Ra'zac forge their weapons.

□ **espada** sword
□ **simple** simple

□ **eficiente** efficient
□ **evadió** he evaded · *evadir* to evade
□ **sangre** *NF* blood

🎬 In the forest, Brom again addresses Eragon.

□ **cabalgata** ride
□ **frontera** border
□ **cordillera** mountain range
□ **descubiertos** discovered · *descubierto*
discovered · *descubrir* to discover
□ **posibilidades** possibilities · *posibilidad*
possibility
□ **área** area
□ **salida** exit

🎬 Eragon and Brom leave the trail and view the
scene below from behind a large rock.

□ **primo** cousin
□ **entrenamos** we trained · *entrenar*
to train
□ **espadas** swords · *espada* sword
□ **he subestimado** I have underestimated ·
*subestimar* to underestimate

🎬 Eragon and Brom practice fighting.

□ **habilidades** abilities · *habilidad* ability
□ **anciano** old man
□ **atácame** *IMP* attack me · *atacar* to attack
□ **efecto** effect
□ **entrenamiento** training
□ **madera** wood

🎬 In the evening, Brom strikes two rocks together.

□ **lastimar** to hurt
□ **escupen** they spit · *escupir* to spit
□ **edad** age
□ **sostener** to sustain
□ **encendí** I lit · *encender* to light
□ **faldas** slopes, hills · *falda* slope, hill
□ **directo** direct

## 10 Fortune Teller    3:43

### Phrase to Listen For

**cerca de** near

### Names

Daret, Angela

🎬 Eragon and Brom arrive at a small village.

□ **aldea** small town
□ **caballos** horses · *caballo* horse
□ **compra** *IMP* buy · *comprar* to buy
□ **pan** *NM* bread

🎬 Eragon enters a hut. A woman approaches.

- ☐ **ha pedido** she has asked for, she has requested · *pedir* to ask for, to request
- ☐ **huesos** bones · *hueso* bone
- ☐ **infancia** infancy
- ☐ **dura** hard, tough · *duro* hard, tough
- ☐ **generaciones** generations · *generación* generation
- ☐ **batallas** battles · *batalla* battle
- ☐ **no logro** I can't manage, I'm unable · *lograr* to manage, to be able, to achieve
- ☐ **condenado** condemned, doomed · *condenar* to condemn, to doom
- ☐ **yace** it lies · *yacer* to lie [POSITION]
- ☐ **se aproxima** he draws near · *aproximarse* to draw near, to get closer
- ☐ **con rapidez** rapidly, quickly
- ☐ **futuro** future

## 11 Instinct    4:00

### Phrases to Listen For
a través de  through
tu lazo con ella  your connection with her
antes de  before
lo que  what

### Name
Urgals

🎬 Eragon leaves the hut.

- ☐ **futuro** future

🎬 Eragon wakes up.

- ☐ **arde** it burns · *arder* to burn, to sting
- ☐ **lento** slow
- ☐ **patearon** they kicked · *patear* to kick
- ☐ **descubriste** you discovered · *descubrir* to discover
- ☐ **instinto** instinct
- ☐ **magia** magic
- ☐ **reacción** reaction
- ☐ **fluye** it flows · *fluir* to flow
- ☐ **a través de** through
- ☐ **montan** they mount, they ride · *montar* to mount, to ride

🎬 Eragon stands up.

- ☐ **suyo** your own
- ☐ **lazo** bond
- ☐ **se celebre** SUBJ it is celebrated · *celebrar* to celebrate
- ☐ **recurso** recourse
- ☐ **reglas** rules · *regla* rule
- ☐ **limitaciones** limitations · *limitación* limitation

- ☐ **ejecutar** to execute
- ☐ **hechizo** spell, enchantment
- ☐ **lengua** tongue, language
- ☐ **antigua** ancient · *antiguo* ancient
- ☐ **duendes** elves · *duende* NM elf
- ☐ **controlar** to control
- ☐ **hechizos** spells · *hechizo* spell, enchantment
- ☐ **física** physical · *físico* physical
- ☐ **resistir** to resist, to oppose
- ☐ **efecto** effect
- ☐ **débil** weak
- ☐ **puente** NM bridge
- ☐ **inconsciente** unconscious
- ☐ **aniquilarán** they will annihilate · *aniquilar* to annihilate
- ☐ **límites** limits · *límite* NM limit
- ☐ **aprenderlos** to learn them · *aprender* to learn

🎬 Eragon points at the tree. He uses words that are not Spanish, *traevam* and *kvistr*.

- ☐ **ramas** branches · *rama* branch

## 12 Finally Flying    3:14

### Phrases to Listen For
ya que  since
hay que  it's necessary
claro que  of course
de nuevo  again
no está tan mal por aquí  it's not so bad here
no está nada mal  it's not bad at all
lo que  what
tal vez  maybe, perhaps
aún no  not yet
eso no es nada  that's nothing

### Name
Brom

🎬 Brom looks out over the valley.

- ☐ **anunciamos** we announced · *anunciar* to announce
- ☐ **espectacularmente** spectacularly
- ☐ **colinas** hills · *colina* hill

🎬 Saphira appears suddenly and lands.

- ☐ **mencionó** mentioned · *mencionar* to mention
- ☐ **agradécele** IMP thank him · *agradecer* to thank
- ☐ **silla** chair

🎬 Saphira and Eragon fly.

- ☐ **inclínate** IMP lean · *inclinarse* to lean
- ☐ **gira** she turns · *girar* to turn, to spin
- ☐ **acelera** she accelerates · *acelerar* to accelerate
- ☐ **sujétate** IMP hold on · *sujetarse* to hold on

□ **combatir** to combat
□ **incluso** including, even
□ **cola** tail
□ **fantástico** fantastic

## 13 A Fellow Rider 4:21

### Phrases to Listen For
**no te preocupes** *IMP* don't worry
**no escuchas nada de lo que te digo** you don't
hear anything I tell you
**con vida** alive (*LIT* with life)
**hay que** it's necessary
**el uno al otro** to each other

### Names
Saphira, Za'roc, Morzan, Galbatorix, Carvajal

🎬 While Eragon and Saphira fly, the Ra'zac pursue
Brom. He uses the word *kvistr* again.

□ **síguelos** *IMP* follow them · *seguir* to follow

🎬 Eragon and Brom attend to Saphira's wounds.

□ **protege** *IMP* protect · *proteger* to protect
□ **irresponsabilidad** irresponsibility
□ **cuesta** it costs · *costar* to cost
□ **permiso** permission

🎬 Eragon joins Brom as he washes up in the stream.

□ **habíamos acordado** we had agreed ·
*acordar* to agree
□ **mentirnos** to lie to each other · *mentir* to lie
□ **asesinada** killed · *asesinado* killed ·
*asesinar* to kill, to murder
□ **espada** sword
□ **asesina de dragones** dragon slayer ·
*asesino* murderer · *dragón NM* dragon
□ **protegerme** to protect me · *proteger* to protect
□ **asesinado** killed · *asesinar* to kill, to murder
□ **encuentro** encounter
□ **encajé** I thrust · *encajar* to thrust, to insert
□ **excepto** except
□ **me oculté** I hid · *ocultarse* to hide
□ **totalmente** totally
□ **ambos** both

## 14 Girl of His Dreams 4:46

### Phrases to Listen For
**no está a discusión** it's not up for discussion,
it's not open to discussion
**tratar de** to try to
**un movimiento en falso** one false move
**a veces** sometimes

**hasta que** until
**igual de fuerte que tú** as strong as you

### Names
Arya, Ellesméra, Gil'ead, Durza, Eragon

🎬 The Ra'zac report to Durza.

□ **sangre** *NF* blood
□ **te acabo de ascender** I've just promoted you ·
*ascender* to promote

🎬 Eragon dreams.

□ **princesa** princess
□ **aliados** allies · *aliado* ally
□ **prisionera** prisoner · *prisionero* prisoner

🎬 After awakening, Eragon talks to Brom in the
morning fog.

□ **presa** prisoner · *preso* prisoner
□ **discusión** discussion
□ **dirección** direction
□ **riesgo** risk
□ **huevo** egg
□ **solamente** only
□ **sacrificio** sacrifice
□ **felizmente** happily
□ **valora** she values · *valorar* to value
□ **suya** her own
□ **movimiento en falso** false move · *movimiento*
move, movement · *falso* false
□ **decisión** decision
□ **inconsciente** irresponsible
□ **valiente** courageous, valiant
□ **sabio** wise

🎬 Eragon surveys Gil'ead.

□ **anochecer** *NM* nightfall
□ **paredes** walls · *pared NF* wall
□ **encierran** they enclose · *encerrar* to enclose
□ **realmente** really

## 15 Saving Arya 4:22

### Phrases to Listen For
**más rápido** faster
**abran paso** *IMP* make way
**porqué** reason
**aun así** even so
**qué interesante** how interesting
**antes de que** before
**tendrás que** you will have to
**hay que** it's necessary

### Name
Za'roc

🎬 Eragon enters Gil'ead. He uses the non-Spanish words *marmor* and *trais*.

☐ **abran paso** *IMP* make way · *abrir paso* to make way · *abrir* to open · *paso* way

🎬 Eragon finds Arya.

☐ **no tenías porqué venir** you had no reason to come · *porqué NM* reason
☐ **bosque** *NM* forest
☐ **mago** magician
☐ **interesante** interesting
☐ **exhala** he exhales · *exhalar* to exhale
☐ **aliento** breath
☐ **gritos** shouts, screams · *grito* shout, scream

🎬 Brom steps in front of the spear.

☐ **sugiero** I suggest · *sugerir* to suggest
☐ **arqueros** archers · *arquero* archer
☐ **disparen** *IMP* shoot · *disparar* to shoot
☐ **techo** roof
☐ **peso** weight

## 16  Dying with Honor                    4:31

### Phrases to Listen For
**hay que** it's necessary
**se muere** he is dying
**no vale nada** it is not worth a thing
**te mueras** *SUBJ* you die
**por mi culpa** because of me (*LIT* for my fault)

🎬 In the night, Arya attends Brom. Eragon joins them. Non-Spanish words include *waise* and *heill*.

☐ **¿atravesaste?** did you pierce? · *atravesar* to pierce
☐ **se aniquila** one destroys · *aniquilar* to destroy
☐ **atraviesas** you pierce · *atravesar* to pierce
☐ **devolviste** you returned · *devolver* to return
☐ **no vale** it is not worth · *valer* to be worth
☐ **porción** portion
☐ **valentía** courage, bravery
☐ **dignidad** dignity

🎬 Eragon and Arya bury Brom.

☐ **escupir** to spit
☐ **no lo dañará** it will not damage · *dañar* to damage, to hurt

## 17  Murtagh                    2:02

### Phrases to Listen For
**tengo que** I have to
**necesitas de mí** you need me

**¿por qué?** why?
**hay que** it's necessary

### Name
Murtagh

🎬 Arya falls to the ground.

☐ **envenenó** he poisoned · *envenenar* to poison
☐ **encuentro** I find · *encontrar* to find, to encounter

🎬 Saphira drops Murtagh in front of Eragon.

☐ **siguiéndonos** following us · *seguir* to follow
☐ **valle** *NM* valley
☐ **arroyo** brook, stream
☐ **sufrirá** she will suffer · *sufrir* to suffer
☐ **arriesgaste** you risked · *arriesgar* to risk
☐ **asesinada** murdered · *asesinado* murdered · *asesinar* to murder
☐ **rumores** rumors · *rumor NM* rumor
☐ **retribución** retribution
☐ **me muestras** you show me · *mostrar* to show
☐ **convencer** to convince

## 18  The Varden                    6:17

### Phrases to Listen For
**tendremos que** we will have to
**hasta que** until
**no tardes** *IMP* don't be too long
**otra vez** again
**ni lo menciones** *IMP* don't mention it
**suelen pasar** they usually happen
**por suerte para ti** lucky for you
**a mi favor** in my favor
**ser penada con la muerte** to be punished by death
**¿por qué?** why?
**ten cuidado** *IMP* be careful
**ya no hay** there is no longer any

### Names
Urgals, Ajihad, Saphira, Morsan

🎬 Eragon and Murtagh dismount.

☐ **a pie** on foot · *pie NM* foot
☐ **ni lo menciones** *IMP* don't even mention it · *mencionar* to mention
☐ **visión** vision

🎬 Eragon leaps into the water beneath the falls. Murtagh follows.

☐ **salta** *IMP* jump · *saltar* to jump

🎬 Galbatorix confronts Durza.

☐ **tarea** assignment
☐ **simplemente** simply
☐ **complicaciones** complications · *complicación* complication
☐ **suelen pasar** they usually happen · *soler* to usually (+ VERB) · *pasar* to happen
☐ **incompetencia** incompetence
☐ **directo** directly
☐ **responsabilidad** responsibility
☐ **hombros** shoulders · *hombro* shoulder
☐ **se resisten** they resist · *resistirse* to resist, to oppose
☐ **reinado** reign
☐ **deslealtad** disloyalty
☐ **penada** punished · *penado* punished · *penar* to punish
☐ **reúne** IMP gather · *reunir* to gather
☐ **síguelos** IMP follow them · *seguir* to follow

🎬 Eragon and Murtagh are captured and brought before the leader.

☐ **bestia** beast
☐ **tráela** IMP bring her · *traer* to bring

🎬 Saphira brings Arya to Eragon and the Varden.

☐ **está luchando** she is fighting, she is struggling · *luchar* to fight, to struggle
☐ **latidos** heart beats, pulse · *latido* heartbeat, pulse
☐ **débiles** weak · *débil* weak
☐ **envenenada** poisoned · *envenenado* poisoned · *envenenar* to poison
☐ **curanderos** healers · *curandero* healer

🎬 Urgals kill the guard. A messenger carries the news to the leader of the Varden.

☐ **escalan** they climb · *escalar* to climb, to scale
☐ **montaña** mountain
☐ **superarán** they will surpass · *superar* to surpass, to overcome
☐ **ejecútenlo** IMP execute him · *ejecutar* to execute
☐ **traidor** traitor
☐ **no elije** he doesn't choose · *elegir* to choose
☐ **odiándolo** hating him · *odiar* to hate
☐ **prisión** prison
☐ **asesínenlo** IMP kill him · *asesinar* to kill, to murder
☐ **escapar** to escape
☐ **suéltenme** IMP let me go, let go of me · *soltar* to let go, to let go of
☐ **arriesgarme** to take a risk · *arriesgarse* to take a risk
☐ **me rodean** they surround me · *rodear* to surround

🎬 Durza surveys his army.

☐ **cobardes** cowards · *cobarde* NMF coward
☐ **no se ocultarán** they will not hide · *ocultarse* to hide
☐ **destruiremos** we will destroy · *destruir* to destroy
☐ **existencia** existence
☐ **aniquílenlos** IMP annihilate them · *aniquilar* to annihilate

## 19 Preparing for Battle 4:05

### Phrases to Listen For

**me tienen miedo** they are afraid of me
**¿por qué no habrían de temer?** why shouldn't they be fearful?
**desde que** since
**¿por qué?** why?
**toda la noche** all night
**en sus puestos** at your posts

### Names

Carvajal, Saphira

🎬 Eragon washes his hands. The daughter of Ajihad enters.

☐ **disculpa** excuse (me) · *disculpar* to excuse, to forgive
☐ **ante** before
☐ **ha respondido** she has responded · *responder* to respond
☐ **curaciones** healing · *curación* healing
☐ **profunda** profound · *profundo* profound
☐ **contestará** she will answer · *contestar* to answer

🎬 Eragon walks with Ajihad.

☐ **huye** he flees · *huir* to flee
☐ **ocultarse** to hide
☐ **sospecha** suspicion
☐ **se esparció** it spread · *esparcirse* to spread
☐ **rumor** NM rumor

🎬 Ajihad shows Eragon his armor.

☐ **armadura** armor
☐ **escudos** shields · *escudo* shield

🎬 Arya helps Eragon with his armor.

☐ **sencillo** simple
☐ **búsqueda** search
☐ **peligrosa** dangerous · *peligroso* dangerous
☐ **hemos cargado** we have carried · *cargar* to carry
☐ **huevo** egg
☐ **memoria** memory
☐ **naciera** SUBJ she is born · *nacer* to be born
☐ **finalmente** finally

- □ **destino** destiny
- □ **simple** simple
- □ **eligió** she chose · *elegir* to choose
- □ **apenas** barely
- □ **reconocer** to recognize

🎬 Arya takes Eragon to Saphira, who is now covered with armor.
- □ **protegiendo** protecting · *proteger* to protect
- □ **esperanza** hope
- □ **guiará** he will guide · *guiar* to guide

🎬 The Vardens prepare for the battle.
- □ **soldados** soldiers · *soldado* soldier
- □ **posiciones** positions · *posición* position
- □ **puestos** placed · *puesto* placed · *poner* to place

## 20 Together as One                   1:41

### Phrases to Listen For
**¿por qué?** why?
**tengo miedo** I'm afraid

🎬 The leaders of the Varden look out over their troops.
- □ **arqueros** archers · *arquero* archer

🎬 As the battle begins, Saphira talks to Eragon.
- □ **se elije** one chooses · *elegir* to choose
- □ **valor** *NM* courage, bravery

## 21 To Win or Die                    6:11

### Phrases to Listen For
**hay que acabar con esto** it is necessary to finish this off
**hay que** it's necessary
**no te preocupes por mí** *IMP* don't worry about me
**lo que** what
**tengo que** I have to

🎬 Aboard Saphira, Eragon flies into battle. Murtagh escapes. Some non-Spanish words are spoken.
- □ **regresarte** to return to you · *regresar* to return

🎬 Durza enters the fray, mounted on his own dragon.
- □ **sangre** *NF* blood
- □ **magia negra** black magic · *magia* magic · *negro* black
- □ **arráncaselo** *IMP* pull it out of him · *arrancar* to pull out

- □ **pecho** chest
- □ **gritar** to shout
- □ **te hirieron** they wounded you · *herir* to wound, to hurt
- □ **concéntrate** *IMP* concentrate · *concentrarse* to concentrate
- □ **visión** vision
- □ **está fallando** it is failing · *fallar* to fail
- □ **herida** wound
- □ **debilita** it weakens · *debilitar* to weaken
- □ **tranquila** *EXP* easy, take it easy, be calm
- □ **lo superaremos** we will overcome it · *superar* to overcome
- □ **estoy debilitándome** I'm weakening · *debilitarse* to weaken

## 22 Losing Strength                   2:12

### Phrase to Listen For
**lo que** what

🎬 After crashing, Eragon approaches Saphira. Eragon again uses the non-Spanish words *waise* and *heill.*
- □ **ambos** both

## 23 A Living Legend                   4:53

### Phrases to Listen For
**por suerte** luckily
**a veces** sometimes
**no hay que** it's not necessary
**orgulloso de ti** proud of you
**el tiempo vuela** time flies
**más pronto de lo que crees** sooner than you think

### Names
Brom, Ellesméra, Galbatorix, Eragon, Shade, Geisha

🎬 Eragon wakes up and sees Murtagh.
- □ **irreemplazables** irreplaceable · *irreemplazable* irreplaceable
- □ **reemplazar** to replace
- □ **imprudente** imprudent
- □ **me alegra** it makes me happy · *alegrar* to make happy
- □ **sabio** wise
- □ **porción** portion, part
- □ **valentía** courage, bravery
- □ **orgulloso** proud
- □ **no lo mencionarías** you would not mention it · *mencionar* to mention
- □ **caballo** horse

Eragon, riding on Saphira, reaches Arya.

☐ **que me despidiera** *SUBJ* for me to say good-bye ·
*despedirse* to say good-bye

☐ **derrota** defeat

☐ **precio** price

☐ **valor** *NM* courage, bravery

☐ **leyenda** legend

☐ **aniquilador** killer, destroyer

☐ **se esparce** it is spread · *esparcirse* to be spread

☐ **ayer** yesterday

☐ **héroe** *NM* hero

## 24 End Titles 6:33

End credits.

# The Chronicles of Narnia: The Lion, the Witch and the Wardrobe

**No somos héroes, señor. Somos de Finchley.**
*We're not heroes, sir. We're from Finchley.*

GENRE       Classic Literature Adaptation/Fantasy/Adventure
YEAR        2005
DIRECTOR    Andrew Adamson
CAST        Tilda Swinton, James McAvoy, Georgie Henley, William Moseley
STUDIO      Disney

The Pevensie children—Peter, Susan, Edmund, and Lucy—meet enchanting fauns, ice-cold witches, talking beavers, and the most noble of lions as they find their way to Narnia through an old wardrobe. When one of them betrays his siblings and the forces of good in Narnia, redemption comes from an unexpected source. For Spanish learners, the pace of conversation is manageable, the sentence structure is usually simple, and the vocabulary—though sprinkled with mythology—is uncomplicated.

## BASIC VOCABULARY

### Names

Lucy, Edmund, Ed, Narnia, Aslan, Susan, Tumnus, Adán, Pevensie

### Nouns

☐ **bosque** *NM* forest · *Ella es la que tiene a Narnia bajo un invierno eterno, y dio órdenes de que si alguien se encontraba un humano vagando en el* ***bosque****, deberíamos entregárselo a ella.* She is the one who has Narnia under an eternal winter and gave orders that if anyone finds a human wandering in the forest, we must turn him over to her.

☐ **bruja** witch · *La* ***bruja*** *llegó a ellos antes que yo.* The witch got to them before I did.

☐ **castillo** castle · *Debe estar en el* ***castillo*** *de la bruja y ya saben lo que dicen.* He must be in the witch's castle, and you all know what they say.

☐ **castor** *NM* beaver · *También el* ***castor*** *me dijo que planeas hacerte un sombrero con él.* The beaver also told me that you plan to make him into a hat for yourself.

☐ **fauno** faun · *Soy un* ***fauno****, y tú, ¿qué eres?* I'm a faun, and you, what are you?

☐ **majestad** *NF* majesty, your majesty · *Perdóneme,* ***Majestad****.* Forgive me, Your Majesty.

☐ **mesa de piedra** stone table · *El castor habló sobre una* ***Mesa de Piedra****, y que Aslan tiene tropas ahí.* The beaver spoke of a Stone Table, and that Aslan has troops there.

☐ **ropero** wardrobe · *Es un* ***ropero*** *bastante amplio.* It's an awfully big wardrobe.

☐ **traidor** traitor · *Majestad, encontramos al* ***traidor****.* Your Majesty, we found the traitor.

☐ **tropas** troops · *tropa* troop · *¿Nuestras* ***tropas****?* Our troops?

## 1 Introduction                    7:09

### Phrases to Listen For

**tenemos que** we have to
**hay que** it's necessary
**¿por qué?** why?
**piensas en** you think about
**ti mismo** yourself
**lo que** what
**tendríamos que** we would have to
**todos a bordo** all aboard
**favor de** please
**todo en orden** everything is in order
**no te preocupes** *IMP* don't worry

### Names

Peter, Edmund, Bampton, Steventon, Milton Road, Huntington, Easton

☐ Edmund is watching the bombing through a window.

☐ **refugio** shelter

☐ **¡agáchate!** *IMP* get down! · *agachar* to get down, to crouch

☐ **nos matas** you kill us · *matar* to kill

☐ **egoísta** selfish

☐ At a train station, Lucy, Susan, Edmund, and Peter say good-bye to their mother.

☐ **personal** *NM* personnel

☐ **evacuación** evacuation

☐ **¿te abriga?** are you dressed warmly? · *abrigarse* to dress warmly

☐ **obligaría** he would force · *obligar* to force, to obligate

☐ **a bordo** on board

☐ **abordar** to board

☐ **pórtate bien** *IMP* behave yourself · *portarse* to behave oneself

☐ The children advance through the crowded train station. A woman in uniform asks for their tickets.

☐ **boletos** tickets · *boleto* ticket

☐ **extrañar** to miss

## 2 Mrs. MacReady                    4:07

### Phrases to Listen For

**tal vez** maybe, perhaps
**por lo tanto** therefore
**sobre todo** above all
**ya verás** you'll soon see
**lo que** what
**en serio** seriously
**por favor** please

### Names

MacReady, Kirke

☐ The children carry their bags. A car crosses the train tracks.

☐ **vendríamos** we would come · *venir* to come

☐ **etiquetas** labels, tags · *etiqueta* label, tag

☐ A horse-drawn wagon stops before the children.

☐ **pertenencias** belongings, possessions · *pertenencia* belonging, possession

☐ **aprecio** I appreciate · *apreciar* to appreciate

☐ The children and Mrs. MacReady enter the house.

☐ **acostumbrado** accustomed, in the habit (of) · *acostumbrarse* to be accustomed, to be in the habit (of)

☐ **unas cuantas** several, a few · *unos cuantos* several, a few
☐ **reglas** rules · *regla* rule
☐ **gritar** to shout
☐ **utilizar** to use, to utilize
☐ **montaplatos** *NM* dumbwaiter
☐ **no toque** *IMP* don't touch · *tocar* to touch
☐ **objetos** objects · *objeto* object
☐ **prohibido** prohibited · *prohibir* to prohibit

🎬 Peter listens to the radio.

☐ **anoche** last night
☐ **fuerza aérea alemana** German Air Force · *fuerza* force · *aérea* air · *alemana ADJ* German
☐ **realizó** it carried out · *realizar* to carry out
☐ **varios** several
☐ **Gran Bretaña** Great Britain
☐ **bombardeos** bombardments, bombings · *bombardeo* bombardment, bombing
☐ **duraron** they lasted · *durar* to last

🎬 Lucy is in bed. Peter and Susan approach her.

☐ **sábanas** sheets · *sábana* sheet
☐ **duras** rough, scratchy · *duro* rough, scratchy
☐ **eternas** forever, eternal · *eterno* forever, eternal
☐ **fantástico** fantastic

🎬 Lucy watches the rain through the window.

☐ **gastro** gastro
☐ **vascular** vascular
☐ **pon atención** *IMP* pay attention · *poner atención* to pay attention
☐ **gastrovascular** gastrovascular
☐ **latín** *NM* Latin
☐ **inventado** invented · *inventar* to invent
☐ **jugar a las escondidas** to play hide-and-seek
☐ **divertido** fun · *divertirse* to have fun

🎬 The children rise to play hide-and-seek. The song "Oh, Johnny" plays.

☐ **once** eleven
☐ **doce** twelve
☐ **trece** thirteen
☐ **catorce** fourteen
☐ **quince** fifteen
☐ **dieciséis** sixteen
☐ **veinticuatro** twenty-four
☐ **veinticinco** twenty-five
☐ **veintiséis** twenty-six
☐ **veintisiete** twenty-seven
☐ **veintiocho** twenty-eight
☐ **veintinueve** twenty-nine

## 3 The Wardrobe 7:08

### Phrases to Listen For
**¿cómo que…?** what do you mean …?
**de verdad** really, truly
**todo lo que** everything that
**lo lamento** I'm sorry
**¿por qué?** why?
**no lo sé** I don't know
**cerca de** near

### Names
Helen, Cair Paravel, Lucy Pevensie

🎬 Lucy enters the room with the wardrobe.

☐ **setenta** seventy
☐ **ochenta** eighty
☐ **noventa** ninety

🎬 Lucy comes out from behind the lamppost and approaches the faun.

☐ **¿te escondías de mí?** were you hiding from me? · *esconder* to hide
☐ **barba** beard
☐ **enano** dwarf
☐ **la más alta** the tallest · *alto* tall
☐ **Eva** Eve
☐ **humana** human · *humano* human
☐ **a partir de** beginning, starting
☐ **farol** *NM* streetlamp
☐ **océano** ocean
☐ **oriente** *NM* east
☐ **roca** rock
☐ **palo** stick
☐ **hielo** ice
☐ **bastante amplio** quite large · *bastante* quite, enough · *amplio* large, ample

🎬 Lucy extends her hand to Tumnus.

☐ **estréchela** *IMP* shake it (my hand), shake hands · *estrechar la mano* to shake hands
☐ **lejana** faraway · *lejano* faraway
☐ **Bitación** Spare Oom [Tumnus' name for the land where Lucy lives]
☐ **te invito** I invite you · *invitar* to invite
☐ **cenar** to eat dinner, to dine
☐ **cálido** warm
☐ **galletas** cookies, crackers · *galleta* cookie, cracker
☐ **té** *NM* tea
☐ **pasteles** cakes · *pastel NM* cake
☐ **sardinas** sardines · *sardina* sardine
☐ **ratito** *DIM* a little while · *rato* a while
☐ **montones** piles · *montón NM* large pile, large amount

## 4   Mr. Tumnus' House      6:11

**Phrases to Listen For**

**después de**  after
**muchas gracias**  thank you very much
**hace años**  years ago
**no importa**  it doesn't matter
**tengo que**  I have to
**tal vez**  maybe, perhaps
**lo siento**  I'm sorry
**no importa lo que pase** *SUBJ*  no matter what
   happens

🎬 Lucy and Tumnus walk through the snow.

☐ **cómodo**  comfortable
☐ **tibio**  warm

🎬 Lucy and Tumnus enter his home.

☐ **cara**  face
☐ **invierno**  winter
☐ **patinas**  you skate · *patinar* to skate
☐ **hielo**  ice
☐ **nieve** *NF*  snow
☐ **cien**  one hundred

🎬 Lucy sits down and takes a cup from Tumnus.

☐ **verano**  summer
☐ **faunos**  fauns · *fauno* faun
☐ **bailábamos**  we danced · *bailar* to dance
☐ **dríadas**  wood nymphs · *dríada*
   wood nymph
☐ **jamás nos cansábamos**  we never got tired ·
   *jamás* never · *cansarse* to get tired
☐ **música**  music
☐ **preciosa**  precious · *precioso* precious
☐ **pieza**  piece
☐ **canción de cuna**  lullaby · *canción* song ·
   *cuna* cradle
☐ **me alegro**  I'm happy · *alegrarse*
   to be happy

🎬 Lucy wakes up in the dark, still inside Tumnus'
   house.

☐ **terrible**  terrible
☐ **gentil**  kind
☐ **cometí**  I committed · *cometer*
   to commit
☐ **secuestrarte**  to kidnap you · *secuestrar*
   to kidnap
☐ **eterno**  eternal
☐ **humano**  human
☐ **vagando**  wandering aimlessly · *vagar*
   to wander aimlessly
☐ **entregárselo**  to give it to her · *entregar*
   to give, to deliver

🎬 Tumnus takes Lucy by the hand and runs through
   the snow.

☐ **espías**  spies · *espía NMF* spy
☐ **disculpa**  forgive (me) · *disculpar* to forgive,
   to excuse
☐ **quédatelo** *IMP*  you keep it · *quedarse* to keep
☐ **no me había sentido**  I hadn't felt · *sentir* to feel

## 5   Just Your Imagination      5:06

**Phrases to Listen For**

**a la vez**  at a time
**ya basta**  enough already
**¿por qué?**  why?
**tienes que**  you have to
**todo lo que**  everything that
**tiene razón**  she's right

**Name**
Lu

🎬 Lucy comes out of the wardrobe and falls.

☐ **noventa**  ninety
☐ **cien**  one hundred
☐ **se trata**  it is about · *tratarse* to be about
☐ **fondo**  back
☐ **imaginación**  imagination
☐ **mentiras**  lies · *mentira* lie
☐ **apoyo**  support
☐ **fútbol** *NM*  football
☐ **gabinete** *NM*  cabinet
☐ **baño**  bathroom
☐ **paz** *NF*  peace
☐ **empeorarlo**  to make it worse · *empeorar*
   to make worse
☐ **chiste** *NM*  joke
☐ **crecerás**  you will grow up · *crecer* to grow,
   to grow up
☐ **arreglas**  you fix · *arreglar* to fix

🎬 Edmund opens the wardrobe door.

☐ **no temas** *SUBJ*  you are not afraid ·
   *temer* to be afraid
☐ **oscuridad**  darkness

## 6   Hail the Queen!      5:14

**Phrases to Listen For**

**por favor**  please
**¿por qué?**  why?
**tal vez**  maybe, perhaps
**¿en serio?**  really?
**hasta entonces**  see you then (*LIT* until then)
**otra vez**  again

**te ves** you look
**hace frío** it's cold
**por aquí** over here

## Name

Ginarrbrik

🎬 Edmund watches in the snow as a sleigh approaches. The White Witch addresses Edmund.

- [ ] **dominios** dominions · *dominio* dominion
- [ ] **persiguiendo** following · *perseguir* to follow, to pursue
- [ ] **te estás congelando** you are freezing · *congelarse* to freeze, to be freezing

🎬 Edmund sits beside the White Witch on the sleigh.

- [ ] **beber** to drink
- [ ] **caliente** hot
- [ ] **crecer** to grow
- [ ] **se te antoje** SUBJ you fancy · *antojarse* to fancy
- [ ] **golosinas** candies, sweets · *golosina* candy, sweet
- [ ] **encantadores** enchanting, charming · *encantador* enchanting, charming
- [ ] **nombrarte** to name you · *nombrar* to name (to a post)
- [ ] **príncipe** NM prince
- [ ] **sirvientes** servants · *sirviente* NM servant
- [ ] **colinas** hills · *colina* hill
- [ ] **palacio** palace
- [ ] **divertirse** to have fun
- [ ] **repletas** full · *repleto* full
- [ ] **arruinar** to ruin, to spoil
- [ ] **apetito** appetite
- [ ] **visitarme** to visit me · *visitar* to visit
- [ ] **esperarte** to expect you, to wait for you · *esperar* to expect, to wait

🎬 As soon as the White Witch leaves Edmund, Lucy finds him.

- [ ] **no se enteró** she was not informed, she did not find out · *enterarse* to be informed, to find out
- [ ] **escapar** to escape
- [ ] **salida** exit

## 7 Peter, Wake Up! 4:34

## Phrases to Listen For

**en realidad** actually
**lo lamento** I'm sorry
**por supuesto** of course
**por lógica** logically
**¿no es así?** isn't that right?

## Name

MacReady

🎬 Lucy wakes up Peter.

- [ ] **solamente** only
- [ ] **fingí** I pretended, I was faking · *fingir* to pretend, to fake
- [ ] **discúlpame** IMP forgive me · *disculpar* to forgive, to excuse
- [ ] **alentarla** to encourage her · *alentar* to encourage
- [ ] **fingir** to pretend, to fake

🎬 Lucy bumps into the professor.

- [ ] **traviesos** mischievous · *travieso* mischievous
- [ ] **no se comportan** you don't behave · *comportarse* to behave
- [ ] **mandar** to send
- [ ] **establo** stable
- [ ] **no lo molestaran** SUBJ they don't bother you · *molestar* to bother
- [ ] **descuide** IMP don't worry · *descuidar* to not worry, to neglect
- [ ] **explicación** explanation
- [ ] **taza** cup

🎬 The professor fills his pipe.

- [ ] **afectaron** they affect · *afectar* to affect
- [ ] **delicada** delicate · *delicado* delicate
- [ ] **estabilidad** stability
- [ ] **emocional** emotional
- [ ] **ama de llaves** housekeeper · *ama* mistress, supervisor · *llave* NF key
- [ ] **no se repetirá** it won't happen again · *repetir* to happen again, to repeat
- [ ] **llanto** crying
- [ ] **yo lo arreglo** I'll fix it (LIT I fix it) · *arreglar* to fix, to mend
- [ ] **noté** I noticed · *notar* to notice
- [ ] **descubrió** she discovered · *descubrir* to discover
- [ ] **lógica** logic
- [ ] **estaban fingiendo** they were faking · *fingir* to fake, to pretend
- [ ] **miente** she lies · *mentir* to lie
- [ ] **actuar** to act

🎬 The children play cricket outside.

- [ ] **anotación** score
- [ ] **Bella Durmiente** Sleeping Beauty · *bello* beautiful · *durmiente* sleeping
- [ ] **jugamos a las escondidas** we play hide-and-seek · *jugar a las escondidas* to play hide-and-seek
- [ ] **aire fresco** fresh air · *aire* NM air · *fresco* fresh
- [ ] **adentro** inside
- [ ] **ruido** noise

## 8  The World of Narnia                         7:21

### Phrases to Listen For

**ten cuidado** IMP  be careful
**lo siento**  I'm sorry
**tal vez**  maybe, perhaps
**ya basta**  enough already
**lo lamento**  I'm sorry
**no importa**  it doesn't matter
**hay que**  it's necessary
**ni siquiera van**  they're not even going
**tenemos que**  we have to
**¿por qué?**  why?
**lo que**  what
**después de que**  after
**tiene razón**  she's right
**¿todo en orden?**  everything all right?
**a salvo**  safe
**no quiero que se nos haga de noche** SUBJ
  I don't want night to fall

### Names

Lu, Tumnus, Jadis, Maugrim, Narnia

The children enter the wardrobe.

☐ **me pisaste**  you stepped on me · *pisar* to step on,
  to walk on
☐ **empujar**  to push
☐ **no te pisé**  I didn't step on you · *pisar* to step on,
  to walk on
☐ **empujando**  pushing · *empujar* to push
☐ **tranquila** EXP  easy, take it easy, be calm
☐ **imaginación**  imagination
☐ **mentiroso**  liar
☐ **oí**  I heard · *oír* to hear
☐ **fingir**  to pretend, to fake
☐ **graciosa**  funny · *gracioso* funny
☐ **visitarlo**  to visit him · *visitar* to visit
☐ **nieve** NF  snow
☐ **analizas**  you analyze · *analizar* to analyze
☐ **lógica**  logic

The children, dressed in full-length coats, walk
through the forest.

☐ **comida**  food
☐ **rica**  excellent · *rico* excellent [FOOD]

The children enter Tumnus' home.

☐ **arresto**  arrest
☐ **alta traición**  high treason · *alto* high ·
  *traición* treason
☐ **imperial**  imperial
☐ **asilar**  to give refuge, to give protection, to harbor
☐ **confraternizar**  fraternizing · *confraternizar*
  to fraternize
☐ **humanos**  humans · *humano* human

☐ **firma**  signature
☐ **policía secreta**  secret police · *policía* police
  force · *secreto* secret
☐ **arrestaron**  they arrested · *arrestar* to arrest
☐ **humano**  human
☐ **descubrió**  she discovered · *descubrir* to discover
☐ **criminal** NMF  criminal
☐ **pájaro**  bird

The children exit Tumnus' house and encounter
a beaver.

☐ **oler**  to smell
☐ **regalé**  I gave · *regalar* to give a gift
☐ **está engañando**  he is deceiving · *engañar*
  to deceive
☐ **charlábamos**  we talked, we chatted · *charlar*
  to talk, to chat
☐ **estar a salvo**  to be safe · *a salvo* safe
☐ **mitad** NF  half
☐ **té** NM  tea
☐ **caliente**  hot
☐ **presa**  dam
☐ **me faltan detalles**  I need to take care of a few
  details (LIT details are lacking to me) · *faltar*
  to lack · *detalle* NM detail
☐ **negocio**  business

## 9  Beavers' Home                         3:32

### Phrases to Listen For

**lo que**  what
**por favor**  please
**con cuidado**  carefully
**todo lo contrario**  quite the opposite
**más vale**  it's better
**tenemos que**  we have to
**¿por qué?**  why?
**tiene razón**  he's right
**lo siento**  I'm sorry
**tal vez**  maybe, perhaps

### Names

Cair Paravel, Finchley

A female beaver steps out of a beaver dam to greet
the male beaver and the four children.

☐ **angustiada**  anxious, distressed · *angustiado*
  anxious, distressed · *angustiarse* to become
  anxious, to get distressed
☐ **descubro**  I discover · *descubrir* to discover
☐ **tejón** NM  badger
☐ **pelo**  hair
☐ **no me diste**  you didn't give me · *dar* to give
☐ **civilizada**  civilized · *civilizado* civilized ·
  *civilizar* to civilize

□ **despacio** slowly
□ **pisen** *IMP* step · *pisar* to step on, to walk on
□ **desorganizado** disorganized · *desorganizar* to disorganize
□ **¿estás disfrutando?** are you enjoying? · *disfrutar* to enjoy
□ **vista** view

▰ Peter and Lucy are seated at a table inside the beaver dam. Susan approaches.

□ **han cruzado** they have crossed · *cruzar* to cross
□ **vuelto** returned · *volver* to return
□ **esperanza** hope

▰ One of the beavers laughs.

□ **simpático** nice, kind, pleasant
□ **verdadero** true
□ **ausente** absent
□ **profecía** prophecy
□ **regreso** return
□ **arrestado** arrested · *arrestar* to arrest
□ **culpan** you blame · *culpar* to blame
□ **culpamos** we blame · *culpar* to blame
□ **todo lo contrario** quite the opposite
□ **carne** *NF* flesh
□ **hueso** bone
□ **trono** throne
□ **rima** it rhymes · *rimar* to rhyme
□ **antigua** ancient · *antiguo* ancient
□ **leyenda** legend
□ **Eva** Eve
□ **derrotar** to defeat
□ **restaurar** to restore
□ **paz** *NF* peace
□ **más vale** *EXP* you'd better, it's a good thing
□ **cometen** you are committing · *cometer* to commit
□ **terrible** terrible
□ **error** *NM* error, mistake
□ **héroes** heroes · *héroe NM* hero
□ **hospitalidad** hospitality
□ **control** *NM* control

▰ Still inside the dam, Peter calls for Edmund.

□ **necesario** necessary
□ **había visitado** he had visited · *visitar* to visit
□ **anteriormente** previously

## 10  Behold the Queen's Castle   6:20

### Phrases to Listen For
**lo que** what
**¿por qué?** why?
**claro que** of course

**antes de que** before
**tiene razón** she's right
**hay que** it's necessary
**tal vez** maybe, perhaps

### Name
Maugrim

▰ After following Edmund for a short while, Peter, Susan, Lucy, and the beaver view the palace of the White Witch.

□ **carnada** bait
□ **evitar** to avoid
□ **profecía** prophecy
□ **asesinará** she will kill you · *asesinar* to kill, to murder

▰ A wolf attacks Edmund.

□ **mil disculpas** a thousand pardons · *disculpa* pardon, apology
□ **afortunado** fortunate
□ **favorito** favorite

▰ Edmund sits on the throne of the White Witch.

□ **sordas** deaf · *sordo* deaf
□ **inteligencia** intelligence
□ **te atreves** you dare · *atreverse* to dare
□ **sencilla** simple · *sencillo* simple
□ **castores** beavers · *castor NM* beaver
□ **presa** dam
□ **inútil** useless
□ **golosinas** candies, sweets · *golosina* candy, sweet

## 11  They're After Us!   4:31

### Phrases to Listen For
**tiene hambre** he's hungry (*LIT* he has hunger)
**lo siento** I'm sorry
**¿qué es lo que pasó aquí?** what happened here?
**es lo que pasa** it's what happens
**en serio** seriously
**tienen que** you have to
**en mente** in mind
**ya basta** enough already

▰ The beaver, followed by the children, enters the dam.

□ **no tardo** I won't be long · *tardar* to be long, to take time
□ **gruñón** *NM* grump, grouch
□ **hambre** *NF* hunger
□ **jalea** jelly
□ **galletas** cookies, crackers · *galleta* cookie, cracker

The children follow the beavers through the tunnel.

- **cavamos** we dug · *cavar* to dig
- **tejón** *NM* badger
- **salida** exit
- **túnel** *NM* tunnel
- **mapa** *NM* map
- **no cupo** it didn't fit · *caber* to fit
- **comida** food

The beavers and the children exit the tunnel.

- **enojar** to anger
- **te haré trizas** I'll rip you to shreds · *trizas NFPL* shreds, small pieces
- **dientes** teeth · *diente NM* tooth
- **feo** ugly
- **desafortunado** unfortunate
- **especies** species · *especie NF* species
- **escapar** to escape
- **mente** *NF* mind

The wolves exit the tunnel.

- **saludos** greetings · *saludo* greeting
- **lealtad** *NF* loyalty
- **humanos** humans · *humano* human
- **información** information
- **valiosa** valuable · *valioso* valuable
- **recompensa** reward
- **fugitivos** fugitives · *fugitivo* fugitive
- **norte** *NM* north
- **huyeron** they fled · *huir* to flee
- **olfatear** to sniff

A campfire burns. Lucy speaks to the fox.

- **daño** damage
- **ladran** they bark · *ladrar* to bark
- **muerden** they bite · *morder* to bite
- **se baña** he bathes · *bañarse* to bathe
- **gentileza** kindness, courtesy
- **curar** to heal, to cure
- **heridas** wounds · *herida* wound
- **honor** *NM* honor
- **corto** short
- **reunir** to gather
- **luchar** to struggle, to fight
- **profecía** prophecy
- **necesarios** necessary · *necesario* necessary

## 12 The Queen's Lair                    11:01

### Phrases to Listen For
**no lo sé** I don't know
**antes de que** before
**hace cien años** a hundred years ago
**otra vez** again

**tener que** to have to
**¿qué pasa?** what's going on?
**por ahí** over there
**hace muchos años** many years ago
**tengas que** *SUBJ* you have to
**apuesto a que sí** I'll bet it is
**feliz navidad** Merry Christmas
**hasta el próximo año** see you next year (*LIT* until next year)
**muchas gracias** thank you very much

Edmund eats, then coughs. Tumnus speaks to him.

- **piernas** legs · *pierna* leg
- **nariz** *NF* nose

The White Witch enters Edmund's cell.

- **destrozó** it tore apart · *destrozar* to tear apart, to ruin, to destroy
- **presa** dam
- **guardia** *NM* guard
- **libre** free
- **delató** he betrayed · *delatar* to betray
- **golosinas** candies, sweets · *golosina* candy, sweet
- **súbanlo** *IMP* take him up · *subir* to take up, to go up
- **trineo** sled, sleigh
- **extraña** he misses · *extrañar* to miss

The children cross a natural bridge.

- **campamento** camp
- **cruzando** crossing · *cruzar* to cross
- **río** river
- **congelado** frozen · *congelar* to freeze
- **cien** one hundred
- **totalmente** totally

The beavers lead Susan, Peter, and Lucy across a vast expanse of ice and snow.

- **humanos** humans · *humano* human
- **peludo** hairy, fluffy
- **sombrero** hat
- **el que manda** he who gives the orders · *mandar* to order
- **detrás** behind

Mr. Beaver sniffs the air as the beavers and the children hide.

- **revisar** to look, to look over, to check out
- **cariño** dear, darling, sweetheart

Mr. Beaver returns.

- **peligro** danger
- **se hayan portado** *SUBJ* you have behaved yourselves · *portarse* to behave oneself

🎬 Father Christmas answers Lucy.

- □ **he soportado** I have put up with · *soportar* to put up with, to tolerate
- □ **he conducido** I have driven · *conducir* to drive
- □ **esperanza** hope
- □ **han brindado** you have brought, you have provided · *brindar* to bring, to provide
- □ **majestades** your majesties · *majestad NF* majesty, your majesty
- □ **se debilite** *SUBJ* it weakens · *debilitarse* to weaken, to become weak
- □ **jugo** juice
- □ **flor** *NF* flower
- □ **gota** drop of liquid
- □ **curar** to heal, to cure
- □ **herida** wound
- □ **valiente** courageous, valiant
- □ **batallas** battles · *batalla* battle
- □ **repugnante** repugnant, disgusting, ugly

🎬 Father Christmas picks up a bow and a quiver of arrows and addresses Susan.

- □ **arco** bow
- □ **nunca falla** it never fails · *fallar* to fail
- □ **confianza** confidence, trust
- □ **sopla** *IMP* blow · *soplar* to blow
- □ **apoyo** support, help, assistance

🎬 Peter pulls a sword from its sheath as Father Christmas addresses them.

- □ **herramientas** tools · *herramienta* tool
- □ **sabiduría** wisdom
- □ **irme** to go · *irse* to go away, to leave
- □ **invierno** winter
- □ **se acumulan** they accumulate, they pile up · *acumularse* to accumulate, to pile up
- □ **te ausentas** you are away, you're gone · *ausentarse* to be away, to be gone

🎬 Father Christmas rides away on his sleigh.

- □ **hielo** ice
- □ **cruzar** to cross
- □ **armar** to build, to put together
- □ **veloz** fast, speedy
- □ **realista** realistic

## 13 Across the Melting River   6:40

**Phrases to Listen For**
- **lo que** what
- **por favor** please
- **todo lo que** everything that

- **tienes que** you have to
- **para siempre** forever
- **no te preocupes** *IMP* don't worry

🎬 Mr. Beaver crosses the ice.

- □ **advertí** I warned · *advertir* to warn
- □ **no siguieras** *SUBJ* you don't continue · *seguir* to continue, to follow
- □ **postres** desserts · *postre NM* dessert
- □ **cena** dinner
- □ **cocinas** you cook · *cocinar* to cook
- □ **se enterara** *SUBJ* she's informed, she learns, she becomes aware · *enterarse* to inform, to learn, to become aware

🎬 A wolf attacks Mr. Beaver.

- □ **lastimar** to hurt
- □ **atraviésalo** *IMP* run him through · *atravesar* to pierce
- □ **lobo** wolf
- □ **traje rojo** red suit · *traje NM* suit · *rojo* red
- □ **espada** sword
- □ **héroe** *NM* hero
- □ **río** river
- □ **¡sosténganse!** *IMP* hold on! · *sostenerse* to hold on

🎬 Peter pierces the ice with his sword. The children float downstream.

- □ **abrigo** overcoat, coat
- □ **cariño** dear, darling, sweetheart

🎬 The White Witch, her henchman, and Edmund view the falls.

- □ **hace demasiado calor** it's too hot · *hacer calor* to be hot · *demasiado* too, too much · *calor NM* heat
- □ **trineo** sled, sleigh
- □ **incitaba** he was rallying, he was inciting · *incitar* to rally, to incite
- □ **tembloroso** shuddering, trembling
- □ **agradable** pleasing, pleasant
- □ **sorpresa** surprise
- □ **anoche** last night
- □ **halagarme** to flatter me · *halagar* to flatter
- □ **grosero** rude
- □ **humanos** humans · *humano* human
- □ **criaturas** creatures · *criatura* creature
- □ **honestidad** honesty
- □ **adelántense** *IMP* go on ahead · *adelantarse* to go ahead, to move forward
- □ **reúnan** *IMP* gather, bring together · *reunir* to gather, to bring together
- □ **súbditos** subjects · *súbdito* subject

## 14  Aslan's Camp                                   5:39

**Phrases to Listen For**

**¿por qué?**  why?
**tal vez**  maybe, perhaps
**te ves**  you look
**a salvo**  safe
**lo que**  what
**no me hagas mucho caso** *IMP*  don't pay much
  attention to me
**¿no es así?**  isn't that right?

**Names**

Oreius, Cair Paravel, Peter, Finchley

🎬  Mr. and Mrs. Beaver, Peter, Susan, and Lucy enter
  the camp.

☐ **cara**  face
☐ **fea**  ugly · *feo* ugly
☐ **afeitarte**  to shave yourself · *afeitarse* to shave
  oneself

🎬  Aslan exits his tent.

☐ **bienvenido** *ADJ*  welcome
☐ **Eva**  Eve
☐ **castores**  beavers · *castor NM* beaver
☐ **humano**  human
☐ **solicitar**  to solicit, to request
☐ **capturado**  captured
☐ **traicionó**  he betrayed · *traicionar* to betray
☐ **explicación**  explanation
☐ **solamente**  only
☐ **empeore** *SUBJ*  it makes worse · *empeorar*
  to make worse
☐ **traición**  betrayal
☐ **sencillo**  simple

🎬  Aslan and Peter view Cair Paravel in the
  distance.

☐ **tronos**  thrones · *trono* throne
☐ **absoluto**  absolute
☐ **profecía**  prophecy
☐ **planeas**  you plan · *planear* to plan
☐ **sombrero**  hat
☐ **magia**  magic
☐ **poderosa**  powerful · *poderoso* powerful
☐ **rige**  he rules · *regir* to rule, to govern
☐ **diferencia**  it differentiates · *diferenciar*
  to differentiate
☐ **correcto**  correct
☐ **incorrecto**  incorrect
☐ **gobierna**  it governs · *gobernar* to govern
☐ **destinos**  destinies · *destino* destiny
☐ **proteger**  to protect
☐ **a salvo**  safe
☐ **necesario**  necessary

☐ **reflexiones** *SUBJ*  you reflect, you consider ·
  *reflexionar*  to reflect, to consider

🎬  Ginarrbrik, the Witch's henchman, addresses
  Edmund, who is bound and gagged.

☐ **príncipe** *NM*  prince
☐ **incómodo**  uncomfortable
☐ **acomode** *SUBJ*  I arrange · *acomodar* to arrange
☐ **almohada**  pillow
☐ **tratamiento**  treatment

🎬  Susan and Lucy stand amid the trees beyond
  a red tent.

☐ **varios**  several
☐ **nos divertíamos**  we had fun · *divertirse* to have
  fun
☐ **aburrida**  boring · *aburrido* boring

## 15  Sir Peter                                      7:13

**Phrases to Listen For**

**por favor**  please
**tal vez**  maybe, perhaps
**tenemos algo que hacer**  we have something to do
**a salvo**  safe
**lo que**  what
**por mi culpa**  because of me
**tengo que**  I have to
**lo siento**  I'm sorry

**Names**

Sir Peter, Oreius, Philip, Aslan, Jadis

🎬  A wolf growls and barks at Susan and Lucy.

☐ **huir**  to flee
☐ **valor** *NM*  courage, bravery
☐ **necesario**  necessary
☐ **guarden** *IMP*  put away · *guardar* to put away
☐ **armas**  weapons · *arma* weapon
☐ **batalla**  battle

🎬  Aslan frees the wolf from beneath his paw.

☐ **guiará**  he will guide, he will lead · *guiar* to guide,
  to lead
☐ **limpia** *IMP*  clean · *limpiar* to clean
☐ **espada**  sword
☐ **¡de pie!** *EXP*  stand!
☐ **terror** *NM*  terror
☐ **lobos**  wolves · *lobo* wolf

🎬  Inside the White Witch's camp, preparations
  are being made for battle. The White Witch listens
  to the battle plan.

☐ **minotauros**  minotaurs · *minotauro* minotaur
☐ **flanco**  flank

□ **gigantes** giants · *gigante* NM giant
□ **de reserva** in reserve
□ **enanos** dwarves · *enano* dwarf
□ **prisionero** prisoner

🎬 Edmund eats. Lucy addresses him.

□ **comida** food
□ **de regreso** return
□ **a salvo** safe
□ **peligroso** dangerous
□ **te ibas a ahogar** you were going to drown · *ahogarse* to drown
□ **sufran** SUBJ they suffer · *sufrir* to suffer

🎬 Susan picks up her bow and arrows.

□ **practicar** to practice
□ **en guardia** on guard
□ **bloquea** IMP block · *bloquear* to block
□ **demanda** she demands · *demandar* to demand
□ **audiencia** audience

## 16  The Lion and the Witch               5:51

### Phrases to Listen For

**a solas** alone
**para siempre** forever
**a partir de** beginning, starting
**tienen que** you have to

🎬 Ginarrbrik leads the White Witch and her entourage into Aslan's camp.

□ **emperatriz** NF empress
□ **islas** islands · *isla* island
□ **Islas Solitarias** Lone Islands
□ **ofensa** offense
□ **daño** damage
□ **se forjó** was forged · *forjarse* to be forged
□ **no recites** IMP don't recite · *recitar* to recite
□ **magia** magic
□ **ante** before
□ **sangre** NF blood
□ **propiedad** property
□ **llevártelo** to take him with you · *llevar* to take, to carry
□ **lograrías** you would accomplish, you would achieve · *lograr* to accomplish, to achieve
□ **negarme** to deny me · *negar* to deny
□ **derecho** right
□ **no recibo** I don't receive · *recibir* to receive
□ **demanda** it demands · *demandar* to demand
□ **devastada** devastated · *devastado* devastated · *devastar* to devastate
□ **perecerá** it will perish · *perecer* to perish

□ **dicta** it dictates · *dictar* to dictate
□ **tradición** tradition
□ **discutiré** I will discuss · *discutir* to discuss

🎬 Aslan enters his tent, followed by the White Witch. Shortly, they exit.

□ **ha renunciado** she has renounced · *renunciar* to renounce
□ **sacrificio** sacrifice
□ **promesa** promise

🎬 At night, Lucy and Susan follow Aslan.

□ **acompañarte** to accompany you · *acompañar* to accompany
□ **rato** while
□ **a partir de** starting, beginning

## 17  Aslan's Sacrifice               8:32

### Phrases to Listen For

**¿por qué no se defiende?** why doesn't he defend himself?
**en serio** really, seriously
**para siempre** forever
**no importa** it doesn't matter
**lo que** what
**hay que** it's necessary
**ya no hay tiempo** there's no more time

🎬 The White Witch holds a dagger as Aslan approaches.

□ **admiren** IMP admire · *admirar* to admire
□ **león** NM lion
□ **comida** food
□ **¿por qué no se defiende?** why doesn't he defend himself?
□ **átenlo** IMP tie him · *atar* to tie
□ **afeitarlo** to shave him · *afeitar* to shave
□ **decepcionada** disappointed · *decepcionado* disappointed · *decepcionar* to disappoint
□ **sacrificarte** to sacrifice yourself · *sacrificarse* to sacrifice oneself
□ **lograrías** you would achieve, you would accomplish · *lograr* to achieve, to accomplish
□ **humano** human
□ **magia** magic
□ **se aplacará** it will be appeased · *aplacar* to placate, to appease
□ **conquistar** to conquer
□ **te enteraste** you were informed · *enterarse* to be informed
□ **desespera** IMP despair · *desesperar* to despair, to give up hope
□ **batalla** battle
□ **dure** SUBJ it lasts · *durar* to last

📽 Susan and Lucy climb onto the table where Aslan was slain.

☐ **avisar** to warn, to advise
☐ **abandonarlo** to abandon him ·
   *abandonar* to abandon

📽 In bed, Peter awakes and draws his sword.

☐ **príncipes** princes · *príncipe NM* prince
☐ **noticia** message

## 18 You Have to Lead Us  3:00

**Phrase to Listen For**
   **tendrás que** you'll have to

📽 Peter exits Aslan's tent.

☐ **ejército** army
☐ **se acerca** it draws near · *acercarse* to draw near

📽 Peter sits on a white horse.

☐ **alteza** your highness
☐ **superan** they surpass · *superar* to surpass, to overcome
☐ **batallas** battles · *batalla* battle

## 19 Battle for Narnia  3:25

**Phrase to Listen For**
   **así que** so

📽 Aboard her chariot, the White Witch gives battle instructions.

☐ **prisioneros** prisoners · *prisionero* prisoner

## 20 Aslan's Resurrection  2:21

**Phrases to Listen For**
   **tengo frío** I'm cold
   **de otro modo** in another way
   **tal vez** maybe, perhaps
   **se dio** it was given
   **tenemos que** we have to

📽 In the morning, Susan and Lucy find the Stone Table broken.

☐ **cuchillo** knife
☐ **significado** meaning
☐ **sacrificio** sacrifice
☐ **habría interpretado** she would have interpreted ·
   *interpretar* to interpret
☐ **magia** magic
☐ **víctima** *NMF* victim

☐ **voluntaria** voluntary · *voluntario* voluntary
☐ **no ha cometido** he hasn't committed ·
   *cometer* to commit
☐ **traición** betrayal, treason
☐ **ejecutada** executed · *ejecutado* executed ·
   *ejecutar* to execute
☐ **dará marcha atrás** it will turn backwards ·
   *dar marcha atrás* to turn backwards
☐ **noticia** news
☐ **batalla** battle
☐ **lomo** back [OF AN ANIMAL]
☐ **recorrer** to cover [DISTANCE]
☐ **se cubran** *SUBJ* you cover · *cubrirse* to cover
☐ **oídos** ears · *oído* ear

## 21 Phoenix  4:29

📽 Mounted on the white horse, Peter shouts instructions.

☐ **rocas** rocks · *roca* rock
☐ **señal** *NF* signal

📽 Susan and Lucy ride atop Aslan.

☐ **sosténganse** *IMP* hold on · *sostenerse* to hold on

📽 Aslan breathes life into Tumnus and the other statues.

☐ **registrar** to search, to examine

## 22 Peter vs. the Witch  6:01

**Phrases to Listen For**
   **tienes que** you have to
   **¿por qué?** why?
   **lo que** what

📽 Edmund draws his sword. Mr. Beaver speaks to Edmund.

☐ **huyeras** *SUBJ* you flee, you get away · *huir* to flee, to get away

## 23 The Royal Coronation  6:03

**Phrases to Listen For**
   **hasta que** until
   **no te preocupes** *IMP* don't worry
   **a su tiempo** in his time
   **ya no** no longer
   **¿qué tienes?** what's the matter?
   **¿qué pasa?** what's going on?
   **lo que** what
   **otra vez** again
   **hay que** it's necessary

## Names

Lucy, Edmund, Susan, Peter, Narnia, Philip, Lu

🎬 At Cair Paravel, Aslan escorts the four children to their thrones.

- □ **océano** ocean
- □ **oriente** *NM* east
- □ **valiente** courageous, valiant
- □ **occidente** *NM* west
- □ **radiante** radiant
- □ **sur** *NM* south
- □ **benévola** benevolent · *benévolo* benevolent
- □ **norte** *NM* north
- □ **magnífico** magnificent
- □ **que su sabiduría nos guíe** *SUBJ* may your wisdom guide us · *sabiduría* wisdom · *guiar* to guide
- □ **estrellas** stars · *estrella* star

🎬 Lucy watches Aslan on the beach in the distance. Tumnus approaches.

- □ **presionarlo** to pressure him · *presionar* to pressure
- □ **domesticado** tamed, domesticated · *domesticar* to tame, to domesticate

🎬 An older Peter, Susan, Edmund, and Lucy ride on horseback through the forest.

- □ **descanso** I rest, I'm resting · *descansar* to rest
- □ **ciervo** stag
- □ **Bitación** Spare Oom [Tumnus' name for the land where Lucy lives]
- □ **ramas** branches · *rama* branch
- □ **abrigos** coats, overcoats · *abrigo* coat, overcoat
- □ **me estás pisando** you're stepping on me · *pisar* to step on, to walk on
- □ **me empujaron** you pushed me · *empujar* to push
- □ **me pisaste** you stepped on me · *pisar* to step on, to walk on
- □ **yo no te pisé** I didn't step on you · *pisar* to step on, to walk on

🎬 Peter, Susan, Edmund, and Lucy fall out of the wardrobe. The professor enters the room.

- □ **escondidos** hidden · *escondido* hidden · *esconder* to hide

## 24 Credits
11:26

### Phrase to Listen For

**aun así** even so

🎬 End credits. Lucy looks inside the wardrobe. The professor stands to address her.

- □ **probablemente** probably

# Tarzan

**¿Qué les dije?**
*What did I say?*

| | |
|---|---|
| GENRE | Classic Literature Adaptation/Adventure/Animation |
| YEAR | 1999 |
| DIRECTORS | Chris Buck, Kevin Lima |
| CAST | Eduardo Palomo, Héctor Emmanuel Gómez, Gabriela Tessier, Lucero |
| STUDIO | Walt Disney Pictures |

Edgar Rice Burroughs' story about a baby boy raised in the jungle by gorillas has captured the imagination of story lovers for generations. This modern animated adaptation features the music of Phil Collins, the comic relief of Tarzan's friend Terk, the romance inspired by the beautiful scientist and explorer Jane, and the danger of two villains—the gorilla hunter Clayton and the dangerous leopard Sabor. The Spanish vocabulary and sentence structure used in the film are simple, but sometimes the animals in the story can be hard to understand, because they speak quickly and with exaggerated cartoon voices. While it may not be a film for those brand-new to Spanish in context, once the animal voices are familiar and easier to understand, it offers a delightful learning experience.

## BASIC VOCABULARY

### Names

Tarzan, Kerchak, Clayton, Terk, Kala, Porter, Tantor

### Nouns

☐ **criaturas** creatures · *criatura* creature ·
*Al contrario, señor Clayton, la teoría de mi padre
es que son criaturas sociales.* On the contrary,
Mr. Clayton, my father's theory is that they are
social creatures.

☐ **elefante** *NM* elephant · *Sí, un pelo. ¡Aja!
Pero de elefante.* Yes, a hair. Aha! But of an
elephant.

☐ **fe** *NF* faith · *Mas con fe y entendimiento
en un hombre convertirás.* But with faith and
understanding, you will become a man.

☐ **gorilas** gorillas · *gorila* gorilla · *Mi padre
y yo hicimos esta expedición para estudiar a los
gorilas.* My father and I made this expedition
in order to study gorillas.

☐ **manada** pack, herd · *¡Viven en manada!*
They live in a pack!

☐ **peligro** danger · *Peligro vas a encontrar.*
You will find danger.

☐ **piraña** piranha · *¡Piraña!* Piranha!

### Verbs

☐ **creas** *SUBJ* you believe · *creer* to believe ·
*Pon tu fe en lo que tú más creas.* Put your faith
in what you most believe in.

☐ **guiará** it will guide · *guiar* to guide ·
*Te guiará tu corazón.* Your heart will guide
you.

### Other

☐ **feo** ugly · *Pero esta vez en verdad vi algo feo.*
But this time I really saw something ugly.

☐ **salvaje** *ADJ* savage, wild · *Todo este tiempo pensé
que eras un bruto salvaje o algo así.* All this time
I thought you were a wild brute or something like
that.

## 1 Main Title/"Two Worlds" 3:22

### Phrase to Listen For

**lo que** what

🎬 Phil Collins sings "Two Worlds." Several scenes
show Tarzan's family surviving a shipwreck and
building a new life in the jungle.

☐ **pon** *IMP* put · *poner* to put, to place
☐ **paraíso** paradise
☐ **paz** *NF* peace
☐ **suaves** smooth, soft · *suave* smooth, soft
☐ **huellas** footprints · *huella* footprint
☐ **arena** sand

☐ **jungla** jungle
☐ **cubrirá** it will cover · *cubrir* to cover
☐ **alerta** alert
☐ **valor** *NM* courage, bravery
☐ **construye** *IMP* construct, build · *construir*
to construct, to build
☐ **protección** protection

🎬 The gorilla's baby is killed.
☐ **llanto** crying
☐ **curar** to heal, to cure
☐ **herida** wound

## 2 Kala's Discovery 2:46

🎬 The gorilla Kala enters the tree house.

## 3 A Narrow Escape 2:09

🎬 Kala holds the baby Tarzan. Later, Kala and Tarzan
escape from the leopard.
☐ **unión** union
☐ **intensa** intense · *intenso* intense

## 4 Adopted 2:44

### Phrases to Listen For

**tuve que** I had to
**¿qué rayos...?** what the heck ...?, what in the
world ...?
**tendrás que** you will have to

### Names

Kala, Terkina, Sabor

🎬 The gorilla clan sees Kala arrive.
☐ **ha vuelto** she has returned · *volver* to return
☐ **desviarme** to take a detour · *desviarse* to take
a detour
☐ **fea** ugly · *feo* ugly
☐ **rara** strange · *raro* strange
☐ **qué rayos** what the heck
☐ **te acostumbras** you get used to it ·
*acostumbrarse* to get used to, to become
accustomed

🎬 Kerchak sniffs the baby Tarzan.
☐ **no repondrá** he will not replace ·
*reponer* to replace
☐ **devolverlo** to take it back, to return it ·
*devolver* to take back, to return
☐ **jungla** jungle
☐ **peligroso** dangerous
☐ **cachorro** cub, puppy, young animal

## 5  "You'll Be in My Heart"  1:38

**Phrases to Listen For**
**te ves** you look
**para siempre** forever
**no importa** it doesn't matter
**dentro de** inside

The baby Tarzan cries. Kala sings.
☐ **calma** *EXP* easy, take it easy, be calm
☐ **me apena** it grieves me · *apenar* to grieve
☐ **siéntela** *IMP* feel it · *sentir* to feel
☐ **protejo** I protect · *proteger* to protect

In the darkness of the jungle, Kala carries Tarzan.
☐ **abrazarte** to embrace you, to hug you · *abrazar* to embrace, to hug
☐ **protegeré** I will protect · *proteger* to protect
☐ **fusión** union
☐ **irrompible** unbreakable

## 6  Young Tarzan  1:41

**Phrases to Listen For**
**qué susto** what a fright
**claro que sí** of course

Flowers bloom. Kala awakens and does not find Tarzan.
☐ **susto** fright
☐ **imitar** to imitate
☐ **animales** animals · *animal NM* animal
☐ **ruidosos** noisy · *ruidoso* noisy
☐ **divertidos** fun · *divertido* fun · *divertirse* to have fun
☐ **imito** I imitate · *imitar* to imitate
☐ **leopardo** leopard
☐ **inventas** you invent · *inventar* to invent
☐ **sonido** sound

Tarzan bumps into Kerchak.
☐ **sabio** wise
☐ **protector** protective
☐ **decírtelo** to tell you that · *decir* to tell, to say
☐ **escarabajo** beetle

## 7  Pest Control  2:25

**Phrases to Listen For**
**hay que** it's necessary
**tengo que** I have to
**tienes que** you have to
**¿no crees?** don't you think?

At the waterfalls, two gorillas play. Terk arrives.
☐ **partir** to cut (into pieces)
☐ **diversión** fun
☐ **tardaste siglos** you took centuries · *tardar* to take (time) · *siglo* century
☐ **plaga** plague
☐ **controlado** controlled, under control · *controlar* to control
☐ **bromitas** *DIM* little jokes · *broma* joke
☐ **maravilla sin pelo** hairless wonder · *maravilla* marvel, wonder · *pelo* hair
☐ **acompañarlos** to accompany you, to go with you · *acompañar* to accompany, to go with
☐ **situación** situation
☐ **complicada** complicated · *complicado* complicated · *complicar* to complicate, to make complicated
☐ **me fascina** it fascinates me · *fascinar* to fascinate
☐ **te consta** *EXP* there's no doubt about you
☐ **convencerlos** to convince them · *convencer* to convince
☐ **absurdo** absurd

Terk and Tarzan observe the elephants.
☐ **humillación** humiliation
☐ **adelántate** *IMP* go ahead · *adelantarse* to go ahead, to move forward
☐ **déjenmelo** *IMP* leave it to me · *dejar* to leave
☐ **arreglo** I'll fix (*LIT* I fix) · *arreglar* to fix, to repair

Tarzan dives toward the elephants.
☐ **le dolió** it hurt him · *doler* to hurt
☐ **genial** terrific
☐ **sobrevive** he survives · *sobrevivir* to survive
☐ **vista** view

## 8  Baby Tantor  1:16

**Phrases to Listen For**
**en verdad** really, truly
**por supuesto** of course
**tiene razón** he's right
**por favor** please
**otra vez** again
**¿qué tienen?** what's the matter?

Tantor, a baby elephant, hesitates about entering the water.
☐ **higiénica** clean, hygienic · *higiénico* clean, hygienic
☐ **turbia** muddy, cloudy · *turbio* muddy, cloudy

- □ **sospechosa** suspect · *sospechoso* suspect
- □ **bacterias** bacteria · *bacteria* bacteria
- □ **está nadando** it is swimming · *nadar* to swim
- □ **directo** directly
- □ **paciencia** patience
- □ **pirañas** piranhas · *piraña* piranha
- □ **África** Africa
- □ **Sudamérica** South America
- □ **detrás de** behind
- □ **trasero** backside

## 9   Piranha!                   0:58

Tarzan comes up for air.

## 10   Outcast                   1:40

**Phrases to Listen For**
¡qué tonto! how dumb!, how foolish!
¿qué pasó? what happened?
lo que what
por poco almost

Terk drags Tarzan on the sand.

- □ **pirañas** piranhas · *piraña* piranha
- □ **devoran** they devour · *devorar* to devour
- □ **infarto** heart attack
- □ **conseguiste** you got · *conseguir* to get
- □ **alboroto** uproar, commotion
- □ **colita** DIM tail · *cola* tail

Kala arrives at the shore. Shortly, Kerchak arrives as well.

- □ **asustaste** you scared · *asustar* to scare
- □ **accidente** NM accident
- □ **excusa** excuse
- □ **no lo defiendas** IMP don't defend him · *defender* to defend

## 11   Hand to Hand                2:00

**Phrases to Listen For**
¿por qué? why?
no importa lo que... it doesn't matter what ...
lo que what
así es that's right

Tarzan smears mud over himself. Kala looks into the water from behind.

- □ **cubierto** covered · *cubrir* to cover
- □ **lodo** mud

- □ **no pertenezco** I don't belong · *pertenecer* to belong
- □ **cierra la boca** IMP shut your mouth, shut up · *cerrar la boca* to shut one's mouth, to shut up
- □ **nariz** NF nose
- □ **orejas** ears · *oreja* ear

## 12   "Son of Man"                2:47

**Phrase to Listen For**
lo que what

Tarzan climbs over Kala.

- □ **simio** ape
- □ **seguramente** surely

The boy Tarzan slips as he climbs a tree.

- □ **sabio** wise
- □ **respuestas** answers · *respuesta* answer
- □ **montaña** mountain
- □ **cima** top
- □ **alma** soul
- □ **libre** free
- □ **orgulloso** proud

Tarzan makes a spear.

- □ **guíe** SUBJ he guides · *guiar* to guide
- □ **entendimiento** understanding
- □ **te convertirás** you will become · *convertirse* to become

Tarzan is just out of reach of the green snake.

- □ **imaginación** imagination
- □ **realiza tu ilusión** IMP make your dream come true · *realizar* to make real, to realize · *ilusión* dream, illusion

## 13   Monkeying Around            0:54

**Phrases to Listen For**
hasta que until
¡ya basta! enough already!

Tarzan sneaks up behind Kala.

- □ **no te atrevas** IMP don't you dare · *atreverse* to dare
- □ **pelaje** NM fur
- □ **brillante** brilliant, shiny
- □ **cuello** neck
- □ **diversión** fun
- □ **se saque un ojo** SUBJ someone loses an eye · *sacar* to take out · *ojo* eye
- □ **lastimado** hurt · *lastimar* to hurt
- □ **quebradora** armlock, hammerlock [WRESTLING]

## 14    Sabor Attacks      4:20

### Phrases to Listen For

**lo siento** I'm sorry
**tal vez** maybe, perhaps
**llamar la atención** to get attention (LIT to call attention)
**lo que pasa es** the situation is (LIT what happens is)
**me di cuenta** I noticed

🎬 Tarzan lets go of Terk.

☐ **animal** NM animal
☐ **últimamente** recently, lately
☐ **subespecie** NF subspecies
☐ **elefantes** elephants · *elefante* NM elephant
☐ **maní** NM peanut

🎬 Tarzan raises Sabor high above his head.

☐ **abran paso** IMP make way · *abrir paso* to make way · *abrir* to open · *paso* way
☐ **costumbre** NF custom, habit
☐ **sepas** SUBJ you know · *saber* to know
☐ **me tropecé** I tripped · *tropezarse* to trip

## 15    Explorers      3:08

### Phrases to Listen For

**¿por qué...?** why ...?
**lo siento** I'm sorry
**al contrario** on the contrary
**ya basta** enough already
**¿qué tal si...?** what if ...?
**tal vez** maybe, perhaps

### Names

Clayton, Porter

🎬 Tarzan finds a bullet shell.

☐ **supe** I knew · *saber* to know
☐ **había nacido** I had been born · *nacer* to be born
☐ **África** Africa
☐ **había sido creada** it had been created · *creado* created · *crear* to create

🎬 The professor finds Clayton.

☐ **hippopotamus anfibius** hippopotamus [LATIN]
☐ **rhinoceros bihornus** rhinoceros [LATIN]
☐ **profesor** NM professor
☐ **disparos** gunshots · *disparo* gunshot

🎬 Jane approaches Clayton.

☐ **expedición** expedition
☐ **ahuyentar** to frighten

☐ **contrataron** you hired · *contratar* to hire
☐ **protección** protection
☐ **parada** standing · *parado* standing · *pararse* to stand up
☐ **nido** nest
☐ **hallazgo** find
☐ **bestias** beasts · *bestia* beast
☐ **evidencia** evidence
☐ **nidos** nests · *nido* nest
☐ **habías predicho** you had predicted · *predecir* to predict

🎬 Clayton leans on the barrel of his gun as Jane and her father inspect the gorilla "nest."

☐ **salvajes** savage, wild · *salvaje* ADJ savage, wild
☐ **arrancarían la cabeza** they would yank your head off, they would tear your head off · *arrancar* to yank off, to tear off · *cabeza* head
☐ **saludarlos** greeting you, saying hello to you · *saludar* to greet, to say hello
☐ **al contrario** on the contrary
☐ **teoría** theory
☐ **sociales** social · *social* ADJ social
☐ **oeste** NM west
☐ **ganoderma ablonatum** herb [PSEUDO LATIN]
☐ **excelente** excellent
☐ **habilidades** abilities, skills · *habilidad* ability, skill
☐ **safari** NM safari

## 16    The Baby Baboon      1:01

### Phrases to Listen For

**por Dios** dear God
**tal vez** maybe, perhaps
**está de lujo** it is a luxury
**por favor** please

🎬 Jane looks down at a baby baboon.

☐ **causó** he caused · *causar* to cause
☐ **alboroto** commotion, racket
☐ **aguarda** IMP wait · *aguardar* to wait
☐ **lindura** beauty

🎬 The baboon steals Jane's book.

☐ **ladronzuelo** little thief
☐ **de lujo** luxurious · *lujo* luxury
☐ **dibujos** drawings · *dibujo* drawing
☐ **babuino** baboon
☐ **papel** NM paper
☐ **bananas** bananas · *banana* banana

## 17 Tarzan to the Rescue 2:38

### Phrases to Listen For
**lágrimas de cocodrilo** crocodile tears
**¿qué rayos...?** what in the world ...?, what the
heck?

🎬 The baby baboon cries.
- **lágrimas de cocodrilo** · crocodile tears,
fake tears · *lágrima* tear · *cocodrilo*
crocodile
- **se enfadarían** they would get upset, they would
get annoyed · *enfadarse* to get upset, to get
annoyed, to get angry
- **paciencia** patience

🎬 Tarzan swings through the air holding on to Jane.
- **¿qué rayos sucede?** what the heck is happening? ·
*suceder* to happen
- **¡auxilio!** *EXP* help!

## 18 Treetop Introductions 4:05

### Phrases to Listen For
**por favor** please
**ya basta** enough already
**muchas gracias** thank you very much
**¿por qué?** why?
**tal vez** maybe, perhaps

🎬 Jane holds on to a tree.
- **monos** monkeys · *mono* monkey
- **empeorar** to worsen, to get worse
- **apártate** *IMP* move away, get away ·
*apartarse* to move away
- **me dan cosquillas** that tickles ·
*dar* to give · *cosquillas NFPL* tickling
- **advierto** I warn · *advertir* to warn

🎬 Jane listens to Tarzan's heart.
- **palpitar** to beat [HEART]
- **peinarme** to fix my hair, to comb my hair ·
*peinarse* to fix one's hair, to comb one's hair
- **humedad** humidity
- **bruto** brute
- **exacto** exactly
- **extraordinario** extraordinary
- **campamento** camp

🎬 Tarzan's friends search the jungle for him.
- **interesante** interesting
- **horror** *NM* horror
- **escóndanme** *IMP* hide me · *esconder*
to hide

- **contrólate** *IMP* control yourself ·
*controlar* to control
- **estás avergonzándome** you are embarrassing
me · *avergonzar* to embarrass

## 19 "Trashin' the Camp" 4:05

### Phrases to Listen For
**otra vez** again
**lo que** what

### Name
Tantor

🎬 Terk inspects a table with scientific equipment.
- **bestia** beast
- **primitiva** primitive · *primitivo* primitive
- **responsable** responsible
- **desastre** *NM* disaster

🎬 The gorillas break plates and tear pages from
books.
- **rásgalo** *IMP* tear it · *rasgar* to tear
- **ritmo** rhythm
- **raro** strange
- **¡ánimo!** *EXP* come on!, get up!, get going!
- **me fascina** it fascinates me · *fascinar*
to fascinate

## 20 Jane's Rant 1:09

### Phrases to Listen For
**por todas partes** everywhere
**al final** in the end
**¿en serio?** seriously?, really?

🎬 In camp, Jane talks to her father and Clayton.
- **babuino** baboon
- **dibujé** I drew · *dibujar* to draw
- **monos** monkeys · *mono* monkey
- **ejército** army
- **estaban gritándome** they were shouting at me,
they were screaming at me · *gritar* to shout,
to scream
- **mandrillus** mandrill [LATIN]
- **imitando** imitating · *imitar* to imitate
- **terrible** terrible
- **lianas** vines · *liana* vine
- **aire** *NM* air
- **rodearon** they surrounded · *rodear* to surround
- **bota** boot
- **volador salvaje** flying savage · *volador* flying ·
*salvaje NM* savage
- **taparrabo** loincloth

- □ **escándalo** commotion, disturbance
- □ **no tengo la menor idea** I don't have the slightest idea · *tener* to have · *menor* least · *idea* idea
- □ **inventaba** she invented, she made up · *inventar* to invent, to make up
- □ **hombre mono** ape man (*LIT* monkey man) · *hombre* man · *mono* monkey

## 21  Tarzan Confronts Kerchak        1:45

### Phrases to Listen For
**no lo sé** I don't know
**tal vez** maybe, perhaps
**¿por qué?** why?
**lo que** what
**¿en serio?** seriously?, really?
**a solas** alone
**ya basta** enough already
**lo importante es** the important thing is
**lo que** what

### Name
Isabel

Kerchak addresses the gorillas.

- □ **evitaremos** we will avoid · *evitar* to avoid
- □ **daño** damage
- □ **intimida** it intimidates · *intimidar* to intimidate
- □ **protege** *IMP* protect · *proteger* to protect
- □ **ruego** I beg · *rogar* to beg
- □ **me ocultaste** you hid from me · *ocultar* to hide, to conceal

In camp, Jane draws a picture of Tarzan on a chalkboard.

- □ **erguido** erect
- □ **encorvado** curved
- □ **soportaba** he supported · *soportar* to support, to bear
- □ **pecho** chest
- □ **nudillos** knuckles · *nudillo* knuckle
- □ **extraordinario** extraordinary
- □ **sorprendente** surprising
- □ **posición** position
- □ **descubrimiento** discovery
- □ **lenguaje** *NM* language
- □ **comportamiento** behavior
- □ **humano** human
- □ **respeto** respect
- □ **espacio personal** personal space · *espacio* space
- □ **acechándome** threatening me · *acechar* to threaten
- □ **confundido** confused · *confundir* to confuse
- □ **al principio** at first, in the beginning · *principio* start, beginning

- □ **intensos** intense · *intenso* intense
- □ **fijos** fixed, set · *fijo* fixed, set
- □ **tales** such · *tal* such
- □ **pizarrón** *NM* blackboard, chalkboard

## 22  Tarzan Drops In        1:41

### Phrases to Listen For
**se ve** he looks
**tal vez** maybe, perhaps
**Dios Salve a la Reina** God Save the Queen
**yo me haré cargo de esto** I'll take care of this

Clayton approaches the professor and Jane at the chalkboard.

- □ **fantasía** fantasy
- □ **infantil** infantile
- □ **real** real
- □ **¡apártense!** *IMP* move away! · *apartarse* to move away
- □ **sonido** sound
- □ **escopeta** shotgun
- □ **espacio** space
- □ **personal** personal
- □ **simio** ape
- □ **eslabón perdido** missing link · *eslabón NM* link · *perdido* missing, lost · *perder* to lose
- □ **guía** *NMF* guide [PERSON]
- □ **gorila** gorilla
- □ **gritar** shouting · *gritar* to shout
- □ **lenguaje** *NM* language
- □ **obligaré** I'll force · *obligar* to force, to make, to obligate

Clayton erases the chalkboard.

- □ **perico** parrot
- □ **Dios Salve a la Reina** God Save the Queen
- □ **dámelo** *IMP* give it to me · *dar* to give
- □ **me haré cargo** I'll take charge · *hacerse cargo* to take charge, to take care of

## 23  "Strangers Like Me"        3:54

### Phrases to Listen For
**lo que** what
**de nuevo** again
**así que** so
**¿por qué no?** why not?

The lamp is lit. Phil Collins sings "Strangers Like Me."

- □ **razonable** reasonable
- □ **mas** but
- □ **imagen** *NF* image
- □ **descubriré** I will discover · *descubrir* to discover

□ **cuan** how
□ **futuro** future
□ **normal** normal

🎬 Tarzan rides a bicycle.

□ **gesto** gesture
□ **atracción** attraction
□ **me invita** it invites me · *invitar* to invite
□ **emociones** emotions · *emoción* emotion
□ **detrás de** behind
□ **horizonte** *NM* horizon
□ **enseñes** *SUBJ* you teach · *enseñar* to teach
□ **mostraré** I will show · *mostrar* to show
□ **guiaré** I will guide · *guiar* to guide

🎬 In camp, Clayton faces Jane and the professor.

□ **arribará** it will arrive · *arribar* to arrive, to reach port

🎬 Terk and Tantor talk.

□ **corta** *IMP* cut · *cortar* to cut
□ **cuerdas** cords · *cuerda* cord

## 24 The Boat Arrives                          2:43

**Phrases to Listen For**

**hay que** it's necessary
**¿qué pasa?** what's happening?, what's going on?
**por favor** please
**hasta que** until
**para nada** for nothing, useless
**de verdad** really, truly
**tengo que** I have to
**lo lamento** I'm sorry

### Names
Jones, Snipes

🎬 The sailors break camp.

□ **quítenlo** *IMP* remove it · *quitar* to remove
□ **recojan** *IMP* gather up, pick up · *recoger* to gather, to pick up
□ **aguarden** *IMP* wait · *aguardar* to wait
□ **no me embarcaría** I wouldn't board, I wouldn't get on board · *embarcar* to board, to get on board
□ **desastre** *NM* disaster

🎬 Clayton pleads with the captain.

□ **falla** failure, breakdown
□ **máquinas** machines · *máquina* machine
□ **espérenos** *IMP* wait for us · *esperar* to wait
□ **puertos** ports · *puerto* port
□ **Londres** London
□ **culpa suya** your fault · *culpa* fault · *suyo* your
□ **instintos** instincts · *instinto* instinct

□ **trampas** traps · *trampa* trap
□ **bestias** beasts · *bestia* beast
□ **me decepciona** it disappoints me · *decepcionar* to disappoint

🎬 Jane bumps into Tarzan in camp. The word *imposible* is used but is cut short.

□ **imposible** impossible
□ **arribó** it arrived · *arribar* to arrive
□ **Inglaterra** England
□ **posibilidad** possibility
□ **acompañaras** *SUBJ* you accompany · *acompañar* to accompany
□ **equipaje** *NM* luggage

🎬 Clayton leans against a crate and addresses Tarzan.

□ **típico** typical
□ **explicación** explanation
□ **decepcionada** disappointed · *decepcionado* disappointed · *decepcionar* to disappoint
□ **hecha trizas** devastated · *hecho trizas* devastated · *estar hecho trizas* to be devastated · *trizas* *NFPL* small pieces, shreds
□ **se reúnan** they meet · *reunirse* to meet
□ **planes** plans · *plan* *NM* plan

## 25 Distracting Kerchak                       1:02

**Phrases to Listen For**

**con mucho gusto** with great pleasure
**lo que** what
**de acuerdo** agreed

🎬 Tarzan follows Terk down the trees.

□ **distraigas** *SUBJ* you distract · *distraer* to distract
□ **distraería** I would distract · *distraer* to distract
□ **cierra** *IMP* shut, close · *cerrar* to shut, to close
□ **trompa** trunk [OF AN ELEPHANT]
□ **tira** he throws, he tosses · *tirar* to throw, to toss
□ **jirafa** giraffe
□ **recién nacida** *ADJ* newborn · *recién* recently · *nacido* born · *nacer* to be born
□ **numerito** *DIM* musical number · *número* number
□ **cara** face
□ **no me obligues** *IMP* don't force me · *obligar* to force, to obligate
□ **vergonzoso** embarrassing, shameful

🎬 Terk wears a dress.

□ **te adelgaza** it makes you look thinner · *adelgazar* to cause to appear thin, to become thin
□ **escote** *NM* neckline
□ **algo atrevido** somewhat daring · *atrevido* daring

## 26 Meeting Tarzan's Family                    3:36

**Phrases to Listen For**
**tenga cuidado** *IMP* be careful
**no lo sé** I don't know
**ya basta** enough already

**Name**
Arquímedes Porter

Tarzan, Jane, the professor, and Clayton face Kala.
- **asustarla** to frighten her · *asustar* to frighten
- **se escapa** she's getting away · *escaparse* to get away, to escape
- **se espantará** she will be frightened · *espantarse* to be frightened
- **huyendo** fleeing · *huir* to flee

The professor is asleep, dreaming.
- **majestad** *NF* majesty
- **coqueta** coquette, flirt
- **servicio** service
- **roce social** social interaction · *roce NM* regular contact · *social* social

## 27 Tarzan Defies Kerchak                    1:53

**Phrase to Listen For**
**hace años** years ago

Kerchak finds Tarzan and the other humans with the gorillas.
- **ejemplar** exemplary
- **suéltala** *IMP* let it go · *soltar* to let go
- **devuélvemela** *IMP* give it back · *devolver* to give back, to return

Tarzan releases Kerchak.
- **proteger** to protect
- **traicionaste** you betrayed · *traicionar* to betray

Kala approaches Tarzan from behind.
- **confundido** confused · *confundir* to confuse
- **acompáñame** *IMP* come with me · *acompañar* to come with, to accompany
- **haberte mostrado** to have shown you · *mostrar* to show

## 28 The Truth                    3:51

**Phrases to Listen For**
**no importa** it doesn't matter
**largo de aquí** go away
**ya no me importas** I don't care about you any more

After Tarzan boards the boat to head for the ship, Terk and Tantor arrive at the shore.
- **no te hubieras detenido** *SUBJ* you shouldn't have stopped · *detener* to stop
- **indicaciones** *NFPL* directions
- **despedirnos** to say good-bye to each other · *despedirse* to say good-bye to one another
- **lampiño** hairless person
- **ingrato** ungrateful person
- **desteñido** colorless item
- **sin pelo** hairless, without hair · *pelo* hair
- **extrañarlo** to miss him · *extrañar* to miss

## 29 Clayton's Trap                    2:05

**Phrases to Listen For**
**lo que** what
**a bordo** aboard
**¿por qué?** why?
**de hecho** in fact
**tengo que** I have to

**Names**
Darwin, Kipling

Before boarding the ship, Jane talks to Tarzan.
- **científicos** scientists · *científico* scientist
- **famosos** famous · *famoso* famous
- **escritores** writers · *escritor NM* writer
- **qué torpe** how clumsy

Clayton puts the barrel of his gun beneath Tarzan's chin.
- **hombre mono** ape man (*LIT* monkey man) · *hombre* man · *mono* monkey
- **bienvenida** welcome
- **a bordo** on board
- **escena** scene
- **peludos** hairy · *peludo* hairy
- **jaulas** cages · *jaula* cage
- **trescientas** three hundred · *trescientos* three hundred
- **libras esterlinas** pounds sterling [BRITISH MONEY] · *libra* pound · *esterlina* sterling
- **agradecértelo** to thank you for it · *agradecer* to thank
- **prisión** prison

## 30 "We Got a Boat to Catch"                    2:23

**Phrases to Listen For**
**ya basta** enough already
**estoy harto de** I'm sick of, I'm up to here with
**tenemos que** we have to

**lo siento** I am sorry
**tenía razón** he was right
**¿qué tal?** what do you think of that?
**a veces** sometimes

🎬 Terk and Tantor hear Tarzan's cry for help.
☐ **estoy harto** I'm fed up · *hartar* to be fed up
☐ **constipación emocional** emotional constipation
☐ **¿lo entendiste?** did you understand? · *entender* to understand
☐ **sujétate** IMP hold on · *sujetarse* to hold on

🎬 Terk and Tantor fall into the ocean.
☐ **me había sentido** I had felt · *sentir* to feel
☐ **preciosa** precious · *precioso* precious

🎬 In the ship's hold, Tarzan jumps from wall to wall.
☐ **traicionó** he betrayed · *traicionar* to betray
☐ **traicioné** I betrayed · *traicionar* to betray
☐ **magníficas** magnificent · *magnífico* magnificent
☐ **temblando** trembling · *temblar* to tremble
☐ **jaulas** cages · *jaula* cage
☐ **ha convertido** it has become · *convertir* to become

🎬 Tantor and Terk fight on deck.
☐ **animal** NM animal
☐ **me avergüenzas** you embarrass me · *avergonzar* to embarrass, to shame

## 31 Ambush                                    3:13

**Phrases to Listen For**
**me acuerdo de ti** I remember you
**¡a la carga!** charge!
**lo que** what
**después de que** after

🎬 Clayton points his gun at Kerchak.
☐ **lucirá mejor** it will look better · *lucir* to look, to look good
☐ **sala de trofeos** trophy room · *sala* room · *trofeo* trophy
☐ **¡a la carga!** EXP charge!

🎬 Tarzan frees Kerchak.
☐ **hogar** NM home
☐ **presa** prey
☐ **aguardando** waiting · *aguardar* to wait
☐ **descuide** IMP don't worry · *descuidar* to not worry, to neglect
☐ **útil** useful

🎬 Clayton wounds Tarzan and shoots Kerchak.
☐ **esconderse** hiding yourself · *esconderse* to hide oneself
☐ **retos** challenges · *reto* challenge
☐ **me deshaga de ti** SUBJ I get rid of you · *deshacerse de* to get rid of
☐ **reunir** to gather, to gather up
☐ **mona** monkey · *mono* monkey
☐ **sencillo** simple

## 32 A Fight to the Finish                      1:42

🎬 Tarzan points the gun at Clayton.
☐ **dispara** IMP shoot · *disparar* to shoot

## 33 "My Son"                                   2:30

🎬 Tarzan approaches Kerchak.
☐ **has formado** you have formed · *formar* to form
☐ **dependerá** it will depend · *depender* to depend

## 34 Good-byes                                  2:22

**Phrase to Listen For**
**todos los días** every day

🎬 At the shore, Tarzan faces Jane.
☐ **Londres** London
☐ **comparado** compared · *comparar* to compare
☐ **extrañar** to miss
☐ **despedirnos** to say good-bye to each other · *despedirse* to say good-bye to one another

🎬 The professor and Jane are in the boat headed for the ship.
☐ **extrañaré** I will miss · *extrañar* to miss
☐ **pertenezco** I belong · *pertenecer* to belong
☐ **Inglaterra** England

🎬 Jane tackles Tarzan.
☐ **rescatar** to rescue
☐ **guante** NM glove

🎬 The professor addresses the captain.
☐ **selva** jungle
☐ **adiosito** DIM good-bye · *adiós* good-bye

## 35 Our Family                                 0:55

**Phrase to Listen For**
**lo que** what

🎬 Jane speaks to the gorillas.

□ **pon** *IMP* place, put · *poner* to place, to put

## 36 End Credits 5:57

🎬 End credits.

### Phrases to Listen For

**te ves** you look
**para siempre** forever
**no importa** it doesn't matter
**dentro de mí** inside me
**tendrás que** you will have to
**por siempre** forever

□ **como me apena** how it hurts me, how it makes me sorry · *apenar* to hurt, to make sorry
□ **siéntela** *IMP* feel it · *sentir* to feel
□ **protejo** I protect · *proteger* to protect
□ **frágil** fragile
□ **sensual** sensual
□ **abrazarte** to hug you, to hold you · *abrazar* to hug, to hold

□ **fusión** fusion
□ **irrompible** unbreakable
□ **proceder** *NM* behavior
□ **diferencias** differences · *diferencia* difference
□ **destino** destiny
□ **mas** but
□ **soledad** loneliness
□ **aguantar** to tolerate, to put up with
□ **no sufras más** *IMP* don't suffer any more · *sufrir* to suffer
□ **pon** *IMP* put · *poner* to put, to place
□ **paraíso** paradise
□ **paz** *NF* peace
□ **ponte alerta** *IMP* be alert · *ponerse* to become · *alerta* alert
□ **valor** *NM* courage, bravery
□ **construye** *IMP* construct, build · *construir* to construct, to build
□ **protección** protection
□ **llanto** crying
□ **curar** to heal, to cure
□ **herida** wound

# Holes

**¿Te enseño a leer?**
*You still want to learn to read?*

GENRE      Drama/Literature Adaptation
YEAR       2003
DIRECTOR   Andrew Davis
CAST       Shia LaBeouf, Sigourney Weaver, Jon Voight
STUDIO     Walt Disney Productions

Stanley Yelnats is unjustly convicted of stealing a pair of baseball shoes and is sentenced to the deceptively named Camp Green Lake. At this desert camp, Stanley (known as "Caveman") encounters three villains (Warden Walker, Mr. Sir, and Mr. Pendanski), a hard-core gang of juvenile delinquents, and the legend of outlaw Kissin' Kate Barlow. Spanish learners will find the vocabulary straightforward and will have many opportunities to develop an ear for phrases that include complex sentence structure.

## BASIC VOCABULARY

### Names

Yelnats, Camp Green Lake, Magnet, Madame Zeroni, Hector

### Nouns

□ **campamento** camp · *Ah, pues nunca he visitado un campamento.* Ah, well, I've never visited a camp.

□ **cavernícola** *NMF* caveman, cave-dwelling person · *En la excavación de Cavernícola apareció algo.* Something appeared in Caveman's excavation.

□ **directora** director · *director NM* director · *Si a la directora le parece, se te dará el resto del día libre.* If it seems like it to the director, she will give you the rest of the day off.

□ **hoyos** holes · *hoyo* hole · *Le encanta hacer hoyos.* He loves to dig holes.

□ **lagartijas** lizards · *lagartija* lizard · *Ah, descuida, lo uso con las lagartijas amarillas, no gastaría una bala en ti.* Ah, don't worry, I use it with the yellow lizards, I wouldn't spend a bullet on you.

□ **lago** lake · *Se fue con el lago.* It went away with the lake.

□ **pala** shovel · *Si no hacen que excaven más rápido, pueden tomar una pala y ayudar.* If you don't make them dig faster, you can both take a shovel and help.

□ **tatara tatarabuelo** great-great-great-grandfather · *Todo es por el indigno y ruin robacerdos de tu tatara tatarabuelo.* All because of your worthless, despicable, pig-stealer of a great-great-great-grandfather.

### Verbs

□ **cavar** to dig · *Ah, es que la verdad yo no sé enseñar, y me canso de cavar todo el día, así que sólo quiero volver y roncar.* Ah, the truth is that I don't know how to teach, and I get tired digging all day, so the only thing I want to do is come back and snore.

□ **disculpa** excuse (me) · *disculpar* to excuse · *Disculpa.* Excuse me.

### Other

□ **torpe** *ADJ* dense · *No soy torpe.* I'm not dense.

### 1 Opening Credits/ The Family Curse 5:15

#### Phrases to Listen For

**ya no sirve** it's no good anymore
**ya basta** enough already
**deja de** *IMP* stop
**maldición familiar** family curse

**qué asco** how gross, how sick, how disgusting
**me alegra** it makes me happy, I'm happy
**¿por qué no?** why not?
**lo que** what
**no tienes que** you don't have to

### Name

Stanley Yelnats

🎬 A boy looks at a rattlesnake.

□ **levántalo** *IMP* pick it up · *levantar* to pick up, to lift

□ **estás quemándote** you are burning yourself, you are getting burned · *quemarse* to burn oneself, to get burned

□ **calentamiento global** global warming

□ **agujero de ozono** ozone hole · *agujero* hole

□ **vómito** vomit

□ **divertido** funny, fun · *divertirse* to have fun

□ **¡reacciona!** *IMP* wake up!, watch out! · *reaccionar* to react

□ **bromas** practical jokes · *broma* practical joke

🎬 A pair of shoes flies through the air and hits Stanley.

□ **incorrecto** incorrect

□ **maldición** curse

□ **familiar** *ADJ* family

□ **salen mal** they turn out badly · *salir* to turn out, to leave

□ **alivia** it helps · *aliviar* to relieve

□ **culpar** to blame

🎬 Stanley smells the baseball shoes.

□ **qué asco** how sick, how disgusting, yuck · *asco* disgust

□ **apestan** they stink · *apestar* to stink

□ **destino** destiny

□ **escrito** written · *escribir* to write

□ **zapatos** shoes · *zapato* shoe

□ **¡detente!** *IMP* stop! · *detenerse* to stop

□ **tenis** tennis shoes, athletic shoes · *teni NM* tennis shoe, athletic shoe

🎬 Stanley rides a bus through the desert.

□ **tercero** third

□ **inventor** *NM* inventor

□ **cura** cure

□ **pie** *NM* foot

🎬 The police knock on the door of Stanley's apartment.

□ **oloroso** smelly, strong-smelling

□ **me alegra** I'm happy (*LIT* it makes me happy) · *alegrar* to make happy

□ **piso** floor

- **apesta** it stinks · *apestar* to stink
- **asqueroso** gross, sickening
- **no te espantes** *IMP* don't be frightened · *espantarse* to be frightened
- **moretón** *NM* bruise
- **fea** ugly · *feo* ugly
- **equivocación** mistake, error
- **consultar** to consult
- **abogado** lawyer
- **se arrepentirán** you all will regret · *arrepentirse* to regret
- **haberse metido** having become involved · *meterse* to become involved
- **no se lo arrebates** *IMP* don't grab it from him · *arrebatar* to grab forcefully
- **pedazo** piece
- **pastel** *NM* cake
- **café** *NM* coffee
- **tacita** *DIM* little cup · *taza* cup
- **olerlos** to smell them · *oler* to smell
- **huelo** I smell · *oler* to smell
- **revisa** *IMP* check · *revisar* to check, to review, to go over
- **válida** valid · *válido* valid
- **corte** *NF* court of law
- **contestar** to answer
- **permanecer** to remain

Stanley's family is seated around the table.
- **indigno** worthless, no-good
- **ruin** despicable, dirty-rotten
- **robacerdos** *NM* pig stealer · *robar* to steal, to rob · *cerdo* pig
- **carpintero** woodpecker (*LIT* carpenter)
- **no cantes** *IMP* don't sing · *cantar* to sing
- **canción** song
- **corteza** bark
- **no canten** *IMP* don't sing · *cantar* to sing
- **mesa** table
- **Ma** Mom
- **tranquila** *EXP* easy, take it easy, be calm
- **costoso** expensive
- **Pa** Dad

Stanley and his family appear in court.
- **te encierro** I lock you up · *encerrar* to lock up
- **cárcel** *NF* jail
- **conciencia** consciousness, conscience
- **vacante** *NF* vacancy, opening
- **juventud** *NF* youth
- **forje** *SUBJ* it forges · *forjar* to forge
- **carácter** *NM* character
- **decisión** decision
- **he visitado** I have visited · *visitar* to visit
- **dieciocho** eighteen

## 2 Welcome to Camp Green Lake 4:53

**Phrases to Listen For**
**darle su bienvenida** welcome him
**no te pases de listo** *IMP* don't get smart
**para nada** not at all
**lo que** what
**tal vez** maybe, perhaps

Stanley steps off the bus.
- **bienvenida** welcome
- **tiernito** *DIM* rookie · *tierno* tender
- **oí** I heard · *oír* to hear

A man eating sunflower seeds in an office tells Stanley to be seated.
- **semillas de girasol** sunflower seeds · *semilla* seed · *girasol* sunflower
- **fumar** smoking · *fumar* to smoke
- **nombran** they name · *nombrar* to name (to a post)
- **al revés** backwards
- **tradición** tradition
- **divertido** funny · *divertirse* to have fun
- **exploradoras** girl scouts · *exploradora* girl scout · *explorador* boy scout
- **caja** box, case
- **sorpresas** surprises · *sorpresa* surprise
- **sed** *NF* thirst
- **acostúmbrate** *IMP* get used to it · *acostumbrarse* to get used to, to get accustomed to
- **sediento** thirsty
- **siguientes** next · *siguiente* next
- **dieciocho** eighteen

Mr. Sir walks with Stanley outside.
- **mira a tu alrededor** *IMP* look at your surroundings, look around you · *mirar* to look at · *alrededor* surroundings
- **torres** towers · *torre* *NF* tower
- **guardias** guards · *guardia* guard
- **cerca eléctrica** electric fence · *cerca* fence
- **huir** to flee, to run away
- **no te lo impediré** I won't stop you · *impedir* to stop, to impede
- **apestas** you stink · *apestar* to stink
- **descuida** *IMP* don't worry, relax · *descuidar* to not worry
- **uso** I use · *usar* to use
- **amarillas** yellow · *amarillo* yellow
- **no gastaría** I wouldn't spend · *gastar* to spend
- **bala** bullet
- **escapar** to escape
- **no encontrarías** you wouldn't find · *encontrar* to find

□ **kilómetros** kilometers · *kilómetro* kilometer
□ **oasis** *NM* oasis
□ **buitres** vultures · *buitre NM* vulture
□ **entero** whole
□ **tercer** third

🎬 Mr. Sir picks up a pair of boots.

□ **desvístete** *IMP* get undressed · *desvestirse* to get undressed, to undress
□ **ropa** clothes
□ **lavada** washed · *lavado* washed · *lavar* to wash
□ **excavarás** you will dig · *excavar* to dig
□ **sesenta** sixty
□ **diámetro** diameter
□ **referencia** reference
□ **cascabel** *NF* rattlesnake
□ **muerda** *SUBJ* it bites · *morder* to bite
□ **mordido** bitten · *morder* to bite
□ **lagartija amarilla** yellow lizard · *lagartija* lizard · *amarillo* yellow
□ **pasarte** to happen to you · *pasar* to happen
□ **agonizarías** you would be dying · *agonizar* to be dying
□ **lenta** slow · *lento* slow
□ **penosamente** painfully

## 3 Boys of D-Tent                    4:00

### Phrases to Listen For
**tal vez** maybe, perhaps
**dado que** since, given that
**de mal humor** in a bad mood
**¿por qué no le enseñas…?** why don't you show him …?
**si tienes alguna duda** if you have any questions
**como tú digas** *SUBJ* whatever you say
**¿qué tal huele?** how's it smell?
**no te creo** I don't believe you

### Names
Pendanski, Louis, Rex, Alan, Theodore, X-ray, Squid, Armpit, Pit, Magnet, Zigzag, Stanley, Ricky, Theodore, Clyde Livingston

🎬 Mr. Pendanski joins Stanley and Mr. Sir.

□ **no te convierte** it doesn't make you · *convertir* to make, to convert
□ **respeto** I respect · *respetar* to respect
□ **bienvenido** *ADJ* welcome
□ **consejero** counselor
□ **sentimentalismos** sentimentalism · *sentimentalismo* sentimentalism
□ **toallas** towels · *toalla* towel
□ **tokens** *ENG* tokens
□ **equípalo** *IMP* equip him · *equipar* to equip

🎬 Carrying his equipment, Stanley accompanies Pendanski.

□ **tienda** tent
□ **de** *NF* D [LETTER]
□ **diligencia** diligence
□ **comedor** dining room
□ **cuarto de diversión** game room · *cuarto* room · *diversión* fun
□ **duchas** showers · *ducha* shower
□ **grifo** faucet
□ **temperatura** temperature
□ **helada** freezing cold · *helado* freezing cold · *helar* to freeze
□ **cabaña** cabin
□ **la cabaña de la dirección** headquarters · *cabaña* cabin · *dirección* management
□ **regla** rule
□ **no importunes** *IMP* don't bother · *importunar* to bother
□ **director** *NM* director
□ **de mal humor** in a bad mood · *humor* mood
□ **fumar** smoking · *fumar* to smoke

🎬 The boys from Tent D join Stanley and Pendanski.

□ **Neandertal** *NM* Neanderthal
□ **vómito** vomit
□ **hospital** *NM* hospital
□ **apodos** nicknames · *apodo* nickname
□ **sociedad** society
□ **litera** bunk

🎬 Stanley's bed is stained with vomit.

□ **hogar** *NM* home
□ **limpia** clean · *limpio* clean
□ **cráneo** cranium, skull
□ **mentor** *NM* mentor
□ **vecinos** neighbors · *vecino* neighbor

🎬 Stanley runs with an empty water bottle in his hand.

□ **llenar** to fill
□ **garrafa** water bottle
□ **¿qué tal huele?** how does that smell? · *oler* to smell
□ **rudo** rough
□ **boca** mouth
□ **no exageres** *IMP* don't exaggerate · *exagerar* to exaggerate

🎬 Stanley walks through the cafeteria line.

□ **menú** *NM* menu
□ **frijoles** beans · *fríjol NM* bean
□ **chile** *NM* chili pepper
□ **refritos** refried · *refrito* refried
□ **garbanzo** garbanzo, chickpea

- □ **verdes** green · *verde* green
- □ **gelatina** gelatin
- □ **banana** banana

🎬 Stanley sits down at a table in the cafeteria.

- □ **no vi que sacaras tierra hoy** *SUBJ* I didn't see you taking dirt out today · *sacar* to take out, to remove
- □ **pan** *NM* bread
- □ **encerraron** they locked up · *encerrar* to lock up
- □ **robo** robbery
- □ **tenis** tennis shoes, athletic shoes · *teni NM* tennis shoe, athletic shoe
- □ **asesinó** he killed · *asesinar* to kill, to murder
- □ **víctima** victim
- □ **detalle** *NM* detail
- □ **apestosos** stinking, smelly · *apestoso* stinking, smelly
- □ **Serie Mundial** World Series · *serie NF* series · *mundial ADJ* world
- □ **récord** *NM* record
- □ **velocidad** velocity, speed
- □ **triples** triples · *triple NM* triple
- □ **donó** he donated · *donar* to donate
- □ **orfanato** orphanage
- □ **roja** red · *rojo* red

## 4 The Legend of Kissin' Kate Barlow                    1:58

### Phrases to Listen For
**de los errores se aprende** you learn from your mistakes
**hay que tener suerte** you have to get lucky (*LIT* it's necessary to have some luck)
**¡vaya suerte!** what luck!
**a cabalgar** let's ride

### Names
Livingston, Kate Barlow

🎬 In court, an attorney is interviewing a witness.

- □ **tenis** tennis shoes, athletic shoes · *teni NM* tennis shoe, athletic shoe
- □ **donados** donated · *donado* donated · *donar* to donate, to give
- □ **conexión** connection
- □ **huérfano** orphan
- □ **crecí** I grew · *crecer* to grow
- □ **hogar** *NM* home
- □ **tipo** type, kind
- □ **fanático** fan

🎬 Stanley's grandfather complains.

- □ **indigno** worthless, no-good
- □ **ruin** despicable, dirty-rotten

- □ **robacerdos** *NM* pig stealer · *robar* to steal, to rob · *cerdo* pig
- □ **selló** he sealed · *sellar* to seal
- □ **destino** destiny
- □ **inventos** inventions · *invento* invention
- □ **Pa** Dad
- □ **errores** mistakes, errors · *error NM* mistake, error
- □ **hábil** able, capable
- □ **carecemos de** we're lacking · *carecer (de algo)* to lack (something)
- □ **amasó** he amassed · *amasar* to amass
- □ **fortuna** fortune
- □ **bolsa** stock market
- □ **cariñosa** loving, affectionate, caring · *cariñoso* loving, affectionate, caring

🎬 Kate Barlow stands on top of a stage coach. Stanley is seated at the dinner table with his family.

- □ **besó** she kissed · *besar* to kiss
- □ **asesinó** she killed · *asesinar* to kill, to murder

🎬 Kate Barlow shouts instructions.

- □ **dénmelo** *IMP* give it to me · *dar* to give
- □ **abandonado** abandoned · *abandonar* to abandon
- □ **desierto** desert
- □ **a cabalgar** let's ride · *cabalgar* to ride a horse

🎬 Stanley's grandfather continues the description.

- □ **comida** food
- □ **dieciséis** sixteen
- □ **si lo hubiera besado** *SUBJ* if she had kissed · *besar* to kiss
- □ **lo habría asesinado** she would have killed him · *asesinar* to kill, to murder
- □ **no habrían nacido** you wouldn't have been born · *nacer* to be born

## 5 Digging the First Hole                    2:36

### Phrases to Listen For
**a ver** let's see
**hay que** it's necessary
**hora de** time to
**todo el día** all day

### Name
Pendanski

🎬 Pendanski addresses the boys as they assemble in the early morning.

- □ **rostros** faces · *rostro* face
- □ **compañero** companion, classmate, co-worker
- □ **agujero** hole

□ **palas** shovels · *pala* shovel
□ **tortillas** tortillas · *tortilla* tortilla
□ **biblioteca** library
□ **dormilandia** dreamland
□ **engendros** deformed creatures · *engendro* deformed creature
□ **flojos** lazy people · *flojo* lazy person

X-Ray steals Stanley's shovel.
□ **corta** short · *corto* short
□ **menor** smaller

Mr. Sir instructs Stanley on where to dig.
□ **inicia** IMP start · *iniciar* to start, to begin
□ **interesante** interesting
□ **reportas** you report · *reportar* to report
□ **resto** the rest, the remainder
□ **libre** free
□ **no se trata** it's not about · *tratarse* to be about
□ **forjará** it will forge · *forjar* to forge
□ **carácter** NM character
□ **elige** IMP choose · *elegir* to choose
□ **ardiente** burning
□ **se convierte** he becomes · *convertirse* to become
□ **filosofía** philosophy
□ **millones** millions · *millón* NM million

Stanley digs.
□ **echar** to throw, to toss
□ **se está metiendo** it's getting in · *meterse* to get in, to go in
□ **fíjate** IMP pay attention · *fijarse* to pay attention
□ **echas** you throw · *echar* to throw, to toss

## 6 Stanley Yelnats the First    5:32

### Phrases to Listen For
**toda la eternidad** for all eternity
**¿qué te pasa?** what's the matter?
**¿por qué?** why?
**¿qué tal?** what about?
**no lo sé** I don't know
**de obsequio** as a gift

### Names
Elya Yelnats, Latvia, Morris Menke, Myra, Madame Zeroni, Igor Barkov

Stanley's face is shown in slow motion as he digs. Shortly, a photo of his great-grandfather anticipates a flashback.
□ **indigno** worthless, no-good
□ **ruin** despicable, dirty-rotten

□ **robacerdos** NM pig stealer · *robar* to steal, to rob · *cerdo* pig
□ **inició** it began · *iniciar* to begin, to start
□ **villa** villa, town, village
□ **afanador** person who cleans, cleaning man
□ **establo** stable
□ **pitonisa** fortuneteller
□ **consejo** counsel
□ **América** America
□ **futuro** future
□ **hueca** empty · *hueco* empty
□ **florero** flower vase

Stanley's great-great-grandfather asks Morris Menke for Myra's hand in marriage.
□ **permiso** permission
□ **enorme** enormous
□ **puerco** pig
□ **mocoso** PEJ snot-nosed child, snot-nosed brat

Madame Zeroni counsels Elya Yelnats.
□ **bruto** brute, idiot
□ **elige** IMP choose · *elegir* to choose
□ **no resuelve** it doesn't solve, it doesn't resolve · *resolver* to solve, to resolve
□ **cima** top
□ **montaña** mountain
□ **río** river
□ **convéncelo** IMP convince it · *convencer* to convince
□ **beba** SUBJ it drinks · *beber* to drink
□ **cantas** you sing · *cantar* to sing
□ **carpintero** woodpecker (LIT carpenter)
□ **corteza** bark

Elya Yelnats stands at the river with a pig.
□ **lobo** wolf
□ **aguardaba** he was waiting · *aguardar* to wait
□ **hambriento** hungry
□ **aúlla** he howls · *aullar* to howl
□ **luna** moon
□ **engordará** he will get fatter · *engordar* to get fatter

Madame Zeroni warns Elya Yelnats about the curse.
□ **eternidad** eternity

Mr. Sir listens to music in Spanish as he drives the water truck.
□ **rosalito** DIM little rosebush · *rosal* NM rosebush
□ **se está secando** it is drying up · *secarse* to dry up

The boys stand in line for water.

- □ **cachorro** puppy
- □ **camioneta** pickup truck
- □ **haga fila** *IMP* form a line · *hacer fila* to form a line
- □ **pon el ejemplo** *IMP* set an example · *poner el ejemplo* to set an example
- □ **tarado** idiot, dummy
- □ **no estorbes** *IMP* stay out of the way, don't get in the way · *estorbar* to get in the way
- □ **empujas** you push · *empujar* to push
- □ **ampollas** blisters · *ampolla* blister
- □ **dedos** fingers · *dedo* finger
- □ **enormes** enormous · *enorme* enormous
- □ **descuida** *IMP* don't worry · *descuidar* to not worry
- □ **callos** calluses · *callo* callus
- □ **siguiente** next

Morris Menke asks Myra to choose her husband.

- □ **eliges** you choose · *elegir* to choose
- □ **pesa** it weighs · *pesar* to weigh
- □ **obsequio** gift
- □ **puercos** pigs · *puerco* pig

Zero finishes digging his hole.

- □ **veloz** fast, speedy
- □ **topo** mole
- □ **se traga** he swallows · *tragarse* to swallow
- □ **gusanos** worms · *gusano* worm

Elya Yelnats carries a sack over his shoulder. He later wakes up aboard ship.

- □ **América** America

## 7  Yellow Spotted Lizards                2:19

### Phrases to Listen For
**lo que** what
**para qué** for what, what for

Mr. Sir shoots a yellow spotted lizard.

- □ **siesta** nap

Stanley is in the tent with his fellow prisoners.

- □ **panza** belly
- □ **te hubieran enterrado** *SUBJ* they would have buried you · *enterrar* to bury
- □ **once** eleven
- □ **manchas** stains · *mancha* stain
- □ **contárselas** to count them · *contar* to count
- □ **guaridas** dens, hide-outs · *guarida* den, hide-out
- □ **ayer** yesterday

- □ **se forja** it is forged · *forjar* to forge
- □ **carácter** *NM* character

## 8  A Letter to Mom                1:34

### Phrases to Listen For
**prueba de natación** swimming test
**tendré que** I will have to
**para que** so that
**no les interesa** they don't care, they're not interested

Reveille wakes up Stanley. Stanley writes his mother.

- □ **rato** while, time
- □ **comida** food
- □ **baño** bathroom, restroom
- □ **elige** *IMP* choose · *elegir* to choose
- □ **prueba de natación** swimming test · *prueba* test · *natación* swimming
- □ **esquiar** to ski
- □ **infierno** hell
- □ **tibia** lukewarm · *tibio* lukewarm
- □ **refrescante** refreshing
- □ **te agradaría** you would like (*LIT* it would please you) · *agradar* to please
- □ **consejero** counselor

Pendanski walks through the recreation building.

- □ **apesta** it stinks · *apestar* to stink
- □ **vómito** vomit
- □ **mula** mule
- □ **hubiera rumiado** *SUBJ* it had chewed · *rumiar* to chew the cud
- □ **espárragos** asparagus · *espárrago* asparagus
- □ **quince** fifteen
- □ **estoy disfrutando** I am enjoying · *disfrutar* to enjoy
- □ **silvestre** wild
- □ **renta** rent
- □ **incorrecto** incorrect
- □ **incorrecta** incorrect · *incorrecto* incorrect
- □ **salúdame** *IMP* say hello · *saludar* to say hello, to greet

Someone grabs the letter Stanley is writing.

- □ **carta** letter
- □ **extrañas** you miss · *extrañar* to miss
- □ **no se angustien** *SUBJ* they don't feel anguish, they don't worry · *angustiarse* to feel anguish, to worry
- □ **les alegra** they are happy (*LIT* it makes them happy) · *alegrar* to make happy
- □ **librarse** to get free

## 9 Onion Sam and Miss Katherine 2:58

### Phrases to Listen For
**a ver** let's see
**de verdad** really
**lo que** what
**no me importa** it doesn't matter to me
**qué lástima** what a pity

### Names
Collingwood, Mary Lou, Sam, Katherine, Green Lake, Texas, Sheriff

🎬 Pendanski gives Zero a bottle of water.
- **hallé** I found · *hallar* to find
- **fósil** *NM* fossil
- **interesante** interesting
- **libre** free
- **fósiles** fossils · *fósil NM* fossil
- **pececito** *DIM* little fish · *pez NM* fish
- **pinturas rupestres** cave paintings · *pintura* painting · *rupestre ADJ* cave
- **probable** probable
- **imaginación** imagination
- **peces** fish · *pez NM* fish
- **dueño** owner
- **pueblo** town

🎬 A boat with several men pulls up to the dock.
- **amarra** *IMP* tie · *amarrar* to tie
- **bote** *NM* boat
- **cebollas** onions · *cebolla* onion
- **curatodo** cure-all · *curar* to cure, to heal · *todo* everything, all
- **elixir** *NM* elixir
- **pociones** potions · *poción* potion
- **tónicos** tonics · *tónico* tonic
- **deliciosos** delicious · *delicioso* delicious
- **vegetales** plants · *vegetal NM* plant
- **mágicos** magic · *mágico ADJ* magic
- **aplíquele** *IMP* apply it · *aplicar* to apply
- **cabellera** long hair
- **gruesa** thick · *grueso* thick
- **melena** hair

🎬 Sam addresses Mary Lou and the schoolchildren.
- **antiguos** ancient · *antiguo* ancient
- **egipcios** Egyptians · *egipcio* Egyptian
- **secretos** secrets · *secreto* secret
- **potentes** powerful · *potente* powerful
- **jugos** juices · *jugo* juice
- **curan** they cure · *curar* to cure, to heal
- **dolor** *NM* pain

- **estómago** stomach
- **muelas** teeth, molars · *muela* tooth, molar
- **malestares** discomforts · *malestar NM* discomfort
- **paperas** *NFPL* mumps
- **reumatismo** rheumatism
- **hemorroides** *NFPL* hemorrhoids
- **no me crean** *IMP* don't believe me · *creer* to believe
- **cien** one hundred
- **edad** age
- **veinticinco** twenty-five
- **magia** magic

🎬 A man steps down from a horse-drawn carriage.
- **oro** gold
- **jugo** juice
- **lagartija** lizard
- **brillante** brilliant
- **qué lástima** what a pity
- **amarillas** yellow · *amarillo* yellow
- **odian** they hate · *odiar* to hate
- **pócimas** potions · *pócima* potion
- **salud** *NF* health
- **aceites** oils · *aceite NM* oil

🎬 Sam gives Katherine a bottle of onion tonic.
- **bolsa** bag
- **paraíso** paradise
- **duraznos** peaches · *durazno* peach
- **creación** creation
- **invito** I invite · *invitar* to invite
- **trago** swallow, drink
- **invítame** *IMP* invite me · *invitar* to invite

## 10 Don't Mess with Caveman 6:21

### Phrases to Listen For
**¿por qué?** why?
**es el colmo** he's the worst, he's over the top
**todo en orden** everything is all right
**tengo que** I have to
**ya es hora** it's already time
**echándola a perder** wasting it
**de campamento** from camp
**así que** so

### Name
José

🎬 X-Ray looks down into the hole that Stanley is digging.
- **patético** pathetic
- **dámelo** *IMP* give it to me · *dar* to give
- **libre** free

- **justicia** justice
- **decisión con bases** informed decision · *decisión* decision · *base NF* foundation
- **cachorro** pup, puppy

🎬 Someone knocks Stanley over.

- **fíjate** *IMP* watch out · *fijarse* to pay attention
- **intención** intention
- **sepárense** *IMP* break it up · *separarse* to separate from one another
- **inicias** you start · *iniciar* to start, to begin
- **dura** tough · *duro* tough
- **relájate** *IMP* relax · *relajarse* to relax
- **payaso** clown
- **es el colmo** he's the worst, he's over the top · *colmo* limit, height
- **nadie se meta con** *SUBJ* nobody messes with · *meterse con* to mess with, to provoke
- **salvaje** *NM* savage
- **con nadie quiero meterme** I don't want to mess with anyone · *meterse con* to mess with, to provoke
- **valiente** brave
- **vómito** vomit

🎬 Mr. Sir steps out of his truck.

- **pececitos** *DIM* little fish · *pez NM* fish
- **lacustre** from a lake
- **gracioso** funny
- **engendros** deformed creatures · *engendro* deformed creature
- **alteza** your highness

🎬 Pendanski directs a counseling session.

- **animales** animals · *animal NM* animal
- **criminal** *NMF* criminal
- **metidos** placed, put · *meter* to place, to put
- **jaulas** cages · *jaula* cage
- **cien** one hundred
- **bolsillo** pocket
- **no hubiera ladrado** *SUBJ* it hadn't barked · *ladrar* to bark
- **echándola a perder** wasting it · *echar a perder* to waste
- **apodo** nickname
- **por causa de** because of
- **indigno** worthless, no-good
- **ruin** despicable, dirty-rotten
- **robacerdos** *NM* pig stealer · *robar* to steal, to rob · *cerdo* pig
- **arruinaste** you ruined · *arruinar* to ruin
- **enmendarla** to fix it, to correct it · *enmendar* to fix, to correct
- **sorprendería** it would surprise · *sorprender* to surprise

- **mente** *NF* mind
- **completo** complete
- **desperdicio** waste
- **adoro** I love, I adore · *adorar* to love, to adore

🎬 Stanley's mother writes to him.

- **cartas** letters · *carta* letter
- **descubrimiento** discovery
- **arrendador** landlord
- **está amenazando** he is threatening · *amenazar* to threaten
- **desalojarnos** to evict us, to kick us out · *desalojar* to evict, to kick out
- **olor** *NM* smell, odor
- **insulta** you insult · *insultar* to insult
- **química** chemistry
- **hedor** stench, stink
- **hervirlo** to boil it · *hervir* to boil
- **tenis** tennis shoes, athletic shoes · *teni NM* tennis shoe, athletic shoe
- **exacto** exactly
- **tristeza** sadness
- **anciana** old woman · *anciano* old man, old person
- **zapato** shoe
- **haber olido** to have smelled · *oler* to smell

🎬 Stanley sits on his bunk reading. Zero sits up.

- **te ríes** you are laughing · *reírse* to laugh
- **te acuerdas** you remember · *acordarse* to remember
- **cuento** story
- **incómodo** uncomfortable
- **hombro** shoulder
- **roncar** to snore

🎬 Armpit dances.

- **apesta** it stinks · *apestar* to stink
- **apestas** you stink · *apestar* to stink
- **bájalos** *IMP* put them down, lower them · *bajar* to put down, to lower
- **brazos** arms · *brazo* arm

## 11 Finding Something Special  6:26

### Phrases to Listen For
**que no se vaya** *SUBJ* don't go
**tal vez** maybe, perhaps
**ten cuidado** *IMP* be careful
**como sea** *SUBJ* however

### Names
X-Ray, Keith Berringer, Zigzag, Rex, Doc, Theodore, Armpit, Lou, Pendanski, Squid

🎬 The boys are digging holes.

- ☐ **nube** *NF* cloud
- ☐ **elefante** *NM* elephant
- ☐ **cubra** *SUBJ* it covers · *cubrir* to cover
- ☐ **nubecita** *DIM* little cloud · *nube NF* cloud
- ☐ **solamente** only
- ☐ **chiquita** *DIM* little one · *chiquito DIM* little one · *chico* little one
- ☐ **dueña** owner · *dueño* owner
- ☐ **sombra** shade, shadow
- ☐ **llueva** *SUBJ* it rains · *llover* to rain
- ☐ **arca** ark
- ☐ **animal** *NM* animal
- ☐ **escorpiones** scorpions · *escorpión NM* scorpion
- ☐ **cascabeles** rattlesnakes · *cascabel NF* rattlesnake
- ☐ **amarillas** yellow · *amarillo* yellow

🎬 Stanley picks up something from inside the hole.

- ☐ **¿qué opinas?** what do you think? · *opinar* to think, to give an opinion
- ☐ **casquillo de bala** bullet shell, bullet case · *casquillo* shell, case · *bala* bullet
- ☐ **delgado** thin, slim
- ☐ **letras** letters · *letra* letter
- ☐ **ka** *NF* K [LETTER]
- ☐ **be** *NF* B [LETTER]
- ☐ **pertenece** it belongs · *pertenecer* to belong
- ☐ **enseñársela** to show it to her · *enseñar* to show
- ☐ **libre** free
- ☐ **guardas** you keep · *guardar* to keep, to save

🎬 Pendanski gives X-Ray his ration of water.

- ☐ **no reconozco** I don't recognize · *reconocer* to recognize
- ☐ **oro** gold
- ☐ **urgente** urgent

🎬 The warden removes her sunglasses.

- ☐ **doble** double
- ☐ **ración** ration
- ☐ **comida** food
- ☐ **ducha** shower
- ☐ **llene** *IMP* fill · *llenar* to fill
- ☐ **garrafas** water bottles · *garrafa* water bottle
- ☐ **llené** I filled · *llenar* to fill
- ☐ **llenó** he filled · *llenar* to fill
- ☐ **por casualidad** by coincidence, by chance
- ☐ **trago** swallow, drink
- ☐ **llenaron** they filled · *llenar* to fill
- ☐ **garrafa** water bottle
- ☐ **dármela** to give it to me · *dar* to give
- ☐ **espacio** space
- ☐ **vacío** empty
- ☐ **llénela** *IMP* fill it · *llenar* to fill
- ☐ **molestia** annoyance, bother

- ☐ **carretillas** wheelbarrows · *carretilla* wheelbarrow
- ☐ **encárgate** *IMP* take charge · *encargarse* to take charge
- ☐ **excavarán** you all will dig · *excavar* to dig

🎬 Pendanski leaves with X-Ray.

- ☐ **ce** *NF* C [LETTER]
- ☐ **efe** *NF* F [LETTER]
- ☐ **músculos** muscles · *músculo* muscle
- ☐ **presentimiento** feeling about the future
- ☐ **complaciente** accommodating
- ☐ **filetes** fillets · *filete NM* fillet
- ☐ **cena** dinner
- ☐ **¡ánimo!** *EXP* keep it up!, keep going!, come on!
- ☐ **roca** rock

## 12  The Deal                                          8:46

### Phrases to Listen For
**aguda paranoia** acute paranoia
**al parecer** it looks like
**a pesar de** in spite of
**no lo creo** I don't think so
**tal vez** maybe, perhaps
**¿qué tanto...?** what all ...?
**canción de cuna** lullaby
**¡qué hombres más inútiles!** what useless men!

### Names
Louise, Katherine, Sam, Annabel Lee, Penn, Walker, Trout, X-Ray, Armpit, Texas

🎬 Back in camp, the boys, dirty from the day's work, walk together.

- ☐ **vigilado** monitored · *vigilar* to monitor, to watch, to keep an eye on
- ☐ **instalados** installed · *instalado* installed · *instalar* to install
- ☐ **micrófonos** microphones · *micrófono* microphone
- ☐ **cámaras** cameras · *cámara* camera
- ☐ **cocina** kitchen
- ☐ **vestidor** dressing room
- ☐ **duchas** showers · *ducha* shower
- ☐ **archivo** file
- ☐ **sufre** he suffers · *sufrir* to suffer
- ☐ **aguda** acute · *agudo* acute
- ☐ **paranoia** paranoia
- ☐ **a diario** daily
- ☐ **microscopios** microscopes · *microscopio* microscope
- ☐ **lárgate** *IMP* go away, get away · *largarse* to go away, to get away

🎬 Miss Katherine and the schoolchildren look out at the rain.

- ☐ **temprano** early
- ☐ **lluvia** rain
- ☐ **gorros** caps · *gorro* cap
- ☐ **cebollas** onions · *cebolla* onion
- ☐ **yo lo reparo** I'll fix it (*LIT* I fix it) · *reparar* to fix, to repair
- ☐ **techo** roof
- ☐ **goteras** leaks · *gotera* leak
- ☐ **fabriqué** I built · *fabricar* to build
- ☐ **bote** *NM* boat
- ☐ **cruzar** to cross
- ☐ **cultivo** crop
- ☐ **en apuros** in a tight situation, in trouble
- ☐ **arreglo** I'll repair, I'll fix (*LIT* I repair, I fix) · *arreglar* to repair, to fix
- ☐ **tarros** jars · *tarro* jar
- ☐ **duraznos** peaches · *durazno* peach
- ☐ **trato** deal

🎬 Sam repairs the schoolhouse roof.

- ☐ **garantizo** I guarantee · *garantizar* to guarantee
- ☐ **se atascaron** they are stuck · *atascarse* to be stuck
- ☐ **ventanas** windows · *ventana* window
- ☐ **aire** *NM* air
- ☐ **pensamiento** thought
- ☐ **reino** kingdom
- ☐ **océano** ocean

🎬 Miss Katherine signals with her pointer to indicate words on the chalkboard.

- ☐ **pato** duck
- ☐ **dueño** owner
- ☐ **practicaré** I will practice · *practicar* to practice
- ☐ **pasear** to go for a ride
- ☐ **bote de motor** motorboat · *bote NM* boat · *motor NM* motor
- ☐ **no remaría** you wouldn't row · *remar* to row

🎬 Mr. Sir and the warden walk through the archways connecting the holes.

- ☐ **hemos excavado** we have dug · *excavar* to dig
- ☐ **alrededor** around
- ☐ **dirección** direction
- ☐ **centro** center, middle
- ☐ **antigua** ancient · *antiguo* ancient
- ☐ **Mesopotamia** Mesopotamia
- ☐ **palas** shovels · *pala* shovel
- ☐ **me alegra** I'm happy (*LIT* it makes me happy) · *alegrar* to make happy
- ☐ **hayas vuelto** *SUBJ* you have returned · *volver* to return
- ☐ **agudos** sharp · *agudo* sharp

- ☐ **burlarte** to mock, to make fun of · *burlarse* to mock, to make fun of
- ☐ **burla** joke
- ☐ **chistecito** *DIM* little joke · *chiste NM* joke
- ☐ **costará** it will cost · *costar* to cost
- ☐ **afuera** outside
- ☐ **resultados** results · *resultado* result

🎬 Miss Katherine, with a daisy in her hair, talks to Sam. The warden paces above the excavation.

- ☐ **inútiles** useless · *inútil* useless
- ☐ **abeja reina** queen bee · *abeja* bee · *reina* queen
- ☐ **excaven** *SUBJ* they dig · *excavar* to dig
- ☐ **arenero** sandbox
- ☐ **esfuerzo** effort
- ☐ **castigo** punishment
- ☐ **no estoy cantándoles** I'm not singing to you · *cantar* to sing
- ☐ **canción de cuna** lullaby · *canción* song · *cuna* cradle

🎬 Several riders torch the schoolhouse. Miss Katherine seeks help from the sheriff.

- ☐ **comisario** sheriff
- ☐ **están destruyendo** they are destroying · *destruir* to destroy
- ☐ **beso** kiss
- ☐ **diste** you gave · *dar* to give
- ☐ **cebollero** the onion seller
- ☐ **ebrio** drunk
- ☐ **ahorcar** to hang
- ☐ **cuelga** you hang · *colgar* to hang
- ☐ **ahórqueme** *IMP* hang me · *ahorcar* to hang
- ☐ **besé** I kissed · *besar* to kiss

## **13** Miss Katherine's Revenge        1:17

**Phrase to Listen For**
  **a cavar** let's dig, let's get digging

🎬 Mr. Sir paces the porch, scolding the boys.

- ☐ **comportamiento** behavior
- ☐ **exhibido** exhibited · *exhibir* to exhibit, to show
- ☐ **carácter** *NM* character
- ☐ **se forjará** it will be forged · *forjarse* to be forged
- ☐ **eficiencia** efficiency

🎬 Miss Katherine enters the sheriff's office.

- ☐ **comisario** chief of police, sheriff
- ☐ **beso** kiss

## 14 Mr. Sir's Sunflower Seeds   2:42

**Phrases to Listen For**
**bien hecho** well done
**¿qué pasó?** what happened?
**no pasa nada** nothing is happening
**tal vez** maybe, perhaps
**a ver que tal se pone** we'll see how she reacts

**Name**
Zig

🎬 Mr. Sir serves water from the back of the truck.

☐ **preciado** prized, valued · *preciar* to prize, to value
☐ **lujo** luxury
☐ **faz** *NF* face
☐ **obsequio** gift
☐ **siguiente** next
☐ **optimistas** optimists · *optimista NMF* optimist
☐ **tormentas** storms · *tormenta* storm
☐ **montañas** mountains · *montaña* mountain
☐ **cuento** story
☐ **niñitas** *DIM* little girls · *niña* girl · *niño* boy
☐ **mágico** *ADJ* magic
☐ **no llovía** it didn't rain · *llover* to rain
☐ **diviértanse** *IMP* have fun · *divertirse* to have fun

🎬 Mr. Sir climbs into his truck and drives away.

☐ **semillas** seeds · *semilla* seed
☐ **girasol** *NM* sunflower
☐ **evitarlo** to avoid it · *evitar* to avoid
☐ **dedos** fingers · *dedo* finger
☐ **magnetos** magnets · *magneto* magnet
☐ **pegajosos** sticky · *pegajoso* sticky
☐ **pásamela** *IMP* pass it to me · *pasar* to pass
☐ **viene de regreso** he's coming back · *venir* to come · *de regreso* back
☐ **escóndelas** *IMP* hide them · *esconder* to hide
☐ **escondan** *IMP* hide · *esconder* to hide
☐ **actúen** *IMP* act · *actuar* to act
☐ **cavando** digging · *cavar* to dig
☐ **¿se están divirtiendo?** are you having fun? · *divertirse* to have fun
☐ **cachorro** pup, puppy

## 15 The Warden's Recipe   2:47

**Phrases to Listen For**
**hay que** it's necessary
**me llevan ventaja** they've put one over on me, they're ahead of me
**echo un vistazo** I take a look

**Names**
X-Ray, Lou

🎬 Mr. Sir and Stanley arrive at the warden's residence.

☐ **excavación** excavation, dig, hole
☐ **se escapa** it's escaping, it's getting out · *escaparse* to be escaping, to be getting out
☐ **aire** *NM* air
☐ **llenando** filling · *llenar* to fill
☐ **garrafas** water bottles · *garrafa* water bottle
☐ **camioneta** pickup truck
☐ **semillas** seeds · *semilla* seed
☐ **estuche** *NM* case
☐ **repisa** shelf, ledge
☐ **barniz de uñas** fingernail polish · *barniz NM* varnish, polish · *uña* fingernail
☐ **condenados** condemned · *condenado* condemned · *condenar* to condemn
☐ **mocosos** snot-nosed children, snot-nosed brats · *mocoso PEJ* snot-nosed child, snot-nosed brat
☐ **espalda** back
☐ **detalle** *NM* detail
☐ **filosofía** philosophy
☐ **recompensa** reward
☐ **castigo** punishment
☐ **escalofrío** goose bump, shudder
☐ **recorre** it runs up, it goes up · *recorrer* to run up, to go up, to cover [DISTANCE]
☐ **reclusos** inmates, prisoners · *recluso* inmate, prisoner
☐ **partida** group, bunch
☐ **desconfiables** untrustworthy people · *desconfiable NMF* untrustworthy person
☐ **ventaja** advantage
☐ **echo un vistazo** I glance · *echar un vistazo* to glance · *echar* to throw · *vistazo* glance

🎬 The warden paints her nails.

☐ **ingrediente** *NM* ingredient
☐ **secreto** secret
☐ **veneno** venom
☐ **cascabel** *NF* rattlesnake
☐ **adoro** I love, I adore · *adorar* to love, to adore
☐ **inofensivo** harmless
☐ **seca** it dries · *secar* to dry
☐ **cubriendo** covering · *cubrir* to cover
☐ **saco** sack
☐ **kilos** kilos, kilograms · *kilo* kilo, kilogram
☐ **comérselas** to eat them · *comerse* to eat, to eat up
☐ **mitad** *NF* half
☐ **revise** *IMP* look, check, see · *revisar* to check, to verify, to review

🎬 The warden scratches Mr. Sir's face.

☐ **respeto** respect
☐ **afecto** affection
☐ **sugiero** I suggest · *sugerir* to suggest
☐ **fumaba** you smoked · *fumar* to smoke

## 16 Stanley Teaches Zero to Read 11:21

### Phrases to Listen For

**no me interesa** I don't care, it doesn't matter to me
**¿qué le pasó?** what happened to him?
**para nada** not at all
**más vale que no** you'd better not
**todo el mundo** everyone
**¿te burlas de mí?** are you making fun of me?
**tienes que** you have to
**lo que** what
**todo el día** all day
**de ahora en adelante** from now on
**dale una lección** IMP teach him a lesson
**a ver** let's see
**tuve que** I had to
**igual que** just like

### Names

Kate Barlow, Pendanski, Squid, Laney Park, Theodore, Armpit, Alan, Ricky, Ziggy, Zigzag, X-Ray

🎬 Stanley returns to the holes.

☐ **excavó** he dug · *excavar* to dig
☐ **China** China
☐ **excavan** they dig · *excavar* to dig
☐ **chinos** Chinese · *chino* ADJ Chinese
☐ **semillas** seeds · *semilla* seed
☐ **ladrón** NM thief

🎬 Mr. Sir is in the cafeteria. The boys walk through the line.

☐ **desaparezca** SUBJ it disappears · *desaparecer* to disappear
☐ **sal** NF salt
☐ **catorce** fourteen
☐ **cebollas** onions · *cebolla* onion
☐ **feo** ugly
☐ **cara** face
☐ **más vale que no** you'd better not
☐ **raro** strange
☐ **rostro** face
☐ **guapo** handsome, good-looking
☐ **limpio** clean

🎬 Pendanski speaks in the cafeteria.

☐ **invaluable** invaluable
☐ **lección** lesson
☐ **sensible** sensitive

🎬 Mr. Sir distributes water.

☐ **siguiente** next
☐ **sediento** thirsty
☐ **ka** NF K [LETTER]
☐ **be** NF B [LETTER]

☐ **borra** IMP erase, wipe off · *borrar* to erase, to wipe off
☐ **sonrisa** smile
☐ **tubo** tube
☐ **lápiz labial** lipstick · *lápiz* NM pencil
☐ **iniciales** initials · *inicial* NF initial
☐ **cariñosa** loving, caring, affectionate · *cariñoso* loving, caring, affectionate

🎬 "I Will Survive" plays through a Kate Barlow scene sequence. Stanley sits next to Zero in the tent, teaching him to read.

☐ **zeta** NF Z [LETTER]
☐ **e** NF E [LETTER]
☐ **erre** NF R [LETTER]
☐ **o** NF O [LETTER]
☐ **lento** slow
☐ **¿te burlas de mi?** are you making fun of me? · *burlarse* to make fun
☐ **me burlo de ti** I'm making fun of you · *burlarse* to make fun
☐ **acabaríamos** we would finish · *acabar* to finish
☐ **sencilla** simple · *sencillo* simple

🎬 Stanley and Zero dig.

☐ **veintiséis** twenty-six
☐ **letras** letters · *letra* letter
☐ **quinto** fifth
☐ **odio** I hate · *odiar* to hate
☐ **contestar** to answer

🎬 X-Ray and Squid look down on Stanley and Zero.

☐ **sencillo** simple
☐ **esclavo** slave

🎬 Zero writes. Stanley is seated next to him.

☐ **eme** NF M [LETTER]
☐ **vago** homeless person
☐ **recuerdo** I remember · *recordar* to remember
☐ **aire** NM air
☐ **adonde** where, to where
☐ **aguardaba** she waited · *aguardar* to wait
☐ **parque** NM park
☐ **edificio** building
☐ **contratar** to hire
☐ **investigadores** investigators · *investigador* investigator
☐ **averiguara** SUBJ it finds out · *averiguar* to find out
☐ **túnel** NM tunnel
☐ **puente** NM bridge

🎬 Armpit walks by Stanley and Zero.

☐ **esclavitud** NF slavery
☐ **varios** several

□ **quesos** cheeses · *queso* cheese
□ **manzanas** apples · *manzana* apple
□ **galletas** cookies · *galleta* cookie
□ **sándwich** NM sandwich
□ **miserables** miserable · *miserable* miserable
□ **groserías** rudeness, vulgarity · *grosería* rudeness, vulgarity
□ **tacaño** stingy

🎬 Zigzag offers Stanley a cracker.

□ **galleta** cookie, cracker
□ **oí** I heard · *oír* to hear
□ **cavaré** I will dig · *cavar* to dig
□ **paz** NF peace

🎬 Zigzag sticks the cracker in Stanley's mouth.

□ **trágatela** IMP swallow it · *tragar* to swallow
□ **golpéalo** IMP hit him · *golpear* to hit
□ **defiéndete** IMP defend yourself · *defenderse* to defend oneself
□ **asfixiar** to suffocate
□ **párenlo** IMP stop him · *parar* to stop

🎬 The warden's car is parked amid the holes. Pendanski explains what happened.

□ **básicamente** basically
□ **estaba ahorcando** he was choking · *ahorcar* to choke
□ **interesante** interesting
□ **ahorcar** to choke
□ **encima** on top
□ **se acaloró** he became upset, he got worked up · *acalorarse* to become upset, to get worked up
□ **sangre** NF blood
□ **hervir** to boil

🎬 Zigzag talks to the warden.

□ **ardiente** burning
□ **ha cavado** he has dug · *cavar* to dig
□ **a diario** daily
□ **no estás cavando** you aren't digging · *cavar* to dig

🎬 Pendanski makes fun of Zero.

□ **suma** IMP add · *sumar* to add
□ **genio** genius

🎬 The warden scolds Stanley.

□ **lecciones** lessons · *lección* lesson
□ **lectura** reading

🎬 Pendanski continues to ridicule Zero.

□ **intención** intention
□ **sana** wholesome, good, healthy · *sano* wholesome, good, healthy

□ **mente** NF mind
□ **estresada** stressed · *estresado* stressed · *estresar* to stress, to cause stress to
□ **causa** it causes · *causar* to cause
□ **cerebro** brain
□ **reto** challenge
□ **hache** NF H [LETTER]
□ **o** NF O [LETTER]
□ **y** NF Y [LETTER] · *y griega* NF Y [LETTER]
□ **ese** NF S [LETTER]

## 17 Zero Runs Away                           3:22

### Phrases to Listen For

**ya lo sé** I already know
**tengo muchas nauseas** I feel really nauseous
**lo que sea** SUBJ whatever
**de todas formas** anyway, in any event
**sentido del humor** sense of humor
**no se lo tomen tan a pecho** IMP don't take it so hard, don't take it to heart so much

🎬 Zero runs away.

□ **no dispare** IMP don't shoot · *disparar* to shoot
□ **investigación** investigation
□ **malinterpretó** you misunderstood · *malinterpretar* to misunderstand, to misinterpret
□ **guardias** guards · *guardia* NMF guard [PERSON]
□ **fuentes** water sources · *fuente* NF water source
□ **siesta** nap
□ **rudo** tough

🎬 Mr. Sir talks to the warden and Pendanski in a tent.

□ **tengo muchas nauseas** I'm feeling queasy · *nausea* nausea
□ **haciendo pucheros** pouting · *hacer pucheros* to pout
□ **arrestado** arrested · *arrestar* to arrest
□ **melindroso** prissy, fussy
□ **consejero** counselor
□ **cuestionarnos** to question us · *cuestionar* to question, to discuss a matter
□ **registros** records · *registro* record
□ **quemados** burned · *quemado* burned · *quemar* to burn
□ **estatales** state · *estatal* ADJ state
□ **computadora** computer
□ **insisto** I insist · *insistir* to insist
□ **reclamar** to complain

🎬 Stanley enters the tent.

□ **sangre** NF blood

🎬 At night, Stanley and the others lie on their cots talking.

☐ **cuerpo** body
☐ **buitres** vultures · *buitre NM* vulture
☐ **qué asqueroso** how sickening
☐ **sentido del humor** sense of humor
☐ **no se lo tomen tan a pecho** *IMP* don't take it so much to heart · *tomar a pecho* to take to heart

🎬 Stanley's grandfather describes Elya Yelnats' ordeal.

☐ **abandonó** she abandoned · *abandonar* to abandon
☐ **desierto** desert
☐ **comida** food
☐ **dieciséis** sixteen
☐ **sobrevivió** he survived · *sobrevivir* to survive
☐ **se refugió** he sought refuge, he took refuge · *refugiarse* to seek refuge, to take refuge
☐ **pulgar** *NM* thumb

## 18 Stanley Goes After Zero  7:10

### Phrases to Listen For
**ya es hora** it's time already
**tienes que** you have to
**estás en líos** you are in trouble
**hay que** it's necessary

### Names
Twitch, Sploosh, Kate Barlow, Mary Lou

🎬 In the cafeteria, new arrival Twitch describes his crime.

☐ **planeé** I planned · *planear* to plan
☐ **no lo resistía** I couldn't resist (*LIT* I didn't resist) · *resistir* to resist
☐ **nervioso** nervous
☐ **volante** *NM* steering wheel
☐ **convertible** *NM* convertible

🎬 Mr. Sir gets out of the truck.

☐ **descanso** rest
☐ **saltes** *SUBJ* you jump · *saltar* to jump
☐ **fila** line
☐ **irritable** irritable
☐ **sensible** sensitive
☐ **lárgate** *IMP* get away · *largarse* to get away, to move away
☐ **me estoy hartando de** I am getting sick of, I am getting tired of · *hartarse de* to be sick of, to be tired of
☐ **te metas en la fila** *SUBJ* you take cuts in line, you cut in line · *meterse en la fila* to take cuts in line, to cut in line (*LIT* to put yourself in the line)
☐ **violentos** violent · *violento* violent

☐ **dura** tough · *duro* tough
☐ **lección** lesson

🎬 Stanley drives away in Mr. Sir's truck.

☐ **mete velocidad** *IMP* accelerate · *meter velocidad* to accelerate · *velocidad* speed
☐ **detén** *IMP* stop · *detener* to stop
☐ **camioneta** pickup truck
☐ **demonio** demon

🎬 After crashing, Stanley runs away.

☐ **sal** *IMP* get out · *salir* to leave, to go out
☐ **¡huye!** *IMP* run!, get away! · *huir* to flee, to run away
☐ **estás en líos** you are in trouble · *estar en líos* to be in trouble
☐ **quinto** fifth
☐ **harto de** sick of, tired of, up to here with

🎬 Pendanski surveys the desert with binoculars.

☐ **correcto** correct
☐ **completen** *IMP* complete, finish · *completar* to complete, to finish
☐ **sección** section
☐ **caven** *SUBJ* you all dig · *cavar* to dig
☐ **respecto a** with respect to
☐ **quince** fifteen
☐ **reportaré** I will report · *reportar* to report
☐ **huida** flight, running away
☐ **helicópteros** helicopters · *helicóptero* helicopter
☐ **área** area
☐ **exacto** exactly

🎬 Stanley finds Zero.

☐ **bolsa** bag
☐ **vacía** empty · *vacío* empty
☐ **rico** excellent [FOOD]
☐ **durazno** peach
☐ **envuélvelo** *IMP* wrap it up · *envolver* to wrap
☐ **mételo** *IMP* put it in · *meter* to put in, to insert
☐ **labial** lipstick

🎬 Stanley and Zero climb out from under the boat.

☐ **inicio** beginning
☐ **montaña** mountain
☐ **figura** figure, shape

## 19 Stanley and Zero Climb "God's Thumb"  6:41

### Phrases to Listen For
**¿en serio?** really?, seriously?
**antes de que** before
**qué bien** excellent

**se me ocurre** what I think of, what occurs to me
**¿qué te pasó?** what happened?
**conejo de pascua** Easter Bunny
**el ratón Pérez** Tooth Fairy

## Names

Mary Lou, Sploosh

🎬 God's Thumb stretches high above the desert. Stanley and Zero hike and climb.

- □ **sobrevivió** he survived · *sobrevivir* to survive
- □ **cima** peak, top
- □ **pulgar** *NM* thumb
- □ **oscurezca** *SUBJ* it gets dark · *oscurecer* to get dark
- □ **tienda** store
- □ **helados** ice cream cones, ice cream · *helado* ice cream cone, ice cream
- □ **se me antoja** I feel like having, I fancy (*LIT* it is fancied by me) · *antojarse* to feel like, to fancy
- □ **bikini** *NM* bikini

🎬 Zero is above Stanley as they climb the face of the mountain.

- □ **no voltees** *IMP* don't look back, don't look down, don't turn around · *voltear* to look back, to turn around
- □ **qué horror** yikes, how horrible · *horror NM* horror
- □ **me duele** it hurts, it hurts me · *doler* to hurt
- □ **estoy sangrando** I am bleeding · *sangrar* to bleed
- □ **aguanta** *IMP* hang on, hold on · *aguantar* to hang on, to hold on
- □ **me arde** it stings me · *arder* to sting, to burn
- □ **trata** *IMP* try · *tratar* to try
- □ **ya me harté** I'm already fed up, I'm already sick (of), I'm already tired (of) · *hartarse* to get fed up, to get sick (of), to get tired (of)

🎬 The boys from camp walk near the holes.

- □ **conejo de pascua** Easter Bunny · *conejo* bunny, rabbit · *pascua* Easter
- □ **ratón Pérez** Tooth Fairy
- □ **trago** drink
- □ **huyó** he fled, he took off · *huir* to flee, to take off, to run away
- □ **estilo** style

🎬 Stanley and Zero continue their climb.

- □ **deletrea** *IMP* spell · *deletrear* to spell
- □ **erre** *NF* R [LETTER]
- □ **ce** *NF* C [LETTER]
- □ **roca** rock
- □ **practicando** practicing · *practicar* to practice

🎬 Zero falls.

- □ **¡ánimo!** *EXP* come on!, get up!, get going!
- □ **desliza ésta** *IMP* slide this · *deslizar* to slide
- □ **cómodo** comfortable
- □ **llenar** to fill

🎬 Stanley carries Zero up the mountain.

- □ **montaña** mountain
- □ **cantas** you sing · *cantar* to sing
- □ **mosquitos** mosquitoes · *mosquito* mosquito

🎬 Stanley drinks water.

- □ **qué delicia** what a delight · *delicia* delight
- □ **fresca** fresh · *fresco* fresh
- □ **prueba** *IMP* try, taste · *probar* to try, to taste
- □ **rica** excellent · *rico* excellent [FOOD]
- □ **cebolla** onion
- □ **carpintero** woodpecker (*LIT* carpenter)
- □ **corteza** bark
- □ **lobo** wolf
- □ **aguarda** he waits · *aguardar* to wait
- □ **hambriento** hungry
- □ **aúlla** he howls · *aullar* to howl
- □ **luna** moon

## 20 A Cure for Stinky Feet 1:08

### Phrase to Listen For

**no huele a nada** it doesn't smell like anything

### Name

Pa

🎬 Stanley's father works on his experiment at the stove.

- □ **oler** to smell
- □ **millón** *NM* million
- □ **olerlo** to smell it · *oler* to smell
- □ **no huele** it doesn't smell · *oler* to smell
- □ **no apesta** it doesn't stink · *apestar* to stink
- □ **hueles** you smell · *oler* to smell
- □ **cebollas** onions · *cebolla* onion
- □ **duraznos** peaches · *durazno* peach
- □ **secreto** secret
- □ **no olemos** we don't smell · *oler* to smell

## 21 Zero Confesses 4:36

### Phrases to Listen For

**ni siquiera** not even
**no me importa** it doesn't matter to me
**lo que** what
**en orden** in order

**qué bien** excellent
**¿qué tal?** what about?

## Names
Twitch, Camp Green Lake

🎬 Onion in hand, Stanley walks toward a sleeping Zero.

□ **levántate** *IMP* get up · *levantarse* to get up, to get out of bed
□ **cebollín** chives
□ **flatulento** flatulent
□ **dormiste** you slept · *dormir* to sleep
□ **tiré** I threw · *tirar* to throw, to throw away
□ **tenis** tennis shoes, athletic shoes · *teni NM* tennis shoe, athletic shoe

🎬 Zero walks by a series of bunks.

□ **donaba** he donated · *donar* to donate
□ **refugio de los indigentes** homeless shelter · *refugio* shelter · *indigente NMF* poverty-stricken person, destitute person
□ **no lo soporté** I couldn't stand it · *soportar* to stand, to tolerate
□ **famoso** famous
□ **recuerdo** I remember · *recordar* to remember
□ **patrullas** police cars, patrol cars · *patrulla* police car, patrol car
□ **tras** behind
□ **siguiente** next
□ **aparador** shop window, store window
□ **destino** destiny

🎬 A car drives across the desert.

□ **cadáver** *NM* cadaver
□ **jaguar** *NM* jaguar
□ **impedir** to stop, to impede
□ **abogada** lawyer, attorney · *abogado* lawyer, attorney
□ **derecho** right
□ **proteger** to protect
□ **firmada** signed · *firmado* signed · *firmar* to sign
□ **corte** *NF* court of law
□ **farsa** farce
□ **advierto** I warn · *advertir* to warn

🎬 After the attorney leaves, the warden, Mr. Sir, and Pendanski talk in the office.

□ **huyó** he fled, he ran away · *huir* to flee, to run away
□ **liberarían** they would free · *liberar* to free, to liberate
□ **frito** fried · *freír* to fry

🎬 At night, on God's Thumb, Stanley talks to Zero.

□ **me alegra** I'm happy (*LIT* it makes me happy) · *alegrar* to make happy
□ **arrojaras** *SUBJ* you threw · *arrojar* to throw
□ **puente** *NM* bridge
□ **por causa de** because of
□ **maldición familiar** family curse · *maldición* curse · *familiar ADJ* family
□ **pulgar** *NM* thumb
□ **rara** strange · *raro* strange
□ **sensación** sensation
□ **estrellas** stars · *estrella* star
□ **exacto** exactly
□ **efecto** effect

## 22 Kissin' Kate's Last Stand          2:35

### Phrases to Listen For
**no hay** there is no
**lo que** what
**hay que** it's necessary

### Names
Sam, Trout, Linda Miller, Linda Walker, Houston, Katherine, Sam

🎬 Kate leans against the boat. Sam arrives.

□ **hace calor** it's hot · *calor NM* heat
□ **yo lo reparo** I'll fix it (*LIT* I fix it) · *reparar* to fix, to repair

🎬 Trout Walker arrives and points a rifle at Kate.

□ **no te asesinaré** I won't kill you · *asesinar* to kill, to murder
□ **no me engañes** *IMP* don't lie to me, don't mislead me · *engañar* to mislead, to deceive
□ **banco** bank
□ **anteriores** previous, last · *anterior* previous
□ **trece** thirteen
□ **estudiante** *NMF* student
□ **no ha llovido** it hasn't rained · *llover* to rain
□ **asesinaron** they killed · *asesinar* to kill, to murder
□ **desesperado** desperate
□ **dispara** *IMP* shoot · *disparar* to shoot
□ **inmenso** immense
□ **cavarán** you all will dig · *cavar* to dig
□ **siguientes** next · *siguiente* next
□ **cien** one hundred

🎬 Kate picks up the lizard.

□ **nena** babe, baby · *nene NM* babe, baby
□ **inicia** *IMP* begin, start · *iniciar* to begin, to start
□ **sondeo** searching

## 23 One More Hole 11:24

### Phrases to Listen For

**claro que** of course
**tengo la culpa** I'm to blame
**delincuentes juveniles** juvenile delinquents
**tal vez** maybe, perhaps
**no creo que** I don't think
**hay que** it's necessary
**¿qué tal si...?** what if ...?
**al menos** at least
**por qué** why
**tan pronto** so soon
**no tendrán que** they won't have to
**nada tiene sentido** nothing makes sense
**por aquí** around here
**qué rayos** what the heck
**tengo que** I have to
**no tiene nada que ver** it has nothing to do with
**no hay nada que hacer** there is nothing to do
**por supuesto** of course
**da gusto verte** great to see you
**de verdad** really
**no se olviden de mí** *IMP* don't forget about me

### Names

Kate Barlow, Earl, Hector, Carla, Walker, Theodore, Marion Sevillo, Pendanski

🎬 Stanley and Zero run from hole to hole.

☐ **segurísimo** positively, absolutely
☐ **tardado** time-consuming, slow · *tardar* to take a long time

🎬 Mr. Sir and Pendanski argue in front of the truck. Zero sneaks by.

☐ **camioneta** pickup truck
☐ **llave** *NF* key
☐ **adentro** inside
☐ **enfrente de** in front of
☐ **banda** gang
☐ **delincuentes juveniles** juvenile delinquents · *delincuente* *NMF* delinquent · *juvenil* juvenile, young
☐ **no me insultes** *IMP* don't insult me · *insultar* to insult
☐ **tanque** *NM* tank
☐ **trajeras** *SUBJ* you bring · *traer* to bring
☐ **labios** lips · *labio* lip
☐ **testarudo** pig-headed person, stubborn person
☐ **traértela** to bring it to you · *traer* to bring
☐ **cara** face
☐ **cortada** cut · *cortado* cut · *cortar* to cut
☐ **Neandertal** *NM* Neanderthal
☐ **mecánico** mechanic

☐ **no me avientes cosas** *IMP* don't throw things at me · *aventar* to throw

🎬 Zero arrives at the hole with a shovel.

☐ **adelantaste** you made progress · *adelantar* to make progress, to move forward, to get ahead
☐ **bastante** a lot, plenty
☐ **diamantes** diamonds · *diamante* *NM* diamond
☐ **cariñosa** loving, affectionate · *cariñoso* loving, affectionate
☐ **enterrara** *SUBJ* she buries · *enterrar* to bury
☐ **tesoro** treasure
☐ **hondo** deep
☐ **ancho** wide
☐ **pandilla** gang

🎬 Stanley and Zero raise the chest.

☐ **horror** *NM* horror

🎬 Pendanski arrives at the hole.

☐ **adivina** *IMP* guess · *adivinar* to guess
☐ **inocente** innocent
☐ **ayer** yesterday
☐ **abogada** lawyer, attorney · *abogado* lawyer, attorney
☐ **recogerte** to get you, to pick you up · *recoger* to get, to pick up
☐ **cadáver** *NM* cadaver
☐ **obsequiarle** to give her · *obsequiar* to give a gift
☐ **varios** several
☐ **elegir** to choose
☐ **dueño** owner
☐ **se secó** it dried up · *secarse* to dry up
☐ **incluso** including, even

🎬 The warden, as a girl, digs in the lake.

☐ **ya me harté de** I'm already fed up with, I'm already tired of, I'm already sick of · *hartarse* to be fed up, to be tired (of), to be sick (of)
☐ **lástima** pity
☐ **cavando** digging · *cavar* to dig

🎬 The next day, the warden, Mr. Sir, and Pendanski stand over Stanley, Zero, and the lizards.

☐ **asesinarlos** to kill them · *asesinar* to kill, to murder
☐ **saltarían** they would jump · *saltar* to jump
☐ **no los han mordido** they haven't bitten you · *morder* to bite
☐ **galletas** cookies · *galleta* cookie
☐ **correcto** correct
☐ **bocas** mouths · *boca* mouth
☐ **severamente** severely

□ **reprendidos** reprimanded · *reprendido* reprimanded · *reprender* to reprimand
□ **imaginación** imagination
□ **corra** *IMP* run · *correr* to run

🎬 The warden and Pendanski leave. Mr. Sir remains.

□ **nada tiene sentido** nothing makes sense · *tener sentido* to make sense
□ **apellido** last name
□ **al revés** backwards

🎬 Several officials walk with Pendanski amid the holes.

□ **teléfono** telephone
□ **disponible** available
□ **riesgo** risk
□ **irrumpió en** he burst in · *irrumpir* to burst
□ **cabaña** cabin
□ **huyendo** fleeing · *huir* to flee
□ **qué rayos** what the heck
□ **han tratado** you have tried · *tratar* to try
□ **sugiere** you suggest · *sugerir* to suggest
□ **hubiera entregado** *SUBJ* you had given · *entregar* to give, to deliver, to hand over
□ **ladrón** *NM* thief
□ **morderán** they will bite · *morder* to bite

🎬 Stanley and Zero climb out of the hole.

□ **suéltelo** *IMP* let it go · *soltar* to let go
□ **ladronzuelo** little thief
□ **atrapé** I caught, I trapped · *atrapar* to catch, to trap
□ **directamente** directly
□ **prisión** prison
□ **cargos** charges · *cargo* charge
□ **en vista de** in sight of · *vista* sight
□ **circunstancias** circumstances · *circunstancia* circumstance
□ **directo** directly

🎬 The chest is in the car trunk. The attorney and the warden argue.

□ **propiedad** property
□ **ladrones** thieves · *ladrón* *NM* thief
□ **pon** *IMP* put · *poner* to put, to place
□ **cajuela** trunk
□ **descuiden** *IMP* relax, don't worry · *descuidar* to not worry
□ **archivo** file

🎬 The boys from the camp spot Stanley and Zero in front of the office.

□ **alimentabas** you were food for, you nourished · *alimentar* to feed, to give nourishment
□ **buitres** vultures · *buitre* *NM* vulture

□ **apestas** you stink · *apestar* to stink
□ **comiste** you ate · *comer* to eat
□ **cebolla** onion
□ **hueles** you smell · *oler* to smell
□ **apestan** they stink, they smell awful · *apestar* to stink

🎬 Mr. Sir and Pendanski exit the office.

□ **archivos** files · *archivo* file
□ **decentes** decent · *decente* decent
□ **investigación** investigation
□ **instalaciones** facilities · *instalación* facility
□ **bolígrafo** ballpoint pen
□ **me preste** *SUBJ* you loan · *prestar* to lend, to loan
□ **lápiz** *NM* pencil
□ **papel** *NM* paper

🎬 Armpit talks to Stanley.

□ **lamenta** he is sorry · *lamentar* to be sorry

🎬 One of the officials recognizes Mr. Sir and places him against the wall.

□ **violas** you are violating, you violate · *violar* to violate
□ **libertad condicional** parole · *libertad* *NF* freedom, liberty
□ **portando** carrying · *portar* to carry
□ **arma** weapon
□ **la menor idea** the slightest idea · *menor* least
□ **bajo arresto** under arrest
□ **instalación** facility
□ **jurisdicción** jurisdiction
□ **payasos** clowns · *payaso* clown
□ **sistema** *NM* system
□ **justicia** justice
□ **despídete** *IMP* say good-bye · *despedirse* to say good-bye

🎬 Clouds roll in. It is soon raining.

□ **nubes** clouds · *nube* *NF* cloud
□ **llover** to rain
□ **afuera** outside
□ **reza** *IMP* pray · *rezar* to pray
□ **te extrañaré** I will miss you · *extrañar* to miss

🎬 An officer reads the warden, Mr. Sir, and Pendanski their rights.

□ **derecho** right
□ **permanecer** to remain
□ **desisten de** you give up · *desistir de* to give up
□ **corte** *NF* court of law
□ **diviértanse** *IMP* have fun · *divertirse* to have fun
□ **lluvia** rain

## 24 | Opening the Chest/ End Credits

9:36

### Phrases to Listen For
**a ver** let's see
**¿cuánto vale?** how much is it worth?
**toda la eternidad** for all eternity

### Names
Hector Zeroni, AT&T, Elya Yelnats,
Madame Zeroni, Sploosh

🎬 Stanley's father stands in front of the chest.

☐ **cofre** *NM* chest
☐ **ábrelo** *IMP* open it · *abrir* to open
☐ **crucen** *IMP* cross · *cruzar* to cross
☐ **dedos** fingers · *dedo* finger
☐ **rudo** tough
☐ **mitad** *NF* half
☐ **que se divida** *SUBJ* it will be split, it will be divided · *dividirse* to be split, to be divided
☐ **boichik** boy [YIDDISH]
☐ **veinticinco** twenty-five
☐ **fecha** date
☐ **mil novecientos cinco** 1905 [DATE], one thousand nine hundred five
☐ **¿cuánto vale?** how much is it worth? · *valer* to be worth
☐ **millones** millions · *millón NM* million

🎬 Hector's mother steps off the bus.

☐ **contratar** to hire
☐ **investigadores** investigators · *investigador* investigator
☐ **resultó** it turned out · *resultar* to turn out, to result

☐ **tatara nieto** great-grandson · *nieto* grandson, grandchild
☐ **vecinos** neighbors · *vecino* neighbor

🎬 Zero jumps into a pool.

☐ **liberaron** they freed · *liberar* to free, to liberate
☐ **consejeros** counselors · *consejero* counselor
☐ **no se preocuparán por** they will not worry about, they will not be worried about · *preocuparse* to worry, to be worried
☐ **cebollas** onions · *cebolla* onion
☐ **función** event
☐ **piscina** pool

🎬 In a commercial, Sweetfeet steps out of a shower, a towel on his shoulder.

☐ **fanáticos** fans, enthusiasts · *fanático* fan, enthusiast
☐ **pie** *NM* foot
☐ **oloroso** smelly
☐ **compañeros** teammates · *compañero* teammate
☐ **aplico** I apply · *aplicar* to apply, to put on
☐ **aroma** *NM* aroma
☐ **disponible** available
☐ **presentación** presentation, format, style
☐ **colección** collection
☐ **producto** product
☐ **industrias** industries · *industria* industry
☐ **ka** *NF* K [LETTER]
☐ **be** *NF* B [LETTER]
☐ **me agrada** I like (*LIT* it pleases me) · *agradar* to please
☐ **olor** smell

🎬 A statue holds a shovel.

☐ **llenarán** you will fill · *llenar* to fill
☐ **eternidad** eternity

# Home Alone

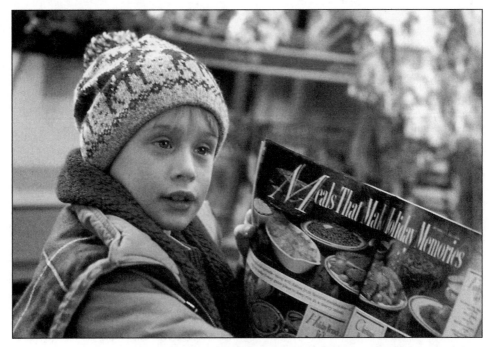

**Señorita, tengo ocho años, ¿cree que estaría aquí solo? Yo creo que no.**
*Ma'am, I'm eight years old. You think I would be here alone? I don't think so.*

| | |
|---|---|
| GENRE | Comedy/Holiday Favorite |
| YEAR | 1990 |
| DIRECTOR | Chris Columbus |
| CAST | Macaulay Culkin, Joe Pesci, Daniel Stern, Catherine O'Hara, John Heard, John Candy |
| STUDIO | Twentieth Century Fox |

"Rockin' Around the Christmas Tree," "Run Rudolph Run," "Have Yourself a Merry Little Christmas" and other Christmas classics provide a nostalgic background for this tale of a young boy who is accidentally left home alone when his entire family travels to Paris for the holidays. Kevin's adventures defending his home against the inept "Wet Bandits," Harry and Marv, balance tender moments with great slapstick comedy. Spanish learners will get good practice with more advanced language rules, and there is rich vocabulary related to Christmas, family, friends, neighbors, and travel.

## BASIC VOCABULARY

### Names
Kevin, McCallister, Buzz (pronounced more like "Boz"), Frank, Peter, Marvin, Harry, Paris, Nueva York

### Nouns
- **aeropuerto** airport · *No fueron al **aeropuerto**.* They didn't go to the airport.
- **cretino** cretin, idiot · *Se comporta como un **cretino**.* He acts like an idiot.
- **inútil** NMF incompetent person · *Kevin, eres un completo **inútil**.* Kevin, you're a complete incompetent.
- **obsequios** gifts · *obsequio* gift · *Quiero por favor decirle que en vez de **obsequios** este año, sólo quiero recuperar a mi familia.* I want to tell him please that instead of gifts this Christmas, I just want to have my family back.
- **rostro** face · *Oye, voy a darte hasta la cuenta de diez para que saques tu feo, cobarde e inútil **rostro** de mi propiedad antes de que te llene los intestinos de plomo.* Hey, I'm going to give you to the count of ten to get your ugly, cowardly, and useless face off my property before I fill your guts with lead.
- **vuelo** flight · *Tomamos el **vuelo** matutino, el que tú no quisiste esperar.* We took the morning flight, the one that you didn't want to wait for.

### Verbs
- **aguarde** IMP wait · *aguardar* to wait · ***Aguarde**, tengo un cupón para eso.* Wait, I have a coupon for that.
- **guarda** he keeps · *guardar* to keep, to save · *Ahí es donde **guarda** a sus víctimas.* That's where he keeps his victims.

### Other
- **feo** ugly, awful · *Es oscuro y hay cosas muy raras ahí, y huele muy **feo**.* It's dark and there are strange things there, and it smells awful.

## 1 Main Titles 3:46

### Phrases to Listen For
- **casi no me falta nada** I don't have much left
- **por favor** please
- **claro que** of course
- **¿por qué?** why?
- **al teléfono** on the telephone
- **ni siquiera es** it's not even
- **fuera de aquí** get out of here
- **¿qué es lo que pasa?** what's happening?
- **así es** that's right
- **no tienes nada que hacer** you have nothing to do
- **otra vez** again

- **has subido de peso** you have gained weight
- **lo siento** I'm sorry
- **¿para qué?** what for?
- **tal vez** maybe, perhaps

### Names
Trish, Montreal, Frank, Kate, Leslie, Fuller, Tracy, Todd

As the film begins, the following actors' names are heard with Spanish pronunciation: Macaulay Culkin, Joe Pesci, Daniel Stern, John Heard, Roberts Blossom, Catherine O'Hara, Angela Goethals, Devin Ratray, Gary Bamman, Hillary Wolf, Larry Hankin.

- **valija** suitcase
- **secadora** hairdryer, dryer
- **adiós** good-bye
- **sala** living room
- **cepillo** brush

Kevin's mother is talking on the telephone.

- **locura** craziness
- **película** movie, film
- **al teléfono** on the telephone
- **adultos** adults · *adulto* adult
- **se comporta** he's behaving · *comportarse* to behave
- **perrera** dog pound
- **cuelga** IMP hang up · *colgar* to hang up [TELEPHONE]
- **oblígame** IMP make me · *obligar* to make, to force, to obligate

Kevin's dad enters the bedroom and talks to his wife, then talks to Kevin.

- **convertidor de voltaje** voltage converter · *convertidor* converter · *voltaje* NM voltage
- **afeitarme** to shave myself · *afeitarse* to shave oneself
- **barba** beard
- **recoge** IMP pick up · *recoger* to pick up, to gather
- **micro-máquinas** micro-machines · *micro-máquina* micro-machine
- **pisó** she stepped on · *pisar* to step on, to walk on
- **cuello** neck
- **cochera** garage
- **pegamento** glue
- **¿quemé...?** did I burn ...?, did I burn down ...? · *quemar* to burn, to burn down
- **adornos** ornaments, decorations · *adorno* ornament, decoration
- **anzuelos** fish hooks · *anzuelo* fish hook
- **lombrices** worms · *lombriz* NF worm
- **secas** dry, dried · *seco* dry, dried

□ **embarradas** smeared · *embarrado* smeared ·
*embarrar* to smear, to spread
□ **peso** weight
□ **empaca** *IMP* pack · *empacar* to pack

🎬 Kevin looks straight ahead and says, "¡Empacar!"

□ **champú** *NM* shampoo
□ **pizzas** pizzas · *pizza* pizza
□ **orfelinato** orphanage

## 2 "I'm Living Alone!" 2:00

### Phrases to Listen For
**lo que** what
**tiene razón** she's right
**¿por qué?** why?
**de todos modos** in any case, anyway
**tienes que** you have to
**un par de semanas** a couple of weeks

### Names
Megan, Jeff, Linnie, Rob, Fuller, Marley

🎬 Kevin talks with family members about how and
what to pack.

□ **empacar** to pack
□ **valija** suitcase
□ **lástima** pity, too bad
□ **bobo** idiot, dummy, fool
□ **idiota** *NMF* idiot
□ **completo** complete
□ **no hayas empacado** *SUBJ* you haven't packed ·
*empacar* to pack
□ **basura** trash, garbage
□ **enano** dwarf
□ **papel sanitario** toilet paper · *papel NM* paper
□ **franceses** French · *francés NM* French
□ **les incompétents** the incompetent ones
[FRENCH]
□ **¡fuera bomba!** bombs away!
□ **posdata** P.S., post script
□ **sofá-cama** sofa bed
□ **bebe** he drinks · *beber* to drink
□ **mojará** he will wet · *mojar* to wet, to make wet
□ **me da asco** it makes me sick, it makes me
nauseous · *dar asco* to make sick, to make one
feel sick, to make nauseous
□ **crezca** *SUBJ* I grow up · *crecer* to grow,
to grow up

🎬 Kevin's brother Buzz is talking with one of the
cousins about feeding the tarantula. Kevin enters
toward the end of the scene.

□ **¿quién alimentará?** who will feed? · *alimentar*
to feed, to give nourishment

□ **tarántula** tarantula
□ **ración** ration, helping
□ **triple** triple
□ **ratones** mice · *ratón NM* mouse
□ **francesas** French · *francesa* French ·
*francés ADJ* French
□ **no se afeitan** they don't shave · *afeitarse* to shave
oneself
□ **axilas** arm pits · *axila* arm pit
□ **playas** beaches · *playa* beach
□ **nudistas** nude · *nudista ADJ* nude
□ **invierno** winter
□ **mocoso** *PEJ* snot-nosed kid, snot-nosed
brat
□ **te pusieras de rodillas** *SUBJ* you were to get
down on your knees · *ponerse de rodillas* to get
down on one's knees · *rodilla* knee

## 3 Old Man Marley 3:02

### Phrases to Listen For
**¿por qué?** why?
**por ahí** over there
**para que** so that
**a lo largo y a lo ancho** the length and the
width
**tal vez** maybe, perhaps
**de vacaciones** on vacation
**de paseo** on a trip
**algo parecido** something like that
**así que** so
**lo que** what

### Names
South Bend, Fuller

🎬 The boys are looking out the window at their
neighbor, "Old Man Marley."

□ **asesino** murderer, killer
□ **pala** shovel
□ **asesinó** he murdered · *asesinar* to murder,
to kill
□ **mitad** *NF* half
□ **pala para nieve** snow shovel · *pala* shovel ·
*nieve NF* snow
□ **se ha ocultado** he has been hidden · *ocultarse*
to be hidden
□ **vecindario** neighborhood
□ **arresta** it arrests · *arrestar* to arrest
□ **evidencia** evidence
□ **condenarlo** to convict him · *condenar*
to convict, to condemn
□ **cuerpos** bodies · *cuerpo* body
□ **cuestión de tiempo** matter of time ·
*cuestión* matter, question · *tiempo* time

□ **a lo largo y a lo ancho** the length and width · *largo* length · *ancho* width
□ **aceras** sidewalks · *acera* sidewalk
□ **trata** he is trying · *tratar* to try
□ **bote de basura** trash can
□ **víctimas** victims · *víctima* victim
□ **convierte** it turns, it changes · *convertir* to turn, to change, to convert
□ **momias** mummies · *momia* mummy

🎬 A "police officer" is talking to two of the youngest children.
□ **actividad** activity
□ **de vacaciones** on vacation · *vacaciones* NFPL vacation
□ **de paseo** on a trip

🎬 The pizza delivery boy enters.
□ **ciento veintidós cincuenta** $122.50, one hundred twenty-two fifty [MONEY]
□ **acertaste** you hit the mark, you answered correctly · *acertar* to hit the mark, to answer correctly
□ **pizza** pizza
□ **platos** plates · *plato* plate
□ **plástico** plastic

🎬 Kevin's dad talks with the "police officer."
□ **arrestado** under arrest · *arrestar* to arrest
□ **época de navidad** Christmas season · *época* season, time [OF THE YEAR] · *navidad* Christmas
□ **robos** robberies · *robo* robbery
□ **estamos revisando** we are checking over · *revisar* to check over, to review
□ **precauciones** precautions · *precaución* precaution
□ **relojes** timers · *reloj* NM timer
□ **automáticos** automatic · *automático* automatic
□ **cerraduras** locks · *cerradura* lock
□ **beber** to drink

**4 Spilled Milk** 2:40

## Phrases to Listen For
**lo que** what
**tiene que** he has to
**¿a qué hora?** at what time?
**tenemos que** we have to
**a las ocho** at eight o'clock
**de la mañana** in the morning
**en punto** on the dot, sharp
**los cheques de viajero** traveler's checks
**tendrá que** he will have to

**ya no hay** there is no more
**¿qué pasa?** what's happening?
**¿qué demonios?** what the devil?, what the heck?
**a propósito** on purpose
**¿por qué?** why?
**buenas noches** good night
**es el colmo** that's over the top
**lo lamento** I'm sorry
**por aquí** over here
**de nada** you're welcome
**echa de menos** he misses
**así que** so
**tengo que** I have to
**enseguida** right away
**no se preocupe** IMP don't worry

## Names
Frank, Francia, Ohio

🎬 Kevin enters the room. Everyone is sitting at the table eating pizza.
□ **vaso de plástico** plastic glass
□ **San Nicolás** St. Nicholas
□ **beber** to drink
□ **aduana** customs, customs office
□ **temprano** early
□ **a las ocho de la mañana en punto** in the morning at eight o'clock sharp · *ocho* eight · *mañana* morning · *en punto* sharp
□ **beban** SUBJ they drink · *beber* to drink
□ **leche** NF milk
□ **repartidor** delivery boy
□ **ciento veintidós dólares** $122.00, one hundred twenty-two dollars
□ **centavos** cents · *centavo* cent
□ **propina** tip [MONEY]
□ **pizzas** pizzas · *pizza* pizza
□ **doce** twelve
□ **cheques de viajero** traveler's checks · *cheque* NM check · *viajero* traveler
□ **efectivo** cash
□ **seguramente** surely
□ **sólo de queso** cheese only · *sólo* ADV only · *queso* cheese
□ **probarla** to taste it · *probar* to taste, to try
□ **no bebas** IMP don't drink · *beber* to drink
□ **refresco** soda, soft drink
□ **plato** plate

🎬 Buzz pretends to throw up and sets off a series of events that lead to total confusion.
□ **¿qué demonios te pasa a ti?** what the heck is the matter with you?, what the devil is the matter with you? · *demonio* demon, devil
□ **a propósito** on purpose
□ **odio** I hate · *odiar* to hate

□ **salchicha** sausage
□ **aceitunas** olives · *aceituna* olive

🎬 There is silence while everyone stares at Kevin.

□ **desastre** *NM* disaster
□ **cierra la boca** *IMP* shut up, be quiet ·
*cerrar la boca* to shut up, to be quiet (*LIT* to close the mouth)
□ **modales** *NMPL* manners
□ **es el colmo** that's the last straw, that's the worst ·
*colmo* extreme case, worst
□ **sucio** filthy

🎬 Kevin's mother walks with Kevin, pays for the pizza, and talks with the "police officer."

□ **basura** trash, garbage
□ **manicomio** insane asylum
□ **cuñado** brother-in-law
□ **locura** craziness
□ **reunión** meeting
□ **transferido** transferred · *transferir* to transfer
□ **echa de menos** he misses · *echar de menos* to miss, to long to see
□ **excelente** excellent
□ **castigar** to punish
□ **no se preocupe** *IMP* don't worry ·
*preocuparse* to worry

## 5 "Everyone in This Family Hates Me." 2:14

### Phrases to Listen For
**tiene que** he has to
**me da miedo** I'm afraid
**en serio** seriously
**nada de eso** not at all

### Name
Fuller

🎬 Kevin and his mother walk upstairs.

□ **quince** fifteen
□ **maltratado** mistreated · *maltratar* to mistreat
□ **se comporta mal** he misbehaves ·
*comportarse* to behave
□ **tercer** third
□ **piso** floor
□ **moja** he wets · *mojar* to wet, to make wet
□ **mojará** he will wet · *mojar* to wet, to make wet
□ **odian** they hate · *odiar* to hate
□ **San Nicolás** St. Nicholas
□ **asco** the worst, the pits
□ **resto** the rest, the remainder
□ **despertaras** *SUBJ* you wake up · *despertar* to wake up

□ **repítelo** *IMP* say it again · *repetir* to say again, to repeat

🎬 Kevin, in the attic, repeats his wish.

□ **desaparezcan** *SUBJ* they disappear ·
*desaparecer* to disappear

## 6 Head Counts Don't Always Count 5:44

### Phrases to Listen For
**no lo sé** I don't know
**a las ocho en punto** at eight o'clock sharp
**en realidad** really
**hace frío** it's cold
**tengo hambre** I'm hungry
**par de días** couple of days
**por acá** over here
**en turista** in coach
**de prisa** quickly
**por favor** please
**de verdad** real

### Names
Mitch Murphy, Orlando, Florida, Missouri, Francia, Megan, Frank, Heather, Laura, Arthur

🎬 A neighbor kid, Mitch Murphy, talks to the Airport Express driver.

□ **no lo sé** I don't know · *saber* to know
□ **a las ocho en punto** at eight o'clock sharp
□ **cruzando la calle** across the street (*LIT* crossing the street) · *cruzar* to cross · *calle NF* street
□ **recoger** to pick up
□ **camionetas** vans · *camioneta* van
□ **kilometraje** *NM* mileage [based on kilometers]
□ **¡esfúmate!** *IMP* get lost! · *esfumarse* to vanish, to disappear
□ **no se enfade** *IMP* don't get upset · *enfadarse* to get upset

🎬 The family hurriedly gets ready to leave.

□ **camioneta** van
□ **pasaportes** passports · *pasaporte NM* passport
□ **pasajes** tickets · *pasaje NM* ticket
□ **microondas** *NM* microwave oven
□ **secarlos** to dry them · *secar* to dry

🎬 The neighbor kid again talks to the driver.

□ **velocidad** speed, velocity
□ **transmisión automática** automatic transmission
□ **transmisión en las cuatro ruedas** four-wheel drive
□ **desaparece** *IMP* disappear · *desaparecer* to disappear

🎬 The children come outside and prepare to board the Airport Express. The first Spanish word easily understood in this scene is *once.*

□ **es una locura** it's crazy · *locura* craziness
□ **tengo hambre** I'm hungry · *tener hambre* to be hungry (*LIT* to have hunger)
□ **fila** line
□ **once** eleven
□ **noventa** ninety
□ **mitad** *NF* half

🎬 The parents leave the house and board the vans.

□ **positivo** positive
□ **realista** realistic
□ **reparada** repaired · *reparado* repaired · *reparar* to repair
□ **líneas telefónicas** telephone lines
□ **repararlas** to repair them · *reparar* to repair
□ **especialmente** especially
□ **incluyéndome** including me · *incluir* to include
□ **choferes** drivers · *chofer NMF* driver
□ **montaña** mountain
□ **valijas** suitcases · *valija* suitcase

🎬 The song "Run Rudolph Run" plays as the family hurries to catch the plane. At the gate, the boarding agent hurries them on board.

□ **apenas** barely, hardly
□ **asientos** seats · *asiento* seat
□ **separados** separated, scattered · *separado* separated, separate · *separar* to separate
□ **turista** coach, tourist
□ **libre** free, open

🎬 The family is now on board the plane.

□ **cinco a y be** 5-A and B
□ **cuatro a y be** 4-A and B
□ **abrigos** coats · *abrigo* coat, overcoat
□ **abrochen** *IMP* fasten · *abrochar* to fasten
□ **cinturones** seat belts · *cinturón NM* seat belt
□ **champaña** champagne
□ **gratuita** complimentary, free · *gratuito* complimentary, free
□ **ojalá** hopefully

🎬 Kevin looks for his family. The jet takes off. Listen for *bolsa* and *bolso*, both of which are words for "purse."

□ **cristal** *NM* crystal, fine glassware
□ **métalas** *IMP* put them in · *meter* to put in
□ **bolsa** purse, bag
□ **bolso** purse, bag
□ **llénela** *IMP* fill it up · *llenar* to fill
□ **se están divirtiendo mucho** they're having a lot of fun · *divertirse* to have fun

## 7 "I Made My Family Disappear!" 5:40

### Phrases to Listen For
**lo que** what
**tiene que** he has to
**no me digas** *IMP* don't tell me
**a cargo** in charge
**para que** in order to
**antes de que** before

### Names
Megan, Rod, Frank, Linnie, Snakes, Johnny, Acey

🎬 Kevin searches the house and pauses to think about things that his family had said to him.

□ **broma** joke, practical joke
□ **imaginación** imagination
□ **desaparecí a mi familia** I made my family disappear · *desaparecer* to disappear, to make disappear
□ **completo** complete, total
□ **franceses** French · *francés NM* French
□ **les incompétents** the incompetent ones [FRENCH]
□ **coma** *SUBJ* she eats · *comer* to eat
□ **tarántula** tarantula
□ **desastre** *NM* disaster
□ **quince** fifteen
□ **causar** to cause
□ **hice desaparecer** I made disappear · *hacer desaparecer* to make disappear

🎬 Kevin runs through the house and goes to Buzz's room.

□ **libre** free
□ **vestida** dressed · *vestido* dressed · *vestir* to dress
□ **qué asco** yuck · *asco* disgusting
□ **cohetes** rockets · *cohete NM* rocket
□ **guardaré** I'll keep · *guardar* to keep, to save
□ **estoy revisando** I'm going through · *revisar* to go through, to review
□ **preciados** precious · *preciado* precious
□ **tesoros** treasures · *tesoro* treasure
□ **novia** girlfriend · *novio* boyfriend

🎬 Kevin views *Angels with Filthy Souls.*

□ **mercancía** merchandise
□ **entrada** entrance
□ **¡lárgate de aquí!** *IMP* get out of here! · *largarse* to get out, to go away
□ **plata** money
□ **lástima** pity
□ **a cargo** in charge
□ **mantecado** bun made with lard

☐ **prohibido** prohibited · *prohibir* to prohibit
☐ **impedirlo** to prevent it · *impedir* to prevent, to impede
☐ **saques** SUBJ you take out, you remove · *sacar* to take out, to remove
☐ **cobarde** cowardly
☐ **propiedad** property
☐ **te llene** SUBJ I fill you · *llenar* to fill
☐ **intestinos** guts, intestines · *intestino* intestine
☐ **plomo** lead [METAL]
☐ **disculpa** excuse (me) · *disculpar* to excuse
☐ **inmundo** filthy
☐ **animal** NM animal

## 8 "What Kind of Mother Am I?" 6:08

**Phrases to Listen For**
**con prisa** in a hurry
**lo que** what
**en cuanto a** concerning
**lo tengo bien estudiado** I have studied it well
**tal vez** maybe, perhaps
**tengo que** I have to
**lo lamento** I'm sorry
**por favor** please

**Names**
Leslie, Frank

📽 On the airplane, Kevin's mother wakes up worried.

☐ **terrible** terrible
☐ **presentimiento** premonition
☐ **apagué** I turned off · *apagar* to turn off, to switch off
☐ **café** NM coffee
☐ **llave** NF key
☐ **cochera** garage

📽 Kevin slides down the staircase. Kevin's mother and the adults talk.

☐ **teléfono** telephone
☐ **averiado** out of order, broken · *averiar* to break
☐ **en cuanto** as soon as
☐ **aterricemos** SUBJ we land · *aterrizar* to land [AIRCRAFT]
☐ **gafas** NFPL glasses

📽 Larry and Marv arrive in the neighborhood in a plumbing truck.

☐ **personalmente** personally
☐ **sencillo** simple
☐ **atiende** IMP pay attention · *atender* to pay attention, to watch

☐ **vacías** empty · *vacío* empty
☐ **relojes automáticos** automatic timers · *reloj* NM timer
☐ **observa** IMP watch · *observar* to observe, to watch
☐ **seiscientos sesenta y cuatro** 664, six hundred sixty-four
☐ **encenderá** it will turn on · *encender* to turn on, to switch on
☐ **exactamente** exactly
☐ **seiscientos setenta y dos** 672, six hundred seventy-two
☐ **lujosa** luxurious · *lujoso* luxurious
☐ **valiosas** valuable · *valioso* valuable
☐ **estéreos** stereos · *estéreo* stereo
☐ **video caseteras** videocassette players, VCRs · *video casetera* videocassette player, VCR
☐ **estupenda** fantastic, outstanding · *estupendo* fantastic, outstanding
☐ **joyería** jewelry
☐ **acciones** stocks [FINANCIAL] · *acción* share of company stock
☐ **vendibles** saleable · *vendible* saleable
☐ **joya** jewel
☐ **herramienta** tool

📽 Kevin watches *How the Grinch Stole Christmas*. The thieves head toward the basement.

☐ **sótano** basement

📽 The family arrives in Paris.

☐ **bienvenidos** welcome · *bienvenido* ADJ welcome
☐ **emergencia** emergency
☐ **créame** IMP believe me · *creer* to believe
☐ **reservaciones** reservations · *reservación* reservation
☐ **agenda** daily planner

## 9 "I'm the Man of the House!" 4:40

**Phrases to Listen For**
**tener miedo** to be afraid
**no tengo miedo** I am not afraid
**en casa** at home
**así que** so
**solo** alone
**no lo sé** I don't know
**no lo creo** I don't think so
**solo en casa** home alone
**para que** so that
**así es** that's right
**por favor** please
**lo siento** I'm sorry
**de nuevo** again

**todo en orden** everything is okay, everything is in order
**lo lamento** I'm sorry
**lo que** what
**¿qué tal...?** how about ...?
**el viernes por la mañana** Friday morning
**a menos que** unless
**¿de acuerdo?** all right?, agreed?
**los echaré de menos** I'll miss you
**feliz navidad** Merry Christmas

## Names
Larry, Rose, Balzak, Chicago, Nueva York, Nashville, Rob

🎬 Kevin gets out from under the bed and goes outside.

□ **miedoso** fraidy cat, coward
□ **se escondería** he would hide · *esconderse* to hide (oneself)
□ **debajo de** under
□ **ladrones** thieves · *ladrón NM* thief

🎬 Kevin's mother talks to the authorities.

□ **departamento** department
□ **teléfono** telephone
□ **averiado** out of order, broken · *averiar* to break
□ **comunicarla** to connect you · *comunicar* to connect, to put in communication
□ **crisis familiares** family crisis · *crisis NF* crisis · *familiar ADJ* family
□ **contestar** to answer
□ **alterada** very upset · *alterado* very upset · *alterarse* to get upset
□ **sargento** sergeant
□ **envuelto** involved · *envolver* to involve
□ **altercados** altercations · *altercado* altercation
□ **violentos** violent · *violento* violent
□ **ebrio** drunk, inebriated
□ **mentalmente enfermo** mentally ill
□ **accidente casero** home accident · *accidente NM* accident · *casero* related to the home
□ **ha ingerido** he has ingested · *ingerir* to ingest
□ **veneno** poison, venom
□ **objeto** object
□ **obstruya SUBJ** it is obstructing · *obstruir* to obstruct
□ **garganta** throat
□ **verificar** to check, to verify
□ **tranquila EXP** easy, take it easy, be calm
□ **ellos me comunicaron** they connected me · *comunicar* to connect, to put in communication with
□ **no cuelgue IMP** don't hang up · *colgar* to hang up [TELEPHONE]

□ **localizar** to find
□ **responden** they answer · *responder* to answer
□ **contestadoras** answering machines · *contestadora* answering machine
□ **responda IMP** answer · *responder* to answer

🎬 The police knock at Kevin's door.

□ **enterado** understood, 10-4 [RADIO COMMUNICATION]

🎬 The McCallisters talk with the agent at the airport ticket counter.

□ **emergencia** emergency
□ **alivio** relief
□ **reservado** reserved, booked, sold out · *reservar* to reserve, to book
□ **vendido** sold out · *vender* to sell
□ **privado** private, charter
□ **reservaciones** reservations · *reservación* reservation
□ **viernes NM** Friday
□ **faltan dos días** two days away · *faltar* to be lacking
□ **agotados** exhausted · *agotado* exhausted · *agotarse* to become exhausted
□ **absolutamente** absolutely
□ **abandonado** abandoned · *abandonar* to abandon
□ **madame** ma'am [FRENCH]
□ **asiento** seat
□ **libre** free, available
□ **posibilidad** possibility
□ **aguardaré** I'll wait · *aguardar* to wait
□ **los echaré de menos** I'll miss you · *echar de menos* to miss

## 10 | I Took a Shower ...     5:13

### Phrases to Listen For
**para que** so that
**por favor** please
**de nuevo** again
**tienes razón** you're right
**no lo sé** I don't know
**tal vez** maybe, perhaps
**tienes que** you have to

### Names
Murphy, Florida, Ted, Jimmy

🎬 Kevin has showered and stands in front of the mirror.

□ **ducha** shower
□ **lavé** I washed · *lavar* to wash
□ **cuerpo** body

□ **jabón** NM soap
□ **principales** main · *principal* main
□ **hendiduras** crevices · *hendidura* crevice
□ **dedos** fingers · *dedo* finger
□ **ombligo** navel, belly button
□ **me agradó** I liked (*LIT* it pleased me) ·
  *agradar* to please
□ **cabello** hair
□ **champú** NM shampoo
□ **adultos** adults · *adulto* adult
□ **enjuague en crema** hair conditioner ·
  *enjuague* NM conditioner for hair
□ **brillara** SUBJ shine · *brillar* to shine
□ **no encuentro** I don't find · *encontrar* to find
□ **cepillo de dientes** toothbrush · *cepillo* brush ·
  *diente* NM tooth

🎬 Kevin enters Buzz's room and climbs the
  shelves.

□ **ahorros** NMPL savings

🎬 Harry and Marv rob the house across the
  street.

□ **ladrones** thieves · *ladrón* NM thief
□ **ruido** noise
□ **mensaje** NM message
□ **señal** NF tone, signal
□ **apartamento** apartment
□ **número telefónico** telephone number
□ **clave del país** country code · *clave* NF code ·
  *país* NM country
□ **anoche** last night
□ **tesoro** treasure

🎬 Kevin goes shopping.

□ **cepillo dental** toothbrush · *cepillo* brush
□ **aprobado** approved · *aprobar* to approve
□ **asociación médica dental** dental association
□ **averiguarlo** to find it out · *averiguar*
  to find out
□ **no lo revisamos** we didn't check it ·
  *revisar* to check, to review
□ **autoridad** authority
□ **no puedo mentirle** I can't lie to him ·
  *mentir* to lie
□ **yo no puedo engañarlo** I can't deceive him ·
  *engañar* to deceive
□ **no tiene ninguna importancia** it's not that
  important · *tener* to have · *ninguna* no ·
  *importancia* importance
□ **detén** IMP stop · *detener* to stop, to restrain

🎬 Kevin runs outside the store.

□ **¡detente!** IMP stop! · *detener* to stop
□ **delincuente** NMF delinquent

## 11 Encounter with the Enemy  10:12

### Phrases to Listen For
**¿dónde está la gracia?** what's so funny?
**¿de qué te ríes?** what are you laughing about?
**¿qué pasa contigo?** what's the matter with you?
**tarjeta de visita** calling card
**tengo que** I have to
**tienes que** you have to
**lo siento** I'm sorry
**feliz navidad** Merry Christmas
**¿qué pasa?** what's the matter?, what's up?
**yo menos** I'm even less likely (*LIT* I less)
**antes de que** before
**de compras** shopping
**el mundo de verdad** the real world
**lárgate de aquí** IMP get out of here
**tiene que** you have to
**¿de verdad?** really?
**para que** so that
**de verdad** real
**por piedad** have mercy
**buenas noches** good night

### Names
American Airlines, Rolex, Irene, Porsche,
Nerón

🎬 Harry plugs the sink and turns the water on.

□ **¿dónde está la gracia?** what's so funny?
□ **¿de qué te ríes?** what are you laughing about? ·
  *reírse* to laugh
□ **tarjeta de visita** calling card
□ **firma** signature
□ **bandidos** bandits · *bandido* bandit
□ **mojados** wet · *mojado* wet · *mojar* to get wet,
  to make wet

🎬 Harry and Marv nearly run over Kevin.
  They follow him.

□ **fijarte** to pay attention · *fijarse* to pay attention
□ **tránsito** traffic
□ **demonios** demons, devils · *demonio* demon,
  devil
□ **San Nicolás** St. Nicholas
□ **¿te diste cuenta?** did you notice?, could you tell? ·
  *darse cuenta* to notice
□ **cien** one hundred
□ **me miró raro** he gave me a strange look
  (*LIT* he looked at me strange) · *mirar* to look at ·
  *raro* strange
□ **iglesia** church

🎬 Kevin comes out from behind the Nativity scene.

□ **sujetos** guys, dudes, fellows · *sujeto* guy, dude,
  fellow

The thieves arrive at Kevin's house. The song "Rockin' Around the Christmas Tree" is playing. Meanwhile, in Paris, the McCallister family watches *It's a Wonderful Life* in French.

- □ **cocina** kitchen
- □ **camarones** shrimp · *camarón NM* shrimp
- □ **déjame en paz** *IMP* leave me alone · *dejar* to leave · *paz NF* peace

Peter McCallister tries to see if the operator speaks English, using the French words *parlez* and *anglais*.

- □ **operadora** operator · *operador* operator
- □ **español** Spanish [LANGUAGE]
- □ **conseguiste** did you get, did you find · *conseguir* to get, to find
- □ **no encuentro** I haven't found, I don't find · *encontrar* to find
- □ **de compras** shopping
- □ **olvídelo** *IMP* forget it · *olvidar* to forget

Buzz and his sister talk about Kevin's plight.

- □ **absurdo** absurd
- □ **encerrados** locked up, closed in · *encerrado* locked up, closed in · *encerrar* to lock up, to close in
- □ **apartamento** apartment
- □ **ha actuado** he has acted · *actuar* to act
- □ **se le volteó** it backfired on him (*LIT* it flipped over on him) · *voltear* to flip, to turn over
- □ **indefenso** defenseless
- □ **detectores de humo** smoke detectors · *detector NM* detector · *humo* smoke
- □ **aburrida** boring · *aburrido* boring
- □ **Estados Unidos de Norteamérica** United States of America
- □ **remotamente** remotely
- □ **peligroso** dangerous

The pizza delivery boy arrives. Kevin plays *Angels with Filthy Souls*.

- □ **Nerón** Nero
- □ **pizza** pizza
- □ **entrada** entrance
- □ **¡lárgate de aquí!** *IMP* get out of here! · *largarse* to get out, to go away
- □ **plata** money
- □ **once** eleven
- □ **ochenta** eighty
- □ **inmundo** filthy
- □ **animal** *NM* animal
- □ **miserable** *ADJ* stingy
- □ **saques** *SUBJ* you take out, you remove · *sacar* to take out, to remove
- □ **cobarde** cowardly

- □ **propiedad** property
- □ **te llene** *SUBJ* I fill you · *llenar* to fill
- □ **intestinos** guts, intestines · *intestino* intestine
- □ **plomo** lead [METAL]
- □ **deliciosa** delicious · *delicioso* delicious
- □ **queso** cheese

Kate McCallister is at the airport in Paris.

- □ **anuncia** it announces · *anunciar* to announce
- □ **salida** departure
- □ **preciosos** precious · *precioso* precious
- □ **quinientos** five hundred
- □ **traductora de bolsillo** pocket translator
- □ **asientos** seats · *asiento* seat
- □ **turista** coach, tourist
- □ **¿quién lo notará?** who will notice? · *notar* to notice
- □ **sortija** ring
- □ **preciosa** precious · *precioso* precious
- □ **están abordando** they are boarding · *abordar* to board
- □ **viernes** *NM* Friday
- □ **reloj** *NM* watch
- □ **pendientes** earrings · *pendiente NM* earring
- □ **caja** box
- □ **zapatos** shoes · *zapato* shoe
- □ **desesperada** desperate · *desesperado* desperate
- □ **se lo suplico** I beg of you · *suplicar* to beg, to plead
- □ **por piedad** have mercy · *piedad* mercy

Kevin watches *The Tonight Show* with Johnny Carson.

- □ **radio** radio
- □ **intención** intention
- □ **molestia** bother, annoyance

## 12 The Man of the House Goes Shopping    6:16

**Phrases to Listen For**
- **favor de** please
- **¿por qué no?** why not?
- **ya basta** enough already
- **lárgate de aquí** *IMP* get out of here
- **no me digas** *IMP* don't tell me
- **a cargo** in charge
- **lo que** what
- **para que** in order to
- **antes de que** before
- **¿qué pasó?** what happened?
- **acaban de** they just finished
- **claro que** of course
- **se veía** it looked like

## Names

Johnny, Snakes

🎬 Kevin pretends to sing "I'm Dreaming of a White Christmas." With the music playing in the background, Kevin goes shopping. At the checkout stand, he talks to the cashier.

- □ **oferta** sale
- □ **personal** *NM* personnel
- □ **limpieza** cleaning
- □ **caja** register, cash register
- □ **cenas** dinners · *cena* dinner
- □ **microondas** *NM* microwave oven
- □ **probarla** to try it · *probar* to try, to taste
- □ **cupón** *NM* coupon
- □ **periódico** newspaper
- □ **diecinueve** nineteen
- □ **ochenta** eighty

🎬 Kevin does the laundry in the basement. Harry and Marv observe the house from the van.

- □ **vacía** empty · *vacío* empty
- □ **anoche** last night
- □ **revisar** to check out, to review

🎬 Kevin plays *Angels with Filthy Souls*.

- □ **¡rayos!** *EXP* holy cow! · *rayo* bolt of lightning
- □ **¡lárgate de aquí!** *IMP* get out of here! · *largarse* to get out, to go away
- □ **plata** money
- □ **lástima** pity
- □ **a cargo** in charge
- □ **ducha** shower
- □ **saques** *SUBJ* you take out, you remove · *sacar* to take out, to remove
- □ **cobarde** cowardly
- □ **propiedad** property
- □ **te llene** *SUBJ* I fill you · *llenar* to fill
- □ **intestinos** guts, intestines · *intestino* intestine
- □ **plomo** lead [METAL]
- □ **disculpa** excuse (me) · *disculpar* to excuse
- □ **inmundo** filthy
- □ **animal** *NM* animal

🎬 Marv talks with Harry in the van.

- □ **se nos adelantó** he beat us, he got there ahead of us · *adelantarse* to beat (in arriving someplace), to get (somewhere) ahead of, to arrive early
- □ **adentro** inside
- □ **discutieron** they argued · *discutir* to argue
- □ **despachó el otro a tiros** he shot the other one · *despachar* to take care of, to deal with · *tiro* shot
- □ **reconocer** to recognize

- □ **voces** voices · *voz NF* voice
- □ **vecindario** neighborhood
- □ **supón** *IMP* suppose · *suponer* to suppose
- □ **crimen** *NM* crime
- □ **zona** area, zone
- □ **víbora** snake

## 13 Everything's Full; Help from a Polka King    5:48

### Phrases to Listen For

**lo lamento mucho** I'm very sorry
**víspera de navidad** Christmas Eve
**todo lo que** everything that
**lo siento** I'm sorry
**¿dónde diablos?** where the devil?, where the heck?
**yo lo lamento** I'm sorry
**nada de eso** not at all
**tengo que** I have to
**lo que sea** *SUBJ* anything
**por favor** please
**con permiso** excuse me (*LIT* with permission)
**mucho gusto** nice to meet you
**no importa** it doesn't matter
**tener que** to have to
**santo cielo** good heavens
**tiene que** you have to
**claro que sí** of course
**¿por qué no?** why not?
**así que** so
**a las nueve de la noche** at nine o'clock at night

### Names

Chicago, Dallas, Scranton, Gus Polinski, Kenosha, Yamakusi, Sheboygan, Milwaukee

🎬 Upon arrival in the United States, Kate McCallister talks with the airline ticket agent.

- □ **vendido** sold, sold out · *venderse* to sell out
- □ **víspera de navidad** Christmas Eve · *víspera* eve of an event · *navidad* Christmas
- □ **aerolínea** airline
- □ **disponible** available
- □ **lo lamento muchísimo** I'm very sorry · *lamentar* to regret · *muchísimo* very much
- □ **le estorbo** I'm in your way · *estorbar* to be in the way
- □ **pasaje** *NM* a ticket
- □ **cuídelo** *IMP* take care of it · *cuidar* to take care of
- □ **sesenta** sixty
- □ **sucia** dirty, filthy · *sucio* dirty, filthy
- □ **¿dónde diablos estoy?** where the devil am I? · *diablo* devil

□ **esperanza** hope
□ **época** season, time [OF THE YEAR]
□ **eterna** eternal · *eterno* eternal
□ **pista** runway
□ **cuesta** it costs · *costar* to cost
□ **vender** to sell
□ **alma** soul
□ **demonio** devil, demon

▥ Gus Polinski interrupts to talk with Kate McCallister.

□ **¿puede disculparnos?** can you excuse us? · *disculpar* to excuse, to forgive
□ **con permiso** excuse me (LIT with permission) · *permiso* permission
□ **evitar** to avoid
□ **dilema** NM dilemma
□ **crisis** NF crisis
□ **polca** polka
□ **oeste** NM west
□ **alegres** happy folks, happy people · *alegre* NMF happy person
□ **había reconocido** you had recognized · *reconocer* to recognize
□ **éxitos** successes · *éxito* success
□ **lagos** lakes · *lago* lake
□ **gemelos** twin · *gemelo* twin
□ **bésame** IMP kiss me · *besar* to kiss
□ **twist** ENG twist
□ **canciones** songs · *canción* song
□ **a principios de** at the beginning of · *principio* beginning
□ **vendimos** we sold · *vender* to sell
□ **seiscientas** six hundred · *seiscientos* six hundred
□ **copias** copies · *copia* copy
□ **éxito** success
□ **estoy divagando** I'm getting sidetracked · *divagar* to get sidetracked
□ **se canceló** it was canceled · *cancelar* to cancel
□ **conducir** to drive
□ **chaqueta** jacket
□ **amarilla** yellow · *amarillo* yellow
□ **barba** beard
□ **alquilar** to rent
□ **camioneta** van, pickup truck
□ **oí** I heard · *oír* to hear

▥ Harry and Marv observe Kevin's house once again.

□ **engañados** deceived, tricked · *engañado* deceived, tricked · *engañar* to deceive, to trick
□ **guardería** day care
□ **bromeando** joking · *bromear* to joke
□ **incluso** including, even
□ **organizaremos** we will organize · *organizar* to organize
□ **plan** NM plan

□ **descargaremos** we will unload · *descargar* to unload
□ **oscuro** dark
□ **oscuridad** darkness
□ **miedoso** coward

## 14 A Message to Santa/ "Somewhere in My Memory" 3:06

### Phrases to Listen For
**víspera de navidad** Christmas Eve
**vacuna contra la rabia** rabies vaccine
**conejo de pascua** Easter Bunny
**por favor** please
**en vez de** instead of
**no hay cuidado** no problem
**tiene que** he has to

### Names
Kate, Megan, Linnie, Jeff, Frank

▥ Kevin visits Santa.

□ **zapatos** shoes · *zapato* shoe
□ **si te urge** if it is urgent · *urgir* to be urgent
□ **demonios** demons, devils · *demonio* demon, devil
□ **multar** to fine, to ticket
□ **San Nicolás** St. Nicholas
□ **víspera de navidad** Christmas Eve · *víspera* eve of an event · *navidad* Christmas
□ **vacuna** vaccine
□ **rabia** rabies
□ **conejo de pascua** Easter Bunny
□ **reunión** meeting
□ **retrasado** late, behind schedule · *retrasar* to make (someone) late
□ **verdadero** real, true
□ **curiosidad** curiosity
□ **ya tengo edad** I'm old enough · *tener* to have · *edad* age
□ **mensaje** NM message
□ **seiscientos setenta y uno** 671, six hundred seventy-one
□ **número telefónico** telephone number
□ **es sumamente importante** it's super important, it's extremely important
□ **recuperar** to recover, to get back
□ **primos** cousins · *primo* cousin
□ **gnomo** gnome
□ **caramelos** caramels · *caramelo* caramel
□ **novio** boyfriend, groom
□ **tímido** shy, timid
□ **toma** IMP take it · *tomar* to take
□ **cenar** to eat dinner, to dine
□ **maldición** EXP darn, damn [CURSE]

## 15 The Real Old Man Marley 7:10

**Phrases to Listen For**

**feliz navidad** Merry Christmas
**no tienes porqué temer** you have no reason to be afraid
**creo que sí** I think so
**a veces** sometimes
**lo que** what
**¿por qué?** why?
**hace años** years ago
**antes de que** before
**no lo sé** I don't know
**tener miedo** to be afraid
**al menos** at least
**no tendrá que** you won't have to
**tener miedo** to be afraid
**ella lo echa de menos** she misses you

Kevin enters the church.

□ **nieta** granddaughter · *nieto* grandson
□ **coro** choir, chorus
□ **pelirroja** redhead · *pelirrojo* redhead
□ **edad** age
□ **saludarme** to say hello to me, to greet me · *saludar* to say hello, to greet
□ **molestia** pest, annoyance
□ **últimamente** lately, recently
□ **no me comporté** I didn't behave · *comportarse* to behave
□ **realmente** really
□ **complicado** complicated · *complicar* to complicate, to make complicated
□ **especialmente** especially
□ **en el fondo** deep down, at heart · *fondo* bottom
□ **lastimarlos** to hurt them · *lastimar* to hurt
□ **iglesia** church
□ **se mudaran** SUBJ you moved · *mudarse* to move [RESIDENCE]
□ **disputa** dispute, argument
□ **adulto** adult
□ **nos disgustamos** we got upset · *disgustarse* to get upset
□ **le apena** it saddens you · *apenar* to sadden, to embarrass
□ **no se ofenda** IMP don't be offended, no offense · *ofender* to offend
□ **sótano** basement
□ **oscuro** dark
□ **raras** strange · *raro* strange
□ **huele** it smells · *oler* to smell
□ **disgusta** it disgusts · *disgustar* to disgust, to upset, to displease

□ **sótanos** basements · *sótano* basement
□ **me obligué** I forced myself · *obligarse* to force oneself
□ **lavar** to wash
□ **ropa** clothes
□ **descubrí** I discovered · *descubrir* to discover
□ **enciende** it turns on · *encender* to turn on, to switch on
□ **lo furioso** how mad, how angry · *furioso* mad, angry, furious
□ **lo echa de menos** she misses you · *echar de menos* to miss, to long to see
□ **envío** I send · *enviar* to send
□ **cheque** NM check
□ **camisa** shirt
□ **enorme** enormous
□ **espantapájaros** NM scarecrow
□ **pijamas** pajamas · *pijama* pajamas
□ **dinosaurios** dinosaurs · *dinosaurio* dinosaur
□ **charlar** to chat, to talk

## 16 "This Is My House— I Have to Defend It!" 1:29

At home, Kevin prepares to defend his house.

□ **defender** to defend
□ **plan** NM plan
□ **batalla** battle

## 17 "Merry Christmas, Little Fella!" 4:14

**Phrases to Listen For**

**tal vez** maybe, perhaps
**feliz navidad** Merry Christmas
**¿qué te pasó?** what happened to you?

Harry and Marv arrive at the McCallister home.

□ **revisar** to look over, to check out, to review
□ **camioneta** van, pickup truck
□ **puerta trasera** back door · *puerta* door · *trasero* back, rear
□ **bobos** fools, idiots, dummies · *bobo* fool, idiot, dummy

Kevin prays. The clock strikes nine.

□ **bendice** IMP bless · *bendecir* to bless
□ **nutritiva** nutritious · *nutritivo* nutritious
□ **cena** dinner
□ **microondas** NM microwave oven

- ☐ **macarrones** macaroni · *macarrón* NM piece of macaroni
- ☐ **queso** cheese
- ☐ **en oferta** on sale · *oferta* sale

🎬 Harry and Marv talk to Kevin through the back door.

- ☐ **completamente** completely
- ☐ **gnomo** gnome
- ☐ **daño** damage
- ☐ **mata** IMP kill · *matar* to kill
- ☐ **mocoso** PEJ snot-nosed kid, snot-nosed brat
- ☐ **armado** armed · *armar* to arm
- ☐ **sótano** basement

### 18 "Do You Do Ironing?"; Too Hot to Handle       3:24

🎬 Harry and Marv attempt to enter the house. Marv gets hit by the iron. Harry mumbles and then shouts when he enters the house.

- ☐ **enano** dwarf
- ☐ **gusano** worm
- ☐ **infierno** hell

### 19 "Come and Get Me!"       3:08

**Phrases to Listen For**

**por favor** please
**¿por qué?** why?
**tienen ganas de** you have desire for
**con cuidado** be careful
**lo que** what

**Names**

Lincoln Boulevard, Murphy

🎬 Harry talks to Kevin through the dining room door.

- ☐ **atraparte** to trap you, to catch you · *atrapar* to trap, to catch
- ☐ **enano** dwarf

🎬 Harry and Marv meet in the dining room.

- ☐ **¿por qué rayos?** why the heck?
- ☐ **zapatos** shoes · *zapato* shoe
- ☐ **gallina** hen, chicken

🎬 Kevin is at the top of the stairs.

- ☐ **soburros** idiots, dummies, fools · *soburro* idiot, dummy, fool
- ☐ **rendir** to surrender

🎬 Harry lands on top of Marvin.

- ☐ **diente** NM tooth
- ☐ **oro** gold

- ☐ **bombardeas** you bomb · *bombardear* to bomb, to bombard
- ☐ **lata** can
- ☐ **arrancaré** I will yank off, I will pull off · *arrancar* to yank off, to pull from the root
- ☐ **orejas** ears · *oreja* ear
- ☐ **herviré** I will boil · *hervir* to boil
- ☐ **aceite** NM oil

🎬 Kevin makes a phone call.

- ☐ **emergencias** emergency · *emergencia* emergency
- ☐ **dirección** address
- ☐ **apellido** last name

### 20 The Slide for Life       2:45

**Phrases to Listen For**

**Dios mío** good heavens (LIT my God)
**tal vez** maybe, perhaps
**por aquí** over here
**antes de que** before
**lo que** what

🎬 Harry and Marv look out the upstairs window.

- ☐ **se suicidó** he killed himself · *suicidarse* to kill oneself, to commit suicide
- ☐ **soburros** idiots, dummies, fools · *soburro* idiot, dummy, fool
- ☐ **tras** after
- ☐ **tendernos una trampa** to lay a trap for us · *tender* to lay out · *trampa* trap
- ☐ **ventana** window

🎬 Harry and Marv climb across the rope.

- ☐ **cállate** IMP shut up, be quiet · *callarse* to shut up, to be quiet

### 21 Outsmarted ... And a Welcome Guest       4:47

**Phrases to Listen For**

**lo que** what
**a la vez** at a time
**desde hace mucho** for a long time
**ni siquiera conoce** he doesn't even know
**alguna vez** sometime, one time
**de vacaciones** on vacation
**todo el día** all day
**por la noche** in the evening
**nos dimos cuenta** we noticed
**después de** after
**de nuevo** again
**tal vez** maybe, perhaps

**lo sé** I know
**lo siento** I'm sorry

## Names
Decker, Cobb, Joe, Ziggy, Eddie

🎬 Kevin climbs down from the tree and runs across the street.

☐ **no me estorbes** *IMP* get out of my way, don't block me · *estorbar* to get in the way

🎬 Harry and Marv catch Kevin.

☐ **exacto** exactly
☐ **quemarle la cabeza** to burn his head · *quemar* to burn · *cabeza* head
☐ **soplete** *NM* welding torch
☐ **aplastaremos** we will smash · *aplastar* to smash
☐ **plancha** iron
☐ **lata** can
☐ **pintura** paint
☐ **meterle un clavo en el pie** to put a nail in his foot · *meter* to put in
☐ **arrancarle** to yank out of him · *arrancar* to yank out, to pull from the root
☐ **deditos** *DIM* little fingers · *dedo* finger

🎬 The police arrive. Kevin views the scene from inside his house.

☐ **por enfrente** through the front · *enfrente ADV* in front
☐ **¡chispas!** *EXP* wow! · *chispa* spark
☐ **grandioso** amazing, terrific, magnificent
☐ **con exactitud** exactly (*LIT* with exactitude)
☐ **bandidos** bandits · *bandido* bandit
☐ **mojados** wet · *mojado* wet · *mojar* to get wet, to make wet
☐ **no me toque** *IMP* don't touch me · *tocar* to touch
☐ **adentro** inside

🎬 "Have Yourself a Merry Little Christmas" is playing. Kate McCallister is still riding with Gus Polinski and the band.

☐ **se está devaluando** you're putting yourself down · *devaluarse* to put oneself down
☐ **mírenos** *IMP* look at us · *mirar* to look at
☐ **mitad** *NF* half
☐ **boca** mouth
☐ **escriba** *SUBJ* he writes · *escribir* to write
☐ **de vacaciones** on vacation · *vacaciones NFPL* vacation
☐ **funeraria** funeral home
☐ **terrible** terrible, awful
☐ **acongojado** worried · *acongojarse* to worry, to become distressed
☐ **suegra** mother-in-law · *suegro* father-in-law

☐ **cadáver** *NM* cadaver
☐ **se recuperó** he recovered · *recuperarse* to recover, to get over
☐ **créame** *IMP* believe me · *creer* to believe
☐ **se recuperan** they recover · *recuperarse* to recover, to get over
☐ **resistentes** resistant, tough · *resistente* resistant, tough
☐ **lo mencionó** you mentioned it · *mencionar* to mention
☐ **animarla** to encourage you · *animar* to encourage

## 22 Christmas Morning 4:26

### Phrases to Listen For
**feliz navidad** Merry Christmas
**lo lamento tanto** I'm so sorry
**de compras** shopping
**¿en serio?** really?, seriously?

🎬 Kevin looks for his mom. Gus Polinski's truck pulls up outside the house. Kevin's mom enters. The rest of the family follows.

☐ **no babeo** I don't drool · *babear* to drool
☐ **sí babeas** you do too drool · *babear* to drool
☐ **cuanto me alegra** how happy I am (*LIT* how happy it makes me) · *alegrar* to make happy
☐ **corto** short
☐ **te felicito** I congratulate you, congratulations · *felicitar* to congratulate
☐ **por no quemar** for not burning down · *quemar* to burn, to burn down
☐ **matutino** morning
☐ **tienda** store
☐ **leche** *NF* milk
☐ **de compras** shopping
☐ **ayer** yesterday
☐ **huevos** eggs · *huevo* egg
☐ **suavizante de ropa** fabric softener · *suavizante NM* conditioner, softener · *ropa* clothes
☐ **gracioso** funny
☐ **desempacar** to unpack

## 23 Another Special Reunion 1:08

🎬 Kevin watches as Mr. Marley's family arrives. Buzz shouts.

## 24 End Titles/"Somewhere in My Memory" Reprise 3:44

🎬 End credits.

# Hoosiers

**Los amo a todos.**
*I love you guys.*

| | |
|---|---|
| GENRE | Drama/Sports |
| YEAR | 1986 |
| DIRECTOR | David Anspaugh |
| CAST | Gene Hackman, Barbara Hershey, Dennis Hopper |
| STUDIO | Orion Pictures |

A volatile coach with a checkered past leads a small Indiana high school basketball team against the team from a much larger school in the 1952 state high school championship game. Inspired by a true story, the journey of this team is a classic tale of redemption. Ranked as one of the top ten sports movies of all time by *Sports Illustrated*, *Hoosiers* has action, romance, religion, politics, fist fights, beautiful scenery, and a terrific musical score. Spanish learners will find that the actors speak clearly at an easily understandable speed. The movie presents a great opportunity to learn Spanish sports vocabulary, especially basketball terms, as well as other vocabulary words associated with failure and success.

## BASIC VOCABULARY

### Names
Jimmy, Indiana, Norman Dale, Hickory, Rade Butcher, Buddy Walker, Everett, Shooter, Cletus, Opal Fleener, Strap

### Nouns
- □ **básquetbol** *NM* basketball · *Fui contratado para entrenar a los muchachos en **básquetbol** y lo hice al máximo de mi habilidad.* I was hired to teach the boys basketball, and I did that to the best of my ability.
- □ **cancha** court · *Dios te quiere en la **cancha**.* God wants you on the court.
- □ **partido** game · *Tal vez esta noche se esté haciendo historia con este **partido**.* Perhaps history is being made tonight with this game.
- □ **pelota** ball · *Earl tiene problema para pasar la **pelota**.* Earl has a problem passing the ball.
- □ **tiro** shot · *¿Crees que el último **tiro** deba hacerlo el cuatro?* Do you believe that number four will take the last shot?

### Verb
- □ **encesta** he shoots · **encestar** to shoot, to score, scoring [BASKETBALL] · *Al menos va a la escuela y **encesta** algunos balones.* At least he goes to school and shoots some baskets. · *Ni **encestar** tampoco.* Not scoring either.

### Other
- □ **doce** twelve · *¿La última vez que entrenó fue hace **doce** años?* The last time you coached was twelve years ago?
- □ **técnica** *ADJ* technical [SPORTS] · *Es una falta **técnica**.* It's a technical foul.

---

## 1   Main Title/Arrival                          3:57

🎬 Coach Dale arrives.

---

## 2   Job to Do                                   2:39

### Phrases to Listen For
**según entiendo** as I understand it (*LIT* according to I understand)
**mala fama** bad name, bad reputation
**lo que** what
**cerramos el trato** we closed the deal

### Names
Cletus Summers, Buffalo

---

🎬 Coach Dale steps into the hallway and views the trophies. The bell rings.
- □ **oficina** office
- □ **decepcionarla** to disappoint you · *decepcionar* to disappoint
- □ **debo haber malentendido** I must have misunderstood · *malentender* to misunderstand
- □ **había contratado** he had hired · *contratar* to hire, to contract
- □ **había entrenado** he had coached · *entrenar* to coach
- □ **preparatoria** high school
- □ **entrenaba** I coached · *entrenar* to coach
- □ **civismo** civics
- □ **según entiendo** as I understand · *entender* to understand
- □ **experiencia** experience
- □ **¿me está entrevistando?** are you interviewing me? · *entrevistar* to interview
- □ **empleo** job
- □ **hospitalidad** hospitality
- □ **adquirir** to acquire
- □ **mala fama** bad name, bad reputation

🎬 Coach Dale opens the door to Cletus' office.
- □ **flotando** floating · *flotar* to float
- □ **no te reconocí** I didn't recognize you · *reconocer* to recognize
- □ **primavera** spring [SEASON]
- □ **mil novecientos treinta y uno** 1931 [DATE], one thousand nine hundred thirty-one
- □ **me costó** it was hard for me (*LIT* it cost me) · *costar* to cost
- □ **localizarte** to find you · *localizar* to find, to locate
- □ **seguías** you continued · *seguir* to continue
- □ **ejército** army
- □ **ayer** yesterday
- □ **anteayer** day before yesterday
- □ **trato** deal
- □ **prácticas** practices · *práctica* practice
- □ **conveniente** advisable
- □ **hace bastante que no entrenas** you haven't coached in a long time (*LIT* it's been quite a while that you don't coach) · *bastante* quite, plenty · *entrenar* to coach
- □ **iniciarás** you will begin · *iniciar* to begin

---

## 3   Jimmy                                       2:13

### Phrases to Listen For
**los viernes por la noche** Friday evenings
**tienen que prepararse** they have to get ready
**tiene que salir bien** it has to turn out okay

## Names
Jimmy Chitwood, Chester

🎬 In the gym, Jimmy ties his shoes. Coach Dale and Cletus enter.

- ☐ **acostumbrado** accustomed · *acostumbrar* to be accustomed, to be used to
- ☐ **orgullosos** proud · *orgulloso* proud
- ☐ **doscientas** two hundred · *doscientos* two hundred
- ☐ **viernes** NM Friday
- ☐ **practican** you practice · *practicar* to practice
- ☐ **sábado** Saturday
- ☐ **amigable** friendly, amicable
- ☐ **granja** farm
- ☐ **cómodo** comfortable

🎬 A young woman lifts a box out of the trunk.

- ☐ **saluda** IMP say hello, greet · *saludar* to say hello, to greet
- ☐ **despídete** IMP say good-bye · *despedirse* to say good-bye
- ☐ **indispensable** indispensable
- ☐ **según** according to
- ☐ **experiencia** experience

## 4   Warm Welcome                    2:57

### Phrases to Listen For
**¿qué tal?** what's up?, how's it going?
**a cargo de** in charge of
**hasta que** until
**así que** so
**de nuevo** again
**lo que** what
**¿no es cierto?** isn't that right?
**¿por qué?** why?
**¿qué tiene que ver con usted?** what does that have to do with you?
**de acuerdo** agreed
**buenos días** good day

### Names
George, Jimmy Chitwood, Terhune, Ítaca, Nueva York

🎬 Coach Dale enters the barbershop.

- ☐ **entrenó** you coached · *entrenar* to coach
- ☐ **Ítaca** Ithaca
- ☐ **Nueva York** New York
- ☐ **marina** navy
- ☐ **a cargo de** in charge of
- ☐ **prácticas** practices · *práctica* practice

- ☐ **se acostumbre** you get used to things · *acostumbrarse* to get accustomed to, to get used to
- ☐ **reunirnos** to meet, to get together · *reunirse* to meet, to get together
- ☐ **recto** good, God-fearing
- ☐ **principios** principles · *principio* principle
- ☐ **morales** NFPL morals
- ☐ **cristianos** Christian · *cristiano* ADJ Christian
- ☐ **ejemplo** example
- ☐ **defensa por zonas** zone defense · *defensa por zona* zone defense
- ☐ **táctica** tactic
- ☐ **quince** fifteen
- ☐ **excepto** except
- ☐ **no logro entender** I can't grasp, I can't understand · *lograr* to be able to, to achieve · *entender* to understand
- ☐ **contratamos** we hired · *contratar* to hire, to contract
- ☐ **no ha entrenado** he hasn't coached · *entrenar* to coach
- ☐ **punto principal** main point · *punto* point · *principal* main

🎬 In the morning, Coach Dale steps out of his car.

- ☐ **oí** I heard · *oír* to hear
- ☐ **generosos** generous · *generoso* generous
- ☐ **anoche** last night
- ☐ **olvido** I forget · *olvidar* to forget
- ☐ **rústico** rural, hick
- ☐ **veinticuatro** twenty-four
- ☐ **enferma** sick · *enfermo* sick
- ☐ **falleció** he passed away, he died · *fallecer* to pass away, to die
- ☐ **vecinos** neighbors · *vecino* neighbor
- ☐ **convencerán** they will convince · *convencer* to convince

## 5   First Practice                   7:10

### Phrases to Listen For
**tal vez** maybe, perhaps
**no me importa** it doesn't matter to me, I don't care about it
**echa a perder** you spoil, you ruin
**me encargaré de** I'll take care of
**¿por qué?** why?
**de baja estatura** short
**para que** so that, in order to
**me encargo de** I'm in charge of
**así que** so
**lo que** what
**por qué** why
**no te quedes atrás** IMP don't get left behind

**todos los días** every day
**hasta que** until
**de acuerdo** all right, agreed

## Names

George, Norm, Whit, Terhune, Tim, Rollin Butcher, Rade

🎬 Coach Dale enters the gym where the boys have begun practice.

☐ **afuera** outside
☐ **he planeado** I have planned · *planear* to plan
☐ **horario** schedule
☐ **rutina** routine
☐ **acostumbrados** accustomed, used to · *acostumbrado* accustomed, used to · *acostumbrar* to be accustomed, to be used to
☐ **confundirlos** to confuse them · *confundir* to confuse
☐ **gradual** gradual
☐ **faltan dos semanas** there are only two weeks · *faltar* to lack
☐ **amigables** friendly, amicable · *amigable* friendly, amicable
☐ **se desnuda** he gets naked · *desnudarse* to get naked, to undress
☐ **nieve** NF snow
☐ **aullando** howling · *aullar* to howl
☐ **luna** moon
☐ **forzado** forced · *forzar* to force
☐ **enfrentarlo** to face it, to deal with it · *enfrentar* to face, to deal with
☐ **tradúzcalo** IMP translate it · *traducir* to translate
☐ **amenaza** threat
☐ **echa a perder** you ruin · *echar a perder* to ruin
☐ **personalmente** personally
☐ **me encargaré de** I'll see to, I'll make sure · *encargarse de* to see to, to make sure
☐ **golpe** NM a hit, a blow
☐ **frontera** border

🎬 Coach Dale calls the team together.

☐ **realmente** really
☐ **no cuento** I don't count · *contar* to count
☐ **de baja estatura** short · *bajo* short · *estatura* height
☐ **practiquen** SUBJ they practice · *practicar* to practice
☐ **me encargo de** I'm in charge of · *encargarse de* to be in charge of
☐ **equipaje** NM equipment
☐ **mayoría** majority
☐ **sesenta** sixty
☐ **banca** bench
☐ **vacía** empty · *vacío* empty
☐ **entrené** I coached · *entrenar* to coach

☐ **abandoné** I abandoned, I gave up · *abandonar* to abandon, to give up
☐ **prácticas** practices · *práctica* practice
☐ **descubrirán** you will discover · *descubrir* to discover
☐ **actividad** activity
☐ **voluntaria** volunteer · *voluntario* volunteer
☐ **requisito** requirement
☐ **invitar** to invite
☐ **avisarme** to let me know · *avisar* to let know, to warn
☐ **sal** IMP get out · *salir* to leave, to go out
☐ **boca** mouth
☐ **gallina** chicken, hen
☐ **se divierta** SUBJ you have fun · *divertirse* to have fun

🎬 Jimmy witnesses the start of the first practice session. Soon they start drills.

☐ **sillas** chairs · *silla* chair
☐ **colóquenlas** IMP place them · *colocar* to place
☐ **divertido** fun · *divertirse* to have fun
☐ **diseñadas** designed · *diseñado* designed · *diseñar* to design
☐ **se diviertan** SUBJ you have fun · *divertirse* to have fun
☐ **consiste** it consists · *consistir* to consist
☐ **principios** fundamentals, principles · *principio* fundamental, principle
☐ **patas** legs · *pata* leg [OF AN ANIMAL]
☐ **elévenlas** IMP get them up, raise them up · *elevar* to raise
☐ **arrójala** IMP throw it · *arrojar* to throw
☐ **deshazte** IMP get rid of it · *deshacerse* to get rid of

🎬 Coach Dale stops the passing drill.

☐ **clara** clear · *claro* clear
☐ **dejen de sonreír** IMP stop smiling · *dejar de* to stop (doing something) · *sonreír* to smile
☐ **unidad** unit
☐ **desháganse** IMP get rid of · *deshacerse* to get rid of
☐ **bola** ball

🎬 The team is quick-stepping in place.

☐ **energía** energy
☐ **oponentes** opponents · *oponente* NM opponent
☐ **no podemos arriesgarnos** we can't take the chance · *arriesgarse* to take a chance, to risk

🎬 Several men from Hickory enter the gym.

☐ **nos enteramos** we learned, we found out · *enterarse* to learn, to find out
☐ **extraña** strange · *extraño* strange

☐ **practicar** to practice
☐ **practicando** practicing · *practicar* to practice
☐ **está actuando** you are acting · *actuar* to act
☐ **condición** condition
☐ **física** physical · *físico* physical
☐ **estupenda** stupendous, excellent · *estupendo* stupendous, excellent
☐ **ejército** army

🎬 Coach Dale addresses the men from town.

☐ **espectadores** spectators · *espectador* spectator
☐ **distracciones** distractions · *distracción* distraction
☐ **derecho** right
☐ **distinto** different
☐ **manda** you give the orders · *mandar* to give an order, to order
☐ **práctica** practice
☐ **cámbiate** *IMP* change your clothes, get changed · *cambiarse* to change (clothes)
☐ **se confunden** they get confused · *confundirse* to get confused, to become confused
☐ **avíseme** *IMP* tell me, let me know · *avisar* to let know, to inform, to advise
☐ **error** *NM* mistake, error

🎬 Practice continues. Coach Dale stands at the free throw line.

☐ **formen** *IMP* form · *formar* to form
☐ **fórmense** *IMP* get in line, line up · *formarse* to line up
☐ **doblen las rodillas** *IMP* bend your knees · *doblar* to bend · *rodilla* knee

## 6  Shooter                                1:16

### Phrases to Listen For
**de tu lado** at your side, right with you
**tener que** to have to

### Names
George, Wilbert, Shooter, Flatch

🎬 In a café, Coach Dale and Cletus eat pie.

☐ **condiciones** *NFPL* condition, shape
☐ **díselo** *IMP* tell him · *decir* to tell, to say
☐ **mil novecientos treinta y tres** 1933 [DATE], one thousand nine hundred thirty-three
☐ **cometieron** they committed · *cometer* to commit
☐ **prestarme** to lend me · *prestar* to lend
☐ **devuélveselo** *IMP* give it back to him · *devolver* to give (something) back, to return
☐ **veinticinco** twenty-five
☐ **centavos** cents · *centavo* cent

## 7  A Chat with Jimmy                      1:39

### Phrases to Listen For
**lo que** what
**no me importa** it doesn't matter to me, I don't care

### Name
Myra Fleener

🎬 Jimmy shoots baskets outside. Coach Dale joins him.

☐ **estuve entrenando** I was coaching · *entrenar* to coach
☐ **aumentar** to add to, to gain, to increase
☐ **ventaja** advantage
☐ **bloquear** to block
☐ **talento** talent

## 8  Only a Game                            2:16

### Phrases to Listen For
**muchos hasta asesinarían** a lot of people would kill
**¿por qué?** why?
**lo que** what

### Name
Wabash

🎬 Coach Dale climbs the stairs and encounters Myra Fleener.

☐ **déjelo en paz** *IMP* leave him alone, leave him in peace · *dejar* to leave · *paz* *NF* peace
☐ **esperanzas** hopes · *esperanza* hope
☐ **se esfuerza** he makes an effort · *esforzarse* to make an effort
☐ **beca** scholarship
☐ **no le conviene** it's not what's best for him · *convenir* to be best for, to be advisable
☐ **sentido** sense
☐ **estrellas** stars · *estrella* star
☐ **centro** center
☐ **antiguos** old · *antiguo* old
☐ **gloria** glory
☐ **diecisiete** seventeen
☐ **asesinarían** they would kill · *asesinar* to kill
☐ **tratados** treated · *tratado* treated · *tratar* to treat
☐ **menosprecian** they undervalue · *menospreciar* to undervalue
☐ **últimamente** recently, lately
☐ **arrojan** they throw · *arrojar* to throw
☐ **aro** hoop
☐ **acero** steel

□ **idolatrados** idolized · *idolatrado* idolized · *idolatrar* to idolize
□ **hostil** hostile
□ **al contrario** on the contrary
□ **mapas** maps · *mapa NM* map
□ **edad** age
□ **huyendo** running away, fleeing · *huir* to run away, to flee
□ **asunto** matter, concern
□ **suyo** of yours

## 9 Pep Rally                                    2:41

### Phrases to Listen For

**darles las gracias** to thank them
**nos estamos relacionando** we're getting to know each other
**lo que** what
**me ha gustado** I've been pleased with (*LIT* it has pleased me)

🎬 Coach Dale stands outside his classroom. Later, in the gym, he is called to the microphone.

□ **calurosa** warm · *caluroso* warm
□ **bienvenida** welcome
□ **nos estamos relacionando** we're getting to know each other · *relacionarse* to get to know one another, to build a relationship
□ **emocionado** excited · *emocionarse* to get excited
□ **apoyaran** *SUBJ* you support · *apoyar* to support
□ **individuos** individuals · *individuo* individual
□ **sacrificarse** to make the sacrifice
□ **veintitrés** twenty-three
□ **siguientes** next, following · *siguiente* next, following
□ **representar** to represent
□ **preparatoria** high school
□ **entrega** devotion
□ **esfuerzo** effort
□ **exige** it demands · *exigir* to demand
□ **respeto** respect

## 10 First Game                                  8:24

### Phrases to Listen For

**tienen que** you have to
**¿de acuerdo?** agreed?, all right?
**no lo sé** I don't know
**antes de que** before
**hasta que** until
**por lo menos** at least
**antes de** before

**hay que** it's necessary
**lo que** what
**tenemos que** we have to
**¿por qué?** why?
**loco de remate** completely crazy

### Names
Ollie, Norm

🎬 In the locker room prior to the first game, Coach Dale dries his face. The team is seated on benches facing each other.

□ **disciplinar** to discipline
□ **no encestarán** you will not shoot · *encestar* to shoot, to score [BASKETBALL]
□ **ajusten** *IMP* adjust, set · *ajustar* to adjust, to set
□ **patrones** patterns · *patrón NM* pattern
□ **anotar** to score

🎬 The minister prays while Coach Dale puts on his coat.

□ **oremos** *SUBJ* let us pray · *orar* to pray
□ **valientes** courageous, valiant · *valiente* courageous, valiant
□ **bendice** *IMP* bless · *bendecir* to bless
□ **temporada** season
□ **aguarden** *IMP* wait · *aguardar* to wait
□ **bienvenido** *ADJ* welcome

🎬 The warm-up period ends. Coach Dale talks to Ollie and the team.

□ **oriéntense** *IMP* get yourself set · *orientarse* to get set, to orient oneself
□ **pistones** pistons · *pistón NM* piston

🎬 Strap arrives. The game starts.

□ **parado** standing still · *parar* to stand
□ **lanza** *IMP* shoot · *lanzar* to shoot, to throw
□ **cuida** *IMP* watch (your defense), take care of (your defense) · *cuidar* to take care of
□ **defender** to defend
□ **zonas** zones · *zona* zone
□ **ofensiva** offensive [SPORTS]
□ **encesten** *IMP* shoot · *encestar* to shoot, to score [BASKETBALL]
□ **bloquéalo** *IMP* block him out · *bloquear* to block
□ **centro** *NMF* center [position, player] [BASKETBALL]
□ **compañero** teammate

🎬 The team enters the locker room for halftime.

□ **espantosa** horrible · *espantoso* horrible
□ **boca** mouth
□ **tonterías** foolishness · *tontería* foolish act

□ **vergonzoso** embarrassing
□ **vestidor** dressing room
□ **mitad del partido** halftime · *mitad* NF half, halfway · *partido* game
□ **mantenlos** IMP keep them · *mantener* to keep
□ **estuvimos practicando** we were practicing · *practicar* to practice

🎬 Ollie enters the game for Rade.
□ **quinta** fifth · *quinto* fifth
□ **veinticinco** twenty-five
□ **loco de remate** completely crazy

## 11  The Law                                    1:46

### Phrase to Listen For
**lo que** what

🎬 The team enters the locker room after the game.
□ **orgulloso** proud
□ **valor** NM courage, bravery
□ **condición** condition
□ **concierne** it concerns · *concernir* to concern
□ **absolutamente** absolutely
□ **discusión** discussion, argument

## 12  Sunday Supper                              3:29

### Phrases to Listen For
**por qué** why
**¿por qué?** why?
**lo siento** I'm sorry

### Names
Opal Fleener, Norm

🎬 Coach Dale refuses a haircut and then helps Opal and Myra Fleener load their truck.
□ **corto** I cut · *cortar* to cut
□ **cabello** hair
□ **cortó** he cut · *cortar* to cut
□ **servidor** servant
□ **negarlo** to deny it, to refuse it · *negar* to deny · *negarse* to refuse
□ **no brilla** it doesn't shine · *brillar* to shine
□ **nublado** cloudy · *nublarse* to cloud over
□ **domingo** Sunday

🎬 Coach Dale holds sugarcane in his hand. Opal asks about the boys.
□ **hábleme** IMP tell me · *hablar* to talk, to tell
□ **mejorar** to improve
□ **talento** talent
□ **disciplina** discipline

□ **al respecto** about that, with respect to that
□ **costumbres** habits, customs · *costumbre* habit, custom
□ **entrenarlos** to train them · *entrenar* to train
□ **madera** wood

🎬 Coach Dale and Myra select cane stalks.
□ **evento** event
□ **noche anterior** night before · *noche* NF night · *anterior* previous
□ **amanecer** NM dawn
□ **extremo** extreme
□ **postgrado** post-graduate degree
□ **sorprende** it surprises · *sorprender* to surprise
□ **enfermó** became sick · *enfermar* to become sick
□ **extrañaba** I missed · *extrañar* to miss
□ **cambien** SUBJ they change · *cambiar* to change
□ **seguridad** security
□ **asuntos** matters · *asunto* matter
□ **personales** personal · *personal* personal
□ **privado** private

## 13  Shooter's Game Plan                        1:48

### Phrases to Listen For
**tiene que hacer lo que tiene que hacer** he has to do what he has to do
**tiene que** you have to

### Names
Rooster, Cedar Knob

🎬 Coach Dale looks in a mirror. Shooter arrives at the door.
□ **visitas** visits · *visita* visit
□ **calor** NM heat
□ **delicioso** delicious, delightful
□ **deporte** NM sport
□ **que se ha inventado** that has been invented · *inventar* to invent
□ **acerca de** about
□ **he observado** I have observed · *observar* to observe
□ **entrena** you train · *entrenar* to train, to coach
□ **insectos** insects · *insecto* insect
□ **táctica** tactic
□ **evasiva** evasive · *evasivo* evasive
□ **presionarlos** to press them · *presionar* to press, to pressure
□ **purgatorio** purgatory
□ **gimnasio** gym, gymnasium
□ **metros** meters · *metro* meter
□ **canasta** basket

Hoosiers · · · · · · · · · · · · · 145 · · · · ·

## 14 Passion on the Road 4:20

### Phrases to Listen For

**vuelve a ser** it changes back to, it becomes again
**lo siento** I'm sorry
**lo sentirás** you will be sorry
**¿de acuerdo?** agreed?, all right?
**de acuerdo a** according to
**tener que** to have to
**para empezar** to begin with
**lo mejor** the best
**lo que** what
**¿no es cierto?** isn't that right?
**así es** yes indeed
**¿por qué?** why?
**tienes que** you have to
**te gusta** you like (*LIT* it pleases you)
**me gusta** I like (*LIT* it pleases me)
**de pie** on your feet, standing

### Names

Nelson, Merle, Everett

🎬 Coach Dale sits next to Strap on the team bus.

☐ **autobús** *NM* bus
☐ **predicador** preacher
☐ **temporada** season
☐ **pintamos** we paint · *pintar* to paint
☐ **peregrinación** series of religious revival meetings (*LIT* pilgrimage)
☐ **otoño** autumn, fall
☐ **rojo** red
☐ **revelación** revelation
☐ **pintara** *SUBJ* he paints · *pintar* to paint

🎬 During the game, Coach Dale talks to Cletus on the bench.

☐ **animales** animals · *animal NM* animal
☐ **ratonera** mouse hole
☐ **no lanza** he doesn't shoot · *lanzar* to shoot, to throw
☐ **suéltenme** *IMP* let go of me, let me go · *soltar* to let go, to release
☐ **déjenme en paz** *IMP* leave me alone, leave me in peace · *dejar* to leave · *paz NF* peace
☐ **burlar** to evade, to get around
☐ **evitarlo** to avoid it · *evitar* to avoid
☐ **banca** bench
☐ **cesta** basket

🎬 Coach Dale crosses the court when one of his players is fouled.

☐ **reglas** rules · *regla* rule
☐ **locales** local, home · *local* local, home
☐ **injusto** unjust, unfair

☐ **cueva** cave
☐ **montón** *NM* large pile, large amount
☐ **gorilas** gorillas · *gorila* gorilla
☐ **estúpido** *OFFENSIVE* fool, idiot
☐ **expulsados** ejected, expelled · *expulsado* ejected, expelled · *expulsar* to eject, to expel
☐ **tranquilícense** *IMP* calm down · *tranquilizarse* to calm down
☐ **basura** trash, garbage
☐ **golpe** *NM* hit, blow

🎬 Coach Dale visits Cletus.

☐ **necesario** necessary
☐ **partidos** games · *partido* game
☐ **de pie** on your feet, standing · *pie NM* foot

## 15 Seeking Assistance 4:31

### Phrases to Listen For

**para que** in order to
**así que** so
**todo lo que** everything that
**¿qué tiene que ver el alcohol con...?** what does alcohol have to do with ...?
**lo que** what
**tienen razón** you're right
**así es** agreed, indeed

### Name

Verdi

🎬 Coach Dale drives his car into the forest and honks his horn.

☐ **identifíquese** *IMP* identify yourself · *identificarse* to identify oneself
☐ **consejero** advisor, counselor, scout

🎬 Coach Dale and Shooter sit in front of the fireplace.

☐ **calor** *NM* heat
☐ **invierno** winter
☐ **me las arreglo** I manage (things) · *arreglarse* to manage, to sort out, to work out
☐ **trago** swallow, drink
☐ **proposición** proposition
☐ **asistente** *NMF* assistant
☐ **prácticas** practices · *práctica* practice
☐ **partidos** games · *partido* game
☐ **condiciones** conditions · *condición* condition
☐ **bañarse** to bathe
☐ **afeitarse** to shave oneself
☐ **corbata** tie
☐ **guardado** stored · *guardar* to store, to keep, to save
☐ **arrugado** wrinkled · *arrugar* to wrinkle

□ **sobrio** sober
□ **alcohol** *NM* alcohol
□ **beber** to drink
□ **aliento** breath
□ **alcohólico** alcoholic
□ **se avergüenza** he is ashamed · *avergonzarse* to be ashamed

Coach Dale talks to his team on the bench. Shooter arrives, dressed in a suit.

□ **presión** pressure
□ **paciencia** patience
□ **ofensiva** offense
□ **te repondrás** you will recover · *reponerse* to recover
□ **maravillosamente** marvelously

## 16 Coach in Question          3:51

**Phrases to Listen For**
**lo que** what
**¿por qué?** why?
**al mando** in charge

In class, Ollie reads his report on "Progress."

□ **electricidad** electricity
□ **progreso** progress
□ **unión** consolidation, unification
□ **escolar** *ADJ* school
□ **remodelación** remodeling
□ **iglesia** church building
□ **tractores** tractors · *tractor NM* tractor
□ **adicionales** additional · *adicional* additional
□ **recogedoras de heno** hay bailers · *recogedora* machine that picks or gathers · *heno* hay
□ **recogedoras de maíz** corn pickers · *recogedora* machine that picks or gathers · *maíz NM* corn
□ **segadoras de grano** grain combines · *segadora* combine, harvester · *grano* grain
□ **tajadoras agrícolas** field chopper · *tajadora* chopper
□ **cañerías** plumbing · *cañería* plumbing
□ **internas** indoor · *interno* indoor

Everett remains after class to talk to Coach Dale.

□ **alcohólico** alcoholic
□ **estúpido** *OFFENSIVE* stupid, foolish

Myra Fleener enters the classroom. Everett leaves.

□ **cargo** position
□ **directora** director, principal · *director NM* director, principal
□ **temporal** temporary, provisional
□ **informarle** to inform you · *informar* to inform

□ **se ha publicado** it has been published · *publicar* to publish
□ **petición** petition
□ **removerlo** to remove you · *remover* to remove
□ **puesto** position
□ **votación** voting
□ **sábado** Saturday
□ **junta** meeting
□ **viernes** *NM* Friday
□ **habilidad** ability
□ **complicado** complicated · *complicar* to complicate, to make complicated

Coach Dale asks for a time-out. The referee calls a technical foul.

□ **cometida** committed · *cometido* committed · *cometer* to commit
□ **solamente** only
□ **suspendido** suspended · *suspender* to suspend
□ **obedece** *IMP* obey · *obedecer* to obey
□ **mando** in charge
□ **triunfo** triumph, victory

## 17 Checkered Past          1:47

**Phrases to Listen For**
**lo siento** I'm sorry
**en vez de** instead of

**Name**
Ithaca

Myra Fleener joins Coach Dale in the field.

□ **atractivo** attractive
□ **luchar** to struggle, to fight
□ **huir** to flee, to run away
□ **nacionales** national · *nacional* national
□ **guerreros** warriors · *guerrero* warrior
□ **suspensión** suspension
□ **vitalicia** lifetime · *vitalicio ADJ* lifetime
□ **impuesta** imposed · *impuesto* imposed · *imponer* to impose
□ **comisión** commission
□ **nacional** national
□ **deportiva** sports · *deportivo ADJ* sports
□ **físicamente** physically
□ **serie** *NF* series
□ **incidentes** incidents · *incidente NM* incident
□ **involucrado** involved · *involucrar* to involve
□ **famoso** famous
□ **violento** violent
□ **asociación** association
□ **atlética** athletic · *atlético* athletic
□ **Nueva York** New York

- □ **firmaría** it would sign · *firmar* to sign
- □ **artículo** article
- □ **biblioteca** library
- □ **curiosidad** curiosity
- □ **esfuerzos** efforts · *esfuerzo* effort
- □ **en relación a** relating to
- □ **nobles** noble · *noble ADJ* noble
- □ **dignos** worthy · *digno* worthy
- □ **admiración** admiration
- □ **junta** meeting
- □ **placentero** pleasant

## 18  Town Vote                                              4:24

### Phrases to Listen For
**en cambio** on the other hand
**lo más rápido posible** as fast as possible
**tenemos que hacer algo al respecto** we have to do something about that
**lo que** what
**tengas que** *SUBJ* you have to
**hay que** it's necessary
**volveremos a votar** we will vote again
**de acuerdo** agreed, all right

### Names
Sam, Rollin

🎬 Inside the church, Coach Dale pleads his case.

- □ **he cometido** I have committed, I have made · *cometer* to commit, to make
- □ **errores** mistakes, errors · *error NM* mistake, error
- □ **tomo** I take · *tomar* to take
- □ **absoluta** absolute · *absoluto* absolute
- □ **responsabilidad** responsibility
- □ **contratado** hired · *contratar* to hire, to contract
- □ **entrenar** to coach
- □ **máximo** maximum, best
- □ **habilidad** ability
- □ **pido disculpas** I apologize · *pedir disculpas* to apologize
- □ **complacidos** pleased · *complacido* pleased · *complacer* to please
- □ **resultados** results · *resultado* result
- □ **orgulloso** proud

🎬 Myra Fleener joins several men up front and speaks to the crowd.

- □ **equivocación** mistake
- □ **voto** I vote · *votar* to vote
- □ **boletas** tickets, ballots · *boleta* ticket, ballot
- □ **votar** to vote

🎬 Jimmy enters and asks to speak.

- □ **cambie** *SUBJ* it changes · *cambiar* to change
- □ **trato** deal
- □ **despedido** fired, dismissed · *despedir* to fire, to dismiss
- □ **votación** voting
- □ **sesenta y ocho** sixty-eight
- □ **se oponen** they are opposed · *oponerse* to be opposed

## 19  Team Turnaround                                      2:37

### Phrases to Listen For
**¿por qué?** why?
**para que** in order to
**lo que** what
**tenemos que** we have to
**a como de lugar** no matter what
**tienes que** you have to
**palabra de explorador** scout's honor (*LIT* word of a scout)

🎬 After a scene sequence of several games, Coach Dale plunges Shooter's head into a sink of water.

- □ **arriesgué** I risked · *arriesgar* to risk
- □ **controlarte** to control yourself · *controlarse* to control oneself
- □ **hospital** *NM* hospital
- □ **te cures** *SUBJ* you are healed · *curarse* to heal, to be healed
- □ **resistir** to hold on, to hang in there
- □ **ejército** army
- □ **nervios** *NMPL* nerves
- □ **destrozados** exhausted, shot · *destrozado* exhausted, shot · *destrozar* to exhaust, to ruin
- □ **pistones** pistons · *pistón NM* piston
- □ **partidos** games · *partido* game
- □ **palabra de explorador** scout's honor (*LIT* word of a scout) · *explorador* boy scout
- □ **prometiste** you promised · *prometer* to promise

## 20  Shooter's Shot                                         4:26

### Phrases to Listen For
**¿de acuerdo?** all right?, agreed?
**por favor** please
**toda la noche** all night
**de acuerdo** agreed, all right

### Names
Rade, Buddy, Merle

🎬 Coach Dale stands up to talk to the referee.

- □ **veintiuno** twenty-one
- □ **uniforme** *NM* uniform
- □ **rojo** red
- □ **discutir** to discuss
- □ **tranquilízate** *IMP* relax, calm down ·
  *tranquilizarse* to calm down
- □ **ciego** blind
- □ **ángulo** angle
- □ **violento** violent
- □ **abuso** abuse
- □ **desgracia** disgrace
- □ **profesión** profession
- □ **sáqueme** *IMP* kick me out, throw me out ·
  *sacar* to throw out, to take out, to remove
- □ **absurdo** absurd
- □ **gritar** to shout, to scream
- □ **demente** *NMF* demented person
- □ **injusto** unjust, unfair
- □ **depende** it depends · *depender* to depend

🎬 With the score tied at 58, a time-out is called, and the team looks to Shooter for guidance.

- □ **probable** probable, likely
- □ **expulsen** *SUBJ* they take out · *expulsar* to take out, to remove from the action, to eject
- □ **ocuparás su lugar** you will take his place · *ocupar* to take, to fill, to occupy
- □ **cierren** *IMP* close · *cerrar* to close
- □ **táctica** tactic
- □ **fantástico** fantastic
- □ **te felicito** I congratulate you · *felicitar* to congratulate

## 21 | Sectional Finals          4:36

### Phrases to Listen For
**¿de acuerdo?** agreed?, all right?
**tiene que** you have to

### Names
Deerlick, Norm

🎬 The team warms up for the Sectional Finals in Deerlick, Indiana.

- □ **división** division
- □ **presión** pressure
- □ **concéntrate** *IMP* concentrate, focus · *concentrarse* to concentrate, to focus
- □ **mentalmente** mentally
- □ **ambos** both
- □ **encima de** on top of
- □ **cometida** committed · *cometido* committed · *cometer* · to commit

- □ **rojo** red
- □ **absurdo** absurd

🎬 Shooter, inebriated, walks onto the court.

- □ **derecho** right
- □ **mentira** lie
- □ **movió** he moved · *mover* to move
- □ **injusticia** injustice
- □ **árbitro** referee
- □ **anteojos** *NMPL* eyeglasses
- □ **controlado** controlled, under control · *controlar* to control
- □ **asistente** *NMF* assistant
- □ **no me discuta** *IMP* don't argue with me · *discutir* to argue
- □ **entrada** entrance

🎬 A fight breaks out on the court.

- □ **apártense** *IMP* break it up, separate, move away · *apartarse* to separate, to move away
- □ **herido** wounded · *herir* to wound, to hurt
- □ **multarlos** to fine them · *multar* to fine
- □ **lastimado** injured · *lastimar* to injure, to hurt
- □ **protesta** protest
- □ **culpable** *NMF* guilty person
- □ **cobarde** cowardly
- □ **salvajes** savages · *salvaje NMF* savage
- □ **reanude** *SUBJ* it resumes · *reanudar* to resume

## 22 | Hospital Visit          2:34

### Phrases to Listen For
**lo que** what
**de acuerdo** all right
**por favor** please
**lo siento** I'm sorry
**tengo mucha sed** I'm very thirsty

### Name
Sahara

🎬 Shortly, Coach Dale visits Shooter in the hospital.

- □ **seco** dry
- □ **desierto** desert
- □ **visitarme** to visit me · *visitar* to visit
- □ **gnomos** gnomes · *gnomo* gnome
- □ **criaturas** creatures · *criatura* creature
- □ **verdes** green · *verde* green
- □ **puntadas** stitches · *puntada* stitch
- □ **excelente** excellent
- □ **regionales** regional · *regional* regional
- □ **orgulloso** proud
- □ **realmente** really
- □ **locales** local · *local* local

□ **me estoy congelando** I'm freezing ·
*congelarse* to freeze, to be freezing
□ **manta** blanket
□ **controlarme** to control myself · *controlarse*
to control oneself
□ **conseguiste** you got · *conseguir* to get,
to acquire
□ **alcohólico** alcoholic
□ **inútil** useless
□ **castigarte** to punish yourself · *castigarse*
to punish oneself
□ **enfermera** nurse · *enfermero* nurse
□ **tengo mucha sed** I'm very thirsty · *tener sed*
to be thirsty (*LIT* to have thirst)

## 23 Regional Finals  6:34

### Phrases to Listen For
**lo mismo** the same
**después de** after
**por supuesto** of course
**más allá de** beyond
**así que** so
**una y otra vez** again and again
**lo más importante** the most important thing
**lo mejor** the best
**tienes que** you have to
**¿de acuerdo?** agreed?, all right?
**no es cierto** that's not right
**a menos que** unless

### Names
Jasper, Indiana, Bobby Rocket

The team arrives at the Regional Finals in Jasper, Indiana.

□ **protegernos** to protect us · *proteger* to protect
□ **gimnasio** gymnasium
□ **ojalá** hopefully
□ **campeonato** championship
□ **regional** regional

Coach Dale arrives in the locker room before the game.

□ **tradición** tradition
□ **competencias** competitions · *competencia*
competition
□ **siguiente** next, following
□ **enfrente** *ADV* in front
□ **tamaño** size
□ **lujosos** luxurious · *lujoso* luxurious
□ **uniformes** uniforms · *uniforme NM* uniform
□ **concéntrense** *IMP* concentrate, focus ·
*concentrarse* to concentrate, to focus

□ **principios** principles · *principio* principle
□ **hemos repasado** we have gone over, we have
reviewed · *repasar* to go over, to review
□ **esfuerzo** effort
□ **concentración** concentration
□ **habilidad** ability
□ **resultado** result
□ **ganadores** winners · *ganador* winner

As the game progresses, Coach Dale paces and shouts.

□ **movimiento** movement, move
□ **ilegal** illegal
□ **bloquéalo** *IMP* block him out · *bloquear* to block
□ **bloquea** *IMP* block · *bloquear* to block
□ **¿quién tira?** who's shooting? · *tirar* to shoot,
to throw

Coach Dale talks to the team on the bench.

□ **impedir** to stop, to impede
□ **no te separes** *IMP* don't move away, don't leave,
don't split up · *separarse* to move away, to leave,
to split up
□ **ofensiva** offense [SPORTS]
□ **pégate a él** *IMP* stick to him · *pegarse*
to stick to
□ **goma de mascar** chewing gum · *goma* gum ·
*mascar* to chew
□ **sabor** *NM* flavor
□ **¡demonios!** *INT* demons! · *demonio* demon
□ **¿qué está usted marcando?** what are you calling
(a foul)? · *marcar* to call (a foul) [SPORTS]
□ **pie** *NM* foot
□ **adentro** inside
□ **obstrucción** obstruction

An opposing player hits Everett in the shoulder, knocking his stitches loose.

□ **absurdo** absurd
□ **puntadas** stitches · *puntada* stitch
□ **tape** *IMP* cover · *tapar* to cover
□ **herida** wound
□ **tápela** *IMP* cover it up · *tapar* to cover
□ **bloqueando** blocking · *bloquear* to block
□ **banca** bench
□ **obedece** *IMP* obey · *obedecer* to obey
□ **cesta** basket
□ **quince** fifteen
□ **paciencia** patience
□ **adecuado** right, correct

After the time-out, Strap concludes his prayer and enters the game for Everett.

□ **jugada** play [SPORTS]
□ **utiliza** *IMP* use · *utilizar* to use, to utilize

□ **rebotar** bouncing · *rebotar* to bounce
□ **catorce** fourteen
□ **¿están bromeando?** are you joking? ·
*bromear* to joke

## 24  Ollie's Opportunity                    4:54

### Phrases to Listen For
**¿de acuerdo?** agreed?, all right?
**lo que** what

### Names
Ollie Collins, Wildcats

On the bench, Coach Dale calls for Ollie to enter the game.

□ **me resbalé** I slipped · *resbalarse* to slip
□ **trece** thirteen
□ **anoten** *IMP* score · *anotar* to score
□ **cometan** *IMP* commit · *cometer* to commit
□ **tiro libre** free throw · *tiro* throw · *libre* free
□ **demuéstrales** *IMP* show them · *demostrar* to show
□ **tiros** shots · *tiro* shot
□ **tiempo fuera** time-out
□ **pedido** asked for, requested · *pedir* to ask for, to request

During the time-out, the band plays. Coach Dale talks to the players on the bench.

□ **meta** *SUBJ* he puts in · *meter* to put in
□ **defensiva** defense [SPORTS]
□ **de inmediato** immediately, right away
□ **disparo** shot
□ **desesperado** *ADJ* desperate, desperation
□ **que dé resultado** *SUBJ* may it give good results · *dar* to give

Ollie steps to the free throw line.

□ **enanos** dwarves, midgets · *enano* dwarf, midget
□ **concéntrate** *IMP* concentrate, focus · *concentrarse* to concentrate, to focus
□ **bloqueen** *IMP* block out · *bloquear* to block

## 25  A Long Time                             2:53

### Phrases to Listen For
**¿siempre está en lo correcto?** is it always right?
**lo que** what, that

### Names
Deerlick, Norman Dale, Ithaca

Myra is turning the soil. Coach Dale walks toward his car and calls to her.

□ **sembrar** to seed, to plant seeds
□ **lodo** mud
□ **almanaque** *NM* almanac
□ **correcto** correct
□ **granjero** farmer
□ **molinero** miller
□ **me cortó el cabello** she gave me a haircut · *cortar* to cut
□ **cabello** hair
□ **dar un paseo** to take a walk

Coach Dale and Myra take a walk among the trees.

□ **primavera** spring [SEASON]
□ **verde** green
□ **Irlanda** Ireland
□ **fotografías** photographs · *fotografía* photograph
□ **postales** postcards · *postal* *NM* postcard
□ **cine** *NM* cinema, movie theater
□ **guerreros** warriors · *guerrero* warrior
□ **suspendido** suspended · *suspender* to suspend
□ **puño** fist
□ **lastimar** to hurt
□ **curioso** curious, strange
□ **época** epoch, time, era
□ **rudo** rough
□ **terco** stubborn
□ **obstinado** obstinate
□ **te besaba** I was kissing you, I kissed you · *besar* to kiss

## 26  Press Conference                        1:00

### Phrases to Listen For
**no lo sé** I don't know
**tal vez** maybe, perhaps
**así que** so
**lo que** what

### Name
Indianapolis

The team walks through the entry tunnel leading to their home court. Ollie is being interviewed by a reporter.

□ **semejante** similar
□ **hazaña** deed
□ **sino** but rather
□ **sorprendido** surprised · *sorprender* to surprise
□ **canasta** basket
□ **se enfrentarán** you will be facing · *enfrentar* to face

- **poderosos** powerful · *poderoso* powerful
- **miden** they measure · *medir* to measure
- **metros** meters · *metro* meter
- **competir** to compete
- **profesionales** professionals · *profesional* professional
- **agricultura** agriculture, farming
- **edificio** building
- **pisos** floors · *piso* floor
- **excepto** except
- **fotografías** photographs · *fotografía* photograph
- **ante** before, in front of
- **quince** fifteen
- **luna** moon

## 27 Redemption 2:26

**Phrases to Listen For**
**¿te sientes bien?** do you feel all right?
**tengo que irme** I have to go

**Name**
Ollie

Shooter is in the hospital, talking to a nurse at her desk. Shortly, Everett arrives.

- **campeonato** championship
- **estatal** *ADJ* state
- **héroe** *NM* hero
- **radio** radio
- **oí** I heard · *oír* to hear
- **cometieron** they committed · *cometer* to commit
- **gritar** to shout, to scream
- **camisa de fuerza** straitjacket
- **vacío** empty
- **alucinaciones** hallucinations · *alucinación* hallucination
- **mejorar** to improve
- **compraremos** we'll buy · *comprar* to buy
- **acompañarte** to accompany you, to go with you · *acompañar* to accompany, to go with
- **despedázalos** *IMP* destroy them, tear them to pieces · *despedazar* to tear to pieces
- **repetir** to repeat

## 28 Same Measurements 2:38

**Phrases to Listen For**
**así que** so
**mucha suerte** good luck (*LIT* much luck)

**Names**
Butcher, Butler, Ollie

The garage door rises. Coach Dale and the team enter the tunnel.

- **bienvenidos** welcome · *bienvenido* *ADJ* welcome
- **gimnasio** gymnasium, gym
- **horario** schedule
- **práctica** practice
- **llevará a cabo** it will take place · *llevar a cabo* to take place
- **avísenme** *IMP* let me know · *avisar* to let know, to warn
- **suceso** event, occurrence
- **emocionante** exciting
- **triunfen** *SUBJ* you triumph, you win · *triunfar* to triumph, to win

The team walks onto the gym floor.

- **debajo de** underneath
- **tablero** backboard
- **¿cuánto mide?** how long is it?, what does it measure? · *medir* to measure
- **metros** meters · *metro* meter
- **hombros** shoulders · *hombro* shoulder
- **aro** hoop
- **notarán** you will notice · *notar* to notice
- **medidas** measurements · *medida* measurement
- **practicar** to practice
- **inmenso** immense

## 29 David & Goliath 3:45

**Phrases to Listen For**
**todo el tiempo** all the time
**tienen que** you have to
**ya que** since

**Names**
South Bend Central, Boyd, David

The crowd cheers as the announcer welcomes them to the championship game.

- **bienvenidos** welcome · *bienvenido* *ADJ* welcome
- **campeonato** championship
- **escuelas preparatorias** high schools · *escuela* school · *preparatoria* preparatory
- **confrontación** confrontation
- **improbable** improbable
- **célebre** celebrated, famous
- **torneos** tournaments · *torneo* tournament

A family listens to the game on the radio.

- **que se lleva a cabo** that is taking place · *llevarse a cabo* to take place
- **diminuta** tiny
- **total** total
- **sesenta y cuatro** sixty-four

□ **alumnos** students · *alumno* student
□ **estatales** state · *estatal* ADJ state
□ **gigantescos** giant
□ **osos** bears · *oso* bear
□ **dos mil ochocientos** two thousand eight hundred
□ **siglo** century

🎬 Shooter listens to the game on the radio.

□ **centrales** central · *central* central
□ **presenciar** to be present for, to witness
□ **versión** version
□ **Cenicienta** Cinderella

🎬 Coach Dale writes on the chalkboard.

□ **repasamos** we reviewed · *repasar* to review
□ **quince** fifteen
□ **anota** he scores · *anotar* to score
□ **promedio** average
□ **mantengan la calma** IMP keep calm ·
   *mantener* to keep · *calma* calm
□ **cierren** IMP close · *cerrar* to close
□ **con rudeza** tough (LIT with toughness) ·
   *rudeza* toughness, roughness
□ **compensar** to compensate
□ **altura** height
□ **reverendo** reverend
□ **discurso** speech

🎬 The team bows for prayer.

□ **batalla** battle
□ **no depende** it doesn't depend · *depender*
   to depend
□ **guerreros** warriors · *guerrero* warrior
□ **sino** but rather, but instead
□ **proveniente** coming (from)
□ **bolsa** bag
□ **piedra** rock
□ **arrojó** he threw · *arrojar* to throw forcefully
□ **filisteo** Philistine
□ **suelo** ground

## 30 Championship Game   10:05

### Phrases to Listen For

**tal vez** maybe, perhaps
**tenemos que** we have to
**de acuerdo** all right
**en cuanto** as soon as
**en marcha** let's go
**para que** in order to

### Names

Buddy, South Bend Central, Buddy Walker, Everett
Flatch, Merle Webb, Jimmy Chitwood, Willy Long,
Wilbert, Steve Aroby, Walker, Earle, Rade Butcher

🎬 The game is under way. Coach Dale calls a time-out.

□ **excelentes** excellent · *excelente* excellent
□ **vergüenza** embarrassment
□ **bloquearlo** to block him out · *bloquear* to block
□ **burlar** to get by, to evade, to get away
□ **cuida** he guards · *cuidar* to guard [BASKETBALL]
□ **distraemos** we distract · *distraer* to distract

🎬 The game resumes after the time-out.
   Coach Dale shouts instructions.

□ **con calma** easy, calmly · *calma* calm
□ **paciencia** patience

🎬 The radio announcer describes the action.

□ **período** period
□ **se la lanza** it is thrown · *lanzar* to throw
□ **salta** he jumps · *saltar* to jump
□ **anota** he scores · *anotar* to score
□ **falla** he misses · *fallar* to miss (a shot)
   [BASKETBALL]

🎬 Coach Dale shouts from the bench.

□ **excelente** excellent
□ **presiónenlos** IMP press them · *presionar*
   to press, to pressure
□ **indica** he calls, he indicates · *indicar* to indicate
□ **jugada** play [SPORTS]
□ **línea lateral** sideline
□ **rebota** it bounces · *rebotar* to bounce
□ **canasta** basket
□ **recuperan** they recover · *recuperar* to recover
□ **bola** ball

🎬 With the score 40-38, Jimmy Chitwood intercepts
   the ball and ties the game.

□ **marcador** scoreboard
□ **sensacional** sensational
□ **intercepta** he intercepts · *interceptar*
   to intercept
□ **empatados** tied · *empatado* tied ·
   *empatar* to tie, to even up
□ **he presenciado** I have been present for,
   I have witnessed · *presenciar* to be present for,
   to witness
□ **presiónalo** IMP pressure him · *presionar*
   to pressure, to press

🎬 Hickory intercepts the ball and calls a time-out.
   Coach Dale outlines a play.

□ **señuelo** decoy
□ **¡en marcha!** EXP let's go!
□ **se recuperó** it recovered · *recuperarse* to recover
□ **diecinueve** nineteen
□ **responsable** responsible
□ **intercepción** interception

## 31  Team! Team! Team!                    1:08

**Phrases to Listen For**

**nos estamos relacionando**  we're getting to know
 each other
**lo que**  what

🎬 Inside the empty gym, a small boy shoots baskets.

☐ **consiste**  it consists · *consistir*  to consist
☐ **fundamental** *ADJ*  fundamental

☐ **nos estamos relacionando**  we're getting to know
 each other · *relacionarse*  to get to know one
 another, to build a relationship
☐ **divertido**  fun · *divertirse*  to have fun
☐ **unidad**  unit

## 32  End Credits                          4:01

🎬 End credits.

# Rocky III

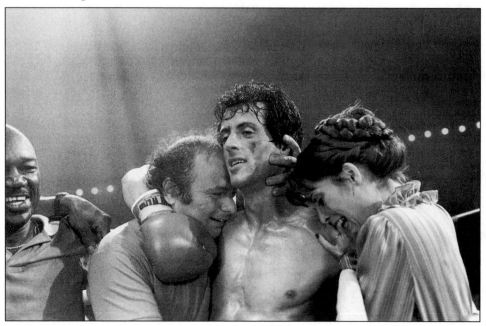

—¿Estás bien? —Mejor que nunca.
*"Are you all right?" "Better than ever."*

GENRE       Drama/Sports
YEAR        1982
DIRECTOR    Sylvester Stallone
CAST        Sylvester Stallone, Mr. T, Talia Shire, Burgess Meredith
STUDIO      MGM

Rocky learns the consequences of trading a dusty gym filled with sweat and blood for the glitter of celebrity and wealth. However, with the help of coach Mickey, wife Adrian, and former opponent Apollo Creed, Rocky discovers how to face many life challenges—the death of a loved one, the cruel reality of being dethroned, and the emptiness of leaving your best work undone. *Rocky III* carries an Intermediate rank because the dialogue is very rapid in some of the boxing scenes, and it can be difficult to understand, yet between these fast and furious scenes are many opportunities to learn vocabulary related to success and failure, victory and defeat, and sports—especially boxing. Beginners or Advanced Beginners shouldn't be put off by the film's ranking if they are familiar with the story.

## BASIC VOCABULARY

### Names
Mickey, Apollo, Clubber, Adrian, Paulie, Rocky

### Nouns
☐ **asaltos** boxing rounds · **asalto** boxing round · *Él jamás ha peleado a quince asaltos.* He's never fought fifteen rounds. · *Creo que Lang no esperaba esto en el primer asalto y veamos qué ocurre en el segundo.* I think Lang wasn't expecting that in the first round and we'll see what happens in the second.

☐ **boca** mouth · *Y cuando lo vea, le cerraré la boca.* And when I see him, I'll shut his mouth.

☐ **boxeador** boxer · *Soy tan bueno como otro boxeador.* I'm as good as any other boxer.

☐ **centro** middle, center · *Esta es una gran batalla, y los dos peleadores están exhaustos en el centro del cuadrilátero.* This is a great battle, and the two fighters are exhausted in the middle of the ring.

☐ **cuadrilátero** boxing ring · *Aquí en el cuadrilátero yo soy el superhombre.* Here in the ring, I am the superman.

☐ **nocaut** knockout · *Damas y caballeros, el ganador por nocaut...* Ladies and gentlemen, the winner by knockout ...

☐ **peso completo** heavyweight · *peso* weight · *completo* complete · *Bienvenidos a la pelea por el título de peso completo.* Welcome to the fight for the heavyweight title.

☐ **semental** stallion · *Lo que tú digas, Semental.* Whatever you say, Stallion.

☐ **título** title · *No quieren que tenga título, porque yo no soy un tipo al que pueda dominar como él.* They don't want me to have the title, because I'm not the kind they can dominate like him.

### Verb
☐ **acábalo** *IMP* finish him, finish it · *acabar* to finish, to finish off · *Acábalo.* Finish him.

### Other
☐ **mundial** *ADJ* world · *Ha defendido su título diez veces y por ahora ha aceptado tener un enfrentamiento con el campeón mundial de lucha.* He has defended his title ten times and as of now he has accepted a match with the world champion of wrestling.

☐ **qué rayos** *INT* what the heck · *¿Qué rayos quieres?* What the heck do you want?

## 1 Title/Champion     3:10

### Phrases to Listen For
**lo que** what
**ya lo tienes** it's all yours, you have it already

**no lo sé** I don't know
**campeón mundial** world champion
**peso completo** heavyweight

### Name
Apollo Creed

🎬 Over titles, an announcer describes the fight between Rocky Balboa and Apollo Creed.

☐ **ciego** blind
☐ **conmoción** shock
☐ **acercamiento** act of moving closer
☐ **intenso** intense
☐ **responde** he responds · *responder* to respond, to answer
☐ **izquierdazo** punch made with the left hand [SPORTS]
☐ **agotados** exhausted · *agotado* exhausted · *agotar* to exhaust, to wear out
☐ **derechazo** punch made with the right hand [SPORTS]
☐ **tremendo** tremendous
☐ **batalla** battle
☐ **peleadores** fighters · *peleador* fighter
☐ **exhaustos** exhausted · *exhausto* exhausted

🎬 Both Rocky and Creed are on the mat while the referee counts.

☐ **retendrá** he will retain · *retener* to retain
☐ **título** title
☐ **trata** he tries · *tratar* to try, to attempt
☐ **piso** floor

🎬 Apollo falls to the mat.

☐ **triunfo** triumph
☐ **ha conmocionado** he has excited, he has emotionally moved · *conmocionar* to excite, to move emotionally
☐ **asombrosa** amazing · *asombroso* amazing
☐ **lo vencí** I beat him · *vencer* to beat, to defeat

## 2 Defender     3:39

### Phrases to Listen For
**así se hace** that's how you do it, that's how it's done
**no puede ser** it can't be
**primer contrincante** top challenger
**lo que** what

### Names
Jaffe, Muppets

🎬 "Eye of the Tiger" plays while Rocky's successes and Clubber Lang's victories are shown.

□ **rodéalo** *IMP* corral him · *rodear* to surround
□ **Bola del Fuego** Ball of Fire
□ **noquea** he knocks out · *noquear* to knock out
□ **alemán** *NM* German
□ **sexta** sixth · *sexto* sixth
□ **asciende** he climbs, he ascends · *ascender* to climb, to ascend
□ **octavo** eighth
□ **peldaño** position, rung, step
□ **golpéame** *IMP* hit me · *golpear* to hit

🎬 Rocky is a guest on the Muppets' television program.

□ **programa** *NM* program
□ **invitado especial** special guest · *invitado* invited guest

🎬 Clubber Lang raises his hands in victory.

□ **contrincante** *NMF* challenger, opponent, rival
□ **tras** after

## 3 ⬛ Credits/Poor Paulie     6:06

### Phrases to Listen For
**toda mi vida** all my life
**campeón mundial** world champion
**tendremos que** we will have to
**lista de espera** waiting list
**¿qué te pasa?** what's the matter with you?
**¿por qué?** why?
**hasta que** until
**cuida la boca** *IMP* watch your mouth
**por favor** please
**de todas formas** anyway
**cállate la boca** *IMP* shut your mouth
**tenías que** you had to

### Names
Clubber Lang, Paulie, Paul

🎬 Clubber Lang is seen on a black-and-white television. Shortly, Paulie is shown watching.

□ **se atreve** he dares · *atreverse* to dare
□ **enfrentarme** to face me · *enfrentar* to face
□ **entreno** I train · *entrenar* to train
□ **evitarme** to avoid me · *evitar* to avoid
□ **esconderse** to hide

🎬 On the black-and-white television, sports announcer Jim Hill comments on Clubber Lang and Rocky Balboa.

□ **peleador** fighter
□ **zurdo** left-handed

□ **ha defendido** he has defended · *defender* to defend
□ **enfrentamiento** match [BOXING]
□ **lucha** wrestling
□ **especie** *NF* kind, type
□ **beneficio** benefit
□ **destinado** designated · *destinar* to designate
□ **fundación** foundation
□ **local** local
□ **crédito** credit
□ **deportista** *NMF* sportsman, sportswoman
□ **contrincante** *NMF* challenger, opponent
□ **estén pendientes** *IMP* be on the lookout, pay attention · *estar pendiente* to be on the lookout, to pay attention

🎬 Paulie leaves the bar where he was watching television. A commercial plays in the background.

□ **asombro** amazement
□ **dispóngase** *IMP* prepare, get ready · *disponerse* to prepare, to get ready
□ **asombrarse** to be amazed
□ **saludar** to greet, to say hello
□ **cerveza** beer
□ **no me saludas** you don't give me your best wishes, you don't greet me · *saludar* to give one's best wishes, to send one's best wishes, to greet
□ **le enviamos saludos** we send him our best wishes, we send greetings · *saludo* greeting

🎬 Paulie throws a bottle at a "Rocky" pinball machine. Outside the jail, Rocky and Paulie walk in a parking garage.

□ **creciera** *SUBJ* she grows up · *crecer* to grow, to grow up
□ **infierno** hell
□ **cuida** *IMP* watch · *cuidar* to watch
□ **no me asustas** you don't scare me · *asustar* to scare, to frighten
□ **mírate** *IMP* look at yourself · *mirar* to look at
□ **rostro** face
□ **luce** it radiates, it shines · *lucir* to radiate, to shine
□ **atractivo** attractive
□ **ropa** clothes

🎬 Paulie removes his watch.

□ **sucio** dirty
□ **miserable** miserable
□ **reloj** *NM* watch
□ **vago** bum
□ **se reían de ti** they laughed at you · *reírse* to laugh

□ **parlotear** to talk, to chat
□ **quién sacó la cara por ti** who stuck his neck out for you · *sacar la cara por* to stick one's neck out for (*LIT* to stick one's face out for)
□ **ambos** both
□ **nadie se reía de mí** nobody laughed at me · *reírse* to laugh
□ **responsable** responsible
□ **embarazada** pregnant
□ **premio** prize

▉ Paulie stops walking and faces Rocky.

□ **compras** you buy · *comprar* to buy
□ **preguntaste** you asked · *preguntar* to ask
□ **sentimientos** feelings · *sentimiento* feeling
□ **piedra** rock
□ **al diablo con todos** to hell with everyone (*LIT* to the devil with everyone) · *diablo* devil
□ **estupideces** nonsense · *estupidez NF* nonsense, stupidity
□ **perdedor** loser
□ **celoso** jealous
□ **holgazán** *NM* lazy person
□ **¿te costó mucho?** did it cost a lot? · *costar* to cost

## 4 | Thunderlips                                    10:09

### Phrases to Listen For

**te importaría?** would you care?, would it matter to you?, would you mind?
**así es** that's it
**estamos de suerte** we're in luck, we're lucky
**estamos de mucha suerte** we're very lucky
**por fortuna** fortunately, luckily
**¿qué rayos...?** what in the world ...?, what the heck ...?
**creo que sí** I think so
**no lo creo** I don't believe it
**campeón mundial** world champion
**Semental Italiano** Italian Stallion
**para qué** what for
**así que** so
**estás en problemas** you are in trouble
**¿qué tal...?** what about ...?
**por supuesto** of course
**santo cielo** good heavens
**Dios mío** good heavens (*LIT* my God)
**está en apuros** he's in a tight spot
**tiene que** he has to
**¿te sientes bien?** do you feel all right?
**ya lo tienes** it's all yours, you have it already
**el año que entra** next year
**de esa forma** like that, in that way

### Names

Dennis James, Jim Healy, Bob Hope, Philadelphia, Mick, Mickey, Rocko, Thunderlips, Relámpago

▉ Rocky, leaning against the headboard of their bed, talks to Adrian.

□ **normal** normal
□ **pelearás** you will fight · *pelear* to fight
□ **luchador** wrestler
□ **divertido** fun · *divertirse* to have fun
□ **canto** I sing · *cantar* to sing
□ **despertarás** you will wake · *despertar* to wake, to wake up
□ **composición** song, tune, composition
□ **por fortuna** fortunately, luckily

▉ Battle of Champions: Rocky Balboa vs. Thunderlips.

□ **aficionados** fans · *aficionado* fan
□ **encuentro** encounter
□ **donado** donated · *donar* to donate
□ **caridad** charity
□ **salúdalo** *IMP* say hello · *saludar* to say hello, to greet
□ **¿qué opinas?** what do you think? · *opinar* to think, to give an opinion
□ **arena** arena
□ **teoría** theory
□ **funciones normales** right mind · *función* function · *normal* normal
□ **criatura** creature
□ **daño cerebral** brain damage · *daño* damage · *cerebral* brain
□ **luchadores** wrestlers · *luchador* wrestler
□ **dinosaurio** dinosaur
□ **últimamente** recently, lately
□ **causarte** to cause you · *causar* to cause
□ **daños** damage, damages, harm · *daño* damage, harm
□ **severos** severe, serious · *severo* severe, serious

▉ Two announcers in black tuxedos talk about Thunderlips' arrival.

□ **lucha** wrestling
□ **realmente** really
□ **vestuario** clothing, wardrobe
□ **espectacular** spectacular
□ **cargando** carrying · *cargar* to carry
□ **beneficio** benefit
□ **anatomía** anatomy

▉ Thunderlips (*Relámpago*) enters the ring.

□ **relámpago** flash of lightning
□ **macho** macho, real man
□ **fiambre** *NM* corpse, dead meat
□ **¡diablos!** *INT* yikes! (*LIT* devils!) · *diablo* devil

- **monstruo** monster
- **¿subirías...?** would you go up ...? · *subir* to go up, to climb up
- **saludarlo** to greet him · *saludar* to greet
- **esquina** corner
- **espectáculo** show, spectacle
- **estatura** height
- **ciento setenta y cinco** one hundred seventy-five
- **kilos** kilos, kilograms · *kilo* kilo, kilogram
- **brazo** arm
- **objeto** object
- **montaña** mountain
- **lujuria** lust, lechery
- **fundida** smelted · *fundido* smelted · *fundir* to smelt, to melt

🎬 Thunderlips points his finger at the crowd.
- **basura** trash, garbage

🎬 The ring announcer introduces Rocky.
- **Filadelfia** Philadelphia
- **Semental Italiano** Italian Stallion
- **coma** SUBJ he eats · *comer* to eat
- **noventa** ninety
- **gramos** grams · *gramo* gram

🎬 Rocky and Mickey walk toward the center of the ring.
- **solo es una diversión** it's just for fun · *diversión* fun
- **posamos** we pose · *posar* to pose
- **fotografía** photograph
- **enano** dwarf
- **me enfadé** I got angry, I got annoyed · *enfadarse* to get angry, to get annoyed
- **partirlo** to cut you · *partir* to cut, to split
- **pedazos** pieces · *pedazo* piece
- **rostro** face
- **alrededor** around
- **corra** SUBJ he runs · *correr* to run
- **me pongo nervioso** I get nervous · *ponerse nervioso* to get nervous

🎬 The bell rings and Thunderlips charges Rocky in his corner.
- **¿por qué no damos vueltas?** why don't we go around and around? · *dar vueltas* to go around
- **balancear** to keep things in balance, to balance
- **asunto** matter
- **¿no te dolió?** didn't it hurt? · *doler* to hurt
- **no finjas** IMP don't fake it · *fingir* to fake
- **totalmente** totally
- **frenético** crazy, out of his mind
- **dura** tough, hard · *duro* tough, hard

- **acuérdate** IMP remember · *acordarse* to remember
- **barrio** barrio, neighborhood
- **espíritu** NM spirit
- **espalda** back
- **¿se divierte?** is he having fun? · *divertirse* to have fun

🎬 Thunderlips leaps in the air and lands on Rocky.
- **hacha** hatchet
- **está en apuros** he's in a jam, he's in a tight spot, he's in trouble · *estar en apuros* to be in a jam, to be in a tight spot, to be in trouble
- **superhombre** superman
- **detenlo** IMP stop him · *detener* to stop
- **saco** sack
- **patatas** potatoes · *patata* potato

🎬 Thunderlips hurls Rocky into the crowd.
- **quinta** fifth · *quinto* fifth
- **fila** row
- **se ha convertido** it has become, it has turned into · *convertirse* to become, to turn into
- **verdadera** true, real · *verdadero* true, real
- **confusión** confusion, mess
- **furioso** furious
- **trapo** washrag
- **sucio** dirty
- **no me estorbe** IMP get out of my way · *estorbar* to be in the way, to block

🎬 Thunderlips throws the referee across the ring.
- **guardias** guards · *guardia* NMF guard [PERSON]
- **intervienen** they intervene · *intervenir* to intervene
- **quítenme** IMP take off (of me) · *quitar* to take off
- **guantes** gloves · *guante* NM glove
- **por los aires** through the air · *aire* NM air
- **zoológico** zoo
- **peligroso** dangerous
- **comisionado** commissioner
- **enseguida** right away, at once
- **demente** NMF demented individual

🎬 Rocky jumps into the ring. Thunderlips joins him.
- **gusanos** worms · *gusano* worm
- **estrangularlo** to strangle him · *estrangular* to strangle
- **perro de caza** hunting dog · *caza* hunting
- **aplica** he applies, he's applying · *aplicar* to apply
- **llave estranguladora** headlock · *llave* NF key · *estrangulador* strangling

□ **cuerpo** body
□ **golpéalo** IMP hit him · *golpear* to hit
□ **desármalo** IMP weaken him, take away his strength · *desarmar* to weaken, to disarm

🎬 Rocky hurls Thunderlips from the ring.

□ **rascacielos** NM skyscraper
□ **humano** human
□ **arrojado** thrown · *arrojar* to throw
□ **no me estorben** IMP get out of my way, stay out of my way, don't block me · *estorbar* to be in the way, to block
□ **empate** NM tie
□ **asistir** attending · *asistir* to attend
□ **anual** annual
□ **doce** twelve
□ **actuaste** you acted · *actuar* to act
□ **duele** it hurts · *doler* to hurt

## 5   One More Fight         10:37

### Phrases to Listen For

**¿por qué?** why?
**claro que** of course
**¿tienes hambre?** are you hungry?
**se ve** you look
**tenemos que** we have to
**lo que** what
**de vez en cuando** from time to time
**por supuesto** of course
**tal vez** maybe, perhaps
**lárgate de aquí** IMP get out of here
**no importa** it doesn't matter
**ya no tiene valor** he's lost his courage (LIT he no longer has courage)
**tiene hambre** he's hungry
**así que** so
**por favor** please

### Names

Paulie, Philadelphia, Mick, Apollo

🎬 The *Bulletin* newspaper reports that Rocky and Thunderlips raised $75,000 for the youth club.

□ **relámpago** flash of lightning
□ **reúnen** they gather · *reunir* to gather
□ **setenta y cinco** seventy-five

🎬 Rocky drives an antique car through a pillared garden.

□ **Pinocho** Pinocchio
□ **mentira** lie
□ **nariz** NF nose
□ **crecer** to grow
□ **crecieron** they grew · *crecer* to grow

□ **orejas** ears · *oreja* ear
□ **pelearás** you will fight · *pelear* to fight
□ **planeado** planned · *planear* to plan
□ **¿tienes hambre?** are you hungry? · *tener hambre* to be hungry (LIT to have hunger)
□ **almorzar** to eat lunch, to eat brunch
□ **donas** donuts · *dona* donut
□ **almuerzan** they eat (for lunch), they eat (for brunch) · *almorzar* to eat lunch, to eat brunch

🎬 In the dining room with Paulie, Rocky reads "The Three Bears" to his son.

□ **oso** bear
□ **frazadas** blankets · *frazada* blanket
□ **expuesta** exposed · *expuesto* exposed · *exponer* to expose
□ **cereal** NM cereal
□ **Ricitos de Oro** Goldilocks · *ricitos* DIM little curls · *rizo* curl · *oro* gold
□ **allanamiento** unlawful entry
□ **cárcel** NF jail
□ **gentil** kind, nice

🎬 Adrian and Mickey enter the dining room.

□ **nos vamos a divertir** we're going to have fun · *divertirse* to have fun
□ **cerveza** beer
□ **carreras** races · *carrera* race
□ **séptima** seventh · *séptimo* seventh

🎬 Mickey, Adrian, and Rocky listen to a band playing "Rocky's Theme."

□ **íntimos** intimate · *íntimo* intimate
□ **desafía** he challenges, he defies · *desafiar* to challenge, to defy
□ **posibilidades** possibilities · *posibilidad* possibility
□ **lógica** logic
□ **ciudadanos** citizens · *ciudadano* citizen
□ **Filadelfia** Philadelphia
□ **han disfrutado** they have enjoyed · *disfrutar* to enjoy
□ **triunfos** triumphs · *triunfo* triumph
□ **participación** participation
□ **espectáculos** spectacles, shows · *espectáculo* spectacle, show
□ **caridad** charity
□ **honor** NM honor
□ **monumento** monument
□ **celebración** celebration
□ **indomable** indomitable
□ **espíritu** NM spirit
□ **saluda** it salutes · *saludar* to salute
□ **predilecto** favorite

🎬 A statue of Rocky is unveiled.

- □ **belleza** beauty
- □ **me tocó muy adentro** it touched me deeply · *tocar* to touch · *adentro* inside
- □ **dañara** *SUBJ* it hurts · *dañar* to hurt, to damage
- □ **deporte** *NM* sport
- □ **generoso** generous
- □ **optar** to choose, to opt

🎬 Clubber Lang calls out to Rocky.

- □ **edad** age
- □ **estatuas** statues · *estatua* statue
- □ **valor** *NM* courage, bravery

🎬 Mickey interrupts and addresses Clubber Lang.

- □ **lárgate de aquí** *IMP* get out of here · *largarse* to go away, to get away
- □ **estás evadiendo** you are avoiding · *evadir* to avoid
- □ **política** politics
- □ **triunfe** *SUBJ* I triumph · *triunfar* to triumph
- □ **tipo** guy
- □ **dominar** to dominate
- □ **ineptos** inept people · *inepto* inept person

🎬 Mickey again speaks to Clubber Lang.

- □ **vergüenza** shame
- □ **provengo** I come from · *provenir* to come from
- □ **has evitado** you have avoided · *evitar* to avoid
- □ **cobarde** cowardly

🎬 As Rocky starts to answer Clubber Lang's challenge, Mickey interrupts.

- □ **enfrentamiento** match [BOXING]
- □ **me alegra** I'm happy (*LIT* it makes me happy) · *alegrar* to make happy
- □ **he ganado** I have won · *ganar* to win
- □ **piel** *NF* skin
- □ **apariencia** appearance
- □ **júzguenme** *IMP* judge me · *juzgar* to judge

🎬 Clubber Lang addresses Adrian.

- □ **verdadero** true, real
- □ **departamento** apartment
- □ **¿entendiste?** did you understand? · *entender* to understand

🎬 Rocky enters Mickey's bedroom.

- □ **corta** short · *corto* short
- □ **vacaciones** *NFPL* vacation
- □ **permanentes** permanent · *permanente* permanent

- □ **sujeto** person, guy
- □ **¡qué novedad!** *EXP* what else is new?
- □ **máquina** machine
- □ **trituradora** shredding, crushing
- □ **he defendido** I have defended · *defender* to defend
- □ **sencillo** simple
- □ **pan comido** easy as pie (*LIT* eaten bread) · *pan* *NM* bread · *comido* eaten
- □ **boxeadores** boxers · *boxeador* boxer
- □ **asesinos** killers, murderers · *asesino* killer, murderer
- □ **despedazar** to break into many pieces

🎬 Rocky sits down on the sofa.

- □ **golpes** hits, blows · *golpe* *NM* hit, blow
- □ **salud** *NF* health

🎬 Mickey joins Rocky on the sofa.

- □ **explicártelo** to explain it to you · *explicar* to explain
- □ **superdotado** very gifted, very talented
- □ **rudo** rough
- □ **temerario** reckless
- □ **mandíbula** jaw
- □ **hierro** iron
- □ **pasarte** to happen to you · *pasar* to happen
- □ **civilizado** civilized · *civilizar* to civilize
- □ **descuida** *IMP* don't worry · *descuidar* to not worry, to neglect
- □ **caballos** horses · *caballo* horse
- □ **pensión** pension
- □ **luchar** to struggle, to fight
- □ **no te obstines** *IMP* don't be stubborn, don't be hardheaded · *obstinarse* to be stubborn, to be hardheaded
- □ **has entrenado** you have trained · *entrenar* to train
- □ **éxito** success
- □ **he protegido** I have protected · *proteger* to protect
- □ **gimnasio** gymnasium, gym
- □ **entrenes** *SUBJ* you train · *entrenar* to train
- □ **no te vendan** *SUBJ* you haven't bought (*LIT* they don't sell to you) · *vender* to sell
- □ **ropa interior** underwear · *ropa* clothes · *interior* interior

**6** **Cross-Training** 4:11

**Phrases to Listen For**
**todo el tiempo** all the time
**¿por qué?** why?
**largo de aquí** get out of here
**así es como** that's how

**de lado a lado** from side to side
**antes de que** before
**no me gusta** I don't like (*LIT* it doesn't please me)
**para nada** at all
**lo que** what
**de acuerdo** agreed
**tal vez** maybe, perhaps

A sign over the training ring says, "Heavyweight Champion of the World."

□ **capas** robes, capes · *capa* robe, cape
□ **coleccionistas** collectors · *coleccionista NMF* collector
□ **aprovechen** *IMP* take advantage (of this) · *aprovechar* to take advantage (of an opportunity)
□ **botones** buttons · *botón NM* button
□ **te depositará** he will place you · *depositar* to place, to deposit
□ **Marte** Mars
□ **rudo** tough

Rocky, dressed in yellow, punches a red bag.

□ **¿cómo demonios…?** how the heck …? (*LIT* how the demons …?) · *demonio* demon
□ **entrenar** to train
□ **algarabía** uproar
□ **especie** *NF* type, kind
□ **reputación** reputation
□ **alquilaste** you rented, did you rent · *alquilar* to rent
□ **estilo** style
□ **pieza** piece
□ **gimnasio** gymnasium, gym
□ **solamente** only
□ **sangre** *NF* blood
□ **sudor** sweat
□ **lágrimas** tears · *lágrima* tear
□ **relájate** *IMP* relax · *relajarse* to relax
□ **disfrútalo** *IMP* enjoy it · *disfrutar* to enjoy

A woman asks to kiss Rocky.

□ **brutal** brutal
□ **beso** kiss
□ **nena** baby · *nene* baby
□ **zoológico** zoo
□ **te entrenas** you train · *entrenarse* to train
□ **besará** he will kiss · *besar* to kiss
□ **foto** *NF* photo · *fotografía* photograph
□ **velocidad** velocity, speed

At the practice ring, Mickey shouts at Rocky from ringside.

□ **arma mortal** deadly weapon · *arma* weapon · *mortal* deadly

□ **pulmonía** pneumonia
□ **ligero** light, slight
□ **masaje** *NM* massage
□ **orgulloso** proud
□ **circo** circus

## 7 Clubber Lang                    10:30

### Phrases to Listen For

**por supuesto** of course
**no lo sé** I don't know
**tal vez** maybe, perhaps
**campeón mundial** world champion
**no lo olvides** *IMP* don't forget it
**de acuerdo** all right, agreed
**¿por qué?** why?
**por favor** please
**no te preocupes** *IMP* don't worry
**¿qué demonios…?** what the devil …?
**por Dios** dear God
**buenas noches** good night
**antes de que** before
**buena suerte** good luck
**ningún comentario** no comment
**Semental Italiano** Italian Stallion
**así que** so
**tenía razón** he was right
**lo que** what
**con cuidado** be careful
**¿me tienes miedo?** are you afraid of me?

### Names

Bill Baldwin, Stu Nahan, Apollo Creed, Mick, Mickey, Chicago, Clubber Lang, Philadelphia, Marty Denkin, Jimmy Lennon

The fight announcers describe the scene.

□ **bienvenidos** welcome · *bienvenido ADJ* welcome
□ **memorable** memorable
□ **campeonato** championship

Rocky answers a reporter's questions. Mickey is at his side.

□ **carrera** career
□ **arma mortal** deadly weapon · *arma* weapon · *mortal* deadly
□ **notar** to notice

Clubber paces back and forth while reporters address him.

□ **baila** *IMP* dance · *bailar* to dance
□ **baile** *NM* dance
□ **larguen** *IMP* go away, get lost, get out of here · *largarse* to go away

🎬 Rocky and Mickey continue to answer questions.

☐ **te retirarás** you will retire · *retirarse* to retire

☐ **definitivo** definite

🎬 Clubber shouts at the reporters.

☐ **parásitos** parasites · *parásito* parasite

☐ **lárguense** *IMP* go away, get lost, get out of here · *largarse* to go away

🎬 Rocky continues the interview.

☐ **circo** circus

☐ **divertido** fun · *divertirse* to have fun

🎬 Cameras flash on Clubber.

☐ **bata** robe

☐ **pronóstico** prediction

🎬 The announcers discuss the fight with Apollo Creed.

☐ **ex-campeón** *NM* ex-champion

☐ **predicción** prediction

☐ **retador** challenger

☐ **experiencia** experience

☐ **más dura** hardest · *duro* hard, difficult

🎬 Mickey advises Rocky in the locker room.

☐ **no te precipites** *IMP* don't get in a hurry, don't rush · *precipitarse* to hurry, to rush

☐ **acósalo** *IMP* wear him down · *acosar* to wear down, to harass, to go after continually

☐ **quince** fifteen

☐ **recuérdalo** *IMP* remember it · *recordar* to remember

🎬 Apollo predicts the outcome of the fight.

☐ **predigo** I predict · *predecir* to predict

☐ **realmente** really

🎬 Photographers await Rocky as he walks downstairs.

☐ **sonría** *IMP* smile · *sonreír* to smile

☐ **periódico** newspaper

🎬 Clubber Lang addresses Rocky from the stairs.

☐ **gusano** worm

☐ **cobarde** cowardly

☐ **campeón de papel** paper champion · *campeón NM* champion · *papel NM* paper

☐ **bocón** *NM* big mouth

☐ **anciano** old man

☐ **suéltenme** *IMP* let me go · *soltar* to let go

☐ **fiambre** *NM* dead meat

☐ **médico** medical doctor

🎬 Rocky and Adrian escort Mickey into the locker room.

☐ **mesa** table

☐ **respira** *IMP* breathe · *respirar* to breathe

☐ **profundo** deep

☐ **información** information

☐ **suspenderse** to be suspended

☐ **respirar** to breathe

☐ **reglas** rules · *regla* rule

☐ **sal ya de aquí** *IMP* get out of here right now · *salir* to leave, to go out

☐ **véncelo** *IMP* defeat him · *vencer* to defeat

☐ **qué demonios** what the devil, what the heck · *demonio* demon

☐ **avergonzado** ashamed · *avergonzarse* to be ashamed

🎬 Rocky walks out of the locker room.

☐ **Amo del Desastre** Master of Disaster · *amo* master · *desastre NM* disaster

☐ **El Rey del Aguijón** the King of Sting · *rey NM* king · *aguijón NM* stinger, thorn

☐ **grandioso** magnificent, awe-inspiring

🎬 Apollo Creed steps into the ring.

☐ **luce** he shines · *lucir* to shine, to radiate

☐ **verdadero** true, real

☐ **vista** sight

☐ **sales** *SUBJ* you spoil, you ruin, you jinx · *salar* to spoil, to ruin, to jinx

☐ **esquina** corner

☐ **gallina** chicken, hen

☐ **complácenos** *IMP* do us a favor, give us the pleasure · *complacer* to give pleasure, to please

☐ **simio** ape

🎬 Apollo steps out of the ring.

☐ **azul** blue

☐ **kilos** kilos, kilograms · *kilo* kilo, kilogram

☐ **setenta y cinco** seventy-five

☐ **gramos** grams · *gramo* gram

☐ **invencible** invincible

☐ **conversaron** you talked · *conversar* to talk

☐ **comentario** comment, commentary

☐ **oponente** *NMF* opponent

☐ **amarilla** yellow · *amarillo* yellow

☐ **presentación** introduction

☐ **noventa** ninety

☐ **orgullo** pride

☐ **Semental Italiano** Italian Stallion

☐ **actualmente** currently, nowadays

☐ **multitud** *NF* crowd

🎬 Rocky and Clubber Lang walk toward center ring.

☐ **instrucciones** instructions · *instrucción* instruction
☐ **limpia** clean · *limpio* clean
☐ **sepárense** IMP separate · *separarse* to separate, to split apart
☐ **obedecer** to obey
☐ **separarse** to separate, to split apart
☐ **campana** bell

🎬 Rocky and Clubber return to their corners.

☐ **peleadores** fighters · *peleador* fighter
☐ **tremendos** tremendous · *tremendo* tremendous
☐ **puños** fists · *puño* fist
☐ **seguramente** surely
☐ **brillante** brilliant

🎬 Rocky crosses himself.

☐ **demonio** demon
☐ **furia** fury
☐ **aparición** appearance
☐ **determinado** determined, resolute
☐ **destruir** to destroy
☐ **al rojo vivo** red-hot
☐ **pégale** IMP hit him · *pegar* to hit
☐ **golpeador** fighter (LIT hitter)
☐ **sube la guardia** IMP get your guard up · *subir* to raise · *guardia* guard
☐ **defiéndete** IMP defend yourself · *defenderse* to defend oneself

🎬 Rocky returns to his corner after Round One.

☐ **sujétalo** IMP hold on to him · *sujetar* to hold on to
☐ **presión** pressure
☐ **golpes** hits, blows · *golpe* NM hit, blow
☐ **eléctricos** electric · *eléctrico* electric
☐ **bambolearse** to be wobbling

🎬 The bell rings for the second round to begin.

☐ **golpéame** IMP hit me · *golpear* to hit
☐ **adentro** inside
☐ **débil** weak
☐ **golpiza** violent beating
☐ **izquierdazo** punch made with the left hand [SPORTS]
☐ **vencí** I defeated · *vencer* to defeat
☐ **sostenerse** to support oneself, to stay, to remain
☐ **ganador** winner

## 8 Mourning Mickey 6:14

### Phrases to Listen For
**hasta que** until
**hay que** it's necessary

**así es** that's right
**no tienes que** you don't have to
**tenemos más cosas que hacer** we have more things to do
**Dios mío** good heavens (LIT my God)

### Names
Mick, Goldmill

🎬 Rocky enters the locker room to join Adrian, Mickey, and the doctors.

☐ **hospital** NM hospital
☐ **de inmediato** immediately
☐ **ganador** winner
☐ **me duele** it hurts · *doler* to hurt

🎬 Mickey's burial service is being held. Some words in Hebrew are spoken: *Israel, Shalom.*

☐ **concluye** it concludes · *concluir* to conclude
☐ **servicio** service
☐ **en recuerdo** in memory · *recuerdo* memory
☐ **amoroso** loving, full of love, tenderhearted

## 9 Eye of the Tiger 4:13

### Phrases to Listen For
**¿por qué?** why?
**así es** that's right, that's the way it is
**para ser honesto** to be honest
**así que** so
**de acuerdo** agreed
**no tenías hambre** you weren't hungry
**tienes que** you have to
**¿para qué?** what for?
**lo que** what
**no tengo que** I don't have to

### Name
Apollo Creed

🎬 Rocky is inside the old gym. Apollo joins him.

☐ **directo** directly
☐ **negocios** business matters · *negocio* business
☐ **diarios** daily newspapers · *diario* daily newspaper
☐ **honesto** honest
☐ **respuesta** answer
☐ **verdadera** true, real · *verdadero* true, real
☐ **toque** NM touch
☐ **promover** to promote
☐ **convertirlo** to turn it into, to make it · *convertir* to turn into, to convert
☐ **involucrarme** being involved, getting involved, dealing · *involucrarse* to be involved, to get involved, to deal

□ **lastimado** hurt · *lastimar* to hurt
□ **nos duele** it hurts us · *doler* to hurt
□ **hazte justicia** *IMP* make it right for yourself ·
  *hacerse justicia* to make (something) right
  for oneself
□ **lamentarlo** to be sorry for it · *lamentar*
  to be sorry
□ **filo** edge
□ **profundo** profound, deep
□ **dolor** *NM* pain
□ **no tenías hambre** you weren't hungry ·
  *tener hambre* to be hungry (*LIT* to have hunger)
□ **tigre** *NM* tiger
□ **principio** beginning
□ **plan** *NM* plan
□ **curiosidad** curiosity

🎬 On television, Clubber answers questions about
a rematch.

□ **desafío** challenge
□ **reencuentro** rematch
□ **rechazo** I reject · *rechazar* to reject

🎬 Paulie, Apollo, Rocky, and Adrian watch Clubber
on television.

□ **ansioso** anxious
□ **opina** you think · *opinar* to think, to give
  an opinion
□ **está entrenando** he is training · *entrenar*
  to train
□ **anciano** old man
□ **animal** *NM* animal
□ **solamente** only
□ **bocón** *NM* big mouth
□ **entrenaré** I will train · *entrenar* to train
□ **noquearé** I will knock out · *noquear* to knock
  out
□ **torturarlo** to torture him · *torturar* to torture
□ **crucificaré** I will crucify · *crucificar*
  to crucify
□ **créanme** *IMP* believe me · *creer* to believe
□ **duras** tough, hard · *duro* tough, hard
□ **posibilidades** possibilities · *posibilidad*
  possibility
□ **recuperar** to recover
□ **realmente** really
□ **pocas** few · *pocos* few
□ **expertos** experts · *experto* expert
□ **naturalmente** naturally
□ **transmitiremos** we will broadcast ·
  *transmitir* to broadcast
□ **cadenas de televisión** television networks ·
  *cadena* network · *televisión* television
□ **disculpa** apology
□ **entrevista** interview

□ **legendario** legendary
□ **falleció** he died, he passed away · *fallecer* to die,
  to pass away

## 10 New Beginning · 4:44

### Phrases to Listen For
**tal vez** maybe, perhaps
**¿por qué?** why?
**hay que** it's necessary
**lo que** what
**no me gusta** I don't like (*LIT* it doesn't please
  me)
**antes de que** before
**tienes que** you have to
**¿de acuerdo?** agreed?
**tenemos que** we have to
**no te gusta** you don't like (*LIT* it doesn't please
  you)

### Names
Rocko, California, Rock, Paulie, Adrian, Duke

🎬 Rocky, dressed in a suit, steps down the stairs.

□ **aeropuerto** airport
□ **suéter** *NM* sweater
□ **caluroso** warm
□ **te portes** *SUBJ* you behave · *portarse* to behave
  oneself
□ **beso** kiss
□ **sorpresa** surprise

🎬 Apollo, Paulie, Adrian, and Rocky step out of a cab
in Los Angeles.

□ **repugnante** repugnant
□ **registrarse** to register
□ **gimnasio** gymnasium, gym
□ **siniestro** sinister, evil, bad
□ **acostumbras** you are used to, you are
  accustomed to · *acostumbrar* to be used to,
  to be accustomed to
□ **nos acostumbraremos** we will get used to it ·
  *acostumbrarse* to get used to, to get accustomed
  to
□ **cerveza** beer
□ **armado** armed · *armar* to arm
□ **daño** damage
□ **cigarrillo** cigarette

🎬 Paulie, Apollo, Rocky, and Adrian walk through
an alley.

□ **diversión** fun
□ **ratas** rats · *rata* rat
□ **sitio** place, site
□ **salud** *NF* health

▣ Inside the gym, several fighters are training. Rocky and his companions enter.

☐ **entrené** I trained · *entrenar* to train
☐ **recuperarlo** to recover it, to get it back · *recuperar* to recover, to get back
☐ **tigre** *NM* tiger
☐ **pesimista** pessimistic
☐ **no me asustas** you don't scare me · *asustar* to scare
☐ **tranquilízate** *IMP* calm down · *tranquilizarse* to calm down
☐ **libre** free
☐ **te trastornes** *SUBJ* you go crazy · *trastornarse* to go crazy
☐ **filosofía** philosophy
☐ **relájate** *IMP* relax · *relajarse* to relax
☐ **negocio** business
☐ **dispuestos** willing · *dispuesto* willing
☐ **entrenar** to train
☐ **reputación** reputation
☐ **aturdido** punchy, stunned, dazed, confused · *aturdirse* to be punchy, to be stunned, to be dazed, to get confused

## 11 No Tomorrow                            7:05

### Phrases to Listen For

**te ves** you look
**tanto como** just like
**de prisa** quickly
**qué asco** how disgusting
**hay que** it's necessary
**tal vez** maybe, perhaps
**¿qué rayos haces?** what the heck are you doing?
**lo que** what
**no has tenido hambre** you haven't been hungry
**¿qué le pasa?** what's wrong with him?
**se acabó** it's over
**¿qué pasa contigo?** what's the matter with you?

▣ Amid leaky pipes and bare lightbulbs, Apollo encourages Rocky.

☐ **concreto** concrete
☐ **salta** *IMP* jump · *saltar* to jump
☐ **balancéate** *IMP* balance yourself, keep your balance · *balancearse* to balance oneself, to keep one's balance
☐ **gracia** grace
☐ **que despeguen del concreto** *SUBJ* get them off the concrete · *despegar* to get off, to unstick

☐ **relájate** *IMP* relax · *relajarse* to relax
☐ **levántalos** *IMP* get them up, raise them up · *levantar* to raise
☐ **entrenar** to train
☐ **selvática** *ADJ* jungle
☐ **música** music
☐ **baile** *NM* dance
☐ **retar** to challenge
☐ **dedos de los pies** toes · *dedo del pie* toe
☐ **cuerpo** body
☐ **ritmo** rhythm
☐ **entrenado** trained · *entrenar* to train
☐ **estúpido** *OFFENSIVE* stupid
☐ **genial** great, terrific
☐ **nadar** to swim
☐ **piedra** rock

▣ Rocky is in the pool.

☐ **vuelta** lap
☐ **atún** *NM* tuna
☐ **gimnasio** gymnasium, gym
☐ **estirándose** stretching · *estirarse* to stretch
☐ **conciencia** awareness
☐ **músculos** muscles · *músculo* muscle
☐ **estírate** *IMP* stretch · *estirarse* to stretch
☐ **aprisa** hurriedly, quickly
☐ **pescado** fish [COOKING]

▣ Paulie gets out of bed.

☐ **trago** swallow
☐ **vagos** bums · *vago* bum
☐ **los encerrarán** they will lock you up · *encerrar* to lock up
☐ **idiota** *NMF* idiot
☐ **gusano** worm
☐ **qué asco** how sick, how gross

▣ Film of Rocky's fight with Clubber is being shown.

☐ **quince** fifteen
☐ **séptimo** seventh
☐ **u** or
☐ **octavo** eighth

▣ Rocky is sitting up on his bed. Adrian, in the bathroom, is speaking.

☐ **caliente** hot
☐ **luna de miel** honeymoon · *luna* moon · *miel* *NF* honey
☐ **esquina** corner
☐ **está en apuros** he's in a jam, he's in a tight spot, he's in trouble · *estar en apuros* to be in a jam, to be in a tight spot, to be in trouble
☐ **lanza** he throws · *lanzar* to throw
☐ **derechazo** punch made with the right hand [SPORTS]

🎬 In the gym, Rocky is training.

- ☐ **vigor** NM vigor, energy
- ☐ **mente** NF mind
- ☐ **clara** clear · *claro* clear
- ☐ **concéntrate** IMP concentrate · *concentrarse* to concentrate

🎬 Rocky spars with Apollo.

- ☐ **diviértete** IMP have fun · *divertirse* to have fun
- ☐ **calma** calm
- ☐ **no te apresures** IMP don't rush, don't hurry, don't get in a hurry · *apresurarse* to rush, to hurry, to get in a hurry
- ☐ **afuera** outside
- ☐ **adentro** inside
- ☐ **mírame** IMP look at me · *mirar* to look at

🎬 Apollo stops sparring and shouts at Rocky.

- ☐ **demonios** demons · *demonio* demon
- ☐ **tipo** guy
- ☐ **te noqueará** he will knock you out · *noquear* to knock out
- ☐ **hospital** NM hospital
- ☐ **hombros** shoulders · *hombro* shoulder
- ☐ **aniquilarte** to annihilate you · *aniquilar* to annihilate

🎬 Apollo and Rocky return to sparring.

- ☐ **dañarte** to get hurt · *dañarse* to get hurt
- ☐ **acorralado** cornered · *acorralar* to corner
- ☐ **cuerdas** ropes · *cuerda* rope
- ☐ **gancho** hook

🎬 Apollo stops sparring again and shouts.

- ☐ **diablos** devils · *diablo* devil

🎬 Rocky and Apollo walk along the beach.

- ☐ **velocidad** velocity, speed
- ☐ **flexibilidad** flexibility
- ☐ **concentrarte** to concentrate, to focus · *concentrarse* to concentrate, to focus
- ☐ **no has tenido hambre** you haven't been hungry · *tener hambre* to be hungry (LIT to have hunger)

# 12 Pep Talk                    4:44

## Phrases to Listen For

**¿por qué?** why?
**lo que** what
**tienes que** you have to
**al menos** at least
**por Dios** dear God

**al principio** at first
**tengo miedo** I'm afraid
**¿de acuerdo?** all right?
**tener miedo** to be afraid
**no importa** it doesn't matter
**alrededor de** around

🎬 Adrian approaches Rocky on the beach.

- ☐ **me alegro** I'm happy · *alegrarse* to be happy
- ☐ **te has rendido** you have given up, you have surrendered · *rendirse* to give up, to surrender
- ☐ **se convirtió en** it turned into · *convertirse* to turn into, to become
- ☐ **arruiné** I ruined · *arruinar* to ruin
- ☐ **estrella** star
- ☐ **me había mentido** he had lied to me · *mentir* to lie
- ☐ **engañó** he deceived · *engañar* to deceive
- ☐ **protegerte** to protect you · *proteger* to protect
- ☐ **protegerme** to protect me · *proteger* to protect
- ☐ **empeoró** it made worse · *empeorar* to make worse
- ☐ **ganador** winner
- ☐ **perdedor** loser
- ☐ **real** real
- ☐ **verdadero** true, real

🎬 Adrian moves close to Rocky, shouting.

- ☐ **obligas** you make · *obligar* to make, to force
- ☐ **al principio** in the beginning, at first · *principio* beginning
- ☐ **arena** arena
- ☐ **reponer** to replace
- ☐ **diablos** devils · *diablo* devil
- ☐ **humano** human
- ☐ **mentiroso** liar
- ☐ **no lo obligaste** you didn't force him · *obligar* to force
- ☐ **simplemente** simply
- ☐ **culpable** guilty
- ☐ **reales** real · *real* real
- ☐ **crea** SUBJ I believe · *creer* to believe
- ☐ **alrededor de** around
- ☐ **cobarde** NMF coward
- ☐ **arráncatelo** IMP get rid of it · *arrancar* to tear out, to pull out
- ☐ **humo** smoke
- ☐ **se disipe** SUBJ it dissipates, it disappears · *disiparse* to dissipate, to disappear
- ☐ **resto** the rest, the remainder
- ☐ **sólidas** solid · *sólido* ADJ solid
- ☐ **excusas** excuses · *excusa* excuse

## 13 Getting Strong                                   3:25

**Phrases to Listen For**

**así es** that's right, that's the way it is
**así se hace** that's how it's done

Several scenes show Apollo instructing Rocky in the gym, in the pool, and on the beach.

☐ **balancéate** IMP maintain your balance · *balancearse* to maintain one's balance
☐ **vueltas** laps · *vuelta* lap
☐ **esquiva** IMP avoid (it) · *esquivar* to avoid
☐ **gancho** hook
☐ **genial** great, terrific
☐ **lento** slow

## 14 "Go for It!"                                     15:38

**Phrases to Listen For**

**campeón de los completos** heavyweight champion
**¿cómo se ven?** how do they look?
**lo que** what
**ya que** since
**para que** so that
**tal vez** maybe, perhaps
**por favor** please
**antes de que** before
**estoy de acuerdo** I agree
**se ve** he looks
**Semental Italiano** Italian Stallion
**campeón mundial** world champion
**peso completo** heavyweight
**ya no tienes que buscarme** you don't have to look for me anymore
**hasta que** until
**de inmediato** immediately, right away
**otra vez** again
**de nuevo** again
**¿qué rayos?** what the heck?, what in the world?
**tienes que** you have to
**a la vez** at the same time
**sin embargo** however
**de todos modos** in any event, in any case
**estás bien?** are you all right?
**mejor que nunca** better than ever (*LIT* better than never)

## Names

Stu Nahan, Bill Baldwin, Madison Square Garden, Rocky Balboa, Clubber Lang, Philadelphia, Chicago, Lou Fillipo

At Madison Square Garden, the announcers discuss the upcoming fight.

☐ **bienvenida** welcome
☐ **emocionante** exciting
☐ **ansiada** long-awaited · *ansiado* long-awaited · *ansiar* to long for, to yearn for
☐ **revanchas** rematches · *revancha* rematch
☐ **ex-campeón** NM ex-champion
☐ **actual** current
☐ **completos** heavyweights · *completo* heavyweight
☐ **vestidores** dressing rooms · *vestidor* dressing room

A reporter interviews Clubber Lang about the fight.

☐ **estrategia** strategy
☐ **predecible** predictable
☐ **estúpido** OFFENSIVE stupid
☐ **directamente** directly
☐ **lastimado** hurt · *lastimar* to hurt
☐ **no odio** I don't hate · *odiar* to hate
☐ **destruiré** I will destroy · *destruir* to destroy

Alone in the locker room, Apollo counsels Rocky.

☐ **costó** it cost · *costar* to cost

The announcers continue their pre-fight commentary.

☐ **temperamentales** temperamental · *temperamental* temperamental
☐ **posibilidades** possibilities · *posibilidad* possibility
☐ **recupere** SUBJ he recovers · *recuperar* to recover

Still in the locker room, Apollo continues counseling Rocky.

☐ **turno** turn

Clubber's interview continues.

☐ **predicción** prediction

The announcers continue their pre-fight commentary.

☐ **cuerpo** body
☐ **contrincante** NMF challenger
☐ **recuperar** to recover
☐ **sicológicamente** psychologically
☐ **tremendo** tremendous
☐ **asestó** he dealt · *asestar* to deal, to deliver
☐ **anterior** previous

🎬 Apollo opens the locker-room door and joins Rocky.

☐ **sala del entrenamiento** training room
☐ **úsalos** *IMP* wear them, use them · *usar* to wear, to use
☐ **mandarlo** to send it · *mandar* to send
☐ **lavar** to wash

🎬 The announcers continue their pre-fight commentary.

☐ **gramo** gram
☐ **devastador** devastating

🎬 Rocky follows Paulie to the doors. Apollo speaks.

☐ **orgulloso** proud

🎬 Rocky and his companions enter the arena.

☐ **guardia** guard
☐ **marina** Navy, Marines
☐ **estupendo** stupendous
☐ **tensión** tension
☐ **rostro** face
☐ **rigidez** *NF* tautness
☐ **ciertamente** certainly
☐ **derrota** defeat
☐ **empate** *NM* tie
☐ **Semental Italiano** Italian Stallion

🎬 Rocky enters the ring.

☐ **increíblemente** incredibly
☐ **delgado** thin, slim
☐ **ha bajado** he has lost (*LIT* he has gone down) · *bajar* to lose, to go down
☐ **kilos** kilos, kilograms · *kilo* kilo, kilogram
☐ **acero** steel
☐ **multitud** *NF* crowd
☐ **determinación** determination
☐ **mira** *IMP* look · *mirar* to look at
☐ **detrás de** behind

🎬 The spotlight focuses on Clubber Lang.

☐ **triturador** shredding machine, grinding machine
☐ **lárgate** *IMP* get lost, get out of here, go away · *largarse* to go away
☐ **lujo** luxury
☐ **agredir** to assault
☐ **espectadores** spectators · *espectador* spectator
☐ **hostil** hostile

🎬 Clubber walks into the ring, his hands in the air. Apollo instructs Rocky.

☐ **debilidades** weaknesses · *debilidad* weakness
☐ **paliza** beating
☐ **gentiles** nice, "cool" · *gentil* nice, "cool"
☐ **vista** sight

☐ **simio** ape
☐ **espalda** back
☐ **gusano** worm
☐ **conato** attempt
☐ **pleito** fight
☐ **campana** bell
☐ **extraoficialmente** unofficially
☐ **ojalá** hopefully
☐ **controlarlos** to control them · *controlar* to control
☐ **gentil** nice, "cool"
☐ **aficionados** fans · *aficionado* fan
☐ **quítenme esta capa** *IMP* take this robe off me · *quitar* to take off, to remove · *capa* robe
☐ **bienvenidos** welcome · *bienvenido ADJ* welcome
☐ **campeonato** championship

🎬 The crowd is shouting "Rocky, Rocky, ..." as the event is about to begin. Apollo claps. Rocky warms up.

☐ **esquina** corner
☐ **roja** red · *rojo* red
☐ **retador** challenger
☐ **ochenta y cinco** eighty-five
☐ **gramos** grams · *gramo* gram
☐ **semi-completo** middleweight

🎬 The bell rings. The ring announcer continues the introduction.

☐ **azul** blue
☐ **sesenta y cinco** sixty-five
☐ **súper** super
☐ **golpeador** fighter, hitter

🎬 The referee calls the boxers to center ring.

☐ **ayer** yesterday
☐ **se acordaron** you agreed · *acordarse* to agree
☐ **reglas** rules · *regla* rule
☐ **repetiré** I will repeat · *repetir* to repeat
☐ **golpes** hits, blows · *golpe NM* hit, blow
☐ **cabezazos** head butts · *cabezazo* head butt, hit with the head
☐ **indique** *SUBJ* I indicate · *indicar* to indicate
☐ **vencerte** to defeat you · *vencer* to defeat, to beat

🎬 Rocky and Clubber return to their corners.
☐ **ritmo** rhythm
☐ **golpéalo** *IMP* hit him · *golpear* to hit

🎬 The bell rings.
☐ **hostilidades** hostilities · *hostilidad* hostility
☐ **de inmediato** immediately
☐ **inicio** beginning
☐ **serie** *NF* series

- **ganchos** hooks · *gancho* hook
- **está bailando** he is dancing · *bailar* to dance
- **fantástico** fantastic
- **derechazo** punch made with the right hand [SPORTS]
- **está descontrolando** it is confusing · *descontrolar* to confuse
- **estilo** style
- **miren** IMP look · *mirar* to look at
- **acorrálalo** IMP corner him · *acorralar* to corner
- **absolutamente** absolutely

Clubber shouts at Rocky.
- **golpéame** IMP hit me · *golpear* to hit
- **martillo** hammer
- **que no te abrace** SUBJ don't let him hold you · *abrazar* to hold, to hug

The referee shouts at the fighters.
- **sepárense** IMP break it up, get away from each other, separate · *separarse* to get away from one another, to separate from one another
- **enardecida** wild, aroused, excited · *enardecido* wild, aroused, excited · *enardecer* to arouse passion, to create excitement
- **combinación** combination
- **está manejando** he is managing, he is handling · *manejar* to manage, to handle

The bell rings, ending Round One.
- **esquinas** corners · *esquina* corner
- **tranquilizarlo** to calm him · *tranquilizar* to calm
- **no enloqueces** you don't go crazy · *enloquecer* to go crazy
- **tipo** guy
- **tranquilízate** IMP calm down · *tranquilizarse* to calm down
- **acorralado** cornered · *acorralar* to corner
- **no escape** SUBJ he doesn't escape · *escapar* to escape
- **merced** NF mercy

The bell rings, beginning Round Two.
- **se miden** they are studying each other · *medirse* to be studying one another
- **están despejándose** they are becoming clear · *despejarse* to become clear
- **está dominando** he is dominating · *dominar* to dominate
- **tiro** swing
- **sal** IMP leave · *salir* to leave

Clubber pushes Rocky back into the corner.
- **aniquilaré** I will annihilate · *aniquilar* to annihilate
- **brazos** arms · *brazo* arm
- **lastimar** to hurt, to injure
- **cúbrete** IMP cover yourself · *cubrirse* to cover oneself
- **salte** IMP get out of there, leave · *salirse* to get out
- **dueño** owner
- **golpe** NM hit, blow

Rocky is knocked down.
- **recupérate** IMP recover, get up · *recuperarse* to recover

Rocky is knocked down a second time.
- **lona** mat, canvas
- **defiéndete** IMP defend yourself · *defenderse* to defend oneself

The bell rings, ending the round.
- **malísimo** very bad, the "baddest"
- **esquinas** corners · *esquina* corner
- **de pie** standing · *pie* NM foot
- **enfrentándolo** facing him · *enfrentar* to face
- **no desperdicies** IMP don't waste · *desperdiciar* to waste
- **manera** manner, way
- **tigre** NM tiger

Round Three begins.
- **inicia** it begins · *iniciar* to begin
- **lento** slow
- **anteriores** previous · *anterior* previous
- **aniquilar** to annihilate
- **le asesta** he deals him · *asestar* to deal, to deliver
- **derechazos** punches made with the right hand · *derechazo* punch made with the right hand [SPORTS]
- **decisión** decision
- **síguelo** IMP follow him · *seguir* to follow

At ringside, Paulie and Apollo discuss Rocky's tactics.
- **enojar** to anger
- **observa** it is watching · *observar* to watch, to observe
- **noquéame** IMP knock me out · *noquear* to knock out
- **noquéalo** IMP knock him out · *noquear* to knock out
- **descontrolar** to cause to lose control

☐ **lo está metiendo en su juego** he's luring him into his trap (*LIT* he's putting him into his own game) · *meter* to put · *juego* game

☐ **cuerdas** ropes · *cuerda* rope

☐ **entero** whole

☐ **sin embargo** however

☐ **espectacular** spectacular

Apollo kisses Paulie.

☐ **boxeadores** boxers · *boxeador* boxer

☐ **espeluznante** hair-raising, frightening, terrifying

☐ **plan** *NM* plan

☐ **perfectamente** perfectly

☐ **concebido** conceived · *concebir* to conceive

☐ **se reservó** he kept, he held in reserve · *reservarse* to keep, to hold in reserve

The referee counts to ten.

☐ **exhausto** exhausted

☐ **ganador** winner

☐ **boxeo** *NM* boxing

## 15 Favor                              1:51

### Phrases to Listen For

**¿en serio?** seriously?, really?

**lo que** what

**por supuesto** of course

**qué pena** what a shame

**te ves** you look

**te lo aseguro** I assure you

Rocky and Apollo, dressed to spar, walk into the gym.

☐ **trato** deal

☐ **locura** craziness

☐ **mentes** minds · *mente NF* mind

☐ **insanas** unhealthy · *insano* unhealthy

☐ **sentido** sense

☐ **verdadera** true, real · *verdadero* real

☐ **ganarías** you would win · *ganar* to win

☐ **inaceptable** unacceptable

☐ **inteligencia** intelligence

☐ **vencí** I defeated · *vencer* to defeat, to beat

☐ **mentí** I lied · *mentir* to lie

☐ **mentiste** you lied · *mentir* to lie

☐ **televisión** television

☐ **periodistas** newspaper reporters · *periodista NMF* newspaper reporter

☐ **edad** age

☐ **belleza** beauty

Rocky and Apollo enter the ring.

☐ **despacio** slowly

☐ **vencerte** to defeat you · *vencer* to defeat, to beat

☐ **boxeas** you box · *boxear* to box

☐ **qué pena** what a shame · *pena* shame

☐ **tocarás** you will ring · *tocar* to ring

☐ **campana** bell

☐ **huir** to flee

## 16 End Credits                        3:11

End credits.

# Anne of Green Gables

**Dentro de unos años, seguiré recordando a Green Gables como un sueño maravilloso que me perseguirá por siempre.**
*In years to come, I'm going to look back on Green Gables as a beautiful dream that will always haunt me.*

| | |
|---|---|
| GENRE | Classic Literature Adaptation |
| YEAR | 1985 |
| DIRECTOR | Kevin Sullivan |
| CAST | Megan Follows, Colleen Dewhurst, Richard Farnsworth |
| STUDIO | Sullivan Entertainment |

After Anne arrives at Green Gables, we follow her continuing search for a bosom friend, her enduring conflict with the handsome Gilbert Blythe, and the touching relationship between Anne and her new family, Matthew and Marilla Cuthbert. *Anne of Green Gables* is probably the most difficult film in our collection because of its length, extensive vocabulary, and higher frequency of complex sentence structure. While challenging, this film will help you develop your ability to carry on graceful conversations on a variety of topics.

## BASIC VOCABULARY

### Names

Avonlea, Diana Barry, Alice Bell, Gilbert Blythe, Green Gables, Cuthbert, Hammond, Phillips, Queens, Charlottetown

### Nouns

☐ **actitud** *NF* attitude · *Qué hermosa **actitud** para alguien que ha trabajado tanto.* What a beautiful attitude for someone who has worked so hard.

☐ **angustia** anguish · *Es una frase que leí hace tiempo y la repito con frecuencia para alentarme en estos momentos de gran **angustia**.* It's a sentence that I read a while ago, and I repeat it frequently to encourage me in these moments of great anguish.

☐ **baile** *NM* dance · *¿Por qué me diste la espalda en el **baile** de navidad?* Why did you turn your back on me at the Christmas dance?

☐ **cabello** hair · *Anne, lamento haberme burlado del color de tu **cabello**.* Anne, I'm sorry for having made fun of the color of your hair.

☐ **comportamiento** behavior · *Un buen **comportamiento** es definitivamente más importante que hacer una actuación para ofrecer disculpas.* Good behavior is definitely more important than a theatrical performance in order to offer apologies.

☐ **equivocación** error, mistake · *No, no hay **equivocación**.* No, there's no mistake.

☐ **estudios** *NMPL* studies · *Jamás podrás ahorrar para tus **estudios**.* You'll never be able to save for your studies.

☐ **examen** *NM* test, exam · *Acabo de ver los resultados del **examen**.* I just saw the exam results.

☐ **huérfana** orphan · *huérfano* orphan · *No podrá ser tan cruel como para prolongar un sufrimiento innecesario a una pobre **huérfana**.* You won't be so cruel as to prolong the unnecessary suffering of a poor orphan girl.

☐ **imaginación** imagination · *Soportaré esta angustia hasta que regreses, aunque tal vez pudiera desmayarme si es que mi **imaginación** actúa como siempre.* I'll tolerate this anguish until you return, although I may faint if my imagination acts as it always does.

☐ **isla** island · *Quisiera poder recordar a ustedes como el grupo más brillante y más empeñoso de toda la **Isla** Príncipe Eduardo.* I want to be able to remember you as the most brilliant and most dedicated group of students on all of Prince Edward Island.

☐ **lengua** tongue · *Por amor de Dios, niña, muérdete la **lengua** y vámonos ya.* For the love of God, child, bite your tongue and let's go right now.

☐ **orfanato** orphanage · *Esa niña tiene que regresar al **orfanato**.* That girl has to return to the orphanage.

### Verbs

☐ **acompañarte** accompanying you · *acompañar* to accompany · *Yo sí, en especial si tengo el honor de **acompañarte** al concierto.* I would, especially if I have the honor of accompanying you to the concert.

☐ **no apruebo** I don't approve of · *aprobar* to approve of · *Pero, yo no **apruebo** los bailes.* But, I don't approve of dances.

☐ **no te angusties** *IMP* don't worry · *angustiarse* to be worried · ***No te angusties**, Diana.* Don't worry, Diana.

### Other

☐ **a prueba** on trial, on a trial basis · *prueba* test, trial · *Tal vez pudieras quedarte **a prueba** durante un tiempo por el bien de todos.* Maybe you could stay on a trial basis for a time for the good of everyone.

☐ **acerca de** about · *Se me ocurrió una hermosa historia **acerca de** nosotros.* A beautiful story about us occurred to me.

☐ **alta** high · *alto* high · *Frank Stockly me dijo que el estudiante que obtenga la calificación más **alta** en literatura ganará la beca Avery.* Frank Stockly told me that the student who earns the highest grade in literature will win the Avery scholarship.

☐ **correcto** correct, right · *No me parece **correcto** llamar a las personas por nombres que les son ajenos.* It doesn't seem right to me to call people by names that are not their own.

☐ **de inmediato** immediately, right away · *Lo sé, pero tenía que decirte algo **de inmediato**.* I know, but I had to tell you something right away.

☐ **probable** probable, likely · *Y es muy **probable** que llegase a la conclusión de que me agradaría por un tiempo, pero al final seguiría prefiriendo el sonido que produce el viento al golpear los abetos, más que el tintineo del cristal.* And it's very likely that I would come to the conclusion that I would like it for a while, but in the end I would continue preferring the sound that the wind makes as it strikes the firs, more than the tinkling of crystal.

☐ **terrible** terrible · *Marilla, no creí que nada podía ser más **terrible** que tener el cabello rojo.* Marilla, I didn't think that anything could be more terrible than having red hair.

## **1** Orphan Children · · · · · · · · · 6:30

### Phrases to Listen For

**ten cuidado** *IMP* be careful
**en lugar de** instead of
**por favor** please
**llevan más de una hora esperando** they have
  been waiting for more than an hour
**¿qué te pasa?** what's the matter with you?
**¿qué pasó?** what happened?
**tal vez** maybe, perhaps
**lo que** what
**¿qué pasará?** what will happen?
**¿no es así?** isn't that right?
**tendrás que** you will have to

### Names

Megan Follows, Colleen Dewhurst, Shalott, Richard
Farnsworth, Camelot, Meg, Peter, Hammond, Tom,
Katie, Nora

🎬 Anne recites "The Lady of Shalott."

- ☐ **oscura** dark · *oscuro* dark
- ☐ **prisión** prison
- ☐ **suave** soft
- ☐ **brisa** breeze
- ☐ **estremecer** to cause to quiver, to cause to
  shudder
- ☐ **cruzando** crossing · *cruzar* to cross
- ☐ **río** river
- ☐ **se desplaza** it flows · *desplazarse* to flow
- ☐ **murallas** large walls · *muralla* large wall
- ☐ **enormes** enormous · *enorme* enormous
- ☐ **torres** towers · *torre NF* tower
- ☐ **flores** flowers · *flor NF* flower
- ☐ **espacio** space
- ☐ **apartada** separate · *apartado* separate ·
  *apartar* to separate
- ☐ **aguarda** she waits · *aguardar* to wait
- ☐ **la Dama de Shalott** the Lady of Shalott
- ☐ **estrella invitada** guest star · *estrella* star ·
  *invitado* invited · *invitar* to invite
- ☐ **serena** peaceful · *sereno* peaceful
- ☐ **sonido** sound
- ☐ **viento** wind
- ☐ **murmura** she whispers · *murmurar* to whisper
- ☐ **voz** *NF* voice
- ☐ **tejer** to weave
- ☐ **de día y de noche** day and night
- ☐ **mágica** magic · *mágico ADJ* magic
- ☐ **telaraña** spider web
- ☐ **alegres colores** cheerful colors · *color NM*
  color
- ☐ **murmullo** whisper
- ☐ **desconoce** she does not know · *desconocer*
  to not know, to fail to recognize, to be unaware

- ☐ **cruel** cruel
- ☐ **castigo** punishment
- ☐ **tejiendo** weaving · *tejer* to weave
- ☐ **sin cesar** without ceasing
- ☐ **ocupación** occupation

🎬 Mrs. Hammond stands on the porch and holds
  a young child in her arms.

- ☐ **en este instante** this instant · *instante NM*
  instant
- ☐ **tranquilízate** *IMP* calm down · *tranquilizarse*
  to calm down
- ☐ **nena** baby girl · *nene* baby boy
- ☐ **no derrames** *IMP* don't spill · *derramar*
  to spill
- ☐ **leche** *NF* milk

🎬 Anne runs into the kitchen. Mrs. Hammond
  follows.

- ☐ **pretendes** you want, you're trying · *pretender*
  to want, to try
- ☐ **cubo** pail, bucket
- ☐ **ración** portion
- ☐ **cámbiales los pañales** *IMP* change their diapers ·
  *cambiar* to change · *pañal NM* diaper
- ☐ **si pusieras más atención** *SUBJ* if you paid more
  attention · *poner atención* to pay attention
- ☐ **labores** chores · *labor NM* chore
- ☐ **meter las narices** to put your nose ·
  *meter* to put · *nariz NF* nose
- ☐ **espantosos** horrible · *espantoso* horrible
- ☐ **librejos** awful books · *librejo PEJ* awful book
- ☐ **interesante** interesting
- ☐ **diabólicos** diabolic · *diabólico* diabolic
- ☐ **criaturas** children · *criatura* child
- ☐ **combustible** *NM* combustible material
- ☐ **estufa** stove
- ☐ **boba** distracted girl, empty-headed girl ·
  *bobo* distracted boy, empty-headed boy
- ☐ **empleados** employees · *empleado* employee
- ☐ **almuerzo** brunch, lunch
- ☐ **adoro** I love · *adorar* to love, to adore
- ☐ **infantes** babies, infants · *infante NMF* baby,
  infant
- ☐ **con moderación** in moderation
- ☐ **gemelos** twins · *gemelo* twin
- ☐ **consecutivas** consecutive · *consecutivo*
  consecutive
- ☐ **si careciera** *SUBJ* if I lacked · *carecer* to lack
- ☐ **no toleraré** I won't tolerate · *tolerar* to tolerate
- ☐ **insultos** insults · *insulto* insult
- ☐ **paliza** beating, series of whacks
- ☐ **si te atreves a decir** if you dare say · *atreverse*
  to dare
- ☐ **aserradero** sawmill

🎬 At the Hammond lumber mill, a bearded man shouts.

☐ **¿adónde diablos...?** where the devil ...? · *diablo* devil

☐ **tablones** planks, boards · *tablón NM* plank, board

☐ **idiota** *NMF* idiot

☐ **furioso** furious

☐ **gritaba** he was shouting · *gritar* to shout

☐ **maldecía** he was cursing · *maldecir* to curse

☐ **carreta** cart, wagon

🎬 Anne looks in the mirror.

☐ **si no me hubiera sumergido** *SUBJ* if I hadn't immersed myself · *sumergirse* to immerse oneself

☐ **belleza** beauty

🎬 At the kitchen table, a woman is consoling Mrs. Hammond. Soon Anne joins them.

☐ **disfrutó de la vida** he enjoyed life · *disfrutar* to enjoy

☐ **vende** *IMP* sell · *vender* to sell

☐ **devolverla** return her · *devolver* to return, to take back

☐ **considero** I consider · *considerar* to consider

☐ **carga** burden

☐ **soportar** to tolerate, to bear

☐ **sin protestar** without protest · *protestar* to protest

☐ **almorzar** to eat brunch, to eat lunch

☐ **preocupación** worry

☐ **se lo suplico** I beg you · *suplicar* to beg, to plead

☐ **huérfanos** orphans · *huérfano* orphan

☐ **defecto** defect

☐ **basura** trash, garbage

☐ **inmunda** filthy · *inmundo* filthy

☐ **orfanatorio** orphanage

## 2 Buried Hopes                                      4:09

### Phrases to Listen For

**acababa de** I just

**tuve que** I had to

**tener que** to have to

**nada hay que valga la pena comentar** *SUBJ* there is nothing that's worth talking about

**lo que** that

**para que** so that

**no importa** it doesn't matter

**como se llama** what he is called

**en tanto** as long as

**tal vez** maybe, perhaps

**así es** that's right

**como a usted guste** *SUBJ* as you like

### Names

Halifax, Walter, Bertha Shirley, Ezequías, Katie, Cadbury, Príncipe Eduardo, Bright River

🎬 Mrs. Hammond and Anne enter the orphanage.

☐ **carta** letter

☐ **dividir** to divide

☐ **adorados** beloved, adored · *adorado* beloved, adored · *adorar* to love, to adore

☐ **gemelos** twins · *gemelo* twin

☐ **familiares** family members · *familiar* family member

☐ **responsabilidad** responsibility

☐ **nada hay que valga la pena comentar** *SUBJ* there is nothing that's worth talking about · *valer* to be worth · *comentar* to talk about, to mention

☐ **interesante** interesting

☐ **doce** twelve

☐ **marzo** March

☐ **nació** she was born · *nacer* to be born

☐ **fiebres** fevers · *fiebre NF* fever

☐ **apenas** barely, hardly

☐ **vecina** neighbor · *vecino* neighbor

☐ **orfanatos** orphanages · *orfanato* orphanage

☐ **criatura** child

☐ **me enorgullece** it makes me proud · *enorgullecerse* to make one proud

☐ **desgracia** disgrace, misfortune

☐ **apropiado** appropriate

☐ **rosa** rose

☐ **aroma** *NM* aroma

☐ **igualmente** equally, just as

☐ **cardo** thistle

☐ **lechuga** lettuce

☐ **chiquilla** girl, young woman · *chiquillo* boy, young man [TERM OF ENDEARMENT]

☐ **inteligente** intelligent

☐ **no le ocasionará** it will not cause you · *ocasionar* to cause, to bring about

☐ **realizan** you perform · *realizar* to perform, to realize a goal

☐ **misión** mission

☐ **auxiliarme** helping me · *auxiliar* to help, to assist

☐ **predicamento** predicament, situation

☐ **firmar** to sign

☐ **varios** several, a few

☐ **documentos** documents, papers · *documento* document, paper

🎬 Anne talks to her imaginary friend in the windowpane.

☐ **me alegra** I'm happy (*LIT* it makes me happy) · *alegrar* to make happy

□ **alma gemela** soul mate, kindred spirit ·
  *alma* soul · *gemelo* twin
□ **camisón** *NM* nightgown
□ **¿no te inspiran respeto?** have you no respect?,
  don't they inspire respect? · *inspirar* to inspire ·
  *respeto* respect
□ **reglas** rules · *regla* rule
□ **códigos** codes, regulations · *código* code,
  regulation
□ **disculpe** *SUBJ* excuse (me) · *disculpar* to excuse,
  to pardon
□ **distraída** absent-minded · *distraído*
  absent-minded · *distraer* to distract
□ **mejoraré** I will improve · *mejorar*
  to improve
□ **se ha convertido** it has become ·
  *convertirse* to become
□ **cementerio** cemetery
□ **esperanzas** hopes · *esperanza* hope
□ **fallidas** failed, vain · *fallido* failed, vain
□ **frase** *NF* sentence
□ **la repito** I repeat it · *repetir* to repeat
□ **con frecuencia** frequently
□ **alentarme** to encourage me · *alentar*
  to encourage
□ **han solicitado** they have requested ·
  *solicitar* to solicit, to request
□ **la Isla del Príncipe Eduardo** Prince Edward
  Island · *isla* island · *príncipe NM* prince
□ **premiar** to give a prize, to reward
□ **rebeldía** rebellion
□ **en aras de** in the interest of, for the sake of
□ **disciplina** discipline
□ **fantasías** fantasies · *fantasía* fantasy
□ **métete a la cama** *IMP* get yourself into bed ·
  *meterse* to get into

🎬 Anne waits at the train station in Bright River.

□ **aguardar** to wait
□ **sala de espera** waiting room
□ **espacio** space, room
□ **ofrecimiento** offer

## 3 Dreams Come True                          15:51

### Phrases to Listen For
  **tal vez** maybe, perhaps
  **hasta que** until
  **lo que** what, that
  **tener que** to have to
  **en tanto** as long as
  **así es** that's right
  **en serio** seriously
  **acerca de** about
  **hace años** years ago

**antes de** before
**después de** after
**a medianoche** at midnight
**tuve que** I had to
**hace seis meses** six months ago
**hace media hora** a half hour ago
**no te preocupes** *IMP* don't worry
**así que** so
**¿no es así?** isn't that right?
**no se moleste** *IMP* don't bother
**por supuesto** of course
**me alegra tanto** I'm so happy (*LIT* it makes me
  so happy)
**buena suerte** good luck
**darse cuenta** to notice
**me he enamorado** I have fallen in love
**cerca del mar** near the sea
**¿por qué?** why?
**ya lo sé** I know that
**a pesar de** in spite of
**por favor** please
**no tienes la culpa** it's not your fault
**¿cómo te llamas?** what is your name?
**a qué te refieres** what you mean
**ya basta** enough already
**ya que** since
**tendremos que** we will have to
**tiene que** she has to
**supongo que sí** I suppose so
**no me hace falta** I don't lack
**tendrá que** she will have to
**buenas noches** good night
**aun siendo así** even so

### Names
Thomas, Matthew Cuthbert, Lyndes, Rachel,
Spencer, Hoptown, Roberta, New Brunswick,
Angus, Charlottetown, Barry, Cordelia,
Anne Shirley

🎬 Rachel Lynde watches Matthew Cuthbert drive
  a horse-drawn carriage.

□ **vereda** path
□ **época** time of year, season
□ **iglesia** church
□ **se haya enamorado** *SUBJ* he's fallen in love ·
  *enamorarse* to fall in love
□ **ha arrebatado** it has snatched away · *arrebatar*
  to snatch away, to seize
□ **paz** *NF* peace
□ **tranquilidad** tranquility
□ **lo que se propone** what he's up to · *proponerse*
  to set out to do, to propose
□ **vestía de traje** he was dressed in a suit,
  he was wearing a suit · *vestir* to dress, to wear ·
  *traje NM* suit

🎬 Marilla carries a tea set.

- □ **sorpresa** surprise
- □ **clan** *NM* clan
- □ **interés** *NM* interest
- □ **fumaba** he was smoking · *fumar* to smoke
- □ **pipa** pipe
- □ **aire libre** open air, outside · *aire NM* air · *libre* open, free
- □ **no inunde** it doesn't inundate · *inundar* to inundate
- □ **nube** *NF* cloud
- □ **humo** smoke
- □ **cocina** kitchen
- □ **no prolongues** *IMP* don't prolong · *prolongar* to prolong
- □ **suspenso** suspense
- □ **estación** station
- □ **Nueva Escocia** Nova Scotia
- □ **criar** to raise [CHILD OR ANIMAL]
- □ **¿quién te ha metido esas ideas en la cabeza?** who put those ideas in your head? · *meter* to put
- □ **no responde** it doesn't respond · *responder* to respond
- □ **nos visitó** she visited us · *visitar* to visit
- □ **nos comentó** she mentioned to us · *comentar* to mention
- □ **primavera** spring [SEASON]
- □ **detenidamente** slowly
- □ **recado** message
- □ **sobrina** niece · *sobrino* nephew
- □ **rogándole** requesting her · *rogar* to request, to beg
- □ **trámites** steps, procedures · *trámite NM* step, procedure
- □ **nada me sorprenderá** nothing will surprise me · *sorprender* to surprise
- □ **le pedimos que buscase** *SUBJ* we asked her to look for · *pedir* to ask for, to request · *buscar* to look for
- □ **once** eleven
- □ **doce** twelve
- □ **con la edad suficiente** old enough · *edad* age · *suficiente* sufficient
- □ **labores** chores · *labor NM* chore
- □ **suficientemente** sufficiently
- □ **educado** educated, taught · *educar* to educate, to teach
- □ **correctamente** correctly
- □ **me precio de** I pride myself on · *preciarse de* to pride oneself on
- □ **están cometiendo** you are committing · *cometer* to commit
- □ **un grave error** a grave error, a serious mistake · *grave* grave, serious · *error NM* error, mistake

- □ **hubieras pedido** *SUBJ* you had asked for · *pedir* to ask for, to request
- □ **la semana pasada** last week
- □ **pareja** couple, husband and wife
- □ **chiquillo** boy, young man [TERM OF ENDEARMENT]
- □ **orfanatos** orphanages · *orfanato* orphanage
- □ **le prendió fuego a la casa** he set the house on fire · *prender* to set, to light
- □ **intencionalmente** intentionally
- □ **carbonizados** burned · *carbonizado* burned · *carbonizar* to burn
- □ **absolutamente** absolutely
- □ **raro** unusual, rare
- □ **se empeñe** *SUBJ* he insists · *empeñarse* to insist
- □ **ceder** to cede, to yield
- □ **huérfano** orphan
- □ **arrojó** he threw · *arrojar* to throw forcefully
- □ **estricnina** strychnine
- □ **pozo** well
- □ **gritos** shouts, cries, screams · *grito* shout, cry, scream
- □ **agonía** agony

🎬 Matthew arrives at the train station.

- □ **pasajeros** passengers · *pasajero* passenger
- □ **andén** *NM* platform
- □ **no creo que muerda** *SUBJ* I don't think she bites · *morder* to bite
- □ **recoger** to pick up
- □ **explicártelo** to explain it to you · *explicar* to explain
- □ **tarabilla** chatterbox

🎬 Anne approaches Matthew at the train station.

- □ **recogerme** to pick me up · *recoger* to pick up
- □ **trepar** to climb
- □ **enorme** enormous
- □ **cerezo** cherry tree
- □ **brilla** shines · *brillar* to shine
- □ **luna** moon
- □ **una espera muy agradable** a very pleasant wait · *espera* wait · *agradable* pleasant
- □ **paisajes** landscapes, scenery · *paisaje NM* landscape, scenery, countryside
- □ **esbelta** thin · *esbelto* thin
- □ **ligera** light · *ligero* light [WEIGHT]
- □ **asa** handle
- □ **se desprende** it comes off · *desprenderse* to come off, to detach, to separate
- □ **evitarlo** to avoid it · *evitar* to avoid
- □ **bolsa de viaje** travel bag · *bolsa* bag · *viaje NM* trip, journey
- □ **fina** fine, exquisite · *fino* fine, exquisite

🎬 Matthew helps Anne into the carriage.

- **tipo** type
- **equipaje** *NM* luggage
- **la Dama de Shalott** the Lady of Shalott
- **carruaje** *NM* carriage
- **tirado** pulled · *tirar* to pull
- **caballos** horses · *caballo* horse
- **me alegra** it makes me happy · *alegrar* to make happy
- **ramas** branches · *rama* branch
- **trecho** stretch, distance
- **me fascina** I'm fascinated by it (*LIT* it fascinates me) · *fascinar* to fascinate, to delight
- **pertenecer** to belong
- **he pertenecido** have I belonged · *pertenecer* to belong
- **sitio** place, site
- **intención** intention
- **boca** mouth
- **solía** I used to · *soler* to used to (+ VERB)
- **la Isla del Príncipe Eduardo** Prince Edward Island · *isla* island · *príncipe NM* prince
- **Canadá** Canada
- **que se ha convertido en una realidad** that has come true (*LIT* that has become a reality) · *convertirse* to become · *realidad* reality
- **peculiar** peculiar, strange
- **rojo** red
- **nos deslumbró** it blinded us · *deslumbrar* to blind with bright light
- **absoluta** absolutely [here, *absoluta* before *totalmente* is short for *absolutamente*]
- **totalmente** totally, completely

🎬 Anne shows Matthew her hair and asks him about it.

- **pelirrojo** red-haired, redheaded
- **delgada** thin · *delgado* thin
- **pecas** freckles · *peca* freckle
- **verdes** green · *verde* green
- **tez** *NF* complexion, facial skin
- **complexión** complexion
- **pétalo de rosa** rose petal
- **violeta** violet [COLOR]
- **pena** embarrassment, shame
- **me agobie** *SUBJ* it is a burden to me, it burdens me · *agobiar* to be a burden, to burden
- **divinamente** divinely
- **deslumbrantemente** amazingly
- **inteligente** intelligent
- **angelicalmente** angelically
- **bondadoso** good, kind
- **bondadosa** good, kind · *bondadoso* good, kind

🎬 Matthew and Anne enter the "avenue" of trees in bloom.

- **avenida** avenue
- **adecuada** appropriate, adequate · *adecuado* appropriate, adequate
- **no la describiría** it wouldn't describe it · *describir* to describe
- **adecuadamente** appropriately, adequately
- **paradisíaco** heavenly
- **significado** meaning
- **vía** way, route, railroad tracks
- **láctea** milky
- **ensueño** daydream, fantasy
- **encantador** enchanting, charming
- **estanque** *NM* pond
- **lago** lake
- **relucientes** shining · *reluciente* shining
- **apropiado** appropriate
- **le causan** they cause you · *causar* to cause
- **emoción** emotion, excitement
- **arrancar** to pull from the root
- **mala hierba** weeds
- **plantío** field of planted vegetables
- **pepinos** cucumbers · *pepino* cucumber
- **emocionante** exciting

🎬 Matthew shows Green Gables to Anne.

- **he pellizcado** I have pinched · *pellizcar* to pinch
- **real** real, true
- **arre** *INT* giddy-up

🎬 Anne and Matthew enter Green Gables.

- **abrumada** overwhelmed · *abrumado* overwhelmed · *abrumar* to overwhelm
- **abandonarla** to abandon her · *abandonar* to abandon
- **resultado** result
- **mensajes** messages · *mensaje NM* message
- **personalmente** personally
- **trágico** tragic
- **bello** beautiful, pretty
- **precisamente** precisely, exactly
- **me fascinaría** it would fascinate me · *fascinar* to fascinate
- **distinguido** distinguished · *distinguirse* to be distinguished
- **tonterías** silliness, foolishness, nonsense · *tontería* silly thing, foolish thing
- **simple** simple
- **prosaicamente** prosaically, mundanely
- **perfectamente** perfectly
- **normal** normal
- **avergonzada** ashamed · *avergonzado* ashamed · *avergonzarse* to be ashamed

☐ **suplicaría** I would implore · *suplicar* to implore
☐ **importancia** importance
☐ **escriba** *SUBJ* one writes · *escribir* to write
☐ **ene** *NF* N [LETTER]
☐ **horriblemente** horribly
☐ **feo** ugly
☐ **humildad** humility
☐ **contéstame** *IMP* answer me · *contestar* to answer
☐ **cabello** hair
☐ **castaño** brown
☐ **parada** standing · *parado* standing · *parar* to stand
☐ **maleta** suitcase
☐ **albergue** *NM* lodging
☐ **sombrero** hat
☐ **hambrienta** hungry · *hambriento* hungry
☐ **me invade la desesperación** I'm in the depths of despair (*LIT* despair invades me) · *invadir* to invade · *desesperación* desperation, despair
☐ **jamás me he sentido así** I've never felt that way · *sentirse* to feel
☐ **invadirla** to overcome you, to overwhelm you, to invade you · *invadir* to overcome, to overwhelm, to invade
☐ **quien se desespera** *SUBJ* whoever despairs · *desesperarse* to despair, to lose hope
☐ **espalda** back

🎞 Marilla opens the door to Anne's bedroom.

☐ **lávate** *IMP* wash up · *lavarse* to wash oneself
☐ **cenar** to eat dinner, to dine

🎞 Matthew washes and dries his hands.

☐ **la devolveré** I will take her back · *devolver* to take back, to return
☐ **temprano** early
☐ **supones** you suppose · *suponer* to suppose
☐ **tierna** tender · *tierno* tender
☐ **lástima** pity
☐ **está ansiosa por quedarse** she's anxious to stay · *ansioso* anxious · *quedarse* to stay
☐ **te ha embrujado** she has bewitched you · *embrujar* to bewitch
☐ **obvio** obvious
☐ **permanezca** *SUBJ* she remains · *permanecer* to remain
☐ **podríamos contratar** we could hire · *contratar* to hire, to contract
☐ **respirar** to breathe
☐ **no nos sería de utilidad** she would not be useful to us · *utilidad* usefulness, utility
☐ **espantosa** horrible · *espantoso* horrible

## 4 | Haunting Beauty 7:53

**Phrases to Listen For**

**date prisa** *IMP* hurry up
**dentro de** within
**por siempre** forever
**el día de hoy** today
**no me digas** *IMP* don't tell me, you don't say
**lo lamento** I'm sorry
**en el momento preciso** at just the right moment, at the exact moment
**¿cuántos años tienes?** how old are you?
**de acuerdo** agreed, all right
**buenas tardes** good afternoon
**en verdad** really
**trataré de** I will try to
**hasta por los codos** way too much (*LIT* up to the elbows)
**¿a qué te refieres?** what do you mean?
**a propósito** by the way
**desde entonces** since then, ever since
**en tanto** as long as
**por supuesto** of course
**enseguida** right away
**en cuanto a** concerning
**te lo pido** I beg you
**me despido de ti** I take leave of you
**lo pasará por alto** he will overlook it
**buenas noches** good night

**Names**

Jerry Moody, Sarah, Roberta, Marilla, Blewett, Spencer, Mathilda, Anne Shirley

🎞 Matthew helps Marilla into the carriage.

☐ **chiquillo** boy, young man [TERM OF ENDEARMENT]
☐ **riachuelo** small river
☐ **lo contrataría** I would hire him · *contratar* to hire, to contract
☐ **verano** summer
☐ **date prisa** *IMP* hurry up · *darse prisa* to hurry up
☐ **se grabe** *SUBJ* it becomes etched · *grabarse* to become etched
☐ **memoria** memory
☐ **me perseguirá** it will follow me · *perseguir* to follow, to pursue
☐ **romántico** romantic
☐ **bondades** kind deeds, kindness · *bondad* kindness, goodness

🎞 Mrs. Spencer and her daughter run to meet Marilla and Anne.

☐ **instalando** getting settled · *instalar* to get settled
☐ **víctima** victim

☐ **trágicos** tragic · *trágico* tragic
☐ **acontecimientos** events · *acontecimiento* event
☐ **insistió** she insisted · *insistir* to insist
☐ **debí tramitarlo** I ought to have taken care of it · *deber* to ought to · *tramitar* to take care of, to handle
☐ **personalmente** personally
☐ **profundamente** profoundly
☐ **devolverla** to return her · *devolver* to return, to take back
☐ **ahora que lo mencionas** now that you mention it · *mencionar* to mention
☐ **visitarme** to visit me · *visitar* to visit
☐ **ayer** yesterday
☐ **extremadamente** extremely
☐ **numerosa** numerous · *numeroso* numerous
☐ **desesperada** desperate · *desesperado* desperate
☐ **gemelos** twins · *gemelo* twin
☐ **¿cómo lo adivinaste?** how did you guess? · *adivinar* to guess
☐ **preciso** perfect, exactly right
☐ **llegada** arrival
☐ **absolutamente** absolutely
☐ **providencial** providential
☐ **trece** thirteen
☐ **eres poca cosa** you're a little thing
☐ **delgada** thin · *delgado* thin
☐ **rinden** they produce · *rendir* to produce
☐ **te ganes** SUBJ you earn · *ganarse* to earn
☐ **alimentos** food · *alimento* food, nourishment
☐ **actúes** SUBJ you act, you behave · *actuar* to act, to behave
☐ **mesura** courtesy, discretion
☐ **respeto** respect
☐ **me quedo con ella** I'll keep her · *quedarse* to keep, to remain
☐ **se han portado mal** they have behaved poorly · *portarse* to behave
☐ **últimamente** recently, lately
☐ **verdaderamente** truly
☐ **agotada** exhausted · *agotado* exhausted · *agotar* to exhaust, to tire
☐ **decisión** decision

🎬 Marilla and Anne drive away from Mrs. Spencer and Mrs. Blewett in the carriage.

☐ **devolverte** to return you · *devolver* to return, to take back
☐ **entregarte** to hand you over · *entregar* to hand over, to deliver
☐ **distinto** distinct, different
☐ **aspecto** look, expression
☐ **bruja** witch
☐ **avergonzada** ashamed · *avergonzado* ashamed · *avergonzarse* to be ashamed

☐ **expresarte** expressing yourself · *expresarse* to express oneself
☐ **extraña** stranger · *extraño* stranger
☐ **cuida tu lengua** IMP watch your tongue · *cuidar* to watch, to take care
☐ **no critiques** IMP don't criticize · *criticar* to criticize

🎬 Matthew milks a cow. Marilla speaks.

☐ **no entregaría** I wouldn't give · *entregar* to give, to deliver
☐ **sarnoso** mangy
☐ **absurdo** absurd
☐ **no interfirieras** SUBJ you didn't interfere · *interferir* to interfere
☐ **métodos** methods · *método* method
☐ **solterona** spinster · *solterón* confirmed bachelor
☐ **educar** to educate
☐ **solterón** confirmed bachelor
☐ **chiquilla** girl, young woman · *chiquillo* boy, young man [TERM OF ENDEARMENT]
☐ **charla** she chatters · *charlar* to chatter, to talk
☐ **hasta por los codos** way too much (LIT up to the elbows) · *codo* elbow
☐ **¿a qué negarlo?** EXP who could deny it?
☐ **poco frecuente** not very common · *frecuente* frequent

🎬 Marilla enters Anne's bedroom.

☐ **terminaste** you finished · *terminar* to finish
☐ **rezar** to pray
☐ **yo no acostumbro** I'm not accustomed · *acostumbrar* to be accustomed
☐ **pelirroja** redheaded · *pelirrojo* redheaded
☐ **a propósito** on purpose
☐ **disgustada** upset, displeased · *disgustado* upset, displeased · *disgustar* to upset, to displease
☐ **diariamente** daily
☐ **si usted así lo manda** if you say so
☐ **¿y cómo se reza?** and how does one pray? · *rezar* to pray
☐ **te arrodillas** you get down on your knees, you kneel · *arrodillarse* to get down on one's knees, to kneel
☐ **enorme** enormous
☐ **pradera** large meadow
☐ **totalmente** totally, completely
☐ **elevaría** I would raise · *elevar* to raise
☐ **mirada** look
☐ **cúpula** dome
☐ **catedral** NF cathedral
☐ **ya tienes edad suficiente** you're old enough · *tener* to have · *edad* age · *suficiente* sufficient
☐ **idear** to think of ideas, to form ideas for

- **plegarias** prayers · *plegaria* prayer
- **bendiciones** blessings · *bendición* blessing
- **humildad** humility
- **misericordioso** merciful
- **celestial** celestial, heavenly
- **anhelo** I desire · *anhelar* to desire
- **excesivamente** excessively
- **numerosas** numerous · *numeroso* numerous
- **tardaría** I would take a long time · *tardar* to take a long time
- **enumerarlas** listing them · *enumerar* to list, to enumerate
- **mencionar** to mention
- **te suplico** I plead with you · *suplicar* to plead, to beg
- **me despido** I take leave of you · *despedirse* to take leave, to say good-bye
- **atentamente** sincerely
- **carta** letter
- **tienda** store
- **oración** prayer
- **lo más cercano a** the closest thing to · *cercano* near
- **hereje** *NMF* heathen

## 5 Bite Your Tongue                    9:19

### Phrases to Listen For

**buenos días** good morning
**hace varias horas** several hours ago
**¿por qué?** why?
**tendré que** I will have to
**antes de** before
**en caso de que** in case
**tener que** to have to
**no lo sé** I don't know
**a prueba** on a trial basis
**de acuerdo** agreed
**así es** that's right
**lo que** what
**guarda silencio** *IMP* keep quiet
**por amor de Dios** for the love of God
**cielo santo** good heavens
**de inmediato** right away
**de ahora en adelante** from now on
**dar cabida a la ira** to allow for any anger, to find room for anger
**en cuanto** as soon as
**tan en serio** so seriously
**tuviste que** you had to
**para que** in order to
**así que** so
**tendrás que** you will have to
**hace cuatro años que** it's been four years since
**antes que** before

**no tienes que** you don't have to
**por supuesto** of course
**tengo que** I have to
**a primera hora** first thing
**lo que usted mande** *SUBJ* whatever you say

### Names

Rachel Lynde, Blewett

🎬 Anne enters the kitchen where Marilla is working.

- **desayunó** he ate breakfast · *desayunar* to eat breakfast
- **varias** several · *varios* several
- **antes de que amanezca** *SUBJ* before dawn · *amanecer* to dawn
- **me había propuesto** I had made up my mind · *proponerse* to make up one's mind, to decide
- **paciente** patient
- **soportar** to tolerate
- **soportarla** to tolerate it · *soportar* to tolerate
- **considera** you consider · *considerar* to consider
- **necesario** necessary
- **preciso** precise, exact
- **estés almorzando** *SUBJ* you are eating brunch · *almorzar* to eat brunch
- **religión** religion
- **desesperadamente** desperately
- **aumentar de peso** to gain weight
- **santificado** hallowed, holy · *santificar* to sanctify
- **letra** lyric
- **melodía** melody
- **oración** prayer
- **apréndetela** *IMP* learn it · *aprender* to learn
- **guarda** *IMP* keep · *guardar* to keep
- **tarjeta** card
- **sala** living room
- **compórtate** *IMP* behave yourself · *comportarse* to behave oneself
- **hereje** *NMF* heathen

🎬 Rachel enters Green Gables.

- **me horroriza** it horrifies me · *horrorizar* to horrify
- **se ha cometido** it has been made, it has been committed · *cometer* to commit
- **superar** to overcome
- **impresión** impression
- **devolverla** to return her · *devolver* to return, to take back
- **error** *NM* error, mistake
- **catastrófico** catastrophic
- **vecina** neighbor · *vecino* neighbor
- **aspecto** look, face
- **flaca** thin · *flaco* thin
- **feúcha** very ugly · *feúcho* very ugly

□ **chiquilla** girl, young woman · *chiquillo* boy, young man [TERM OF ENDEARMENT]

□ **zanahoria** carrot

□ **¿cómo se atreve?** how dare you? · *atreverse* to dare

□ **grosera** rude person, vulgar person · *grosero* rude person, vulgar person

□ **maleducada** ill-mannered person · *maleducado* ill-mannered person

□ **insensible** unfeeling

□ **la odio** I hate you · *odiar* to hate

□ **se expresaran** SUBJ they expressed, they spoke · *expresar* to express, to speak

□ **gordinflona** very fat person · *gordinflón* PEJ very fat person

□ **fea** ugly · *feo* ugly

□ **bruja** witch

□ **chismosa** gossip · *chismoso* gossip [PERSON]

□ **las que arrojan** those who throw · *arrojar* to throw forcefully

□ **estricnina** strychnine

□ **pozos** wells · *pozo* well

□ **expresarte** express yourself · *expresarse* to express oneself

□ **no estoy justificando** I'm not justifying · *justificar* to justify

□ **fuiste muy dura con ella** you were very hard on her · *duro* hard, tough

□ **no te lo reprocho** I don't reproach you for it · *reprochar* to reproach

□ **dar cabida** to make room · *dar* to give · *cabida* room to fit, capacity for more

□ **ira** ire

□ **pensamientos** thoughts · *pensamiento* thought

□ **obvio** obvious

□ **sentido común** common sense

□ **admiré** I admired · *admirar* to admire

□ **desapareció** it disappeared · *desaparecer* to disappear

□ **cruzó por esta puerta** she passed through this doorway, she came in this door · *cruzar* to cross

□ **visítame** IMP visit me · *visitar* to visit

🎬 Anne sits on a bench outside. Marilla approaches.

□ **insultar** to insult

□ **derecho** right

□ **franca** frank · *franco* frank

□ **extraña** stranger · *extraño* stranger

□ **invitada** guest · *invitado* guest

□ **sin mencionar** not to mention, without mentioning · *mencionar* to mention

□ **excelentes** excellent · *excelente* excellent

□ **te hubieras mordido** SUBJ you had bitten · *morderse* to bite (oneself)

□ **disculpa** apology

□ **ofrecérsela** to offer it to her · *ofrecer* to offer

□ **aplicarme** to apply to me, to give me · *aplicar* to apply

□ **castigo** punishment

□ **encerrarme** to lock me up · *encerrar* to lock up

□ **oscuro** dark

□ **calabozo** jail cell, prison

□ **habiten** SUBJ they live · *habitar* to live in a place, to inhabit

□ **serpientes** serpents · *serpiente* NF serpent

□ **sapos** toads · *sapo* toad

□ **pan** NM bread

□ **protestar** to protest

□ **pretendes** you expect · *pretender* to expect, to want

□ **permanecer** to remain

□ **techo** roof, ceiling

□ **disculparte** to apologize · *disculparse* to apologize

🎬 Matthew climbs the stairs and enters Anne's bedroom.

□ **humillante** humiliating

□ **convencer** to convince

□ **lamentar** to be sorry for

□ **aparentar** to seem

□ **despiadada** cruel, merciless, wicked · *despiadado* cruel, merciless, wicked

□ **detenidamente** slowly

□ **complacerlo** to please you · *complacer* to please

□ **causa** cause

□ **sinceridad** sincerity

□ **borrar** to erase

□ **mancha** stain

□ **derramé** I spilled · *derramar* to spill

□ **estoy interfiriendo** I am interfering · *interferir* to interfere

□ **ni aunque me colgaran se enterará por mí** SUBJ not even if they hang me will anyone find out from me · *aunque* although · *colgar* to hang · *enterarse* to learn of

🎬 Matthew and Marilla sit at the table. Anne enters the room.

□ **no debí haberme enfurecido** I shouldn't have lost my temper · *enfurecerse* to lose one's temper

□ **estoy dispuesta** I'm willing · *dispuesto* willing

□ **sabia** wise · *sabio* wise

□ **decisión** decision

□ **plegarias** prayers · *plegaria* prayer

□ **lo que usted mande** SUBJ as you wish (LIT whatever you order) · *mandar* to order

□ **recuperaría la cordura** she would come to her senses · *recuperar* to recover · *cordura* sanity, common sense

## 6 Strong Discipline 10:33

### Phrases to Listen For

**date prisa** IMP hurry up
**lo que** what
**así es como** that's how
**hasta que** until
**de verdad** real
**por amor de Dios** for the love of God
**buenos días** good morning
**a pesar de** in spite of
**por favor** please
**por supuesto** of course
**todo mundo** everyone
**no te preocupes** IMP don't worry
**para que** so that
**a la mitad** in the middle
**tal vez** maybe, perhaps
**a prueba** on trial
**darte de baja** to remove you
**ya que** since
**tenía que** I had to
**antes que** before
**alma gemela** soul mate, kindred spirit
**mangas de campana** puffed sleeves
**no tenías porqué haber tomado mi broche**
    you had no reason to have taken my brooch
**nada de eso** not at all
**día de campo** picnic, outing
**tengo que** I have to
**amiga íntima** bosom friend, close friend
**tuve razón** I was right
**de pronto** suddenly
**en tanto** as long as
**antes de que** before
**tenía razón** she was right
**¿por qué?** why?
**así que** so

### Names

Lynde, Cuthbert, Katie Morris, Thomas, Marilla,
Lady Cordelia Fitzgerald, Camelot, Blewett

🎬 Marilla enters Anne's room.

☐ **date prisa** IMP hurry up · *darse prisa* to hurry up
☐ **estás murmurando** you are muttering ·
    *murmurar* to mutter, to whisper, to murmur
☐ **elegante** elegant
☐ **no se efectúa** one doesn't carry out ·
    *efectuar* to carry out, to bring about
☐ **visita** visit
☐ **ropa de trabajo** work clothes
☐ **amatistas** amethysts · *amatista* amethyst
☐ **preciosas** precious · *precioso* precious
☐ **diamantes** diamonds · *diamante* NM
    diamond

☐ **muérdete la lengua** IMP bite your tongue ·
    *morderse* to bite (oneself)

🎬 Anne and Marilla walk onto the Lynde porch.

☐ **profundamente** profoundly, deeply
☐ **absurdo** absurd
☐ **he avergonzado** I have shamed · *avergonzar*
    to shame
☐ **hospedarme** to stay, to dwell · *hospedarse*
    to stay, to dwell
☐ **desagradecida** ungrateful · *desagradecido*
    ungrateful
☐ **infierno** hell
☐ **flaca** thin, skinny · *flaco* thin, skinny
☐ **feúcha** very ugly · *feúcho* very ugly
☐ **pelirroja** redheaded · *pelirrojo* redheaded
☐ **cruel** cruel
☐ **prolongar** to prolong
☐ **sufrimiento** suffering
☐ **innecesario** unnecessary
☐ **le suplico** I beg you · *suplicar* to beg,
    to plead
☐ **me excedí** I overdid it · *excederse* to overdo
☐ **no debes ofenderte** you mustn't be offended ·
    *ofenderse* to be offended
☐ **con franqueza** frankly, with frankness
☐ **creció** she grew up · *crecer* to grow,
    to grow up
☐ **adquiriendo** acquiring · *adquirir* to acquire
☐ **castaño oscuro** dark brown · *castaño* brown ·
    *oscuro* dark
☐ **me ha devuelto** you have returned to me ·
    *devolver* to return
☐ **fe** NF faith
☐ **la consideraré** I will consider you ·
    *considerar* to consider
☐ **benefactora** benefactress · *benefactor* NM
    benefactor
☐ **disciplina** discipline
☐ **educación** education
☐ **adecuada** adequate, appropriate ·
    *adecuado* adequate, appropriate
☐ **la escuela dominical** Sunday School
☐ **se impartirá** it will be given · *impartir* to give,
    to impart
☐ **civilizados** civilized · *civilizado* civilized ·
    *civilizar* to civilize
☐ **edad** age
☐ **partida** split · *partido* split · *partir* to split
☐ **mitad** NF middle
☐ **esperanza** hope

🎬 Anne and Marilla walk along the road.

☐ **definitivo** definitive, definite
☐ **inscribirte** to enroll you · *inscribir* to enroll

- **proporcionarme** to give me · *proporcionar* to give
- **alientos** encouragement · *aliento* encouragement
- **comportarte** behaving yourself, to behave yourself · *comportarse* to behave oneself
- **motivos** reasons · *motivo* reason
- **temperamento** temperament
- **definitivamente** definitely
- **actuación** performance
- **disculpas** apologies · *disculpa* apology
- **reserva** IMP save · *reservar* to save, to hold in reserve
- **energía** energy
- **rezos** prayers · *rezo* prayer
- **plegarias** prayers · *plegaria* prayer
- **valen** they have value · *valer* to have value, to be worth
- **sinceras** sincere · *sincero* sincere
- **egoísta** selfish, egotistical
- **verdadera** true · *verdadero* true
- **vitrina** glass showcase
- **descubrí** I discovered · *descubrir* to discover
- **librero** bookcase
- **cristal** glass
- **no había despedazado** he hadn't shattered · *despedazar* to shatter, to break into many pieces
- **alcohólico** alcoholic
- **marido** husband
- **solía** I used to · *soler* to used to (+ VERB)
- **hechizo** spell
- **penetrar** to penetrate
- **conveniente** proper
- **amiga íntima** bosom friend, close friend
- **alma gemela** soul mate, kindred spirit · *alma* soul · *gemelo* twin
- **ladera** slope, hillside
- **orquídeas** orchids · *orquídea* orchid
- **patrocinan** they sponsor · *patrocinar* to sponsor
- **lago** lake
- **relucientes** shining · *reluciente* shining
- **desperdicias** you waste · *desperdiciar* to waste
- **inventar** inventing · *inventar* to invent
- **simplemente** simply
- **ajenos** not belonging to · *ajeno* not belonging to

🎬 Anne is having a dress fitted by Marilla.

- **semejante** similar
- **tontería** foolish act, silly act
- **alimentar** to feed, to give nourishment
- **vanidad** vanity
- **cómodos** comfortable · *cómodo* comfortable
- **sencillos** simple · *sencillo* simple
- **domingos** Sundays · *domingo* Sunday
- **mangas** sleeves · *manga* sleeve

- **campana** bell
- **no desperdiciaré** I won't waste · *desperdiciar* to waste
- **tela** cloth, material
- **adornos** adornments, decorations, ornaments · *adorno* adornment, decoration, ornament
- **volantes** frilly · *volante* frilly
- **drapeados** draped · *drapeado* draped · *drapear* to drape
- **cómodo** comfortable
- **sencillo** simple
- **mayoría** majority
- **confórmate** IMP get used to it · *conformarse* to get used to
- **broche** NM brooch
- **amatista** amethyst
- **ayer** yesterday
- **como lucía** how it looked · *lucir* to look
- **alhajero** jewelry box
- **entrometida** meddling · *entrometido* meddling · *entrometerse* to meddle
- **cualidades** characteristics, qualities · *cualidad* characteristic, quality
- **repetir** to repeat
- **mentira** lie
- **confieses** SUBJ you confess · *confesar* to confess
- **encerrada** locked up · *encerrado* locked up · *encerrar* to lock up, to enclose

🎬 Matthew sits at the table. Marilla stands next to him.

- **rincón** NM corner
- **rendija** crack
- **confesarlo** to confess it · *confesar* to confess
- **eso me duele** that hurts me · *doler* to hurt
- **cómoda** dresser [FURNITURE]
- **revisé** I looked carefully · *revisar* to look carefully
- **hendiduras** cracks · *hendidura* crack
- **piso** floor
- **dispuesta** willing · *dispuesto* willing
- **concederte** to concede to you, to grant you · *conceder* to concede, to grant
- **precipitado** hasty
- **ladrona** thief · *ladrón* NM thief
- **mentirosa** liar · *mentiroso* liar

🎬 Marilla enters Anne's room with a tray.

- **confesar** to confess
- **defenderte** to defend yourself · *defender* to defend
- **me invadió** I was overcome by (LIT it invaded me) · *invadir* to invade
- **tentación** temptation
- **irresistible** irresistible
- **portar** to carry

□ **cruzar** to cross
□ **puente** NF bridge
□ **viento** wind
□ **despeinaba** it messed up · *despeinar* to mess up [HAIR]
□ **devolvería** I would return · *devolver* to return, to take back
□ **me incliné** I leaned · *inclinarse* to lean
□ **reflejada** reflected · *reflejado* reflected · *reflejar* to reflect
□ **se me escapó** it got away from me, it slipped away · *escapar* to get away, to slip away, to escape
□ **se hundió** it sank · *hundirse* to sink, to be sinking
□ **profundas** deep · *profundo* deep
□ **he asimilado** I've come to understand · *asimilar* to understand
□ **importancia** importance
□ **recuerdo** keepsake, remembrance
□ **romance** NM romance
□ **frustrado** frustrated · *frustrarse* to be frustrated
□ **confesaba** I confessed · *confesar* to confess
□ **empacar** to pack

▰ Marilla walks downstairs.

□ **afecto** affection
□ **furiosa** furious · *furioso* furious
□ **haber tolerado** having tolerated · *tolerar* to tolerate

▰ Marilla enters Anne's room and shows her the brooch.

□ **¿por qué inventaste...?** why did you make up ...?, why did you invent ...? · *inventar* to make up (story, lie), to invent
□ **permanecería** I would remain · *permanecer* to remain
□ **hasta que confesara** SUBJ until I confessed · *confesar* to confess
□ **inventé** I made up · *inventar* to make up (story, lie), to invent
□ **confesión** confession
□ **interesante** interesting
□ **templo** church building

## 7  Bosom Friends                          4:47

### Phrases to Listen For

**¿qué tal?** greetings
**mucho gusto** nice to meet you
**por amor de Dios** for the love of God
**lo que** what
**acerca de** about
**a punto de** about to

**por primera vez** for the first time
**tal vez** maybe, perhaps
**un poco de** a little bit of
**día de campo** picnic, outing
**haremos un buen papel** we'll make a good showing, we'll perform well
**¿no te parece?** don't you think?
**la abeja reina** the queen bee

### Names

Anne, Allan, Elizabeth, Cuthbert, Diana, Gilbert, Moody, Prissy Andrews, Queens, Josie Pye

▰ Anne shakes hands with Mr. Barry.

□ **jardín** NM garden
□ **procura calmarte** IMP try to calm down, try to get hold of yourself · *procurar* to try · *calmarse* to calm (oneself) down
□ **tarabilla** chatterbox
□ **emocionada** excited · *emocionado* excited · *emocionarse* to get excited, to become emotional
□ **helado** ice cream
□ **reverendo** reverend
□ **hospedaje** NM lodging
□ **físicamente** physically
□ **considerablemente** considerably
□ **afectada** affected, ruffled · *afectado* affected, ruffled · *afectar* to affect
□ **espiritualmente** spiritually
□ **disminuir** to diminish
□ **tensiones** jitters, feelings of stress · *tensión* tension
□ **té** NM tea
□ **visitarnos** to visit us · *visitar* to visit
□ **se han mudado** they have moved · *mudarse* to move [RESIDENCE]
□ **casa parroquial** parsonage · *parroquial* parochial
□ **maravillas** marvels, wonders, wonderful things · *maravilla* marvel, wonder
□ **habilidades** abilities, skills · *habilidad* ability, skill
□ **repostera** dessert maker, dessert seller
□ **ansiosa** anxious, eager · *ansioso* anxious, eager
□ **secretos** secrets · *secreto* secret
□ **limonada** lemonade
□ **encantadora** charming, enchanting · *encantador* charming, enchanting
□ **definitiva** definitive · *definitivo* definitive
□ **apartarse** to keep oneself away, to separate oneself
□ **catástrofes** catastrophes · *catástrofe* NF catastrophe
□ **meditarlo** to think about it · *meditar* to think about, to meditate

🎬 Anne walks with Diana Barry.

- □ **instrucciones** instructions · *instrucción* instruction
- □ **precisas** specific, precise, exact · *preciso* specific, precise, exact
- □ **costumbre** *NF* habit, custom
- □ **charlar** to chat
- □ **ave** *NF* bird
- □ **probable** probable, likely
- □ **urraca** magpie
- □ **participar** to participate
- □ **carrera de tres pies** three-legged race · *carrera* race · *pie NM* foot
- □ **honor** *NM* honor
- □ **compañera** partner, companion · *compañero* partner, companion
- □ **apariencia** appearance, look
- □ **sana** healthy · *sano* healthy
- □ **veloz** fast, speedy
- □ **haremos un buen papel** we'll make a good showing, we'll perform well · *papel* role

🎬 Anne and Diana line up at the starting line.

- □ **en sus marcas** on your mark · *marca* mark
- □ **las felicito** I congratulate you · *felicitar* to congratulate
- □ **ha derrotado** she has defeated · *derrotar* to defeat
- □ **varones** men · *varón NM* man
- □ **orgulloso** prideful, proud

🎬 Anne and Diana are in a rowboat.

- □ **verdaderas** true, real · *verdadero* true, real
- □ **heroínas** heroines · *heroína* heroine
- □ **lástima** pity
- □ **¿no opinas...?** don't you think ...? · *opinar* to think, to give an opinion
- □ **guiñarle el ojo** to wink
- □ **desconocida** strange, unknown · *desconocido* strange, unknown · *desconocer* to not know, to be unaware of
- □ **hubiera guiñado** *SUBJ* he had winked · *guiñar* to wink
- □ **dieciséis** sixteen
- □ **enfermo** sick, ill
- □ **me alegro** I'm happy · *alegrarse* to be happy
- □ **atrasada** behind schedule · *atrasado* behind schedule · *atrasarse* to fall behind
- □ **abeja** bee
- □ **ingresar** to enroll
- □ **profesa** he professes · *profesar* to profess
- □ **desmedido** unlimited
- □ **está enamorada de** she is in love with · *estar enamorado de* to be in love with
- □ **se ahogue** *SUBJ* she drowns · *ahogarse* to drown

- □ **experiencia** experience
- □ **romántica** romantic · *romántico* romantic
- □ **ahogarse** to drown
- □ **extraña** strange · *extraño* strange
- □ **presentimiento** feeling about the future

## 8 Red Hair Curse    8:59

### Phrases to Listen For
- **¿cómo te llamas?** what's your name?
- **tenemos mucho en común** we have a lot in common
- **lo que** what
- **tuve la culpa** I was to blame, it was my fault
- **hasta que** until
- **antes de que** before
- **tienes que** you have to
- **¿por qué?** why?
- **se burla de** he makes fun of
- **cabeza de cuervo** crow head
- **por favor** please
- **de inmediato** immediately
- **por amor de Dios** for the love of God
- **alma gemela** soul mate, kindred spirit
- **después de todo** after all
- **no te preocupes** *IMP* don't worry
- **ni siquiera** I don't even
- **trato de** I'll try to
- **lo contrario** the opposite
- **lo sé** I know
- **tenía que** I had to
- **acerca de** about
- **hace muchos años** many years ago
- **desde entonces** since then
- **así que** so
- **que tengas suerte** *SUBJ* good luck

### Names
Gilbert Blythe, Halifax, Blair

🎬 Anne stands in front of Mr. Phillips, the school teacher.

- □ **nos enorgullecemos** we are proud of · *enorgullecerse* to be proud of
- □ **nivel** *NM* level
- □ **educación** education
- □ **te esfuerces** *SUBJ* you make the effort · *esforzarse* to make the effort
- □ **he impartido** I've given, I've taught · *impartir* to give, to teach, to impart
- □ **convencida** convinced · *convencido* convinced · *convencer* to convince
- □ **en común** in common
- □ **te sentarás** you will sit · *sentarse* to sit
- □ **asiento** seat

☐ **lección** lesson
☐ **asesorar** to advise
☐ **alumnas** students · *alumno* student
☐ **cuadernos** notebooks · *cuaderno* notebook
☐ **memoricen** IMP memorize · *memorizar* to memorize
☐ **dicté** I dictated · *dictar* to dictate
☐ **ayer** yesterday
☐ **zanahoria** carrot
☐ **¿cómo te atreves?** how dare you? · *atreverse* to dare
☐ **actitud** NF attitude
☐ **te colocarás** you will put yourself, you will place yourself · *colocarse* to put oneself, to place oneself
☐ **tolerar** to tolerate
☐ **elementos** elements · *elemento* element
☐ **vengativos** vindictive, vengeful · *vengativo* vindictive, vengeful
☐ **alumnos** students · *alumno* student
☐ **carácter** NM character
☐ **controlarlo** to control it · *controlar* to control
☐ **cien** one hundred

🎬 Diana waits for Anne by a tree outside the schoolhouse. When Anne exits, Gilbert approaches.

☐ **haberme burlado** having made fun of · *burlarse* to make fun
☐ **quisiera que me perdonaras** SUBJ I would like you to forgive me · *querer* to want · *perdonar* to forgive
☐ **se burla de** he makes fun of · *burlarse de* to make fun of
☐ **cabeza de cuervo** crow head
☐ **disculpa** apology
☐ **diferencia** difference
☐ **llamada** called · *llamado* called · *llamar* to call
☐ **hierro** iron
☐ **ha penetrado** it has penetrated · *penetrar* to penetrate
☐ **alma** soul
☐ **pelirroja** redhead · *pelirrojo* redhead
☐ **tragedia** tragedy

🎬 Marilla attempts to open the door to Anne's room.

☐ **en este instante** at this instant
☐ **me encuentro** I find myself · *encontrar* to find
☐ **sumida** in the depths, submerged · *sumido* in the depths, submerged · *sumirse* to plunge, to submerge
☐ **desesperación** despair, desperation
☐ **pamplinas** EXP nonsense, fiddlesticks
☐ **enferma** sick · *enfermo* sick
☐ **inocente** innocent
☐ **avergonzada** ashamed · *avergonzado* ashamed · *avergonzarse* to be ashamed

☐ **te atreviste** you dared · *atreverse* to dare
☐ **pizarra** writing slate
☐ **no tenías porqué perder los estribos** you had no reason to lose your temper · *porqué* NM reason · *perder* to lose · *estribo* stirrup
☐ **rojo** red
☐ **verde** green
☐ **desconsolada** disconsolate, heartbroken · *desconsolado* disconsolate, heartbroken
☐ **me lo teñí** I dyed it · *teñirse* to dye (one's)
☐ **¿te lo teñiste?** you dyed it? · *teñirse* to dye (one's)
☐ **juró solemnemente** he solemnly swore · *jurar* to swear, to take an oath
☐ **negro como el azabache** jet black · *azabache* jet [a velvet-black coal]
☐ **te estás refiriendo** are you referring · *referirse* to be referring
☐ **vendedor** salesman
☐ **prohíbo** I forbid · *prohibir* to forbid, to prohibit
☐ **categóricamente** categorically
☐ **vanidad** vanity
☐ **acarrear** to carry one, to lead one
☐ **superar** to overcome
☐ **cara** face
☐ **derecho** right
☐ **¿le dolió?** did it hurt him? · *doler* to hurt
☐ **enojada** angry · *enojado* angry · *enojarse* to get angry
☐ **furiosa** furious · *furioso* furious
☐ **comportarte** to behave yourself · *comportarse* to behave oneself
☐ **decisión** decision
☐ **gemela** twin · *gemelo* twin

🎬 Marilla cuts Anne's hair. Matthew is at her side.

☐ **espejo** mirror
☐ **tonterías** silliness, foolishness

🎬 Diana picks flowers as Anne speaks.

☐ **heroínas** heroines · *heroína* heroine
☐ **enfermedad** infirmity, sickness
☐ **venden** they sell · *vender* to sell
☐ **haberlo teñido** having dyed it · *teñir* to dye
☐ **verano** summer
☐ **penitencia** penitence
☐ **fea** ugly · *feo* ugly
☐ **trato** I try · *tratar* to try
☐ **lo contrario** the contrary

🎬 Anne looks out her window. Diana is signaling her with flags.

☐ **burbuja** bubble
☐ **dríade** NF wood nymph
☐ **utilicé** I used · *utilizar* to use, to utilize

□ **banderas** flags · *bandera* flag
□ **recuperar el aliento** to catch one's breath · *recuperar* to recover · *aliento* breath
□ **despensa** pantry
□ **galletas** cookies, crackers · *galleta* cookie, cracker
□ **comentaban** she was mentioning · *comentar* to mention, to comment
□ **te parecías** you are like · *parecerse* to be like
□ **comentó** she mentioned · *comentar* to mention, to comment
□ **comprometida** engaged · *comprometido* engaged · *comprometerse* to get engaged
□ **discusión** argument
□ **compromiso** engagement
□ **ha padecido** she has suffered · *padecer* to suffer
□ **romance** NM romance
□ **destinado** destined
□ **fracaso** failure
□ **estaré vigilando** I will be watching · *vigilar* to watch
□ **irme** to go, to leave · *irse* to go away, to leave
□ **exámenes** exams, tests · *examen* NM exam, test

## 9  School Competition          8:17

### Phrases to Listen For

**al lado de** to the side of, beside
**sin embargo** however
**antes de que** before
**su primer lugar** his first place
**tal vez** maybe, perhaps
**por el campo** through the field
**por aquí** through here
**antes de que** before
**de una vez por todas** once and for all
**no vale ni la mitad** you are not worth even half
**lo que** what
**buenos días** good morning
**ya que** since
**se trataba de un juego** I thought you were kidding
**muy en serio** very seriously
**al menos** at least
**pasar de largo** to pass by at a distance
**así que** so
**¿por qué?** why?
**en vez de** instead of
**no tengo que hacer trampas** I don't have to cheat
**no tiene que hacer trampas** she doesn't have to cheat
**date prisa** IMP hurry up
**príncipe azul** prince charming

**a veces** sometimes
**primer lugar** first place
**de acuerdo a** according to

### Names
Gilbert Blythe, Anne Shirley, Prissy Andrews, Charlie Sloan, Sadler, Diana, Josie Pye, Geraldine, Avonlea, Spurgeon, Moody

🎬 Mr. Phillips rings a bell.
□ **coloquen** IMP place · *colocar* to place
□ **lápices** pencils · *lápiz* NM pencil
□ **pruebas** tests · *prueba* test
□ **recogeré** I will pick up · *recoger* to pick up, to gather, to collect
□ **sin embargo** however
□ **almorzar** to eat brunch, to eat lunch
□ **comunicarles** to communicate to them · *comunicar* to communicate
□ **resultado** result
□ **examen** NM exam
□ **matemáticas** NFPL mathematics
□ **calificaciones** grades · *calificación* grade
□ **pertenecen** they belong · *pertenecer* to belong
□ **tercero** third
□ **ha mejorado** she has improved · *mejorar* to improve
□ **considerablemente** considerably
□ **supervisión** supervision
□ **sonrió** he smiled · *sonreír* to smile
□ **felicitarte** to congratulate you · *felicitar* to congratulate
□ **vanagloriarse** to brag

🎬 Several boys are standing in the road as Anne and Diana approach.
□ **prepárenlos** IMP get ready · *preparar* to get ready, to prepare
□ **cruzar** to cross
□ **no temas** IMP don't be afraid · *temer* to fear
□ **bravucones** bullies · *bravucón* NM bully
□ **civilizadas** civilized · *civilizado* civilized · *civilizar* to civilize
□ **vereda** path, trail
□ **intenciones** intentions · *intención* intention
□ **sin aliento** out of breath
□ **bravucón** NM bully
□ **cobarde** NMF coward
□ **no atravesar** EXP no trespassing · *atravesar* to cross, to pass through
□ **se atrevan** SUBJ you dare · *atreverse* to dare
□ **propiedad** property
□ **vacas** cows · *vaca* cow
□ **leche** NF milk
□ **había puesto** I had placed · *poner* to place, to put

- □ **pie** *NM* foot
- □ **propósito** purpose
- □ **evitar** to avoid
- □ **se torturara** *SUBJ* she is tortured · *torturar* to torture
- □ **criaturas** creatures · *criatura* creature
- □ **agradables** pleasing, pleasant · *agradable* pleasing, pleasant
- □ **dolor** *NM* pain
- □ **me provoca** it causes me · *provocar* to cause
- □ **haberlas intimidado** to have frightened them · *intimidar* to frighten, to intimidate
- □ **te arrepentirás** you will be sorry · *arrepentirse* to be sorry
- □ **márchate** *IMP* get moving, leave, go away · *marcharse* to get moving, to leave, to go away
- □ **paciencia** patience
- □ **situación** situation

🎬 Inside the schoolhouse, Mr. Phillips stands next to Anne as Mr. Sadler scolds him.

- □ **educación** education
- □ **está usted impartiendo** you are imparting, you are giving · *impartir* to impart, to give
- □ **disciplina** discipline
- □ **escandalosa** scandalous · *escandaloso* scandalous
- □ **no vale** you are not worth · *valer* to be worth
- □ **mitad** *NF* half
- □ **cobra** you charge · *cobrar* to charge
- □ **perfectamente** perfectly
- □ **no habría obtenido** you wouldn't have obtained · *obtener* to obtain
- □ **consejeros** board members · *consejero* board member
- □ **sugiero** I suggest · *sugerir* to suggest
- □ **empleo** job
- □ **discipline** *IMP* discipline · *disciplinar* to discipline
- □ **alumnos** students · *alumno* student
- □ **no se metan** *SUBJ* they don't get into · *meterse* to get into

🎬 Mr. Sadler leaves. Mr. Phillips addresses Anne.

- □ **interés** *NM* interest
- □ **varones** men · *varón NM* man
- □ **resto** the rest, the remainder
- □ **pupitre** *NM* student desk
- □ **obedece** *IMP* obey · *obedecer* to obey

🎬 Mr. Phillips sits at his desk with a book open.

- □ **se inicia** it is beginning · *iniciarse* to begin
- □ **ortografía** spelling
- □ **crisantemo** chrysanthemum

- □ **pecosa** freckled, freckle-faced · *pecoso* freckled, freckle-faced
- □ **feúcha** very ugly · *feúcho* very ugly

🎬 Gilbert follows Anne and Diana as they walk down the road.

- □ **te felicito** I congratulate you · *felicitar* to congratulate
- □ **haber ganado** having won · *ganar* to win
- □ **no me ignoras** you don't ignore me · *ignorar* to ignore
- □ **triunfo** triumph
- □ **saludar** to greet
- □ **he saludado** I have greeted · *saludar* to greet
- □ **bien educada** well-mannered · *educado* polite, educated
- □ **¿por qué no desciendes?** why don't you come down? · *descender* to come down, to descend
- □ **torre** *NF* tower
- □ **felicitación** congratulations
- □ **informarle** to inform you · *informar* to inform
- □ **valor** *NM* courage, bravery
- □ **zorra** fox · *zorro* fox
- □ **gallinero** hen house, chicken coop
- □ **elije** he chooses · *elegir* to choose, to select
- □ **amistad** *NF* friendship
- □ **celosa** jealous · *celoso* jealous
- □ **inteligente** intelligent
- □ **limonada** lemonade
- □ **pretendía** he wanted · *pretender* to want, to expect
- □ **insultarme** to insult me · *insultar* to insult
- □ **hacer trampas** to cheat
- □ **se apellida** her last name is · *apellidarse* to have as a last name, to be surnamed

🎬 Anne and Diana run on the sand.

- □ **date prisa** *IMP* hurry up · *darse prisa* to hurry up

🎬 Anne and Diana walk along a bridge.

- □ **príncipe azul** prince charming · *príncipe NM* prince · *azul* blue
- □ **princesa** princess

🎬 Mr. Phillips walks through the classroom.

- □ **comparten** they share · *compartir* to share
- □ **resultados** results · *resultado* result
- □ **exámenes** exams · *examen NM* exam
- □ **noticias** *NFPL* news
- □ **marcharme** to leave, to move · *marcharse* to leave, to move
- □ **guiar** to guide
- □ **mentes** minds · *mente NF* mind
- □ **alturas** heights · *altura* height
- □ **estudio** study [EDUCATION]

□ **despedidas** farewells, good-byes · *despedida* farewell, good-bye
□ **natural** natural
□ **aliviar** to relieve
□ **sufrimiento** suffering
□ **experimentan** you experience · *experimentar* to experience
□ **noticia** news
□ **temprano** early
□ **dirigiremos** we will head out · *dirigirse* to head out
□ **granja** farm
□ **amablemente** kindly
□ **han organizado** they have organized · *organizar* to organize
□ **convivio** get-together
□ **con motivo de** in honor of · *motivo* reason, purpose

## 10 Dangerous Games          7:20

### Phrases to Listen For

**hasta luego** see you later (*LIT* until later)
**claro que sí** of course
**que tenga suerte** *SUBJ* good luck
**cuídese mucho** *IMP* take care
**a toda costa** no matter what
**a pesar de** in spite of
**por encima de** on top of
**lejos de** far from
**tenías que** you had to
**¿por qué?** why?
**¿por aquí?** through here?
**no importa** it doesn't matter
**no tengas miedo** *IMP* don't be afraid
**hace dos años** two years ago
**tal vez** maybe, perhaps
**tengo miedo** I am afraid
**hasta que** until
**tener miedo** to be afraid
**ten valor** *IMP* be brave
**así es como** that's how
**en primer lugar** in first place

### Names

Sadler, Phillips, Prissy, Charlottetown, Marysville, Gilbert Blythe, Josie, Green Gables, Charlie Sloan, Hammond, Marilla, Spurgeon, John Barry

🎬 Mr. Phillips kisses Prissy Andrews on the cheek.
□ **escríbanos** *IMP* write us · *escribir* to write
□ **comentó** he mentioned · *comentar* to mention, to comment
□ **había propuesto** he had made up his mind · *proponerse* to make up one's mind, to decide

□ **deshacerse** to get rid of
□ **a toda costa** at all costs, no matter what
□ **aparentemente** apparently
□ **directores** directors, board members, trustees · *director NM* director, board member, trustee
□ **obligaron** they forced · *obligar* to force, to obligate
□ **evitar** to avoid
□ **lástima** pity
□ **empleo** job, employment
□ **particular** private

🎬 Josie Pye walks along the rail fence and jumps into Gilbert's arms.
□ **consideran** they consider · *considerar* to consider
□ **triunfo** triumph
□ **por encima de** on top of
□ **valla** fence
□ **madera** wood
□ **caballete** ridge (of a roof)
□ **tejado** roof
□ **sabelotodo** know-it-all
□ **arriesgado** at risk, risky · *arriesgar* to risk
□ **¿te atreverías?** would you dare? · *atreverse* to dare
□ **capaz** capable
□ **cocina** kitchen
□ **perjudicarte** to harm you · *perjudicar* to harm, to hurt
□ **pereceré** I will perish · *perecer* to perish

🎬 Anne walks along the rooftop.
□ **perder el sentido** to faint
□ **pediré prestado** I will borrow · *pedir prestado* to borrow
□ **carruaje** *NM* carriage
□ **necesario** necessary
□ **estoy en perfectas condiciones** I'm perfectly fine, I'm in good shape · *condiciónes NFPL* condition, shape
□ **por ese rumbo** in that direction
□ **apoyarte en mí** lean on me · *apoyarse en* to lean on
□ **direcciones** directions · *dirección* direction
□ **totalmente** totally, completely
□ **opuestas** opposite · *opuesto* opposite

🎬 Diana holds Anne as they walk together.
□ **elegir** to choose
□ **te lastimaste el tobillo** you hurt your ankle · *lastimarse* to hurt oneself · *tobillo* ankle
□ **satisfacción** satisfaction
□ **cruzamos** we cross · *cruzar* to cross
□ **corto** short

☐ **bosque** *NM* forest
☐ **embrujado** bewitched · *embrujar* to bewitch
☐ **tinieblas** darkness · *tiniebla* darkness
☐ **fantasmas** ghosts · *fantasma* ghost
☐ **romántica** romantic · *romántico* romantic
☐ **¿viste algo?** did you see something? · *ver* to see
☐ **me tropecé con una piedra** I tripped on a rock · *tropezar* to trip · *piedra* rock
☐ **paseando** walking · *pasear* to go for a walk
☐ **vacas** cows · *vaca* cow
☐ **vestida** dressed · *vestido* dressed · *vestir* to dress
☐ **rondaba** she was making rounds · *rondar* to make rounds
☐ **aserradero** sawmill
☐ **difunto** dead
☐ **retorciendo** writhing · *retorcerse* to writhe
☐ **gimiendo** moaning, groaning · *gemir* to moan, to groan, to howl
☐ **la acompañe** *SUBJ* he accompanies her · *acompañar* to accompany
☐ **almuerzo** brunch, lunch
☐ **deliciosamente** deliciously
☐ **fantasma** ghost
☐ **asesinada** murdered · *asesinado* murdered · *asesinar* to murder
☐ **espalda** back
☐ **dedos** fingers · *dedo* finger
☐ **helados** freezing, frozen · *helado* freezing, frozen · *helar* to freeze
☐ **haya mentido** *SUBJ* she has lied · *mentir* to lie
☐ **cabaña** cabin

🎬 Anne falls into a pit.

☐ **no te angusties** *IMP* don't worry · *angustiarse* to worry
☐ **contrólate** *IMP* calm down, control yourself · *controlarse* to calm down, to control oneself
☐ **me lastimé el otro tobillo** I hurt my other ankle · *lastimarse* to hurt oneself · *tobillo* ankle
☐ **valor** *NM* courage, bravery
☐ **soportaré** I'll tolerate · *soportar* to tolerate
☐ **desmayarme** to faint · *desmayarse* to faint
☐ **actúa** it acts · *actuar* to act
☐ **valiente** courageous, valiant

🎬 Mr. Barry carries Anne. Marilla runs to meet them.

☐ **no temas** *IMP* don't be afraid · *temer* to fear
☐ **techo** roof
☐ **pozo** well
☐ **abandonado** abandoned · *abandonar* to abandon
☐ **iniciarías** you would begin · *iniciar* to begin
☐ **verano** summer
☐ **apenas** barely, hardly

☐ **positivo** positive
☐ **pude haberme roto** I could have broken · *romper* to break
☐ **cuello** neck
☐ **hubieran desafiado** *SUBJ* they would dare · *desafiar* to dare, to challenge
☐ **habría permanecido** I would have remained · *permanecer* to remain
☐ **firme** *ADJ* firm
☐ **olvidándome** forgetting · *olvidarse* to forget
☐ **desafío** dare, challenge
☐ **dura** hard · *duro* hard
☐ **sufrimiento** suffering
☐ **físico** physical
☐ **consideramos** we consider · *considerar* to consider
☐ **obtuvo** she obtained · *obtener* to obtain
☐ **finalizar** to finalize
☐ **curso** course
☐ **honor** *NM* honor
☐ **compartido** shared · *compartir* to share

## 11 Perfect Hostess · 13:16

**Phrases to Listen For**

**a diario** daily
**así que** so
**buenas tardes** good afternoon
**hacia acá** toward here
**tuvimos la suerte** we were lucky (*LIT* we had luck)
**para que** in order to
**lo que** what
**así que** so
**hasta que** until
**me puse a llorar** I started crying
**por favor** please
**hasta que** until
**¿qué te pasa?** what's the matter?
**de inmediato** immediately
**tal vez** maybe, perhaps
**en cuanto a** concerning
**de acuerdo con** in agreement with
**tengas la culpa** *SUBJ* you are to blame
**en contra mía** against me
**no tuviste la culpa** you weren't to blame, it wasn't your fault
**a pesar de** in spite of
**de verdad** really
**por supuesto** of course
**amiga íntima secreta** secret bosom friend, secret close friend
**íntima amiga** bosom friend, close friend
**en tanto** as long as
**de acuerdo** agreed

**hasta siempre** farewell
**a partir de** beginning

## Names

Matthew, Allan, Jerry, Lily Sands, Anne, Marilla,
Cuthbert, Lynde

🎬 Marilla walks downstairs.

- □ **has adornado** you have decorated ·
  *adornar* to decorate, to adorn, to beautify
- □ **flores** flowers · *flor* NF flower
- □ **jardín** NM garden
- □ **impresionar** to impress
- □ **juego de té de porcelana** porcelain tea set ·
  *té* NM tea · *porcelana* porcelain
- □ **a diario** daily
- □ **apropiado** appropriate
- □ **pastel** NM cake
- □ **fruta** fruit
- □ **mermelada** jelly, jam
- □ **cereza** cherry
- □ **botella** bottle
- □ **licor** NM liqueur
- □ **frambuesa** raspberry
- □ **despensa** pantry
- □ **cocina** kitchen
- □ **acompañarme** to accompany me · *acompañar*
  to accompany
- □ **reunión** meeting
- □ **sociedad** society
- □ **cena** dinner

🎬 Diana enters the house.

- □ **sepas** SUBJ you know · *saber* to know
- □ **atender** to attend to, to take care of
- □ **invitada** guest · *invitado* guest
- □ **anfitriona** hostess
- □ **ideal** ideal
- □ **guardar** to put away
- □ **sombrilla** parasol, umbrella for sun
- □ **hayas invitado** SUBJ you have invited ·
  *invitar* to invite
- □ **patatas** potatoes · *patata* potato
- □ **remolcador** tugboat
- □ **cosecha** crop
- □ **excelente** excellent
- □ **contratar** to hire, to contract
- □ **manzanas** apples · *manzana* apple
- □ **muchísimas** a great many · *muchísimo* a great
  many, a great deal of
- □ **ha estado cocinando** she has been cooking ·
  *cocinar* to cook
- □ **pasteles** cakes · *pastel* NM cake
- □ **tartas** tarts · *tarta* tart, cake
- □ **conservas** preserves
- □ **varios** several

- □ **invitados** guests · *invitado* guest
- □ **beber** to drink

🎬 Anne pulls a bottle out of the pantry.

- □ **favorito** favorite
- □ **admitir** to admit
- □ **vigilar** to watch over
- □ **estufa** stove
- □ **responsabilidades** responsibilities ·
  *responsabilidad* responsibility
- □ **asumir** to assume
- □ **estupendo** stupendous
- □ **superior** superior
- □ **ufanándose** bragging, boasting · *ufanarse*
  to brag, to boast
- □ **no me sorprende** it doesn't surprise me ·
  *sorprender* to surprise
- □ **en lo más mínimo** in the least · *mínimo*
  minimal, minute, tiny
- □ **estupenda** stupendous · *estupendo* stupendous
- □ **cocinera** cook · *cocinero* cook
- □ **cocinar** to cook
- □ **margen** NM margin, leeway
- □ **imprescindible** indispensable
- □ **apegarse** to stick to
- □ **recetas** recipes · *receta* recipe
- □ **agregarle** to add to it · *agregar* to add
- □ **harina** flour
- □ **gravemente** gravely
- □ **enferma** sick · *enfermo* sick
- □ **viruela** smallpox
- □ **habían abandonado** they had abandoned ·
  *abandonar* to abandon
- □ **te cuidaba** I took care of you, I cared for you ·
  *cuidar* to take care of, to care for
- □ **sanabas** you were healing · *sanar* to heal
- □ **enfermaba** I was sick · *enfermar* to become sick,
  to get sick
- □ **plantabas** you were planting · *plantar* to plant
- □ **rosal** NM rose bush
- □ **tumba** tomb
- □ **regabas** you were watering · *regar* to water
- □ **lágrimas** tears · *lágrima* tear
- □ **juventud** NF youth
- □ **había sacrificado** she had sacrificed ·
  *sacrificar* to sacrifice
- □ **patética** pathetic, moving · *patético* pathetic,
  moving
- □ **piedra** rock
- □ **ingrediente** NM ingredient
- □ **esencial** essential
- □ **furiosa** furious · *furioso* furious
- □ **reto** challenge
- □ **mareada** dizzy · *mareado* dizzy ·
  *marearse* to feel dizzy

□ **pedazo** piece
□ **vaso** glass
□ **enfermarte** to get sick · *enfermarse* to get sick, to become sick
□ **recuéstate** *IMP* lie down · *recostarse* to lie down
□ **¿dónde te duele?** where does it hurt (you)? · *doler* to hurt
□ **debió desatarse** it must have broken out (*LIT* it must have been unleashed) · *desatarse* to break out [EPIDEMIC], to be unleashed
□ **epidemia de viruela** smallpox epidemic
□ **no te angusties** *IMP* don't worry · *angustiarse* to worry
□ **no me apartaré de ti** I won't forsake you · *apartarse* to forsake, to leave, to move away
□ **te recuperes** *SUBJ* you recover, you recuperate · *recuperarse* to recover, to recuperate

🎬 Diana arrives at her house drunk.

□ **ebria** drunk · *ebrio* drunk
□ **pamplinas** *EXP* nonsense
□ **salida** exit
□ **destilería** distillery
□ **liga para abstinencia** abstinence league
□ **cruel** cruel
□ **despiadada** cruel, merciless, wicked · *despiadado* cruel, merciless, wicked
□ **amistad** *NF* friendship
□ **he comprobado** I have realized · *comprobar* to realize, to prove
□ **abandona** *IMP* get off, leave, vacate · *abandonar* to get off, to leave, to vacate
□ **propiedad** property

🎬 Marilla smells an empty bottle.

□ **bebió** she drank · *beber* to drink
□ **vasos** glasses · *vaso* glass
□ **embriagarse** to become inebriated, to become intoxicated
□ **habilidad** ability
□ **atraer** to attract
□ **guardé** I kept · *guardar* to keep, to save
□ **sótano** basement
□ **explicación** explanation

🎬 Marilla and Anne are in the Barry house.

□ **mentirosa** liar · *mentiroso* liar
□ **manipuladora** manipulator · *manipulador* manipulator
□ **ha puesto** she has placed, she has put · *poner* to place, to put
□ **venda** bandage
□ **advertí** I warned · *advertir* to warn
□ **que no prepararas** *SUBJ* that you not prepare, you not to prepare · *preparar* to prepare

□ **asqueroso** disgusting
□ **embriagar** to inebriate, to intoxicate
□ **beberse** to drink up
□ **lentamente** slowly
□ **tras** after
□ **insensata** senseless · *insensato* senseless
□ **ebrio** drunk, intoxicated
□ **paliza** beating, series of whacks
□ **culpable** guilty
□ **demonio** demon
□ **bebida** drink
□ **no hubieras insistido** *SUBJ* you hadn't insisted · *insistir* to insist
□ **famoso** famous
□ **perfectamente** perfectly
□ **reverendo** reverend
□ **visitarnos** to visit us · *visitar* to visit
□ **virtudes** virtues · *virtud* *NF* virtue
□ **cristianas** Christian · *cristiano ADJ* Christian
□ **mesa** table
□ **grave** grave, serious
□ **entrometerse** to intrude, to interfere, to meddle

🎬 Marilla walks along the porch of the Barry house and joins Anne and the minister's wife.

□ **obstinadas** obstinate · *obstinado* obstinate
□ **autosuficientes** self-sufficient · *autosuficiente* self-sufficient
□ **entrometidas** interfering · *entrometido* interfering · *entrometerse* to interfere
□ **expresarte** to express yourself · *expresarse* to express oneself
□ **no involucraras** *SUBJ* you didn't involve · *involucrar* to involve
□ **haberte expresado** to have expressed yourself · *expresarse* to express oneself

🎬 Marilla scrubs the floor.

□ **excusa** excuse
□ **han criticado** they have criticized · *criticar* to criticize
□ **vino familiar** homemade wine · *vino* wine · *familiar ADJ* family
□ **emergencia** emergency
□ **despedazado** broken · *despedazar* to break into pieces, to shatter
□ **curso** course, path
□ **estrellas** stars · *estrella* star
□ **semejante** similar
□ **tontería** foolishness

🎬 Diana waves. Anne joins her.

□ **no ha cedido** she hasn't yielded · *ceder* to yield, to cede
□ **inútil** useless

□ **exceptuando** excepting, with the exception of · *exceptuar* to except
□ **amiga íntima** bosom friend, close friend
□ **secreta** secret · *secreto* secret
□ **pecado** sin
□ **juro solemnemente** I solemnly swear · *jurar* to swear, to take an oath · *solemnemente* solemnly
□ **permaneceré** I will remain · *permanecer* to remain
□ **fiel** faithful
□ **luna** moon
□ **alumbrándonos** shining on us · *alumbrar* to shine light on
□ **no lo averigüe** SUBJ she doesn't find out · *averiguar* to find out
□ **sospechar** to suspect
□ **rizo** curl
□ **debo irme** I must go, I have to leave · *irse* to go away, to leave
□ **bondadosa** kind · *bondadoso* kind
□ **a partir de** beginning, starting
□ **extrañas** strangers · *extraño* stranger
□ **serte fiel** to be faithful to you

**12** SIDE B 1 **Future Foundation** 11:37

## Phrases to Listen For

**tenemos que** we have to
**buenos días** good morning
**en cuanto a** concerning
**sin embargo** however
**no tan de prisa** not in such a hurry
**por favor** please
**antes de** before
**algún día** someday
**ni siquiera** not even
**en cuanto** as soon as
**amigas íntimas** bosom friends, close friends
**lo que** what
**en tanto** as long as
**no importa** it doesn't matter
**tienes que** you have to
**tal vez** maybe, perhaps
**cielo santo** good heavens
**buenas noches** good night
**nada de eso** not at all
**después de** after
**¿por qué?** why?
**a punto de** about to
**se encargó de** she took care of, she took charge of
**¿en serio?** really?
**tener que** to have to
**de nada** you're welcome
**en vez de** instead of

## Names
Megan Follows, Colleen Dewhurst, Stacy, Phillips, Príncipe Eduardo, Ben Hur

In front of the schoolhouse, Anne stands alone while Diana talks to several girls. The new teacher approaches.
□ **salón** NM classroom
□ **asiento** seat
□ **injusto** unjust
□ **formulan** they formulate · *formular* to formulate
□ **enseñanzas** teachings · *enseñanza* teaching
□ **interés** NM interest
□ **abrumen** SUBJ you overwhelm · *abrumar* to overwhelm
□ **esfuerzo** effort
□ **nivel** NM level
□ **calidad** quality
□ **establecido** established · *establecer* to establish
□ **advertir** to warn
□ **inflexible** inflexible
□ **estricta** strict · *estricto* strict
□ **puntualidad** punctuality
□ **sin embargo** however
□ **convencida** convinced · *convencido* convinced · *convencer* to convince
□ **guía** NMF guide [PERSON]
□ **dispuestos** willing · *dispuesto* willing
□ **consejos** advice, counsel · *consejo* piece of advice
□ **formarse** to form for yourself · *formarse* to form for oneself
□ **ideales** ideals · *ideal* NM ideal
□ **cimiento** foundation
□ **futuras** future · *futuro* ADJ future
□ **brillante** brilliant
□ **empeñoso** diligent, hardworking
□ **isla** island

Miss Stacy leads the class through the field.
□ **magnífico** magnificent
□ **bosque** NM forest

Anne is reading during geometry class. Miss Stacy approaches Anne.
□ **charlar** to chat
□ **novelas** novels · *novela* novel
□ **geometría** geometry
□ **uso** use
□ **burla** mockery
□ **penitencia** penitence
□ **averiguaré** I will find out · *averiguar* to find out
□ **concluyó** concluded, finished · *concluir* to conclude, to finish
□ **carrera** race

□ **regresártelo** to return it to you · *regresar* to return
□ **lecciones** lessons · *lección* lesson
□ **alentar** to encourage
□ **literatura** literature
□ **alimentar** to feed, to give nourishment
□ **cualidad** quality, characteristic
□ **lección** lesson
□ **supe** I knew · *saber* to know
□ **sufrimiento** suffering
□ **humano** *ADJ* human
□ **padeces** you suffer, you undergo · *padecer* to suffer, to undergo
□ **solíamos** we used to · *soler* to used to (+ VERB)
□ **amigas íntimas** close friends, bosom friends · *amigo* friend · *íntimo* close, intimate
□ **prohibido** prohibited, forbidden · *prohibir* to prohibit, to forbid
□ **visita** visit
□ **he soportado** I have tolerated · *soportar* to tolerate
□ **incomprensión** incomprehension
□ **me rodea** it surrounds me · *rodear* to surround
□ **huérfana** orphan · *huérfano* orphan
□ **espantosa** horrible · *espantoso* horrible
□ **injusticia** injustice
□ **acusada** accused · *acusado* accused · *acusar* to accuse
□ **falsedad** falsehood

🎬 Anne and Miss Stacy exit the schoolhouse and walk along the road.

□ **en ocasiones** on occasion · *ocasión* occasion
□ **se niegan** they refuse · *negarse* to refuse
□ **produce** it produces · *producir* to produce
□ **temor** *NM* fear
□ **edifican** they build · *edificar* to build
□ **muros** walls · *muro* wall
□ **protegerse** to protect themselves · *protegerse* to protect oneself
□ **injusticias** injustices · *injusticia* injustice
□ **tribulaciones** tribulations · *tribulación* tribulation
□ **afirmarán** they will build, they will strengthen · *afirmar* to build, to strengthen
□ **carácter** *NM* character
□ **equivocaciones** mistakes · *equivocación* mistake
□ **inmenso** immense
□ **consuelo** consolation
□ **fresco** fresh
□ **esperanza** hope
□ **haya acusado** *SUBJ* he has accused · *acusar* to accuse

□ **te devolverá** it will return to you · *devolver* to return
□ **libertad** *NF* liberty

🎬 Anne finds a mouse in the pudding.

□ **pudín** *NM* pudding
□ **revisar** to check
□ **demora** delay
□ **ciruela** plum
□ **salsa** sauce
□ **qué ocurrencia** *EXP* what an idea
□ **anoche** last night
□ **cubrirla** to cover it · *cubrir* to cover
□ **estopilla** cheesecloth
□ **novicia** nun
□ **altar** *NM* altar
□ **confirmar** to confirm
□ **votos** vows · *voto* vow
□ **ratones** mice · *ratón* *NM* mouse
□ **merienda** supper

🎬 Miss Stacy enters Green Gables.

□ **visitar** to visit
□ **aproveché** I took advantage · *aprovechar* to take advantage, to make the most of
□ **afectando** affecting · *afectar* to affect
□ **todo lo contrario** completely to the contrary
□ **está realizando** she is doing, she is accomplishing · *realizar* to do, to accomplish
□ **magnífica** wonderful · *magnífico* wonderful
□ **labor** *NF* job
□ **créame** *IMP* believe me · *creer* to believe
□ **asistir** to attend
□ **adicionales** additional · *adicional* additional
□ **después de la salida** after hours, after school · *salida* leaving, exit
□ **admisión** admission
□ **empeñosa** hardworking, eager, diligent · *empeñoso* hardworking, eager, diligent
□ **energía** energy
□ **obstinada** obstinate · *obstinado* obstinate
□ **inestable** unstable
□ **merendar** to eat supper
□ **mesa** table
□ **tonterías** foolishness, nonsense · *tontería* foolish thing, silly thing
□ **cena** dinner
□ **deliciosa** delicious · *delicioso* delicious
□ **se encargó** she was responsible (for) · *encargarse* to be responsible (for)
□ **enseguida** right away, at once, immediately
□ **ratón** *NM* mouse
□ **se ahogó** it drowned · *ahogarse* to drown
□ **confesarle** to confess to you · *confesar* to confess

□ **fantasías** fantasies · *fantasía* fantasy
□ **me estoy esforzando** I'm making an effort ·
  *esforzarse* to make an effort
□ **superar** to overcome
□ **fallas** faults · *falla* fault
□ **perico** parrot
□ **cuantas** how many · *cuantos* how many
□ **romántica** romantic · *romántico* romantic

🎬 At the schoolhouse, Diana accepts a paper from
Miss Stacy.

□ **ingresar** to enroll
□ **concentrarme en** to concentrate on, to focus on ·
  *concentrarse* to concentrate, to focus
□ **has ingerido** you have ingested · *ingerir*
  to ingest
□ **veneno** venom, poison
□ **verbos** verbs · *verbo* verb
□ **latín** NM Latin
□ **repasaremos** we will review · *repasar* to review
□ **álgebra** algebra
□ **abran** IMP open · *abrir* to open
□ **página** page

**13** SIDE B **2** **Friendship Rekindled** 11:22

## Phrases to Listen For

**antes de que** before
**tiene algo que ver en ello** she has anything to do
  with it
**estar de acuerdo** to be in agreement, to agree
**¿por qué no?** why not?
**qué cosas dices** what things you say
**ni siquiera** not even
**lo que** what
**se acabó** it ran out
**hasta que** until
**buenos días** good morning
**buenas tardes** good afternoon
**según se dice** so I'm told (LIT according to what
  is said)
**pastel de humildad** humble pie
  (LIT humble cake)
**de una vez por todas** once and for all
**por supuesto** of course
**en serio** seriously
**pasar la noche** to spend the night
**tendrá que** it will have to
**buenas noches** good night
**cambie de opinión** SUBJ I change my mind
**de acuerdo** agreed
**mangas de campana** puffed sleeves
  (LIT bell sleeves)
**cambiar de opinión** to change one's mind

## Names

Matthew, Príncipe Eduardo, Lynde, Gil, Ruby Gillis,
Minnie May, Diana, Mary Joe, Hammond, Barry,
Carmody

🎬 Marilla, wearing a red ribbon, looks out the
window.

□ **alimentos** food · *alimento* food, nourishment
□ **anochezca** SUBJ it gets dark · *anochecer*
  to get dark
□ **que se divierta** SUBJ you have fun ·
  *divertirse* to have fun
□ **muchísimo** very much
□ **primer ministro** prime minister
□ **obligado** obligated, forced · *obligar* to obligate,
  to force
□ **enterarse de** to learn of
□ **males** evils, wrongs · *mal* NM evil, wrong
□ **isla** island
□ **pórtate bien** IMP behave yourself · *portarse*
  to behave oneself

🎬 Anne and Matthew sit by the fireplace.

□ **se irá a pique** it will go to the dogs, it will go
  down the tubes, it will go under · *irse a pique*
  to go to the dogs, to go down the tubes,
  to go under, to fail
□ **gobierno** government
□ **modifica** it changes · *modificar* to change,
  to modify
□ **votar** to vote
□ **conservador** conservative
□ **me alegro** I'm happy · *alegrarse* to be happy
□ **compañeros** classmates, companions ·
  *compañero* classmate, companion
□ **oposición** opposition
□ **corteja** he courts · *cortejar* to court
□ **religión** religion
□ **política** politics
□ **experta** expert · *experto* expert
□ **menesteres** tasks, jobs · *menester* NM task, job
□ **cortejó** did you court · *cortejar* to court
□ **rotos** broken · *roto* broken · *romper* to break
□ **situación** situation
□ **séquito** entourage
□ **pretendientes** suitors · *pretendiente* NM
  suitor
□ **cuerdo** sensible, in his right mind

🎬 Diana runs into Green Gables seeking help from
Anne and Matthew.

□ **ha enfermado** she has become sick · *enfermar*
  to become sick
□ **difteria** diphtheria, the croup
□ **localizar** to find, to locate

☐ **nos identificamos** we're such kindred spirits, we think alike · *identificarse* to be kindred spirits, to think alike, to be alike

☐ **respirar** to breathe

☐ **abrigo** overcoat

☐ **exactamente** exactly

☐ **ipecacuana** ipecac

☐ **expectorar** to spit up, to cough up

☐ **gemelos** twins · *gemelo* twin

☐ **padecían** they suffered · *padecer* to suffer

☐ **con regularidad** regularly

☐ **curaba** I treated · *curar* to treat, to cure

Anne and Diana enter the Barry house, where Minnie May is being cared for by Mary Joe.

☐ **pon** *IMP* put · *poner* to put, to place

☐ **leños** logs · *leño* log

☐ **estufa** stove

☐ **hierve** *IMP* boil · *hervir* to boil

☐ **herir** to hurt, to wound

☐ **sentimientos** feelings · *sentimiento* feeling

☐ **ropa limpia** clean clothes

☐ **calienta** *IMP* heat up · *calentar* to heat, to heat up

☐ **cataplasma de mostaza** mustard plaster · *cataplasma* plaster, poultice · *mostaza* mustard

Matthew and the doctor arrive at the Barry house.

☐ **administré** I administered · *administrar* to administer

☐ **frasco** bottle

☐ **arrojó las flemas** she coughed up the phlegm · *arrojar las flemas* to cough up phlegm

☐ **mejorar** to improve

☐ **emoción** emotion

☐ **expresan** they express · *expresar* to express

Anne enters the kitchen.

☐ **dormiste** you slept · *dormir* to sleep

☐ **derecho** right

☐ **según se dice** so I'm told, they say (*LIT* according to what is said) · *según* according to · *decir* to say, to tell

☐ **¿qué aspecto tiene?** what does he look like?

☐ **no se convirtió** he didn't become · *convertirse* to become

☐ **galanura** looks, physical attractiveness

☐ **orador** orator, speaker

☐ **estrechó mi mano** he shook my hand · *estrechar la mano* to shake hands

☐ **emocionante** exciting

☐ **excitación** excitement

☐ **suplicando** begging, pleading · *suplicar* to beg, to plead

☐ **obviamente** obviously

☐ **despertarte** to wake you up · *despertar* to wake

☐ **han invitado** they have invited · *invitar* to invite

☐ **cenar** to eat dinner, to dine

☐ **impresión** impression

☐ **pastel** *NM* cake

☐ **humildad** humility

☐ **ansiosa** anxious · *ansioso* anxious

Anne sits with Diana, Mrs. Barry, and Minnie May by the fireplace.

☐ **avergonzada** ashamed · *avergonzado* ashamed · *avergonzarse* to be ashamed

☐ **no albergo** I don't harbor · *albergar* to harbor

☐ **sentimientos negativos** ill feelings · *sentimiento* feeling · *negativo* negative

☐ **embriagar** to inebriate, to intoxicate

☐ **acompañarnos** to accompany us · *acompañar* to accompany

☐ **nos honraría** we'd be honored, it would honor us · *honrar* to honor

☐ **ocasión** occasion

☐ **invitada** guest · *invitado* guest

☐ **honor** *NM* honor

Matthew and Marilla sit by the fireplace. Anne stands behind them.

☐ **tranquilizarte** to calm down · *tranquilizarse* to calm down, to calm oneself

☐ **se opone** she is opposed · *oponerse* to oppose

☐ **fabricación** fabrication

☐ **mesa** table

☐ **me sorprende** it surprises me · *sorprender* to surprise

☐ **asistir** to attend

☐ **bailes** dances · *baile* *NM* dance

☐ **adultos** adults · *adulto* adult

☐ **presente** *NM* present

☐ **pronunciar un discurso** to give an address · *discurso* address, speech

☐ **sermón** *NM* sermon

☐ **invitaron** they invited · *invitar* to invite

☐ **declinar** to decline, to refuse

☐ **herida** wound

☐ **sanar** to heal

Anne walks slowly out of the room. Matthew and Marilla continue by the fireplace.

☐ **te habría enorgullecido** it would have filled you with pride, it would have made you proud · *enorgullecer* to fill with pride, to make proud

☐ **presencia de ánimo** presence of mind

☐ **atendió** she attended · *atender* to attend to, to help

☐ **acordamos** we agreed · *acordar* to agree, to make a deal, to come to an accord

- □ **yo la educaría** I would raise her · *educar* to raise, to educate
- □ **pretende** she wants, she desires · *pretender* to want, to desire
- □ **tranquilizar** to calm, to ease
- □ **conciencia** conscience
- □ **protestas** protests · *protesta* protest
- □ **suspiros** sighs · *suspiro* sigh
- □ **cambie** SUBJ I change · *cambiar* to change
- □ **luna** moon
- □ **llenarían** they would fill · *llenar* to fill
- □ **ridiculeces** nonsense · *ridiculez* NF ridiculousness, absurdity
- □ **aterrorizada** terrified · *aterrorizado* terrified · *aterrorizar* to terrify, to terrorize
- □ **criatura** child
- □ **amargada** bitter · *amargado* bitter · *amargarse* to become bitter
- □ **interferir** to interfere

🎬 Anne is washing dishes in the kitchen. Marilla enters.

- □ **intervención** intervention
- □ **me lavo** I wash · *lavarse* to wash oneself
- □ **te resfrías** you catch cold · *resfriarse* to catch a cold
- □ **enfermas** you become sick · *enfermar* to get sick, to become sick
- □ **pulmonía** pneumonia
- □ **anoche** last night
- □ **mangas** sleeves · *manga* sleeve
- □ **campana** bell
- □ **sorprendían** they were surprised · *sorprenderse* to be surprised
- □ **elegancia** elegance
- □ **innata** natural, inborn, innate
- □ **pamplinas** EXP nonsense
- □ **estás regando** you are pouring, you are dripping · *regar* to pour, to water
- □ **sucia** dirty · *sucio* dirty
- □ **grasosa** greasy · *grasoso* greasy
- □ **piso** floor
- □ **recién lavado** clean, recently washed · *recién* recently · *lavado* washed · *lavar* to wash
- □ **comentario** comment, commentary

## 14 SIDE B 3 Christmas Ball 14:17

### Phrases to Listen For

**¿qué tal?** what's up?, how are you?
**el día de hoy** today
**tal vez** maybe, perhaps
**por supuesto** of course
**ya que** since

**mangas de campana** puffed sleeves (LIT bell sleeves)
**cielo santo** good heavens
**¿por qué?** why?
**desde un principio** from the beginning
**tendrás que** you will have to
**de lado** sideways
**darle las gracias** to thank, to give thanks, to say thank you
**buenas noches** good night
**para siempre** forever
**me da mucho gusto verla** pleased to see you, nice to see you
**se ve** it looks, she looks
**hacia acá** over here
**de acuerdo** agreed, all right
**feliz navidad** Merry Christmas
**por amor de Dios** for the love of God
**por favor** please
**lo lamento** I'm sorry
**cambiaré de opinión** I will change my mind
**en cuanto a** concerning
**en cuanto** as soon as
**no me importa** it doesn't matter, I don't care
**por culpa mía** because of me (LIT for my fault)
**no te preocupes** IMP don't worry
**lo que** what
**no lo sé** I don't know
**desde hace cuarenta y siete años** for forty-seven years
**nos dio un gran susto** you gave us a great fright
**para que** so that, in order to
**temo que no** I'm afraid not
**a cambio de** in exchange for
**cambiara de opinión** SUBJ you change your mind
**buenos días** good day
**alma gemela** soul mate, kindred spirit (LIT twin soul)

### Names

Cuthbert, George, Martha, Alice Bell, Gilbert, Josie Pye, Diana, Josephine, Minnie May

🎬 Matthew looks at a dress in the shop window. He then enters the store.

- □ **rastrillos de jardín** garden rakes · *rastrillo* rake · *jardín* NM garden
- □ **no acostumbramos** we aren't accustomed to, we don't usually · *acostumbrarse* to be accustomed to, to usually (+ VERB)
- □ **almacenar** to store
- □ **diciembre** NM December
- □ **verificaré** I will check · *verificar* to check, to verify
- □ **almacén** NM warehouse
- □ **existencia** existence

- ☐ **semilla**  seed
- ☐ **heno**  hay
- ☐ **se vende**  it is sold · *vender*  to sell
- ☐ **primavera**  spring [SEASON]
- ☐ **qué ocurrencia**  EXP  what was I thinking
- ☐ **setenta**  seventy
- ☐ **centavos**  cents · *centavo*  cent
- ☐ **rastrillo**  rake
- ☐ **azúcar refinada**  white sugar · *azúcar* NMF sugar · *refinado*  refined
- ☐ **moscabado**  brown sugar
- ☐ **¿qué me aconseja?**  what do you suggest?, what do you advise? · *aconsejar*  to advise, to suggest
- ☐ **excelente**  excellent
- ☐ **kilos**  kilos, kilograms · *kilo*  kilo, kilogram
- ☐ **mangas**  sleeves · *manga*  sleeve
- ☐ **campana**  bell
- ☐ **principio**  beginning
- ☐ **me acompaña**  you accompany me, you come with me · *acompañar*  to accompany, to come with
- ☐ **aparador**  store window

🎬 Marilla is working in the kitchen. Anne enters, wearing a light blue dress.

- ☐ **tramaba**  he was plotting · *tramar*  to plot
- ☐ **absurdo**  absurd
- ☐ **cruzar las puertas**  to get through the doors · *cruzar*  to cross
- ☐ **satisfecha**  satisfied · *satisfecho*  satisfied · *satisfacer*  to satisfy
- ☐ **recorras**  SUBJ  you walk around · *recorrer*  to walk around
- ☐ **vanagloriándote**  boasting · *vanagloriarse*  to boast
- ☐ **pavo real**  peacock · *pavo*  turkey · *real* ADJ royal
- ☐ **esperpento**  an ugly thing, a ridiculous thing
- ☐ **virgen**  NF  virgin

🎬 Matthew is working in the barn when Anne enters in her new dress.

- ☐ **lucirlo**  to wear it · *lucir*  to wear
- ☐ **exquisito**  exquisite
- ☐ **impecable**  impeccable
- ☐ **elegancia**  elegance
- ☐ **se te ensucie**  SUBJ  it gets you dirty · *ensuciarse*  to get dirty

🎬 Anne and Diana walk downstairs.

- ☐ **diviértanse**  IMP  have fun · *divertirse*  to have fun
- ☐ **quedará grabada en mi mente**  I will never forget it, it will be etched on my mind · *grabarse*  to be remembered, to be etched · *mente* NF  mind

- ☐ **peinarme**  to wear my hair, to comb my hair
- ☐ **diecisiete**  seventeen
- ☐ **dieciocho**  eighteen
- ☐ **luce**  he looks · *lucir*  to look
- ☐ **no lo he observado**  I haven't noticed him · *observar*  to notice, to observe
- ☐ **pena**  shame
- ☐ **hayas tratado**  SUBJ  you have treated · *tratar*  to treat
- ☐ **haberte invitado**  to have invited you · *invitar*  to invite
- ☐ **bailar**  to dance
- ☐ **ha vuelto a mirar**  he's looked again · *volver*  to do again, to return · *mirar*  to look at
- ☐ **insistes**  you insist · *insistir*  to insist
- ☐ **nos vamos a divertir**  we're going to have fun · *divertirse*  to have fun
- ☐ **tobogán**  NM  toboggan
- ☐ **ponche**  NM  punch [DRINK]
- ☐ **deslumbrante**  dazzling, wonderful
- ☐ **no te ha pedido**  he hasn't asked you · *pedir*  to ask, to request
- ☐ **bailes**  SUBJ  you dance · *bailar*  to dance

🎬 Anne and Diana dance.

- ☐ **carnet de baile**  dance card
- ☐ **gesto**  gesture
- ☐ **romántico**  romantic
- ☐ **admirador secreto**  secret admirer · *admirador*  admirer · *secreto*  secret
- ☐ **regañarnos**  to scold us · *regañar*  to scold
- ☐ **habitación de huéspedes**  guest room · *habitación*  room · *huésped* NMF  guest
- ☐ **emocionante**  exciting
- ☐ **quién se acuesta**  who lies down · *acostarse*  to lie down

🎬 Anne and Diana run into the guest room and jump into the bed, where they encounter Aunt Josephine.

- ☐ **atropello**  outrage
- ☐ **vendrías**  you would come · *venir*  to come
- ☐ **visitarnos**  to visit us · *visitar*  to visit
- ☐ **maleducada**  ill-mannered · *maleducado*  ill-mannered
- ☐ **enterar**  to learn, to find out about
- ☐ **atentado**  attack
- ☐ **culpable**  NMF  guilty person
- ☐ **sugerí**  I suggested · *sugerir*  to suggest
- ☐ **carrera**  race
- ☐ **motivo**  reason
- ☐ **piano**  piano
- ☐ **pagarte**  to pay for you · *pagar*  to pay
- ☐ **urbanidad**  good manners, civility
- ☐ **anciana**  old woman · *anciano*  old man

🎬 Aunt Josephine pulls the covers over her head.

☐ **espantoso** frightening
☐ **pagármelas** to pay for them for me ·
  *pagar* to pay
☐ **furiosa** furious · *furioso* furious
☐ **en cuanto amanezca** SUBJ as soon as it dawns,
  first thing in the morning · *amanecer* to dawn
☐ **divertido** fun · *divertirse* to have fun
☐ **¿te fijaste...?** did you notice ...? ·
  *fijarse* to notice, to pay attention to
☐ **cara** face
☐ **lecciones** lessons · *lección* lesson
☐ **experiencia** experience
☐ **disculpas** apologies · *disculpa* apology

🎬 Aunt Josephine is writing at a table. Anne enters
  the room.

☐ **rematar** to finish off
☐ **víctima** victim
☐ **confesar** to confess
☐ **confesiones** confessions · *confesión* confession
☐ **asesinas** murderers · *asesina* murderer
☐ **inocentes** innocent · *inocente* innocent
☐ **responsable** responsible
☐ **saltar** to jump
☐ **educada** polite, well-mannered · *educado* polite,
  well-mannered · *educar* to bring up, to raise
☐ **huérfana** orphan · *huérfano* orphan
☐ **desconoce la urbanidad** she is unfamiliar with
  polite behavior · *desconocer* to be unfamiliar ·
  *urbanidad* courtesy
☐ **considero** I consider, I think · *considerar*
  to consider, to think
☐ **mademoiselle** mademoiselle [FRENCH]
☐ **privada** deprived · *privado* deprived ·
  *privar* to deprive
☐ **pocas** few · *pocos* few
☐ **conciliar** to get (sleep)
☐ **chiquillas** girls, young women · *chiquillo* boy,
  young man [TERM OF ENDEARMENT]
☐ **frenéticas** frenetic, wild · *frenético* frenetic, wild
☐ **salvajes** savages · *salvaje* NMF savage
☐ **saltan** they jump · *saltar* to jump
☐ **realmente** really
☐ **pavorosa** frightening · *pavoroso* frightening
☐ **ápice** NM bit, small amount
☐ **carece de** you lack · *carecer de* to lack
☐ **edad** age
☐ **amenaza** threat
☐ **susto** fright
☐ **reservada** reserved · *reservado* reserved ·
  *reservar* to reserve
☐ **cuento** I tell · *contar* to tell
☐ **patea** she kicks · *patear* to kick
☐ **profundamente** profoundly, deeply

☐ **amargados** bitter · *amargado* bitter ·
  *amargarse* to become bitter
☐ **obligada** forced, obligated · *obligado* forced,
  obligated · *obligar* to force, to obligate
☐ **había arruinado** I had ruined · *arruinar* to ruin
☐ **famosa** famous · *famoso* famous
☐ **pianista** NMF pianist
☐ **explicación** explanation
☐ **válida** valid · *válido* valid
☐ **carta** letter
☐ **expreso** I express · *expresar* to express
☐ **descontento** discontent, dissatisfaction

🎬 Aunt Josephine places her pen on the table and
  tears up the letter she was writing.

☐ **se ha desvanecido** it has vanished, it has
  disappeared · *desvanecerse* to vanish,
  to disappear
☐ **sugerir** to suggest
☐ **causa** it causes · *causar* to cause
☐ **pavor** NM horror, fear
☐ **visitarme** to visit me · *visitar* to visit
☐ **visitarla** to visit you · *visitar* to visit
☐ **me diviertes** you amuse me · *divertir* to amuse,
  to entertain
☐ **divertirme** to amuse me · *divertir* to amuse,
  to entertain
☐ **agradable** pleasing, pleasant
☐ **gritona** loud-mouthed, screaming, yelling ·
  *gritón* loud-mouthed, screaming, yelling
☐ **gruñona** grump, grouch · *gruñón* NM grump,
  grouch
☐ **ofenderla** to offend you · *ofender* to offend
☐ **desmentirme** to contradict me ·
  *desmentir* to contradict
☐ **concertista** NMF concert musician
☐ **rápidamente** rapidly
☐ **alma gemela** soul mate, kindred spirit ·
  *alma* soul · *gemelo* twin

## 15 │ SIDE B 4 │ Trip to Town    9:52

### Phrases to Listen For

  **almas gemelas** soul mates, kindred spirits
  **no te preocupes** IMP don't worry
  **ni siquiera** not even
  **así que** so
  **para que** so that, in order to
  **hasta que** until
  **lo que** what
  **parece que** it looks like
  **¿qué opinas?** what do you think?
  **después de** after
  **hace mucho tiempo** a long time ago
  **tal vez** maybe, perhaps

**desde que** since
**desde cuando** since when
**te deseo suerte** I wish you luck

## Names

Jo, John, Nancy, Stacy, Gilbert, Halifax, Avonlea, Madame Selitsky, Bell, Gil, Moody

🎬 Anne and Diana are in a rowboat. Diana reads.

□ **adjunto a la presente** enclosed with this letter · *adjunto* enclosed
□ **brazaletes** bracelets · *brazalete NM* bracelet
□ **plata** silver
□ **visitarme** to visit me · *visitar* to visit
□ **hospedarlas** to put you up · *hospedar* to put up, to host
□ **habitación para huéspedes** guest room · *habitación* room · *huésped NMF* guest
□ **más amplia** largest · *amplio* large, roomy
□ **saludo** greeting
□ **cariñoso** caring, affectionate
□ **almas gemelas** soul mates, kindred spirits · *alma* soul · *gemelo* twin
□ **escasas** scarce · *escaso* scarce

🎬 In the schoolhouse, Anne looks back at Gil.

□ **se realiza** it is completed · *realizarse* to be completed, to be accomplished

🎬 Anne and Diana ride in a carriage driven by Mr. Barry.

□ **mitiga** it lessens, it mitigates · *mitigar* to lessen, to mitigate
□ **ansiedad** anxiety

🎬 Diana, Anne, and Mr. Barry enter Aunt Josephine's house.

□ **ambas** both · *ambos* both
□ **lucen** you look · *lucir* to look
□ **equipaje NM** luggage
□ **límpiense IMP** clean · *limpiarse* to clean, to wipe
□ **tía** aunt · *tío* uncle
□ **agotadas** exhausted · *agotado* exhausted · *agotarse* to become exhausted
□ **baño** bath
□ **atenderá** she will assist · *atender* to assist
□ **nervios NMPL** nerves
□ **traicionaran SUBJ** they betray · *traicionar* to betray
□ **disfrutaremos** we will enjoy · *disfrutar* to enjoy
□ **deliciosa** delicious · *delicioso* delicious
□ **cena** dinner
□ **al concluir** at the conclusion of, on concluding · *concluir* to conclude
□ **sorpresa** surprise
□ **salón NM** room, classroom

□ **palmas** palms · *palma* palm
□ **visitarla** to visit her · *visitar* to visit
□ **rica** rich · *rico* rich
□ **carece de** she lacks · *carecer de* to lack
□ **consuelo** consolation
□ **belleza** beauty
□ **apoyo** support

🎬 In the guest room at Aunt Josephine's house, Anne and Diana talk.

□ **nerviosa** nervous · *nervioso* nervous
□ **desaparece** it disappears · *desaparecer* to disappear
□ **vacío** emptiness
□ **ahoga** it drowns, it suffocates · *ahogar* to drown, to suffocate
□ **confianza** confidence, trust, faith
□ **aprobarás** you will pass · *aprobar* to pass [EDUCATION]
□ **reprobar** to fail [EDUCATION]
□ **mitad NF** half
□ **desgracia** disgrace
□ **te superara SUBJ** he beat you · *superar* to beat, to surpass
□ **me conformaría con** I would settle for, I would be content with · *conformarse* to settle, to be content
□ **derrotar** to defeat
□ **necesario** necessary

🎬 A man in a suit places a paper on the desk.

□ **exámenes** exams · *examen NM* exam
□ **repartidos** distributed · *repartido* distributed · *repartir* to distribute, to hand out
□ **descalificará** it will disqualify · *descalificar* to disqualify

🎬 A bell rings. Anne stands at the top of the stairs with Miss Stacy.

□ **pálida** pale · *pálido* pale
□ **lógico** logical
□ **apruebe SUBJ** I pass · *aprobar* to pass [EDUCATION]
□ **fracase SUBJ** I fail · *fracasar* to fail
□ **extrañarla** to miss you · *extrañar* to miss
□ **terriblemente** terribly
□ **digna** worthy · *digno* worthy
□ **éxito** success
□ **abandonar** to abandon
□ **espíritu NM** spirit
□ **cimentar** to lay a foundation
□ **futuro** future
□ **despedirse** to say good-bye
□ **fresco** fresh
□ **equivocaciones** mistakes · *equivocación* mistake

🎬 Anne and Diana sit at an elegant table with Aunt Josephine.

☐ **nací** I was born · *nacer* to be born
☐ **sofisticada** sophisticated · *sofisticado* sophisticated
☐ **¿qué opinas?** what do you think? · *opinar* to think, to give an opinion
☐ **nunca había reparado** I had never thought seriously · *reparar* to think seriously, to consider
☐ **tema** NM theme, subject
☐ **conclusión** conclusion
☐ **me agradaría** I would like (LIT it would please me) · *agradar* to please
☐ **sonido** sound
☐ **produce** it produces, it makes · *producir* to produce, to make
☐ **viento** wind
☐ **abetos** firs · *abeto* fir
☐ **tintineo** ringing
☐ **cristal** NM crystal
☐ **reanudar** to resume
☐ **normal** normal

🎬 Anne, Diana, and Aunt Josephine walk inside Aunt Josephine's house.

☐ **rostro** face
☐ **alabastro** alabaster
☐ **¿y no te fijaste...?** and didn't you notice ...?
☐ **pavoneándose** showing off · *pavonearse* to show off
☐ **nariz** NF nose
☐ **no me atrevería** I wouldn't dare · *atreverse* to dare
☐ **piadosa** pious · *piadoso* pious
☐ **comparando** comparing · *comparar* to compare
☐ **vanidad** vanity
☐ **me felicitó** she congratulated me · *felicitar* to congratulate
☐ **mundano** worldly
☐ **contratarte** to hire you · *contratar* to hire, to contract
☐ **bufón** NM clown
☐ **particular** private
☐ **no pretendía** I wasn't trying · *pretender* to try, to want
☐ **graciosa** funny · *gracioso* funny
☐ **hayan disfrutado** SUBJ they have enjoyed · *disfrutar* to enjoy
☐ **celebración** celebration
☐ **enormemente** enormously
☐ **inolvidable** unforgettable
☐ **bienvenidas** welcome · *bienvenido* ADJ welcome
☐ **no me había divertido tanto** I hadn't had so much fun · *divertirse* to have fun

☐ **solterona** spinster · *solterón* confirmed bachelor
☐ **me enteré** I found out, I learned · *enterarse* to find out, to learn
☐ **adoptada** adopted · *adoptado* adopted · *adoptar* to adopt
☐ **huérfana** orphan · *huérfano* orphan

🎬 Mr. Barry, Diana, and Anne encounter Gil along the road.

☐ **de regreso** on the way back
☐ **estación** station

## 16 SIDE B 5   Gilbert to the Rescue    16:24

### Phrases to Listen For

**no se ve** it doesn't look
**¿en serio?** really?
**de acuerdo** agreed
**tengo miedo** I'm afraid
**antes de que** before
**en tanto** as long as
**tienes razón** you are right
**hay que** it's necessary
**por favor** please
**dense prisa** IMP hurry up
**tenía que** I had to
**aun cuando** even when
**al pensar que** thinking that
**aguarda un minuto** IMP wait a minute
**acabo de** I just
**primer lugar** first place
**¿no te parece?** don't you think?
**lo siento** I'm sorry
**hace años** years ago
**en forma atroz** atrociously
**¿por qué?** why?
**hace más de un año** over a year ago
**lo que** what
**tuve que** I had to
**por supuesto** of course
**tener que** to have to
**claro que** of course
**estamos orgullosos de ti** we are proud of you
**buenas tardes** good afternoon
**lo sé** I know
**a pesar de** in spite of
**tal vez** maybe, perhaps
**después de** after
**qué diablilla** you little devil
**¿qué tal?** what's up?
**tienes razón** you are right
**tan de prisa** in such a hurry
**no te preocupes** IMP don't worry
**para que** so that

**tendrás que**  you'll have to
**ya tienes edad suficiente**  you are old enough already
**he tenido edad**  I have been old enough
**de toda confianza**  trustworthy
**desde un principio**  from the beginning
**por favor**  please
**tienes toda la razón**  you are completely right
**no importa**  it doesn't matter
**me parece que**  it seems to me

## Names

Ruby, Elaine, Tennyson, Diana, Jane Andrews, Lynde, Camelot, Shalott, Anne Shirley, Avonlea, John Barry, Laura Spencer, White Sands, Charlottetown, Alice Lawson, Stacy

Anne and three girls stand beside a boat.

- □ **acostarme** to lie down · *acostarse* to lie down
- □ **pelirroja** redhead · *pelirrojo* redhead
- □ **interpretar** to play the role
- □ **se pondría furioso** he would be furious · *ponerse* to become · *furioso* furious
- □ **piel** *NF* skin
- □ **oscuro** dark
- □ **rojo** red
- □ **castaño** brown
- □ **rubio** blond
- □ **auténtico** authentic

Anne lies down in the boat.

- □ **cubrirme** to cover me · *cubrir* to cover
- □ **carpeta** cover
- □ **piano** piano
- □ **actuación** acting
- □ **pecado** sin
- □ **callarte** to be quiet · *callarse* to be quiet
- □ **estás arruinando** you are ruining · *arruinar* to ruin
- □ **efecto** effect
- □ **naciera** *SUBJ* she was born · *nacer* to be born
- □ **encárgate** *IMP* take charge, take care · *encargarse* to take charge, to take care
- □ **flores** flowers · *flor* *NF* flower
- □ **sonreír** to smile
- □ **yacía** she was lying down · *yacer* to lie [POSITION]
- □ **esbozando una sonrisa** giving a trace of a smile, giving a hint of a smile · *esbozar* to sketch · *sonrisa* smile

The girls kiss Anne's forehead and launch the boat.

- □ **tumba** tomb
- □ **acuática** aquatic · *acuático* aquatic
- □ **tejiendo** weaving · *tejer* to weave
- □ **prenda** garment, item of clothing

- □ **mágica** magic · *mágico* *ADJ* magic
- □ **voz** *NF* voice
- □ **rumor** *NM* murmur
- □ **maldición** curse
- □ **arroyo** creek
- □ **obligó** it forced · *obligar* to force, to obligate
- □ **apartarse** to separate herself, to move away, to distance herself · *apartarse* to separate oneself, to move away, to distance oneself
- □ **bote** *NM* boat
- □ **rumbo** direction
- □ **entonar** to sing
- □ **canción** song
- □ **la Dama de Shalott** the Lady of Shalott

Anne takes hold of a pillar of the bridge as the waterlogged boat continues downstream.

- □ **divertido** fun · *divertirse* to have fun
- □ **se ahoga** she's drowning · *ahogarse* to drown
- □ **se está ahogando** she is drowning · *ahogarse* to drown

Gilbert encounters Anne as he rows a boat.

- □ **qué rayos** *EXP* what the heck · *rayo* ray, bolt of lightning
- □ **estaba pescando** I was fishing · *pescar* to fish
- □ **truchas** trout · *trucha* trout
- □ **se ha ahogado** she has drowned · *ahogarse* to drown
- □ **dense prisa** *IMP* hurry up · *darse prisa* to hurry up
- □ **hundir** to sink
- □ **pilotes** pilings · *pilote* *NM* piling
- □ **hundirme** to sink · *hundirse* to sink
- □ **orilla** edge, shore
- □ **aguardaba** I was waiting · *aguardar* to wait
- □ **paciencia** patience
- □ **necesario** necessary
- □ **si me disculpa** if you will excuse me · *disculpar* to excuse, to forgive
- □ **sufren** they suffer · *sufrir* to suffer
- □ **aguarda** *IMP* wait · *aguardar* to wait
- □ **oficina de correos** post office · *oficina* office · *correo* mail
- □ **resultados** results · *resultado* result
- □ **triunfo** triumph, victory
- □ **empatamos** we tied · *empatar* to tie
- □ **aprobamos** we passed · *aprobar* to pass [EDUCATION]
- □ **íntegro** whole
- □ **doscientos** two hundred
- □ **compartirlo** to share it · *compartir* to share
- □ **superarte** to surpass you, to beat you · *superar* to surpass, to beat
- □ **niñería** childishness

- **el que me rescataras** *SUBJ* the fact that you rescued me · *rescatar* to rescue
- **difícilmente** not easily
- **borra** it erases · *borrar* to erase
- **equivocaciones** mistakes · *equivocación* mistake
- **pasadas** past · *pasado ADJ* past
- **haberme burlado** having made fun of · *burlarse* to make fun of
- **heriste** you hurt · *herir* to hurt, to wound
- **sentimientos** feelings · *sentimiento* feeling
- **en forma atroz** atrociously · *forma* form · *atroz* atrocious
- **me diste la espalda** you turned your back on me · *dar la espalda* to turn one's back on
- **humillación** humiliation
- **deliberada** deliberate · *deliberado* deliberate
- **perfectamente** perfectly
- **inteligente** intelligent
- **sabrías** you would know · *saber* to know
- **respuesta** answer, response
- **me ahogué** I drowned · *ahogarse* to drown

🎬 Anne runs into Diana's arms. Shortly, several others join them.

- **culpables** guilty · *culpable* guilty
- **histérica** hysterical · *histérico* hysterical
- **puente** *NM* bridge
- **qué romántico** how romantic
- **mencionar** to mention
- **romance** *NM* romance
- **normal** normal
- **aplicar** to apply
- **culpable** *NMF* guilty person
- **dueño** owner
- **remedio** remedy
- **sensata** sensible · *sensato* sensible
- **posibilidades** possibilities · *posibilidad* possibility
- **se ampliarán** they will broaden · *ampliarse* to broaden
- **desgracia** disgrace, misfortune
- **empaté** I tied · *empatar* to tie
- **jamás niego** I never deny · *negar* to deny
- **has honrado** you have honored · *honrar* to honor
- **orgullosos** proud · *orgulloso* proud

🎬 Gilbert is fishing near a covered bridge. Marilla approaches him in a horse-drawn carriage.

- **te has convertido** you have become · *convertirse* to become
- **orgullosa** proud · *orgulloso* proud
- **reto** challenge
- **superarla** to surpass her · *superar* to surpass

- **talento** talent
- **convertirse** to become

🎬 Anne converses with Alice Lawson in Lawson's Mercantile.

- **recitar** to recite
- **declamar** to recite, to perform
- **salteador** highwayman
- **patético** pathetic, moving
- **pieza** piece
- **cómica** comic · *cómico ADJ* comic
- **nerviosa** nervous · *nervioso* nervous
- **en público** in public
- **varias** several · *varios* several
- **tela** cloth
- **organdí** *NM* organdy
- **lucirá** it will look · *lucir* to look
- **exquisita** exquisite · *exquisito* exquisite
- **eléctricas** electric · *eléctrico* electric
- **hotel** *NM* hotel
- **convencerme** to convince me · *convencer* to convince
- **participara** *SUBJ* I participate · *participar* to participate
- **violín** *NM* violin
- **no he practicado** I haven't practiced · *practicar* to practice
- **hospital** *NM* hospital
- **causa** cause
- **noble** *ADJ* noble
- **dispuesta** willing · *dispuesto* willing
- **sufrir** to suffer
- **semejante** similar
- **aficionados** amateurs · *aficionado* amateur
- **se arrepientan** *SUBJ* they'll be sorry, they'll change their minds · *arrepentirse* to be sorry, to change one's mind
- **habernos invitado** having invited us · *invitar* to invite
- **función** event
- **obtener** to obtain
- **daño** damage
- **comunidad** community, fellowship
- **se desprende** he parts with · *desprenderse* to part with
- **facilidad** facility, ease of doing something
- **informo** I inform, I tell · *informar* to inform, to tell
- **está de moda** it is in fashion · *estar de moda* to be in fashion
- **diablilla** *DIM* little devil · *diablo* devil
- **abusar** to abuse
- **generosidad** generosity
- **exquisito** exquisite
- **concierto** concert

🎬 Anne drops a package as she walks. Gilbert approaches her in a horse and buggy.

☐ **prometiste** you promised · *prometer* to promise
☐ **complicado** complicated · *complicar* to complicate, to make complicated
☐ **gentil** kind, nice
☐ **me estoy especializando** I'm specializing · *especializar* to specialize
☐ **librarte** saving you · *librar* to save
☐ **situaciones** situations · *situación* situation
☐ **descortés** discourteous
☐ **marcharme** leaving · *marcharse* to leave
☐ **emocionada** excited · *emocionado* excited · *emocionarse* to get excited, to become emotional
☐ **calificación** grade
☐ **resentimientos** grudges · *resentimiento* grudge
☐ **valiente** courageous
☐ **conservando** keeping · *conservar* to keep, to conserve
☐ **al ingresar** on enrolling · *ingresar* to enroll
☐ **título** title, degree
☐ **sugerencia** suggestion
☐ **magnífica** magnificent, wonderful · *magnífico* magnificent, wonderful
☐ **actriz** NF actress · *actor* NM actor
☐ **declamarás** you will perform, you will recite · *declamar* to perform, to recite
☐ **recital** NM recital
☐ **confesión** confession
☐ **almacén** NM warehouse
☐ **aplaudiré hasta rabiar** I will applaud like crazy · *aplaudir hasta rabiar* to applaud like crazy
☐ **repitas** SUBJ you repeat · *repetir* to repeat
☐ **recitación** recitation
☐ **pedírmelo** to ask it of me · *pedir* to ask for, to request
☐ **honor** NM honor
☐ **ya tienes edad suficiente** you are old enough · *tener* to have · *edad* age
☐ **decisiones** decisions · *decisión* decision
☐ **invitación** invitation
☐ **mostrarle** to show her · *mostrar* to show

🎬 Marilla looks out the window.

☐ **cause** SUBJ it causes · *causar* to cause
☐ **alboroto** fuss, uproar
☐ **visitar** to visit
☐ **le fascinó** it fascinated her · *fascinar* to fascinate
☐ **elegiste** you chose · *elegir* to choose
☐ **informar** to inform
☐ **de toda confianza** trustworthy
☐ **opina** she thinks · *opinar* to think, to give an opinion
☐ **principio** beginning

☐ **te pedí que no te inmiscuyeras** SUBJ I asked you not to interfere, I asked that you not interfere · *pedir* to ask, to request · *inmiscuirse* to interfere
☐ **educación** education, upbringing

🎬 Marilla enters Anne's room.

☐ **control** NM control
☐ **te molestaras** SUBJ you would be bothered, it would bother you · *molestarse* to be bothered
☐ **distinguida** distinguished · *distinguido* distinguished · *distinguirse* to be distinguished
☐ **ya no perteneces** you no longer belong · *pertenecer* to belong
☐ **tristeza** sadness
☐ **vas a aventurarte** you are going to venture out · *aventurarse* to venture out
☐ **forjarte** to forge for yourself · *forjarse* to forge for oneself
☐ **futuro** future
☐ **ataduras** hindrances · *atadura* hindrance
☐ **cambie** SUBJ I change · *cambiar* to change

🎬 With trees in the background, Anne speaks. Shortly, Diana opens a letter and reads.

☐ **entregues** SUBJ you deliver · *entregar* to deliver, to give
☐ **atentamente** sincerely
☐ **absurda** absurd · *absurdo* absurd
☐ **desafió** he challenged · *desafiar* to challenge
☐ **explicación** explanation

## 17 | SIDE B 6 | Recital Jitters          9:26

### Phrases to Listen For

**buena suerte** good luck
**de todas formas** anyway
**cambiar de opinión** to change your mind
**en cuanto** as soon as
**en la medianoche** at midnight
**de verdad** really
**acaba de** she just
**muchas gracias** thank you
**otra vez** again
**de nuevo** again
**dentro de** within
**en medio del** in the middle of the
**tengo que** I have to
**por supuesto** of course
**claro que sí** of course
**es preciso** it's important, it is urgent
**date prisa** IMP hurry up
**tenemos dieciséis años** we are sixteen years old
**a pesar de** in spite of
**me conformo con** I'm satisfied with, I'm content with

## Names

Matthew, Jane, Diana, Queens, Hesperus, Norman, Amelia Evans, Charlottetown

🎬 Anne looks in the mirror.

- □ **te arruines** SUBJ you ruin · *arruinarse* to be ruined
- □ **armatoste** NM monstrosity, large object
- □ **delgado** thin, slim
- □ **época** season
- □ **convencerme** to convince me · *convencer* to convince

🎬 Matthew fastens a pearl necklace around Anne's neck.

- □ **inútil** useless
- □ **razonar** to reason
- □ **perlas** pearls · *perla* pearl
- □ **lucen** they look · *lucir* to look
- □ **totalmente** totally
- □ **que no se te atore** SUBJ don't let your dress get caught · *atorarse* to become caught
- □ **rueda** wheel
- □ **público** public, audience

🎬 Elegantly dressed men and women descend the stairs.

- □ **precioso** precious
- □ **contestación** answer
- □ **recado** message
- □ **concierto** concert
- □ **entrometido** meddling · *entrometerse* to meddle
- □ **derecho** right
- □ **personalmente** personally
- □ **considerándome** considering me · *considerar* to consider
- □ **atentamente** sincerely
- □ **nadie me tachará de** nobody will accuse me of · *tachar* to accuse, to judge
- □ **cobarde** NMF coward
- □ **disponible** available
- □ **avergonzada** ashamed · *avergonzado* ashamed · *avergonzarse* to be ashamed
- □ **escenario** stage
- □ **despiadados** unmerciful · *despiadado* unmerciful
- □ **fracasar** to fail
- □ **jamás has fracasado** you have never failed · *jamás* never · *fracasar* to fail
- □ **¡ánimo!** EXP come on!, get up!, get going!

🎬 Several elegantly dressed people are listening to a presentation. Some are standing, some are seated.

- □ **naufragio** shipwreck
- □ **gritó** he shouted · *gritar* to shout

- □ **vigía** NMF lookout [PERSON]
- □ **había descendido** it had descended · *descender* to descend
- □ **enorme** enormous
- □ **manto** cover, blanket
- □ **luna** moon
- □ **doncella** lady [POETIC]
- □ **aferrada** clutching, holding on tightly · *aferrado* clutching, holding on tightly · *aferrar* to seize
- □ **grueso** thick
- □ **madero** plank
- □ **sal** NF salt
- □ **congelada** frozen · *congelado* frozen · *congelar* to freeze
- □ **pecho** chest
- □ **lágrimas** tears · *lágrima* tear
- □ **saladas** salty · *salado* salty · *salar* to salt, to add salt to
- □ **hierba acuática** seaweed
- □ **olas** waves · *ola* wave
- □ **invierno** winter
- □ **proteja** SUBJ he protects · *proteger* to protect
- □ **semejante** similar
- □ **arrecife** NM reef
- □ **punta** point

🎬 The audience applauds at the conclusion of an actress's presentation.

- □ **realizar** to complete, to accomplish
- □ **recorrido** tour · *recorrer* to tour, to travel
- □ **Europa** Europe
- □ **excepcional** exceptional
- □ **me emocioné** I was moved · *emocionarse* to be moved emotionally, to become excited
- □ **hospital** NM hospital
- □ **por obsequiarnos** for giving us · *obsequiar* to give a gift
- □ **emotiva** emotionally stirring · *emotivo* emotionally stirring
- □ **actuación** performance
- □ **apoyo** support
- □ **función** event

🎬 The actress steps offstage.

- □ **estudiantes** students · *estudiante* NMF student
- □ **destacadas** outstanding · *destacado* outstanding · *destacar* to stand out
- □ **ha obtenido** she has obtained · *obtener* to obtain
- □ **calificación** grade
- □ **el examen de nuevo ingreso** placement exam · *examen* NM exam · *nuevo ingreso* new enrollment
- □ **pertenecer** to belong
- □ **academia** academy
- □ **bienvenida** welcome

☐ **aficionada** amateur · *aficionado* amateur · *aficionarse* to become interested in
☐ **superar** to overcome, to surpass

🎬 Anne looks out at the audience as she stands before them. She uses many words that are poetic and not used in common speech, such as *vetustos* and *salteador*.

☐ **viento** wind
☐ **torrente** *NM* torrent
☐ **oscuridad** darkness
☐ **vetustos** ancient · *vetusto* ancient
☐ **galeón fantasma** ghost ship · *galeón NM* galleon, ship · *fantasma* ghost, enchanted
☐ **flotando** floating · *flotar* to float
☐ **un mar encrespado** choppy sea · *mar NM* sea · *encresparse* to be choppy [SEA]
☐ **vereda** trail, path
☐ **listón** *NM* ribbon
☐ **páramo** swamp
☐ **púrpura** purple
☐ **salteador** highwayman
☐ **cabalgando** riding · *cabalgar* to ride a horse
☐ **posada** inn
☐ **caballo** horse
☐ **silencioso** silent
☐ **penumbra** semi-darkness
☐ **previa** before, prior · *previo* before, prior
☐ **se ocultan** they are hidden · *ocultarse* to be hidden
☐ **reconocibles** recognizable · *reconocible* recognizable
☐ **rayos** rays · *rayo* ray
☐ **protegidos** protected · *protegido* protected · *proteger* to protect
☐ **infierno** hell
☐ **destino** destiny
☐ **cabalgó** he rode · *cabalgar* to ride a horse
☐ **demente** *NMF* demented person
☐ **profiriendo** uttering · *proferir* to utter
☐ **insultos** insults · *insulto* insult
☐ **firmamento** firmament

🎬 Anne raises her gloved arm.

☐ **humeante** smoking
☐ **rastro** sign, mark
☐ **espadín** *NM* rapier
☐ **blandiendo** brandishing · *blandir* to brandish
☐ **ensangrentadas** bloodstained · *ensangrentado* bloodstained · *ensangrentar* to stain with blood
☐ **espuelas** spurs · *espuela* spur
☐ **teñida** dyed · *teñido* dyed · *teñir* to dye
☐ **rojo** red
☐ **casaca de terciopelo** velvet coat · *casaca* coat, riding jacket · *terciopelo* velvet

☐ **dispararon** they shot · *disparar* to shoot
☐ **tirado** sprawled · *tirarse* to throw oneself
☐ **charco** puddle
☐ **sangre** *NF* blood
☐ **puñado** handful
☐ **cuello** neck

🎬 Anne sits down.

☐ **espléndida** splendid · *espléndido* splendid
☐ **felicitarte** to congratulate you · *felicitar* to congratulate
☐ **gratamente** pleasantly
☐ **sorprendida** surprised · *sorprendido* surprised · *sorprender* to surprise
☐ **poemas** poems · *poema NM* poem
☐ **favoritos** favorite · *favorito* favorite

🎬 Anne and Gilbert approach each other, but Marilla and her friends intercept Anne.

☐ **admitir** to admit
☐ **satisfecha** satisfied · *satisfecho* satisfied · *satisfacer* to satisfy
☐ **compararse** to be compared
☐ **profesional** professional
☐ **no niegues** *IMP* don't deny · *negar* to deny
☐ **suspendido cabello** upswept hairdo · *suspendido* upswept · *cabello* hair
☐ **rojizo** reddish · *rojo* red
☐ **estaba declamando** she was reciting · *declamar* to recite
☐ **pelirrojo** redhead
☐ **elegante** elegant
☐ **magnífica** magnificent · *magnífico* magnificent
☐ **robo** I rob · *robar* to rob
☐ **ansiosas** anxious · *ansioso* anxious
☐ **descortés** discourteous
☐ **preciso** necessary
☐ **enseguida** at once, right away
☐ **date prisa** *IMP* hurry up · *darse prisa* to hurry up

🎬 Anne and Diana look out to sea.

☐ **culpable** guilty
☐ **diamantes** diamonds · *diamante NM* diamond
☐ **rica** rich · *rico* rich
☐ **verano** summer
☐ **hotel** *NM* hotel
☐ **ensalada de pollo** chicken salad
☐ **helados** ice cream · *helado* ice cream
☐ **ricas** rich · *rico* rich
☐ **dieciséis** sixteen
☐ **experiencia** experience
☐ **ambas** both · *ambos* both
☐ **poseemos** we possess · *poseer* to possess
☐ **disfrutar** to enjoy
☐ **belleza** beauty

□ **cofres** chests · *cofre NM* chest
□ **me conformo con** I'm satisfied with, I'm content with · *conformarse* to be satisfied, to be content
□ **collar de perlas** pearl necklace · *collar NM* necklace · *perla* pearl
□ **obsequió** he gave · *obsequiar* to give a gift
□ **joyas** jewels · *joya* jewel
□ **impedirlo** to stop it, to get in the way of it · *impedir* to stop, to get in the way of

## 18 | SIDE B 7 | Queen's College Scholar    9:31

### Phrases to Listen For

**date prisa** *IMP* hurry up
**me preocupa mucho** she worries me a lot, I'm worried about her
**a pesar de** in spite of
**así que** so
**en lugar de** instead of
**para que** in order to, so that
**por lo tanto** therefore
**te ves** you look
**lo que** what
**tomé la decisión** I made the decision
**por todos lados** everywhere
**tal vez** maybe, perhaps
**la riqueza de nada sirve** riches aren't worth anything
**a punto de** about to
**todo el mundo** everyone

### Names

Spencer, Beechwood, Anne Shirley, Josie, Jane, Ruby, Gilbert Blythe, White Sands, Frank Stockly, Avery, Redmond, Lynde, Emily Clay, Barry

🎬 At the train station, Matthew turns to Marilla, who then turns to Anne at the ticket window.

□ **date prisa** *IMP* hurry up · *darse prisa* to hurry up
□ **esperarte** to wait for you *esperar* to wait
□ **emocionándote** becoming emotional · *emocionarse* to become emotional
□ **por naderías** over nothing
□ **exceso** excess
□ **sensiblería** mushiness, excessive display of emotion
□ **lo beses** *SUBJ* you kiss him · *besar* to kiss
□ **pasajeros** passengers · *pasajero* passenger

🎬 Anne sits down aboard the train. Marilla addresses Matthew on the platform.

□ **se ausentará** she will be gone · *ausentarse* to be gone, to be absent
□ **permaneciera** *SUBJ* she stayed, she remained · *permanecer* to stay, to remain

□ **cometió** she committed · *cometer* to commit
□ **equivocación** mistake
□ **afortunada** fortunate · *afortunado* fortunate
□ **sino** but
□ **providencial** providential
□ **extraña** strange · *extraño* strange

🎬 Anne rides in a carriage with Aunt Josephine.

□ **me agradan** they please me · *agradar* to please
□ **me obligan** they force me · *obligar* to force, to obligate
□ **me ahorran** they save me · *ahorrar* to save
□ **molestia** annoyance
□ **obligarme** to force me · *obligar* to force, to obligate
□ **aceptaras** *SUBJ* you accept · *aceptar* to accept
□ **hospedarte** to stay · *hospedarse* to stay
□ **práctico** practical
□ **dueña** owner · *dueño* owner
□ **pensión** boarding house
□ **bondadosa** kind · *bondadoso* kind
□ **protegida** safe, protected · *protegido* safe, protected · *proteger* to keep safe, to protect

🎬 A woman wearing a white housekeeping apron stands in front of a door and addresses Anne.

□ **creativa** creative · *creativo* creative
□ **asigné** I assigned · *asignar* to assign
□ **gentil** nice
□ **decenas** tens, multiples of ten · *decena* a set of ten
□ **estudiantes** students · *estudiante NMF* student
□ **no dudes en decírmelo** *IMP* don't hesitate to tell it to me · *dudar* to hesitate
□ **animarme** to cheer me up · *animarse* to cheer up
□ **miserable** miserable

🎬 At Queens College, a professor addresses the new group of students.

□ **colegio** academy, secondary school
□ **programa** *NM* program
□ **asignado** assigned · *asignar* to assign
□ **enfrentar** to face
□ **una época muy difícil** a difficult time
□ **capaces** capable · *capaz* capable
□ **periodo** period
□ **prueba** test
□ **realmente** really
□ **estancia** stay, time spent (in a place)

🎬 A bell rings. Josie Pye approaches Anne.

□ **qué mal aspecto tienes** you look awful · *aspecto* look, appearance

- **se te enrojecen** they become red · *enrojecerse* to become red
- **nariz** *NF* nose
- **roja** red · *rojo* red
- **francés** *NM* French [LANGUAGE]
- **bigote** *NM* mustache
- **sensacional** sensational
- **acompáñame** *IMP* come with me · *acompañar* to come with, to accompany
- **almorzar** to eat brunch
- **reuniré** I'm going to meet up with · *reunir* to meet, to get together
- **compañeras** classmates · *compañero* classmate
- **idiota** *NMF* idiot
- **comportamiento** behavior
- **concierto** concert
- **decisión** decision
- **ignorarlo** to ignore him · *ignorar* to ignore
- **definitivamente** definitely
- **apuestos** handsome, good-looking · *apuesto* handsome, good-looking
- **me sorprende** it surprises me · *sorprender* to surprise
- **descortés** discourteous

🎬 Two young women join Anne and Josie Pye.

- **hubieran elegido** *SUBJ* you had chosen · *elegir* to elect, to choose
- **ingresar** to enroll
- **aprobaré** I will pass · *aprobar* to pass [EDUCATION]
- **estudiante** *NMF* student
- **obtenga** *SUBJ* he or she obtains · *obtener* to obtain
- **calificación** grade
- **literatura** literature
- **beca** scholarship
- **doscientos** two hundred
- **anuales** annually · *anual* annual
- **ganador** winner
- **nadando** swimming · *nadar* to swim
- **profundas** deep · *profundo* deep
- **ganadores** winners · *ganador* winner
- **becas** scholarships · *beca* scholarship
- **meter** to put, to stick
- **narices** noses · *nariz* *NF* nose

🎬 Anne drinks tea with Aunt Josephine.

- **graduarte** graduating · *graduarse* to graduate
- **arte** *NM* art
- **ambiciosa** ambitious · *ambicioso* ambitious
- **excepción** exception
- **ambicionaba** I aspired to · *ambicionar* to aspire to
- **diciéndolo** saying it · *decir* to say, to tell

- **riqueza** riches
- **compartirla** to share it · *compartir* to share
- **ambicionaban** they aspired to, they were chasing after · *ambicionar* to aspire to, to chase after
- **interesantes** interesting · *interesante* interesting
- **amistades** friendships · *amistad* *NF* friendship
- **círculo** circle
- **práctica** practical · *práctico* practical
- **romance** *NM* romance
- **me convierta** *SUBJ* it turns me into · *convertir* to turn into, to convert
- **solterona** spinster · *solterón* confirmed bachelor
- **ofenderla** to offend you · *ofender* to offend
- **grave** grave, serious
- **casada** married · *casado* married · *casarse* to marry, to get married
- **malhumorada** grouchy, ill-tempered · *malhumorado* grouchy, ill-tempered
- **recomendarte** to recommend to you · *recomendar* to recommend
- **reservar** to reserve
- **espacio** space
- **planes** plans · *plan* *NM* plan
- **diplomas** diplomas, degrees · *diploma* *NM* diploma, degree
- **suplirán** they will substitute for, they will take the place of · *suplir* to substitute for, to take the place of
- **carencia** lack

🎬 Anne approaches an elderly man behind a counter.

- **entregárselo** to deliver it to him · *entregar* to deliver, to give
- **salón** *NM* classroom
- **claramente** clearly

🎬 At Green Gables, Marilla reads a letter to Matthew.

- **curso** term, course
- **me he involucrado** I have been preoccupied, I have buried myself · *involucrarse* to be preoccupied, to bury oneself, to involve oneself
- **noción** notion, sense
- **exámenes** exams · *examen* *NM* exam
- **solía** she used to · *soler* to used to (+ VERB)
- **naciendo** rising · *nacer* to rise, to be born
- **ocultándose** setting · *ocultarse* to set, to hide
- **apruebe** *SUBJ* I pass · *aprobar* to pass [EDUCATION]
- **geometría** geometry
- **repruebo** I fail · *reprobar* to fail [EDUCATION]

🎬 Outside Queens Academy, Anne walks with Jane Andrews. Both wear hats.

- □ **anímate** IMP cheer up · *animarse* to cheer up
- □ **premios** prizes · *premio* prize
- □ **importancia** importance
- □ **todo el mundo comenta** everyone says · *comentar* to say, to comment
- □ **ganadora** winner · *ganador* winner
- □ **medalla de oro** gold medal
- □ **revisar** to check
- □ **pizarrón de avisos** bulletin board · *pizarrón* NM chalk board · *aviso* notice, warning
- □ **directo** directly
- □ **tocador** dressing room
- □ **he reprobado** I have failed · *reprobar* to fail [EDUCATION]
- □ **lástima** pity
- □ **genial** terrific
- □ **felicitar** to congratulate

## 19 SIDE B 8 Lament for Matthew 11:53

### Phrases to Listen For

**así que** so
**tendrá que** he will have to
**en cuanto a** concerning
**¿por qué?** why?
**enamorada de** in love with
**¿qué tienes?** what's wrong?, what's the matter?
**desde el primer día** from the first day
**muy orgulloso de ti** very proud of you
**lo que** what
**en resumen** in sum, in short
**buenos días** good morning
**por aquí** around here
**así es** that's right, indeed
**en forma impecable** in impeccable shape
**que se vaya a pique** SUBJ that it goes downhill, that it goes under
**el momento preciso** the exact moment
**hace tiempo** a long time ago, a while ago, a while back
**tuviera que** SUBJ I'd have to
**de alguna forma** somehow
**porqué** reason, reason why
**¿a qué te refieres?** what are you talking about?
**hasta que** until
**tengo dieciséis años** I'm sixteen years old
**tenía esa edad** I was that age
**hace años** years ago
**¿qué pasó?** what happened?

### Names

Moody, Diana Barry, Jesus, Carmody, Sadler, Spencer, Redmond

🎬 Near a lighthouse, Anne walks with Diana.

- □ **aroma** NM aroma
- □ **menta** mint
- □ **delicioso** delicious
- □ **no soporto** I can't stand · *soportar* to stand, to tolerate
- □ **canosa** gray-haired · *canoso* gray-haired
- □ **casada** married · *casado* married · *casarse* to marry, to get married
- □ **extraordinariamente** extraordinarily
- □ **interesarte** to be interested · *interesarse* to be interested
- □ **rendido** surrendering · *rendir* to surrender
- □ **ante** before
- □ **aclarar** to clarify, to explain
- □ **malentendido** misunderstanding
- □ **empeñoso** hardworking, diligent
- □ **en cuanto a ti concierne** EXP as far as you are concerned · *concernir* to concern
- □ **libre** free
- □ **estaba enamorada de** she was in love with · *estar enamorado de* to be in love with
- □ **preferible** preferable
- □ **inteligente** intelligent

🎬 Matthew falls to the ground.

- □ **brega** hard work, struggle
- □ **he envejecido** I have grown old · *envejecer* to grow old
- □ **labores del campo** field chores · *labor* NM chore · *campo* field, farmland
- □ **no cambies** IMP don't change · *cambiar* to change
- □ **orgulloso** proud

🎬 Several people are gathered around a casket.

- □ **nos hemos reunido** we have met · *reunirse* to meet, to get together
- □ **respetuoso** respectful
- □ **tumba** tomb
- □ **aferrarnos** to grasp · *aferrarse* to grasp
- □ **misterio** mystery
- □ **sufren** they suffer · *sufrir* to suffer
- □ **evidencia** evidence
- □ **en resumen** in summary · *resumen* NM summary
- □ **encomendamos** we commend · *encomendar* to commend, to entrust
- □ **alma** soul
- □ **profundamente** deeply
- □ **pérdida** loss

🎬 Marilla hears Anne crying.

- □ **tranquilízate** IMP calm down · *tranquilizarse* to calm down

□ **no lo remedias** you won't fix it, you won't remedy it · *remediar* to fix, to remedy
□ **protégeme** *IMP* protect me · *proteger* to protect
□ **brazos** arms · *brazo* arm
□ **duele** it hurts · *doler* to hurt
□ **vacío** emptiness
□ **estricta** strict · *estricto* strict
□ **presencia** presence
□ **menor** less
□ **interior** *NM* interior, inside
□ **integrante** integral
□ **correcto** correct
□ **lloremos** *SUBJ* we cry · *llorar* to cry

🎬 Mr. Sadler stops in front of Green Gables and speaks to Marilla.

□ **¿cómo marcha...?** how are things working out with ...?, how is (it) doing? · *marchar* to work out, to go, to move forward
□ **negocios** business, business activities · *negocio* business
□ **absorben** they absorb · *absorber* to absorb
□ **se disfruta** one enjoys · *disfrutar* to enjoy
□ **paisaje** *NM* countryside, landscape
□ **se comenta** it is said · *comentar* to say, to comment
□ **granja** farm
□ **zona** zone
□ **norte** *NM* north
□ **cuidaba** he took care of · *cuidar* to take care of
□ **propiedad** property
□ **impecable** impeccable
□ **se vaya a pique** *SUBJ* it gets run down, it goes down the tubes · *irse a pique* to get run down, to go down the tubes, to go to the dogs
□ **valor** *NM* value
□ **preciso** right, exact, precise
□ **considerar** to consider
□ **venderla** selling it · *vender* to sell
□ **obtener** to obtain
□ **precio** price
□ **no puedo negarle** I can't deny to you · *negar* to deny
□ **ha cruzado** it has crossed · *cruzar* to cross
□ **mente** *NF* mind

🎬 As Mr. Sadler leaves, Anne joins Marilla in front of the house.

□ **pretendió** he desired, he wanted · *pretender* to desire, to want
□ **vista** sight, eyesight
□ **se va debilitando** it is growing weaker · *debilitarse* to weaken

□ **jaquecas** headaches · *jaqueca* headache
□ **persisten** they persist · *persistir* to persist
□ **definitivamente** definitely
□ **ha pedido** she has asked · *pedir* to ask for, to request
□ **vender** to sell
□ **surgiera** *SUBJ* it arises · *surgir* to arise, to come up
□ **vacaciones** *NFPL* vacation
□ **sobreviviremos** we will survive · *sobrevivir* to survive
□ **beca** scholarship
□ **rentará** he will rent · *rentar* to rent
□ **personal** *NM* personnel
□ **diario** daily
□ **clima** *NM* climate, weather
□ **los fines de semana** weekends · *fin de semana* weekend · *fin NM* end · *semana* week
□ **sacrifiques** *SUBJ* you sacrifice · *sacrificar* to sacrifice
□ **educación** education
□ **dieciséis** sixteen
□ **obstinada** obstinate · *obstinado* obstinate
□ **bendita seas** *SUBJ* bless you · *bendito* blessed
□ **imponerme** to impose · *imponerse* to impose
□ **obligarte** to force you · *obligar* to force, to obligate
□ **interponerme** to get in the way · *interponerse* to get in the way
□ **se ha convertido en** he has become · *convertirse* to become
□ **edad** age
□ **solíamos** we used to · *soler* to used to (+ *VERB*)
□ **novio** boyfriend
□ **discutimos** we argued · *discutir* to argue
□ **disculparlo** to forgive him · *disculpar* to forgive
□ **sufrir** to suffer
□ **lamenté** I was sorry · *lamentar* to be sorry
□ **haber actuado** having acted · *actuar* to act

**20** SIDE B **9** | **Loving Partnership/ Credits** 4:12

**Phrases to Listen For**
**en asuntos ajenos** in other people's matters
**déjala en paz** *IMP* leave her alone
**acerca de** about
**no digas nada** *SUBJ* don't say anything (*LIT* don't say nothing)
**tendrás que** you will have to
**por correspondencia** by correspondence
**¿no tienes miedo?** you aren't afraid?

## Names
Carmody, Green Gables, Gilbert Blythe,
Anne Shirley, Avonlea

🎬 Marilla sits with Rachel Lynde on the porch.
Anne leans against the railing.

☐ **me alegra** I'm glad (*LIT* it makes me happy) ·
*alegrar* to make happy
☐ **hayas recuperado** *SUBJ* you have recovered ·
*recuperar* to recover
☐ **cordura** common sense
☐ **curso** course
☐ **se llenen** *SUBJ* they fill · *llenar* to fill
☐ **latín** *NM* Latin
☐ **griego** Greek
☐ **cursos** courses · *curso* course
☐ **correspondencia** correspondence
☐ **recapacitar** to reflect, to think over
☐ **no te entrometas** *IMP* mind your own
business, don't meddle, don't interfere ·
*entrometerse* to meddle, to interfere
☐ **asuntos** matters · *asunto* matter
☐ **ajenos** belonging to others · *ajeno* belonging
to others
☐ **déjala en paz** *IMP* leave her alone ·
*dejar en paz* to leave alone · *paz NF*
peace
☐ **estudio** study [EDUCATION]

☐ **obstinación** obstinacy
☐ **provoca** it provokes, it brings about ·
*provocar* to provoke, to bring about

🎬 Gilbert rides on horseback toward Anne.

☐ **atajo** shortcut
☐ **ábrela** *IMP* open it · *abrir* to open
☐ **dispuestos** willing · *dispuesto* willing
☐ **acceder** to agree
☐ **propuesta** proposal, suggestion
☐ **contrato** contract
☐ **puesto** position
☐ **pública** public · *público ADJ* public
☐ **plaza** place, spot
☐ **libertad** *NF* liberty
☐ **directores** trustees, board members ·
*director NM* trustee, board member
☐ **acerca de** about
☐ **hospedaje** *NM* lodging
☐ **ahorrar** to save
☐ **ahorraré** I will save · *ahorrar* to save
☐ **renunciar** resigning · to resign
☐ **gentil** kind
☐ **sepas** *SUBJ* you know · *saber* to know
☐ **tareas** assignments, work · *tarea* assignment,
work, homework
☐ **pizarra** chalkboard, writing slate
☐ **zanahoria** carrot

# Finding Nemo

**Oye, ¡yo vi un bote! ¡Pasó por aquí hace un instante!**
*Hey, I've seen a boat! And it passed by not too long ago!*

| | |
|---|---|
| GENRE | Comedy/Animation |
| YEAR | 2003 |
| DIRECTORS | Andrew Stanton, Lee Unkrich |
| CAST | Herman López, Patricia Palestino, Memo Aponte Jr., Arturo Mercado |
| STUDIO | Pixar |

Marlin, an overprotective and not-very-funny clownfish, loses his son Nemo to an Australian scuba diver who collects interesting fish. Though fearful of life beyond the reef, Marlin sets out for Sydney determined to rescue Nemo; along the way he encounters all sorts of frightening and funny sea creatures. Dory, a colorful reef tang who becomes his companion, has short-term memory loss that provides great comedy. For the Spanish learner, *Finding Nemo* has simple grammar and easy vocabulary on a wide range of topics, but at times the dialogue is very rapid. Because of the rapid speech, the film is ranked as Advanced and is recommended for those who have gained some experience listening to conversational Spanish.

## BASIC VOCABULARY

### Names
Sydney, Gill, Sherman, Wallaby

### Nouns
- **aleta** fin · *¿Qué le pasó en la **aleta**?* What happened to the fin?
- **arrecife** NM reef · *Sí, yo sufrí mucho cuando el mayor fue al **arrecife**.* Yes, I suffered a lot when the oldest one went to the reef.
- **bote** NM boat · *Es un gran **bote**.* It's a large boat.
- **burbujas** bubbles · *burbuja* bubble · *Te vas a cenar mis **burbujas**.* You're going to eat my bubbles for dinner.
- **océano** ocean · *Porque nadie en el **océano** entero quiere ayudarme.* Because nobody in the entire ocean wants to help me.
- **peces** fish · **pez** NM fish · *Cuidado, los tiburones comen **peces**.* Careful, sharks eat fish. · *Tres semanas ya son desde mi último **pez**, palabra de honor o que me hagan filete y me sirvan en sopa.* It's already been three weeks since my last fish, word of honor or may they cut me into fillets and serve me in soup.
- **pez payaso** clownfish · *pez* NM fish · *payaso* clown · *Soy un **pez payaso**.* I'm a clownfish.
- **tanque** NM tank · *Lo que tienes que hacer es poner una piedra adentro y atascar los engranes, así el **tanque** se irá ensuciando minuto a minuto.* What you have to do is to place one rock inside and jam the gears, so that the tank will grow filthier minute by minute.
- **Tiburoncín** DIM Little Shark [nickname given to Nemo; "Sharkbait" in English] · *Tu turno, **Tiburoncín**.* Your turn, Little Shark.

### Verb
- **nadaremos** we will swim · **nadando** swimming · *nadar* to swim · ***Nadaremos**, **nadaremos** en el mar.* Just keep swimming, just keep swimming in the sea. (LIT We will swim, we will swim in the sea.) · *Está **nadando** hacia el filtro.* He's swimming toward the filter.

## 1  New Parents                                    3:28

### Phrases to Listen For
**de veras** really
**¿te gusta o no te gusta?** do you like it? (LIT does it please you or does it not please you?)
**¡qué lindos!** how beautiful!
**tenemos que nombrarlos** we have to name them
**ya está** done already (LIT it already is)
**trato de no hacerlo** I try not to, I try not to do it

**tiene que** you have to
**están a salvo** they are safe

### Names
Marlin, Coral, Junior

🎬 Two clownfish view the deep ocean from their home in a sea anemone.

- **vista** view
- **respira** it breathes · *respirar* to breathe
- **marido** husband
- **paraíso** paradise
- **vecindario** neighborhood
- **adoro** I love, I adore · *adorar* to love, to adore
- **fabuloso** fabulous
- **espacio** space
- **ballena** whale
- **ventana** window
- **ruido** noise

🎬 Marlin and Coral view their eggs.

- **nombrarlos** to name them · *nombrar* to name, to give a name
- **mitad** NF half
- **cuatrocientos** four hundred
- **trato** I try · *tratar* to try
- **anzuelo** fish hook
- **labio** lip
- **adentro** inside
- **galán** NM gallant young man

🎬 Marlin and Coral spot a predator.

- **están a salvo** they are safe · *estar a salvo* to be safe

## 2  Main Titles                                    1:17

🎬 Marlin finds one egg.

- **te cuida** he'll take care of you (LIT he takes care of you) · *cuidar* to take care of

## 3  First Day of School                            5:42

### Phrases to Listen For
**¿tienes náuseas?** are you nauseated?
**a ver** let's see
**¿qué tal si...?** what if ...?
**por allá** over there
**qué gusto** what pleasure
**lo que** what
**hay que** it's necessary
**tal vez** maybe, perhaps
**algún día** some day

**no te vayas a poner histérico** *IMP* don't get
hysterical
**se veía** it looked
**por favor** please
**se ve** it looks
**todos a bordo** all aboard
**tienen que** they have to
**¿por qué?** why?

## Names
Carlos Plancton, Martín, Marlin, Bocter, Tim,
Sheldon, Mollano, López

Nemo leaves the sea anemone. Marlin frees Nemo.

□ **fractura** break, broken bone
□ **fluidos** fluids · *fluido* fluid
□ **área** area
□ **¿tienes náuseas?** are you nauseated? ·
*tener* to have · *nausea* nausea
□ **franjas** stripes · *franja* stripe
□ **contesta** *IMP* answer · *contestar* to answer
□ **francamente** frankly
□ **grave** grave, serious
□ **pocas** few · *pocos* few
□ **aleteando** flapping fins · *aletear* to flap fins,
to flap wings
□ **cepillarte** to brush yourself · *cepillarse* to brush
oneself
□ **anémona** anemone
□ **cepíllate** *IMP* brush yourself · *cepillarse* to brush
oneself
□ **te faltó** you missed (*LIT* it was lacking to you) ·
*faltar* to be missing, to lack

Marlin and Nemo look out of the anemone.

□ **emoción** excitement
□ **educación** education
□ **respecto a** with respect to
□ **peligro** danger

Marlin and Nemo swim to school.

□ **escuela** school
□ **tiburón** *NM* shark
□ **no lo planeo** I don't plan on it · *planear*
to plan
□ **edad** age
□ **tortugas** turtles · *tortuga* turtle
□ **vecino** neighbor
□ **marinas** sea · *marino ADJ* sea
□ **cien** one hundred
□ **preguntaré** I will ask · *preguntar* to ask
□ **¡precaución!** *EXP* watch out!

Fish traffic stops. Marlin holds Nemo's fin.

□ **histérico** hysterical
□ **zoológico** zoo

□ **caracol** *NM* snail
□ **agresivo** aggressive
□ **entrada** entrance
□ **salida** leaving, departure, exit
□ **déjenme en paz** *IMP* leave me alone ·
*dejar* to leave · *paz NF* peace
□ **devuélvanmelo** *IMP* give it back to me ·
*devolver* to give back, to return
□ **acusar** to tell on, to accuse

Marlin and Nemo approach Bob, Ted, and Bill.

□ **miren** *IMP* look · *mirar* to look at
□ **raro** strange
□ **simpático** nice, pleasant
□ **chiste** *NM* joke
□ **simple** simple
□ **confusión** confusion
□ **comediantes** comedians · *comediante NMF*
comedian
□ **payasito** *DIM* little clown · *payaso* clown

Marlin tells a joke to Bob, Ted, and Bill.

□ **molusco** mollusk
□ **nadaba** he was swimming · *nadar* to swim
□ **pepino** cucumber

Bob the seahorse interrupts Marlin's joke.

□ **sal** *IMP* get out · *salir* to leave, to go out
□ **jardín** *NM* garden
□ **esponja** sponge

Three young fish join Marlin, Nemo, Bob, Ted,
and Phil.

□ **gracioso** funny
□ **educado** polite, well-mannered · *educar*
to bring up, to raise
□ **nacimiento** birth
□ **tentáculo** tentacle
□ **nota** he notices · *notar* to notice
□ **bailar** to dance
□ **intolerante** intolerant
□ **hache, dos, o** $H_2O$, water
□ **hiperodioso** super-hateful

The teacher, Mr. Ray, swims into view.

□ **nombrar** to name
□ **zonas** zones · *zona* zone
□ **raya** ray [ANIMAL]
□ **mesopelágico** mesopelagic
□ **batial** bathyal
□ **abisopelágico** abyssopelagic
□ **resto** the rest, the remainder
□ **profundas** deep · *profundo* deep
□ **todos a bordo** all aboard
□ **exploradores** explorers · *explorador* explorer

☐ **conocimiento** knowledge
☐ **divertido** fun · *divertirse* to have fun
☐ **ignorancia** ignorance
☐ **aburrido** boring

🎬 Nemo introduces himself to Mr. Ray.

☐ **contestar** to answer
☐ **tipo** type, kind
☐ **hogar** NM home
☐ **anémona** anemone
☐ **no te trabes** IMP don't get tongue-tied ·
 *trabarse* to get tongue-tied
☐ **pausa** pause
☐ **descuide** IMP don't worry · *descuidar* to not
 worry, to neglect
☐ **órbitas ópticas** eyes [UNCOMMON]
☐ **ganglio** ganglion
☐ **supraesofágico** supraesophogeal
☐ **ciencia** science
☐ **maravilla** marvel, wonder

🎬 Marlin watches Nemo leave with Mr. Ray.
 Bob, Ted, and Bill approach.

☐ **primerizo** first-time father, novice ·
 *primeriza* first-time mother
☐ **sufrí** I suffered · *sufrir* to suffer
☐ **madurar** to mature
☐ **freímos** we fry · *freír* to fry
☐ **servimos** we serve · *servir* to serve
☐ **salsa** salsa, sauce
☐ **cara** face
☐ **pony** ENG pony

## 4  Field Trip                                0:58

### Phrases to Listen For
**hay que** it's necessary
**qué lindas** how beautiful

🎬 Mr. Ray continues singing as his students ride
 on top. He sings a series of scientific terms very
 rapidly.

☐ **nombrar** to name
☐ **especies** species · *especie* NF species
☐ **poríferos** sponges, poriferans · *porífero* sponge,
 poriferan
☐ **coelenterados** coelenterates · *coelenterado*
 coelenterate
☐ **hidrozoos** hydrozoas · *hidrozoo* hydrozoa
☐ **moluscos** mollusks · *molusco* mollusk
☐ **gasterópodos** gastropods · *gasterópodo*
 gastropod
☐ **artrópodos** arthropods · *artrópodo* arthropod
☐ **equinodermos** echinoderms · *equinodermo*
 echinoderm

☐ **canten** IMP sing · *cantar* to sing
☐ **aletas** fins · *aleta* fin
☐ **algas marinas** sea algae · *alga* alga ·
 *marino* ADJ sea
☐ **comida** food
☐ **rayo** ray

🎬 The student fish get off Mr. Ray's back.

☐ **explorar** to explore
☐ **cianobacterias** blue-green algae, blue-green
 bacteria · *cianobacteria* blue-green alga,
 blue-green bacteria
☐ **ecosistema** NM ecosystem
☐ **infinitesimal** infinitesimal
☐ **átomo** atom
☐ **proteínas** proteins · *proteína* protein
☐ **bacteria** bacteria
☐ **granos** grains · *grano* grain
☐ **arena** sand

## 5  The Drop Off                              1:53

### Phrases to Listen For
**a ver** let's see
**tenía miedo** he was afraid
**tenía razón** I was right
**tienes miedo** you are afraid
**hasta que** until
**para que** to, in order to
**está a salvo** he's safe

### Name
Carlos Plancton

🎬 Nemo catches up to his three friends. They view
 the Drop Off.

☐ **espérenme** IMP wait for me · *esperar*
 to wait
☐ **tinta** ink

🎬 Marlin arrives as Nemo swims on the edge
 of the Drop Off.

☐ **superficie** NF surface
☐ **no es cosa suya** it's none of your concern
 (LIT it's not your thing)
☐ **hallé** I found · *hallar* to find
☐ **capaz** capable
☐ **odio** I hate · *odiar* to hate

🎬 Mr. Ray arrives to offer help.

☐ **reúnense** IMP get together · *reunirse* to get
 together
☐ **científico** scientist
☐ **interrupción** interruption
☐ **supervisión** supervision

□ **está a salvo** he is safe · *estar a salvo* to be safe
□ **instante** *NM* instant
□ **desaparecer** to disappear
□ **se distrae** you are distracted · *distraerse* to be distracted, to get distracted
□ **se distraiga** *SUBJ* you get distracted · *distraerse* to get distracted, to be distracted

## 6  Nemo Lost                                      2:20

**Phrases to Listen For**
**tener que** to have to
**antes de que** before
**estás en problemas** you're in trouble
**por favor** please

Nemo swims toward the boat.

□ **movimiento** movement
□ **no te atrevas** *IMP* don't you dare · *atreverse* to dare
□ **bote** *NM* boat
□ **aletitas** *DIM* little fins · *aleta* fin
□ **de regreso** return, back, on the way back

## 7  Meeting Dory                                   2:21

**Phrases to Listen For**
**por favor** please
**tengo que** I have to
**¿de veras?** really?
**por aquí** this way, here
**no hay problema** there's no problem, no problem
**¿qué te pasa?** what's the matter with you?
**¿qué tienes?** what's wrong?
**¿por dónde?** where?, which way?
**¿qué te sucede?** what's with you?
**corto plazo** short-term
**de inmediato** immediately

Marlin swims through schools of fish heading in the opposite direction. He bumps into Dory.

□ **instante** *NM* instant, moment
□ **bastante** enough
□ **qué miedote** *PEJ* what awful fear · *miedo* fear
□ **me enseñabas** you were showing me · *enseñar* to show
□ **broma** joke
□ **simpática** nice · *simpático* nice
□ **simpatía** sympathy
□ **sufro** I suffer · *sufrir* to suffer
□ **memoria** memory
□ **corto plazo** short-term · *corto* short · *plazo* term

□ **olvido** I forget · *olvidar* to forget
□ **de inmediato** immediately

## 8  Sharks                                         6:41

**Phrases to Listen For**
**de veras** really, truly
**en serio** seriously
**no hay nada que hacer** there's nothing to do
**tengo hambre** I'm hungry
**hay que** it's necessary
**palabra de honor** word of honor
**así que** so
**tiene que** it has to
**otra vez** again
**¡qué lindo!** how beautiful!

**Names**
Bruce, Marlin, Ancla, Chum

Marlin encounters Bruce the shark.

□ **tiburones** sharks · *tiburón* *NM* shark
□ **bocadillos** appetizers, snacks · *bocadillo* appetizer, snack
□ **zona** zone, area
□ **postrecitos** *DIM* little desserts · *postre* *NM* dessert
□ **reunioncita** *DIM* little meeting · *reunión* meeting
□ **divertidas** fun · *divertido* fun · *divertirse* to have fun
□ **insisto** I insist · *insistir* to insist
□ **globos** balloons · *globo* balloon
□ **revientan** they burst · *reventar* to burst
□ **provocar** to provoke, to cause
□ **migraña** migraine
□ **ancla** anchor
□ **hambre** *NF* hunger
□ **frenesí** *NM* frenzy
□ **alimenticio** nutritious

A bell rings.

□ **oficialmente** officially
□ **junta** meeting
□ **iniciar** to begin
□ **promesa** promise
□ **tiburón** *NM* shark
□ **máquina** machine
□ **imagen** *NF* image
□ **comida** food
□ **excepto** except
□ **delfines** dolphins · *delfín* *NM* dolphin
□ **delfincito** *DIM* little dolphin · *delfín* *NM* dolphin
□ **aletear** to flap fins

□ **tema** *NM* theme, subject
□ **quinto** *ADJ* fifth
□ **invita** *IMP* invite · *invitar* to invite
□ **invitaron** you invited · *invitar* to invite
□ **acompañarte** to accompany you ·
 *acompañar* to accompany
□ **compañero** companion
□ **inicio** I begin · *iniciar* to begin
□ **testimonios** testimonies · *testimonio* testimony
□ **honor** *NM* honor
□ **filete** *NM* fillet
□ **sopa** soup

■ The sharks clap.

□ **inspiras** you inspire · *inspirar* to inspire
□ **amén** *NM* amen
□ **nena** babe, pretty girl, baby girl ·
 *nene NM* babe, baby boy, little one
□ **remordimiento** remorse
□ **negación** denial
□ **inicia** *IMP* begin · *iniciar* to begin
□ **chiste** *NM* joke
□ **molusco** mollusk
□ **pepino de mar** sea cucumber ·
 *pepino* cucumber · *mar NM* sea
□ **normalmente** normally

■ Marlin spots the diver's mask.

□ **gracia** grace, humor
□ **buzos** underwater divers · *buzo* underwater
 diver
□ **humanos** humans · *humano* human
□ **dueños** owners · *dueño* owner
□ **banqueros** bankers · *banquero* banker
□ **marcas** marks · *marca* mark
□ **te duele** it hurts you · *doler* to hurt
□ **sangre** *NF* blood

■ Dory bleeds.

□ **delicioso** delicious, delightful
□ **intervención** intervention
□ **mordida** bite
□ **contrólate** *IMP* control yourself · *controlarse*
 to control oneself
□ **cena** dinner
□ **repite** *IMP* repeat · *repetir* to repeat
□ **salida** exit, way out
□ **escapar** to escape
□ **escape** *NM* escape, escape hatch
□ **bloqueado** blocked · *bloquear* to block
□ **concéntrate** *IMP* concentrate, focus ·
 *concentrarse* to concentrate, to focus
□ **sujeto** guy
□ **visor** *NM* mask
□ **naden** *IMP* swim · *nadar* to swim

## 9  The Tank Gang                        5:23

### Phrases to Listen For
 **por favor** please
 **¿qué tal?** what's up?
 **¡qué raro!** how strange!
 **lo que** what
 **los rayos equis** x-rays
 **claro que** of course
 **otra vez** again
 **cumple ocho años** she turns eight years old
 **tengo que** I have to
 **tienes que** you have to

### Names
Barbara, Deb, Flo, Peach, Schilder, Nigel, Tucker,
Chuckles

■ Nemo bumps into the glass wall of a fish tank.
 The dentist speaks.

□ **prepáralo** *IMP* prepare him · *preparar*
 to prepare
□ **corona** crown
□ **algodón** *NM* cotton
□ **pececito** *DIM* little fish · *pez NM* fish
□ **bello** beautiful
□ **luchando** struggling · *luchar* to struggle
□ **hizo efecto** it took effect · *hacer efecto*
 to take effect
□ **anestesia** anesthesia

■ Bubbles enter the water from a treasure chest.
 The fish name several invented pet stores:
 Peces Pepe, Animalandia, Pecerama, Interpez.

□ **burbujitas** *DIM* little bubbles · *burbuja* bubble
□ **burbujotas** large bubbles · *burbuja* bubble
□ **bonjour** good day, good morning [FRENCH]
□ **despacio** slowly
□ **aterrado** frightened · *aterrar* to frighten
□ **nene** *NM* babe, baby boy, little one
□ **tienda de mascotas** pet store · *tienda* store ·
 *mascota* pet
□ **correo** mail
□ **descontaminado** decontaminated ·
 *descontaminar* to decontaminate
□ **oui** yes [FRENCH]
□ **limpieza** cleaning
□ **mer** sea [FRENCH]
□ **bon** good [FRENCH]
□ **enorme** enormous
□ **azul** blue
□ **raro** rare, strange
□ **endodoncia** root canal
□ **rayos equis** x-rays · *rayo* ray · *equis NF* X
 [LETTER]

■ The dentist operates the drill.
- □ **hule** *NM* plastic
- □ **instalados** installed · *instalado* installed · *instalar* to install
- □ **taladro Gator-Glidden** Gator-Glidden drill · *taladro* drill [DENTAL INSTRUMENT]
- □ **últimamente** recently, lately
- □ **técnica** technique
- □ **tiranervios** *NM* barbed broach [DENTAL INSTRUMENT]
- □ **excavador** spoon-shaped tool [DENTAL INSTRUMENT]
- □ **gota** drop (of liquid)
- □ **yo lo desinflo** I'll deflate him (LIT I deflate him) · *desinflar* to deflate

■ The dentist sprays water into the patient's mouth.
- □ **enjuáguese** *IMP* rinse · *enjuagar* to rinse
- □ **boca** mouth
- □ **humana** human · *humano* human
- □ **asquerosa** gross, sickening · *asqueroso* gross, sickening
- □ **cavidad** cavity
- □ **horrorosa** horrifying
- □ **sellador** sealant
- □ **no manche** *SUBJ* it doesn't stain · *manchar* to stain
- □ **esmalte** *NM* enamel
- □ **recién llegado** recent arrival, newly arrived · *recién* recently · *llegado* arrived · *llegar* to arrive
- □ **dentista** *NMF* dentist
- □ **forastero** stranger
- □ **nadan** they swim · *nadar* to swim
- □ **aves** birds · *ave NF* bird

■ The dentist shows the picture of Darla to the fish in the tank.
- □ **sobrina** niece · *sobrino* nephew
- □ **saluda** *IMP* say hello · *saludar* to say hello, to greet
- □ **viernes** *NM* Friday
- □ **secretito** *DIM* little secret · *secreto* secret
- □ **seca** it dries · *secar* to dry
- □ **visitar** to visit
- □ **pits** *ENG* bathroom [SLANG]
- □ **enseguida** at once, right away
- □ **agitar** to shake, to stir, to agitate
- □ **bolsa** bag
- □ **dio un paseo** he took a ride, he went for a ride · *dar un paseo* to take a ride, to go for a ride
- □ **tobogán** *NM* water slide
- □ **porcelana** porcelain

■ The dentist leaves the bathroom.
- □ **matapeces** *NM* fish killer
- □ **nadie lo toque** *IMP* nobody touch it · *tocar* to touch
- □ **te metiste** you got yourself in · *meterse* to get in
- □ **agita** *IMP* flap · *agitar* to flap
- □ **alternando** alternating · *alternar* to alternate
- □ **aletas** fins · *aleta* fin
- □ **concéntrate** *IMP* concentrate, focus · *concentrarse* to concentrate, to focus
- □ **mirada** look
- □ **bienvenida** welcome

## 10 The Abyss 2:06

### Phrases to Listen For
**¿por qué se te fue?** why did you let go of it?, why did you let it get away from you?
**se ha ido** it has gone
**hay que** it's necessary
**todo el día** all day

■ Marlin and Dory sleep.
- □ **pala** shovel
- □ **piraña** piranha
- □ **azul** blue
- □ **tiburones** sharks · *tiburón NM* shark
- □ **visor** *NM* mask

■ The mask sinks.
- □ **eco** echo
- □ **pista** clue
- □ **malhumorado** bad-tempered person
- □ **derrota** it defeats · *derrotar* to defeat
- □ **nadaremos** we will swim · *nadar* to swim
- □ **no cantes** *IMP* don't sing · *cantar* to sing
- □ **nades** *SUBJ* you swim · *nadar* to swim
- □ **cancioncita** *DIM* little song · *canción* song
- □ **dándome vueltas en la cabeza** spinning inside my head · *dar vueltas* to spin

## 11 Anglerfish 3:12

### Phrases to Listen For
**lo que sea** *SUBJ* whatever
**otra vez** again

### Names
Sherman, Wallaby

■ Marlin and Dory speak in the dark.
- □ **conciencia** conscience
- □ **no me quejo** I can't complain (LIT I don't complain · *quejarse* to complain

□ **visor** *NM* mask
□ **oí** I heard · *oír* to hear
□ **humor** *NM* mood
□ **no te presiones** *IMP* don't worry, don't hurry, don't put pressure on yourself, relax · *presionarse* to worry, to hurry, to put pressure on oneself
□ **¡presiónate!** *IMP* worry!, hurry!, feel the pressure! · *presionarse* to worry, to hurry, to put pressure on oneself
□ **presión** pressure
□ **cruel** cruel
□ **fallaste** you failed · *fallar* to fail
□ **cenaste** you dined, you ate dinner · *cenar* to dine, to eat dinner
□ **a dieta** on a diet
□ **olvido** I forget · *olvidar* to forget

## 12   Nemo's Initiation                    4:06

### Phrases to Listen For
**a partir de este momento** beginning this moment
**de acuerdo** agreed, all right
**lo que** what
**hay que** it's necessary
**por favor** please
**tienes que** you have to
**a prueba de bobos** foolproof

Inside the fish tank, Jacques wakes up Nemo.
□ **suivez-moi** follow me [FRENCH]
□ **globo** balloon
□ **proceda** *IMP* proceed · *proceder* to proceed
□ **novato** beginner, rookie, newcomer
□ **naranja** *ADJ* orange [COLOR]
□ **cima** top
□ **monte** *NM* mountain
□ **¿quiquirisquihaga?** what do you want me to do? [playful use of *qué quieres que haga*]
□ **vínculos fraternos** bonds of brotherhood · *vínculo* bond · *fraterno* brotherly
□ **tanquedad** tankhood [INVENTED WORD]
□ **club** *NM* club
□ **capaz** capable, able
□ **aro** ring, hoop
□ **enciende** *IMP* light · *encender* to light (a fire)
□ **burbujeante** bubbling

Nemo swims through the stream of bubbles.
□ **a partir de** beginning with, starting from, from
□ **bienvenido** *ADJ* welcome
□ **evitaremos** we will avoid · *evitar* to avoid

□ **sacrifiquen** *SUBJ* they sacrifice · *sacrificar* to sacrifice
□ **escape** *NM* escape
□ **escapatorias** escapes · *escapatoria* escape
□ **disculpa** excuse (me) · *disculpar* to excuse
□ **filtro** filter
□ **piedra** rock
□ **adentro** inside
□ **atascar** to block, to jam
□ **engranes** gears · *engrane* *NM* gear
□ **ensuciando** getting dirtier · *ensuciarse* to get dirty
□ **dentista** *NMF* dentist
□ **limpiar** to clean
□ **bolsas** bags · *bolsa* bag
□ **individuales** individual · *individual* *ADJ* individual
□ **nos rodaremos** we will roll · *rodarse* to roll
□ **mueble** *NM* piece of furniture
□ **ventana** window
□ **toldo** awning
□ **arbustos** bushes · *arbusto* bush
□ **cruzando** crossing · *cruzar* to cross
□ **bahía** bay
□ **prueba de bobos** foolproof · *prueba* test · *bobo* fool, silly person
□ **no te ofendas** *IMP* no offense, don't be offended · *ofenderse* to be offended
□ **no nadas** you don't swim · *nadar* to swim

## 13   Fish Impressions                    4:38

### Phrases to Listen For
**por favor** please
**¿por qué?** why?
**por mi cuenta** on my own
**claro que** of course
**la punta de mi lengua** the tip of my tongue
**hablo en serio** I'm serious (*LIT* I speak seriously)
**¿qué me pasa?** what's the matter with me?
**no importa** it doesn't matter
**otra vez** again
**así es** that's right
**lo que hay que hacer** what must be done (*LIT* what it is necessary to do)
**te luciste** you did great
**de nada** thank you
**tengo que** I have to
**a través** through
**ya basta** enough already

### Names
Sherman, Chencho, Fabio, Wallaby, Sydney

■ Marlin and Dory swim in the deep blue sea.

- □ **oí** I heard · *oír* to hear
- □ **repetírtelo** to repeat it to you · *repetir* to repeat
- □ **herirte** to hurt you · *herir* to hurt
- □ **retrasos** delays · *retraso* delay
- □ **causa** it causes · *causar* to cause
- □ **en ocasiones** on occasion, occasionally · *ocasión* occasion
- □ **retrapeces** NM delayfish [INVENTED WORD]
- □ **emoción** emotion
- □ **complicada** complicated · *complicado* complicated · *complicar* to complicate, to make complicated

■ Dory cries.

- □ **imitaciones** imitations · *imitación* imitation
- □ **ensayamos** we practiced, we rehearsed · *ensayar* to practice, to rehearse
- □ **adivine** IMP guess · *adivinar* to guess
- □ **nariz** NF nose
- □ **espada** sword
- □ **payasín** DIM little clown · *payaso* clown
- □ **mantequilla** butter
- □ **punta** tip
- □ **lengua** tongue
- □ **langosta** lobster
- □ **patas** feet · *pata* foot [OF AN ANIMAL]
- □ **almeja** clam
- □ **borrachos** drunk · *borracho* drunk
- □ **machos** macho, manly · *macho* macho, manly
- □ **grandiosos** magnificent · *grandioso* magnificent
- □ **hallar** to find
- □ **dirección** address

■ Marlin swims away from Dory and the fish that do imitations. Dory intercepts.

- □ **frustrante** frustrating
- □ **entero** entire, whole
- □ **parientes** relatives · *pariente* NMF relative
- □ **ce** NF C [LETTER]
- □ **a** NF A [LETTER]
- □ **o** NF O [LETTER]
- □ **Corriente Australiana Oriental** East Australian Current · *corriente* NF current · *australiano* Australian · *oriental* east, eastern

■ The fish that do imitations point the way to Sydney.

- □ **¿qué opinan?** what do you think? *opinar* to think, to give an opinion
- □ **leguas** leagues · *legua* league [DISTANCE]
- □ **directo** directly, straight
- □ **grandioso** awesome
- □ **¡te luciste!** you did great! · *lucirse* to do well
- □ **apoyo** help, support, assistance

- □ **apoyando** helping · *apoyar* to help, to support, to assist
- □ **relájate** IMP relax · *relajarse* to relax
- □ **compañero** companion, partner
- □ **imitan** you imitate · *imitar* to imitate
- □ **fosa** trench
- □ **naden** IMP swim · *nadar* to swim
- □ **a través** through, across
- □ **no lo olvido** I won't forget it (LIT I don't forget it) · *olvidar* to forget
- □ **señal** NF signal, sign
- □ **alarma** alarm
- □ **brillante** shiny
- □ **nadó** it swam · *nadar* to swim

## 14 Jellyfish                                    3:14

### Phrases to Listen For

**por aquí** over here
**¿qué tal...?** what's up ...?
**a través de** through
**¿por qué?** why?
**así que** so
**al mismo tiempo** at the same time
**¿tienes hambre?** are you hungry?
**tienes que** you have to

### Names

Squishy, Wallaby

■ Marlin and Dory swim upward to go over the trench.

- □ **exacto** exactly
- □ **corriente** NF current
- □ **chiquitín** DIM little one, little boy · *chico* boy
- □ **a través de** through, across
- □ **fosa** trench
- □ **medusa** jellyfish
- □ **anémona** anemone
- □ **aguantar** to tolerate, to put up with, to handle
- □ **entendiste** you understood · *entender* to understand
- □ **chiquita** DIM little one, small one · *chiquito* DIM little one, small one · *chico* small one

■ Dory bounces on top of the jellyfish.

- □ **no brinques** IMP don't jump · *brincar* to jump
- □ **puntas** ends, points, tips · *punta* end, point, tip
- □ **pican** they sting · *picar* to sting
- □ **¡gáname!** IMP beat me! · *ganar* to win, to beat
- □ **brinque** SUBJ he jumps · *brincar* to jump
- □ **reglas** rules · *regla* rule
- □ **tentáculos** tentacles · *tentáculo* tentacle
- □ **en sus marcas** on your mark · *marca* mark
- □ **suicida** suicidal

□ **de eso se trata** that's what it's about · *tratarse* to be about, to deal with
□ **nos divertimos** we had fun · *divertirse* to have fun
□ **ríndete** *IMP* surrender, give up · *rendirse* to surrender, to give up
□ **evolución** evolution
□ **nací** I was born · *nacer* to be born
□ **veloz** fast
□ **hambre** *NF* hunger
□ **cenar** to eat dinner, to dine
□ **rebasa** *IMP* pass · *rebasar* to pass

🎬 Marlin escapes the jellyfish.

□ **ganador** winner
□ **mírennos** *IMP* look at us · *mirar* to look at
□ **descalificada** disqualified · *descalificado* disqualified · *descalificar* to disqualify

## 15 The Filter                              3:16

### Phrases to Listen For
**parada técnica** official time-out
**hay que** it's necessary
**es plancton comido** easy as pie (*LIT* it's eaten plankton [a play on the expression *es pan comido* it's eaten bread])
**con cuidado** be careful
**no tengas miedo** *IMP* don't be afraid

### Name
Peach

🎬 Gill approaches Nemo.

□ **afuera** outside
□ **buscándote** looking for you · *buscar* to look for
□ **movimiento** movement
□ **tazas** cups · *taza* cup
□ **café** *NM* coffee
□ **sigue vigilando** *IMP* keep watching · *vigilar* to watch
□ **escape** *NM* escape
□ **utensilios** utensils · *utensilio* utensil
□ **dentales** dental · *dental* dental
□ **doble u, ce** *NF* W. C. [LETTERS]
□ **drenaje** *NM* drainage
□ **escapar** to escape
□ **caja** box, case

🎬 The bubbles flow from the treasure chest.

□ **parada técnica** official time-out [SPORTS]
□ *Selecciones* Reader's Digest
□ **turno** turn
□ **nene** *NM* babe, baby boy
□ **adentro** inside

□ **fondo** bottom
□ **cámara** chamber
□ **resto** the rest, the remainder
□ **plancton** *NM* plankton
□ **oírme** to hear me · *oír* to hear
□ **piedra** rock
□ **abertura** opening
□ **ventilador** fan
□ **gira** it spins · *girar* to spin
□ **mete** *IMP* put, place · *meter* to put, to place
□ **despacio** slowly

🎬 Nemo places the pebble that stops the filter.

□ **grandioso** magnificent, awesome
□ **tubo** tube
□ **sal** *IMP* get out, leave · *salir* to leave, to get out
□ **sostente** *IMP* hold on · *sostenerse* to hold on
□ **¡ánimo!** *EXP* come on!, hang in there!, get up!, get going!
□ **no lo obligues** *IMP* don't force him · *obligar* to force

## 16 Sea Turtles                             4:38

### Phrases to Listen For
**¿qué pasó?** what happened?
**¿qué cosa?** what's happening?, what's that?
**¡qué cosa!** wow!
**lo lamento** I'm sorry
**hay que** it's necessary
**¿te diste cuenta?** did you notice?
**lo que** what
**¡qué gran onda!** terrific!, that's really cool!
**el camino de vuelta** the return path
**uno a la vez** one at a time
**por favor** please

### Names
Crush, Chiqui, Medusín

🎬 Marlin is asleep on top of a sea turtle.

□ **concéntrate** *IMP* concentrate, focus · *concentrarse* to concentrate, to focus
□ **medusas** jellyfish · *medusa* jellyfish
□ **emociones** emotions · *emoción* emotion
□ **estómago** stomach
□ **no ensucies** *IMP* don't get dirty · *ensuciar* to get dirty
□ **espalda** back
□ **encerar** to polish, to wax
□ **tortuga** turtle
□ **Corriente Australiana Oriental** East Australian Current · *corriente NF* current · *australiano* Australian · *oriental* east, eastern

☐ **gózala** *IMP* enjoy it · *gozar* to enjoy
☐ **soltarte** to let go · *soltarse* to let go
☐ **azul** blue
☐ **piso** floor

🎬 Marlin joins Dory as she lies atop a different turtle.

☐ **veintinueve** twenty-nine
☐ **grandioso** magnificent, awesome
☐ **te diste cuenta** did you notice · *darse cuenta* to notice
☐ **onda** wave
☐ **choque** *NM* head-butt, crash
☐ **suave** cool, soft, smooth
☐ **medusín** *DIM* jellyfish [nickname; "Jelly Man" in English] · *medusa* jellyfish
☐ **exacto** exactly
☐ **deslízate** *IMP* slide · *deslizarse* to slide, to flow
☐ **huevos** eggs · *huevo* egg
☐ **playa** beach
☐ **cascarón** *NM* eggshell
☐ **el camino de vuelta** the road back · *de vuelta* back · *volver* to go back, to return
☐ **montaña** mountain

🎬 The tiny sea turtles pile on Marlin.

☐ **divagué** I got off track, I digressed · *divagar* to get off track, to digress
☐ **detalles** details · *detalle* *NM* detail

## 17 News Travels                    4:49

### Phrases to Listen For

**esto se pone interesante** this is getting interesting
**tal vez** maybe, perhaps
**tan duro con él** so hard on him
**no lo sé** I don't know
**así que** so
**desde entonces** since then
**¿qué tal?** what's up?, how's it going?
**tuvieron que** they had to
**en cuestión de días** in a matter of days
**lo que** what
**tenía tantas ganas** I had such great desire
**tengo que** I have to
**¿en serio?** seriously?, really?
**después de que** since
**otra vez** again
**hay que** it's necessary
**¡qué agallas!** what guts! (*LIT* what gills!)

### Names

Mateo, Sydney, Nigel

🎬 Marlin tells his story to the sea turtles and Dory.

☐ **interesante** interesting
☐ **nadó** he swam · *nadar* to swim
☐ **superficie** *NF* surface
☐ **buzos** scuba divers · *buzo* scuba diver
☐ **nadé** I swam · *nadar* to swim

🎬 The sea turtles continue the story.

☐ **se topó con** he ran into · *toparse con* to run into
☐ **feroces** ferocious · *feroz* ferocious
☐ **tiburones** sharks · *tiburón* *NM* shark
☐ **impresionante** impressive
☐ **he nadado** I have swum · *nadar* to swim
☐ **metros** meters · *metro* meter
☐ **oscuridad** darkness
☐ **horrendo** horrendous, horrifying, horrible
☐ **criatura** creature
☐ **filosos** sharp · *filoso* sharp
☐ **dientes** teeth · *diente* *NM* tooth
☐ **huyendo** fleeing · *huir* to flee
☐ **Corriente Australiana** Australian Current · *corriente* *NF* current · *australiano* Australian
☐ **costa** coast, shore
☐ **cuestión** matter
☐ **ejemplar** exemplary

🎬 Seagulls cry "Mine, mine, mine."

☐ **mine** *ENG* mine
☐ **ratas** rats · *rata* rat
☐ **alas** wings · *ala* wing
☐ **contentos** happy, content · *contento* happy, content
☐ **repite** *IMP* repeat · *repetir* to repeat
☐ **oí** I heard · *oír* to hear
☐ **bahía** bay
☐ **brillante** brilliant, shiny
☐ **no mencionen** *IMP* don't mention · *mencionar* to mention

🎬 Nemo approaches Gill inside the skull.

☐ **tiburoncín** *DIM* little shark · *tiburón* *NM* shark
☐ **filtro** filter
☐ **peligro** danger
☐ **nada vale** nothing is worth · *valer* to be worth

🎬 Nigel hits the window. The dentist pulls a tooth.

☐ **diente** *NM* tooth
☐ **correcto** correct
☐ **primer ministro** prime minister
☐ **extracción** extraction
☐ **ligamento periodontal** periodontal ligament
☐ **elevador** elevator
☐ **ha luchado** he has struggled · *luchar* to struggle
☐ **entero** entire, whole
☐ **buscándote** looking for you · *buscar* to look for

- □ **kilómetros** kilometers · *kilómetro* kilometer
- □ **ha combatido** he has battled · *combatir* to battle
- □ **medusas** jellyfish · *medusa* jellyfish
- □ **tipo** type, kind
- □ **pesca** fishing
- □ **deportiva** sport · *deportivo* ADJ sport
- □ **atún** NM tuna
- □ **trucha** trout
- □ **Marlin** ENG Marlin
- □ **tiburón** NM shark

🎬 Nigel holds up three feathers.

- □ **cuatro mil ochocientos** 4,800 · *cuatro* four · *mil* thousand · *ochocientos* eight hundred
- □ **nene** NM babe, baby boy, little one
- □ **buzo** scuba diver
- □ **gigantes** giant · *gigante* ADJ giant
- □ **capturaron** they captured · *capturar* to capture
- □ **persiguió** he pursued · *perseguir* to pursue
- □ **monstruo** monster
- □ **ató** he tied · *atar* to tie
- □ **demonio** demon
- □ **roca** rock
- □ **recompensa** reward
- □ **batalla** battle
- □ **tortugas marinas** sea turtles · *tortuga* turtle · *marino* ADJ sea
- □ **Corriente Australiana Oriental** East Australian Current · *corriente* NF current · *australiano* Australian · *oriental* east, eastern

🎬 Nemo carries a pebble toward the filter.

- □ **por delante** ahead, in front
- □ **punta** point, tip
- □ **cubierto** covered · *cubrir* to cover
- □ **gérmenes** germs · *germen* NM germ
- □ **agallas** gills · *agalla* gill

## 18 Off Ramp                                    4:25

### Phrases to Listen For

**menos de** less than
**antes de que** before
**tenemos que** we have to
**tendrá que** he will have to
**¿te refieres…?** are you referring to …?
**tenía que** it had to
**así que** so
**lo que** what
**en serio** really, truly
**me gustó** I liked (LIT it pleased me)
**hay que** it's necessary
**en línea recta** straight ahead, in a straight line
**¿qué tal si…?** what if …?

**pensando en** thinking about
**a ver** let's see
**por aquí** this way, here
**¿por qué?** why?
**claro que sí** of course
**en lugar de** in place of, instead of

### Names
Crush, Chiqui

🎬 Darla's picture is in the background. Gill gives instructions.

- □ **ensuciarse** to get dirty
- □ **oui** yes [FRENCH]
- □ **no limpies** IMP don't clean · *limpiar* to clean
- □ **resistiré** I will resist · *resistir* to resist
- □ **sucios** dirty · *sucio* dirty
- □ **den asco** SUBJ you disgust · *dar asco* to disgust, to make sick, to cause to gag
- □ **dentista** NMF dentist

🎬 Marlin and Dory continue with the sea turtles.

- □ **listos** ready · *listo* ready
- □ **salida** exit, off-ramp
- □ **turbulento vórtice del terror** swirling vortex of terror · *vórtice* NM vortex · *terror* NM terror
- □ **técnica** technique
- □ **apropiada** proper · *apropiado* proper
- □ **bienvenidos** welcome · *bienvenido* ADJ welcome
- □ **brinco** jump
- □ **pared** NF wall
- □ **corten** IMP cut · *cortar* to cut
- □ **giren** IMP spin · *girar* to spin
- □ **vuelta aguda** sharp turn · *vuelta* turn · *agudo* sharp
- □ **rueden** IMP roll · *rodar* to roll
- □ **rolen** IMP spin · *rolar* to spin, to roll
- □ **encantador** enchanting, charming
- □ **repite** IMP repeat · *repetir* to repeat
- □ **medusín** DIM jellyfish · *medusa* jellyfish

🎬 Marlin and Dory are outside the current.

- □ **divertido** fun · *divertirse* to have fun
- □ **tortugas** turtles · *tortuga* turtle
- □ **excelente** excellent
- □ **aletas** fins · *aleta* fin
- □ **relájate** IMP relax · *relajarse* to relax
- □ **¿qué edad tienes?** how old are you? · *tener* to have · *edad* age
- □ **línea recta** straight line
- □ **nadaremos** we will swim · *nadar* to swim
- □ **vaya** EXP wow
- □ **comienzo** I'm starting · *comenzar* to start, to begin
- □ **naranja** ADJ orange [COLOR]
- □ **adivinar** to guess

□ **sabelotodo** know-it-all
□ **franjas** stripes · *franja* stripe
□ **siguiente** next
□ **definitivamente** definitely
□ **mancha** stain
□ **nadamos** we are swimming · *nadar* to swim
□ **círculos** circles · *círculo* circle
□ **superficie** NF surface
□ **respira** IMP breathe · *respirar* to breathe
□ **hondo** deep

Dory and Marlin each take a deep breath.
□ **indicaciones** directions
□ **tontín** DIM silly one · *tonto* silly one, foolish one
□ **no te creas único** IMP don't think you're the only one · *creerse* to believe oneself to be
□ **turno** turn
□ **misterioso** mysterious
□ **tragará** he will swallow · *tragar* to swallow
□ **escupirá** he will spit out · *escupir* to spit, to spit out
□ **espinas** bones · *espina* bone [FISH]
□ **escena** scene

## 19  Dory Speaks Whale            1:41

**Phrases to Listen For**
**a ver** let's see
**tal vez** maybe, perhaps
**¿y qué tal si...?** and what if ...?
**¿qué tal?** what's going on?

**Name**
Pancho

Marlin and Dory approach a whale.
□ **cortés** courteous, polite
□ **importancia** importance
□ **ballena** whale
□ **cetáceo** whale, cetacean [LANGUAGE]

Dory speaks whale.
□ **ofendiste** you offended · *ofender* to offend
□ **dialecto** dialect
□ **infección** infection
□ **estomacal** ADJ stomach
□ **tiburones** sharks · *tiburón* NM shark
□ **cantan** they sing · *cantar* to sing
□ **charros** Mexican cowboys · *charro* Mexican cowboy
□ **orca** killer whale
□ **orcaleano** orcan [LANGUAGE]
□ **hambrienta** hungry · *hambriento* hungry
□ **ballenas** whales · *ballena* whale
□ **krill** krill

## 20  Algae            1:28

**Phrases to Listen For**
**tengo que** I have to
**antes de que** before
**Names**
Jacques, Flo, Barbara, Dave Reynolds

The fish tank is green inside. Gill talks to Nemo.
□ **sucio** dirty
□ **absolutamente** absolutely
□ **no limpiaras** SUBJ you don't clean · *limpiar* to clean
□ **perdonez-moi** pardon me [FRENCH]
□ **miren** IMP look · *mirar* to look at
□ **mugre** filth
□ **se acerca** it's getting close · *acercarse* to get close
□ **mueble** NM piece of furniture
□ **llaves** keys · *llave* NF key
□ **globo** balloon
□ **asqueroso** sickening
□ **voltea** IMP turn around · *voltear* to turn around
□ **guac** gross, sick

The dentist opens the top of the fish tank and looks inside.
□ **qué asco** how sickening, how revolting
□ **cita** appointment
□ **limpiar** to clean
□ **¿oíste...?** did you hear ...? · *oír* to hear
□ **limpios** clean · *limpio* clean
□ **nene** NM babe, baby boy, little one
□ **no me sorprendería** it would not surprise me · *sorprender* to surprise
□ **bahía** bay

## 21  Inside the Whale            4:49

**Phrases to Listen For**
**¿por qué?** why?
**tengo que** I have to
**claro que sí** of course
**no te rindas** IMP don't give up
**por supuesto** of course
**lo que** what
**ya basta** enough already
**claro que** of course

**Names**
Moby, Dorivio

The whale swims in the bay. Marlin tries to escape.
□ **ballena** whale
□ **cetáceo** whale, cetacean [LANGUAGE]
□ **edad** age

🎬 Marlin lies down inside the whale.
- **no te rindas** *IMP* don't give up · *rendirse* to give up, to surrender
- **simpática** kind, nice · *simpático* kind, nice
- **promesa** promise
- **impedir** to stop, to prevent, to impede
- **empeorar** to worsen
- **ruido** noise
- **desciende** it's coming down · *descender* to come down
- **está descendiendo** it's coming down · *descender* to come down
- **vacío** empty
- **nos coloquemos** *SUBJ* we put ourselves · *colocarse* to put ourselves
- **garganta** throat
- **capuchino helado** frozen cappuccino · *helado* ice-cold, frozen
- **saborearnos** to taste us, to savor us · *saborear* to taste, to savor
- **sabor** *NM* flavor, taste
- **almuerzo** brunch
- **cetáceo** whale, cetacean [LANGUAGE]
- **capaz** capable, able

## 22 Sydney Harbour 0:56

### Phrases to Listen For
**tenías razón** you were right
**hay que** it's necessary

### Name
Sydney

🎬 Marlin and Dory rise out of the water.
- **ojalá** if only, I wish
- **cetáceo** whale, cetacean [LANGUAGE]

## 23 The Aquascum 1:44

### Phrases to Listen For
**qué lindo** how beautiful
**falsa alarma** false alarm
**¿qué pasa?** what's going on?

### Name
Peach

🎬 Inside the fish tank, the starfish speaks.
- **amaneció** the sun rose, it dawned · *amanecer* to dawn
- **soleado** sunny
- **aseado** cleaned up
- **limpiaron** they cleaned · *limpiar* to clean
- **limpio** clean

- **instalarlo** to install it · *instalar* to install
- **anoche** last night
- **dormíamos** we slept · *dormir* to sleep

🎬 The starfish reads the filter manual.
- **Aquamugre** *NM* Aquascum (*LIT* filthy water)
- **filtro** filter
- **purificador** purifying
- **multiusos** multipurpose · *multiuso* multipurpose
- **autolimpiable** self-cleaning
- **libre** free
- **mantenimiento** maintenance
- **garantiza** it guarantees · *garantizar* to guarantee
- **extender** to extend
- **programado** programmed · *programar* to program
- **escanear** to scan
- **ambiente** *NM* environment
- **temperatura** temperature
- **veintiocho** twenty-eight
- **grados** degrees · *grado* degree
- **pe, hache** *NF* pH [LETTERS]
- **normal** normal
- **odio** hate
- **plan** *NM* plan
- **escape** *NM* escape
- **se arruinó** it was ruined · *arruinarse* to be ruined
- **ocúltate** *IMP* hide · *ocultarse* to hide

🎬 The door to the dentist's office opens.
- **falsa** false
- **alarma** alarm
- **nervios** *NMPL* nerves
- **soportan** they tolerate · *soportar* to tolerate
- **métanse** *IMP* put yourselves · *meterse* to put oneself
- **allí** there
- **rueda** *IMP* roll · *rodar* to roll
- **inclínate** *IMP* lean · *inclinarse* to lean
- **ventana** window
- **fea** ugly · *feo* ugly
- **panza** belly

## 24 Pelicans 2:42

### Phrases to Listen For
**para que** so that, in order to
**no se pelean** *IMP* don't fight
**a ver** let's see
**¿qué tienes?** what's wrong?, what's the matter?
**tengo que** I have to

### Names
Nigel, Gerald

▆ Darla opens the door. Marlin and Dory survey the boats in the harbor.

☐ **botes** boats · *bote* NM boat
☐ **familiar** familiar
☐ **energía** energy
☐ **cisne** NM swan
☐ **pelícano** pelican
☐ **me almuercen** SUBJ they eat me for brunch · *almorzar* to eat brunch, to eat lunch

▆ Nigel and his friends watch a pelican struggle on the dock.

☐ **apenas** barely, hardly
☐ **lengua** tongue
☐ **compadre** NM close friend
☐ **ha recorrido** he has covered · *recorrer* to cover [DISTANCE]

▆ Nigel talks in a low voice to Marlin and Dory on the dock.

☐ **brinquen** IMP jump · *brincar* to jump
☐ **boca** mouth
☐ **naranja** ADJ orange [COLOR]
☐ **aletita** DIM little fin · *aleta* fin
☐ **ajusten** IMP tighten · *ajustar* to tighten
☐ **cinturones** seat belts · *cinturón* NM seat belt
☐ **¡sujétense!** IMP hold on! · *sujetarse* to hold on

## 25 Darla! 3:16

**Phrases to Listen For**
¿qué tal...? what about ...?
¿qué pasa? what's happening?
lo que what
¡claro que sí! of course!
¡a la carga! charge!

**Names**
Darla, Nigel

▆ Darla taps the fish tank.

☐ **ruido** noise
☐ **estrellita** DIM little star · *estrella* star
☐ **revisarte** to check you · *revisar* to check, to examine
☐ **dientes** teeth · *diente* NM tooth
☐ **porcelana** porcelain
☐ **piraña** piranha
☐ **Amazonas** NM Amazon River
☐ **se ahogó** he drowned · *ahogarse* to drown
☐ **nena** babe, baby girl, little one · *nene* NM babe, baby boy, little one
☐ **¿qué es lo que pretende?** what is he trying to do? · *pretender* to try
☐ **tirar** to throw away

☐ **doble u, ce** NF W. C. [LETTERS]
☐ **basura** trash

▆ Nigel arrives with Marlin and Dory at the dentist's office.

☐ **dentista** NMF dentist
☐ **¡a la carga!** EXP charge!
☐ **no huyas** IMP don't flee · *huir* to flee
☐ **no te voy a hacer daño** I'm not going to hurt you · *hacer daño* to hurt

▆ Darla picks up the plastic bag with Nemo in it.

☐ **pececito** DIM little fish · *pez* NM fish
☐ **punta** peak
☐ **monte** NM mount, mountain
☐ **¿quiquirisquihaga?** what do you want me to do? [playful use of *qué quieres que haga*]
☐ **globo** balloon
☐ **aro de fuego** ring of fire · *aro* ring · *fuego* fire

▆ Gill lands on Darla's head.

☐ **animales** animals · *animal* NM animal
☐ **se han vuelto locos** they have gone crazy · *volverse loco* to go crazy
☐ **mando** I send · *mandar* to send
☐ **saludos** greetings · *saludo* greeting
☐ **drenaje** NM drainage
☐ **pececito** DIM little fish · *pez* NM fish

## 26 Good-bye Dory 2:31

**Phrases to Listen For**
lo lamento I'm sorry
¡no te vayas! IMP don't go!
por favor please
lo siento I'm sorry

▆ Nigel places Marlin and Dory in the bay.

☐ **memoria** memory
☐ **hogar** NM home
☐ **maná del cielo** manna from heaven
☐ **néctar** NM nectar
☐ **entendiste** you understood · *entender* to understand

## 27 Nemo and Dory 2:25

**Phrases to Listen For**
se me olvidó I forgot
¿qué tal si...? what if ...?

▆ Nemo encounters Dory.

☐ **disculpa** excuse (me) · *disculpar* to excuse
☐ **tranquila** EXP easy, take it easy, be calm

□ **testigo** witness
□ **naranja** *ADJ* orange [COLOR]
□ **azulita** *DIM* little blue one · *azul* blue

🎬 Dory lifts the crab out of the water.

□ **zona** zone, area
□ **pesca** fishing
□ **no estorbes** *IMP* don't block, stay out of the way · *estorbar* to block, to be in the way
□ **papi** *NM* daddy
□ **den vuelta** *IMP* turn around · *dar vuelta* to turn around
□ **en sentido contrario** against traffic, wrong way · *sentido* way · *contrario* opposite

## 28 Fishing Net                          2:32

### Phrases to Listen For
**otra vez** again
**hay que** it's necessary
**hacia abajo** downward
**lo que** what

🎬 A net scoops up the fish.

□ **se acerca** it's getting close · *acercarse* to get close
□ **auxilio** help
□ **sáquennos** *IMP* get us out · *sacar* to take out, to remove
□ **sal** *IMP* get out · *salir* to leave, to get out
□ **nadaremos** we will swim · *nadar* to swim
□ **fondo** bottom

## 29 Reunion                               1:25

### Phrases to Listen For
**tiene ciento cincuenta años** he is one hundred fifty years old (*LIT* he has one hundred fifty years)
**para que** so that

### Name
Carlos

🎬 Nemo is lying on the sand groaning.

□ **te cuida** he'll take care of you (*LIT* he takes care of you) · *cuidar* to care for, to take care of
□ **no te odio** I don't hate you · *odiar* to hate
□ **adivina** *IMP* guess · *adivinar* to guess
□ **tortugas** turtles · *tortuga* turtle
□ **plancton** *NM* plankton
□ **cien** one hundred
□ **cruzaría** I would cross · *cruzar* to cross

## 30 Back on the Reef                      1:51

### Phrases to Listen For
**claro que no** of course not
**a bordo** on board, aboard
**estudiante de intercambio** exchange student
**lo que** what
**a salvo** safe
**próxima parada** next stop
**hasta luego** see you later (*LIT* until later)
**buen día** good day

### Names
Martín, Timón

🎬 Marlin wakes up Nemo.

□ **a bordo** on board
□ **exploradores** explorers · *explorador* explorer

🎬 Marlin tells a joke to Bob, Ted, and Bill.

□ **pepino de mar** sea cucumber · *pepino* cucumber · *mar NM* sea
□ **molusco** mollusk
□ **anémona** anemone
□ **anónima** anonymous · *anónimo* anonymous

🎬 A sea turtle climbs aboard Mr. Ray.

□ **estudiante de intercambio** exchange student · *estudiante NMF* student · *intercambio* exchange
□ **ce, a, o [CAO]** *NF* CAO [LETTERS], *Corriente Australiana Oriental* East Australian Current · *corriente NF* current · *australiano* Australian · *oriental* east, eastern
□ **suave** smooth, cool
□ **exacto** exactly

🎬 Bruce the shark approaches Marlin and his friends.

□ **no se alarmen** *IMP* don't be alarmed · *alarmarse* to be alarmed
□ **compañero** companion
□ **a salvo** safe
□ **entrante** next
□ **programa** *NM* program
□ **comida** food

🎬 Mr. Ray swims away with his students.

□ **sujétense** *IMP* hold on · *sujetarse* to hold on
□ **parada** stop
□ **sabiduría** wisdom
□ **diviértete** *IMP* have fun · *divertirse* to have fun
□ **raya** ray [ANIMAL]

🎬 Nemo hugs his father.

□ **aventura** adventure

## 31 Tank Escape 0:42

### Phrases to Listen For

**garantía de por vida** lifetime guarantee
**tengo que** I have to
**y ahora, ¿qué?** and now what?

### Names

Barbara, Peach

🎬 The dentist examines the filter.

☐ **garantía** guarantee
☐ **se descompone** it breaks down ·
  *descomponerse* to break down

☐ **limpiar** to clean
☐ **bolsas** bags · *bolsa* bag

🎬 Gill and the other fish are in plastic bags in the bay, encouraging Peach.

☐ **¡ánimo!** *EXP* come on!, get up!, get going!
☐ **rueda** *IMP* roll · *rodar* to roll
☐ **luz roja** red light · *luz NF* light · *rojo* red
☐ **corta** short · *corto* short

## 32 End Credits 7:28

🎬 End credits.

# The Incredibles

**¡Vaya! Creo que hoy papá ha tenido un gran progreso.**
*Well, I think Dad has made some excellent progress today.*

| | |
|---|---|
| GENRE | Adventure/Animation |
| YEAR | 2004 |
| DIRECTOR | Brad Bird |
| CAST | Victor Trujillo, Consuelo Duval, Leyla Rangel, Memo Aponte, Jr. |
| STUDIO | Pixar |

An out-of-shape superhero and family man, Mr. Incredible, now relegated to the unexciting routine of daily life in suburbia, longs for the adventure of days gone by. When a stunning blonde offers him the chance to return to his life of glory, he jumps at the opportunity, and the action doesn't let up. As his daughter Violet says, "Mom and Dad's lives could be in jeopardy. Or worse, their marriage." This film is ranked Advanced because of the rapid pace of the dialogue, which will help develop your ability to understand fast-paced conversational Spanish.

## BASIC VOCABULARY

### Names

Bob, Dash, Parr, Violeta, Helen, Robert, Elastigirl, Síndrome

### Nouns

☐ **control** NM control · *Oye, escucha, si te refieres a lo que pasó en la base de detención, ya tenía bajo control todo.* Listen, listen, if you are referring to what happened at the containment unit, I already had everything under control.

☐ **héroe** NM hero · *Echas de menos tu vida de héroe.* You miss your life as a hero.

☐ **identidad** identity · *Entiende, no deben saber nuestra identidad.* Understand, they must not know our identity.

☐ **isla** island · *Tuvimos que evacuar a todo el personal de la isla por seguridad.* We had to evacuate all personnel from the island for safety reasons.

☐ **Mister Increíble** Mr. Incredible · *mister* Mr. · *increíble* incredible · *Dígame, Mister Incréible, ¿tiene una identidad secreta?* Tell me, Mr. Incredible, do you have a secret identity?

### Other

☐ **a salvo** safe · *Le aseguro que su secreto está a salvo.* I assure you that your secret is safe.

☐ **divertido** fun · *divertirse* to have fun · *Ay, no creas que no es divertido, pero voy a recorrer el lugar.* Ay, don't think that this isn't fun, but I'm going to check out the place.

☐ **respecto a** with respect to · *Dash, ¿debes hablar de algo con tu padre respecto a la escuela?* Dash, should you talk about something with your father with respect to school?

☐ **súper** super · *Otros niños no poseen súper poderes.* Other children don't possess superpowers.

---

## 1 | Golden Age

9:15

### Phrases to Listen For

**no se preocupe** IMP don't worry
**todo el tiempo** all the time
**claro que** of course
**¿qué te pasa?** what's up with you?, what are you thinking?
**ir de compras** to go shopping
**no importa** it doesn't matter
**a salvo** safe
**por favor** please
**¿cómo te llamas?** what's your name?
**me llamo** my name is
**no te preocupes** IMP don't worry

**tal vez** maybe, perhaps
**no hace falta** it's not necessary
**algún día** someday
**plan de vuelo** flight plan
**todo el día** all day
**no me digas** IMP don't tell me
**no tienes nada que ver conmigo** you have nothing to do with me

### Names

Incrediboy, Buddy, Frozono, Bomb Voyage, Skippy, Rechinidos

🎬 A film reel is scratching. Mr. Incredible fiddles with his microphone.

☐ **revisa** IMP check · *revisar* to check
☐ **cámara** camera
☐ **nivel** NM level
☐ **panel** NM panel
☐ **encendido** turned on · *encender* to turn on, to switch on
☐ **paredes** walls · *pared* NF wall
☐ **encender** to turn on, to switch on
☐ **identidad secreta** secret identity
☐ **superhéroe** NM superhero
☐ **presión** pressure

🎬 Elastigirl answers questions.

☐ **supermercado** supermarket
☐ **ir de compras** to go shopping

🎬 Frozone is interviewed.

☐ **relación** relationship
☐ **se formaliza** it is formalized, it is strengthened · *formalizar* to formalize, to strengthen
☐ **manejas** you manage · *manejar* to manage
☐ **alter ego** alter ego
☐ **mega** mega
☐ **ultra** ultra

🎬 Mr. Incredible continues his interview.

☐ **peligro** danger
☐ **sirviente** NM servant
☐ **limpiar** to clean
☐ **histérica** hysterical · *histérico* hysterical
☐ **simple** simple

🎬 Mr. Incredible is driving.

☐ **interrumpimos** we interrupt · *interrumpir* to interrupt
☐ **noticia** news item
☐ **peligrosa** dangerous · *peligroso* dangerous
☐ **persecución** pursuit
☐ **armados** armed · *armado* armed · *armarse* to arm oneself
☐ **avenida** avenue

- **San Pablo**  San Pablo, St. Paul
- **dirección**  direction
- **norte** *NM*  north

🎬 A woman steps into the street to stop Mr. Incredible.

- **madame**  madam, ma'am [FRENCH]
- **rechinidos**  squeaks · *rechinido* squeak
- **sugiero**  I suggest · *sugerir* to suggest

🎬 Two policemen thank Mr. Incredible.

- **unidades**  units · *unidad* unit
- **robo**  robbery
- **autobús** *NM*  bus
- **ka** *NF*  K [LETTER]
- **acudan** *IMP*  go · *acudir* to go
- **inmediatamente**  immediately

🎬 Buddy is sitting in Mr. Incredible's car.

- **despegue** *NM*  take-off [AIRCRAFT]
- **club** *NM*  club
- **admiradores**  fans · *admirador* fans, admirers
- **atento**  attentive
- **pose** *IMP*  pose · *posar* to pose
- **fotos**  photos · *foto NF* photograph · *fotografía* photograph
- **papelito** *DIM*  little paper · *papel NM* paper
- **firmé**  I signed · *firmar* to sign
- **por entrenarme**  about training me, about teaching me · *entrenar* to train, to teach
- **maniobras**  moves, maneuvers · *maniobra* move, maneuver
- **expresiones**  expressions · *expresión* expression
- **favoritas**  favorites · *favorito* favorite

🎬 A thief is going through a woman's purse.

- **contenido**  contents
- **bolso**  purse
- **mente** *NF*  mind
- **lo atrapé**  I caught him · *atrapar* to catch, to capture, to trap
- **lo atrapaste**  you caught him · *atrapar* to catch, to capture, to trap
- **apoyo**  help, support
- **trato**  deal
- **equitativo**  fair
- **flexible**  flexible
- **me comprometí**  I made a commitment, I have an appointment, I have a date · *comprometerse* to make a commitment, to have an appointment, to have a date, to be committed
- **recogen**  they collect · *recoger* to collect, to pick up, to gather
- **normalmente**  normally
- **basura**  trash, garbage

🎬 A helicopter flies overhead. Frozone follows.

- **monsieur**  sir [FRENCH]

🎬 Buddy joins Mr. Incredible as he detains Bomb Voyage.

- **aerobotas**  aeroboots, rocket boots · *aerobota* aeroboot, rocket boot
- **honesto**  honest
- **finalmente**  finally
- **descubrí**  I discovered · *descubrir* to discover
- **protegido**  protégé
- **oficialmente**  officially
- **inventé**  I invented · *inventar* to invent
- **vuelas**  you fly · *volar* to fly
- **bomba**  bomb
- **afectas**  you're affecting · *afectar* to affect
- **plan de vuelo**  flight plan · *plan NM* plan · *vuelo* flight
- **aterrizar**  to land [AIRCRAFT]
- **maquiné**  I plotted · *maquinar* to plot
- **capa**  cape

🎬 Mr. Incredible escorts Buddy to the police.

- **de vuelta**  back · *volver* to go back, to return
- **no cometas** *IMP*  don't commit · *cometer* to commit
- **brincar**  to jump
- **paramédicos**  paramedics · *paramédico* paramedic
- **hospital** *NM*  hospital
- **explosión**  explosion
- **edificio**  building
- **bóveda**  vault
- **perímetro**  perimeter
- **huyó**  he got away, he fled · *huir* to get away, to flee
- **ocasionó**  he caused · *ocasionar* to cause, to bring about
- **no sufran** *IMP*  don't worry, don't trouble yourselves (*LIT* don't suffer) · *sufrir* to suffer

## 2 Weddings & Lawsuits 2:18

### Phrases to Listen For

**¿qué tal estoy?**  how do I look?
**en realidad**  really
**hay que**  it's necessary
**hasta que la muerte los separe** *SUBJ*  until death do you part (*LIT* until death separates you)
**no importa lo que pase** *SUBJ*  no matter what happens
**¿qué ha de pasar?**  what could happen?
**todo el mundo**  everyone

**para que** for
**a cambio de** in exchange for

## Name

Oliverio Sanito

🎬 Mr. Incredible enters the church.

☐ **galán** *NM* gallant man, handsome gentleman
☐ **máscara** mask
☐ **legítima** legitimate, lawful · *legítimo* legitimate, lawful
☐ **preguntaste** you asked · *preguntar* to ask
☐ **olvidarías** you would forget · *olvidar* to forget
☐ **estabas bromeando** you were joking · *bromear* to joke
☐ **flexible** flexible
☐ **separe** *SUBJ* it separates · *separar* to separate
☐ **declaro** I declare · *declarar* to declare
☐ **pareja** couple
☐ **marido** husband
☐ **superhéroes** superheroes · *superhéroe NM* superhero

🎬 Newspapers spiral onto the screen.

☐ **sorprendente** surprising
☐ **suceso** event, occurrence
☐ **superhéroe** *NM* superhero
☐ **demandado** sued · *demandar* to sue
☐ **aparentemente** apparently
☐ **demandante** *NMF* plaintiff in a lawsuit
☐ **frustrado** frustrated · *frustrar* to frustrate
☐ **intento** attempt, try
☐ **suicidio** suicide
☐ **cargos** charges · *cargo* charge
☐ **afamado** famed · *afamar* to be famous, to be well known
☐ **Suprema Corte de Justicia** Supreme Court · *justicia* justice

🎬 A lawyer and his client are being interviewed.

☐ **cliente** *NMF* client
☐ **lesión** wound, injury
☐ **acciones** actions · *acción* action
☐ **muchísimo** very much
☐ **dolor** *NM* pain
☐ **arruinaste** you ruined · *arruinar* to ruin
☐ **pedazo** piece
☐ **comentarios** comments · *comentario* comment
☐ **demanda** lawsuit

🎬 A train hangs suspended over a destroyed bridge.

☐ **víctimas** victims · *víctima* victim
☐ **accidente** *NM* accident
☐ **derrotas** defeats · *derrota* defeat
☐ **cuesta** it costs · *costar* to cost
☐ **millones** millions · *millón NM* million

☐ **gobierno** government
☐ **docenas** dozens · *docena* dozen
☐ **demandas** lawsuits · *demanda* lawsuit
☐ **identidad secreta** secret identity

🎬 Several people carry protest signs with messages like "Down with Supers."

☐ **tremenda** tremendous · *tremendo* tremendous
☐ **presión** pressure
☐ **pública** public · *público ADJ* public
☐ **aplastante** crushing
☐ **carga** charge, cost
☐ **financiera** financial · *financiero* financial
☐ **serie** *NF* series
☐ **discretamente** discreetly
☐ **inició** it began, it started · *iniciar* to begin, to start
☐ **programa** *NM* program
☐ **reubicación** relocation

🎬 A newspaper headline reads "Government Hides Heroes."

☐ **amnistía** amnesty
☐ **responsabilidad** responsibility
☐ **pasadas** past · *pasado ADJ* past
☐ **promesa** promise
☐ **actividades** activities · *actividad* activity
☐ **heroicas** heroic · *heroico* heroic

🎬 Crowds of people walk the streets.

☐ **ciudadanos** citizens · *ciudadano* citizen
☐ **comunes** common · *común* common
☐ **héroes** heroes · *héroe NM* hero
☐ **discreta** discreet · *discreto* discreet
☐ **anónimamente** anonymously

## 3 15 Years & 50 Pounds                    1:58

### Phrases to Listen For

**¿por qué?** why?
**a la vez** at a time
**tengo que** I have to
**hasta la noche** see you tonight (*LIT* until the night)
**es que** it's just that, the reason is that

### Names

Angustias, Norma Wilcox, Don Tragedias, Doña Penas, Seguritas, Señor Rabia

🎬 "Denied" is being stamped on a document. Mr. Incredible is at his desk talking to an elderly woman.

☐ **rechazada** rejected, denied · *rechazado* rejected, denied · *rechazar* to reject, to deny

□ **reclamación** complaint
□ **cobertura** coverage
□ **amplia** full
□ **angustias** anguish, distress · *angustia* anguish, distress
□ **se especifica** it is specified · *especificarse* to specify
□ **párrafo** paragraph
□ **diecisiete** seventeen
□ **claramente** clearly

🎬 Mr. Incredible answers the telephone. Elastigirl is calling from home.

□ **reclamaciones** complaints · *reclamación* complaint
□ **celebración** celebration
□ **memorable** memorable
□ **ocasión** occasion
□ **mudanza** move [RESIDENCE]
□ **noticia** news item
□ **desempaqué** I unpacked · *desempacar* to unpack
□ **caja** box
□ **guardamos** we kept · *guardar* to keep, to save
□ **basura** trash, garbage
□ **cliente** *NMF* client, customer
□ **póliza** policy

🎬 Mr. Incredible hangs up the telephone and turns his attention to the elderly lady seated across from him.

□ **pensión** pension, retirement income
□ **fija** fixed · *fijo* fixed
□ **copia** copy
□ **doble u** *NF* W [LETTER]
□ **i** *NF* I [LETTER]
□ **ele** *NF* L [LETTER]
□ **ce** *NF* C [LETTER]
□ **o** *NF* O [LETTER]
□ **equis** *NF* X [LETTER]
□ **tercer** third
□ **piso** floor
□ **aconsejo** I advise · *aconsejar* to advise, to counsel
□ **completar** to complete
□ **hoja** page
□ **veintinueve** twenty-nine
□ **jurídico** legal, legal department
□ **respondan** *SUBJ* they respond · *responder* to respond
□ **apoyarla** to help you · *apoyar* to help
□ **indicado** correct, appropriate
□ **desesperada** desperate · *desesperado* desperate

□ **finja** *IMP* fake · *fingir* to fake
□ **desesperación** desperation

🎬 The boss enters Mr. Incredible's office.

□ **autorizaste** you authorized · *autorizar* to authorize
□ **rabia** anger
□ **cubre** it covers · *cubrir* to cover
□ **robo** robbery
□ **coberturas** coverage · *cobertura* coverage
□ **cheques** checks · *cheque NM* check
□ **tragedias** tragedies · *tragedia* tragedy
□ **penas** hardships · *pena* hardship, grief
□ **descanso** rest, break

## 4  After School                                  3:37

### Phrases to Listen For
**¿qué es lo que pasa?** what's happening?
**se burla de mí** he makes fun of me
**creo que no** I don't think so
**no lo sé** I don't know
**lo que** what
**no lo creo** I don't think so, I don't believe it
**otra vez** again
**se ve** you can see it, it shows (*LIT* it is seen)
**hay que** it's necessary
**de verdad** really
**todo el mundo** everyone
**se fijó en mí** he noticed me, he paid attention to me
**¿qué pasa?** what's going on?

### Names
Bernie, Dashiell Robert Parr, Tony Rydinger

🎬 Elastigirl enters the principal's office.

□ **aprecio** I appreciate · *apreciar* to appreciate
□ **influencia** influence
□ **se burla de** he makes fun of · *burlarse de* to make fun of
□ **enfrente de** in front of
□ **chinches** thumbtacks · *chinche NF* thumbtack
□ **asiento** seat
□ **cámara** camera
□ **atrapé** I caught · *atrapar* to catch, to trap
□ **silla** chair
□ **chinche** *NF* thumbtack
□ **coincidencia** coincidence
□ **no me sermonee** *IMP* don't preach to me, don't lecture me · *sermonear* to preach, to lecture
□ **ratita** *DIM* little rat · *rata* rat
□ **delincuente** *NMF* delinquent
□ **molestia** bother, inconvenience

□ **culpable** guilty
□ **carita** *DIM* little face · *cara* face
□ **satisfacción** satisfaction

🎬 Elastigirl and Dash ride in the car.

□ **tercera** third · *tercero* third
□ **mandan** they send · *mandar* to send
□ **dirección** main office, principal's office
□ **solución** solution
□ **constructiva** constructive · *constructivo* constructive
□ **deportes** sports · *deporte* *NM* sport
□ **despacio** slowly
□ **competitivo** competitive
□ **presumido** vain · *presumir* to show off
□ **desafíe** *SUBJ* he challenges · *desafiar* to challenge
□ **integrarnos** for us to become integrated · *integrarse* to integrate
□ **sociedad** society
□ **actuar** to act
□ **no deben avergonzarnos** we shouldn't be ashamed (*LIT* they shouldn't make us feel ashamed) · *avergonzar* to shame, to make (someone) feel ashamed

🎬 Violet waits outside the school building.

□ **rana** frog
□ **pantalón** *NM* pair of pants
□ **risa** laughter
□ **hamburguesas** hamburgers · *hamburguesa* hamburger
□ **cargo** I carry · *cargar* to carry
□ **fútbol** *NM* football
□ **nadar** to swim
□ **se fijó** he noticed · *fijarse* to notice

🎬 Mr. Incredible parks in the driveway.

□ **estacionamiento** driveway
□ **rayos** *INT* jeepers, heck

## 5  Family Dinner                                3:36

### Phrases to Listen For

otra vez  again
de verdad  really
qué gusto  how nice
aun así  even so
hay que  it's necessary
para que  in order to
¿qué tal la escuela?  how's school?
no tengo hambre  I'm not hungry
¿de qué tienes hambre?  what are you hungry for?
¡ya basta!  enough already!
tienen que ir  you have to go

saluda a Nena de mi parte  say hello to Nena for me
claro que sí  of course
buenas noches  good night

### Names

Tony Rydinger, Simon J. Paladino, Lucio, Nena

🎬 The Parr family eats dinner.

□ **caras** faces · *cara* face
□ **raras** strange · *raro* strange
□ **necesario** necessary
□ **mesa** table
□ **bocados** bites of food · *bocado* bite of food
□ **carnívoro** carnivore
□ **cortar** to cut
□ **carne** *NF* meat
□ **rana** frog
□ **disecamos** we dissected · *disecar* to dissect
□ **director** *NM* principal
□ **citó** he summoned · *citar* to summon
□ **silla** chair
□ **chinche** *NF* thumbtack
□ **video** video
□ **no lo notaron** they didn't notice it · *notar* to notice
□ **debiste haber volado** you must have flown · *volar* to fly
□ **velocidad** velocity, speed
□ **no se trata** it's not about · *tratarse* to be about
□ **incitarlo** to incite him, to encourage him · *incitar* to incite, to encourage negative behavior
□ **no lo incito** I'm not inciting him, I'm not encouraging him · *incitar* to incite, to encourage negative behavior

🎬 Cutting Dash's meat, Mr. Incredible breaks the plate.

□ **demonios** *INT* darn, rats (*LIT* demons) · *demonio* demon
□ **plato** plate
□ **reportar** to report
□ **comida** food
□ **no tengo hambre** I'm not hungry · *tener hambre* to be hungry (*LIT* to have hunger)
□ **filete** *NM* steak
□ **recalentado** leftovers (*LIT* reheated) · *recalentar* to reheat
□ **pasta** pasta

🎬 Dash speaks up to tease Violet.

□ **cara** face
□ **insecto** insect

□ **no se grita** you're not supposed to shout, one doesn't shout · *gritar* to shout

□ **obedezcan** *IMP* obey · *obedecer* to obey

🎬 Violet attacks Dash.

□ **freír** to fry

□ **cargas de fuerza** force fields · *carga de fuerza* force field

🎬 Mr. Incredible opens the newspaper and reads.

□ **defensor** *NM* defense attorney

□ **derechos** rights · *derecho* right

□ **superhéroes** superheroes · *superhéroe NM* superhero

□ **ha desaparecido** he has disappeared · *desaparecer* to disappear

□ **telescopio** telescope

🎬 Mr. Incredible's reading is interrupted as Elastigirl calls to him from the dining room table.

□ **involucrarte** to get yourself involved · *involucrarse* to get involved, to become involved

□ **intervengas** *SUBJ* you intervene · *intervenir* to intervene

□ **intervenga** *SUBJ* I intervene · *intervenir* to intervene

□ **intervengo** I intervene · *intervenir* to intervene

🎬 The doorbell rings. Dash answers the door.

□ **torpedo** torpedo

□ **hielo darte la bienvenida** ice of you to drop by [a play on the standard greeting "nice of you to drop by" (*quiero darte la bienvenida* I want to welcome you)] · *hielo* ice · *bienvenida* welcome

□ **se deshace** it shatters · *deshacerse* to shatter

□ **miércoles** *NM* Wednesday

□ **bolos** *NMPL* bowling

□ **saluda** *IMP* say hello, greet · *saludar* to say hello, to greet

🎬 Mr. Incredible and Frozone leave the house. Elastigirl and their children continue talking at the dinner table.

□ **no creas** *IMP* don't think, don't believe · *creer* to think, to believe

□ **visita** visit

□ **oficina** office

□ **discutir** to discuss

□ **asuntito** *DIM* little matter · *asunto* matter

□ **no poseen** they don't possess · *poseer* to possess

□ **normal** normal

□ **ir al baño** to go to the bathroom · *baño* bathroom

## 6 | 2 Ex-Supers 6:09

### Phrases to Listen For

**así que** so

**de veras** really, truly

**¿qué te parece?** what do you think?, how about …?

**lo que** what

**por ejemplo** for example

**¿hace cuánto?** how long since?

**es que** the reason is, it's just that

**me dio sed** I'm thirsty

**esto no se hace ya** no more of that

**más tarde** later

**al respecto** about that

**de todas formas** in any case, in any event

**lo que pasa** what's happening

**está bien** that's fine

**lo siento** I'm sorry

**no pasa nada** nothing's going on, nothing is happening

**buenas noches** good night

### Names

Norma, Municiberg, Frozono

🎬 Mr. Incredible and Frozone listen to a police scanner in a car.

□ **rayo** ray, bolt

□ **sepultan** they bury · *sepultar* to bury

□ **varón** *NM* man

□ **fontanero** plumber

□ **monologar** to deliver a monologue, to talk at length

□ **inicia** he begins, he starts · *iniciar* to begin, to start

□ **discurso** speech

□ **débil** weak

□ **comparado con** compared with · *comparar* to compare

□ **inevitable** unavoidable, inevitable

□ **derrota** defeat

□ **patético** pathetic

□ **plato** plate

□ **veintitrés** twenty-three

□ **cincuenta y seis** fifty-six

□ **robo** robbery

□ **qué desgracia** how unfortunate

□ **agarrar** to grab

□ **rufián** *NM* ruffian

□ **sincero** sincere, frank

□ **bolos** *NMPL* bowling

□ **hay que darle un giro a las cosas** you have to shake things up, just to shake things up · *hay que* you have to, it's necessary · *giro* complete turn · *cosa* thing

🎬 Mirage observes Mr. Incredible and Frozone from another car.

☐ **gordo** fat one
☐ **charlan** they chat, they are chatting · *charlar* to chat

🎬 Mr. Incredible and Frozone continue their discussion in the car.

☐ **protegemos** we protect · *proteger* to protect
☐ **invitación** invitation
☐ **ejemplo** example
☐ **telescopio** telescope
☐ **periódico** newspaper
☐ **adaptarse** adapting oneself · *adaptarse* to adapt oneself
☐ **sociedad** society
☐ **costó** it cost, it was hard, it was difficult · *costar* to cost, to be hard, to be difficult
☐ **arriesgado** risky · *arriesgar* to risk
☐ **al principio** in the beginning, at first
☐ **unidades** units · *unidad* unit
☐ **disponibles** available · *disponible* available
☐ **reporte** NM report
☐ **cuarta** fourth · *cuarto* fourth

🎬 Mr. Incredible and Frozone are inside a burning building.

☐ **apagarlo** to turn it off · *apagar* to turn off, to switch off
☐ **hielo** ice
☐ **denso** dense, hard
☐ **se evapora** it evaporates · *evaporarse* to evaporate
☐ **calor** NM heat
☐ **me deshidraté** I'm dehydrated (LIT I became dehydrated) · *deshidratarse* to become dehydrated
☐ **aire** NM air
☐ **excusa** excuse
☐ **músculos** muscles · *músculo* muscle
☐ **atravesar** to go across, to move through
☐ **estructura** structure
☐ **edificio** building
☐ **se debilita** it's getting weak, it's weakening · *debilitarse* to weaken
☐ **nos va a caer encima** it's going to fall on top of us · *caer* to fall · *encima* on top of
☐ **se calienta** it's getting hot · *calentarse* to get hot

🎬 Mr. Incredible and Frozone escape to the next building before the burning building collapses.

☐ **confundirán** they will confuse · *confundir* to confuse
☐ **maleantes** criminals · *maleante* NMF criminal

☐ **incompetentes** incompetent · *incompetente* ADJ incompetent

🎬 A police officer points his gun at Mr. Incredible and Frozone.

☐ **me dio sed** I'm thirsty, it made me thirsty · *dar sed* to make one feel thirsty · *sed* thirst

🎬 Mirage continues her surveillance.

☐ **verifica** IMP verify · *verificar* to verify
☐ **sujetos** subjects, targets, persons · *sujeto* subject, target [PERSON], person

🎬 Mr. Incredible enters his house and takes a bite of cake.

☐ **once** eleven
☐ **asumí** I assumed · *asumir* to assume
☐ **vendrías** you would come · *venir* to come
☐ **si hubieras vuelto** SUBJ if you had come back · *volver* to come back, to return

🎬 Elastigirl stands up and finds rubble on Mr. Incredible's jacket.

☐ **escombro** debris, rubble
☐ **entrenar** to train
☐ **relajante** relaxing
☐ **opino** I think, I believe · *opinar* to think, to believe, to give an opinion
☐ **tiraste** you tore down, you knocked down · *tirar* to tear down, to knock down
☐ **se incendiaba** it was burning, it was burning down · *incendiarse* to be burning, to burn down
☐ **se dañó** it got damaged · *dañarse* to get damaged
☐ **créelo** IMP believe it · *creer* to believe
☐ **radio** radio
☐ **brindé** I offered · *brindar* to offer
☐ **servicio** service
☐ **público** ADJ public
☐ **en riesgo** at risk · *riesgo* risk
☐ **revivas** SUBJ you relive · *revivir* to relive
☐ **gloria** glory
☐ **revivirlos** reliving them · *revivir* to relive
☐ **negar** to deny
☐ **graduación** graduation
☐ **promovido** promoted · *promover* to promote
☐ **grado** grade
☐ **quinto** fifth
☐ **ceremonia** ceremony
☐ **sicótico** psychotic
☐ **excusas** excuses · *excusa* excuse
☐ **celebrar** to celebrate
☐ **mediocridad** mediocrity
☐ **genuinamente** genuinely

- **excepcional** exceptional
- **compita** SUBJ he competes · *competir* to compete
- **practique** SUBJ he practices · *practicar* to practice
- **deportes** sports · *deporte* NM sport
- **no me conviertas** IMP don't turn me · *convertir* to turn (one thing into another), to change, to convert
- **impresionante** impressive

🎬 Mr. Incredible and Elastigirl stop arguing when they hear Dash and Violet rustling.

- **sal** IMP get out, go out · *salir* to leave, to get out, to go out
- **afuera** outside, out
- **discusión** discussion
- **ruidosa** noisy · *ruidoso* noisy
- **intransigencia** intransigence, pigheadedness
- **maldad** evil

## 7 A Super Defeated          3:48

### Phrases to Listen For
**¿por qué?** why?
**antes de** before
**por qué** why
**de acuerdo** agreed
**en primer lugar** in the first place
**qué bueno** that's great
**de inmediato** immediately
**¿cómo está?** how is he?
**en problemas** in trouble
**tenía que hacer algo** I had to do something
**hay que** it's necessary
**para que** so that
**a partir de** starting

### Names
Seguritas, Rick, Señor Rabia

🎬 Mr. Incredible types on his computer.

- **solicitud** NF application
- **pago** payment
- **reclamación** complaint
- **rabia** anger
- **oficina** office
- **entregar** to give, to deliver, to turn in
- **reportes** reports · *reporte* NM report
- **piso** floor

🎬 Mr. Incredible sits down across from his boss.

- **infeliz** unhappy
- **específico** specific

- **clientes** clients, customers · *cliente* NMF client, customer
- **quejas** complaints · *queja* complaint
- **manejar** to manage
- **funcionamiento** operations
- **interno** internal
- **expertos** experts · *experto* expert
- **desafían** they challenge · *desafiar* to challenge
- **excusas** excuses · *excusa* excuse
- **evaden** they avoid · *evadir* to avoid
- **obstáculos** obstacles · *obstáculo* obstacle
- **han penetrado** they have penetrated · *penetrar* to penetrate
- **burocracia** bureaucracy
- **ilegal** illegal
- **apoyo** support, help, assistance
- **requiere** it requires · *requerir* to require
- **conteste** SUBJ I answer · *contestar* to answer
- **accionistas** shareholders, stockholders · *accionista* shareholder, stockholder

🎬 The boss adjusts a piece of paper on his desk.

- **enorme** enormous
- **reloj** NM clock
- **engranes** cogs, gear teeth · *engrane* NM cog, gear tooth
- **se ajustan** they fit together · *ajustarse* to fit together, to fit
- **limpiarse** to be cleaned
- **lubricarse** to be lubricated
- **ajustarse** to be adjusted
- **relojes** clocks · *reloj* NM clock
- **máquinas** machines · *máquina* machine
- **finas** fine, high quality, elegant · *fino* fine, high quality, elegant
- **cooperan** they cooperate, they work together · *cooperar* to cooperate, to work together
- **diseño** design
- **metafórico** metaphorical

🎬 Mr. Incredible witnesses a robbery taking place outside the window.

- **corporativos** corporate · *corporativo* corporate
- **estoy hablándote** I am speaking to you · *hablar* to speak
- **tema** NM theme, subject
- **discuto** I discuss, I am discussing · *discutir* to discuss
- **actitud** NF attitude
- **enseguida** right away
- **detente** IMP stop · *detenerse* to stop
- **despido** I dismiss, I fire · *despedir* to dismiss, to fire
- **cierra** IMP close · *cerrar* to close

🎬 Mr. Incredible closes the door.

☐ **ladrón** NM thief

☐ **huye** he's fleeing, he's getting away · *huir* to flee, to get away

🎬 The boss is lying in a hospital bed in traction. Mr. Incredible walks with Rick.

☐ **sala de operaciones** operating room · *sala* room · *operación* operation

☐ **de inmediato** immediately

☐ **sanará** he will heal · *sanar* to heal

☐ **me despidieron** they fired me, they dismissed me · *despedir* to fire, to dismiss

☐ **dineral** fortune, great deal of money

☐ **contribuyentes** contributors · *contribuyente* NMF contributor

☐ **averías** damages · *avería* damage

☐ **deshacer** to undo

☐ **memorias** memories · *memoria* memory

☐ **reubicar** to relocate

☐ **plata** money

☐ **se aprecia** it is appreciated · *apreciar* to appreciate

☐ **gloria** glory

☐ **a partir de** starting, beginning

☐ **reubico** I'll relocate (LIT I relocate) · *reubicar* to relocate

☐ **glorias** glories · *gloria* glory

## 8 Help Wanted 4:12

### Phrases to Listen For

**a salvo** safe
**ponga atención** IMP pay attention
**dentro de** inside
**sí mismo** itself
**¿de veras?** really?
**a propósito** on purpose
**echas de menos** you miss
**así es** that's right

### Name

Mirage

🎬 Mr. Incredible pulls a package out of his trash can.

☐ **compatible** compatible

☐ **mensaje** NM message

☐ **secreto** secret

☐ **en común** in common

☐ **según** according to

☐ **gobierno** government

☐ **clasificado** classified · *clasificar* to classify

☐ **no se repetirá** it will not be repeated · *repetir* to repeat

☐ **represento** I represent · *representar* to represent

☐ **división** division

☐ **ultrasecreta** ultrasecret · *ultrasecreto* ultrasecret

☐ **diseña** it designs · *diseñar* to design

☐ **a prueba de balas** bulletproof

☐ **tecnología** technology

☐ **experimental** experimental

☐ **habilidades** abilities · *habilidad* ability

☐ **área** area

🎬 Elastigirl is heard talking about supper being ready as Mr. Incredible continues to view the message.

☐ **cena** dinner

☐ **oí** I heard · *oír* to hear

☐ **zona** zone, area

☐ **aislada** isolated · *aislado* isolated · *aislar* to isolate

☐ **causar** to cause

☐ **daños** damages · *daño* damage

☐ **incalculables** incalculable · *incalculable* incalculable

☐ **instalaciones** facilities, installations · *instalación* facility, installation

☐ **arriesgando** risking · *arriesgar* to risk

☐ **millones** millions · *millón* NM million

☐ **televisión** television

☐ **intento** I'm trying, I try · *intentar* to try, to attempt

☐ **delicadísima** highly sensitive · *delicado* sensitive, delicate, difficult

☐ **naturaleza** nature

☐ **misión** mission

☐ **cenar** to eat dinner, to dine

☐ **pago** payment

☐ **triple** ADJ triple

☐ **actual** ADJ current

☐ **salario** salary

☐ **anual** annual

☐ **tarjeta** card

☐ **identificador de voz** voice identification device, voice identifier · *identificador* identification device · *voz* NF voice

☐ **seguridad** security

☐ **radio** radio

☐ **veinticuatro** twenty-four

☐ **responder** to respond

🎬 Mr. Incredible views memorabilia from "the glory days."

☐ **autodestruirá** it will self-destruct · *autodestruirse* to self-destruct

🎬 Mr. Incredible uses a blow dryer on their books after the sprinkler system was activated.

☐ **distraído** distracted · *distraerse* to get distracted

☐ **a propósito** on purpose

□ **echas de menos** you miss · *echar de menos* to miss

□ **frustrante** frustrating

□ **comento** I mention, I comment · *comentar* to mention, to comment

□ **conferencia** conference

□ **noticias** *NFPL* news

□ **reconocen** they recognize · *reconocer* to recognize

□ **talentos** talents · *talento* talent

□ **promovieron** they promoted · *promover* to promote

## 9 Nomanisan 6:32

### Phrases to Listen For

**por desgracia** unfortunately
**se pasó de listo** it got too smart
**tuvimos que** we had to
**a trabajar** to work, off to work
**hay que** it's necessary
**de vuelta** back
**lo más importante** the most important thing
**en realidad** really, truly
**por supuesto** of course
**¿por qué?** why?
**se ve** it looks
**tal vez** maybe, perhaps
**¿qué le parece?** what do you think?, how does it seem?

### Name

Omnidroide 9000

■ Aboard an aircraft, Mirage explains the challenge to Mr. Incredible.

□ **robot** *NM* robot

□ **batalla** battle

□ **prototipo** prototype

□ **secreto** secret

□ **inteligencia artificial** artificial intelligence

□ **capaz** capable

□ **resolver** to resolve, to solve

□ **se le presente** *SUBJ* it is presented to him · *presentar* to present

□ **por desgracia** unfortunately

□ **jungla** jungle

□ **amenaza** threat

□ **evacuar** to evacuate

□ **personal** *NM* personnel

□ **seguridad** security

□ **altura** height

□ **escudo desvanecedor** cloaking device · *escudo* shield · *desvanecedor* disappearing, vanishing

□ **dificultar** to make difficult

□ **rastreo** tracking

□ **sur** *NM* south

□ **obvio** obvious

□ **representa** it represents · *representar* to represent

□ **inversión** investment

□ **significativa** significant · *significativo* significant

□ **desconectarlo** to disconnect it · *desconectar* to disconnect

□ **evitando** avoiding · *evitar* to avoid

□ **destruirlo** to destroy it · *destruir* to destroy

■ Mirage speaks to Mr. Incredible inside his landing pod.

□ **advertirle** to warn you · *advertir* to warn

□ **inteligente** intelligent

□ **agilidad** agility

□ **grandioso** magnificent

■ Standing next to the molten lava, Mr. Incredible hurts his back.

□ **espalda** back

■ Mirage and her boss watch Mr. Incredible destroy the robot.

□ **sorprendente** surprising

□ **de vuelta** back · *volver* to come back, to return

□ **invítalo** *IMP* invite him · *invitar* to invite

□ **cenar** to eat dinner, to dine

□ **relajadas** relaxed · *relajado* relaxed · *relajar* to relax

□ **alábalo** *IMP* praise him · *alabar* to praise

□ **apreciamos** we appreciate · *apreciar* to appreciate

□ **habilidades** abilities · *habilidad* ability

■ Mirage opens the door; Mr. Incredible enters.

□ **¿me vestí?** did I dress? · *vestir* to dress

□ **formal** formal

□ **elegante** elegant

□ **anfitrión** *NM* host

□ **usualmente** usually

□ **anonimato** anonymity

□ **perfectamente** perfectly

□ **residir** to reside

□ **volcán** *NM* volcano

□ **atrae** it attracts · *atraer* to attract

□ **inestable** unstable

□ **incomprendido** misunderstood

□ **suelo** soil

□ **volcánico** volcanic

□ **fértil** fertile

□ **cena** dinner

□ **cultivado** cultivated · *cultivar* to cultivate

□ **delicioso** delicious

## 10 New & Improved 4:35

### Phrases to Listen For

**que tengas un buen día** *SUBJ* have a good day
**que no falte el pan** *SUBJ* bring home the bacon
  (*LIT* may the bread not be lacking)
**¿qué tal?** what's up?, what's going on?
**tienen que** they have to
**las cosas andan bien** things are going fine
**para nada** not at all
**tal vez** maybe, perhaps
**por las noches** in the evenings, at night
**hace quince años** fifteen years ago
**¿qué tiene de malo?** what's wrong with that?
**de veras** really, truly
**me falta tiempo** I don't have time
**así que** so
**antes de que** before
**a salvo** safe
**no hay que** it's not necessary
**respecto a** about
**¡anda ya!** come on!, cheer up!
**henos aquí** here we are
**lo sé** I know

### Names

Rolf, Praga, Milán, Dynaguy, Testarrayo,
Estratochica, Metaman, Salpicón

🎬 Mr. Incredible finds a tear in his superhero suit.

☐ **clientes** clients, customers · *cliente NMF* client, customer
☐ **que no falte el pan** *SUBJ EXP* bring home the bacon (*LIT* may the bread not be lacking) · *faltar* to be lacking · *pan NM* bread

🎬 Mr. Incredible stops in front of a security gate.

☐ **saludar** to greet, to say hello
☐ **visitantes** visitors · *visitante NMF* visitor
☐ **revisa** *IMP* check · *revisar* to check
☐ **eléctrica** electric · *eléctrico* electric
☐ **gordo** fat

🎬 Mr. Incredible walks with Edna.

☐ **no me quejo** I can't complain (*LIT* I don't complain) · *quejarse* to complain
☐ **noticias** *NFPL* news
☐ **desfile** *NM* fashion show, parade
☐ **nene** *NM* darling, babe
☐ **modelos** models · *modelo* model
☐ **poseen** they possess · *poseer* to possess
☐ **mimadas** spoiled · *mimado* spoiled · *mimar* to spoil
☐ **bobas** silly · *bobo* silly
☐ **larguiruchas** stick figures, gangling, lanky · *larguirucho* stick figure, gangling, lanky

☐ **labios** lips · *labio* lip
☐ **inflados** full, inflated · *inflado* full, inflated · *inflar* to inflate
☐ **solía** I used to · *soler* to used to (+ VERB)
☐ **diseñar** to design
☐ **reto** challenge
☐ **sorpresa** surprise
☐ **llamaras** *SUBJ* you call · *llamar* to call
☐ **compostura** repair
☐ **megamalla** megamesh
☐ **de moda** in fashion
☐ **resistente** resistant
☐ **atravesaste** you tore through · *atravesar* to tear through, to move through, to cross

🎬 Mr. Incredible hands Edna his torn superhero suit.

☐ **vagos** hobos · *vago* hobo
☐ **quince** fifteen
☐ **diseñaste** you designed · *diseñar* to design
☐ **no volteo** I don't look back · *voltear* to look back
☐ **distrae** it distracts · *distraer* to distract
☐ **te urge** you need, you urgently need, it's urgent for you · *urgir* to be urgent
☐ **recupere** *SUBJ* I recover · *recuperar* to recover
☐ **fabricarme** to make me · *fabricar* to make
☐ **presionas** you pressure · *presionar* to pressure

🎬 Edna sketches a new design for a suit for Mr. Incredible.

☐ **intrépido** intrepid
☐ **dramático** dramatic
☐ **heroico** heroic
☐ **clásico** *ADJ* classic
☐ **diseño** design
☐ **capa** cape
☐ **botas** boots · *bota* boot

🎬 A wad of paper hits Mr. Incredible in the face.

☐ **capas** capes · *capa* cape
☐ **decisión** decision
☐ **tormenta** storm
☐ **atento** attentive, courteous
☐ **noviembre** *NM* November
☐ **se atoró** it got caught, it got stuck · *atorarse* to get caught, to get stuck
☐ **aleta** fin
☐ **misil** *NM* missile
☐ **brillante** brilliant
☐ **abril** *NM* April
☐ **veintitrés** twenty-three
☐ **succionada** sucked up · *succionado* sucked up · *succionar* to suck up
☐ **turbina** turbine
☐ **jet** *NM* jet
☐ **generalizar** to generalize

☐ **ascensor express** express elevator ·
*ascensor NM* elevator
☐ **se atasca** he gets stuck, he gets snagged ·
*atascarse* to get stuck, to get snagged
☐ **despegar** to take off [AIRCRAFT]
☐ **remolino** vortex, whirlwind

🎬 Edna walks on the coffee table.

☐ **misión** mission
☐ **henos aquí** here we are
☐ **sentimental** sentimental
☐ **arreglo** I'll repair, I'll fix (*LIT* I repair, I fix) ·
*arreglar* to repair, to fix

## 11 Helen Suspects                     2:52

**Phrases to Listen For**
**hasta pronto** see you soon (*LIT* until soon)
**así es** that's how it is
**hay que** it's necessary
**¿qué pasa?** what's going on?
**que tengas buen viaje** *SUBJ* have a good trip
**favor de** please
**hasta entonces** see you then (*LIT* until then)

**Names**
Elastigirl, Palos Locos

🎬 Elastigirl finds a blond hair on Mr. Incredible's coat.

☐ **no contestes** *IMP* don't answer · *contestar*
to answer
☐ **misión** mission
☐ **oficina** office
☐ **conferencia** conference

🎬 Mr. Incredible is aboard a private jet.

☐ **automático** automatic
☐ **mimosa** mimosa [DRINK]
☐ **temperatura** temperature
☐ **veintiséis** twenty-six
☐ **grados** degrees · *grado* degree
☐ **Palos Locos** Crazy Sticks [name of an island;
"Nomanisan" in English] · *palo* long stick ·
*loco* crazy
☐ **clima** *NM* weather
☐ **ajustar** to fasten
☐ **cinturón de seguridad** seat belt · *cinturón NM*
belt · *seguridad* security, safety
☐ **iniciamos** we are beginning, we are starting ·
*iniciar* to begin, to start
☐ **descenso** descent

🎬 The jet door opens. Mirage greets Mr. Incredible.

☐ **informar** to inform
☐ **siguiente** next

☐ **sala de conferencias** conference room ·
*sala* room · *conferencia* conference
☐ **ala** wing
☐ **de** *NF* D [LETTER]
☐ **trece** thirteen

## 12 Helen & E                          1:08

**Phrases to Listen For**
**después de** after
**¡qué milagro!** what a miracle!

**Names**
Edna, Telescopio

🎬 Elastigirl finds the repair on Mr. Incredible's
superhero suit.

☐ **cariño** darling
☐ **milagro** miracle
☐ **componer** to fix, to repair
☐ **pijama** pajamas
☐ **obligarme** to force me · *obligar* to force
☐ **rogarte** to beg you · *rogar* to beg
☐ **rogarme** to beg me · *rogar* to beg

🎬 Elastigirl mistakenly says *sabor* and corrects herself
to say *saber.*

☐ **sabor** *NM* flavor, taste
☐ **insisto** I insist · *insistir* to insist

## 13 An Important Meeting               3:59

**Phrases to Listen For**
**para que** in order to
**después del** after the
**no puedes contar con nadie** you can't depend
on anybody
**no tenía que tratarte así** I shouldn't have treated
you like that (*LIT* I didn't have to treat you like
that)
**así es cómo** that is how
**a ver** let's see

**Names**
Buddy, Incrediboy, Telescopio, Kronos

🎬 Mr. Incredible enters the conference room at
2:00 P.M. A wall opens and the robot appears.

☐ **muchísimo** very much

🎬 Syndrome lands on the robot.

☐ **derrotarte** to defeat you · *derrotar* to defeat
☐ **destruiste** you destroyed · *destruir* to destroy
☐ **modificaciones** modifications ·
*modificación* modification

□ **requieres** you require · *requerir* to require
□ **admirador** admirer
□ **apoyo** helper
□ **contestación** answer

🎬 A flashback shows Mr. Incredible rejecting Buddy.

□ **me decepcionó** it disappointed me · *decepcionar* to disappoint
□ **lección** lesson
□ **héroes** heroes · *héroe* NM hero
□ **respetas** you respect · *respetar* to respect
□ **peligro** danger
□ **completos** complete · *completo* complete
□ **respeto** respect
□ **nariz** NF nose
□ **riqueza** riches
□ **inventé** I invented · *inventar* to invent
□ **armas** weapons · *arma* weapon

🎬 Mr. Incredible hurls a log at Syndrome. Syndrome responds by capturing Mr. Incredible in a field of energy.

□ **astuto** astute
□ **monologar** to deliver a monologue, to talk at length
□ **genial** ingenious
□ **energía** energy
□ **reservé** I reserved · *reservar* to reserve
□ **inventos** inventions · *invento* invention
□ **uso** use
□ **nemesis** NF nemesis
□ **brillante** brilliant
□ **talla** size
□ **enorme** enormous

🎬 In a cave, Mr. Incredible encounters the remains of Telescopio.

□ **telescopio** telescope
□ **lectura** reading
□ **negativa** negative · *negativo* negative
□ **eliminado** eliminated · *eliminar* to eliminate

## 14 E's Lab                                    3:07

### Phrases to Listen For
**tenía que** I had to
**qué gusto** how nice
**así que** so
**más de** more than
**a prueba de balas** bulletproof
**hay que** it's necessary
**lo básico** the basics
**a mis espaldas** behind my back

**creí que estabas enterada** I thought you knew (LIT I thought you were informed)
**por supuesto** of course

### Name
Edna Moda

🎬 Elastigirl walks downstairs with Edna.

□ **ha confiscado** it has taken over, it has confiscated · *confiscar* to take over, to confiscate
□ **completamente** completely
□ **cariño** darling
□ **admitir** to admit
□ **simple** simple
□ **elegante** elegant
□ **intrépido** intrepid, daring
□ **discurso** speech
□ **inútil** useless
□ **moda** fashion

🎬 Elastigirl and Edna pass through security doors and sit down.

□ **crema** cream
□ **azúcar** NMF sugar
□ **inicié** I started · *iniciar* to start, to begin
□ **iniciaste** you started, you began · *iniciar* to start, to begin
□ **corté** I cut · *cortar* to cut
□ **holgado** relaxed, comfortable
□ **libertad** NF liberty, freedom
□ **movimiento** movement
□ **piel** NF skin
□ **sensible** sensitive
□ **tela** cloth
□ **ideal** ADJ ideal
□ **soporta** it tolerates · *soportar* to tolerate
□ **temperatura** temperature
□ **grados** degrees · *grado* degree
□ **a prueba de balas** bulletproof
□ **se lava en lavadora** it's machine washable, it's washed in the washing machine · *lavar* to wash · *lavadora* washing machine
□ **novedad** innovation
□ **cubrí** I covered · *cubrir* to cover
□ **básico** basic
□ **fabuloso** fabulous

🎬 Edna shows Dash's low-friction superhero suit to Elastigirl.

□ **diseñé** I designed · *diseñar* to design
□ **fricción** friction
□ **calentarse** heating up · *calentarse* to heat up
□ **desgastarse** wearing out · *desgastarse* to wear out
□ **útil** useful

🎬 Edna shows Violet's superhero suit to Elastigirl.

☐ **finalmente** finally
☐ **material** *NM* material
☐ **resistente** resistant
☐ **desaparece** it disappears · *desaparecer* to disappear

🎬 Edna shows Elastigirl the suit she designed for her.

☐ **estirarse** to be stretched
☐ **lastimarte** injuring you · *lastimar* to injure
☐ **prácticamente** practically
☐ **indestructible** indestructible
☐ **fresco** cool
☐ **algodón** *NM* cotton
☐ **egipcio** Egyptian

🎬 Edna hands Elastigirl a device for locating the superhero suit anywhere in the world.

☐ **artefacto** device
☐ **posición** position
☐ **global** global
☐ **precisa** exact, precise · *preciso* exact, precise
☐ **botón** *NM* button
☐ **oculta** hidden, in hiding · *oculto* hidden, in hiding
☐ **a mis espaldas** behind my back · *espalda* back
☐ **enterada** informed · *enterado* informed · *enterarse* to become informed, to find out
☐ **raro** strange
☐ **secretos** secrets · *secreto* secret
☐ **edad de la inestabilidad** mid-life crisis, age of instability · *edad* age · *inestabilidad* instability
☐ **tentaciones** temptations · *tentación* temptation

## 15 Secrets Revealed                    3:26

### Phrase to Listen For
**todo en orden** all's well, everything in order

🎬 Mr. Incredible lands on the roof of the security detail tram car.

☐ **perímetro** perimeter
☐ **sección** section
☐ **orgullo** pride

🎬 Mr. Incredible hits one of the guards in the head with a rock.

☐ **guardia** *NMF* guard [PERSON]
☐ **suspendan** *IMP* suspend · *suspender* to suspend
☐ **vigilancia** surveillance
☐ **intervengan** *IMP* intervene · *intervenir* to intervene

## 16 Suiting Up                         4:28

### Phrases to Listen For
**¿de qué habla?** what are you talking about?, what are you saying?
**así que** so
**se puso en forma** he got in shape
**¿de qué estás hablando?** what are you talking about?
**por favor** please
**estar a cargo** to be in charge
**hasta entonces** until then
**¿por qué?** why?
**otra vez** again
**estoy a cargo** I'm in charge
**hay que** it's necessary
**tal vez** maybe, perhaps
**antes de que** before
**tengo que** I have to
**yo qué sé** what do I know

### Names
Seguritas, Justino

🎬 Elastigirl is talking on the telephone.

☐ **hotel** *NM* hotel
☐ **hospedado** staying, lodging · *hospedarse* to stay, to lodge
☐ **no conecta** it doesn't connect · *conectar* to connect
☐ **conferencia** conference
☐ **registros** records · *registro* record
☐ **despedido** dismissed, fired · *despedir* to dismiss, to fire

🎬 Elastigirl hangs up the telephone.

☐ **averiguarlo** to find out about it · *averiguar* to find out
☐ **intruso** intruder
☐ **alerta** alert

🎬 Elastigirl sobs.

☐ **cabello** hair
☐ **rubio** blond
☐ **mentiras** lies · *mentira* lie
☐ **revivir** to relive
☐ **mírate** *IMP* look · *mirar* to look at
☐ **pon** *IMP* put · *poner* to put, to place
☐ **demuéstrale** *IMP* demonstrate to him · *demostrar* to demonstrate
☐ **enfrenta** *IMP* face · *enfrentar* to face
☐ **cariño** darling
☐ **adoro** I love, I adore · *adorar* to love, to adore
☐ **visitas** visits · *visita* visit

🎬 Elastigirl pulls a bag out of the closet.
- ☐ **comida** food
- ☐ **recalentar** to reheat
- ☐ **estar a cargo** to be in charge
- ☐ **ropa** clothes
- ☐ **disfraz** *NM* disguise

🎬 Elastigirl answers the phone. Dash shortly uses the word *disfrash* in place of *disfraz* because it rhymes with Dash.
- ☐ **responder** responding, answering · *responder* to respond, to answer
- ☐ **disfraz** *NM* disguise, costume
- ☐ **empacaste** you packed · *empacar* to pack
- ☐ **¿estás escondiendo…?** are you hiding …? · *esconder* to hide
- ☐ **empacar** to pack
- ☐ **esconderlo** to hide it · *esconder* to hide
- ☐ **jet** *NM* jet

## 17 Missile Lock 5:49

### Phrases to Listen For
**de veras** really, truly
**debajo de** under
**tenías que** you had to
**¿qué pasa?** what's up?
**no es cierto** that's not true
**cien por ciento** one hundred percent
**muchas gracias** thank you very much
**está bien** that's fine
**estoy en onda** I've got it wired, I'm cool
**no tienen que** they don't have to
**ya que** since
**por eso** for that reason, that's why
**a veces** sometimes
**de qué rayos** what in the world, what the heck
**todo lo que** everything that
**ya es tarde** it's too late
**un campo de fuerza** a force field
**a bordo** aboard, on board
**no hay que hacer** it's necessary not to do, it's imperative not to do

### Names
Kari, Mozart

🎬 Elastigirl pilots a jet.
- ☐ **golf** *NM* golf
- ☐ **reportando** reporting · *reportar* to report
- ☐ **reglas** rules · *regla* rule
- ☐ **vuelo** flight
- ☐ **torre** *NF* tower
- ☐ **solicito** I request, I solicit · *solicitar* to request, to solicit

- ☐ **vectores** vectors · *vector* *NM* vector
- ☐ **acercamiento** approach
- ☐ **tranquila** *EXP* easy, take it easy, be calm
- ☐ **no sobreactúes** *IMP* don't overreact · *sobreactuar* to overreact
- ☐ **café** *NM* coffee

🎬 Syndrome approaches Mr. Incredible.
- ☐ **idolatrarte** idolizing you · *idolatrar* to idolize
- ☐ **rudo** tough
- ☐ **truco** trick
- ☐ **esfumarte** to disappear, to vanish · *esfumarse* to disappear, to vanish
- ☐ **debajo de** under
- ☐ **huesos** bones · *hueso* bone
- ☐ **envidia** envy
- ☐ **arruinarlo** to ruin it · *arruinar* to ruin
- ☐ **malísimo** very bad · *mal* bad
- ☐ **contacto** contact
- ☐ **anoche** last night
- ☐ **veintitrés** twenty-three
- ☐ **andabas de curioso** you were snooping · *andar de curioso* to snoop
- ☐ **mensaje** *NM* message
- ☐ **posición** position
- ☐ **gobierno** government
- ☐ **solicita** it requests · *solicitar* to request, to solicit
- ☐ **permiso** permission
- ☐ **aterrizaje** *NM* landing [AIRCRAFT]
- ☐ **pon** *IMP* put · *poner* to put
- ☐ **transmisión** transmission

🎬 Mirage presses the button that plays the transmission from Elastigirl to the island.
- ☐ **reportando** reporting · *reportar* to report
- ☐ **saludo** greeting

🎬 Elastigirl tosses her bag onto a seat.
- ☐ **me culparía** he would blame me · *culpar* to blame
- ☐ **colarse** to sneak in
- ☐ **averiguar** to find out
- ☐ **cien** one hundred
- ☐ **torpe** stupid, slow, clumsy
- ☐ **niñera** babysitter
- ☐ **irresponsable** *NMF* irresponsible person
- ☐ **¿quién lo cuida?** who is taking care of him? · *cuidar* to take care of

🎬 Kari the babysitter talks on the phone with Elastigirl.
- ☐ **estoy en onda** I've got it wired, I'm cool
- ☐ **cursos** courses, classes · *curso* course, class

- □ **erre, ce, pe** [RCP] *NF* CPR [LETTERS], cardiopulmonary resuscitation
- □ **excelentes** excellent · *excelente* excellent
- □ **calificaciones** grades · *calificación* grade
- □ **certificados** certificates · *certificado* certificate
- □ **mostrarle** to show you · *mostrar* to show
- □ **expertos** experts · *experto* expert
- □ **qué rayos** *EXP* what the heck
- □ **cómoda** comfortable · *cómodo* comfortable
- □ **pago** I'll pay (*LIT* I pay) · *pagar* to pay
- □ **servicio** service
- □ **no hay necesidad** it's not necessary, there is no need · *necesidad* need
- □ **controlar** to control

🎬 An alarm signals. Elastigirl sees missiles heading toward the aircraft.

- □ **transmite** it transmits, it is transmitting · *transmitir* to transmit
- □ **respuesta** answer, response
- □ **desistan** *IMP* stop, desist · *desistir* to stop, to desist
- □ **repito** I repeat · *repetir* to repeat
- □ **detén** *IMP* stop · *detener* to stop
- □ **misiles** missiles · *misil NM* missile
- □ **quince** fifteen
- □ **millas** miles · *milla* mile
- □ **sur** *NM* south
- □ **suroeste** *NM* southwest
- □ **ruta** route
- □ **alrededor de** around
- □ **May Day** *ENG* May Day
- □ **aborten** *IMP* abort · *abortar* to abort
- □ **a bordo** on board
- □ **nave** *NF* ship
- □ **tamaño** size

🎬 The plane explodes. Elastigirl takes the form of a parachute.

- □ **permanezcan** *IMP* stay, remain · *permanecer* to stay, to remain
- □ **pánico** panic

## 18 Out to Sea                                    2:04

### Phrases to Listen For
**¿qué pasa?** what's happening?
**ya basta** enough already

🎬 Elastigirl, Violet, and Dash are in the ocean.

- □ **ahogarnos** to drown · *ahogarse* to drown
- □ **explotó** it exploded · *explotar* to explode
- □ **sobrevivir** to survive
- □ **llorones** crybabies · *llorón NM* crybaby
- □ **castigo** I punish · *castigar* to punish

🎬 As the captured Mr. Incredible watches, Mirage reports the destruction of the plane to Syndrome.

- □ **hemos confirmado** we have confirmed · *confirmar* to confirm
- □ **impacto** impact
- □ **destruido** destroyed · *destruir* to destroy
- □ **preferías** you would prefer · *preferir* to prefer

🎬 As Mr. Incredible is about to capture Syndrome, Mirage intervenes and he takes her prisoner instead.

- □ **trizas** *NFPL* pieces, shreds
- □ **cruel** cruel
- □ **mondadientes** *NM* toothpick
- □ **rompiéndose** breaking · *romperse* to break

🎬 Mr. Incredible releases Mirage.

- □ **débil** weak
- □ **te he superado** I have surpassed you · *superar* to surpass, to overcome

🎬 Elastigirl, Violet, and Dash continue to float in the ocean.

- □ **misiles de corto alcance** short-range missiles · *misil NM* missile · *corto* short · *alcance* reach
- □ **opción** option
- □ **matones** thugs · *matón NM* thug
- □ **nademos** *SUBJ* we swim · *nadar* to swim

## 19 Good Guys/Bad Guys                          3:29

### Phrases to Listen For
**me siento muy orgullosa** I'm very proud (*LIT* I feel very proud)
**aquí la cosa está que arde** the danger is right here
**estar a cargo** to be in charge
**cuento contigo** I have faith in you, I trust you
**lo que pasó** what happened
**de mi parte** on my part
**bajo control todo** everything under control

🎬 Elastigirl, Violet, and Dash arrive on shore.

- □ **tropa** troop
- □ **orgullosa** proud · *orgulloso* proud
- □ **si no lo notaste** if you didn't notice · *notar* to notice
- □ **aquí la cosa está que arde** *EXP* the danger is right here (*LIT* here the thing is that stings) · *arder* to sting, to burn
- □ **estar a cargo** to be in charge
- □ **pónganselos** *IMP* put them on · *ponerse* to put on
- □ **posesión** possession

□ **valiosa** valuable · *valioso* valuable
□ **protéjanla** *IMP* protect it · *proteger* to protect
□ **tipos malos** bad guys · *tipo* guy
□ **salen en la tele** they appear on television · *salir en la televisión* to appear on television · *tele NF* television
□ **programas** programs · *programa NM* program
□ **no se detendrían** they wouldn't stop · *detenerse* to stop
□ **cuento contigo** I'm counting on you · *contar con* to count on
□ **récord** *NM* best mark, record
□ **escóndanse** *IMP* hide · *esconderse* to hide

🎬 Violet follows Elastigirl outside the cave.

□ **exigirte** to demand of you · *exigir* to demand
□ **lujo** luxury
□ **no sufras** *IMP* don't worry, don't trouble yourself (*LIT* don't suffer) · *sufrir* to suffer
□ **sangre** *NF* blood

🎬 Sitting at a console of electronic equipment, Mirage address Syndrome.

□ **débil** weak
□ **apreciar** to appreciate
□ **debilidad** weakness
□ **base de detención** containment unit · *base NF* base, unit · *detención* detention, containment
□ **despreciarla** to despise it · *despreciar* to despise
□ **medir** to measure
□ **agallas** *NFPL* guts
□ **intuía** I knew · *intuir* to know by intuition
□ **no se atrevería** he wouldn't dare · *atreverse* to dare
□ **apuesta** *IMP* bet, wager · *apostar* to bet, to wager

## 20 Elastigirl Returns                    2:52

🎬 Elastigirl enters the base.
□ **cohete** *NM* rocket

## 21 Caves & Rockets                    1:54

### Phrase to Listen For
**así que** so

🎬 Violet practices her powers on a campfire while Dash watches.

□ **no creas** *IMP* don't think, don't believe · *creer* to think, to believe
□ **recorrer** to check out, to look over
□ **vacaciones** *NFPL* vacation
□ **peligra** it is in danger · *peligrar* to be in danger, to be threatened

□ **matrimonio** marriage
□ **arruinar** to ruin
□ **inmaduro** immature boy, immature man
□ **escóndanse** *IMP* hide · *esconderse* to hide
□ **cueva** cave

## 22 Lost & Found                    2:46

### Phrases to Listen For
**¿qué hay que hacer?** what needs to be done?, what do we have to do?
**no lo hay** there isn't (any), there's none
**de hecho** in fact
**tal vez** maybe, perhaps
**¿por qué?** why?
**no creo que...** I don't think ...

🎬 Elastigirl looks down into a room where two men are monitoring several control panels.

□ **arribo** arrival
□ **coordenadas** coordinates · *coordenada* coordinate
□ **determinadas** determined · *determinado* determined · *determinar* to determine
□ **confirma** *IMP* confirm · *confirmar* to confirm
□ **transmisión** transmission
□ **contrainteligencia** counter-intelligence
□ **situación** situation
□ **normal** normal
□ **no respondemos** we are not responding, we are not answering · *responder* to respond, to answer
□ **saludos** greetings · *saludo* greeting
□ **medidas** measures, measurements · *medida* measure, measurement
□ **infrarrojas** infrared · *infrarrojo* infrared
□ **condiciones** conditions · *condición* condition
□ **apropiadas** suitable, appropriate · *apropiado* suitable, appropriate

🎬 Dash wakes up next to Violet.

□ **identificación** · identification
□ **voz** *NF* voice
□ **clave** *NF* password
□ **incorrecta** incorrect
□ **intruso** intruder
□ **alerta** alert

🎬 Mirage releases Mr. Incredible.

□ **humillarme** to humiliate me · *humillar* to humiliate
□ **escapar** to escape
□ **mentiroso** liar
□ **infiel** *NMF* unfaithful person
□ **traicionar** to betray

□ **activaron** they activated · *activar* to activate
□ **seguridad** security
□ **jungla** jungle
□ **peligro** danger
□ **peligroso** dangerous
□ **se colaron** they snuck in · *colarse* to sneak in
□ **tono** tone
□ **apropiado** appropriate, suitable

## 23 100 Mile Dash 3:06

🎬 Violet and Dash run through the jungle.

□ **atrápenlo** IMP catch him, trap him · *atrapar* to catch, to trap
□ **muéstrate** IMP show yourself · *mostrar* to show

## 24 Reunited 3:24

**Phrases to Listen For**
**hay que** it's necessary
**a salvo** safe
**yo qué sé** what do I know
**lo que sea** SUBJ whatever
**tiempo fuera** time-out
**por favor** please
**tienen que** you have to
**de lo que** than
**para que** so that
**todo el mundo** everyone

🎬 Mr. Incredible and Elastigirl run through the jungle.

□ **despedido** fired · *despedir* to fire, to dismiss
□ **admito** I admit · *admitir* to admit
□ **inquietarte** to worry you · *inquietar* to worry
□ **inquietarme** to worry me · *inquietar* to worry
□ **jungla** jungle
□ **desconocida** unfamiliar · *desconocido* unfamiliar · *desconocer* to be unfamiliar with, to not know
□ **peleemos** SUBJ we fight · *pelear* to fight

🎬 An enemy guard fires his weapon. An invisible Violet picks up a stick.

□ **desaparecida** disappeared · *desaparecido* disappeared · *desaparecer* to disappear
□ **no te esconderás** you will not hide · *esconderse* to hide

🎬 Mr. Incredible's family is reunited in the jungle. Syndrome arrives and captures the family.

□ **uniformes** uniforms · *uniforme* NM uniform
□ **premio mayor** top prize, jackpot

🎬 Syndrome shows Mr. Incredible and his family several TV channels.

□ **diseño** design
□ **nave** NF ship
□ **víctimas** victims · *víctima* victim
□ **admitir** to admit
□ **genial** ingenious
□ **película** film, movie
□ **robot** NM robot
□ **emerge** it emerges · *emerger* to emerge
□ **dramáticamente** dramatically
□ **destruye** it destroys · *destruir* to destroy
□ **pánico** panic
□ **esperanza** hope
□ **héroes** heroes · *héroe* NM hero
□ **reales** real · *real* real
□ **fingirte** to pretend to be · *fingirse* to pretend to be
□ **real** real
□ **vencerte** to defeat you · *vencer* to defeat, to conquer
□ **preciados** precious
□ **actos** acts · *acto* act
□ **heroicos** heroic · *heroico* heroic
□ **espectaculares** spectacular · *espectacular* spectacular
□ **inventos** inventions · *invento* invention
□ **venderé** I will sell · *vender* to sell
□ **superhéroe** NM superhero
□ **se convertirá** it will become · *convertirse* to become

## 25 Bob's Confession 2:17

**Phrases to Listen For**
**disparen a voluntad** IMP fire at will
**a salvo** safe
**hay que** it's necessary
**no tienes que** you don't have to
**por favor** please

🎬 The robot is activated.

□ **¡despliéguense!** IMP spread out! · *desplegarse* to spread out
□ **tanques** tanks · *tanque* NM tank
□ **cúbranse** IMP take cover · *cubrirse* to take cover
□ **¡disparen a voluntad!** IMP fire at will! · *disparar* to fire, to shoot · *voluntad* NF will
□ **dispara** it shoots, it fires · *disparar* to shoot, to fire
□ **especie** NF type, kind
□ **rayo** ray
□ **ha abatido** it has demolished · *abatir* to demolish
□ **por completo** completely

🎬 Mr. Incredible apologizes to his family.

☐ **fracaso** failure
☐ **obsesionado** obsessed · *obsesionarse* to become obsessed
☐ **valorado** appreciated, valued · *valorar* to appreciate, to value
☐ **no los valoré** I didn't appreciate you, I didn't value you, I undervalued you · *valorar* to appreciate, to value
☐ **no interrumpas** IMP don't interrupt · *interrumpir* to interrupt
☐ **aventura** adventure
☐ **progreso** progress
☐ **sesión** session

🎬 The family runs through the tunnel.

☐ **superficie** NF surface
☐ **hangar** NM hangar
☐ **guardias** guards · *guardia* NMF guard [PERSON]
☐ **jet** NM jet
☐ **cohete** NM rocket
☐ **coordenadas** coordinates · *coordenada* coordinate
☐ **lanzamiento** launch
☐ **anterior** previous
☐ **cambió** he changed · *cambiar* to change
☐ **clave** NF password
☐ **acceso** I access · *accesar* to access
☐ **computadora** computer

## 26 Frozone & Honey                    0:46

### Phrase to Listen For
**el público está en riesgo** the public is at risk

### Name
Nena

🎬 Frozone puts on aftershave.

☐ **huir** to flee, to take off
☐ **hemos planeado** we have planned · *planear* to plan
☐ **cena** dinner
☐ **público** public
☐ **en riesgo** at risk
☐ **velada** evening out
☐ **hazaña** deed, exploit, feat, important task

## 27 Omnidroid Attacks                  0:57

### Name
Fierónico

🎬 The robot picks up a tanker truck.

☐ **han vuelto** they have returned · *volver* to return
☐ **se viste** he dresses · *vestir* to dress
☐ **superhéroe** NM superhero
☐ **pedazo** piece
☐ **metal** NM metal
☐ **modales** NMPL manners

## 28 Road Trip                          2:33

### Phrases to Listen For
**hay que** it's necessary
**tengo que** I have to
**así que** so
**otra vez** again
**no hay que** it's not necessary
**lo que pase** SUBJ what's happening
**¿qué ha de pasar?** what could happen?

### Name
Tracción

🎬 Elastigirl holds the motor home suspended from the aircraft.

☐ **contestar** to answer
☐ **dura** rough · *duro* rough
☐ **robot** NM robot
☐ **zona** zone, district
☐ **financiera** financial · *financiero* financial
☐ **salida** exit
☐ **centro** downtown
☐ **tomo** I take · *tomar* to take
☐ **preguntaste** you asked · *preguntar* to ask
☐ **sal** IMP get off, exit · *salir* to leave, to get off, to exit
☐ **haz la señal** IMP switch on the turn signal · *hacer la señal* to switch on the turn signal
☐ **no sales** SUBJ you don't exit, you don't get off · *salir* to exit, to get off, to leave

🎬 The motor home rolls into a parking space.

☐ **súper duper** ADJ super-duper
☐ **ocúltense** IMP hide out, hide yourselves · *ocultarse* to hide oneself
☐ **contesto** I answer · *contestar* to answer
☐ **escena** scene
☐ **ejercicios** exercises · *ejercicio* exercise
☐ **no resistiría** he wouldn't oppose, he wouldn't resist · *resistir* to oppose, to resist
☐ **superhéroes** superheroes · *superhéroe* NM superhero

## 29 The Incredibles vs. the Omnidroid 4:54

### Phrases to Listen For
**en serio** seriously, really
**¿para qué?** what for?
**¿qué pasó?** what happened?
**¡ya está!** done!
**no cuentes con eso** IMP don't count on it

### Names
Frozono, Lucio, Zono

🎬 The robot crushes the motor home.

- □ **aparato** apparatus, device
- □ **controla** it controls · *controlar* to control
- □ **robot** NM robot
- □ **lánzalo** IMP throw it · *lanzar* to throw
- □ **destruye** IMP destroy · *destruir* to destroy
- □ **armas** weapons · *arma* weapon

🎬 Violet shows Elastigirl the remote control.

- □ **remoto** remote
- □ **controlas** you control · *controlar* to control
- □ **dámelo** IMP give it to me · *dar* to give
- □ **penetrarlo** to penetrate it · *penetrar* to penetrate
- □ **se acerca** it's getting close · *acercarse* to get close
- □ **trata** IMP try · *tratar* to try
- □ **botón** NM button
- □ **presiona** IMP press · *presionar* to press
- □ **refugio** shelter
- □ **tiro** shot
- □ **cúbranse** IMP take cover · *cubrirse* to take cover

🎬 The robot falls into the river and is destroyed.

- □ **escuela antigua** old school
- □ **dolía** it hurt · *doler* to hurt

## 30 Past vs. Future 3:39

### Phrases to Listen For
**acerca de** about
**¡qué cosa!** wow!
**tiene que** you have to
**lo que** what
**hay que** it's necessary
**¿qué pasa?** what's happening?, what's going on?
**otra vez** again
**¡eso sí que es otra onda!** that's something else!

### Name
Kari

🎬 Mr. Incredible and his family ride in a limousine.

- □ **fondos** NMPL funds
- □ **congelados** frozen · *congelado* frozen
- □ **simple** simple
- □ **estornudo** sneeze
- □ **esposarlo** to handcuff him · *esposar* to handcuff
- □ **población** people
- □ **en deuda** in debt
- □ **escondernos** to hide (ourselves) · *esconderse* to hide
- □ **políticos** politicians · *político* politician
- □ **nos encargaremos** we'll take charge · *encargarse* to take charge
- □ **resto** the rest, the remainder
- □ **correcto** correct

🎬 Inside the limousine, Elastigirl checks telephone messages. Mr. Incredible, Violet, and Dash talk.

- □ **limo** NF limo, limousine · *limusina* limo, limousine
- □ **recogiste tu cabello** you're wearing your hair back, you pulled your hair back · *recoger* to gather · *cabello* hair
- □ **genial** ingenious
- □ **agarraste** you grabbed · *agarrar* to grab
- □ **brazo** arm
- □ **aplastaste** you crushed, you smashed · *aplastar* to crush, to smash
- □ **mensajes** messages · *mensaje* NM message
- □ **raras** strange · *raro* strange
- □ **me estoy aterrando** I'm becoming frightened · *aterrarse* to be frightened
- □ **asesinarnos** to kill us · *asesinar* to kill
- □ **vacaciones** NFPL vacation
- □ **requiere** he requires · *requerir* to require
- □ **reemplazo** replacement
- □ **controlarlo** to control him · *controlar* to control

🎬 Syndrome holds Jack-Jack in his arms and captures Mr. Incredible's family.

- □ **futuro** future
- □ **devolverte** to return to you · *devolver* to return, to give back
- □ **mentor** NM mentor
- □ **apoyador** supportive
- □ **alentador** encouraging
- □ **faltó** it lacked, it was lacking · *faltar* to lack
- □ **secuaz** NM henchman
- □ **está huyendo** he is fleeing, he is getting away · *huir* to flee, to get away
- □ **lanza** IMP throw · *lanzar* to throw
- □ **objeto** object
- □ **herir** to wound, to injure
- □ **lánzame** IMP throw me · *lanzar* to throw
- □ **nene** NM baby boy

🎬 Violet shields the family.

□ **mudarnos** to move · *mudarse* to move [RESIDENCE]

□ **eso sí que es otra onda** that was really cool!

## 31 Happy Endings                          1:56

### Phrases to Listen For

**dentro de** inside
**tienen que** they have to
**lo que** what
**¿te gustó?** did you like it? (*LIT* did it please you?)
**me gustan** I like (*LIT* they please me)
**no te rindas** *IMP* don't give up
**abajo de** below

🎬 A sign announces the Elementary School City Track Finals.

□ **apoyen** *IMP* support · *apoyar* to support
□ **atletismo** track and field
□ **cuadernos** notebooks · *cuaderno* notebook
□ **edición** edition
□ **tienda** store

🎬 Violet is talking with a girlfriend. Soon Tony Rydinger arrives.

□ **porristas** cheerleaders · *porrista NMF* cheerleader

□ **competencia** competition
□ **común** common
□ **grandioso** magnificent, terrific
□ **películas** movies · *película* movie
□ **invito** I invite · *invitar* to invite
□ **palomitas** *NFPL* popcorn
□ **viernes** *NM* Friday

🎬 The gun fires to start the race.

□ **acelera** *IMP* accelerate, go faster · *acelerar* to accelerate, to go faster
□ **despacio** slow
□ **no te rindas** *IMP* don't give up, don't surrender · *rendirse* to give up, to surrender
□ **cierra** *IMP* finish, end up · *cerrar* to finish, to end

🎬 The Parr family walks through the parking lot.

□ **orgullosa** proud · *orgulloso* proud
□ **gradas** *NFPL* stands
□ **subterráneo** subterranean
□ **declaro** I declare · *declarar* to declare
□ **paz** *NF* peace
□ **temblará** it will tremble · *temblar* to tremble
□ **ante** before

## 32 End Credits                          7:50

🎬 End credits.

# Mary Poppins

**¿Recuerdan qué se los dije? Tienen todo el mundo a sus pies.**
*What did I tell you? There's the whole world at your feet.*

GENRE      Musical/Literature Adaptation
YEAR       1964
DIRECTOR   Robert Stevenson
CAST       Julie Andrews, Dick Van Dyke
STUDIO     Walt Disney Productions

"Practically Perfect in Every Way" is a marvelous description of this classic Academy Award–winning film. It's easy to get caught up in the fun as Julie Andrews, Dick Van Dyke, and the rest of the cast dance across the rooftops of London. We've ranked this as Advanced because, for both musical and poetic reasons, the Spanish used in the musical numbers includes less common vocabulary, moves along quickly, and is sometimes difficult to catch. The conversational dialogue, however, is easy to follow.

## BASIC VOCABULARY

### Names

Michael, Banks, Ellen, Bert, George,
Cherry Tree Lane

### Nouns

- ☐ **azúcar** NMF sugar · *Un poquito de azúcar toda purga endulzará.* Just a spoonful of sugar helps the medicine go down. (*LIT* A little bit of sugar sweetens every medicine.)
- ☐ **banco** bank · *Es el presidente del banco, el anciano Señor Dawes, el gigante del mundo financiero.* He's the president of the bank, old Mr. Dawes, the giant of the financial world.
- ☐ **canción** song · *Las señoras ahí en la prisión están esperándome para cantar nuestra canción.* The ladies there in the prison are waiting for me in order to sing our song.
- ☐ **céntimos** pennies · *céntimo* penny · *Pero si tú inviertes tus céntimos con fe en el banco, a salvo estos estarán.* But if you invest your pennies with faith in the bank, they will be safe.
- ☐ **chimenea** chimney · *Chim, chimenea, chim, chimenea, chim chim cheró.* Chim, chimney, chim, chimney, chim, chim, cher-oo.
- ☐ **cometa** kite · *Una buena cometa necesita una buena cola, ¿no es cierto?* A good kite needs a good tail, isn't that right?
- ☐ **diecisiete** seventeen · *El número diecisiete es más adelante.* Number seventeen is up ahead.
- ☐ **pan** NM bread · *No pisen el pan.* Don't step on the bread.
- ☐ **té** tea · *¿Tomar el té en el techo es lógico?* Does drinking tea on the ceiling make sense?
- ☐ **tonterías** EXP nonsense · *Ah, tonterías, no hay porqué lamentarlo.* Ah, nonsense, there's no reason to be sorry about it.
- ☐ **viento** wind · *Nos prometió quedarse hasta que el viento cambiara.* She promised to stay until the wind changes.

### 1 | Opening Credits          6:04

#### Phrases to Listen For

**suerte tendrán** lucky they will be
**tendrá suerte** she'll be lucky
**al vuelo** on the fly
**¿qué tal?** what's up?, how is it?
**lo que** what

#### Names

Lark, Andrew, Cory, Persimmon,
Cherry Tree Lane

🎬 Opening credits.

- ☐ **tipo** type
- ☐ **deshollinador** chimney sweep
- ☐ **besa** she kisses · *besar* to kiss

🎬 Bert is a one-man band.

- ☐ **poemas** poems · *poema* NM poem
- ☐ **cómicos** comical, funny · *cómico* comical, funny
- ☐ **ocasión** occasion
- ☐ **inventados** invented · *inventado* invented · *inventar* to invent
- ☐ **al vuelo** on the fly
- ☐ **vigía** NMF security guard, watchman
- ☐ **verso** verse
- ☐ **carrito** NM little car · *carro* car
- ☐ **crecieron** they grew · *crecer* to grow
- ☐ **brisa** breeze
- ☐ **están proclamando** they are proclaiming · *proclamar* to proclaim
- ☐ **novedad** novelty, something new
- ☐ **mas** but

🎬 Bert's audience claps.

- ☐ **cooperación** cooperation
- ☐ **generosidad** generosity
- ☐ **gratis** free

### 2 | Cherry Tree Lane          3:02

#### Phrases to Listen For

**a la orden** on your order
**buenas tardes** good afternoon
**a remolque** in tow
**mal tiempo** bad weather
**tenía razón** he was right
**sin duda alguna** without a doubt
**¿quién tiene que...?** who has to …?
**¿no es cierto?** isn't that right?
**eso no es cuenta mía** that's not my concern, that's not my affair
**hay que** it's necessary
**por todo el camino** the whole way

#### Names

Cherry Tree Lane, Boom, Bristol, Greenwich, Katie Nanna, Brill, Bourne-Allen, Ainslie

🎬 Bert approaches a lamppost and the street.

- ☐ **bello** beautiful, pretty
- ☐ **imponente** imposing
- ☐ **edificio** building
- ☐ **hogar** NM home
- ☐ **Marina Real** Royal Navy · *marina* navy · *real* ADJ royal
- ☐ **estilo** style

☐ **navío** a very large ship
☐ **en orden** in order · *orden* NM order
☐ **moda** custom
☐ **cañón** NM cannon
☐ **cargado** loaded · *cargar* to load
☐ **famoso** famous
☐ **puntualidad** punctuality
☐ **navega** you navigate · *navegar* to navigate
☐ **a remolque** in tow
☐ **anótelo** IMP note it · *anotar* to note, to write down
☐ **bitácora** ship's log
☐ **advertencia** warning
☐ **está amenazando** it is threatening · *amenazar* to threaten
☐ **tormenta** storm
☐ **formarse** to form, to be formed
☐ **alerta** alert

Bert walks down the sidewalk.

☐ **residencia** residence
☐ **niñera** nanny
☐ **cara** face
☐ **modales** NMPL manners
☐ **espantaría** she would frighten · *espantar* to frighten
☐ **demonio** demon, devil
☐ **oiga** IMP listen · *oír* to hear, to listen
☐ **riquezas** riches · *riqueza* wealth
☐ **apártate** IMP move away · *apartarse* to move away
☐ **abandona** you abandon · *abandonar* to abandon
☐ **salvajes** wild · *salvaje* ADJ wild
☐ **se me escaparon** they got away from me · *escaparse* to get away, to escape
☐ **zoológico** zoo
☐ **parque** NM park
☐ **león** NM lion
☐ **jaula** cage
☐ **discutir** to argue, to discuss
☐ **no se tropiece con** IMP don't bump into · *tropezarse* to bump into, to run into
☐ **escalón** NM stair step
☐ **cadenas** chains · *cadena* chain
☐ **afuera** outside
☐ **derechos** rights · *derecho* right
☐ **defender** to defend
☐ **gritarán** they will shout · *gritar* to shout
☐ **socias sufragistas** sister suffragettes · *socio* associate · *sufragista* ADJ suffragette

Mrs. Banks walks in the front door.

☐ **glorioso** glorious
☐ **meeting** ENG meeting

☐ **se encadenó** she chained herself · *encadenarse* to chain oneself
☐ **rueda** wheel
☐ **carruaje** NM carriage
☐ **primer ministro** prime minister
☐ **prisión** prison
☐ **cantó** she sang · *cantar* to sing
☐ **repartió** she delivered · *repartir* to deliver, to distribute
☐ **propaganda** propaganda
☐ **me alegro** I'm happy, I'm glad · *alegrarse* to be happy, to be glad
☐ **he luchado** I have struggled · *luchar* to struggle

## 3 Mrs. Banks' Cause ("Sister Suffragette")  3:41

### Phrases to Listen For
**poco razonables** not very reasonable
**hay que** it's necessary
**por favor** please
**tendrá que** she will have to
**tendremos que** we will have to
**de nuevo** again
**¿a qué hora?** at what time?
**ya es bastante con que llegue a la casa...** SUBJ it's quite enough that I arrive home ...
**a sus puestos** to your posts
**¿qué tal...?** what about ...?
**mal tiempo** bad weather

### Names
Kensington, Billingsgate, Katie Nanna

Mrs. Banks champions her women's causes with the housekeeper and the nanny.

☐ **simpatizan** you sympathize · *simpatizar* to sympathize
☐ **causa** cause
☐ **soldados** soldiers · *soldado* soldier
☐ **votar** to vote
☐ **en lo personal** as an individual, personally
☐ **razonables** reasonable · *razonable* reasonable
☐ **cadenas** chains · *cadena* chain
☐ **derechos** rights · *derecho* right
☐ **defender** to defend
☐ **gritarán** they will shout · *gritar* to shout
☐ **socias sufragistas** sister suffragettes · *socio* associate · *sufragista* ADJ suffragette
☐ **grito** shout
☐ **luchar** to struggle
☐ **derecho** right
☐ **igualdad** equality

- ☐ **humillaciones** humiliations · *humillación* humiliation
- ☐ **sufrir** suffering · *sufrir* to suffer
- ☐ **sufragio** suffrage
- ☐ **exigir** to demand
- ☐ **lucha** struggle

🎬 Mrs. Banks stops singing and pays attention to Katie Nanna.

- ☐ **respecto a** with respect to
- ☐ **precisa** precise, exact · *preciso* precise, exact
- ☐ **desaparecieron** they disappeared · *desaparecer* to disappear
- ☐ **descuido** neglect
- ☐ **tercera** third · *tercero* third
- ☐ **cuarta** fourth · *cuarto* fourth
- ☐ **suplico** I beg · *suplicar* to beg, to plead
- ☐ **salario** salary
- ☐ **bastante** enough
- ☐ **esconde** *IMP* hide · *esconder* to hide
- ☐ **odia** he hates · *odiar* to hate
- ☐ **reconsiderar** to reconsider
- ☐ **estaba acostumbrándose** he was getting used to · *acostumbrarse* to get used to, to become accustomed

🎬 The clock is about to strike six.

- ☐ **puestos** positions, stations · *puesto* position, station

🎬 Mr. Banks passes by Admiral Boom's house.

- ☐ **se adelantó** you are ahead · *adelantarse* to be ahead, to be fast [TIME]
- ☐ **exacto** exact
- ☐ **finanzas** *NFPL* finances
- ☐ **de maravilla** wonderful
- ☐ **plata** money
- ☐ **circula** it circulates · *circular* to circulate
- ☐ **créditos** credits · *crédito* credit
- ☐ **continuamente** continually
- ☐ **libra Británica** British pound
- ☐ **admiración** admiration
- ☐ **peligrosas** dangerous · *peligroso* dangerous
- ☐ **soplar** to blow
- ☐ **barómetro** barometer
- ☐ **va en descenso** it's falling, it's dropping · *descenso* fall, drop, descent
- ☐ **excelente** excellent
- ☐ **no me sorprendería** it wouldn't surprise me · *sorprender* to surprise
- ☐ **navegara** *SUBJ* you are heading, you are sailing · *navegar* to head, to sail, to navigate

## 4 Mr. Banks Returns Home ("The Life I Lead") 5:59

### Phrases to Listen For

**horario preciso** exact schedule
**¿cómo que...?** what do you mean ...?
**enseguida** at once, right away
**por favor** please
**lo que** what
**lo siento** I'm sorry
**tal vez** maybe, perhaps
**hasta pronto** see you soon (*LIT* until soon)
**buenas noches** good night
**claro que sí** of course
**lo lamento** I'm sorry
**hay que** it's necessary

### Names

Katie Nanna, Eduardo, Winifred, Cherry Tree Lane, Times

🎬 Mr. Banks bumps into Katie Nanna.

- ☐ **sombrero** hat
- ☐ **alegre** happy
- ☐ **satisfecho** satisfied · *satisfacer* to satisfy
- ☐ **aclamado** acclaimed · *aclamar* to acclaim
- ☐ **retorno** I return · *retornar* to return
- ☐ **hogar** *NM* home
- ☐ **luchar** struggling · *luchar* to struggle
- ☐ **cuan** how
- ☐ **grata** pleasant · *grato* pleasant
- ☐ **horario** schedule
- ☐ **preciso** precise, exact
- ☐ **cruzo** I cross · *cruzar* to cross
- ☐ **dintel** *NM* lintel
- ☐ **exacto** exactly, exact
- ☐ **copa** glass
- ☐ **jerez** *NM* sherry
- ☐ **sólida** solid · *sólido ADJ* solid
- ☐ **espléndido** splendid
- ☐ **grato** pleasant
- ☐ **inglés** *NM* English
- ☐ **mil novecientos diez** 1910 [DATE], one thousand nine hundred ten
- ☐ **trono** throne
- ☐ **lord** *ENG* lord
- ☐ **castillo** castle
- ☐ **soberano** sovereign
- ☐ **trato** I treat · *tratar* to treat
- ☐ **vasallos** vassals · *vasallo* vassal
- ☐ **sirvientes** servants · *sirviente NM* servant
- ☐ **firmeza** firmness
- ☐ **gentileza** gentleness
- ☐ **noble** *ADJ* noble
- ☐ **herederos** heirs · *heredero* heir

- **bañados** bathed · *bañado* bathed · *bañar* to give a bath
- **palmaditas** DIM little pats, soft little slaps · *palmada* pat, soft slap
- **cariño** care
- **alcoba** bedroom
- **los envío** I send them · *enviar* to send

◼ Mr. Banks stops singing and addresses Mrs. Banks.

- **enseguida** at once, right away
- **claridad** clarity
- **faltó** she failed, she was absent from · *faltar* to fail, to be absent from
- **puesto** position
- **abandonó** she abandoned · *abandonar* to abandon
- **asunto** matter
- **urgente** urgent
- **inmediatamente** immediately
- **servicio** service

◼ Mr. Banks hangs up the telephone.

- **recorriendo** going over, traveling across · *recorrer* to go over, to travel across
- **parque** NM park
- **tropecé con** I bumped into · *tropezar con* to bump into
- **invaluables** invaluable · *invaluable* invaluable
- **valores** valuables · *valor* NM valuable
- **extraviados** lost · *extraviado* lost · *extraviarse* to get lost
- **sentimentalismos** sentimentalism · *sentimentalismo* sentimentalism
- **aproxímense** IMP come here · *aproximarse* to come closer, to approach, to draw near
- **nos arrastró** it dragged us · *arrastrar* to drag
- **se extravió** it got lost · *extraviarse* to get lost, to become lost
- **recuerdo** I remember · *recordar* to remember
- **aprecio** I appreciate · *apreciar* to appreciate
- **molestias** troubles · *molestia* trouble
- **cocina** kitchen
- **cocinera** cook · *cocinero* cook

◼ Mrs. Banks closes the door.

- **discutirlo** to discuss it · *discutir* to discuss
- **obligación** obligation
- **trabajadora** hardworking · *trabajador* hardworking
- **honrada** honored · *honrado* honored · *honrar* to honor
- **carcelera** jailer · *carcelero* jailer

- **contraté** I hired · *contratar* to hire
- **firme** ADJ firm
- **consideré** I considered · *considerar* to consider
- **eficiente** efficient
- **no confundas** IMP don't confuse · *confundir* to confuse
- **eficiencia** efficiency
- **mal hepático** liver disease, liver complaint · *mal* NM disease · *hepático* liver
- **ocasión** occasion
- **ayas** nannies · *aya* nanny
- **positivo** positive
- **desastre** NM disaster
- **escoger** to choose
- **delicada** delicate · *delicado* delicate, sensitive
- **tarea** task
- **requiere** it requires · *requerir* to require
- **inteligencia** intelligence
- **perspicacia** insight
- **hábil** able
- **lectura de carácter** reading of character, evaluation of character · *lectura* reading · *carácter* NM character
- **circunstancias** circumstances · *circunstancia* circumstance
- **apropiado** appropriate
- **proceda** SUBJ I proceed · *proceder* to proceed
- **escogerla** to select her, to choose her · *escoger* to select, to choose
- **anuncio** announcement, advertisement
- **anota** IMP take notes, write (this) down · *anotar* to take notes, to write down
- **respetable** respectable
- **honorable** honorable

◼ Mr. Banks, wearing his red coat, begins to sing.

- **niñera** nanny
- **futuro** future
- **educar** to educate
- **mandar** to order
- **¿anotaste eso?** did you write that down? · *anotar* to write down
- **precisión** precision
- **disciplina** discipline
- **precisos** essential · *preciso* essential
- **desorden** NM disorder
- **catástrofe** NF catastrophe
- **anarquía** anarchy
- **total** NM total, all
- **lío** mess
- **fatal** fatal
- **inspirado** inspired · *inspirar* to inspire

## Jane and Michael Compose an Advertisement for "The Perfect Nanny"

**5**    4:21

### Phrases to Listen For

**mi hermano y yo sentimos lo que sucedió hoy** my brother and I are sorry for what happened today

**no estoy muy de acuerdo con eso** I don't agree very much with that, I'm not very much in agreement with that

**ni siquiera** not even

**lo que** what

**manos a la obra** hands to the task

**dentro de** within

**a sus puestos** to your posts

### Names

Katie, Winifred, Times, George Banks, Cherry Tree Lane, Binnacle

▬ Michael stands next to Jane, who holds a piece of paper.

□ **hemos discutido** we have discussed · *discutir* to discuss
□ **asunto** matter
□ **acción** action
□ **escaparnos** escaping · *escaparse* to escape
□ **aya** nanny
□ **razonable** reasonable
□ **apreciaré** I will appreciate · *apreciar* to appreciate
□ **cooperación** cooperation
□ **anuncio** announcement, advertisement
□ **se solicita** *EXP* help wanted, now hiring · *solicitar* to solicit
□ **adorables** adorable · *adorable* adorable

▬ Jane reads the paper, singing.

□ **paciencia** patience
□ **experiencia** experience
□ **gentil** kind
□ **verrugas** warts · *verruga* wart
□ **formal** formal
□ **jovial** jovial
□ **cara** face
□ **afectuosa** affectionate
□ **bello** beautiful, pretty
□ **pelo** hair
□ **ricos** excellent · *rico* excellent [FOOD]
□ **pasteles** cakes · *pastel NM* cake
□ **aceite de ricino** castor oil · *aceite NM* oil · *ricino* castor-oil plant
□ **oler** to smell
□ **se bañe** *SUBJ* she bathes · *bañarse* to bathe
□ **perfume** *NM* perfume

□ **nunca apeste** *SUBJ* she never smells bad, she never stinks · *apestar* to smell bad, to stink
□ **basurero** garbage collector
□ **si no pretende** if she doesn't try · *pretender* to try, to attempt
□ **dominarnos** to dominate us · *dominar* to dominate
□ **nos portaremos** we will behave · *portarse* to behave
□ **obedientes** obedient · *obediente* obedient
□ **lentes** *NMPL* glasses
□ **ranas** frogs · *rana* frog
□ **bolso** purse
□ **esconder** to hide
□ **sus servidores muy sinceramente** very truly yours (*LIT* your servants very sincerely) · *servidor* servant · *sinceramente* sincerely
□ **interesante** interesting

▬ Jane and Michael leave the room, leaving Mr. and Mrs. Banks to talk alone.

□ **solamente** only
□ **felicito** I congratulate · *felicitar* to congratulate
□ **cante** *SUBJ* she sings · *cantar* to sing
□ **obra** work, task
□ **brillante** brilliant
□ **columnas** columns · *columna* column

▬ The wind changes direction.

□ **cargado** loaded · *cargar* to load
□ **cañón** *NM* cannon
□ **reporte** *NM* report
□ **cambió** it changed · *cambiar* to change
□ **dirección** direction
□ **rumbo** direction
□ **babor** *NM* port side
□ **tripulación** crew
□ **brujas** witches · *bruja* witch

▬ Ellen looks out the window.

□ **afuera** outside
□ **niñeras** nannies · *niñera* nanny
□ **aguardando** waiting · *aguardar* to wait
□ **doce** twelve
□ **puestos** posts, positions · *puesto* post, position
□ **numerosas** numerous · *numeroso* numerous
□ **puntualidad** punctuality

## Mary Poppins Arrives on the East Wind

**6**    8:40

### Phrases to Listen For

**sirvió de algo** was good for something

**¿no es así?** isn't that right?

**a la vez** at the same time
**lo que** that, what
**un periodo de prueba** a trial period
**tienes que** you have to
**de modo que** so
**por supuesto** of course
**de inmediato** immediately, right away
**al mismo tiempo** at the same time
**vamos a ver** let's see
**¿para qué?** what for?
**tiene que** it has to be
**tal como** just like

## Names
Winifred, Mary Poppins

🎬 The wind blows the potential nannies away.

□ **bruja** witch
□ **escobas** brooms · *escoba* broom
□ **niñera** nanny
□ **anuncio** announcement, advertisement
□ **cara** face
□ **gentil** kind

🎬 Mary Poppins enters the Banks house.

□ **referencias** references · *referencia* reference
□ **no acostumbro** I am not accustomed · *acostumbrar* to be accustomed
□ **anticuado** antiquated, old-fashioned
□ **atributos** attributes · *atributo* attribute
□ **afectuosa** affectionate
□ **me enojo** I get angry · *enojarse* to get angry, to become angry
□ **a la vista** in sight
□ **divertidos** fun · *divertido* fun · *divertirse* to have fun
□ **papel** *NM* paper
□ **arrojé** I threw · *arrojar* to throw forcefully
□ **jovial** jovial, cheerful
□ **firme** *ADJ* firm
□ **ayer** yesterday
□ **anunció** you announced · *anunciar* to announce
□ **enfermo** sick, ill
□ **respecto a** with respect to
□ **salario** salary
□ **aclararlo** to clarify it, to make it clear · *aclarar* to clarify, to make clear
□ **jueves** *NM* Thursday
□ **periodo de prueba** trial period
□ **prudente** prudent, wise

🎬 Mary Poppins slides upstairs.

□ **cierra** *IMP* close · *cerrar* to close
□ **boca** mouth

🎬 George bumps his head on the fireplace.

□ **estabas entrevistando** you were interviewing · *entrevistar* to interview
□ **niñeras** nannies · *niñera* nanny
□ **seleccionaste** you selected, you chose · *seleccionar* to select, to choose
□ **seleccioné** I selected · *seleccionar* to select
□ **de inmediato** immediately
□ **habría arruinado** I would have ruined · *arruinar* to ruin
□ **deba** *SUBJ* she should, she ought · *deber* should, ought
□ **realmente** really
□ **gobernarlos** to govern them · *gobernar* to govern
□ **moldear** to mold, to shape
□ **despida** *SUBJ* she dismisses · *despedir* to dismiss
□ **aspirantes** applicants · *aspirante* *NMF* applicant
□ **puesto** position

🎬 Mary Poppins and the children examine the messy nursery.

□ **cueva** cave
□ **monos** monkeys · *mono* monkey
□ **maleta** suitcase
□ **rara** strange · *raro* strange
□ **alfombra** carpet
□ **alfombras** carpets · *alfombra* carpet
□ **adentro** inside
□ **ventana** window
□ **parque** *NM* park
□ **precisamente** exactly, precisely
□ **palacio** palace
□ **real** *ADJ* royal
□ **aseado** straightened up, tidied up, cleaned · *asear* to straighten up, to tidy up, to clean
□ **resultará** it will turn out, it will be · *resultar* to turn out, to be, to result in
□ **bastante** enough
□ **cómodo** comfortable
□ **toquecitos** *DIM* touch-ups, small improvements, details · *toque* touch

🎬 Mary Poppins opens her carpetbag.

□ **colgar** to hang
□ **sombrero** hat
□ **clavijero** hat stand
□ **nunca juzgues** *IMP* never judge · *nunca* never · *juzgar* to judge
□ **apariencias** appearances · *apariencia* appearance
□ **alegran** they make happy · *alegrar* to make happy
□ **vigilemos** *SUBJ* we watch closely · *vigilar* to watch closely

☐ **hechicera** sorceress, witch · *hechicero* sorcerer, wizard
☐ **raro** strange
☐ **cinta métrica** measuring tape · *cinta* tape
☐ **miden** you measure · *medir* to measure
☐ **ambos** both

🎬 Mary Poppins sits down on the bed with the measuring tape.

☐ **derecho** straight
☐ **no te encorves** IMP don't slouch · *encorvar* to slouch, to bend
☐ **caprichudo** capricious
☐ **suspicaz** suspicious
☐ **mentira** lie, falsehood
☐ **risitas** DIM giggles · *risa* laughter
☐ **innecesarias** unnecessary · *innecesario* unnecessary
☐ **meticulosa** meticulous · *meticuloso* meticulous
☐ **mídete** IMP measure · *medirse* to measure
☐ **prácticamente** practically
☐ **perfección** perfection

## 7 Tidying the Nursery with the Help of "A Spoonful of Sugar" 4:30

### Phrases to Listen For

**lo que** what
**hay que** it's necessary
**¿verdad que sí?** isn't that right?
**tiene que** it has to
**por favor** please
**¿a qué hora?** at what time?

🎬 Mary Poppins removes her coat.

☐ **limpiar** to clean
☐ **truco** trick
☐ **depende** it depends · *depender* to depend
☐ **labor** NF job, work, chore
☐ **u** or
☐ **ocupación** occupation
☐ **elemento** element
☐ **diversión** fun
☐ **snap** ENG snap

🎬 Mary Poppins snaps her fingers and sings "A Spoonful of Sugar."

☐ **penoso** difficult, hard
☐ **quehacer** NM chore, task, work
☐ **medicina** medicine
☐ **amargo** bitter
☐ **sabrosa** tasty, delicious · *sabroso* tasty, delicious
☐ **poquito** DIM little bit · *un poco* a little
☐ **purga** medicine

☐ **endulzará** it will sweeten · *endulzar* to sweeten
☐ **saborear** to savor
☐ **nido** nest
☐ **fabricar** to build
☐ **ave** NF bird
☐ **luchar** to struggle
☐ **ramitas** DIM twigs, small branches · *rama* branch
☐ **entona** he sings · *entonar* to sing
☐ **quehacer** NM chore, task, work
☐ **convierte** it turns into, it changes into · *convertir* to turn into, to change into
☐ **rica** tasty, excellent · *rico* tasty, excellent [FOOD]
☐ **abeja** bee
☐ **néctar** NM nectar
☐ **flor** NF flower
☐ **colmenar** NM bee hive
☐ **diligente** diligent
☐ **ardor** NM fervor
☐ **se guarda** she saves, she puts away, she keeps · *guardarse* to save, to put away, to keep
☐ **sorbito** DIM sip · *sorbo* sip
☐ **fresco** cool, fresh
☐ **sutil** subtle, delicate
☐ **chistosa** funny · *chistoso* funny
☐ **no demoren** IMP don't delay · *demorar* to delay

## 8 Time for an Outing 5:28

### Phrases to Listen For

**es hora de** it's time to
**otra vez** again
**a ver** let's see
**no hay tiempo que perder** there's no time to lose
**lo que** what
**por favor** please
**me alegro de volver a encontrarte** I'm happy to run into you again
**¿no es cierto?** isn't that right?
**antes de lo que se dice** before one can say
**por aquí** over here
**da vuelta** IMP turn
**¿les parece bien?** does it seem fine to you?

🎬 Mary Poppins opens the closet.

☐ **abrigos** coats · *abrigo* coat
☐ **sombreros** hats · *sombrero* hat
☐ **parque** NM park
☐ **bastante** enough
☐ **poquito** DIM little bit · *un poco* a little
☐ **purga** medicine
☐ **endulzará** it will sweeten · *endulzar* to sweeten
☐ **amargo** bitter
☐ **sabrosa** tasty, delicious · *sabroso* tasty, delicious
☐ **deleitará** it will delight · *deleitar* to delight

Bert paints the sidewalk and sings.

- □ **pintura** painting
- □ **ambulante** mobile
- □ **artista** *NMF* artist
- □ **genial** ingenious
- □ **talento** talent
- □ **Real Academia** Royal Academy
- □ **no cobro** I don't charge · *cobrar* to charge
- □ **afición** interest, hobby
- □ **mas** but
- □ **aprecia** it appreciates · *apreciar* to appreciate
- □ **gorra** cap

Bert traces the silhouette of Mary Poppins.

- □ **reconocería** I would recognize · *reconocer* to recognize
- □ **silueta** silhouette
- □ **me alegro** I'm happy · *alegrarse* to be happy
- □ **tras** after
- □ **niñeras** nannies · *niñera* nanny
- □ **de repente** suddenly
- □ **raro** strange
- □ **la menor idea** the slightest idea
- □ **probablemente** probably
- □ **planea** she is planning · *planear* to plan
- □ **divertido** fun · *divertirse* to have fun
- □ **paseo** excursion
- □ **no me sorprendería** it wouldn't surprise me · *sorprender* to surprise
- □ **bogando** rowing · *bogar* to row
- □ **Támesis** *NM* Thames River
- □ **navegar** to sail
- □ **circo** circus
- □ **leones** lions · *león* *NM* lion
- □ **tigres** tigers · *tigre* *NM* tiger
- □ **famosos** famous · *famoso* famous
- □ **artistas** artists · *artista* *NMF* artist
- □ **dispuestos** willing · *dispuesto* willing
- □ **afrontar** to face
- □ **proezas** exploits · *proeza* exploit
- □ **destreza** dexterity
- □ **habilidad** ability
- □ **ante** before

Mary Poppins claps.

- □ **típica** typical · *típico* typical
- □ **campiña** countryside
- □ **inglesa** English · *inglés* *ADJ* English
- □ **pintada** painted · *pintado* painted · *pintar* to paint
- □ **experto** expert
- □ **amante** loving
- □ **pincel** *NM* paintbrush
- □ **no se distingue** you can't make it out · *distinguir* to make out, to distinguish

- □ **feria** fair
- □ **detrás de** behind
- □ **sendero** trail, path
- □ **colina** hilltop
- □ **da vuelta** it turns · *dar vuelta* to turn
- □ **aventuras** adventures · *aventura* adventure
- □ **intención** intention
- □ **magia** magic
- □ **sencillo** simple
- □ **guiño** wink
- □ **doble** *ADJ* double
- □ **parpadeo** blinking
- □ **cierren** *IMP* close · *cerrar* to close
- □ **cuántas** so many · *cuántos* so many

## 9 A "Jolly Holiday" in the Country

5:43

### Phrases to Listen For

**¿por qué?** why?
**¿de veras?** really?
**alguna vez** one time, ever
**¡qué cosas dices!** such things you say!
**tú no tienes juicio** you're silly
**hay razón** there is a reason

Mary Poppins steps over the sidewalk paintings and joins Bert and the children.

- □ **complicas** you complicate · *complicar* to complicate, to make complicated
- □ **no te encorves** *IMP* don't slouch · *encorvar* to slouch, to bend
- □ **jurártelo** to swear it to you · *jurar* to swear
- □ **feria** fair
- □ **detrás de** behind
- □ **sendero** trail, path
- □ **colina** hilltop
- □ **carrusel** *NM* carousel
- □ **se mancharía** it would get smudged · *mancharse* to get smudged, to be stained
- □ **dibujo** drawing

Mary Poppins opens her parasol and takes Bert's arm. Bert sings.

- □ **azul** blue
- □ **glorioso** glorious
- □ **gris** gray
- □ **encanto** charm
- □ **brillar** to shine
- □ **alegría** happiness
- □ **flores** flowers · *flor* *NF* flower
- □ **lucen** they shine, they radiate · *lucir* to shine, to radiate
- □ **proximidad** proximity
- □ **vibrar** to vibrate

□ **no tienes juicio** you're silly, you're out of your mind · *tener juicio* to be sane · *tener* to have · *juicio* judgment

Bert taps his cane and points to the animals. The animals sing.

□ **alegra** she makes happy · *alegrar* to make happy
□ **deprimente** depressing
□ **en torno a** around
□ **ilumina** she illuminates · *iluminar* to illuminate

Mary Poppins steps off the backs of the turtles. She sings.

□ **nací** I was born · *nacer* to be born
□ **molde** *NM* mold
□ **cual diamante sin pulirte** a diamond in the rough · *diamante NM* diamond · *pulir* to polish
□ **brillo** shine
□ **en pos** in pursuit
□ **acosan** they pursue · *acosar* to pursue
□ **circunstancias** circumstances · *circunstancia* circumstance
□ **adversas** adverse · *adverso* adverse
□ **fabricas** you make, you manufacture · *fabricar* to make, to manufacture, to build
□ **reír** to laugh
□ **fe** *NF* faith
□ **honradez** *NF* honor
□ **gentileza** kindness
□ **clara** evident · *claro* evident

## 10 | Mary and Bert Stop for Tea          9:30

### Phrases to Listen For

**lo que** what
**en lo cierto estás** you are right
**no hay que** it's not necessary
**enseguida** right away, at once
**lo siento** I'm sorry
**hay que** it's necessary
**por favor** please
**buenos días** good morning
**otra vez** again
**no les tengo miedo** I'm not afraid of them
**por favor** please
**desde luego** of course
**no hay de que** you're welcome
**muchas gracias** thank you very much

### Names

Silvia, Maria, Prudencia, Clemencia, May, Patty, Eliza, Alicia, Cynthia, Emilia, Sofía, Priscilla, Veronica, Melissa, Agnes, Dora, Flora, Diana, Johnny

Bert and Mary Poppins are seated at a table.

□ **camarero** waiter
□ **nieve** *NF* ice cream
□ **fresa** strawberry
□ **limón** *NM* lemon
□ **pastel** *NM* cake
□ **no se cobrará** there will be no charge, it will not be charged for · *cobrar* to charge
□ **gentiles** kind · *gentil* kind
□ **favorita** favorite · *favorito* favorite
□ **atractivas** attractive · *atractivo* attractive
□ **cautivadoras** captivating · *cautivador* captivating
□ **deliciosa** delicious, delightful · *delicioso* delicious, delightful
□ **nobles** noble · *noble ADJ* noble
□ **elegante** elegant
□ **amante** loving
□ **constante** *ADJ* constant
□ **compañeras** companions · *compañero* companion
□ **fama** fame
□ **primor** *NM* angel, beauty

Bert dances with the penguins. He picks up his hat and cane.

□ **proximidad** proximity
□ **vibrar** to vibrate
□ **glorioso** glorious

Bert, Mary Poppins, Jane, and Michael ride the carousel.

□ **arre** *EXP* giddy-up
□ **carrusel** *NM* carousel
□ **guardia** *NMF* attendant, guard [PERSON]
□ **enseguida** at once, right away
□ **cuerpos** lengths · *cuerpo* length [HORSE RACING]
□ **tercero** third
□ **so** *EXP* whoa
□ **detente** *IMP* stop · *detenerse* to stop
□ **divertirse** to have fun
□ **contrólense** *IMP* control yourself · *controlarse* to control oneself
□ **hipódromo** racetrack

The hunter and his dogs come to an abrupt halt.

□ **zorra** vixen, female fox · *zorro* fox
□ **efectivamente** quite, indeed
□ **casacas rojas** red coats · *casaca* coat · *rojo* red
□ **protejan** *SUBJ* they protect · *proteger* to protect
□ **caballo** horse
□ **cochinos** filthy · *cochino* filthy

🎬 Mary Poppins crosses the finish line.

☐ **excelente** excellent
☐ **informe** *NM* report
☐ **pajarito** *DIM* little bird · *pájaro* bird

## 11 Mary's Winning the Race is Simply "Supercalifragilistic-expialidocious" 5:12

### Phrases to Listen For

**muchas gracias** thank you very much
**claro que no** of course not
**hay que** it's necessary
**tienen que** they have to
**¿no es cierto?** isn't that right?
**hasta que** until
**es hora de** it's time to
**después de** after
**tanta cosa** so many things
**haz memoria** *IMP* try to remember

🎬 Several reporters interview Mary Poppins.

☐ **haber ganado** to have won, having won · *ganar* to win
☐ **fama** fame
☐ **fortuna** fortune
☐ **fotografía** photograph
☐ **diarios** daily newspapers · *diario* daily newspaper
☐ **halagada** flattered · *halagado* flattered · *halagar* to flatter
☐ **probablemente** probably
☐ **describir** to describe
☐ **emoción** emotion
☐ **al contrario** on the contrary
☐ **adecuada** right, correct, appropriate · *adecuado* right, correct, appropriate

🎬 Mary Poppins removes her hat and sings "Supercalifragilisticexpialidocious."

☐ **supercalifragilísticoexpialidoso** supercalifragilisticexpialidocious
☐ **enredoso** difficult, confusing
☐ **con fluidez** fluently · *fluidez NF* fluency
☐ **se juzga** he is judged · *juzgarse* to be judged
☐ **talentoso** talented
☐ **tímido** timid, shy
☐ **nariz** *NF* nose
☐ **pellizcó** he pinched · *pellizcar* to pinch
☐ **desquició** it drove (him) mad · *desquiciar* to drive mad
☐ **verbo** verb
☐ **oí** I heard · *oír* to hear

☐ **se pronuncia** it is pronounced · *pronunciar* to pronounce
☐ **licenciado** certified professional
☐ **príncipes** princes · *príncipe* prince
☐ **maharajás** maharajas · *maharajá* maharaja
☐ **solía** I used to · *soler* to used to (+ VERB)
☐ **invitaban** they invited · *invitar* to invite
☐ **cenar** to eat dinner, to dine
☐ **al revés** backwards
☐ **lengua** tongue
☐ **torpe** uncoordinated
☐ **ensayen** *IMP* practice, rehearse · *ensayar* to practice, to rehearse
☐ **recitar** to recite

🎬 The moustached man playing the bass drum taps Mary Poppins on the shoulder.

☐ **ejemplo** example
☐ **novia** girlfriend · *novio* boyfriend
☐ **encantadora** charming, enchanting · *encantador* charming, enchanting

🎬 It rains. The four return to Bert's sidewalk in the park.

☐ **se arruinaron** they got ruined, they were ruined · *arruinarse* to be ruined
☐ **dibujos** drawings · *dibujo* drawing
☐ **oficio** job, occupation
☐ **lluvias** rains · *lluvia* rain
☐ **resulta** it turns out to be · *resultar* to turn out to be, to result in
☐ **desastre** *NM* disaster

🎬 Clothes, shoes, and an umbrella are drying by the fire.

☐ **medicina** medicine
☐ **se mojan** they got wet, they became wet · *mojarse* to get wet, to become wet
☐ **limón** *NM* lemon
☐ **real** real
☐ **delicioso** delicious
☐ **frambuesa** raspberry
☐ **ponche** *NM* punch [DRINK]
☐ **satisfactorio** satisfactory
☐ **pañuelo** handkerchief
☐ **almohada** pillow
☐ **frágil** fragile
☐ **promesa** promise
☐ **fácilmente** easily
☐ **cambie** *SUBJ* it changes · *cambiar* to change
☐ **brincamos** we jumped · *brincar* to jump
☐ **paisaje** *NM* landscape
☐ **carrusel** *NM* carousel
☐ **caballos** horses · *caballo* horse
☐ **caza** hunting, hunt

☐ **zorra** vixen, female fox · *zorro* fox
☐ **haz memoria** *IMP* remember · *hacer memoria*
to try to remember
☐ **carrera** race
☐ **respetable** respectable
☐ **se atreven** you dare · *atreverse* to dare
☐ **recuérdalo** *IMP* remember it · *recordar*
to remember
☐ **obligarán** you will force · *obligar* to force
☐ **excitados** excited · *excitado* excited ·
*excitarse* to get excited

## 12 Mary Sings the Children to Sleep ("Stay Awake")   7:28

### Phrases to Listen For

**no hay que** it's not necessary
**a la orden** on your order
**así es** that's right
**¿qué le pasa?** what's the matter with her?
**no me digas** *IMP* don't tell me
**en toda la mañana** all morning
**¿de veras?** really?
**muchas gracias** thank you very much
**ya basta** enough already
**tengo que** I have to
**de una vez por todas** once and for all
**lo que** what
**a sus puestos ya** to your posts now
**claro que** of course
**cruzar de brazos** to cross my arms
**no tiene nada que ver** it has nothing to do
with it
**en absoluto** at all, not at all
**por favor** please
**¿qué tal?** what's up?
**buenos días** good morning
**por supuesto** of course
**de nada** you're welcome
**de prisa** quickly
**¿por qué?** why?

### Names

Binnacle, Albert Hall, Winifred, Cory, Andrew

🎬 Michael and Jane sit up in their beds.
Mary Poppins sings.

☐ **bostezar** to yawn
☐ **luna** moon

🎬 Admiral Boom joins Mr. Binnacle near the cannon.

☐ **glorioso** glorious
☐ **doble** *ADJ* double
☐ **carga** charge
☐ **pólvora** gunpowder

☐ **sacudiremos** we will shake · *sacudir* to shake
☐ **caserío** hamlet, group of houses

🎬 Mrs. Banks places flowers in a vase.

☐ **huevos** eggs · *huevo* egg
☐ **podridos** rotten · *podrido* rotten ·
*pudrir* to rot, to decay
☐ **carro** car
☐ **meeting** *ENG* meeting
☐ **todas juntas** all together
☐ **arrojarle** to throw at him · *arrojar* to throw
forcefully
☐ **primer ministro** prime minister
☐ **distinguido** distinguished · *distinguirse*
to be distinguished

🎬 Mr. Banks enters the room.

☐ **espantosos** frightening · *espantoso* frightening
☐ **maullidos** meowing, howling · *maullido*
meowing, howling
☐ **cocina** kitchen
☐ **cocinera** cook · *cocinero* cook
☐ **cantando** singing · *cantar* to sing
☐ **grillo** cricket
☐ **a propósito** by the way
☐ **extraordinario** extraordinary
☐ **hogar** *NM* home
☐ **no ha roto** she hasn't broken · *romper*
to break
☐ **plato** plate
☐ **están discutiendo** they are arguing · *discutir*
to argue
☐ **gentil** kind
☐ **ofensivo** offensive
☐ **graznido** squawking
☐ **cierra** *IMP* close · *cerrar* to close
☐ **ventana** window
☐ **pájaro** bird
☐ **irrita** it irritates · *irritar* to irritate
☐ **canto** song
☐ **odiosamente** detestably, horribly
☐ **alegres** happy · *alegre* happy

🎬 Jane and Michael join their parents at the table.

☐ **expresión** expression
☐ **divertirse** to have fun

🎬 The children leave the room. Mrs. Banks holds
yellow flowers.

☐ **infernal** infernal
☐ **alboroto** ruckus, disturbance
☐ **obvio** obvious
☐ **nervioso** nervous
☐ **aclaremos** *SUBJ* we clear up · *aclarar* to clear up,
to clarify, to explain

- □ **me encuentro** I find myself · *encontrarse* to find oneself
- □ **inmejorable** excellent
- □ **humor** *NM* humor
- □ **alegre** happy
- □ **placentero** pleasant
- □ **enorme** enormous
- □ **diferencia** difference
- □ **atolondrada** foolish · *atolondrado* foolish
- □ **irresponsabilidad** irresponsibility

🎬 After noticing that the clock is about to strike eight o'clock, Mrs. Banks interrupts.

- □ **disculpa** excuse (me), pardon (me) · *disculpar* to excuse, to pardon
- □ **puestos** positions, places, posts · *puesto* position, place, post
- □ **insisto** I insist · *insistir* to insist
- □ **decoro** decorum
- □ **cruzar** to cross
- □ **brazos** arms · *brazo* arm
- □ **disciplina** discipline
- □ **sepas** *SUBJ* you know · *saber* to know
- □ **he notado** I have noticed · *notar* to notice

🎬 Mr. Banks plays three notes on the piano.

- □ **sugiero** I suggest · *sugerir* to suggest
- □ **mandes** *SUBJ* you order · *mandar* to order
- □ **reparar** to repair
- □ **piano** piano
- □ **instrumento** instrument
- □ **bien afinado** well tuned · *afinar* to tune
- □ **en absoluto** at all, not at all

🎬 Mary Poppins, Jane, and Michael walk out the front door.

- □ **afinador** tuner
- □ **pianos** pianos · *piano* piano
- □ **tienda** store
- □ **jengibre** *NM* ginger
- □ **pescadería** fish market
- □ **camarones** shrimp · *camarón NM* shrimp
- □ **travesuras** mischief · *travesura* bit of mischief
- □ **osada** daring · *osado* daring · *osar* to dare
- □ **aventura** adventure
- □ **nos enfrentaremos** we will face · *enfrentarse* to face
- □ **hotentotes** *NMPL* Hottentots
- □ **tesoro** treasure
- □ **enterrado** buried · *enterrar* to bury
- □ **pescado** fish [FOOD]
- □ **procedan** *IMP* proceed · *proceder* to proceed
- □ **según** according to
- □ **instrucciones** instructions · *instrucción* instruction

- □ **lavar** to wash
- □ **brillo** energy
- □ **limpieza** cleaning

🎬 Mary Poppins, Jane, and Michael pause when they hear a dog bark.

- □ **salud** *EXP* bless you (*LIT* health)
- □ **inmediatamente** immediately
- □ **planes** plans · *plan NM* plan

## 13 A Visit to Uncle Albert's ("I Love to Laugh") 10:10

### Phrases to Listen For
**en cuanto** as soon as
**válgame Dios** *SUBJ* dear Lord, oh my goodness
**me da mucho gusto verte** I'm glad to see you
**de veras** really
**lo saben todos** everyone knows it
**lo que pasa es** the situation is, what's happening is
**me encanta a mí** I love it
**me río de mí** I laugh at myself
**cosa que** something that
**me acuerdo de** I remember
**todo el día** all day
**por favor** please
**es que** it's just that
**tal vez** maybe, perhaps
**muchas gracias** thank you very much
**hay de todo** there is a little of everything
**cuánto me alegra** that makes me so happy
**no hay modo de bajar** there's no way to go down
**lo siento** I'm sorry
**es hora de** it's time to
**lo más triste** the saddest thing
**de prisa** quickly
**¿por qué?** why?
**no se preocupe** *IMP* don't worry
**en cuanto** as soon as
**de nuevo** again
**desde luego** of course

### Name
Albert

🎬 Bert opens the door.

- □ **me enteré** I was informed, I learned · *enterarse* to be informed
- □ **contagioso** contagious
- □ **manchas** stains · *mancha* stain
- □ **válgame Dios** *SUBJ* dear Lord, oh my goodness
- □ **prometiste** you promised · *prometer* to promise
- □ **reír** to laugh

- □ **evitarlo** to avoid it · *evitar* to avoid
- □ **me río** I laugh · *reírse* to laugh

🎬 Jane giggles.

- □ **no te rías** IMP don't laugh · *reírse* to laugh
- □ **portarse** behave yourselves · *portarse* to behave oneself
- □ **tardamos** it took us, we were delayed · *tardar* to take time, to be delayed
- □ **ocasión** occasion

🎬 Uncle Albert sings.

- □ **jocoso** jocular, playful
- □ **divertido** funny · *divertirse* to have fun
- □ **penoso** embarrassing

🎬 Mary Poppins sings.

- □ **nariz** NF nose
- □ **ríen** they laugh · *reír* to laugh
- □ **sonido** sound
- □ **feo** ugly
- □ **dientes** teeth · *diente* NM tooth
- □ **silbando** whistling · *silbar* to whistle
- □ **serpientes** serpents, snakes · *serpiente* NF serpent, snake

🎬 Bert sings.

- □ **risa** laughter
- □ **explosión** explosion
- □ **imita** he imitates · *imitar* to imitate
- □ **gorrión** NM sparrow
- □ **adoptar** to adopt

🎬 Uncle Albert sings again.

- □ **contento** happy, content
- □ **adentro** inside
- □ **discretos** discreet individuals · *discreto* discreet individual

🎬 Bert joins Uncle Albert in the air.

- □ **alegría** happiness
- □ **te elevaras** SUBJ you rise up · *elevarse* to rise up, to go up

🎬 Jane and Michael join Bert and Uncle Albert in the air.

- □ **grato** pleasant, nice
- □ **pónganse cómodos** IMP make yourselves comfortable · *ponerse cómodo* to make oneself comfortable
- □ **asiento** seat
- □ **espectáculo** spectacle
- □ **empleo** job, position
- □ **fábrica** factory
- □ **colchones** mattresses · *colchón* NM mattress

- □ **probándolos** testing them · *probar* to test
- □ **inventaste** you invented, you made up · *inventar* to invent, to make up
- □ **comportamiento** behavior
- □ **desagradable** disagreeable, unpleasant
- □ **bochornoso** embarrassing
- □ **ojo de cristal** glass eye · *ojo* eye · *cristal* NM crystal
- □ **horario** schedule
- □ **interrumpido** interrupted · *interrumpir* to interrupt
- □ **mesa** table
- □ **delicioso** delicious
- □ **se está enfriando** it is getting cold · *enfriarse* to get cold, to become cold

🎬 The table rises.

- □ **espléndido** splendid
- □ **no pisen** IMP don't step on · *pisar* to step on, to walk on
- □ **magnífico** magnificent
- □ **seguramente** surely
- □ **remedio** remedy

🎬 Mary Poppins joins Uncle Albert, Bert, Jane, and Michael.

- □ **ojalá** hopefully
- □ **montón** NM large pile, large amount
- □ **terrones** lumps · *terrón* NM lump
- □ **me alegro** I'm happy, I'm glad · *alegrarse* to be happy, to be glad
- □ **leche** NF milk
- □ **época** season
- □ **establo** stable
- □ **ordeñar** to milk
- □ **vaca** cow
- □ **sabrosísimo** delicious, very tasty · *sabroso* delicious, tasty
- □ **helado** ice cream
- □ **fresa** strawberry
- □ **contrólate** IMP control yourself · *controlarse* to control oneself
- □ **correctamente** correctly
- □ **me estoy divirtiendo** I am having fun · *divertirse* to have fun
- □ **mencionarlo** to mention it · *mencionar* to mention
- □ **tristeza** sadness
- □ **ayer** yesterday
- □ **atropellar** to run over
- □ **reemplazar** to replace
- □ **cazando** hunting · *cazar* to hunt
- □ **ratones** mice · *ratón* NM mouse
- □ **resulta** it turns out · *resultar* to turn out
- □ **gracioso** funny

■ Mary Poppins looks at her watch. The five sink to the floor.

- □ **visitarme** to visit me · *visitar* to visit
- □ **se divierten** they have fun · *divertirse* to have fun
- □ **cuida** IMP take care · *cuidar* to take care, to care for
- □ **un rato** a while
- □ **chiste** NM joke
- □ **he guardado** I have saved · *guardar* to save, to keep
- □ **correcto** correct
- □ **inventor** NM inventor
- □ **inventó** he invented · *inventar* to invent
- □ **perfume** NM perfume
- □ **¿cómo traes tan locas a las mujeres?** how do you drive the women so crazy? · *traer loco* to drive crazy
- □ **aroma** NM aroma
- □ **huele** it smells · *oler* to smell

■ Mr. Banks enters the house.

- □ **paseo** excursion
- □ **ojo de vidrio** glass eye · *ojo* eye · *vidrio* glass
- □ **invitaron** they invited · *invitar* to invite
- □ **flotando** floating · *flotar* to float
- □ **techo** ceiling
- □ **suplico** I request, I beg · *suplicar* to request, to beg

## 14 Mr. Banks Has a Few Words with Mary Poppins          4:11

### Phrases to Listen For

**por supuesto** of course
**por eso** that's why
**lo que** what
**desde luego** of course
**de acuerdo** agreed
**no importa** it doesn't matter
**después de todo** after all
**sin par** without match
**por la mañana** in the morning
**pensar en** to think about
**buenas noches** good night
**¿por qué no?** why not?
**qué bueno** how good
**por favor** please
**dar vueltas** to go around and around
**así es** that's right
**qué impertinencias** what impertinence

### Names

Hamstead, Winifred

■ Mr. Banks and Mary Poppins join Mrs. Banks.

- □ **vestirme** to get dressed · *vestirse* to get dressed, to dress oneself
- □ **presente** ADJ present
- □ **confesar** to confess
- □ **decepcionado** disappointed · *decepcionar* to disappoint
- □ **discurso** speech
- □ **no niego** I don't deny · *negar* to deny
- □ **responsable** responsible
- □ **inútiles** useless · *inútil* useless
- □ **frivolidades** frivolities · *frivolidad* frivolity
- □ **seriedad** seriousness
- □ **en vista de** in view of

■ Mr. Banks begins to reprise "The Life I Lead."

- □ **bancos** banks · *banco* bank
- □ **precisión** precision
- □ **hogares** homes · *hogar* NM home
- □ **disciplina** discipline
- □ **reglamento** regulations, following the rules
- □ **elementos** elements · *elemento* element
- □ **desorden** NM disorder
- □ **caos** NM chaos
- □ **desintegración** disintegration
- □ **moral** moral
- □ **total** NM total, all
- □ **lío** mess
- □ **fatal** fatal
- □ **moldearse** to be molded, to be formed
- □ **vigor** NM vigor
- □ **combate** NM combat
- □ **se afronta** one faces · *afrontar* to face
- □ **valor** NM courage
- □ **penetran** they penetrate, they go inside · *penetrar* to penetrate, to go inside
- □ **paisajes** landscape · *paisaje* NM landscape
- □ **pintados** painted · *pintado* painted · *pintar* to paint
- □ **pavimento** pavement
- □ **caballo** horse
- □ **cazando** hunting · *cazar* to hunt
- □ **zorras** vixens, female foxes · *zorro* fox
- □ **caza** hunting, hunt
- □ **tradición** tradition
- □ **inglesa** English · *inglés* ADJ English
- □ **techo** ceiling
- □ **lógico** logical
- □ **flotando** floating · *flotar* to float
- □ **excursiones** excursions · *excursión* excursion
- □ **perjudiciales** harmful · *perjudicial* harmful
- □ **propósito** purpose
- □ **provechoso** beneficial

🎬 Mr. Banks struggles with the word "supercalifragilisticexpialidocious."

☐ **pingüinos** penguins · *pingüino* penguin
☐ **bailantes** dancing · *bailante* dancing
☐ **uso** use
☐ **pura** pure · *puro* pure
☐ **fantasía** fantasy
☐ **real** real
☐ **educación** education

🎬 Mary Poppins begins to sing a verse of "The Life I Lead."

☐ **exacto** exactly (LIT exact, precise)
☐ **pasión** passion
☐ **función** function
☐ **exactamente** exactly
☐ **ante** before
☐ **balance** NM balance
☐ **arroje** SUBJ it yields · *arrojar* to yield
☐ **utilidad** profit
☐ **rebose** SUBJ it overflows · *rebosar* to overflow
☐ **emoción** emotion
☐ **honradez** NF honesty
☐ **temprano** early
☐ **bañados** bathed · *bañado* bathed · *bañar* to give a bath
☐ **peinados** with hair in place, with hair combed, with hair brushed · *peinado* with hair in place, with hair combed, with hair brushed · *peinar* to brush, to comb [HAIR]
☐ **irán** they will go · *ir* to go
☐ **espléndido** splendid
☐ **propuso** you proposed · *proponer* to propose
☐ **propuse** I proposed · *proponer* to propose
☐ **si me disculpa** if you'll excuse me (LIT if you excuse me) · *disculpar* to excuse, to pardon

🎬 Mary Poppins leaves. Mr. and Mrs. Banks remain.

☐ **diste a entender** you gave that impression · *dar a entender* to give the impression, to imply
☐ **magnífica** magnificent · *magnífico* magnificent
☐ **medicina** medicine
☐ **almibaradas** overly sweet · *almibarado* overly sweet
☐ **poco prácticas** not very practical · *práctico* practical
☐ **femeninas** feminine · *femenino* feminine
☐ **absorben** they absorb · *absorber* to absorb
☐ **hogar** NM home

🎬 Mary Poppins enters Jane and Michael's nursery.

☐ **despidieron** they dismissed, they fired · *despedir* to dismiss, to fire
☐ **despedida** dismissed, fired · *despedido* dismissed, fired · *despedir* to dismiss, to fire

☐ **dar vueltas** going in circles · *dar vuelta* to go around, to spin
☐ **a mi alrededor** around me
☐ **ladran** they bark · *ladrar* to bark
☐ **aves** birds · *ave* NF bird
☐ **metiste** you put · *meter* to put
☐ **impertinencias** impertinent things · *impertinencia* impertinence
☐ **metí** I put · *meter* to put
☐ **interesantes** interesting · *interesante* interesting

## 15 Little Things That Are Quite Important ("Feed The Birds") 6:45

### Phrases to Listen For

**muchas veces** many times
**muy a pesar suyo** through no fault of his own
**no logran ver más allá de su nariz** they aren't able to see beyond the end of their nose
**todos los días** every day
**tan solo dos** only two
**tendrán que** they will have to
**no se vea** SUBJ it is not seen, nobody sees
**así que** so
**en cierto modo** in a certain way, in a way
**¿verdad que sí?** isn't that right?
**claro que** of course
**no veo más allá de mi nariz** I don't see beyond the end of my nose
**lo que** what
**dar a comer** to feed
**qué buena idea** what a good idea

### Name
Dawes

🎬 Mary Poppins talks with the children in the nursery.

☐ **nariz** NF nose
☐ **catedral** NF cathedral
☐ **papa** dad, father

🎬 Mary Poppins sings "Feed the Birds."

☐ **sombra** shadow
☐ **templo** church building, temple
☐ **cómprenme** IMP buy from me · *comprar* to buy
☐ **migajas** crumbs · *migaja* crumb
☐ **polluelos** fledglings · *polluelo* fledgling
☐ **hambrientos** hungry · *hambriento* hungry
☐ **compra** you buy · *comprar* to buy
☐ **pregón** NM hawker's cry
☐ **aves** birds · *ave* NF bird
☐ **rodeándola** surrounding her · *rodear* to surround
☐ **adornan** they adorn · *adornar* to adorn
☐ **sonríen** IMP smile · *sonreír* to smile

□ **alguien se acerca** somebody draws near ·
*acercarse* to draw near
□ **sencillo** simple
□ **alimento** food, nourishment
□ **calor** *NM* warmth, heat
□ **cómprenles** *IMP* buy for them · *comprar* to buy

🎬 Mr. Banks walks with Jane and Michael.

□ **decoroso** with decorum, with dignity
□ **portarnos** to behave ourselves · *portarse*
to behave oneself
□ **correctamente** correctly
□ **dueño** owner
□ **vendedora** seller, saleswoman · *vendedor* seller,
salesman
□ **está pregonando** she is calling, she is crying out ·
*pregonar* to call, to cry out [AS A HAWKER]
□ **pregona** she calls, she cries out · *pregonar*
to call, to cry out [AS A HAWKER]
□ **objeto** object, purpose
□ **guardaba** I saved · *guardar* to save, to keep
□ **alcancía** piggy bank, savings box
□ **desperdiciar** to waste
□ **pajarracos** lousy birds · *pajarraco* *PEJ* lousy bird
□ **mencionar** to mention
□ **resto** the rest, the remainder
□ **derroches** *SUBJ* you throw away, you waste,
you squander · *derrochar* to throw away, to waste,
to squander
□ **emplear** to use
□ **interesante** interesting

🎬 Mr. Banks, Jane, and Michael enter the bank.

□ **precisamente** precisely, exactly
□ **anciano** old
□ **gigante** *NM* giant
□ **financiero** financial
□ **excelente** excellent

## 16 Mr. Dawes, Sr. Explains the Advantages of Investing in "The Fidelity Fiduciary Bank" 8:29

### Phrases to Listen For

**conque** so
**dar de comer** to feed
**a salvo** safe
**se verán** they will be seen
**fíjate bien** *IMP* pay attention
**por falta de** for lack of
**¿qué pasa?** what's going on?
**a ver** let's see
**por favor** please
**¿qué les sucede?** what's the matter with you?

**no sé qué** I don't know what
**día tras día** day after day
**de veras** really
**a veces** sometimes

### Names

Tomes, Mousley, Grubbs, Fidelity, Morgan, Jones

🎬 Mr. Dawes, Sr. walks toward Jane and Michael.
He addresses Michael.

□ **conque** so
□ **aves** birds · *ave* *NF* bird
□ **disparate** *NM* folly, silliness
□ **alimentando** feeding · *alimentar* to feed,
to give nourishment
□ **gordas** fat · *gordo* fat
□ **inviertes** you invest · *invertir* to invest
□ **fe** *NF* faith
□ **a salvo estos estarán** these will be safe
(*LIT* safe these will be) · *estar a salvo* to be safe
□ **reinvertidos** reinvested · *reinvertido*
reinvested · *reinvertir* to reinvest
□ **ventaja** advantage
□ **capitalizar** to capitalize
□ **adquirirás** you will acquire · *adquirir* to acquire
□ **sentido** feeling
□ **conquista** conquest
□ **caudal** abundance
□ **expertos** experts · *experto* expert
□ **invierten** they invest · *invertir* to invest
□ **sabiamente** wisely
□ **capital** *NM* capital

🎬 Mr. Banks asks permission to continue the song.

□ **continúa** *IMP* continue · *continuar* to continue
□ **fíjate bien** *IMP* pay close attention · *fijarse*
to pay attention, to notice
□ **acciones** company stocks · *acción* share of
company stock
□ **ferrocarriles** trains · *ferrocarril* *NM* train
□ **África** Africa
□ **exacto** exactly
□ **presas** dams · *presa* dam
□ **Nilo** Nile River
□ **flotas** fleets · *flota* fleet
□ **trasatlánticos** transatlantic · *trasatlántico*
transatlantic
□ **majestuosos** majestic · *majestuoso* majestic
□ **canales** channels, currents · *canal* channel,
current
□ **interoceánicos** interoceanic · *interoceánico*
interoceanic
□ **sobrepasa** it surpasses · *sobrepasar* to surpass
□ **imaginación** imagination
□ **plantaciones** plantations · *plantación* plantation
□ **tabaco** tobacco

☐ **pasión** passion
☐ **visión** vision

🎬 Mr. Dawes, Sr. extends his hand for Michael's money.

☐ **depositas** you deposit · *depositar* to deposit
☐ **no tardarás** you won't take a long time, you won't wait long · *tardar* to take time
☐ **dividendos** dividends · *dividendo* dividend
☐ **crédito** credit
☐ **aumentarán** they will increase, they will add to · *aumentar* to increase, to add to, to augment
☐ **renta** interest income
☐ **semestral** semiannual
☐ **fama** fame
☐ **riquezas** riches · *riqueza* wealth
☐ **influencia** influence
☐ **elevarán** they will rise · *elevar* to rise
☐ **estrata** stratum, level
☐ **financiera** financial · *financiero* financial
☐ **precisa** it needs · *precisar* to need
☐ **cualidad** quality, characteristic
☐ **hipotecas** mortgages · *hipoteca* mortgage

🎬 Mr. Dawes, Sr. advances. Jane and Michael retreat.

☐ **acciones preferentes** preferred stock · *acción preferente* share of preferred stock
☐ **utilidades** NFPL profits
☐ **bonos** bonds · *bono* bond
☐ **inmuebles** properties · *inmueble* NM property
☐ **dividendos** dividends · *dividendo* dividend
☐ **títulos** titles, deeds · *título* title, deed
☐ **desfalcos** mismanagement of money, embezzlement · *desfalco* mismanagement of money, embezzlement
☐ **remates** auctions · *remate* NM auction
☐ **empresas** enterprises, businesses · *empresa* enterprise, business
☐ **privadas** private · *privado* private
☐ **astilleros** shipyards · *astillero* shipyard
☐ **minas** mines · *mina* mine
☐ **diamantes** diamonds · *diamante* NM diamond
☐ **factorías** factories · *factoría* factory
☐ **joyerías** jewelry stores · *joyería* jewelry store
☐ **sociedades** societies · *sociedad* society
☐ **en quiebra** broke
☐ **bancos** banks · *banco* bank
☐ **banca** banking system
☐ **inglesa** English · *inglés* ADJ English
☐ **Inglaterra** England
☐ **para ser precisos** to be exact, to be precise · *preciso* precise

🎬 Mr. Dawes, Sr. seizes Michael's money.

☐ **bienvenido** ADJ welcome
☐ **numerosa** numerous · *numeroso* numerous

☐ **inversionistas** investors · *inversionista* NMF investor
☐ **suéltelo** IMP let go of it, let it go · *soltar* to let go, to release

🎬 Two ladies stand in front of a bank teller.

☐ **devolverle** to return to him · *devolver* to return, to give back
☐ **centavo** cent
☐ **pagos** payments · *pago* payment
☐ **abran** IMP open · *abrir* to open

🎬 Jane and Michael run into Bert.

☐ **suéltela** IMP let go of her · *soltar* to let go, to release
☐ **daño** harm
☐ **sucio** dirty
☐ **ahumado** smoky · *ahumar* to cover with smoke, to fill with smoke
☐ **limpiando** cleaning · *limpiar* to clean
☐ **chimeneas** chimneys · *chimenea* chimney
☐ **se encargará** he will look after, he will take charge · *encargarse* to look after, to take charge
☐ **¿quién los persigue?** who is chasing you? · *perseguir* to chase, to pursue
☐ **terrible** terrible
☐ **persiguiera** SUBJ it chases, it pursues · *perseguir* to chase, to pursue
☐ **ejército** army
☐ **exagerado** excessive · *exagerar* to be excessive, to exaggerate
☐ **seguramente** surely
☐ **error** NM error
☐ **cara** face

🎬 Bert, Jane, and Michael sit down on some steps.

☐ **lastimarlos** to hurt you · *lastimar* to hurt
☐ **tras** after
☐ **rodeado de** surrounded by · *rodear* to surround
☐ **montones** large piles · *montón* NM large pile, large amount
☐ **cruel** cruel
☐ **ser humano** human being
☐ **enjaulado** caged · *enjaular* to cage, to put in a cage
☐ **fabrican** they make, they build, they construct · *fabricar* to make, to build, to construct
☐ **jaulas** cages · *jaula* cage
☐ **tamaños** sizes · *tamaño* size
☐ **alfombras** carpets · *alfombra* carpet
☐ **dificultades** difficulties · *dificultad* NF difficulty
☐ **mírenlo** IMP look at it · *mirar* to look at
☐ **cuida** she cares for, she looks after · *cuidar* to care for, to look after
☐ **guardián** NM constable, guard

- □ **defenderse** defending himself · *defenderse* to defend oneself
- □ **cuitas** problems, difficulties · *cuita* problem, difficulty
- □ **solamente** only
- □ **lamentarse** feeling sorry for himself · *lamentarse* to feel sorry for oneself
- □ **silencioso** silent

## 17 Today Bert Is a Chimney Sweep ("Chim Chim Cher-ee") 5:22

### Phrases to Listen For

**mi suerte tendrán** you will be lucky

**ya se me hizo tarde** it's gotten late (*LIT* it's gotten late for me)

**¿no es cierto?** isn't that right?

**hace falta** it's needed, it's lacking

**qué bueno** how great, it's so good

**es que** it's just that

**hasta pronto** see you soon (*LIT* until soon)

**de lo superior** of the best quality

**a veces** sometimes

**lo que** what

**se ve** it is seen

**qué belleza** what beauty

**con razón** quite right, you're right

**ten cuidado** *IMP* be careful

**enseguida** at once, right away

**tener miedo** to be afraid

**de inmediato** immediately

**sin querer** by accident

**ya no hay remedio** there's nothing to be done about it

**¿por qué no?** why not?

**si hemos de ir** if we have to go

### Name

Abril

🎬 Bert, Jane, and Michael walk up the stairs. Bert sings "Chim Chim Cher-ee."

- □ **tipo de suerte** lucky guy · *tipo* guy · *suerte* luck
- □ **deshollinador** chimney sweep
- □ **besa** she kisses · *besar* to kiss
- □ **deshollina** he sweeps out the chimney · *deshollinar* to sweep out the chimney
- □ **mísero** poor, unfortunate
- □ **ahumado** smoky · *ahumar* to cover with smoke, to fill with smoke

🎬 Jane rings the bell to their house.

- □ **despídelo** *IMP* send him away · *despedir* to send away, to say good-bye, to dismiss

- □ **estreches su mano** *SUBJ* you shake hands · *estrechar la mano* to shake hands
- □ **se volvieron a escapar** they got away again · *escaparse* to escape
- □ **afecta** it affects · *afectar* to affect
- □ **no escaparon** they didn't escape, they didn't get away · *escapar* to escape
- □ **hace falta que los atiendan** *SUBJ* they need someone to look after them · *hacer falta* to be necessary · *atender* to look after, to attend to
- □ **jueves** *NM* Thursday
- □ **quehaceres** chores · *quehacer NM* chore
- □ **abril** *NM* April
- □ **gobernador** governor
- □ **limpie** *SUBJ* you clean · *limpiar* to clean
- □ **sala** living room
- □ **condiciones** *NFPL* condition, state, shape
- □ **humea** it smokes · *humear* to smoke
- □ **sin cesar** endlessly (*LIT* without stopping) · *cesar* to stop, to cease
- □ **se divertirán** they will have fun · *divertirse* to have fun
- □ **seguramente** surely
- □ **enojar** to get angry
- □ **prisión** prison
- □ **no tardaré** I won't be long · *tardar* to be long [TIME]

🎬 By the fireplace, Bert reprises "Chim Chim Cher-ee."

- □ **escojo** I choose · *escoger* to choose
- □ **implementos** tools · *implemento* tool
- □ **de lo superior** superior, of superior quality
- □ **escoba** broom
- □ **fina** fine
- □ **cepillo** brush
- □ **adentro** inside
- □ **oscuro** dark
- □ **feo** ugly
- □ **amplia** wide · *amplio* wide
- □ **tejados** roofs · *tejado* roof
- □ **se asoma** it suddenly appears · *asomarse* to appear suddenly
- □ **luna** moon
- □ **penumbra** partial light
- □ **humo** smoke
- □ **estrellas** stars · *estrella* star
- □ **goza** he enjoys · *gozar* to enjoy
- □ **Londres** London
- □ **belleza** beauty
- □ **chimeneas** chimneys · *chimenea* chimney
- □ **sobresale** it sticks out · *sobresalir* to stick out, to protrude
- □ **tejado** roof
- □ **favorable** favorable

☐ **soplar** to blow
☐ **extrae** it draws, it pulls out · *extraer* to draw, to pull out
☐ **tiro** chimney flue
☐ **estira** it stretches · *estirar* to stretch
☐ **aire** *NM* air, wind
☐ **hubieras pescado** *SUBJ* you had caught (fish) · *pescar* to catch (fish), to fish
☐ **ballena** whale

📽 Mary Poppins joins Bert, Jane, and Michael in the drawing room.

☐ **peligrosas** dangerous · *peligroso* dangerous
☐ **enseguida** at once, right away
☐ **cometí** I committed · *cometer* to commit
☐ **torpeza** blunder
☐ **metieras** *SUBJ* you put · *meter* to put
☐ **correteen** *SUBJ* they run around · *corretear* to run around
☐ **de inmediato** immediately
☐ **conque** so
☐ **remedio** remedy
☐ **afortunada** fortunate · *afortunado* fortunate
☐ **circunstancia** circumstance
☐ **selva** jungle
☐ **virgen** *ADJ* virgin
☐ **explorarla** to explore it · *explorar* to explore

## 18 A March over the Rooftops of London
3:04

### Phrases to Listen For
**de prisa** quickly
**vuelta a la derecha** right turn
**en marcha** march
**claro que no** of course not
**todo el mundo** everyone
**hace frío** it's cold

📽 Mary Poppins stands on the rooftop with Bert and the children. Jane and Michael pick up their brooms.

☐ **fila** line
☐ **alinearse** get in line · *alinearse* to get in a straight line, to form a straight line
☐ **armas** weapons · *arma* weapon
☐ **hombro** shoulder
☐ **vuelta** turn
☐ **en marcha** march

📽 Mary Poppins, Bert, Jane, and Michael march.

☐ **hollín** *NM* soot
☐ **limpio** clean
☐ **pájaros** birds · *pájaro* bird

☐ **estrellas** stars · *estrella* star
☐ **deshollinadores** chimney sweeps · *deshollinador* chimney sweep

## 19 The Chimney Sweeps "Step in Time"
9:10

### Phrases to Listen For
**a bailar al compás** dance to the beat
**no hay ninguna rima** there is no rhyme
**sólo ritmo hay** there is only rhythm
**¿verdad que es maravillosa?** isn't it wonderful?
**¡qué demonios!** what in the world!, what the devil!
**a la orden** at your order
**hay que** it's necessary
**¿qué sucede?** what's happening?
**buena suerte** good luck
**qué fiestón hicimos** what a big party we had
**te dieron la mano** they shook your hand
**que me haga el favor de explicar todo esto** *SUBJ* will you do me the favor of explaining all of this, will you please explain all of this

### Name
Binnacle

📽 Bert waves to his fellow chimney sweeps. They sing "Step in Time."

☐ **compañeros** companions, co-workers · *compañero* companion, co-worker
☐ **bailar** to dance
☐ **al compás** to the rhythm, to the beat, in musical time
☐ **bailen** *IMP* dance · *bailar* to dance
☐ **rima** rhyme
☐ **ritmo** rhythm
☐ **rodillas** knees · *rodilla* knee
☐ **alas** wings · *ala* wing
☐ **cornisa** cornice, ledge, railing
☐ **tejados** roofs · *tejado* roof
☐ **lacen brazos** *IMP* link arms · *lazar* to rope, to lasso · *brazo* arm

📽 Bert dances with Mary Poppins.

☐ **baila** *IMP* dance · *bailar* to dance
☐ **turno** turn
☐ **adorable** adorable

📽 Admiral Boom spies the chimney sweeps.

☐ **hotentotes** *NMPL* Hottentots
☐ **qué demonios** *EXP* what the devil · *demonio* demon, devil
☐ **dispáreles** *IMP* fire on them, shoot them · *disparar* to fire, to shoot

□ **valor** *NM* courage
□ **lección** lesson
□ **cañón** *NM* cannon
□ **cargado** loaded · *cargar* to load
□ **buen tiro** good shot

🎬 The chimney sweeps dance inside the Banks' house.

□ **al compás** to the rhythm, to the beat, in musical time
□ **voten** *IMP* vote · *votar* to vote
□ **patrón** *NM* employer, boss
□ **fiestón** *NM* big party · *fiesta* party
□ **que se divierta** *SUBJ* have a good time · *divertirse* to have a good time, to have fun

🎬 Mary Poppins, Jane, and Michael stand on the staircase. Mr. Banks stands below them.

□ **deshollinadores** chimney sweeps · *deshollinador* chimney sweep
□ **intrusión** intrusion
□ **aclaremos** *SUBJ* we clear up, we clarify · *aclarar* to clear up, to clarify

## 20 A Phone Call from the Bank    8:44

### Phrases to Listen For

**lo que** what
**sin falta** without missing, without fail
**después de todo** after all
**antes que** before
**a las nueve** at nine o'clock
**en plena juventud** in the fullness of youth
**¡qué tontería!** what foolishness!
**cosa grande es** it's a great thing
**para que** in order to
**sentimos lo de los céntimos** we're sorry about the pennies

### Name

Dawes

🎬 Mr. Banks answers the phone.

□ **créame** *IMP* believe me · *creer* to believe
□ **me apena** it embarrasses me · *apenar* to embarrass
□ **asunto** matter
□ **lamentamos** we are sorry · *lamentar* to be sorry
□ **decisión** decision

🎬 Mr. Banks joins Bert in the drawing room. He sings "A Man Has Dreams."

□ **triunfar** triumphing · *triunfar* to triumph
□ **gigantes** giants · *gigante NM* giant

□ **esculpir** carving, engraving · *esculpir* to carve, to engrave
□ **pilar** *NF* pillar
□ **finanzas** *NFPL* finances
□ **ante** before
□ **cumbre** *NF* hilltop, mountaintop
□ **triunfo** triumph
□ **arrebata** he snatches, he grabs · *arrebatar* to snatch, to grab forcefully
□ **se opaca** it loses its shine · *opacarse* to lose its shine
□ **arruina** he ruins · *arruinar* to ruin
□ **plena** full · *pleno* full
□ **juventud** *NF* youth
□ **lío** mess
□ **patrón** *NM* boss, employer
□ **ideal** *ADJ* ideal
□ **ejemplar** exemplary
□ **se destrozó** it was ruined · *destrozarse* to be ruined
□ **ambición** ambition
□ **se desplomó** it collapsed · *desplomarse* to collapse
□ **castigo** punishment
□ **amargo** bitter
□ **cruel** cruel

🎬 Bert walks toward the fireplace.

□ **azucarones** sweets [UNCOMMON]
□ **torna** it turns · *tornar* to turn
□ **pastel** *NM* cake
□ **qué tontería** what nonsense, what foolishness, how silly
□ **no me extraña** it's not strange to me · *extrañar* to be strange, to seem strange
□ **revuelto** mixed up · *revolver* to mix up, to stir up
□ **probarla** to try it · *probar* to try, to test
□ **remedio** remedy
□ **dificultades** difficulties · *dificultad NF* difficulty
□ **engatusó** she charmed, she sweet-talked, she tricked · *engatusar* to charm, to sweet-talk, to trick
□ **prestigio** prestige
□ **alterna** he mixes, he associates · *alternar* to mix (with people), to associate
□ **nobleza** nobility
□ **lágrimas** tears · *lágrima* tear
□ **enjugar** to wipe, to wipe away
□ **caritas** *DIM* little faces · *cara* face
□ **sonriéndole** smiling at him · *sonreír* to smile
□ **contemplar** to contemplate
□ **admito** I admit · *admitir* to admit
□ **luchar** to struggle
□ **infancia** childhood

□ **se esfuma** it vanishes, it disappears ·
  *esfumarse* to vanish, to disappear
□ **habrán crecido** they will have grown ·
  *crecer* to grow
□ **nido** nest
□ **endulzará** it will sweeten · *endulzar* to sweeten
□ **confortará** it will comfort · *confortar* to comfort
□ **alentará** it will encourage · *alentar* to encourage

📽 After Bert leaves, Jane and Michael approach
  Mr. Banks.

□ **causaría** it would cause · *causar* to cause

## 21 Mr. Banks Is Discharged                7:58

### Phrases to Listen For

**buenas noches** good evening
**con poco juicio** with poor judgment
**lo que** what
**hay que** it's necessary
**tenía razón** she was right
**qué tontería** what foolishness
**en realidad** in reality, really
**así que** so
**con todo respeto** with all due respect
**ya que** since
**qué impertinencia** what impertinence
**se ha vuelto loco** he has gone crazy
**no lo sé** I don't know
**loco de remate** completely crazy
**hasta que** until
**por favor** please
**capaz de hacer** capable of doing
**un momento de abatimiento** a moment of
  depression
**al parecer** it seems
**de buenas costumbres** of good habits
**al menos** at least
**hasta donde se sabe** as far as anyone knows,
  as far as one can tell
**qué bueno** how good
**por supuesto** of course
**así parece** that's how it seems
**¿qué pasó?** what happened?
**qué tristeza** how sad

### Names

Boston, George W. Banks, Smith, Dawes,
Cherry Tree Lane, Southwark, Ellen

📽 Mr. Banks slowly opens the door.

□ **sombrero** hat
□ **mil setecientos setenta y tres** 1773 [DATE],
  one thousand seven hundred seventy-three
□ **empleado** employee

□ **con poco juicio** with poor judgment ·
  *juicio* judgment
□ **prestó** loaned · *prestar* to loan, to lend
□ **suma** sum
□ **cargamento** cargo, shipment
□ **colonias** colonies · *colonia* colony
□ **americanas** American · *americano* American
□ **puerto** port
□ **partida** group, party
□ **colonos** colonists · *colono* colonist
□ **abordó** it boarded · *abordar* to board
□ **nave** NF ship
□ **se portaron** they behaved themselves ·
  *portarse* to behave oneself
□ **rudamente** rudely, roughly
□ **arrojaron** they threw, they hurled · *arrojar*
  to throw forcefully
□ **precisamente** precisely
□ **invadió** it invaded · *invadir* to invade
□ **pánico** panic
□ **recinto** place
□ **causado** caused · *causar* to cause
□ **ignominiosa** disgraceful · *ignominioso*
  disgraceful
□ **conducta** conduct
□ **niegas** you deny · *negar* to deny
□ **no lo niego** I don't deny it · *negar* to deny
□ **dispuesto** willing
□ **asumir** to assume, to take on
□ **responsabilidad** responsibility

📽 Mr. Dawes, Jr. punches a hole in Banks' hat.

□ **supercalifragilísticoexpialidoso**
  supercalifragilisticexpialidocious
□ **extraordinaria** extraordinary ·
  *extraordinario* extraordinary
□ **tontería** foolishness
□ **mágica** magic · *mágico* ADJ magic
□ **respeto** respect
□ **impertinencia** impertinence
□ **chiste** NM joke
□ **genial** terrific
□ **adorables** adorable · *adorable* adorable
□ **ojo de cristal** glass eye · *ojo* eye ·
  *cristal* NM crystal
□ **se ha vuelto loco** he has gone crazy ·
  *volverse loco* to go crazy
□ **guardias** guards · *guardia* NMF guard
  [PERSON]
□ **no se atreva** IMP don't you dare ·
  *atreverse* to dare
□ **guárdelos** IMP guard them, keep them ·
  *guardar* to guard, to keep
□ **adiós** good-bye
□ **meterme** to put myself · *meterse* to put oneself

- □ **paisaje** *NM* landscape
- □ **pintado** painted · *pintar* to paint
- □ **pavimento** pavement
- □ **bailar** to dance
- □ **pingüinos** penguins · *pingüino* penguin
- □ **montarme** to mount up, to climb on, to get on · *montarse* to mount up, to climb on, to get on
- □ **caballo** horse
- □ **carrusel** *NM* carousel
- □ **cazar** to hunt
- □ **zorras** vixens, female foxes · *zorro* fox
- □ **empinar** to raise, to fly [AS A KITE]
- □ **niñera** nanny
- □ **poquito** *DIM* little bit · *un poco* a little
- □ **purga** medicine
- □ **endulzará** it will sweeten · *endulzar* to sweeten
- □ **amargo** bitter
- □ **loco de remate** completely crazy

🎬 The wind changes directions.

- □ **está soplando** it is blowing · *soplar* to blow
- □ **oeste** *NM* west
- □ **clavijero** hat stand
- □ **me despido** I say good-bye · *despedirse* to say good-bye

🎬 A policeman talks on the telephone.

- □ **mide** he measures · *medir* to measure
- □ **uno ochenta** one meter, eighty centimeters [about 5 foot 11 inches] (*LIT* one eighty) · *ochenta* eighty
- □ **temprano** early
- □ **averiguamos** we found out, we ascertained · *averiguar* to find out, to ascertain
- □ **destituyeron** they dismissed, they fired · *destituir* to dismiss, to fire
- □ **anoche** last night
- □ **capaz** capable
- □ **abatimiento** depression
- □ **dragaran** *SUBJ* they dredge · *dragar* to dredge
- □ **río** river
- □ **puente** *NM* bridge
- □ **popular** popular
- □ **suicidas** suicide victims · *suicida NMF* suicide victim
- □ **calla** *IMP* quiet · *callar* to be quiet
- □ **finísimo** very fine · *fino* fine
- □ **vicios** vices · *vicio* vice
- □ **costumbres** habits · *costumbre NF* habit
- □ **sabrosa** tasty · *sabroso* tasty
- □ **suplico** I plead, I beg · *suplicar* to plead, to beg
- □ **guarden** *SUBJ* you keep · *guardar* to keep
- □ **inspector** *NM* inspector

🎬 Mr. Banks enters the room.

- □ **amargura** bitterness
- □ **no te arrojaste** you didn't throw yourself · *arrojarse* to throw oneself
- □ **olvídelo** *IMP* forget it · *olvidar* to forget
- □ **extraviado** missing [PERSON] · *extraviarse* to go missing, to get lost
- □ **está besando** he is kissing · *besar* to kiss
- □ **me despidieron** they fired me, they dismissed me · *despedir* to fire, dismiss
- □ **me echaron** they threw me out · *echar* to throw, to throw out
- □ **está loco de remate** he is completely crazy · *estar loco de remate* to be completely crazy
- □ **tristeza** sadness
- □ **sótano** basement

## 22 "Let's Go Fly a Kite" 3:00

### Phrases to Listen For

**por el firmamento en raudo vuelo** through the heavens in swift flight

**por entre nubes de tul** through clouds of tulle

**vamos ya a volar** let's go fly right now

**¿no es cierto?** isn't that right?

**lo que** what

**lo siento** I'm sorry

**no hay porqué** there's no reason

**muchísimas gracias** thank you very very much

### Name

Jones

🎬 Mr. Banks holds a kite for Jane and Michael to see.

- □ **remendó** he repaired, he mended · *remendar* to repair, to mend

🎬 Mr. Banks sings "Let's Go Fly a Kite."

- □ **alas** wings · *ala* wing
- □ **hilo** thread
- □ **papel** *NM* paper
- □ **pon** *IMP* put · *poner* to put
- □ **suelo** ground
- □ **gozarán** you will enjoy · *gozar* to enjoy
- □ **vuelo** flight
- □ **empinar** to raise, to fly [AS A KITE]
- □ **firmamento** firmament
- □ **raudo vuelo** swift flight · *raudo* swift · *vuelo* flight
- □ **azul** blue
- □ **nubes** clouds · *nube NF* cloud
- □ **tul** *NM* tulle
- □ **cola** tail

🎬 Bert hands a kite to a girl and sings.

- ☐ **gozar**  to enjoy
- ☐ **ligero**  light [WEIGHT]
- ☐ **elevar**  to elevate, to raise up

🎬 Mr. Dawes, Jr. flies a kite and addresses Mr. Banks.

- ☐ **felicitarte**  to congratulate you · *felicitar* to congratulate
- ☐ **chiste** NM  joke
- ☐ **ojo de cristal**  glass eye · *ojo* eye · *cristal* NM crystal
- ☐ **se rió**  he laughed · *reírse* to laugh
- ☐ **lamentarlo**  to be sorry for it · *lamentar* to be sorry
- ☐ **puesto**  position
- ☐ **vacante**  vacant
- ☐ **socio**  partner
- ☐ **te felicito**  I congratulate you · *felicitar* to congratulate
- ☐ **muchísimas gracias**  thank you very very much · *muchísimo* very very much

## 23 Mary Poppins Departs                 1:16

### Phrases to Listen For

**ni siquiera te dijeron adiós**  they didn't even tell you good-bye
**ni se acuerdan de ti**  they don't even remember you
**así es**  that's right, indeed
**cual debe ser**  as it should be
**¿no te importa?**  doesn't it bother you?
**claro que sí**  of course
**no te olvides de nosotros** IMP  don't forget us

**por el firmamento en raudo vuelo**  through the heavens in swift flight
**por entre nubes de tul**  through clouds of tulle
**vamos ya a volar**  let's go fly right now

🎬 The parrot speaks to Mary Poppins, and Mary Poppins flies away.

- ☐ **malagradecidos**  ungrateful · *malagradecido* ungrateful
- ☐ **míralos** IMP  look at them · *mirar* to look at
- ☐ **ni se acuerdan**  they don't even remember · *acordarse* to remember
- ☐ **sentimientos**  feelings · *sentimiento* feeling
- ☐ **interfieran** SUBJ  they interfere · *interferir* to interfere
- ☐ **engañarme**  to deceive me, to trick me · *engañar* to deceive, to trick
- ☐ **perfectamente**  perfectly

## 24 Closing Credits                 1:31

### Phrases to Listen For

**por el firmamento en raudo vuelo**  through the heavens in swift flight
**por entre nubes de tul**  through clouds of tulle
**vamos ya a volar**  let's go fly right now

🎬 End credits.

- ☐ **empinar**  to raise, to fly [AS A KITE]
- ☐ **firmamento**  firmament
- ☐ **raudo vuelo**  swift flight · *raudo* swift · *vuelo* flight
- ☐ **azul**  blue
- ☐ **nubes**  clouds · *nube* NF cloud
- ☐ **tul**  tulle